Second Edition

BEHAVIOR DISORDERS
OF
CHILDHOOD

Rita Wicks-Nelson
West Virginia Institute of Technology
Montgomery, West Virginia

Allen C. Israel
University at Albany
State University of New York

PRENTICE HALL
Englewood Cliffs, New Jersey 07632

Library of Congress Cataloging-in-Publication Data

Wicks-Nelson, Rita
    Behavior disorders of childhood / Rita Wicks-Nelson, Allen C.
Israel.
      p.   cm.
    Includes bibliographical references and index.
    ISBN 0-13-084070-X
    1. Child psychopathology. I. Israel, Allen C. II. Title.
    [DNLM: 1. Child Behavior Disorders. 2. Child Development.
    3. Mental Disorders—in infancy & childhood. WS 350.6 W637b]
    RJ499.W45   1991
    618.92′89—dc20
    DNLM/DLC
    for Library of Congress   90-14292
                             CIP

Acquisition editor: *Susan Finnemore*
Editorial/production supervision: *Edith Riker/Chris Nassauer*
Cover design: *Carol Ceraldi*
Prepress buyer: *Debra Kesar*
Manufacturing buyer: *Mary Ann Gloriande*

Printed in the United States of America

10 9 8 7 6 5 4 3

ISBN   0-13-084070-X

Prentice-Hall International (UK) Limited, *London*
Prentice-Hall of Australia Pty. Limited, *Sydney*
Prentice-Hall Canada Inc., *Toronto*
Prentice-Hall Hispanoamericana, S.A., *Mexico*
Prentice-Hall of India Private Limited, *New Delhi*
Prentice-Hall of Japan, Inc., *Tokyo*
Simon & Schuster Asia Pte. Ltd., *Singapore*
Editora Prentice-Hall do Brasil, Ltda., *Rio de Janeiro*

To **Leonard C. Nelson,**
Mary Wicks,
the memory of **William Wicks**
RW-N

To **Sara** and **Daniel,**
Helen Israel,
the memory of **Karlton Israel**
ACI

A special dedication to the memory of
Alice Israel

CONTENTS

2 THE DEVELOPMENTAL CONTEXT

3 PERSPECTIVES AND MODES OF TREATMENT

4 RESEARCH: ITS ROLE AND METHODS

5 CLASSIFICATION AND ASSESSMENT

6 INTERNALIZING PROBLEMS: ANXIETY DISORDERS

7 INTERNALIZING PROBLEMS: DEPRESSION AND PEER RELATIONS

132

8 CONDUCT DISORDERS

155

9 ATTENTION-DEFICIT HYPERACTIVITY DISORDER

10 MENTAL RETARDATION   210

12 AUTISM AND CHILDHOOD SCHIZOPHRENIA

PREFACE

At times one has the good fortune to engage in work permeated by the excitement of progress. Such good fortune applies to the writing of this second edition of *Behavior Disorders of Childhood*. In only a few short years efforts to understand behavioral problems in the young have taken a leap forward. This is not to refute the oft-heard statement that although much has been learned, much is yet to be learned. Indeed, both parts of that statement are true. We have tried in this edition to capture the excitement in the field and to convey both what is known and what is still to be known.

This text shares the fundamental characteristics of the first edition. Designed as a relatively comprehensive introduction to the field of behavior disorders of childhood, it includes central issues, theoretical and methodological underpinnings, descriptions and discussion of many disorders, clinical and research data, and treatment approaches. As is often the case, space limitation demands some selectivity of content.

The three major themes, or predilections, that were evident in the first edition are again woven throughout this book. Indeed, we believe that their importance has become more firmly established. The first is the assumption that the developmental context can contribute much to understanding childhood behavior problems. As normal developmental sequences and processes are increasingly elucidated, they are being brought to bear on identifying and explaining the growth of disordered development. The text reflects our interest in relating normal and disturbed growth.

Obvious throughout the book is the view that behavioral problems are the result of interactions among variables. With few if any exceptions, behavior stems from multiple influences and their continuous interactions. Biological structure and function, inheritance, cognition, social and emotional factors, family, social class, and culture can be expected to come into play.

Our third bias is toward empirical approaches and the theoretical frameworks that rely heavily on the scientific method. We believe that the complexity of human behavior calls for systematic conceptualization and observation, data collection, and hypothesis testing. The methods and results of research thus are critical components of virtually all chapters.

Problems of the young are intricately tied to broad social, cultural, and ethical issues. Many of these are addressed, including the ethics of treatment, the use of medications in treating children, educational mainstreaming, and the impact of television, parental divorce, and chronic disease. Discussions of such topics often make clear the importance of research in informing social and ethical choices.

The text is not formally broken into sections, but it will be apparent that the first five chapters present broad underpinnings of the field: historical context, developmental context, theoretical perspectives, research methodology, and classification/diagnosis. All of these chapters draw heavily on the psychological literature, but they also show the multidisciplinary nature of the study of childhood problems. We assume that most readers will have some background in psychology, but we have also made an effort to serve those who may have relatively limited background and experience.

Chapters 6 through 14 discuss specific behavior disorders: phobias, depression, conduct problems, attention deficit-hyperactivity, learning disabilities, and autism, to name a few. Definition and description, prevalence, causal hypotheses, identification, and treatment are discussed in detail. The chapters are similar but not identical in organization. Chapter variations reflect what is currently of most interest and what is best established. Chapter 15, the closing chapter, focuses on concerns for children, including the enormous need for prevention of behavior disorders.

We extend sincere thanks to several individuals who helped in various ways in this project: Jed Baker, Donna Crane, Irene Farruggio, Michael O'Neill, Debra Salzman, Elana Zimand. The staff of the Vining Library of West Virginia Institute of Technology lent a willing hand. And particular thanks to Sara and Daniel for their patience, cooperation, and delay of gratification.

Finally, we note that the order of authorship of our work was originally decided by a flip of the coin to reflect our equal contributions. In this edition too have we shared equally.

Rita Wicks-Nelson   *Allen C. Israel*

1

INTRODUCTION

This book is written for all those concerned with behavioral or psychological problems displayed by the young. Disordered behavior attracts attention because it is often atypical, strange, or annoying. We may react to it with confusion, embarrassment, fear, repulsion, or sadness. And we may be motivated to change it because it does not easily fit into the fabric of social life. For the most part, though, the desire to understand and treat childhood problems is fueled by the belief that all children should have the opportunity for ideal growth and fulfillment.

Central to the concern about disordered behavior is the question of its origins and maintenance. Why is a child excessively shy, fearful, or aggressive? Why do some youngsters have difficulty in developing the usual patterns of eating and sleeping? What processes underlie intellectual deficiencies, severe social isolation, and self-mutilation? When we ask these questions, we raise the fundamental issues of how people develop and how normal development goes awry.

Much progress is now being made in describing normal development and in understanding the processes that bring it about. This knowledge serves as a guide to identifying, describing, treating, and preventing behaviors that fall short of normative standards. Conversely, the study of disordered behavior increases our understanding of normal development. Interest in problem behavior and development thus go hand in hand.

DEFINING DISORDERED BEHAVIOR

There is no concise and simple way to define and identify disordered functioning. Behavioral repertoires come in endless varieties. Box 1.1 provides actual examples of a few kinds of problem behaviors observed in children. We will examine many more throughout this book, and also see that behavioral disorders are evaluated and treated from several perspectives.

Frequently problem behavior is viewed

BOX 1.1 The faces of problem behaviors

The boy, who was born with two extra chromosomes, was a happy baby who was somewhat slow in walking and did not speak until age four. In nursery school he was easily victimized by other children. Throughout childhood he was fearful, had a short attention span and low tolerance for frustration, and did not want to attend school. By adolescence he was acting antisocial: He set fires and stole. He also displayed some bizarre behaviors, such as putting on many layers of clothing and smearing his mother's clothes with catsup and mayonnaise. (From Mansheim, 1979, pp. 366–67)

Karen was a nine-year-old girl with a history of refusal to eat solid foods. Six weeks earlier, she had choked on a piece of popcorn, with coughing and gagging. From then on, she had refused to eat solid foods and had lost about 15 pounds. Karen had also developed multiple fears concerning choking. She refused to brush her teeth for fear a bristle would come out and choke her. She slept propped on pillows for fear a loose tooth would come out and that she would choke and suffocate. She was afraid to go to sleep and wanted to sleep with her mother because of her fears. She also had nightmares and vivid dreams of choking. (From Chatoor, Conley, and Dickson, 1988, p. 106)

Five-year-old Kraig had a history of dressing in girls' clothes since age two. At that time, he also began to play with cosmetics. He continually displayed feminine mannerisms, gestures, and gait. He was unable and unwilling to play the rough-and-tumble games played by boys in the neighborhood. In fact, he preferred to play with girls, and when playing house with the girls, wanted to play the part of "mother." Kraig was excessively dependent on his mother, and he could manipulate her in ways that satisfied his feminine interests. For example, he would "help" her by carrying her purse. Kraig rigidly insisted on being like a girl and he refused to engage in masculine-like activities. (From Rekers and Lovaas, 1974, p. 174)

as "abnormal." *Ab* means "away," or "from," while *normal* refers to the average or standard. Thus, *abnormal* simply means something that deviates from the average, but common usage also assumes that the deviation is negative or pathological. Psychological or behavioral problems are therefore often referred to as *psychopathology*. Unfortunately, the terms *abnormal* and *psychopathology* are often associated with the idea that problem behavior is caused by disease or other biological factors. We make no such assumption in this book, since the causes of problem behavior are complex, include psychosocial factors, and usually cannot be traced directly to biological factors.

Regardless of terminology, judgments are always required to determine whether or not behavior is "abnormal." We must establish some behavioral standard, and decide whether the behavior of interest does or does not meet the standard in quality or quantity. Of course, dramatic differences are easy to identify. Most of us would agree that individuals who cannot learn to speak or to feed and dress themselves are "abnormal." Less dramatic instances are harder to judge. Children may display behaviors that are quite common and only slightly deviant—and yet appear maladaptive. In these instances parents, teachers, other adults, and occasionally children themselves, rely on numerous criteria to make the judgment that "something is wrong."

Sociocultural Norms

The role of *sociocultural norms*, perhaps the broadest criterion for judging behavior, was tellingly discussed many years ago by the anthropologist Ruth Benedict. After studying widely diverse cultures, Benedict (1934b) proposed that each society selects certain behaviors that are of value to it and socializes its members to act accordingly. Individuals who do not display these behaviors, for whatever reasons, are considered deviant by the society. Deviance is always relative to cultural norms. Benedict noted, for example, that the suspiciousness typically exhibited in one Melanesian culture would be considered pathological in our society. The Melanesians would not leave their cooking pots for fear of the food being poisoned by others (Benedict, 1934a). Further, Melanesians who displayed the helpfulness, kindness, and cheerfulness that is viewed as positive in our society were considered abnormal in their culture.

Cultural norms are applied to children as well as to adults. Youngsters in the United States are expected to be assertive and aggressive, unlike children in some other parts of the world. Thus, we might tolerate higher levels of aggression before we judge such behavior as problematic. We also might be relatively more likely to express concern about the quiet, passive child. Similarly, in technologically advanced societies that value certain intellectual skills special concern would be voiced about the child who does not measure up to these standards of intellectual development.

A study by Weisz et al. (1988) showed that culture might influence the degree to which adults view childhood problems as serious. Adults in the United States and Thailand read descriptions of problems relating to children and then answered questions about them. As Figure 1–1 shows, the Thai adults were clearly less worried than the U.S. adults. This finding appears consistent with the tenets of Thai Buddhism, which teaches that every condition changes and that behavior does not reflect enduring personality.

In a society as complex as that of the United States, *subcultural* norms are also found. Consider, for example, a study that compared two groups of New York City families: well-educated, middle-class families and working class Puerto Rican families (Korn and Gannon, 1983). For their five-year-old sons, the middle-class families reported two-and-one-half times as many problems as the Puerto Rican families. The families set different behavioral standards,

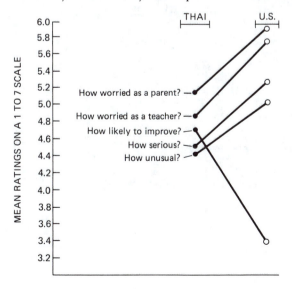

FIGURE 1–1 Thai and U.S. adults' rating of concern about childhood behavior problems. Weisz et al., 1988. Copyright 1988 by the American Psychological Association.

The behavior that is expected of or considered appropriate for a child varies across cultures. (Laima Druskis) (Michael Heron)

and the middle-class families were more psychologically oriented. The kind of problems reported also differed in the two groups of families, and they seemed related to subcultural values and child management. For example, many more middle-class than Puerto Rican families set a standard bedtime and did not allow their children to take a bottle to bed with them. They also reported more sleep problems. In contrast, Puerto Rican families placed high value on "good" behavior, disciplined their children more severely, and reported more discipline problems.

Sociocultural norms also depend on other variables. One of these is the social setting. Energetic running may be quite acceptable on the playground, but would create havoc in the classroom or a dental office. Singing aloud might well be tolerated at home, but rarely allowed in the library. Children are expected to act in certain ways in certain situations—in short, to meet *situational* norms.

Norms are also specified according to *gender*. In most societies males are expected to be relatively more aggressive, dominant, active, and adventurous; females to be more passive, dependent, quiet, and sensitive (Bem 1985; D'Andrade, 1966). These sex stereotypes strongly guide judgments about normality. We would probably be less inclined to worry about the hypersensitive, shy girl and the excessively dominant boy than about their opposite-sex counterparts.

Finally, it must be noted that sociocultural norms may change over time, due to broad societal changes or changes in ideas about mental health. For example, in the 1800s childhood disturbances could be attributed to "masturbatory insanity," but that label no longer exists (Rie, 1971). And nail biting, once seen as a sign of degeneration, is considered quite harmless today (Kanner, 1960, cited by Anthony, 1970).

Developmental Age Norms

Because children change rapidly, their functioning cannot be adequately assessed without developmental norms. The typical rates and sequences of the growth of skills, knowledge, and social-emotional behavior serve as developmental standards to evaluate the possibility that "something is wrong." Adults would be mistaken to worry about the one-year-old who is not yet walking, because many children of this age do not walk. However, if the same child is unable to sit alone, concern would be appropriate, because virtually all babies can sit up before their first birthday.

It is not only failure to initially reach developmental age norms that identifies psychopathology. Children sometimes "act their age" but then fail to progress. For example, temper tantrums in a three-year-old would less likely be labeled a problem than tantrums in a seven-year-old. Children may also reach age norms and then seem to regress.

When age norms are used, caution is appropriate. Adults tend to believe that every child should meet at least the average standards. But when an average is calculated, individuals fall on both sides of it, and a range of values must be considered. Table 1–1 demonstrates this point by showing the range of ages at which certain percentages of children successfully perform three different behaviors. For example, 50 percent of the children assessed used two-word sentences by 20.6 months, but 30 months was the time required for 95 percent of them to do so.

TABLE 1–1 Months at Which Children Perform Certain Behaviors

	5%	50%	95%
Sits alone steadily	5.0	6.6	9.0
Repeats performance laughed at	8.0	10.8	17.0
Sentence of two words	16.0	20.6	30.0

Adapted and reproduced by permission from the Bayley Scales of Infant Development Manual. Copyright © 1969 by the Psychological Corporation. All rights reserved.

Other Developmental Criteria

Several other factors may be considered in evaluating children's behaviors. Behavior that meets age norms may still be judged as disturbed if it occurs too frequently or infrequently, is too intense or insufficiently intense, or endures over too long or too short a period of time. It is not unusual for a child to display fear, for example, but fearfulness may be a problem if it occurs in an excessive number of situations, is extremely intense, and does not weaken over time. Concern might also be expressed for the child whose reactions change, such as when a friendly, outgoing girl turns shy and solitary. Adults are rightly concerned too when a child displays several questionnable behaviors or seems troubled by several things.

More rarely, children exhibit behaviors that appear qualitatively different from the norm (Wenar, 1982). For example, most children become socially responsive to their caretakers soon after birth, but children diagnosed as autistic display unresponsive behaviors.

The Role of Others

Finally, the subjective feelings of others play a role in identifying problem behaviors. The labeling of a problem is likely to occur when others are disturbed, for example, when a sibling complains of being physically attacked or when a teacher is made uncomfortable by a child's social withdrawal. Because childhood disorders are often identified by adults, adult attitudes, sensitivity, tolerance, and ability to cope are bound to influence how children are perceived and treated.

In fact, several research studies show the influence of various factors on parental identification of childhood problems and referral to clinics (McMahon and Forehand, 1988). There is limited evidence that first-born and only children are more readily identified as having problems than other children (Jensen et al., 1990). This issue of adult attitudes was also examined in a study that distinguished two groups among children referred to a clinic for acting-out problems (Rickard et al., 1981). Group 1 showed more actual acting-out behaviors than non-clinic children. Group 2 did not. What further differentiated the groups was parental depression. The parents of group 1 children were not depressed, while those of group 2 children exhibited depression. This suggests that parental depression, rather than children's actual behavior, had led to clinic referral for group 2 children. Yet another investigation indicated that parents who abused their children tended to overestimate problem behaviors emitted by the offspring (Reid, Kavanagh, and Baldwin, 1987).

In summary, then, we can see that defining and identifying behavior or psychological disorders is a complex matter that depends on many factors. Disordered behavior is not an entity carried around in the child. It is best thought of as a judgment about the child's behavior based on society's values, the social context, and an understanding of how most children develop.

HOW COMMON ARE CHILDHOOD DISORDERS?

A frequent question about childhood disorders is: How common are they? *Prevalence* is determined by counting the number of children with a disorder at any one time. It is expressed as the number of such children in the population, or as a percentage (for example, there are 2,000 children suffering from the disorder or 1 percent of all children). *Incidence* is determined by counting the number of new cases within a specific time period. There is good reason for wanting to determine prevalence and incidence: Both suggest the extent to which prevention, treatment, and research are needed. However, they must be considered cautiously.

If one wanted to determine the presence of childhood disorders in a population, it would seem reasonable to survey children's mental health setting—clinics, residential homes, hospitals, private professional offices, and the like. This tactic is often taken. But mental health services may not be sought due to denial, neglect, shame, fear, stigma, or how well certain behaviors are tolerated by adults. On the other hand, increased interest in a disorder—sometimes with media publicity—can result in its being overreported. Another serious matter is that diagnostic categories are not always used in a consistent manner: One mental health worker may diagnose a child as hyperactive and another diagnose the same child as learning disabled. Such unreliability casts doubt on the frequency of specific disorders.

A second way in which the extent of problem behaviors can be determined is by examining all children in a geographic area, or a representative sample of the area. Such *epidemiologic* studies can be extremely useful as they often collect other information that sheds light on the disorders (Richardson and Koller, 1985). Nevertheless, studies differ in the populations examined, quality of sampling, measures, and criteria for disorders. They often rely on adult reports rather than observations of children. Unsurprisingly, the results vary a good deal (Vikan,

1985), so it is difficult to draw general conclusions. The extensive Isle of Wight study indicated that 6.8 percent of 10- to 11-year-olds was reported as needing clinical services (Rutter, 1989b; Rutter, Tizard, and Whitmore, 1970). From a review of studies, Cotler (1986) estimated that in middle childhood about 7 percent of all children show severe to moderate disorders and about 15 percent show mild behavioral problems. Another review reported 14 to 20 percent as an estimate of moderate to severe disorders in children and adolescents (Brandenburg, Friedman, and Silver, 1990).

Population studies also reveal that many children show specific, less severe behaviors that may or may not be considered signs of disturbance. In one of the earliest systematic investigations, almost 500 mothers of a sample of all 6- to 12-year-olds in Buffalo, New York, evaluated their children's behavior in detail (Lapouse and Monk, 1958). They reported among other things that 49 percent of their offspring were overactive, 48 percent lost their tempers twice weekly, and 28 percent experienced nightmares. Recent studies from various countries confirm that such behavioral problems are commonly reported (Cotler, 1986). Problems that are isolated or are only moderately disruptive, or those that spontaneously decrease or disappear, are viewed as transient developmental crises that may or may not require professional consultation. An important task for researchers is to understand better when behavior problems will be transient crises and when they will persist or predict later disturbance (Campbell, 1987).

Sex Differences

A common finding about disorders that are severe enough to be clinically reported is that many occur more frequently in boys than in girls. These include severe mental dysfunctions, hyperactivity, bed wetting, antisocial behavior, and learning difficulties (Eme, 1979; Rutter, 1986a). When prevalence is greater in girls, the problems tend

to involve shyness, fear, and other emotions (Rutter and Gould, 1985).

Sex differences can be attributed to several factors. In general, boys appear to be more biologically vulnerable than girls: They have higher death rates from the moment of conception and seem more affected by major diseases, malnutrition, and poverty (Birns, 1976; Eme, 1979). Some vulnerabilities may stem from the Y chromosome carried by males, others to the male child's being relatively less physically mature (Rutter, 1986a).

Social factors undoubtedly play a role in creating sex differences in prevalence. Boys, more than girls, are adversely affected by family discord, divorce, mental illness and job stress (Zaslow and Hayes, 1986). Parents are more likely to argue in front of boys; they also respond more negatively to boys' oppositional reactions to stress than to girls' emotional reactions to stress (Rutter, 1986a). Sex role socialization may encourage aggression in boys and anxiety in girls.

The picture is even more complex because adults seem to report proportionately more male deviance. They expect misbehavior in boys and are less tolerant of male hyperactivity, disruption, and lack of persistence (Chess and Thomas, 1972; Huston, 1983; Serbin and O'Leary, 1975). Of course, adult tolerance may be lower for boys because males are more difficult to handle from early life. It is possible, then, that biological endowment interacts with socialization and social expectation to create a vicious cycle for the male child (cf. Earls and Jung, 1987; Jensen et al., 1990).

Age of Onset

Investigations into the prevalence of disorders indicate a general trend for behavioral disorders to decrease throughout childhood. But disorders can arise at almost any age and increase and decrease in frequency across age (Kashani et al., 1989; Rutter and Gould, 1985).

A relationship exists between age of onset and certain disorders (Rutter and Gould, 1985). Developmental delays in language and speech are usually seen early in life when children are first acquiring these skills. Deficiencies in attention are typically diagnosed when children begin school. Emotional disorders, such as fears and anxieties, arise at all ages, but their exact nature varies with age. Aggression, noncompliance, stealing, and the like can also arise at any age. Depression and drug abuse often first occur with the approach of adolescence, but they are seen earlier.

The link between age of onset and certain dysfunctions is not coincidental, of course. Chronological age is correlated with chil-

dren's developmental level. In turn, developmental level makes some behavioral problems more or less likely than others. For example, the cognitive and emotional levels of four-year-olds make it unlikely that preschoolers experience the thoughts and feelings that are labeled depression.

The age at which disorders seem to arise may sometimes actually be the ages at which disorders are first noticed or identified. Systematic environmental demands play a role here. A clear example concerns mental retardation, which is defined as children's intellectual functioning being below that of their age-mates. Although mental retardation is identified throughout childhood, it is especially identified when children begin school (Cytryn and Lourie, 1980). The demands of the classroom—and school policy to evaluate intellectual performance—filter out children who previously appeared to function adequately in their home environments.

SOME HISTORICAL INFLUENCES

Humans have long speculated on behavioral dysfunction, but early efforts focused primarily on adults. The first recordings of specific childhood problems appeared in the

early 1800s (Rie, 1971). By the end of the century a few attempts had been made to classify childhood disorders and causes had been proposed. Mental retardation received the most attention, but psychoses, aggression, hyperactivity, and "masturbatory insanity" had all been noted.

Several developments then radically altered views of children, how their development might go awry, and how they might be treated. We will now look at these major developments, many of which will be discussed further in later chapters.

The Influence of Sigmund Freud

Prior to the twentieth century most theories of disordered behavior emphasized biological causes or etiologies. Freud's work helped change this (Chess, 1988).

As a young neurologist, Freud collaborated with others, especially Joseph Breuer, who believed that certain disorders could be caused by psychological events. Freud was particularly interested in the fact that psychological experiences in childhood appeared connected to later symptoms such as paralysis and blindness for which no physical cause was evident. These problems seemed to be alleviated when the patient was able to talk emotionally about earlier experiences. Such observations set Freud on a lifelong course to construct a grand theory of development and a treatment method for disordered behavior.

Based on his study of adults, Freud was convinced that childhood psychological conflicts were the key to understanding behavior. He also hypothesized that all children pass through the same developmental stages that he associated with later behavior. In *Three Essays on the Theory of Sexuality*, published in 1905, and in his 1909 lectures at Clark University in Massachusetts, Freud introduced his radical ideas about the importance of childhood (Evans and Koelsch, 1985; Rie, 1971). His views were controversial from the start, but they came to provide a systematic framework for conceptualizing both childhood and adult behavior.

By the 1930s, Freud's ideas had been widely interpreted by Melanie Klein, Erik Erikson, Heinz Hartmann, and others. Freud's daughter, Anna, elaborated on his ideas and applied them especially to children (Fine, 1985). These efforts helped establish psychiatry as a major discipline in the study and treatment of childhood disorders. In 1935 Leo Kanner published the first child psychiatry text in the United States.

Behaviorism and Social Learning Theory

While Freud was stirring up the academic world with his innovative ideas, a school of psychology that would rival Freud's ideas (Sears, 1975) was being introduced in the United States. Behaviorism was launched by John B. Watson's essay *Psychology As a Behaviorist Views It* (1913). Unlike Freud, Watson placed little value on describing developmental stages and on early psychological conflicts. Instead, he drew on theories of learning to emphasize that most behavior originates through learning processes. Watson thought that people's behavior, whether good or bad, could be explained by learning experiences. He stated enthusiastically:

Give me a dozen healthy infants, well-formed, and my own specified world to bring them up in and I'll guarantee to take any one at random and train him to become any type of specialist I might select—doctor, lawyer, merchant, chief and yes, even beggar-man and thief, regardless of his talents, penchants, tendencies, abilities, vocations, and race of his ancestors. (Watson, 1924, reprinted 1963, p. 104)

E. L. Thorndike (1905) also made an early contribution to behaviorism by formulating the *Law of Effect*. Simply put, this law states that behavior is shaped by its consequences. If the consequence is satisfying, the behavior will be stregthened in the future; if the consequence is discomforting, the behavior will be weakened. Thorndike considered the Law of Effect a fundamental principle of learning and teaching; later researchers substantiated his claim. Of special note is B. F. Skinner, who wrote widely on the application of behavioral consequences to the shaping of behavior (Skinner, 1948, 1953, 1968).

Behaviorism thrived in the United States during the first half of this century. Its impact on childhood psychopathology came gradually as Mowrer, Bijou, Baer, Bandura, and others applied learning principles to children's behavior. Their work focused on different aspects of learning, but they all emphasized the importance of the social context. Their approach is thus often described as the social learning perspective. When applied explicitly to the assessment and treatment of behavior problems, it is called behavior modification or behavior therapy.

The Mental Hygiene and Child Guidance Movements

Despite the interest in adult psychopathology by the early twentieth century, much remained to be learned, and treatment often consisted of custodial hospital care. The mental hygiene movement in the United States aimed to increase understanding, improve treatment, and prevent disorders from occurring at all.

In 1908 Clifford Beers wrote an autobiographical account, *A Mind That Found Itself*, telling of the insensitive and ineffective treatment he had received as a mental patient. Beers proposed reform and obtained support from renowned professionals, including Adolf Meyer. Recognizing both psychological and biological causes of behavior disorders, Meyer believed that disorders stemmed from failure to adapt, and he proposed a "commonsense" approach to studying the patient's environment and to counseling. He set the course for a new professional role—psychiatric social worker (Achenbach, 1974).

Beers' efforts also led to the establishment of the National Committee for Mental Hygiene to study mental dysfunctions, support treatment, and encourage prevention. Because childhood experiences were viewed as influencing adult mental health, children became the focus of study and guidance (Rie, 1971).

By 1896, Lightner Witmer, at the University of Pennsylvania, had already set up the first child psychology clinic in the United States (McReynolds, 1987; Ross, 1972). This clinic primarily assessed and treated children who had learning difficulties. Witmer also founded the journal *Psychological Clinic* and began a hospital school for long-term observation of children. He related psychology to education, sociology, and other disciplines.

An interdisciplinary approach was also taken by psychiatrist William Healy and psychologist Grace Fernald in Chicago in 1909, when they founded the Juvenile Psychopathic Institute. The focus of the Institute was delinquent children, and its approach became the model for child guidance. Healy was convinced that antisocial behavior could be treated by psychological means, by helping youngsters adjust to the circumstances in which they lived (Santostefano, 1978). This required understanding the whole personality and the multiple causes of behavior. Freudian theory provided the central ideas for dealing with psychological conflicts, and attempts were made to gather information about family and other important relationships (Santostefano, 1978; Strean, 1970). The psychiatrist, psychologist, and social worker formed a collaborative team that met to discuss cases.

Healy and his wife, psychologist Augusta Bronner, continued to use this approach when they opened the Judge Baker Guidance Center in Boston. The National Committee for Mental Hygiene subsequently established several other child clinics, adopt-

Both Sigmund Freud (center) and his daughter Anna Freud (foreground) were influential in the development of the psychodynamic conceptualizations of childhood disorders. (AP/Wide World Photos)

John B. Watson was a highly influential figure in the application of the behavioral perspective. (The Bettmann Archive)

ing the same approach. The cases now also included personality and emotional problems. These clinics flourished in the 1920s and 1930s.

In 1924 the child guidance movement was formally represented by the formation of the American Orthopsychiatric Association, with Healy as its first president and Bronner as its second. To this day the association includes a variety of professionals concerned about children.

The Scientific Study of the Child

It was also during the early twentieth century that the systematic study of children became widespread. A central figure in this endeavor was G. Stanley Hall. Like many others of this period, Hall knew little about children's development so he collected questionnaire data about fears, dreams, preferences, play, and the like (Grinder, 1967; Sears, 1975). He wrote extensively and trained students who later became leaders in child study. As president of Clark University, Hall invited Freud to lecture in 1909. He also helped establish the American Psychological Association, and was its first president.

At about the same time, an important event occurred in Europe: Alfred Binet and Theophil Simon were asked to design a test to identify children who were in need of special education (Tuddenham, 1963). They presented children of various ages with different tasks and problems, thereby establishing age-norms by which intellectual performance could be evaluated. The 1905 Binet-Simon test became the basis for the development of intelligence tests. It also encouraged professionals to search for ways to measure other psychological attributes.

Another outstanding figure was Arnold Gesell, who observed children's motor and social behavior at Yale University. Gesell relied heavily on photography, using hundreds of thousands of feet of film to examine the actions of infants and children (Knobloch and Pasamanick, 1974). The organizing concept of his work was *maturation*, the intrinsic unfolding of development relatively independent of environmental influences. Gesell charted normal maturational sequences and deviations from them; today his followers still study and diagnose developmental deviations.

Beginning around 1920 child study began to benefit from several longitudinal research projects that evaluated children as they developed over many years. Research centers existed at the Universities of Michigan, California, Colorado, Minnesota, Ohio, and Washington; the Fels Research Institute; Columbia Teachers College; Johns Hopkins University; and the Iowa Child Welfare Station. A body of knowledge about normal development that was eventually applied to the study of childhood disorders began to accumulate.

Today the study and treatment of childhood disorders consist of multidisciplinary and diverse efforts. The events described above remain influential, some more than others. Many new influences are also evident. Research into all areas of child development has reached new heights of sophistication and complexity and is being brought to bear on the questions of abnormality. Of special influence are a renewed interest in human cognition, emphasis on the social context, advances in the biological sciences, and a joining of developmental psychology, child clinical psychology, child psychiatry, and child medicine (pediatrics). These influences and others bring new excitement and innovation.

CHILDREN AS SPECIAL CLIENTS

The Interdisciplinary Approach

Notable among professionals who work to ameliorate childhood behavioral problems are psychologists, psychiatrists, social workers, and special education teachers.

Most psychologists working with childhood behavior problems have specialized in clinical psychology. Others may have specialized in developmental, school, or educational psychology. They usually hold the doctoral degree (Ph.D. or Psy.D.), which demands four to five years of university graduate study. Psychology has sturdy roots in the laboratory and an interest in both normal and abnormal behavior. Training in

psychology thus includes psychological research as well as direct contact with troubled individuals. Many psychologists have a strong background in assessing behavior by psychological testing.

Psychiatrists, on the other hand, hold the doctorate in medicine (M.D.); they are physicians who have specialized in the care of the mentally disturbed. Psychiatrists make a unique contribution to childhood psychopathology by conducting medical evaluations and prescribing medication when appropriate.

Social workers generally hold the Mas-

TABLE 1–2 Some Early Historical Landmarks

1896	The first child clinic in the U.S. was established at the University of Pennsylvania by Lightner Witmer.
1905	Alfred Binet and Theophil Simon developed the first intelligence tests to identify feebleminded children.
1905	Sigmund Freud's *Three Essays on the Theory of Sexuality* described a startlingly different view of childhood development.
1908	In *A Mind That Found Itself,* Clifford Beers recounted his mental breakdown and advocated an enlightened view of mental disorders, initiating the mental hygiene and child guidance movements.
1909	G. Stanley Hall invited Sigmund Freud to Clark University to lecture on psychoanalysis.
1909	William Healy and Grace Fernald established the Juvenile Psychopathic Institute in Chicago, which would become the model for the child guidance clinics.
1911	The Yale Clinic of Child Development was established for child development research under the guidance of Arnold Gesell.
1913	John B. Watson introduced behaviorism in his essay *Psychology as a Behaviorist Views It.*
1917	William Healy and Augusta Bronner established the Judge Baker Guidance Center in Boston.
1922	The National Committee on Mental Hygiene and the Commonwealth Fund initiated a demonstration program of child guidance clinics.
1924	The American Orthopsychiatric Association was established.
1928–1929	Longitudinal studies of child development began at Berkeley and Fels Research Institute.
1935	Leo Kanner authored *Child Psychiatry,* the first child psychiatry text published in the U.S.

ter's degree in social work. Like psychologists and psychiatrists, they may counsel and conduct therapy, but historically their special focus has been working with the family and other social systems in which children are enmeshed.

Special education teachers, who usually have obtained the Master's degree, emphasize the importance of providing needy children with optimal educational experiences. They are able to plan and implement individualized educational programs, thus contributing to the treatment of many disorders.

Troubled children also come to the attention of nurses, general physicians, teachers in regular classrooms, and professionals in the legal system. Thus, interdisciplinary consultation commonly occurs and often is ideal. A good amount of coordination is necessary if this approach is to be effective. Who functions as the coordinator may depend on the type of disorder, the developmental level of the child, the first point of professional contact, and the treatment setting.

Working with Parents

Dealing with childhood disorders frequently demands working closely with parents, who vary greatly in their motivation and capacity to participate.

Parents seek help for their children for many reasons. Of course, most are truly concerned about the child's welfare. They may also want to alleviate their worries and conflicts with the child. Or they may be referred by schools or the courts to have

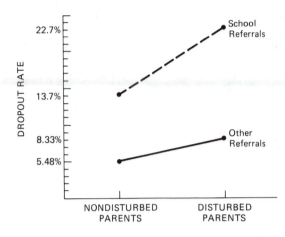

FIGURE 1-2 Dropout rate after initial screening at a child psychiatry clinic. From M. S. Gould, D. Shaffer, & D. Kaplan, The characteristics of dropouts from a child psychiatric clinic, Journal of the American Academy of Child Psychiatry, 24(3), 316–328, 1985, © by Am. Acad. of Child & Adolescent Psychiatry.

the child evaluated, sometimes against their own wishes. All these factors can influence motivation for treatment. So too may other variables, such as family stress and parental dysfunction. For example, Figure 1–2 shows that dropping out of treatment in one psychiatric center was related to both the referral source and parental dysfunction (Gould, Shaffer, and Kaplan, 1985). The dropout rate was especially high for families that had both disturbed parents and school referrals.

As therapy proceeds, parents vary in the ability to understand, support, and carry out recommendations. Some parents fear that they will be blamed for their child's problems (Kraemer, 1987), which may lead to defensiveness. Some have inappropriate goals; for example, authoritarian parents may desire the child to be excessively obedient. Parents can resent professional suggestions, be overly dependent, or expect therapists to "fix up" the child without their involvement. But parental involvement, including that of fathers, is often critical (Webster-Stratton, 1985b). Indeed, parents may provide a unique perspective that would otherwise be missed by the professional (e. g., Deaton, 1985). Thus, the competent and sensitive professional works toward optimizing the quality of parental participation.

Working with and for the Child

Direct interaction with the young is both rewarding and demanding. Since children may be incapable of identifying problems and seeking treatment, they often enter treatment at the suggestion or coercion of adults. Professionals must be sensitive to the child's perspective and create and maintain the child's motivation.

They must also pay special attention to the child's developmental level. Chronological age is a rough indicator of developmental level, but actual measurement of functioning is desirable. Such knowledge can be helpful in judging the significance of problems. Understanding a child's de-

velopmental competencies and failures also provides guidelines for treatment (Campbell, 1989). An example concerns training children to control their own behavior by giving themselves verbal directions. Impulsive children may be taught problem-solving steps and encouraged to say the steps to themselves. But developmental status influences the success of this method: Children under age six may not be capable of performing this task.

Finally, children's rights must be recognized and protected (Rekers, 1984; Erlen, 1987). To the extent that they are able, children have a right to participate in decisions about the goals of treatment and to understand how the goals will be attempted. Moreover, mental health workers often face tough questions concerning social values.

A clear demonstration of the complexities that can arise in working with children was described by Rekers and Lovaas (1974). When the parents of Kraig (described in Box 1.1) sought professional help, Rekers and Lovaas constructed a therapy plan involving social reinforcement for masculine mannerisms, activities, and interests. They justified the intervention on the grounds that the parents had requested help, that Kraig was being socially rejected, and that without treatment Kraig was at risk for developing gender disorders later in life. Not all professionals agreed with the ethics of this position. Some argued that a diversity of behaviors is valuable and that sex stereotypes are questionable guides for behavior (Nordyke et al. 1977; Wolfe, 1979). Others felt that greater attention should have been given to Kraig's involvement in treatment decisions (Ollendick and Cerny, 1981).

While ethical dilemmas regarding behavioral disorders are common, they are of special concern when children are involved. Judgments about social values are often central to these dilemmas, and children are limited in speaking for themselves.

SUMMARY

Childhood behavioral disturbance often elicits emotional reactions as well as motivations in others to help children reach their potential. Central to questions about psychopathology are basic issues of how people develop and how normal development goes awry.

The identification of behavior disorders rests on several criteria, including sociocultural and developmental norms. Because children's problems are commonly identified by parents and other adults, the attitudes, sensitivities, and tolerance of adults are important in determining whether or not a child is labeled as having a problem.

The occurrence of childhood disorders (that is, prevalence and incidence) is assessed by surveying mental health settings or the general population of children. Each method has weaknesses.

Behaviors that are frequently viewed as signs of disturbances are actually quite prevalent in the general child population. It is important to understand when these disturbances are transient developmental crises and when they may persist or predict future problems.

Many disorders occur more frequently in boys than in girls, but girls show a higher occurrence of emotional difficulties. Gender differences may be determined by biological or environmental factors or their interaction.

Interest in childhood disorders evolved gradually. Several historical influences became important early in this century: Freud's work, the rise of behaviorism/social learning theories, the mental hygiene and child guidance movements, and a dramatic increase in child study. These events brought new knowledge and conceptualizations of childhood and childhood disorders. Today, many new influences are evident.

Professional care of children is interdisciplinary, involving psychologists, psychiatrists, social workers, education specialists, and others.

Children's care requires special consideration of their motivation for treatment and level of development. Parental participation is important and parents' needs, motivations, and abilities cannot be ignored. Working with the child client also raises special ethical dilemmas. Professionals must protect the child's rights because children are often limited in advocating for themselves.

2

THE DEVELOPMENTAL CONTEXT

Among the most exciting current happenings in the study of childhood disorders is the coming together of developmental psychology and clinical child psychology/psychiatry. Only since the 1970s has this meeting been meaningful enough to warrant recognition and a new label—developmental psychopathology (Cicchetti, 1984, 1989). Developmental psychopathology is the study of disordered behavior within the context of biological, cognitive, socioemotional, and any other ongoing developmental influences (Rolf and Read, 1984). Thus, it attempts to integrate findings from diverse fields of study. It is interested not only in the origins and developmental course of disordered behavior (Sroufe, 1986), but also in individual adaptation and success.

The developmental approach makes several specific contributions to the study of childhood problems. Perhaps the most obvious is that descriptions of the usual course of growth provide a standard by which abnormality can be judged and conceptualized. Research findings and developmental theories offer hypotheses, too, as to how change occurs and thus how it might go awry. Since no one theory is likely to account for the numerous changes that take place during early life, diverse explanations should be considered. The study of development also examines specific issues, such as the stability of behavior over time, that may be critical for understanding, treating, and preventing childhood disorders.

WHAT IS DEVELOPMENT?

If we were to ask strangers passing on the street to define the term development, many would surely offer "growth" as a synonym. And most would note that development requires time. These are sound ideas. Development does indeed include growth, and it occurs over time. For example, children gradually become physically larger and display a larger number of social responses.

But childhood development also implies direction—a change toward greater complexity and organization. Within a relatively short period of time, the fertilized egg typically becomes the infant who smiles, crawls, and says "da-da," then the preschooler who relates to friends and speaks in complex ways and otherwise acts socially "grown-up." These changes proceed in an orderly fashion, with early structures and competencies laying the groundwork for later, more advanced ones.

Although the direction and orderliness of development are widely agreed upon, the way in which change occurs is debated. For example, some theorists view development as occurring in qualitatively different steps or stages that appear in the same order in all normal children. Others believe that development is best described as a very gradual process of change in which stages cannot be identified. Despite such divergent opinions, many theorists accept the following as guiding principles (Cicchetti and Schneider-Rosen, 1986; Santostefano, 1978; Sroufe and Rutter, 1984).

1. There is a common general course of development of the physical, cognitive, and social-emotional systems in all individuals. Within each system early global behaviors become more finely differentiated, and then integrated. Integration occurs across systems as well.
2. Development proceeds in a coherent pattern; that is, for each individual earlier development is systematically and logically linked to later development. Present behaviors are thus viewed as connected to the past as well as to the future, although this path might be complex and indirect.
3. New and higher modes of functioning, as well as new goals, are attained, and older forms of behavior may also remain available. Thus, development brings higher order functioning and flexibility.
4. The meaning of behavior must be interpreted according to the individual's developmental level. (For example, crying in public is different for four-year-olds than it is for ten-year-olds.)
5. The meaning of behavior must also be interpreted according to the psychological context. Similar behaviors can have quite different meanings; for example, crying can indicate sadness or happiness. And dissimilar behaviors can be equivalent; for example, scowling and social withdrawal appear very different in form but both may express anger.
6. Development results from transactions—ongoing interactions—among biological, psychological, and sociocultural variables.

Later in this chapter we will apply some of these principles to dysfunctional behavior. First, normal development will be overviewed. For readers already possessing knowledge about development, the overview serves as a reminder of the developmental context; for others, the overview provides important concepts and facts about children's growth.

AN OVERVIEW OF NORMAL DEVELOPMENT

Normal development encompasses a wide array of complex processes. Our purpose is thus a modest one: to survey aspects of development as a broad framework within which we can consider behavioral problems of the young.

The Genetic Context

Genetic contributions to behavioral development operate in complex ways, at both the species and individual levels. Through evolutionary processes all humans are biologically programmed to develop in certain ways and have certain characteristics in common. However, there is room for much individual variation.

That humans are biological beings is a truism, but only in this century have we come to understand basic biological processes. All body cells contain *chromosomes*, segments of which are called *genes*. Chromosomes are composed of deoxyribonucleic acid (DNA), the hereditary material, which directs development and cell activity. Most cells have 23 pairs of chromosomes. One pair, the sex chromosomes, differs in females and males: Females have two X chromosomes and males have an X and a Y chromosome. The Y chromosome has fewer genes and is smaller and lighter.

In contrast to other cells, the ovum and sperm (the gametes) undergo a special maturational process, *meiosis*, that results in each having only 23 single chromosomes, one from each of the original pairs. Thus, at conception each prospective parent contributes half of the chromosome complement to the offspring. Prospective mothers contribute an X chromosome, whereas prospective fathers can contribute either an X or a Y.

The processes of meiosis and conception assure billions of possible chromosome combinations for any one individual. Other genetic mechanisms result in even greater variability. Chromosomes may exchange genes, break and reattach to each other, and change by mutation, which is spontaneous alteration of the DNA molecule. Environmental interactions contribute further to produce an infinite variety of humans.

Hereditary influences on behavioral characteristics are often misunderstood, even today. In general, they are much more indirect and flexible than is often believed. Genes act indirectly by guiding the biochemistry of cells. They are best thought of as helping to set a range within which characteristics will develop. Characteristics for which genetic influence has been established can be altered to some degree by the environment. Many traits can be altered substantially; for example, height is genetically influenced but it is also affected by diet and disease. Furthermore, hereditary effects are often not set over time; in fact, genes program change as well as stability (Plomin and Thompson, 1988).

The Child as a Physical Being

Conception takes place in the Fallopian tube. Within a few days the zygote attaches itself to the wall of the uterus. The developing mass floats freely in the amniotic sac except for its attachment by the umbilical cord to the placenta of the prospective mother (Figure 2–1). If all goes uneventfully, birth occurs about 38 weeks after conception. These weeks of prenatal growth, or gestation, are crucial in that the organism can be dramatically affected by biological and environmental factors.

From the moment of conception, growth occurs in a quite predictable manner, following general principles. Growth takes place from the head to the tail regions (the cephalocaudal direction). Thus the head develops earliest, and at birth it is about one-fourth the total body length; by late adolescence this has changed to one-eight (Jones, Garrison, and Morgan, 1985). Growth also occurs from the center of the body to the extremities (the proximodistal direction). This is illustrated in prenatal development by the growth of the chest and trunk prior to the limbs, fingers, and toes.

Throughout life, different body parts develop at different rates. For example, the skeleton, muscles, and internal organs grow rapidly during infancy and early childhood, slow down in middle childhood, and then accelerate in adolescence. In contrast, the reproductive system develops slowly until adolescence, when it grows rapidly (Tanner, 1970).

The nervous system. The nervous system begins to develop shortly after conception when a group of cells called the neural plate thickens, folds inward, and forms the neural tube. This tube differentiates into the nervous system, and most brain cells are produced prenatally (Nowakowski, 1987). At birth the brain is about 25 percent of its

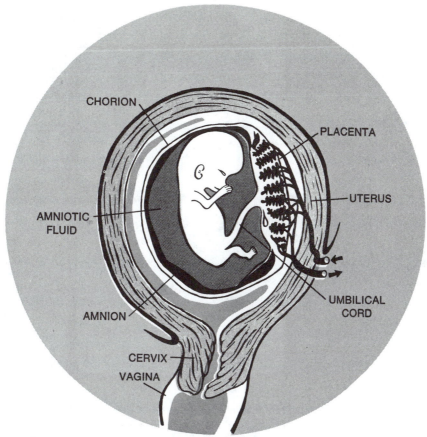

FIGURE 2–1 Schema of the developing child showing indirect contact with the mother's circulatory system.

adult weight, making it proportionately larger than most other organs (Tanner, 1978). (see figure 2-2.)

Further growth occurs after birth. By age five the brain reaches about 95 percent of its adult weight. Neurons (nerve cells) grow in size and in number of synaptic connections to other neurons. Myelin, a fatty cover, continues to be laid down on the axons of some neurons; it speeds up nerve transmission. Different parts of the nervous system develop in spurts more rapidly than others, and the pattern is related to functioning (Greenough, Black, and Wallace, 1987; Prechtl, 1981; Wolfe, 1981). For example, nerves that control reflexes are well developed at birth, but areas that control voluntary movement grow considerably during the first year or life and later.

Brain development depends on biological programming, but also on experience (Bertenthal and Campos, 1987; Greenough et al., 1987). Rats and other animals, for example, which have had opportunity to explore object-filled, enriched environments, develop more brain synapses than animals reared in simple environments. Experience may shape early nervous system growth not only by encouraging new cell connections but also by eliminating connections that are not useful to the organism.

Movement. Like physical growth, early motor development is quite predictable. In-

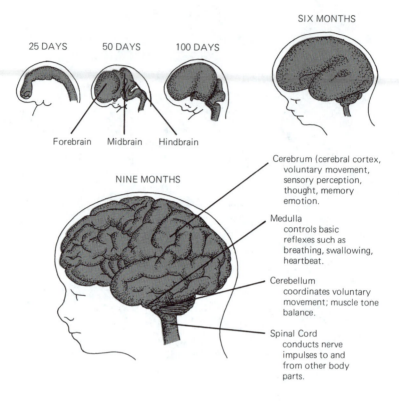

25 DAYS   50 DAYS   100 DAYS

SIX MONTHS

Forebrain   Midbrain   Hindbrain

NINE MONTHS

Cerebrum (cerebral cortex, voluntary movement, sensory perception, thought, memory emotion.

Medulla controls basic reflexes such as breathing, swallowing, heartbeat.

Cerebellum coordinates voluntary movement; muscle tone balance.

Spinal Cord conducts nerve impulses to and from other body parts.

FIGURE 2–2 Prenatal development of the brain, a side view. The brain originates at the head end of the neural tube. Adapted from The development of the brain, W. Maxwell Cowan. Copyright © (1979) by SCIENTIFIC AMERICAN, Inc. All rights reserved.

fants display many involuntary reflexes. Some are related to vital bodily functioning, such as the blinking and sucking reflexes. Others seem of little importance, but perhaps they played a role in human evolution. Many reflexes persist into adulthood, while others disappear early or are transformed into voluntary action (Capute et al., 1978; Thelen, 1986). The absence of reflexes at birth or their persistence beyond certain times are signs of nervous system dysfunctioning. Abnormal reflexes may thus give early warnings of developmental problems.

Movement develops in a particular sequence in children all over the world. It generally follows the head-to-tail principle; for example, babies gain control of their arms more quickly than their legs. Children also control the center of the body before the extremities, and large areas before small muscle groups. Thus, when they begin to use crayons they first use the entire arm and only gradually acquire hand control. Once control is gained over specific muscle groups, children begin to integrate many operations into complex movements. Table 2–1 shows the average age at which some of the basic motor milestones are achieved. As with reflexes, deviations from the timing and pattering of these milestones may indicate nervous system dysfunctioning.

Between the ages of 6 and 12 years, there is a noticeable increase in children's ability to jump rope, skate, climb, ride bicycles, and the like. Indeed, such skills often soon peak in the teen years.

TABLE 2–1 Some Early Gross Motor Milestones

Rolls over	2–4 months
Sits without support	5–7
Stands holding on to furniture	8–9
Creeps on hands and knees	9–10
Stands without support	10–13
Walks alone	11–14
Walks upstairs alone, two feet per step	21–25

On what does physical and motor development depend? Biological programming is suggested by the facts that growth follows a standard sequence and is similar for almost all children. Body shape, height, and weight are influenced by inheritance. And voluntary movement is based on certain muscles being biologically coordinated to work together as a self-correcting unit (Goldfield, 1989; Thelan, Skala, and Kelso, 1987). In fact, it is likely that children would sit, stand, use their hands, and walk even if the environment failed to encourage such behaviors.

Still, environmental effects are obvious. Children who consume excessive calories are likely to be overweight. And learning plays a role in complex movements: Most people can hop and skip but few are gymnastic whizzes. Observing others and practicing activities are important (Adams, 1984). So is feedback from others and from one's own body. Since using a sewing machine is not identical to running an electric saw, specific skills must be practiced. Children probably learn "motor programs"—mental representations of what acts follow other acts—and try to match these programs. Motor development thus has cognitive components (Pick, 1989). In general, the degree to which complex skills are acquired depends on hereditary tendencies, maturation level, motivation, and opportunities to learn and practice (Jones et al., 1985).

When motor development goes awry, the child may be considerably disadvantaged in manipulating and learning about the world. Physical handicaps also can lessen motivation for mastering the environment (Jennings, Connors, and Stegman, 1988). And slow motor development may influence how the child is perceived by others and the self.

Other aspects of physical growth, such as the timing of maturation and attractiveness, can affect psychosocial development (Carron and Bailey, 1974; Siegel, 1982). Overall, boys appear to benefit from early growth: They are rated as more popular, posed, and attractive than late maturers, who are seen as anxious and lacking in self-esteem. The picture is less clear for early maturing girls but may be somewhat negative: Some select older peers, tend to break social norms, and drop out of school (Magnusson, Stattin, and Allen, 1988).

Physically attractive people are viewed as smarter, more likeable, and good (Patzer and Burke, 1988; Stephan and Langlois, 1984). In contrast, physical abnormality is often avoided or reacted to with a mix of sympathy, contempt, and embarrassment. Individuals may be overly polite because they are unsure how to act with handicapped people. In turn, the handicapped may be further disadvantaged because they do not receive appropriate feedback about their behavior.

The Child as an Intellectual Being

The newborn may seem quite unaware of its surroundings and unable to profit from experience, but this is far from true.

Infants cannot report their experiences, but researchers are now able to determine exactly what they are looking at, whether their heart rates and muscle activity change in response to different odors, and the like. Such measures confirm that infants come into the world with considerable capacity to sense their surroundings. Seeing, hearing, smelling, tasting, and touching—all of which develop rapidly during the first years of life—are the sensory basis for experiencing the environment. When these are disturbed, children's abilities to function are interfered with. In the normal course of events, though, information is accurately

Practice plays an important role in the development of complex motor skills. A child's motor development is likely to impact on other areas of functioning and to influence the child's self-concept. (Ken Karp)

perceived and processed through learning and cognition.

Three basic learning processes are widely recognized: classical conditioning, operant learning, and observational learning. These processes operate soon after birth and become more complex as the higher mental processes develop. Memory, attention, mediation, imagery, and concept formation all enable children to better understand their environments. Learning and thinking will be discussed throughout this text. In this section, we present an overview of Piaget's theory and the growth of language.

Piaget's theory of cognition. Piaget was interested in both biology and epistemology, which is the philosophical study of how humans know the world. He worked with the young in hopes of better understanding cognition (Flavell, 1963; Petersen, 1982). Piaget began by studying his own children when they were infants. He eventually constructed a theory of cognition that became one of the most influential psychological theories of this century.

Piaget viewed the child as a biological organism that adapts to its environment by actively organizing and interpreting experiences. In so doing, the child's mind moves from quite simple mental structures, called *schemas*, to more sophisticated ones. Some experiences can be interpreted by already existing schemas; this is referred to as *assimilation*. But some new experiences also require *accommodation*, the modification and growth of schemas. Through these reciprocal functions the child develops increasingly advanced schemas of the world. Both maturation and experience are necessary for cognitive development.

Piaget hypothesized that cognitive growth occurs in four distinct periods or stages, roughly correlated with chronological age (Table 2–2). Consistent with all stage theories, it was assumed that the stages occur in a particular sequence and build on the preceding ones. At any one stage intelligence is qualitatively different than it is at any other stage. This has implications for how children might perceive the world at any particular stage, what they are prepared to learn, and how developmental problems might be interpreted.

Not all of Piaget's many specific propositions are supported, and Piaget seemed to

TABLE 2–2 Piaget's Stages of Cognitive Growth

Sensorimotor birth to 2 yrs.	World is first known through innate sensorimotor reflexes. Behavior becomes voluntary, refined, integrated, planful. Ability develops to mentally represent the world in images and words.
Preoperational 2 to 7 yrs.	Broadened view of the world is achieved as concepts of space, number, color, etc. develop. World is re-created in play. Children can deal with varied situations.
Concrete operational 7 to 11 yrs.	Ability develops to see the world from others' viewpoints. Ability develops to understand that processes can reverse, and that objects can change in form without change in mass (conservation of mass). Ability develops to simultaneously hold in mind several dimensions of a problem. There is increased understanding of relationships.
Formal operational 12 yrs. onward	Truly logical thinking appears: Child can better abstract, think about possibilities, form and evaluate hypotheses, deduce and induce principles.

have underestimated what children can do at certain ages. However, the theory has encouraged much research and has been fruitfully applied to understanding development.

Language and communication. The growth of language, a dramatic process by any standard, is closely linked to learning and cognition. Among the skills required are the abilities to distinguish, produce, and assign meanings to sounds; string sounds into words and words into grammatical sentences; and grasp the social context in which a message is being sent. Table 2–3 presents some of the widely recognized steps in early language acquisition. By age five, the major period of language growth is over (Nelson, 1981), but skills continue to be perfected for many years.

The processes that underlie the development of language are still hotly debated in spite of the fascination they have long held for philosophers and scientists. Perspectives range from an extreme focus on biological programming to a focus on environmental input (Whitehurst and Valdez-Menchaca, 1988). The biological system is obviously constructed so that language can be comprehended and expressed, but language development relies heavily on social input. Social stimulation facilitates early language acquisition, and the child's babbling and talking attract the attention of caretakers. Although language is clearly related to intellectual functioning, it is also a social activity, and communication skills are related to other social competencies and difficulties.

The Child as a Social and Emotional Being

Developmental theorists and researchers have much to say about the growth of the child as a social-emotional being. Our discussion highlights only three areas of continuing interest: temperament, emotional growth, and social relationships.

Temperament. The word *temperament* refers to basic disposition, makeup, or personality. The concept of temperament is an old one, certainly going back to the classical Greek era. The recent surge of interest in temperament can be traced to a longitudinal

TABLE 2–3   Early Acquisition of Language and Communication

	Reception	Expression
Birth to 6 months	Reacts to sudden noise Is quieted by a voice Locates sound Recognizes name and words like "bye-bye."	Cries Babbles, laughs Initiates vocal play Vocalizes to self Experiments with voice
6 to 12 months	Stops activity to *no* Raises arms to *come up* Obeys simple instructions Understands simple statements	Makes sounds of the culture's language Combines vowel sounds Imitates adult sounds Says first words
12 to 18 months	Carries out two consecutive commands Understands new words Listens to nursery rhymes	Uses ten words Requests by naming objects Connect sounds so that they flow like a sentence
18 to 24 months	Recognizes many sounds Understands action words like *show me*	Uses short sentences Uses pronouns Echoes last words of a rhyme
24 to 36 months	Follows commands using *in, on, under* Follows three verbal commands given in one utterance	Uses possessive, noun-verb combinations Mother understands 90% of communications
36 to 48 months	Increases understanding of others' messages and social context of communication	Uses increasingly complex language forms, such as conjunctions and auxiliary verbs

Based on Bryant, 1977; Whitehurst, 1982.

study of New York City children conducted by Chess and Thomas (1977; Thomas and Chess, 1984). These investigators were especially interested in explaining the development of problem behaviors. They recognized environmental influences on development, but were struck by the individual differences in how infants behaved from the first days of life. Based on parental interviews and actual observations, they found that young babies showed distinct individual differences in temperament, defined by nine categories of behavior (Table 2–4). They also found some stability of temperament over time.

Although other researchers have focused on slightly different behaviors, temperament is generally viewed as individual differences in emotional expression, motor activity, and sensitivity to stimulation (Bornstein, Gaughran, Homel, 1986). Most researchers believe that temperament is based

in the biological makeup of the person, is somewhat stable across time and situations, and provides a foundation for the developing personality (Goldsmith et al., 1987; Rothbart, 1986).

There is evidence for moderate hereditary influence on these characteristics (Buss and Plomin, 1986; Wilson and Matheny, 1986). For example, identical twins have more similar temperament than fraternal twins and tend to follow a more similar developmental path.

While twin studies suggest hereditary influence, they do not rule out environmental impact. The stability of temperament over time is only modest to moderate (Bates, 1987; Persson-Blennow and McNeil, 1988), and some of the instability is undoubtedly due to environmental influences. The infant's way of behaving apparently enters immediately into social interactions that, in turn, influence the general environment

TABLE 2–4 Thomas and Chess's Categories of Temperament

1. Activity level
2. Regularity of biological functioning (e.g., eating, sleeping)
3. Approach/withdrawal to new stimuli. Approach is positive, such as smiling. Withdrawal is negative, such as crying.
4. Adaptability to changing situations
5. Level of stimulation necessary to evoke a response
6. Intensity of reaction
7. Mood (e.g., pleasantness, friendliness)
8. Distractibility to extraneous stimuli
9. Attention span and persistence in an activity

and the child's behavioral tendencies. Thus, temperament can be expected to be transformed, and the child's changing characteristics continue to play a role in how the child develops.

Emotional growth. Emotional expression is a part of temperament, but it is worthwhile to ask further about the nature and growth of the emotions (e.g., Izard, 1986). Emotions consist of three components: outward expression, subjective feelings, and physiological changes such as in heart rate. Even very young infants show emotional expressions. Of course, it is impossible to know exactly what they are experiencing. Perhaps specific facial expressions are interpreted by the brain so that infants experience feelings that are akin to the pleasure, anger, and disgust felt by older people. But infant emotions can hardly be expected to be identical to later emotions, because emotional "feelings" depend on experiences in the world and cognitive ability to interpret these experiences.

Nevertheless, many emotions and their expression seem to be present in some form by the time children are two or three years of age. Toddlers also are well on the way to interpreting the emotional expressions of others; for example, in others' voices and faces (Campos et al., 1983; Nelson, 1987). By age five or six, the ability to express and interpret emotional cues becomes quite refined (Bullock and Russell, 1986). Humans are biologically prepared for such growth,

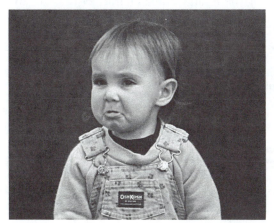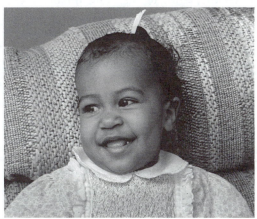

From their facial expressions, it appears that very young children experience basic emotions such as happiness and unhappiness. (Barbara Rios/Photo Researchers) (Jim Whitmer/Stock, Boston)

which is shaped by socialization through learning and cognition (Ekman and Friesen, 1975; Malatesta et al., 1986). The intensity and quality of the emotions enter into most childhood behavioral difficulties, either as a central factor (such as in extreme fears) or as a side effect (such as unhappiness resulting from academic failure).

Social relationships. Regardless of individual disposition, virtually all infants and their caretakers seem biologically prepared to interact in ways that foster their relationship. Most parents are remarkably adept in understanding their babies' signals and needs, and they optimize social interactions (Papousek and Papousek, 1983). Infants, in turn, are sensitive to parental emotional-social signals, so that early child-parent interactions flow like a dance or conversation, in which each partner's behaviors depend on and are coordinated with the other partner's behaviors (Elias, Hayes, and Broerse, 1988; Maccoby and Martin, 1983). Such interactions are the basis for the special social-emotional bond, called *attachment*, that becomes evident when the child is seven to nine months of age.

Early attachment is indicated by the child's staying close to the adult but feeling secure enough to explore the environment. Attachment is also indicated by being upset when the adult leaves. The quality of attachment varies, depending on several factors. Parental sensitivity, emotional intensity, and tender loving care are critical factors (Ainsworth et al., 1978; Belsky, Rovine, and Taylor, 1984). But infant temperament, and how it interacts with parental characteristics, may also play a role in determining attachment (Goldsmith, Bradshaw, and Reiser-Danner, 1986; Thompson, 1986; Thompson, Connell, and Bridges, 1988). The child who meets parental expectations, is easy to feed and otherwise care for, and readily smiles and vocalizes is likely to foster positive feelings and behaviors in the adult. The social context also matters; for example, attachment of stressed mothers and their temperamentally difficult babies is of higher quality when the mothers feel that they are receiving support from other adults (Crockenberg, 1988).

Until quite recently studies of attachment focused on the mother, since she is often the primary caretaker. However, children clearly become attached to fathers, grandparents, siblings, and others early in life. The child's social world rapidly encompasses ever broadening relationships and experiences.

Researchers and theorists continue to explore early attachment as a root of social development. They also continue to study how children develop gender role and become aggressive, kind, achievement oriented, self-disciplined, and impulsive. All of these, and other characteristics, are important in children's socioemotional development, and many will turn up in various discussions throughout this text.

The Social-Cultural Context

The sociocultural context of development includes the family, peers, the school, social class, and culture. It is within these domains that social as well as physical and intellectual attributes are shaped.

The family. In most, if not all societies, the family is considered central to the child's growth. Family influence begins immediately, appears especially strong and pervasive, and may endure over the lifetime. Parental influences on the child are obviously important, but the child impacts family members as well, and it is useful to look at the family as an interacting unit.

Important views of the family have been offered by psychoanalytic and social learning theories (Lynn, 1974; Rutter and Cox, 1985). Psychoanalytic theory views development as the result of the child's moving through psychosexual conflicts that are largely played out with the parents. Many of the specific hypotheses made by this theory have not been borne out (Rutter and Cox, 1985). Social learning theorists rely

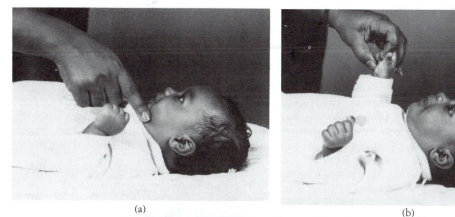

(a)   (b)

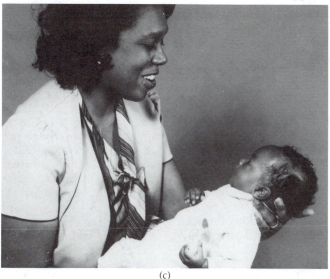

(c)

Many parents interact competently with their infants. Parents touch their infant to test the infant's condition (a) (b). They also hold the infant at the distance that maximizes visual fixation (c). (After Papousek and Papousek (1983). Courtesy A. Russell and R. Molla.)

heavily on learning principles to conceptualize family influence. Parents are seen as shaping their children's development through reinforcement and punishment and by serving as behavioral models. Children in turn are seen as shaping the behavior of their parents. The effects of these crucial processes depend at least in part on the child's cognitive level, expectations, and beliefs (Kagan, 1984).

FAMILY INTERACTIONS. Theories about the family have long offered "food for thought," but the last few decades have provided descriptions and analyses of specific family interactions.

Direct observations of parent-child pairs show that early interaction depends partly on the sex of the parent (Hodapp and Mueller, 1982). Fathers spend less time with their infants and provide less care (Belsky,

Gilstrap, and Rovine, 1984; Ninio and Rinott, 1988). They tend to engage in active, physical, individualistic play with the children. Mothers display more nurturance, vocalize more, emphasize intellectual stimulation, and play conventional games like pat-a-cake (Maccoby and Martin, 1983). Another difference, seen as time passes, is that fathers treat their children in more gender-stereotypic ways than do mothers; for example, they encourage gender-related play and more readily accept dependency in girls (Snow, Jacklin, and Maccoby, 1983).

Studies of how parents interact with their older children suggest the importance of parenting styles (Dubow, Heusmann, and Eron, 1987; Maccoby and Martin, 1983). Table 2–5 describes a view of parenting styles and the child characteristics thought to be associated with them. An additional aspect is the degree to which parents are involved with their children. Parents low in involvement give little time, attention, or emotional commitment to their offspring. High involvement includes many parental behaviors, some more beneficial than others. It is reasonable to assume that the optimal amount of involvement lessens as children become older. But some degree of parental involvement throughout children's lives seems to be associated with positive development.

Research shows that the nuclear family is a complex interacting system. The presence of a third family member changes social interaction between two other members. For example, mother-child interaction decreases when the father is present, and mothers give less attention to their firstborn children after another child arrives (Barnes, 1985; Clarke-Stewart, 1978; Stewart et al., 1987). Patterson's (1986) description of families of antisocial children indicates the complexity of family interaction in the genesis and maintenance of problem behavior.

FAMILY STRUCTURE AND ROLES. A quite recent change in family life is that most women, even mothers of young children, work outside the home. This has created interest in the possible effects of parental employment, which could influence parents' investment in their children, perceptions and expectations for children's behavior, and parenting styles (Greenberger and Goldberg, 1989). What does research tell us about the influence of maternal employment? Overall, effects depend on specific factors (Lerner and Galambos, 1986). These include maternal factors (e.g., mothers' attitudes), the work situation (e.g., prestige of the job), family factors (e.g., fathers' involvement), and child characteristics (e.g., temperament, age, gender). These variables can combine to foster or hinder optimal development. For example, positive outcomes are associated with less maternal stress, greater maternal acceptance of the dual role of mother and worker, and greater maternal satisfaction with the job (Gottfried and Gottfried, 1988).

TABLE 2–5 Patterns of Parental Behavior and Related Child Characteristics

Authoritarian: Parents set rules with little input from children and forbid children to challenge them. Rule deviation results in fairly severe punishment, often physical.	Children tend to withdraw and show little social interaction. They have low self-esteem, and lack spontaniety and internal locus of control.
Indulgent/permissive: Parents tolerate childrens' impulses, make few demands for mature behavior, use little punishment, allow children to regulate their own lives.	Children tend to be impulsive, aggressive, and lack independence and ability to take responsibility.
Authoritative: Parents expect mature behavior, set standards and enforce them, encourage children to express ideas, recognize both parental and children's rights, encourage independence and individuality.	Children tend to be independent, socially responsible, able to control aggression, self-confident and of high self-esteem.

Based on Maccoby and Martin, 1983.

When we consider family structure, we tend to think of the nuclear family of two parents and their offspring. But children in the United States experience divorce, and often live in step-families and other family arrangements. Almost 50 percent will spend part of their lives in a single-parent family (Rutter and Cox, 1985). In most cases the single parent is the mother. Children in these families are at some risk for developing intellectual, social, and emotional problems (Emery, 1982; Shinn, 1978; Wallerstein and Blakeslee, 1989). However, single-parent families vary a great deal—in what brought about the situation, material resources, child-rearing practices, age of the children, and the like. It is not the family structure itself that matters, but the way in which the family is able to function (Emery, Hetherington, and DiLalla, 1984).

Finally, it is important to consider the general finding that children living in the same family grow up to be quite different from each other, partly because their experiences are different (Plomin and Daniels, 1987). Many things make this so. Each child has a unique place and unique interactions in the family. Particular events, whether a divorce or change of residence, occur at a different age for each child. And each child probably has a unique perspective of family events and functioning. In addition, of course, young people are shaped by forces outside the family.

Peers. In all societies children are exposed to other young people and peer relationships contribute to development. Prior to preschool age, children begin to distinguish between what is "adult" and "child," and peer relationships grow in complexity and importance throughout childhood (Brownell, 1986; Hartup, 1983).

Relationships with peers differ qualitatively from those with adults, and they do not serve the exact same functions. This is an important area for further research, in part because some children show relatively strong preference for peers over adults (Harper and Huie, 1987). Moreover, with so many parents working outside the home,

children spend much time with peers in day care and the neighborhood.

Peers can influence each other in many ways. They provide opportunities for learning social skills, help set social values, serve as standards against which children judge themselves, and give or withhold emotional support. Peers reinforce behavior, serve as behavioral models, and enter into friendships and other social groups.

Some children are more accepted and popular with their peers than others. This favored position is related to their being socially competent, friendly, intelligent, and attractive (Hartup, 1983). On the other hand, rejection is related to aggression, noncompliance, snobbishness, and disruptive action. Poor peer relationships are linked to both childhood and later behavior problems in complex ways (Boivin and Begin, 1989; Parker and Asher, 1987). This does not mean that peer relationships directly cause behavioral problems, but unsatisfactory relationships, once began, can have a negative effect.

School. The primary function of the school is to teach intellectual skills and knowledge accumulated by society. Formal education is also charged with broader tasks of socialization (Busch-Rossnagel and Vance, 1982). Schools in the United States are expected to transmit social, moral, and political values consonant with democratic ideals. The messages given about these values can act powerfully on development. Further, schools operate as a social system in and of themselves. Classroom structure, pedagogy, rules, methods of discipline, standards, and expectations all play a role in shaping individual children.

Some schools are linked more strongly than others to student achievement. Of course, schools vary in the characteristics of the students who enter them, but this does not completely explain the school-achievement link (Wolkind and Rutter, 1985; Rutter, 1983a). Certain qualities of school climate and practice appear to foster scholastic and positive social behaviors. Among these are:

1. Organizational structures that encourage staff to work together on agreed upon goals and values
2. Goals that include the fostering of positive attitudes toward education, prosocial group behavior, social cohesiveness, and opportunities for all students
3. Pleasant working conditions
4. Positive teacher-student relationships, and teachers who model positive behaviors
5. Opportunities for students to act responsibly and to participate in the running of the school
6. Good discipline, with appropriate praise and encouragement and little use of punishment
7. Efficient instruction and clear feedback to students

Teachers' expectations for performance are also critical to the school environment. Expectations can rest on factors other than the child's achievement. For example, teachers have more negative perceptions of children of single parents than children from intact homes (Entwisle and Stevenson, 1987). They also have stereotypic gender expectations for students (Minuchin and Shapiro, 1983).

School experiences may influence children's futures by setting into motion particular events that continue the shaping process (Rutter, 1983a). By helping the child achieve academically, schools may open career doors. By instilling values, work habits, and self-esteem, schools may continue to impact learning and social development.

Social class and culture. Social class, or socioeconomic status (SES), is determined by factors such as family income, educational achievement, and occupational level, which correlate with each other. Virtually all societies are stratified according to social class, and social class is marked by differences in many facets of life—environmental conditions, social interactions, values, attitudes, expectations, and opportunities.

For example, there is evidence that economically insecure families believe that they have little control over their lives; they thus may socialize their children in ways that ensure job security, acceptance by others,

and sensitivity to being exploited by others (Kagan, 1984). Middle-class families seem to emphasize choice, intellectual challenges, and job status; they expect their children to have control over their lives and influence others. These differences may translate into how children are managed. In fact, child-rearing practices do vary by social class (Rutter and Cox, 1985). In general, lower SES parents tend to be more restrictive, use more physical punishment, anticipate less independence, and rear children to be more compliant.

The adverse influence of social class is especially notable in lower-class families. Children of poor families are more likely to die and to suffer from disease and disability. Figure 2–3 shows the death rate of infants under one year for the total U.S. population, and the white and black populations. The disadvantage of black people is due at least in part to their disproportionate rate of poverty. Birth weight—a factor in infant death, deformity, and later developmental problems—is directly related to social class. Poor maternal and medical care probably underlie this unfortunate association. Poverty also works against family stability and increases stress. Upon reaching school, children of poor families do less well, and as

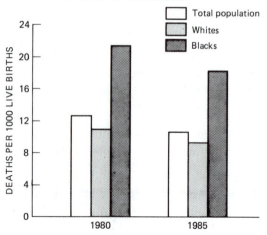

FIGURE 2–3 Death rate of infants under one year of age. *Statistical Abstract of the United States, 1988,* Bureau of the Census.

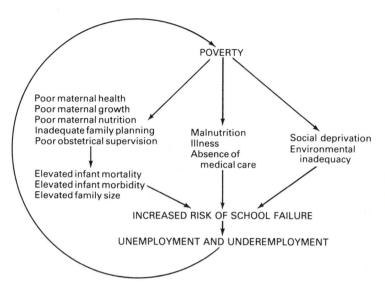

FIGURE 2–4 The cycle of poverty, school failure, and unemployment. Adapted from H. G. Birch and J. D. Gussow, Disadvantaged Children: Health, Nutrition and School Failure. New York: Grune & Stratton, 1970, by permission.

adults they acquire less desirable jobs and have higher rates of unemployment (Figure 2–4). This disadvantageous pattern often repeats itself over generations.

The influence of social class—and all the other social influences we have examined—operates within some broader cultural context. As we previously saw, a society's beliefs and values enter into judgments about normality and abnormality (p. 3–5). Culture also affects the goals toward which societies shape their children and how these goals are attained.

It is probably quite obvious that the several social influences we have examined are not independent of each other. Rather, they overlap and one social context impacts others (Bronfenbrenner, 1986). Children's social worlds are complex, dynamic, and challenging. Developmental psychologists believe it is important both to describe these worlds and to understand the processes that operate.

So far this chapter has offered descriptions and theories about normal growth and its implication for both childhood competencies and difficulties. Inherent in much of what has been said are several related issues that offer a framework for viewing childhood disorders. We now turn to these issues

HOW DEVELOPMENT OCCURS: THE TRANSACTIONAL MODEL

Today most developmentalists view growth as the result of ongoing interactions among biological, psychological, and sociocultural variables. This was not always the case.

Nature and Nurture

For many years a dichotomy was often made between biological and environmental determinants of development. Some argued that biological influences, especially genetic programming, primarily determined how children would "turn out." Others argued that environmental experiences and learning played the critical role in development.

Virtually all theorists now reject this dichotomy. They recognize biological programming for the entire human species, and genetic influence on individual differences in temperament, social behavior, and intelligence (Buss and Plomin, 1986; De-Fries, Plomin, and LaBuda, 1987). But they emphasize that biological influences continuously interact with other influences to produce development.

The environment plays a role in the development even of what is considered basic biological functioning. For example, we have seen that brain growth in rats is enhanced when they are exposed to enriched environments (p. 19). And the development of the visual system of cats is influenced by exposure to light, with biochemical events being involved (Aoki and Siekevitz, 1988). Thus, each individual "in spite of being formed by inexorable genetic processes, is also the unique product of experience" (p. 64).

An especially telling example of the interplay of biology and environment in humans is provided by studies of children who are born prematurely or suffer medical complications just before or after birth (Sameroff and Chandler, 1975; Greenberg and Crnic, 1988). These biological conditions may stem from genetic and/or environmental influences. Overall, the infants have more neurological and intellectual difficulties later in life than full-term infants. Still, many do well and it has been hard to predict outcome. It turns out that an important predictor is social class/home environment. For example, children living on the Hawaiian island of Kauai who suffered relatively severe birth complications and who were reared in middle-class families developed intellectually as well as children with no birth complications who lived in lower class homes (Werner, 1980). The effects of biological adversity depend on the quality of care children receive, which is related to family resources, parenting skills, and social support.

The many examples of biological-environmental interactions that now exist leave no doubt of the importance of research to help us better understand how genes and environment work together to produce development. (See Box 2.1.)

Conceptualizing Developmental Influences

An enormous number of variables obviously play a role in the transactional model of development. There is no one ideal way to conceptualize all of them. However, it is helpful to look at some of the ideas that address this issue. We will begin with an overall scheme to organize developmental variables and then examine a few specific points that are relevant to behavioral disorders.

Table 2–6 shows one way in which developmental factors can be organized. The table is based on the work of Gerrity, Jones, and Self (1983), who relied on Baltes and

TABLE 2–6 Examples of Normative Age-graded, Normative History-graded, and Nonnormative Influences on Development

Determinant	Normative Age-graded	Normative History-graded	Nonnormative
Biological	Puberty	War-time diet	Illness
Psychological	Parent-infant attachment	Consciousness raising in minority groups	Death of significant other
Sociocultural	School attendance	Availability of drugs for recreational use	Birth into upper social class

Adapted from K. M. Gerrity, F. A. Jones, & P. A. Self, Developmental psychology for the clinical child psychologist. In C. W. Walker & M. C. Roberts (Eds.), *Handbook of clinical child psychology*. Copyright © 1983, John Wiley & Sons, Inc.

BOX 2.1   How genetic and environmental influences are linked

It is one thing to cite examples of gene-environment interactions, but quite another to understand how genes and environmental influences might interact over the lifespan. Building on previous work, Scarr and McCartney (1983) argue that these influences are systematically linked from the first days of life. They suggest three on-going ways in which genetic endowment and the environment are related, and they label the relationships *passive*, *evocative*, and *active*.

1. Parents provide environments for their offspring. Their choice of environments is due partly to their own genetic disposition, half of which each shares with the offspring. For example, parents who are genetically predisposed toward particular intellectual abilities may provide their children with books and otherwise expose them to intellectually stimulating environments. In this way, children's genetic endowments are linked to their environments from the beginning of life. Since no action is required by the child, the relationship is called *passive*.

2. Children's characteristics, which are partly determined by genes, *evoke* reactions in others. In our example, adults may react to a

child in a particular way due to the child's easily mastering certain intellectual tasks. Thus, the child's genetic disposition is tied to the child's environment.

3. As children mature, they *actively select* their own environments. Selection is partly based on the child's genetic disposition. The intellectually talented child may choose to spend time in libraries and museums, enhancing the genetic disposition for intellectual ability. Or, perhaps because the child does not like being called an "egghead," he or she may deliberately avoid intellectual settings and thus work against genetic endowment. In either case, genetic endowment and the selected environmental niche are systematically linked.

Scarr and McCartney also propose that the importance of these three processes changes over the lifespan. Parental influence lessens and the child's active niche building becomes stronger. Thus, children increasingly shape their own development, based on both their genes and experiences. This interesting proposal has received both support and criticism, and is stimulating research.

Riegel's work. The developmental determinants are three-fold. Biological determinants include species-wide and individual genetic influences and ways in which the individual's physical being is otherwise affected. Psychological determinants are mental processes and behaviors. Sociocultural determinants are environmental variables embedded in the social and cultural context.

These determinants are interwoven across the lifespan. Some are related to the age of the developing person: They are age graded. Others are related to the historical time in which the person is living: They are

history graded. Both age- and history-graded determinants can affect virtually all individuals, and are thus called normative. But other determinants, although not unusual, may occur only to certain individuals, at unpredictable times and circumstances, and are thus called nonnormative. They are the chance events that affect development. The table gives examples of these several kinds of determinants (the content of some will vary across cultures). In considering the determinants within a transactional model, multiple interacting factors are seen as the causes of any developmental outcome.

Permissive and Efficient Causes of Behavior Problems

The transactional view applies, of course, to maladaptive as well as adaptive outcomes. As Cicchetti and Schneider-Rosen (1986)

note, causation of problem behaviors cannot be reduced to a single cause. They discuss causes as either permissive or efficient. *Per-*

missive causes are dispositions toward certain behaviors. *Efficient* causes bring these dispositions to realization. Take the example of Down's Syndrome, which in most cases requires that the child have a particular chromosome abnormality. This abnormality is a strong pemissive cause, and the child has Down's Syndrome. Nevertheless, even in this extreme case, the *specific* developmental outcome will depend somewhat on factors that realize the condition (efficient causes), many of which will probably be social and psychological, such as the quality of care the child receives.

It is easy to think about biological factors as permissive causes, but it is not necessarily the nature of the variables that determines their function. A variable may be permissive or efficient, depending on the situation.

To take a complex instance, the causes of depression may include biological, psychological, and sociocultural variables. In some cases, a genetic biological factor may act as a permissive cause by predisposing the child to depression; depression may then be realized by an immediate psychological event, such as the death of a friend. The psychological event is the efficient cause. In other cases, the permissive cause may be psychological, such as a pattern of thinking negative thoughts; depression may then occur due to an immediate social event and/or biochemical changes (the efficient cause). It is thus clear that the variations of causation require careful analysis. To add to the complexity, causative factors—and whether they are permissive or efficient—may vary according to the individual's developmental level.

Moreover, there may be causes in which no factor is clearly permissive. Here, different influences may add or multiply and reach a threshold to produce an adverse outcome. In any event, a permissive-efficient analysis provides a framework for thinking about causation. Such an analysis often makes its way into explanations of disordered behavior.

The Timing of Experience

It is widely held that the timing of experience is important in development. There are several reasons for this (Rutter, 1989c). How the nervous system is affected by experience depends on the developmental status of the system; for example, the effects of damage to the brain can vary with the age of the person. The effects of experience also depend on the psychological processes that emerge at different times. Thus, children's being separated from their parents is probably less impactful at five months of age than at three years, because attachment is not yet formed at five months. Timing may also be important in that events occurring at nonnormative times (for example, late physical maturation or teenage marriage) can result in heightened stress or altered opportunities.

Developmentalists have been especially interested in the influence of *early* experience on the origin of behavior problems. This interest derives in part from animal research showing that early exposure to temperature changes, electric shock, and enriched environments impact brain and behavioral developmental (Denenberg, 1987; Thompson and Grusec, 1970). In addition, theoretical propositions have been put forth as to why early experience might crucially influence human growth. For example, Freud (1949) regarded the infant's love for its mother as the prototype for all later love relationships, and thus crucial for social-personality development. Social learning theorists suggested that early learning might be especially important simply because it is the basis for later learning.

The extreme position about early experience argues that the first few years of life are critical in that they *set* much later development. The more moderate and popular view asserts that early life may be a sensitive period, but that no experience sets

BOX 2.2   The importance of early relationships

Interest in early experience is reflected in several lines of research. One is the infant-child attachment that occurs almost universally when infants are about seven to nine months of age. Some infants appear *securely attached*. When tested with a laboratory procedure called the Strange Situation, they seek contact with the parent, explore the environment, become upset when the parent leaves, and react positively when the parent returns. Other infants are *insecurely attached*; they avoid or act ambiguously toward the returning parent when observed in the Strange Situation.

Researchers have tested the hypothesis that the secure-insecure quality of attachment is related to later behavior. In general, insecurely attached infants show less peer competence, self-reliance, control, flexibility, and other adaptive behaviors when they reach the toddler and preschool years (Lewis et al., 1984; Sroufe, 1979; Sroufe and Fleeson, 1986). This association suggests but does not prove that early insecure attachment causes later maladaptive behavior (p. 74). If causation is involved, it likely occurs through a chain of influences. Importantly, the link between early attachment and later behavior is not always present.

Another line of research examining early relationships has looked at children who were reared in orphanages or who were severely abused by being isolated in closets, poorly fed, and the like (Hodges and Tizard, 1989a, b; Skuse, 1984). The specific experiences of these children varied a great deal, and so did the outcomes. Among the negative outcomes were deficits in intelligence, language, and motor and social behaviors. Still, many of the children, when placed in better environments, developed reasonably well.

The Hodges and Tizard (1989a, b) study is an example of this. They followed the growth of children who were placed in residential homes in England at less than four months of age. The homes were of high quality in many ways, but there was little opportunity to form continuous relationships with caretakers. Between the ages of two to seven years, most of the children were adopted or restored to their families. Evaluations were conducted when the children were about 4, 8, and 16 years old. No differences in intelligence existed between the children and a comparison group of children who had lived continuously with their families. But about half of the ex-institutionalized children were more sensitive to adult approval and more likely to have difficulties in peer relationships. A particularly interesting finding was that the quality of family attachments and relationships depended on the family setting: Adoptive families were no different than comparison families but restored families showed difficulties. Thus, less than optimal early rearing in residential homes was associated with both normal and problem development. Moreover, outcome depended on several variables, including the quality of the new environment. This finding is consistent with results from other studies (Rutter, 1989c). Along with the research on security of attachment, it argues that early experience is certainly important but does not set development on an inevitable path.

---

an irretrievable path through life (e.g., Ramey and Campbell, 1987; Rutter and Garmezy, 1983). Humans are malleable, most developmental outcomes are determined by many variables, and later experience can often moderate what has gone before (see Box 2.2). This is not to say, of course, that effort should not be made to provide children with optimal early environments.

Direct and Indirect Effects

In addition to examining the nature and timing of developmental influences, it is fruitful to recognize that effects may be direct or indirect. When a direct effect is operating, variable X leads to outcome Y straight-on. Indirect effects are operating when X influences one or more variables, which eventually leads to Y. It is usually more difficult to establish indirect effects because a pathway of influence must be traced. The pathway may be complex and involve interacting variables.

From all that has been said about the elaborate influences on development, it is not surprising that much is yet to be learned about the causes of disordered behavior.

BEHAVIOR DISORDERS: RISK, VULNERABILITY, PROTECTION

There is enormous interest today in understanding the factors that make it more or less likely that a child will develop disordered behavior. Clearly, such information might increase knowledge about etiology and could be valuable in preventing problems.

In examining this issue, researchers have focused on risk, vulnerability, and protective factors. These terms are sometimes used in slightly different ways. For our purposes, *risk* factors are variables that increase the chance of behavior problems. *Vulnerability* factors intensify the effects of risk. *Protective* factors, often referred to as resiliencies, lessen or ameliorate the effects of risk. How a factor is conceptualized depends on its potential influence and also on where in the chain of events it occurs.

For example, a child's difficult temperament may interact with parental behaviors in ways that produce negative child-parent interactions, which in turn produce poor developmental outcomes. In this case, difficult temperament is functioning as a risk factor. In other circumstances, difficult termperament may act as a vunerability factor. In families at risk due to divorce, children's temperament may interact with parental problems and stress to produce childhood behavior disturbance. In this example, family divorce is the risk factor and temperament is the vulnerability factor that increases the negative effects of divorce (e.g., Hetherington, 1989). Easy child temperament, on the other hand, might be a protective factor in that it might diminish the negative effects of divorce on the child.

Risk Factors

Given that variables can function in different ways, what puts a child at risk for behavior disorders in general, or for a particular disorder? Models of development and psychopathology provide hypotheses about risk factors. So also do astute observations and research with children who do and do not develop problems. Table 2–7 lists factors that are proving fruitful in conceptualizing risk. To some extent all have been implicated in childhood behavior disturbance.

Risk factors may be viewed as having two aspects (Garmezy, 1975; Sameroff, 1987).

One is life events that in some way bring stress to the child. The other is individual disposition to respond maladaptively to life experiences. Disposition may arise through genetic or other biological mechanisms, and also through past experiences. In either case, it is important to consider several points made by researchers (Kopp, 1983; Lambert, 1988; Rutter, 1987).

1. Some risk factors are more influential than others, depending on the disorder involved. For example, genetic and prenatal factors are relatively strong factors in severe mental retardation.

TABLE 2–7 Some Factors That May Increase Risk of Behavior Disorders

Hereditary influences; gene abnormalities
Prenatal influences
Birth defects, complications, prematurity
Postnatal disease and damage, especially to the nervous system
Inadequate nutrition
Poverty
Detrimental early social experiences
Family psychopathology, stress, negative interactions
Child abuse, neglect
Poor peer relationships
Behavioral/psychological patterns (e.g., low self-esteem, depressive thinking, difficult temperament)
Specific stress (e.g., loss of a parent)

2. Children are perhaps more vulnerable to risk factors at certain times in development. And perhaps at any one time they are more affected by some factors than others.

3. Risk factors may work together. Their influence may add, multiply, or otherwise work in complex ways to produce stronger impact.

4. Risk may accumulate over development, so it may be helpful to think in terms of pathways of risk. The pathways may be different for different outcomes, even within a specific disorder. For example, for children displaying hyperactivity, biological/disposition factors may be more involved in behavioral outcomes while family factors may be more involved in educational outcomes (Lambert, 1988).

Vulnerability and Protection

Fascination with why some individuals succumb to risks while others overcome them is not new, but systematic research on the topic is a relatively recent happening. It has taken time and effort for researchers to establish that organisms react differently to apparently similar risk events, and that vulnerability/protection is also related to characteristics of the psychosocial environment (Anthony, 1987). In animal research, for example, the lethal effects of certain poisons on laboratory rats are smaller when the animals are grouped rather than isolated. In humans, self-understanding and the ability to think and act independently appear to protect adolescents from the negative effects of their parents being psychiatrically disturbed (Beardslee and Podorefsky, 1988).

Many variables have been identified as making children more or less vulnerable to risk; they include age, temperament, gender, self-esteem, social comprehension, relationships with significant others, family cohesion and accord, and social networks that support the child and family (e.g., Anthony and Cohler, 1987; Garmezy, 1983; Rutter, 1983b, 1987).

Protection is often conceptualized as arising from the child's competence and adaptability. Garmezy (1975) suggests that competence is indicated by self-esteem, self-discipline, belief that events can be controlled, regulation of impulsive behavior, and ability to think abstractly and flexibly. Waters and Sroufe's (1983) view of competence is consistent with this. They see competence as the ability to (1) generate and coordinate flexible responses to demands and (2) generate and capitalize on environmental opportunities. They hypothesize that competence at one developmental period prepares the child to deal with later challenges and opportunities. Importantly, their definition emphasizes environmental interactions, so that competence depends in part on the environmental variables that children experience.

Rutter (1987) points out that protection may come about in various ways. As shown in Table 2–8, he describes four mechanisms that can operate at key turning points in people's lives to minimize or redirect the influence of risk factors. For Rutter, protection resides in the ways in which people deal with life changes and in what they do about their stressful or disadvantageous circumstances.

Continued research in this area is bound to lead to better knowledge of why and how

TABLE 2–8 Rutter's Description of Four Protective Mechanisms

Reduction of Risk Impact
  The impact of risk can be reduced by:
    providing the child with practice in coping
    reducing demands of the risk factor
    preparing the child for the situation
    exposing the child when he/she can cognitively handle the situation
    decreasing exposure to the risk factor

Reduction of Negative Chain Reactions
  Exposure to risk often sets up a chain of reactions that perpetuates risk effects into the future. Interventions
    that prevent such chains are protective.

Development of Self-esteem and Self-efficacy
  People's concepts and feelings about their social environments, their worth, and their ability to deal with life's
    challenges are important. Positive development results from satisfying social relationships and success in
    accomplishing tasks.

Opening of Opportunities
  Many events, particularly at turning points in people's lives, reduce risk by providing opportunities for adaptive
    growth. Examples are changes in geographic location, chance to continue one's education, shifts in family
    roles.

Adapted from Rutter, 1987.

vulnerable children succumb to risk in varying degrees while resilient children react in constructive ways—even in the face of seemingly overwhelming adversity. Even very young children begin to acquire skills to cope with stress (Band and Weisz, 1988), but little is known about the process. The answer to this riddle does not simply rest within the child, however; it lies in the child's interactions with the environment.

PREDICTING BEHAVIOR DISORDERS: CHANGE AND CONTINUITY

Central to any consideration of behavior disorders is the issue of change and continuity in development.

By definition change occurs in development, and humans certainly are malleable. But there are limits to malleability and so some continuity over time might be expected (Lerner, 1987). This is exemplified in physical aging. When a man reaches old age, his face appears both similar to and different from how it looked at age 10, 20 and 40. However, it may be quite difficult to describe specifically how the transformation occurred and to predict appearance at old age from appearance in youth.

Developmental psychologists have been interested in the possible links between early and later social, emotional, and intellectual behaviors. There is little doubt that both change and continuity can be anticipated as individuals travel along life's pathways. However, specific outcomes probably vary with the behavior being observed as well as other variables, such as gender and environmental demands for change or stability.

When this issue is applied to the study of behavior disorders, a central question is: Do children who display behavior problems still show them or other disturbances later in childhood or into adulthood? The question is important for understanding the development of behavior problems, and it also has implications for treatment and prevention. Childhood behavior problems are always of concern to the degree that they cause discomfort and unhappiness and close the door of opportunities for growth. But when they continue into adulthood in some fashion, they have even graver implications.

What then is known about the continuity of problem behavior? Although subsequent chapters detail the answer to this question, we now present an overview of the data and examine broad aspects of this matter.

It should first be noted, however, that it is difficult to trace the course of any disorder over time. At different developmental levels behaviors that appear quite different from each other may actually fall into the same class. For example, the five-year-old may demonstrate aggression by slapping a playmate, while the adolescent is more likely to use subtle sarcasm. Slapping and verbal abuse seem quite different but may represent the same class of behavior—aggression—whose form was transformed over time by socialization and developmental processes. In a similar vein, actions that seem to fall into different classes may actually serve the same function. For example, consider reactions to feelings of fear. A young child may act timid in a fearful situation but later, due to social experience, may try to overcome fear by behaving overly courageous or assertive. Timidity and extreme courageousness are dissimilar in form, but in this case are functionally equivalent. Would it be correct, then, to conclude that the child's fear had disappeared, or that it had merely taken another maladaptive form? Such issues make it difficult to analyze continuity of behavior.

Nevertheless, the evidence indicates that some behavior problems are quite transitory. The frequency of enuresis (bed wetting past four or five years of age) drops considerably after childhood. There is less evidence regarding signs of emotional disturbance, such as nail biting, nervousness, fears, and depression. Specific links to later emotional problems are not well established, but some linkages do exist (Hersov, 1985; Kohlberg, LaCrosse, and Ricks, 1972). Children who show hyperactivity tend to display academic and social deficits in adolescence and many display some continuation of mal-

adaptive behaviors into adulthood (e.g., Weiss and Hechtman, 1986). Childhood aggression and antisocial behavior are relatively stable over time into adulthood (McMahon and Forehand, 1988). And many severely disordered children (e.g., as in autism) clearly do not escape dysfunction later in life (Meisbov et al., 1989). Thus, both continuity and discontinuity of problem behaviors exist.

Researchers are interested in the factors and processes by which continuity may occur. Let us look at the study conducted by Caspi, Elder, and Bem (1987) in which the continuity of behavior of eight- to ten-year-olds was traced across 30 years. The behavior examined was an ill-tempered interactional style, represented in childhood by temper tantrums (biting, kicking, striking) and verbal explosions (swearing, screaming, shouting). For boys, an association was found between this behavior and adult undercontrol, moodiness, irritability, and lower dependability, production, and ambition. The men experienced erratic work patterns and downward occupational mobility and were likely to divorce. For girls, childhood tantrums were related to marriage to men of low occupational status, unhappy marriage and divorce, and ill temperedness as mothers.

The researchers suggest two processes by which maladaptive behavior is maintained over time. *Cumulative continuity* stems from children's channeling themselves into environments that perpetuate the maladaptive style. For example, the ill-tempered boy may limit opportunity by dropping out of school, thereby creating frustrating situations, to which he responds with more irritability, undercontrol, and the like. *Interactional continuity* originates in the transaction between the person and the environment. The person acts, others respond accordingly, and the person reacts to this. It is assumed that the coercive, ill-tempered style of the child pays off in the short run so that through reinforcement it is maintained, only to eventually be destructive. We note here that the processes suggested by Caspi et al. are similar to the active niche building and evocative processes described in Box 2.1. Caspi et al. make no explicit assumption that ill-temperedness has genetic origins, but both experiential and biological variables may well play a role in linking early and later behaviors.

Rutter (1985b), too, recognizes the processes of cumulative and interactional continuity. Further, he suggests that in some situations an acute event might have long-term consequences. For example, children's maladaptive reactions to the death of a parent might often be transient except that the event could lead to a new family structure or poor mental health of the surviving parent. It is these consequences of the acute event that may bring new overwhelming stress, and with it a continuance of maladaptive behavior.

Rutter's thinking about the processes that lead to the continuity of behavior disturbance provides a framework for thinking about protective mechanisms. As Table 2–8 indicates, many protective mechanisms would weaken the links between early dysfunctional responses to risk and later maladaptive behavior.

SUMMARY

The developmental approach to the study of childhood behavior disorders offers developmental hypotheses and a framework within which to understand children's problems. Development is the progressive, coherent process of growth that results in higher levels of functioning. It is the product of transactions among biological, psychological, and sociocultural variables.

The biological basis of development is the chromosomes, which direct the biochemistry of the body. Hereditary influence, which is complex and indirect, sets a range within which characteristics develop. It programs change as well as stability.

Physical and motor growth occur in an orderly sequence. The nervous system, which grows from the neural plate, is relatively well developed at birth; further development depends on both biological and environmental influences. Motor capacity changes from simple, reflexive to voluntary, coordinated functioning. Complex motor skills depend on hereditary tendencies, motivation, and opportunities to learn and practice. Motor development, the timing of maturation, and physical attractiveness can influence psychosocial growth.

At birth, children have the ability to perceive the environment and to learn. Learning and thinking develop gradually. Piaget's theory of cognitive development proposed that through assimilation and accommodation children develop increasingly sophisticated schemas of the world. Growth occurs in four distinct stages.

By age five, basic language skills are acquired. The capacity for language clearly is programmed into the human species; equally clear is that interaction with others shapes development. Language skill has implications for both intellectual and social functioning.

Among the many facets of socioemotional growth that researchers study are temperament and the emotions. Temperament refers to biologically based, modifiable individual differences in emotional expression, activity level, and sensitivity to stimulation. The rudiments of emotion are present from early life and by age five or six, children show considerable ability to interpret the emotions of others. Both temperament and the emotions play a role in social interaction and behavior problems.

Attachment, the early socioemotional bond between infants and their caretakers, has also been studied extensively. Parental sensitivity to the infant, infant temperament, and the social context influence attachment. From this first relationship, the child's social environment broadens to include an array of other relationships.

The social context for development consists of the family, peers, the school, social class, and culture. Family influence is considered especially powerful and family interaction is complex. Appropriate parental involvement and the authoritative parenting style may foster favorable outcome for children. Analyses of family life must consider current changes in family structures and roles. And it is important to recognize that children growing up in the same family are quite different from each other.

Peers influence each other in many ways. Some children are more readily accepted by their peers than others. Poor peer relationships are associated with childhood and later problem behaviors. Schools that foster positive academic and social behaviors appear to have certain characteristics. Children's development is influenced by the knowledge and skills they acquire, and also by the values, work habits, and self-concepts that schools might provide.

The impact of social class operates in part through family socialization practices that vary with social class. Low SES disadvantages children due to less than optimal health care, higher family stress, and lower school achievement. Whether social class or some other social influence is at issue, influence operates within a larger cultural context of values and structure. In fact, the social context of development is best viewed as several social influences that are interdependent.

The transactional model of development assumes that biological and environmental variables continuously interact to bring about development. There are clear examples of biological-environmental interactions. Scarr and McCartney (1983) have proposed a model of how genetic influence is linked to children's environments by three processes. One way to conceptualize developmental variables is to view them as bio-

logical, psychological, and sociocultural determinants that are interwoven. These determinants may be normative age-related or history-related or they may be nonnormative influences. With regard to the development of behavior problems, the concepts of permissive and efficient causation are useful.

Within the developmental approach to behavior disorders attention has been given to the timing of experience, especially to the effects of early social experience. Research indicates that positive attachments foster development but that human malleability makes it unlikely that early experience irretrievably sets development.

When analyzing developmental effects, it is also useful to recognize that influence may be direct or indirect, with indirect effects more difficult to establish.

There is increasing understanding of the factors that put children at risk for developing dysfunctional behavior. Vulnerability factors make it more probable that children will succumb to risk; protective factors make it less probable. Protection is often viewed in terms of the child's competence, family accord, and support from other social systems. Rutter (1987) suggests four protective mechanisms, that allow risk factors to be minimized or redirected to adaptive pathways.

The issue of change and continuity of behavior is a central concern of developmentalists. The task of tracing change over time is not easy, but it appears that both change and continuity occur in problem as well as adaptive behavior. Among the processes by which maladaptive behavior is maintained are cumulative and interactional continuity.

3

PERSPECTIVES AND MODES
OF TREATMENTS

In Chapter 2 we examined developmental processes and how the developmental view might help us understand behavior disorders of childhood. We now turn to perspectives, or paradigms, that have more traditionally been brought to bear on behavioral disorders. The biological, the psychodynamic, and the behavioral/social learning perspectives are three major viewpoints that have been used to understand aberrant behavior. This chapter also looks at some additional approaches. Before turning to particular viewpoints, however, let us look at the meaning of the terms *perspective* and *paradigm*.

TAKING DIFFERENT PERSPECTIVES

Much of what we now know about children's behavior problems comes from applying the objective methods of science. However, the writings of Thomas Kuhn (1962) and others have made us increasingly aware that science is not a completely objective endeavor. To understand this point it is best to remember that scientists, like other people, must think about and deal with a complex world. To do this they make assumptions and form concepts. When a set of assumptions is shared by a group of investigators, Kuhn refers to them as a paradigm. We employ the terms *perspective*, *paradigm*, and *view* interchangeably to refer to this percep-tual/cognitive "set" that the scientist takes in order to study and understand phenomena.

What are the implications of adopting a particular perspective? Perspectives help make sense out of a puzzling and complex universe. They enable us to view new information in the context of previous experience and to have a basis for reacting to it. Taking a perspective is thus adaptive and functional. At the same time, perspectives limit us as well. They guide us in "selecting" the issues chosen for investigation, but may preclude us from asking certain questions. Then, once a question is selected for investigation, a decision must be made: What will be observed in order to answer this question? All things are not observed, just some things. Perspectives influence this choice, and also how observations are done. In turn, particular methods and instruments help in detecting certain phenomena but result in our missing others. Once information is collected, the adoption of a paradigm affects the interpretations we make of the "facts". we have collected. Overall then, perspective-taking strongly organizes how a problem is approached, investigated, and interpreted.

THE BIOLOGICAL VIEW

In its most general form the biological or physiological, perspective holds that biology plays a central role in the development of behavioral disorders in children. The conjecture that psychopathology is due to a defective or malfunctioning biological system can be traced in the Western world to Greek culture. Hippocrates (460–370 B.C.), who is considered the father of medicine, was an advocate of somatogenesis ("soma" refers to body, "genesis" means origin). He postulated that proper mental functioning relied on a healthy brain and that deviant thinking or behavior was thus the result of brain pathology.

The physiological paradigm initially assumed that biology directly causes abnormal behavior. The original psychiatric classification system developed by Kraeplin in the late 1800s, and the forerunner of current systems, was clearly based on this assumption. Early discoveries of biological causes for particular behavioral problems (for example, the revelation that a spirochete caused syphilis and the mental deterioration of its late stages) led to the hope that similar causes would be found for all abnormal behavior. With limited exception, this has not proven to be the case.

Today a widely employed conceptualization of the role of biology is the notion of diathesis-stress—that a biological predisposition toward a disorder (a diathesis) interacts with environmental or life events (stress) to produce a particular behavioral problem. This is a variant of the more broadly conceived notion that biological factors transact with psychological and socio-cultural influences.

As we saw in Chapter 2, the influence of biological factors on a child's behavior can occur through a variety of mechanisms. Here we will examine three: genetic influences, biochemical malfunctioning, and structural damage or malfunction caused by disease or trauma.

Genetic Influences

The study of genetic influences on human behavior is extremely complex and currently expanding in several directions (Rutter et al., 1990a). Its application to childhood disorders is still comparatively underresearched, however. One likely reason for this is that for many practitioners heredity was not something that could be remediated. As evidence for the role of genetic factors in childhood disorders accumulates, however, it is clear that a fatalistic view of heredity is unwarranted. Treatments of inherited disorders are possible and knowledge about inheritance can be important for prevention (Waisbren et al., 1987). Furthermore, genetic research can tell us subtle things about etiology; for example, whether all or only some cases of a disorder are likely to have a genetic component. Genetic research can even confirm the role of environment in causation and point to characteristics of the environment that might be especially important (Plomin, 1989).

A complete discussion of genetic influence on childhood disorders is not possible here. The topics selected for examination are intended to introduce the reader to this area and to facilitate understanding of later discussions of the role of genetics in specific behavior disorders.

Inheritance through single genes. Beginning with the work of Gregor Mendel scientists have sought to describe the inheritance of certain characteristics controlled by one gene pair. Mendel correctly hypothesized that each parent carries two hereditary factors (later called genes), but passes on only one to the offspring. He also noted that one form of the factor is *dominant,* in that its transmission by either parent leads to the display of that form of the characteristic. The other form, the *recessive,* displays itself only when it is transmitted by both parents. Both of these patterns, and the sex-linked pattern described below, are involved in the inheritance of many human attributes and disorders.

Huntington's chorea is an example of a disease transmitted by a dominant gene. This disease causes death but does not show up until adulthood, when limb spasms, mental deterioration, and psychotic behavior become evident. Many people became aware of this inherited disease and its devasting deterioration due to the death of Woody Guthrie, a well-known folk singer and father of Arlo Guthrie.

The inheritance of Tay-Sachs disease provides an example of a disorder carried by one gene pair and transmitted recessively. Tay-Sachs is a degenerative disease of the nervous system that is evident very early in life. It results in progressive deterioration of mental abilities, motor capacities, and vision. No treatment exists, and death typically ensues by the age of one to three years. An estimated 60 to 90 percent of all cases of Tay-Sachs is found among children of Ashkenazic Jewish extraction.

The *sex-linked* pattern of inheritance involves genes on the sex chromosomes. Of special interest is the situation in which the relevant gene is recessive and carried on the X chromosome, such as in red-green color blindness, hemophilia, and Lesch-Nyhan Syndrome.

Lesch-Nyhan Syndrome is a rare, untreatable X-linked disorder that results in unusual motor development, mental retardation, and extreme self-mutilation in children (Rainer, 1985). Children suffering from the disorder compulsively and repetitively bite their lips, tongue, and fingers. The disorder is found only in males. Since the condition is so severe, causing death before adulthood, Lesch-Nyhan males do not have offspring. The Lesch-Nyhan child has a normal father and a mother who carries the disorder, having one normal X chromosome and one affected X chromosome. Sons received their only X chromosome from their mothers. Those who receive the recessive defective gene will develop the disorder, since the Y chromosome transmitted from the father carries no gene at all to offset the defective gene. Daughters receive one X chromosome from each parent. If a girl receives the defective recessive gene from her mother, it will be offset by the dominant normal gene from her father; she has no affliction herself but could carry Lesch-Nyhan to her son.

Researchers continue to explore the effects of single gene pairs or a small number of genes on specific behavior disorders. Indeed, such research has been greatly facilitated by the emergence of new methods of investigation. For example, advances in understanding Huntington's chorea have come about through what has been termed the "new genetics" (cf. McGuffin, 1987).

Linkage analysis is one such research development. It explores whether the pattern in which a specific disorder appears among family members is the same as for genetic markers. The approximate chromosome location is known for the genetic markers. For example, inherited disorders, such as color blindness, that are linked to a particular chromosome have been used as markers. If the behavior disorder and color blindness appear in family members in the same pattern then it can be presumed that they are close neighbors on the same chromosome. The problem is that there are few such markers. However, advances in molecular genetics such as recombinant DNA techniques have identified hundreds of genetic markers, called restriction fragment length polymorphisms and variable tandem repeats, for which chromosomal location is known. They can serve as genetic markers for linkage analysis in the same way as indicated for color blindness. In the future such advances may lead to many discoveries of single gene effects or instances in which disorders are due to a small number of genes.

Investigating the effects of multiple genes. In contrast to effects due to a single gene pair, most of the behaviors we are concerned with in studying childhood behavior disorders are thought to involve many genes as well as environmental influences.

. . . . genetic effects on behavior are polygenic and probabilistic, not single gene and deterministic. The characteristics in the pea plant that Mendel studied and a few diseases such as Huntington's disease and sickle-cell anemia are due to single genes that have their effects regardless of the environment or the genetic background of the individual. The complexity of behaviors studied by psychologists makes it unlikely that such a deterministic model and the reductionistic approach that it suggests will pay off. There is yet no firm evidence for a single-gene effect that accounts for a detectable amount of variation for any complex behavior. (Plomin, 1989, p. 110).

Such multifactorial inheritance is much more difficult to trace than the single gene effects described above. Accordingly, the study of genetic influences on complex human behavior relies on a combination of evidence from a variety of research methods. Let us turn now to a brief examination of the major research methods employed.

Children with behavior disorders often have parents, siblings, and other family members with similar problems. However, such aggregation of behavior problems in families does not necessarily mean a genetic influence is operating. Family environment may also be operating. One of the goals of research methods is, thus, to determine the degree of genetic influence operating in specific behavior disorders.

The three major research strategies of behavior genetics that have been applied to childhood behavior disorders are the twin, family, and adoption methodologies (Plomin, 1990). The basic aspects of each of these methods are described below. These methods are employed to assess *heritability*, a statistic that indicates the degree to which genetic influence accounts for variance in behavior among individuals in the population studied. While the degree of genetic contribution to behavior is the main focus of such research, an appreciation of the contribution of environmental influences can also be obtained.

The essence of *twin designs* is a comparison of identical twin resemblance to fraternal twin resemblance. Identical or monozygotic (MZ) twins have identical genes, while fraternal or dizygotic (DZ) twins are on the average only 50 percent alike genetically. In fact, they are no more alike genetically than any two siblings. In its most basic form, the twin method suggests a genetic influence if there is greater concordance among identical twins than among fraternal twins. That is, genetic influence is indicated when a disorder occurs more frequently in both members of MZ twin pairs than it does in both members of DZ twin pairs. Various statistical methods, however, allow for more than just a comparison of different concordance rates. For example, estimates can be made of the degree of genetic determination. In addition, variations on the basic twin methodology can be employed to expand the information obtained.

Family studies expand upon the logic of twin studies. The relatives of an individual (the proband) identified as exhibiting a certain behavior or disorder can be examined to determine whether or not they exhibit the same behavior or problem. Identical twins are 100 percent genetically related. First degree relatives' (parents and their offspring and siblings) average genetic relatedness is 50 percent. Half-siblings and other second degree relatives are 25 percent genetically related. Third degree relatives, such as cousins, are only 12.5 percent genetically related. If there is a genetic influence, family members who are genetically more similar to the proband should be more likely to exhibit the same or related difficulties. Statistical estimates of heritability are possible.

Adoption studies are designed to evaluate the relative contributions of genetics and environment by studying genetically related individuals reared apart and genetically unrelated individuals reared together. Several variations on this basic strategy exist. One strategy is to start with adopted children who display a particular behavior disorder and to examine rates of that disorder in members of the children's biological families compared to rates in their adoptive families. Alternatively one could compare biological relatives of adoptees with the specified disorder and biological relatives of control adoptees. Another strategy is to start with biological parents who exhibit a particular disorder and examine the rate of disorder in offspring separated from the parent in early childhood and raised in another household. Rates of disorder in these children can then be compared to a number of comparison groups (e.g., siblings not given for adoption and raised by the biological parent).

There are a number of limitations and potential confounds for each of these strategies. For example, in adoption studies, prenatal as well as genetic factors are part of the biological parent's "contribution." Thus, greater rates of disorder among biological relatives than adoptive relatives could be due to such influences. Combinations of methods, refinements of the basic methods, and more sophisticated methods of quantitative analysis seek to address many of the concerns with individual methods. They also permit the evaluation of hypothetical models that attempt to describe the mechanism of genetic transmission and interaction with environmental influences (Plomin, DeFries, and McClearn, 1990). A convergence of evidence from different sources is most likely to shed light on the problem being studied (Rutter et al., 1990a).

Chromosome abnormalities. Approximately 40 percent of spontaneously aborted fetuses are known to have chromosomal abnormalities. Among live births it has been estimated that 3.52 infants per 1,000 are born with an abnormal number of chromosomes and 2.23 with structural abnormalities (Gath, 1985).

Chromosomes that are aberrant in either number or structure have been shown to cause death or a variety of deficiencies. These "accidents" are often not inherited, so they influence only the specific developing embryo. Abnormality in the number of chromosomes, for example, is thought to occur during maturation of the ova and sperm (meiosis) or in early cell division in the fertilized ova (mitosis). The chromosome pair fails to separate, resulting in either an extra chromosome or the loss of a chromosome in cells.

A large number of such chromosomal anomalies have been described. Mental retardation is commonly associated with many of them. Perhaps the most widely recognized disorder attributed to a chromosome aberration is Down's Syndrome. Characterized by mental deficiency, it is usually caused by an extra #21 chromosome. A group of abnormalities resulting from sex chromosome aberrations has also been discovered. These disorders are often characterized by below-average intelligence, atypical sexual development, and other difficulties.

Newer methods of chromosomal analysis, such as staining methods, allow the identification of quite subtle differences in size, shape, and characteristics of portions of chromosomes. Also, the discovery of a group of structural features known as fragile sites should prove helpful in understanding the origins of certain disorders. For example, the fragile X anomaly is due to a fragile site on the X chromosome. This condition is responsible for about one in ten cases of severe mental retardation (Rutter et al., 1990a).

Biochemical Influences

Much of both early and current thinking about the role of biological influences on disordered behavior implicates imbalances in body chemistry. Hippocrates speculated

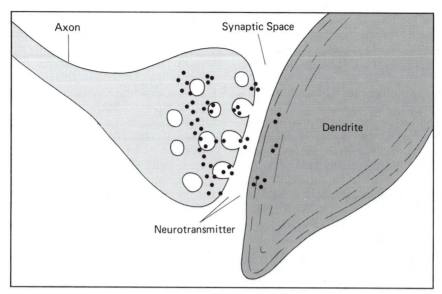

FIGURE 3–1 Neurotransmitters are substances that are released by one neuron and relay the neutral impulse across the synapse to the special receptor of the next neuron.

that adequate mental functioning relied on a proper balance of the four bodily humors: blood, phlegm, yellow bile, and black bile. Thus, for example, excessive black bile was thought to produce melancholia, or what we would today label depression.

While current proposals about specific mechanisms for specific disorders are often questioned, there is fairly broad agreement that biochemistry in some form contributes to some disturbed behaviors. For example, it has been suggested that differences in biochemistry may contribute to the severe loss of appetite characteristic of anorexia nervosa (e.g., Mitchell, 1986).

A great deal of the thinking and theorizing about biochemistry has centered around the role of neurotransmitters. These chemicals are involved in the transmission of impulses across the synapse from one neuron to the next (Figure 3–1). It has been suggested, for example, that neurotransmitters such as norepinephrine are involved

in some complex way in depression (e.g., McNeal and Cimbolic, 1986).

Much contemporary research on biochemical factors emphasizes genetic influences. The chemistry of the body, however, can be affected by a number of other variables: infection, diet, stress, ingestion of foreign substances, and drug and alcohol abuse. It has been postulated that these influences contribute to several disorders. For example, a biochemical theory of hyperactivity was offered by Feingold (1975). Through his work on allergies, Feingold suggested that hyperactivity might be caused by a sensitivity to certain food additives. Still other examples are the possible contribution of lead poisoning to hyperactivity and of prenatal viral infections to the development of childhood psychosis. Like many genetic-biochemical explanations, the presence and role of these factors are being investigated.

Structural and Physiological Damage

Actual damage to the structural or physiological integrity of the biological system, particularly the nervous system, may also

produce a variety of intellectual and behavioral difficulties. These known or presumed influences may occur prenatally, at about the time of birth (perinatal effects), or during later development (postnatal effects).

Prenatal influences. Damage to the developing fetus by a variety of toxic substances is currently receiving a great deal of public and professional attention. At one time it was believed that the placenta protected the fetus from harmful substances that might enter the mother's blood stream. We now know that a variety of such *teratogens* (e.g., radiation, viral or bacterial infections, drugs such as thalidomide and alcohol, and environmental contaminants such as polychlorinated biphenyls-PCBs appear to be related to fetal death, disease, malformation, or functional/behavioral effects (Jacobson, Jacobson, and Fein, 1986). Table 3–1 presents some of the major principles that have emerged regarding the effects of teratogens. Clearly many of the findings regarding teratogenic effects produce much controversy because they are related to sensitive economic, social, and political issues. Indeed, caution is appropriate in interpreting the findings since ethical considerations do not permit research that would provide clear conclusions, such as studies in which pregnant women would be intentionally exposed to any of these conditions. We must thus rely on animal studies, the results of which may not hold for humans, and on investigations of humans under natural (uncontrolled) conditions.

Nevertheless, a case report illustrates why there is reason for concern. Jacobson et al. (1986) present the case of a New Mexico pig farmer who inadvertently used feed treated with a methylmercury fungicide. The mother, who was three months pregnant, exhibited no signs of mercury poisoning. When the baby was born there were elevated levels of mercury in his urine. However, the infant appeared normal and a number of evaluations detected no abnormalities. At three months of age mercury was no longer excreted in the urine; however, a number of problems had begun to emerge. A disturbed pattern of brain waves was observed, as were poor muscle tone, irritability, and the absence of visual fixation. A six-year follow-up found this child with severe neurological impairments. The child was blind, experienced seizures, was unable to speak, and was only minimally aware of his environment. Neurological damage was severe in all family members, but greater at the younger ages and most extensive in the youngest child. One of the important findings of this and other cases is that the effects of teratogens may not appear until sometime later. Such a finding is the basis for rulings that a family's legal rights to seek compensation not be limited to the time surrounding exposure to potentially damaging substances. From a scientific viewpoint the need for long-term research is clear.

Since a wide variety of potential teratogens exist (Kopp and Kaler, 1989), it may

TABLE 3–1 Principles Regarding Effects of Teratogens

1. Teratogens may, particularly at low levels, cause subtle behavioral changes rather than gross defects.

2. Teratogens that result in gross central nervous system malformations at higher doses are more likely to produce congenital behavioral problems.

3. The type of substance and the stage at which exposure occurs both affect the nature of the behavioral problems that occur.

4. The fetus is susceptible throughout gestation—there is no "safe period."

5. The behavioral effects are a result of the interaction of the genotype and the specific teratogen.

6. The degree of behavioral effects appears to depend on the amount of exposure.

7. Exposure may have different effects in different individuals and multiple effects in the same individual. The individual's developmental level at the time of exposure may be important in determining these effects.

Adapted from Jacobson, Jacobson, and Fein, 1986.

not be entirely possible to avoid exposure. Indeed, as women increasingly enter the workplace they may increase their risk of exposure to toxic agents. However, a pregnant woman does have some control over her environment; she can take special care not to expose herself to disease, and to obtain treatment if a disease is contracted.

In addition to teratogens, several other variables such as maternal age and stress have been associated with infant death and developmental difficulties. One possible risk factor that has received considerably less attention is exposure of the father to harmful conditions. The effects of teratogens, in this case, would be transmitted through the father's sperm cells. There is some evidence that birth defects may be unusually high for the children of males who are exposed to certain agents before their offspring are conceived (Kolata, 1978). One example involved men who, as operating room personnel, had been exposed to anesthetic gases. Wives of these men, compared to those of men not so exposed, had a higher prevalence of miscarriages, and their infants were more likely to have birth defects. Another kind of evidence for a paternal risk factor is Abel and Lee's (1988) report of differences in the behavior of mice offspring as a function of the father's exposure to alcohol.

Perinatal and later influences. It is important to note that nervous system damage may also occur during or after birth. At the time of birth, experiences such as excessive medication given to the mother, unusual delivery, and anoxia may result in damage to the newborn. There is evidence to suggest that the frequency of such perinatal complications is greater in lower SES children (see Table 3–2). Further, as noted in Chapter 2, perinatal complications and SES factors have an interactive effect on the infant's subsequent development (e.g., Gray, Dean, and Lowrie, 1988). Postnatal damage may occur as a result of experiences such as accident, illness, malnutrition, or accidental poisoning (e.g., Cohen et al., 1989). Exposure of children to lead, even at relatively

TABLE 3–2 Some Pregnancy and Birth Variables Found to Differ for Low Compared to High SES Infants

Child's birth weight
Maternal stress during pregnancy
Length of labor
Maternal weight gain
Maternal age
Forceps use
Time from membrane rupture to labor

Adapted from Gray, Dean, and Lowrie, 1988.

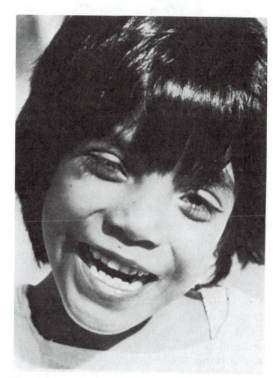

The girl pictured above is one of two daughters born to a, since deceased, alcoholic mother. On the basis of history, mental deficiency, and physical findings, both were diagnosed as having *fetal alcohol syndrome.* Several key features of the syndrome are visible in this girl, including narrow eye openings, underdeveloped-thin upper lip, flattening or absence of the usual indentation under the nose, and possible drooping of the upper eyelids. Behavioral deficits are also implicated in this syndrome. (Courtesy of March of Dimes Birth Defects Foundation)

Mentions of lead poisoning in children often evoke pictures of children in homes containing leaded paint from old flaking walls. Recent studies suggest that there are a variety of other sources of lead exposure and also that damaging effects may be produced at even low levels of exposure. Lead glazes on food containers, exhaust from leaded gasoline, and drinking water (which picks up lead from pipes) may be common sources. Health officials now warn of the importance of prevention and of screening children for lead exposure. (Alan Carey, The Image Works)

low levels, is one example of accidental poisoning that has received recent attention (e.g., Fergusson et al. 1988a; Silva et al. 1988).

Regardless of when biological insult occurs, both the site and the severity of brain damage help determine the nature of the difficulties. A precise description of the relationship between damage and dysfunction cannot always be made, however. Thus, the link between brain damage and psychopathology is unclear and in many ways controversial (Werry, 1979b; Shaffer, 1985). Perhaps most controversial is the concept of minimal brain damage or dysfunction (Chiland, 1988). Problems such as hyperactivity and learning disabilities, for example, are often presumed to be caused by minimal degrees of brain damage that are undetectable with current clinical methods.

One of the major concerns of those who work with children is whether problems arising from brain dysfunction or damage can be remediated. A controversial issue is whether the child's immature central nervous system is highly "plastic," that is, it is more likely to recover after injury than the adult system. Younger systems are more plastic in general, but age is only one factor affecting recovery. Size, location, and progression of the lesion, severity of the insult, secondary complications such as infection, and degree of environmental support are some others (Fletcher, 1988). An emphasis on plasticity encourages efforts to develop lost or unachieved functioning, but it may have some negative consequences. Frustration for the child, parent, and teacher may result where complete plasticity is assumed but is not realized. The assumption that the young brain is highly plastic may also lead to imprecise forms of intervention. On the other hand, identification of loss and realistic expectations for recovery can lead to advances in our understanding and to improved remediation (Duffy et al., 1984; St. James-Roberts, 1979).

We will have numerous opportunities throughout this text to return to hypotheses about the role of biology in determining or influencing behavior disorders. It is probably fair to say that little *definitive* knowledge currently exists. At the same time, the array of hypotheses is fascinating and clearly deserving of investigation. Particularly crucial is understanding how biological influences might interact with psychosocial factors.

THE PSYCHODYNAMIC VIEW

The psychoanalytic theory of Sigmund Freud was the first modern systematic attempt to understand mental disorders in psychological terms. Freud's theory also drew heavily on biology. Freud was a physician who had trained to be a neurologist. His thinking about how the psychic system operated was formulated to parallel the workings of biological systems and to reflect the then-current developments in the natural sciences. Freud's ideas went through a number of transitions during his lifetime. The evolution of his conceptualizations has come to be known as classical psychoanalytic theory. Only a brief description of this complex and highly systematized theory will be given here. More elaborate and detailed summaries have been provided by a number of writers (e.g., Kessler, 1988; Wolman, 1972).

Freud's theory of the human mind has at its core two biologically given instincts. *Eros* is the impulse to seek pleasure and gratification; the energy associated with this sexual instinct is referred to as *libido*. *Thanatos* is the destructive, aggressive instinct that aims to destroy life. These instincts serve as the energy sources of all psychological activity.

Freud's theory is *deterministic*—there is a specific cause for all behavior, even the most trivial. The principles that describe how behavior is determined are universal, applying to both "normal" and "abnormal" behavior. Emphasis is also given to intrapsychic factors rather than environmental or social influences in explaining behavior. Equally important is the idea that mental processes are *unconscious*; that is, determined by forces that are inaccessible to rational awareness. The analogy of an iceberg, nine-tenths of which is below the surface, illustrates the importance placed on unconscious influences. The theory thus emphasizes instinctual-irrational forces, over rational problem solving.

Although Freud based his theory on clinical observations of adults, he came to view personality as being essentially set during the first five to six years of life. Since the child is viewed as moving through a series of distinct stages of growth, Freud's theory is *developmental*, with a distinct emphasis on early childhood. Psychological difficulties in children as well as in adults are seen as the result of problems experienced during these first few years of life.

To move through early development and beyond, the individual is provided with a fixed amount of psychic energy. The theory describes a dynamic process of transfer of this energy among various aspects of the personality. To explain this ongoing transfer, psychoanalytic theory employs a *structural* and *conflict* model as a metaphor for this process.

In this brief discussion, we seek to provide an overview of the framework Freud used in talking about the structural-conflict model, stages of development, and the development of psychopathology. We first describe the structural system.

The Structures of the Mind

Freud hypothesized three parts of the mental apparatus: the *id*, the *ego*, and the *superego*. Each of these "structures" describes part of a system of psychic functioning. The id, present at birth, is the earliest structure and is the source of all psychic energy. Operating entirely at an unconscious level, the id seeks immediate and unconditional gratification of all instinctual urges (the *pleasure principle*). If this cannot be done directly, the id employs *primary process* thinking—obtaining what is desired through fantasy.

The other psychic structures, the ego and superego, both evolve from the id and must obtain their energy from it. The ego is primarily conscious, and its principle task is to mediate between instinctual urges and the outside world. The mature ego employs its cognitive and decision-making functions to test reality. The superego develops when the immature ego cannot handle all conflicts. In order to deal with some of these, the ego incorporates or introjects the parents' standards, and this is the beginning of a separate superego. The superego sets ideal standards for behavior and is the conscience, or self-critical part, of the individual. In trying to satisfy the id's instinctual urges, the ego must consider not only reality but also the ideals of the superego. The *psychodynamics* of the Freudian perspective arise out of the attempts of these three systems to achieve their frequently conflicting goals.

Psychosexual Stages

The psychoanalytic perspective relies on a stage theory of development. As the child develops, the focus of psychic energy passes from one bodily zone to the next. The process leads the individual through stages of psychosexual development in a fixed order. Each stage derives its name from the bodily zone that is the primary source of gratification during the period.

The *oral stage* extends from birth through approximately the first year of life. The mouth is the center of pleasure and the infant is highly dependent on the mother for nurturance. Thus, the themes of this stage are not only oral pleasure but also dependency and taking in. The crucial conflict that ends this period is weaning, when the infant must give up some oral pleasures and dependencies.

During the second and third years of life the locus of satisfaction shifts to the anal zone. The retention and explusion of feces are the major sources of stimulation and pleasure during this *anal stage*, and toilet training is the major task for this period. The period has several themes that derive from the source of stimulation and the developmental task. Primary among them are holding and giving, which may be reflected, for example, in an ungenerous and inward-directed personality. These psychological themes also have gender-related implications. Presumed sexual roles of masculine-active-expulsion and feminine-passive-reception begin to be distinguished during this stage (Wolman, 1972).

During the next period, the *phallic stage*, the genitals become the focus of pleasure, as indicated in the young child's masturbation, curiosity, and inspection of the sexual organs. The chief conflict of this period is the desire to possess the opposite-sex parent and the fear of retaliation from the same-sex parent. For the boy this conflict is called the *Oedipus complex*. The parallel process for the girl is known as the *Electra complex*. The resolution of the Oedipal and Electra complexes is central to both sex-role and moral (superego) development.

The final two periods are the *latency and genital stages*. Following the resolution of the conflicts of the phallic stage, the child enters the latency stage. As the name suggests, this is a period of relative stability, in which the sexual and aggressive impulses of the child are subdued. With puberty, however, these impulses are revived, and the adolescent enters the genital stage, during which heterosexual interests predominate. This stage continues for the remainder of the individual's life. These final two stages are less important to the understanding of behavioral disorders, since Freud suggested that the basic personality structure is laid down by the end of the phallic stage.

According to Freud, each of these stages of development involves a developmental crisis, and the child is hindered in development by not more-or-less resolving the conflicts at any one stage. Failure to reach resolution results in the individual's becom-ing psychologically fixated at the stage. Two situations are at the root of *fixation*. The child may not be able to meet the demands of the environment while also satisfying its own needs—and may thus be psychologically frustrated. Alternatively, needs may be met so well that the child is unwilling to leave the stage, and behaviors associated with the stage continue inappropriately. Thus either frustration or the results of overindulgence can fixate the child at a particular stage, adversely affecting development at all subsequent stages.

Anxiety and the Defense Mechanisms

From the psychoanalytic perspective, the concept of anxiety is crucial to the development of disordered behavior. Anxiety is the danger signal to the ego that some unacceptable id impulse is seeking to gain consciousness. As this signal begins to reach consciousness, the ego creates defense mechanisms such as repression, projection, displacement, and reaction formation to deal with the anxiety. For example, reaction formation is a defense in which the child develops a behavior that is the opposite of the original impulse. Symptoms arising from defense mechanisms are a compromise between impulses seeking expression and the demands of the ego. Thus, symptoms are disguised expressions of unacceptable impulses. One of Freud's most frequently cited cases illustrates the latent (disguised) meaning of a child's symptoms. These symptoms occurred when the child experienced the Oedipal conflict of the phallic stage.

The case of a five-year-old boy, Hans, who was afraid of horses, has served as a model for the psychoanalytic interpretation of childhood phobias (Freud, 1909, 1953). Freud actually saw Hans only once, and the case is based on treatment by the boy's father under Freud's direction. Hans was very affectionate toward his mother and enjoyed spending time "cuddling" with her. When Hans was almost five, he returned from his daily walk with his nursemaid frightened, crying, and wanting to cuddle with his mother. The next day, when the mother took him for the walk herself, Hans expressed fear of being bitten by a horse and that evening insisted upon cuddling with his mother. He cried about having to go out the next day and expressed considerable fear concerning the horse. These symptoms, which continued to worsen, were interpreted by Freud as reflecting the child's sexual impulses toward his mother and his fear of castration by the father. The ego began its defenses against these unacceptable impulses by *repressing* Hans's wish to attack his father, his rival for his mother's affection. This was an attempt to make the unacceptable impulse unconscious. The next step was *projection*: Hans believed that his father wished to attack him, rather than his wishing to attack his father. The final step was *displacement*: The horse was viewed as dangerous, not the father. According to Freud, the choice of the horse as a symbol of the father was due to numerous associations of horses with Hans's father, danger, and penises. For example, the black muzzle and blinders on the horse were viewed as symbolic of the father's mustache and eyeglasses. The fear Hans displaced onto the horse permitted the child's ambivalent feelings toward the father to be resolved. He could now love his father. In addition, thinking of horses as the source of anxiety allowed Hans to avoid anxiety by simply avoiding horses (Kessler 1966).

Criticisms and Modifications of Psychoanalytic Theory

The classical psychoanalytic theory has been modified by a number of workers. Probably the best known of these are the so-called neo-Freudians who minimized the importance of sexual forces and stressed the importance of social influences; they include Karen Horney, Erich Fromm, Harry Stack Sullivan, and Erik Erikson. Others, such as Freud's daughter Anna, remained more loyal to the orthodox tradition, but elaborated and emphasized the role of the ego in development.

Despite the many modifications of Freud's original theory, this general perspective has been severely criticized on both conceptual and methodological grounds. For example, psychoanalytic formulations rest primarily on the impressions and recollections of clinical cases. They also involve large inferential leaps from what is observed to what is interpreted as existing. In addition, the mechanisms Freud postulated are intrapsychic and often unconscious and are therefore difficult, if not impossible, to investigate. Thus, much of the criticism of psychoanalytic theory has rested on its untestability. However, criticism has come on other grounds as well, and specific assumptions, such as the universality of the psychosexual stages, have been questioned.

Those working within the psychoanalytic tradition today have attempted to expand their methodologies. For example, the use of systematic observation has been attempted. Some have also tried to incorporate recent research findings on infant and child development into their conceptualizations (Zeanah et al., 1989). As newer ideas and methods have been put into testable form, they have tended to be less recognizably psychoanalytic. Thus these efforts have been acknowledged by some to have placed considerable strain on psychoanalytic notions (e.g., Dare, 1985; Tyson, 1986).

Psychoanalytic theory certainly has an important place in the history of childhood disorders, and their treatment. Professional activity based on the conceptualizations and treatments derived from this viewpoint also continues (cf. Marans, 1989; Sholevar et al., 1989). However, many feel that rather than viewing ideas derived from psychoanalytic treatment as scientific facts they should be viewed as rich sources of hypotheses for research. The strong influence of the psychoanalytic perspective in drawing attention to the importance and intensity of infantile and early childhood experiences, the importance of relationships with parents, and the phases of child development has been noted. However, some authors also point out how this perspective has led to a deemphasis of the father's role, to a "mother-blaming" bias, and to a lack of interest in how psychological health develops (e.g., Tyson, 1986).

THE BEHAVIORAL/SOCIAL LEARNING VIEW

The central concept of the behavioral/social learning perspective is that childhood disorders are learned in the same way that other behaviors are learned. As indicated in Chapter 1, the publication of John B. Watson's essay *Psychology as a Behaviorist Views It* (1913) set into motion a perspective that would serve as the major rival to the psychoanalytic position. While this perspective was also deterministic, it differed from the psychoanalytic paradigm in a number of key ways. Unlike Freud, Watson emphasized observable events rather than unconscious intrapsychic conflicts. Developed in the psychological laboratory rather than in a clinical setting, the behavioral perspective heavily emphasized objective empirical verification. Learning and the influence of the environment were seen as the appropriate focus of study. Furthermore, development was viewed as a continuous process rather than as a fixed sequence of stages. The assumption was made that learning continues throughout the life span, and therefore that "personality" is not set by a certain age. Finally, unlike classical psychoanalytic theory, the behavioral perspective did not develop as a single comprehensive theory aimed at explaining all behavior. Rather, a number of theories, often employing similar language but each describing a different aspect of the learning process, were suggested.

Classical Conditioning

Pavlov's demonstrations of dogs learning to salivate to previously neutral stimuli served to focus attention on the process of classical conditioning. Two early studies based on this model stand out because of the impact they had on the application of classical conditioning to human problems. Watson and Rayner's (1920) now famous case of Little Albert was an illustration of the conditioning of fear. Albert, an 11-month-old child, initially showed no fear reactions to a variety of objects, including a white rat. He did, however, exhibit fear when a loud sound was produced by the striking of a steel bar. Watson and Rayner attempted to condition fear of the white rat by producing the loud clanging sound each time Albert reached for the animal. After several of these pairings, Albert reacted with crying and avoidance when the rat was presented without the noise (see Figure 3–2). Thus, it appeared that fear could be learned through classical conditioning. Needless to say, there are significant ethical difficulties with conducting studies such as Watson and Rayner's, and therefore behavioral researchers have tended to focus their attention on applying classical conditioning principles to the treatment of disorders.

The second landmark study was Mary Cover Jones's (1924) demonstration that the principles of classical conditioning could be applied to the removal of fearful responses. Peter, a boy of two years and ten months, exhibited a fear of furry objects. Jones first attempted to treat Peter by placing him with a rabbit and children who liked the rabbit and petted it. The treatment appeared to be working but was interrupted when Peter became ill for nearly two months. Just prior to his return to treatment, he was also frightened by a large dog. With Peter's fear back at its original level, Jones decided to treat Peter with a counterconditioning procedure. This involved allowing Peter to eat some of his favorite foods while the animal was moved progressively closer, thus pairing the feared stimulus with pleasantness. The

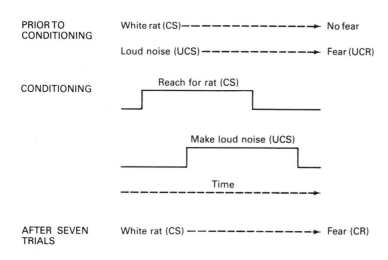

PRIOR TO CONDITIONING

White rat (CS) ––––––––––––––→ No fear

Loud noise (UCS) ––––––––––––→ Fear (UCR)

CONDITIONING

Reach for rat (CS)

Make loud noise (UCS)

Time

AFTER SEVEN TRIALS

White rat (CS) ––––––––––––––→ Fear (CR)

FIGURE 3–2 Watson and Rayner's case of Little Albert. The repeated pairing of an unconditioned stimulus (noise) that produced fear with a previously neutral stimulus (rat) resulted in the rat itself producing a conditioned response of fear.

procedure was apparently successful in reducing the boy's fears, and he was ultimately able to hold the animal by himself.

This case demonstration lacks sufficient control, and we cannot draw conclusions regarding the effectiveness of the procedures derived from classical conditioning. Of additional concern is Jones's inclusion of nonfearful children in treatment sessions.

Did the presence of the children, like the food, make the situation pleasant, or did they also serve as models for nonfearful behavior? Despite these limitations, Jones's contribution was important, and stimulated the development of numerous treatments based on the principles of classical conditioning.

Operant Conditioning

The approach to learning set forth in Thornkide's *Law of Effect* and in the work of B. F. Skinner and his followers is probably the behavioral perspective most extensively applied to children's disorders. Operant, or instrumental, conditioning emphasizes the antecedents and consequences of behavior. Behavior is acquired or reduced, and is emitted in some circumstances but not in others, through reinforcement, extinction, punishment, and other learning processes (see Table 3–3). As for classical conditioning, the majority of efforts derived from operant conditioning have focused on the treatment rather than the etiology of disordered behavior.

Williams's (1959) report on altering a 21-month-old child's tantrums is an early, oft-cited example of the use of operant principles for the treatment of childhood

TABLE 3–3   Some Frequently Employed Instrumental Conditioning Terms

Term	Definition	Example
Positive reinforcement	A stimulus is presented following a response (*contingent* upon the response), increasing the frequency of that response.	Praise for good behavior increases the likelihood of good behavior.
Negative reinforcement	A stimulus is withdrawn contingent upon a response, and its removal increases the frequency of that response.	Removal of mother's demands following a child's tantrum increases the likelihood of tantrums.
Extinction	A weakening of a learned response is produced when the reinforcement that followed it no longer occurs.	Parents ignore bad behavior, and it decreases.
Punishment	A response is followed by either an unpleasant stimulus or the removal of a pleasant stimulus, thereby decreasing the frequency of the response.	A parent scolds a child for hitting, and the child stops hitting; food is removed from the table after a child spits, and the spitting stops.
Generalization	A response is made to a new stimulus that is different from, but similar to, the stimulus present during learning.	A child is fearful of all men with mustaches like that of a stern uncle.
Discrimination	The process by which a stimulus comes to signal that a certain response is likely to be followed by a particular consequence.	An adult's smile indicates that a child's request is likely to be granted.
Shaping	A desired behavior that is not in the child's repertoire is taught by rewarding responses that are increasingly similar to (*successive approximations* of) the desired response.	A mute child is taught to talk by initially reinforcing any sound, then something that sounds a little like the word, and so on.

disorders. Following a long illness the child had developed severe tantrums. It was assumed that the parents had been reinforcing this behavior by attending to it. For example, the child's screaming as the parents left his bedroom was reinforced by their remaining in the room. After determining that there were no medical problems, a program of removing the reinforcement for the tantrum behavior (extinction) was begun. After leisurely putting the child to bed, the parents left and did not reenter the room. Although the child cried for 45 minutes the first night, by the tenth occasion he no longer fussed when left alone. No negative side effects occurred, and the child was reported to be well adjusted at three years of age.

The principles of operant conditioning have increasingly been applied to a broad range of difficult and complex problems, and the treatment procedures themselves have become more varied and complex. The specific application of these procedures will be discussed throughout the succeeding chapters of this book. They all share the assumption that problem behavior can be changed through a learning process and that the focus of treatment should be on the antecedents and consequences of behavior.

Observational Learning

The investigator most widely associated with *observational learning*, or *modeling*, is Albert Bandura, who, along with his associates, has conducted a large number of studies that bear upon the genesis and treatment of childhood disorders. It has been demonstrated that children can acquire a variety of behaviors—aggression, cooperation, delay of gratification, sharing—by watching others perform them. These studies suggest how observational learning can lead to both the acquisition and removal of problem behaviors.

Studies by Bandura and his colleagues on children's imitation of aggressive behavior illustrate how a deviant behavior may be acquired through the observation of a model. In one well known experiment, Bandura (1965) showed nursery school children a five-minute film in which an adult exhibited a number of unusual, aggressive behaviors toward a Bobo doll. The behaviors were also accompanied by distinctive verbalizations. One group of children saw a final scene in which the model was rewarded for aggression; another group saw a final scene in which the model was punished; and the remaining group did not see any final scene. Later, each child was left alone to play in a room containing the Bobo doll and other toys. The child could engage in imitative aggressive behavior or in nonimitative behavior. As you might expect, the children who had seen the model punished exhibited fewer imitative aggressive responses in the playroom. The experimenter then reentered the room and told each child that for each aggressive behavior like the model's he or she could reproduce, a treat would be given. All three groups now showed the same high level of imitative aggression. The study demonstrated that acquisition of the aggressive behavior had occurred and, moreover, that its performance depended on certain environmental "payoffs."

While the phenomenon of observational learning seems straightforward and simple, it is actually quite complex. Numerous variables influence the process. For example, multiple models, conflicting models, and attributes of the models themselves can affect whether learning will occur. In addition to direct imitation of modeled behavior, observation can lead to generalized inhibition or disinhibition of behavior. For example, a child who observes another child being scolded for running about may become quieter in other ways (inhibition). Observing a great deal of shooting and fighting on television, in contrast, may lead a child to exhibit other forms of aggression,

Children often provide models for each other. For example, research indicates that observation of an aggressive model can lead to direct imitation of that behavior or more generalized imitation of a whole class of aggressive behaviors. (Judy Gelles/Stock, Boston)

such as verbal abuse and physical roughness, with peers (disinhibition). In neither case is the exact behavior of the model imitated; rather, a class of behaviors becomes less or more likely to occur due to observation of a model.

Whether imitation is specific or generalized, complex processes are required for observational learning to occur (Bandura, 1977b). Such learning relies on the child's attending to the salient features of the model's behavior. The child must also organize and encode this information and remember it. The acquired behavior must then be performed when it is anticipated that it will meet with desired consequences. The process of learning by observation is viewed by Bandura and others as more than a simple mimicking of behavior. The social learning perspective that has developed from this and other research has placed increasing emphasis on cognitive processes such as attention, memory, and problem solving (Rosenthal, 1984).

OTHER IMPORTANT PERSPECTIVES

Other perspectives on childhood behavioral disorders have expanded on existing paradigms or have added some distinct and different viewpoints to the field. Some of these perspectives are briefly described in the next sections; further detail is provided in later chapters, where their application to specific disorders is illustrated.

The Cognitive-Behavioral Perspective

Quite recent trends in American psychology have resulted in increased emphasis on cognitive processes. One outgrowth of this trend was the direct application of knowledge of cognitive development to applied problems (cf. Gholson and Rosenthal, 1984; Perlmutter, 1986). In addition, some behaviorally oriented clinicians suggested that increased attention be paid to the role of cognitive processes (cf. Bandura, 1977b; Kendall, 1985; Meichenbaum, 1977). From this perspective, behaviors are learned and maintained by interacting systems of external events and cognitions, and cognitive factors influence whether environmental events are attended to, how events are perceived, and whether these events affect future behavior. Table 3–4 presents some basic principles of a cognitive-behavioral perspective.

In recent years a number of investigators have incorporated thinking, imagining, self-statements, self-control, and problem solving into treatments for various behavior

TABLE 3–4 Some Basic Principles of a Cognitive-Behavioral Perspective

1. A person responds primarily to cognitive representations of experiences rather than to the environment or the experiences per se.

2. Most human learning is cognitively mediated.

3. There is a causal interrelationship between thoughts, feelings, and behavior.

4. Cognitive events, processes, products, and structures are important in understanding behavior disorders and therapeutic interventions.

5. Cognitive events, processes, products, and structures can be articulated in a testable manner and integrated into behavioral paradigms. It is desirable to combine cognitive interventions with treatments that involve actual performance of behaviors and with behavioral contingency management.

6. The cognitive-behavioral therapist acts as a diagnostician, educator, and consultant. The therapist assesses distorted or deficient cognitions and dysfunctional behavior patterns, and works with the client to design learning experiences to remediate them.

Adapted from Kendall, 1985b.

disorders (cf. Ingram and Scott, 1990; Kendall, 1987). Meichenbaum and Goodman's (1971) multifaceted training program to teach hyperactive children to "think before they act" is the prototype of much of this work. An important component of the program is to teach children to employ self-statements to help direct their behavior. The steps in such training are outlined in Table 3–5. Self-statement patterns may be quite varied. Researchers have found that children with different behavior problems may exhibit different patterns of self-statements (e.g., Stefanak et al., 1987). Interest has not been limited to self-statements, however. Attention has also been given to other cognitive processes. For example, Dodge (1985) found that some types of aggressive children exhibited distortions in processing social information, seeing provocation in accidental incidents.

Various illustrations of the ways in which a cognitive-behavioral perspective has contributed to the understanding and treatment of childhood behavior disorders are presented throughout the book. The major goal of this perspective is to identify various deficits and distortions in cognitions that contribute to specific childhood problems and to develop interventions matched to these needs (Kendall, 1986).

TABLE 3–5 Sequence of Steps Employed in Meichenbaum and Goodman's Self-Instructional Training

1. While the child watches, an adult model self-instructs aloud while performing the desired task.

2. The child performs the task as the adult instructs aloud.

3. The child self-instructs aloud while performing the task.

4. The child whispers the instructions while doing the task.

5. The child uses private speech to guide performance.

6. The number of self-statements employed by the child is then enlarged over several training sessions.

Adapted from Meichenbaum and Goodman, 1971.

The Psychoeducational Perspective

What we refer to as the psychoeducational perspective is a view that arises out of an approach to working with children rather than a particular conceptual paradigm. Children's problems are viewed within an educational context, and commitment to reeducation is what characterizes the variety of approaches that fall within this rubric (cf. Maher and Zins, 1987).

The term *special education* has also been used to describe school-based efforts to deal with the problems of atypical children. That the vast majority of children receive extended formal education as a right rather than as a privilege is a given in today's society. This has not always been the case, nor has education always been assigned an important role in dealing with children's problems.

Lilly (1979c) has provided an overview of the history of special education. The initial view of the special education approach, particularly for the mentally retarded, was optimistic. Residential treat-ment centers were developed to prepare handicapped individuals to return to the community. Residential schools evolved, however, into permanent residences for more severely handicapped children. Moreover, little attention was given to persons whose problems were milder. Compulsory education laws then forced the educational systems to provide services for the less severely handicapped.

Another development—the construction of general tests of intelligence—had a long-lasting and far-reaching impact on special education. These tests defined a new group of mildly handicapping conditions. The presence of children with "milder" conditions in the school systems led to the development of special classes. With expansion of services, legislation for mandatory special education, and the development of university-based research and training programs, special educational services experienced rapid growth beginning in the 1950s.

More recent changes in special education

Working with children in an educational context and a commitment to education as a means of intervention characterize the psychoeducational approach.

have occurred as a result of court cases and legislation. Many of these changes initially arose out of concern for the mentally retarded (cf. MacMillan, 1982). However, the principles evolved have been extended to other problems. In 1975 the delivery of special services was dramatically affected by P.L. 94–142—The Education for All Handicapped Children Act. This influential law and the application of the psychoeducational perspective will be discussed in more detail later in the book. However, it is appropriate to recognize here two matters that have been of particular importance (Lilly, 1979a; MacMillan and Kavale, 1986). One is that special educators have been prominent in questioning the need to employ traditional categories or special labels with children. They have often led the fight against the use of categorization and for recognition of the role of social and environmental factors in the etiology of childhood problems.

The second issue is whether children should be placed in special classes. Although special classes were originally developed to help children who were not succeeding in regular classrooms, a number of educators began to question their efficacy (e.g., Dunn, 1968). The question of whether children with problems should be placed in special classrooms or "mainstreamed" into the regular school system remains a complex and controversial one, with far-reaching implications. Drawing attention to this concern is one of the continuing contributions of the psychoeducational approach (Hallahan and Kauffman, 1978; Lilly, 1979a; MacMillan and Kavale, 1986).

The Family Systems Perspective

The family systems perspective, like the psychodynamic perspective, was largely developed in the context of treatment. Virtually all approaches to behavior disorders acknowledge the family as having a major impact. A variety of viewpoints might describe how a family factor (for example, parental conflict) contributes to a problem in the child (for example, acting out or aggressive behavior). The focus in the majority of these approaches, however, has remained on the designated child. The family's role is to assist the child in achieving change. In contrast, family systems theorists view the family unit, rather than the individual, as the appropriate "organism" to study and treat.

Several different conceptualizations of the relationship between family interaction and psychopathology have been offered. These conceptualizations vary in the degree to which they are concerned with the etiology of disordered behavior versus family patterns that maintain such behavior and allow dysfunction to continue. In fact, family systems conceptualizations tend to be more concerned with maintenance than with initial etiology (Levant, 1984). This emphasis is based on the principle of *equifinality*—that a number of different casual paths may lead to the same end state. Studying the paths that led a family to its current state is thus of less interest than understanding what maintains the current family system.

No one theory guides all family systems work and, indeed, a number of different approaches exist (cf. Barnes, 1985; Levant, 1984). There are, however, commonalities in these approaches. One central thesis is that families are more complicated than the sum of their parts (Bowen, 1980). The family is viewed as a complex social system that has designated the child as the "identified patient." The child's symptoms play a role in maintaining this system. Therapy, from such a perspective, must address family themes and methods of communication rather than individual child behaviors and parental reactions (see Box 3–1). Therefore, there are two key concepts involved in this viewpoint: a nonlinear systems theory of family influences and a focus on the family as the problem unit rather than the individual.

Most non-systems explanations of family influences are linear; that is, A is seen as causing B. For example, it might be reasoned that family stress operating on a child with a certain psychological and biological makeup may cause a particular psychosomatic disease. The systems perspective, in contrast, suggests a circular relationship of parts, with complex and interrelated feedback mechanisms. Figure 3–3 illustrates how Minuchin, a family systems therapist, views the problem of psychosomatic disease differently from the linear model described above. The central argument of the systems perspective is that the behavior of any child cannot be attributed to biology or merely to a *reaction* in the family system. It is the system's interactions that are problematic and that maintain the child's "symptomatic" behavior.

BOX 3.1   Revisiting Little Hans and his family

Differences between a family systems perspective and viewpoints that focus on the individual child have been illustrated by examining a case that we described earlier, Freud's famous case of Little Hans (Combrinck-Graham 1986). Freud's case would not be considered family therapy from a systems perspective. The father's treating the child under the direction of a therapist is not sufficient to meet the definition of a family intervention. A systems perspective requires more than talking to other family members. Also, in Freud's treatment of Hans the focus remained on Hans's fears. Interactions among family members was not the focus of treatment. Combrinck-Graham points out, for example, that the father's manner of dealing with his wife's threats to cut off Hans's "widdler" (if he didn't stop masturbating) is not discussed. This is not to say that the family may not have changed during Freud's discussions with the father. Combrink-Graham suggests that the father, as a function of becoming active in the child's treatment, may have changed his role in the family. He may have become more centrally involved in parenting. However, such change was not the intent of treatment.

In contrast, Haley (1976), a family therapist, described the treatment of a childhood phobia from a systems perspective. Haley called his case "A Modern Little Hans." This eight-year-old boy's fear of dogs resulted in his being afraid to go out and, thus, paralleled Hans's fear of horses. The family system rather than the phobia was seen as the focus of conceptualization and treatment. The mother was viewed as overinvolved with the boy and overly concerned with his fears. The father's role was more peripheral and he and the mother spent little time together and didn't communicate. The exclusive focus of treatment was not on the boy and his problems. Rather, the therapist explicitly made use of the father-son relationship to change the fear. The father was used as an expert on dogs and he helped the boy overcome his fears. This also served to rearrange the family patterns of interaction. In addition, working at the reestablishment of a relationship between the mother and father not only improved their marriage but altered patterns within the family that had contributed to maintaining the boy's fears. A two-year follow-up revealed that the boy no longer had any fears and was doing well in all respects. The parents' relationship had also improved.

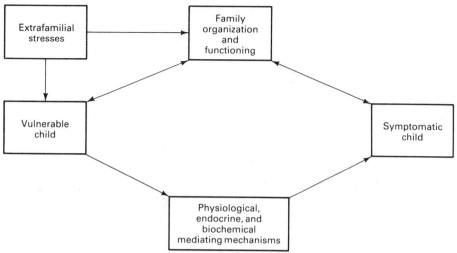

FIGURE 3–3 The model of psychosomatic disease described by Minuchin illustrates a family systems perspective on psychological dysfunction. Reprinted by permission of the publishers, from Psychosomatic Families: Anorexia Nervosa in Context by Salvador Minuchin et al., Cambridge, MA: Harvard University Press, Copyright © 1978 by the President and Fellows of Harvard College.

MODES OF TREATMENT

As indicated earlier, the perspective that a therapist adopts affects the style of the therapy offered. Thus, for example, a professional with a social-learning perspective is likely to offer treatments that are action-oriented, focus on present problems, and assume that therapy is a learning process governed by principles common to all learning situations.

Another dimension by which one can categorize treatments is by what we term the *mode of treatment*, that is, how services are delivered. For example, as we indicated above, therapists operating from a variety of theoretical perspectives advocate for the inclusion of the family in treatment. Thus, working with the family is a mode of treatment employed by therapists from a variety of perspectives. Treatment of children is delivered in a variety of other modes as well. Indeed, research suggests that any one therapist is likely to employ several different modes of treatment and in treating a par-

ticular child may use a combination of these modes (e.g., Tuma and Pratt, 1982).

Therapists may see the child in individual one-to-one sessions. These sessions may resemble the verbal interchanges of adult sessions, or particularly with young children, play may be the primary mode of interaction between the therapist and the child. But therapists may also spend relatively little time with the child and focus instead on training the parents to work with the child. Such parent training may have the added benefit of providing general parenting skills that will be useful in other situations or with other children. Sometimes various members of the family are seen in separate individual treatment. Alternatively, the therapist may choose to work with the family as a unit. Various forms of treatment may also be delivered in a group rather than an individual format. Recent reviews of research on the effectiveness of psychotherapy with children suggest such interventions are successful, particularly those based on a behavioral or cognitive-behavioral perspective, and that there does not seem to be a particular mode of treatment that is consistently more effective (Casey and Berman, 1985; Weisz, Weiss, Alicke, and Klotz, 1987).

The modes indicated above are only some of the forms of treatment employed in working with children. Often consultation is given to significant other adults who work with the child—a teacher, for example. In this section we briefly present an overview of some of the most commonly used modes of treatment. In later chapters we will present specific examples of these modes as they are employed with particular problems.

Individual and Group Psychotherapy

The most common view of psychotherapy is that it is a one-to-one and verbal experience. Indeed, with adults this is the most frequent mode of treatment. Treatment in groups, like individual psychotherapy, has been offered by therapists from a variety of theoretical perspectives. The same assumptions and methods that guide individual therapies are used, but in a group format. While the group format may be selected for convenience or in order to provide services to larger numbers of children, there are also some other rationales for this choice (Johnson, Rasbury, and Siegel, 1986). Groups offer the opportunity for socialization experiences that do not exist in the individual mode. Also, group treatment may be more appealing to the child because it is less threatening, demonstrates that peers have difficulties, and often includes opportunities for activities not likely to occur in one-to-one relationships with an adult therapist.

Play Therapy

Whether in individual or group format, treatments that would be described as verbal forms of psychotherapy are a major form of intervention, particularly with older children and adolescents. However, the need to alter treatment procedures to fit the child's level of cognitive and emotional development is one factor that has produced nonverbal modes of working with children.

A common mode is the use of play as a therapeutic vehicle. This is consistent with the importance of play in the development of young children (Rubin, Fein, and Vandenberg, 1983). Play as a mode of therapy is for many therapists a solution to the lesser verbal abilities of the child. Rather than relying exclusively on abstract verbal means, the therapist uses play to help concretize communications. In this form, as a means of communication, play is used in therapy by most practitioners. However, play therapy as a more structured and distinct approach to treatment also exists. The two best known perspectives on play therapy are derived from the psychodynamic and client-centered perspectives.

Play therapy was the focus of a controversy between two of the principal and early developers of child treatment from a psychoanalytic perspective. Early analysts agreed that change was needed in analytic techniques in order to treat children effectively. This led to the use of play as a mechanism for children to express their thoughts and feelings. However, among the controversies that arose was whether to view children's play as the equivalent of verbal free association in adults. Also there was disagreement over the psychoanalytic interpretation of children's play.

Melanie Klein (1932) was one of the first therapists to emphasize play in the treatment of children and her ideas gained wide popularity. She used the term play therapy to refer to the process whereby the child's play was used as the basis for psychoanalytic interpretation much as free association was used in the psychoanalysis of adults. Anna

Freud (1946) disagreed with the emphasis and significance given to play by Klein and others. She viewed play as only one potential mode of expression. Anna Freud also felt that although the child did express emotions and thoughts through play, these should not be cognitively equated with the purposeful production of free association by adults.

The two women also disagreed on the interpretation of the material derived from play. Here again Klein placed heavy emphasis on symbolic interpretation of play and gave it a prominent role throughout the psychoanalytic process. Anna Freud, in contrast, gave less emphasis to play interpretation and did not see it as always symbolizing conflict. She, for example, disagreed with Klein that a child's opening a lady's handbag symbolically expresses curiosity regarding the contents of the mother's womb. Rather the child may be responding to an experience on the previous day when someone brought a present in a similar receptacle (A. Freud, 1946). The contemporary psychoanalytic position tends to favor Anna Freud's positions on play and other issues (Johnson, Rasbury, and Siegel, 1986). Indeed, the term "play therapy" as it is used today refers to child treatment in

which play is the major mode of expression, regardless of the therapist's orientation, rather than Melanie Klein's more narrow definition.

Another major influence on the evolution of play therapy was the work of Virginia Axline. Axline developed her approach from the client-centered perspective associated with Carl Rogers. The eight basic principles outlined by Axline (1947) remain the guidelines for contemporary client-centered play therapy. They are described in Table 3–6. Therapy with children from a client-centered perspective remains much the same today as when Axline described it (Johnson, Rasbury, and Siegel, 1986). The principles of the client-centered approach are the same for adults and children of varying ages. The therapist makes adjustments in communication style to create the appropriate therapeutic environment. The use of play with young children helps to create such an environment.

Play therapy has been widely employed by child clinicians and much has been written about it (cf. Schaefer and O'Connor, 1983). Only a small portion of this literature, however, would be considered research if one excludes case studies. The research that does exist can often be critiqued on meth-

The use of play as a mode of therapy is common with younger children. Play allows for the establishment of rapport, but also provides for a means of communication more age-appropriate than predominantly verbal forms of therapy. (Judy Gelles/Stock, Boston)

TABLE 3–6   Axline's Eight Basic Principles for Client-Centered Treatment of Children

1. The therapist must develop a warm, friendly rapport as soon as possible.

2. The therapist accepts the child exactly as she or he is.

3. The therapist develops a feeling of permissiveness in the relationship so that the child feels free to express completely her or his feelings.

4. The therapist recognizes the feelings expressed by the child and reflects those feelings back to the child in a manner that allows the child insight into his or her behavior.

5. The therapist maintains a deep respect for the child's ability to solve her or his own problems when given the chance to do so. The responsibility to make choices and to institute change is the child's.

6. The therapist does not attempt to direct the child's talk or behavior in any manner. The child leads the way and the therapist follows.

7. The therapist recognizes that therapy is a gradual process and does not attempt to hurry it along.

8. The therapist establishes only those limitations that are necessary to anchor therapy to the world of reality and to make the child aware of her or his responsibility to the relationship.

Adapted from Axline, 1947.

odological grounds and often does not support the efficacy of play therapy. Where play is a successful mode it is often combined with other components such as cognitive-behavioral procedures (Casey and Berman, 1985; Phillips, 1985).

Parent Training

Many professionals have taken the position that change in the child's behavior may best be achieved by producing changes in the way that the parents manage the child. This viewpoint is consistent with the observation that it may often be the parent's perception, rather than actual differences in child behavior, that results in children's being referred for treatment.

Parent training procedures have been applied to a wide variety of childhood problems. A number of approaches have emerged and a number of popular books have appeared on the shelves of bookstores everywhere. However, in terms of systematic applications and research, most work has come from the social learning-behavioral approach.

Behavioral parent training has received a great deal of clinical and research attention and a number of reviews and discussions have appeared (e.g., Dangel and Polster, 1984; McBurnett, Hobbs, and Lahey, 1989; Twardosz and Nordquist, 1987). Original efforts focused on teaching parents to manage contingencies they applied to children's behavior. More recent approaches include a wider variety of skills such as communication training and expression of emotion (Twardosz and Nordquist, 1987). In addition, investigators have found that a number of stressors such as socioeconomic disadvantage, single-parent status, social isolation, and maternal depression are related to poorer outcomes of parent training (e.g., Forehand, Furey, and McMahon, 1984; Israel, Silverman, and Solotar, 1986; Webster-Stratton, 1985a; Wahler and Dumas, 1984). This has led to the examination of a variety of modifications to existing programs. In addition, parent training is frequently employed as one part of a multifaceted approach to treatment. Other components may include additional therapeutic work with the parent, direct work with the child, or work with the teacher and school.

Treatment in Residential Settings

Residential treatment is usually considered a mode of intervention for children with severe behavior problems. The problem itself may be so difficult to treat that working with the child on an outpatient basis does not provide enough contact or control. Also, there may be a concern that children may harm themselves or others and, therefore, that closer supervision is necessary. The child may also be removed from the home because circumstances there are highly problematic, suggesting that successful interventions could not be achieved at home. Unfortunately, the lack of available alternative placements can result in children's being institutionalized when interventions in less restrictive environments, like group or foster homes, might still be successful. On the other hand, treatment in residential settings is often undertaken when other modes of intervention have not proven successful.

Residential treatment may occur in group homes, child psychiatry units in medical hospitals, units in non-medical settings, and in juvenile facilities that are part of the legal/judicial system. Treatment in such settings usually involves a variety of services including therapeutic, educational, and vocational interventions. Because programs differ so much in their actual content, they have been difficult to evaluate and therefore we know less than we would like about their effectiveness (cf. Kazdin, 1985).

SUMMARY

In this chapter we have attempted to introduce the major views or perspectives that have guided investigators of childhood behavior disorders. Perspectives provide general assumptions that direct both researchers and practitioners. They help explain why a particular disorder may be seen differently or similarly by different investigators and why therapists may suggest different interventions.

The biological/physiological view has attended to, among other influences, the role of genetics (particularly polygenetic inheritance), chromosomal abnormalities, biochemical influences, and structural and physiological damage. In the latter case the role of teratogens has received a great deal of attention.

The psychodynamic view has its roots in the work of Sigmund Freud. The developmental and structural model that Freud proposed has influenced many workers. While the psychoanalytic position has been the subject of much criticism, modern versions of the classical psychoanalytic approach and several derivatives remain popular among many professionals.

The behavioral/social learning view developed as a major rival to the psychoanalytic position. Derived from learning theories, it presents a very different view of children's behavior and results in a different and more active approach to treatment. Principles of classical and operant conditioning and observational learning have all contributed to the application of this perspective to children's problems.

The contribution of several other perspectives will also be seen throughout the book. These include the cognitive-behavioral, psychoeducational, and family systems perspectives.

In addition to differentiating treatments based on the perspective from which they are derived, modes of treatment that cut across these perspectives can also be seen. Individual therapy, group therapy, play, parent training, and residential placement are all modes of treatment that have been applied to a variety of childhood problems.

4

RESEARCH: ITS ROLE
AND METHODS

In preceding chapters we have seen how the developmental approach and theoretical perspectives of psychopathology provide a framework and specific hypotheses that can be brought to bear on the investigation of childhood problems. An enormous amount of research is being conducted to test various hypotheses and otherwise study childhood dysfunction. This chapter discusses the role and major methods of research in the field. Basic research designs are described and examples are given of their applications. Although research methods vary along several dimensions, they all aim to go beyond common-sense speculation to objective reliable knowledge.

THE NATURE OF SCIENCE

The word science comes from the Latin word for knowledge, or to know, but refers to knowledge gained by a particular method of inquiry. The application of the scientific method to human behavior is a relatively recent historical event. Humans have long considered themselves special creatures, too complicated and mysterious for scientific study. Even today we hear that scientific inquiry might be inappropriate or perhaps even dangerous when applied to humans. For the most part, though, psychology and related disciplines are committed to the view that the scientific method can provide the most valid information about disordered behavior.

The overall purpose of science is to describe phenomena and to offer explanations for them. Investigators may wonder: How many parents use physical punishment as a means of disciplining their children? What will happen if a learning disabled child is provided with an enriched school experience? Why are particular children socially withdrawn? Sometimes it is necessary only to describe or count to answer such questions. At other times it is necessary to determine the exact conditions under which a phenomenon occurs or its relationship to other variables. Determining cause-and-effect relationships can be especially helpful to understanding behavior.

Theoretical concepts and assumptions are likely to guide research goals, choice of variables, procedures, analyses, and conclusions. In the early stage of research, theoretical concepts may be little more than hunches or guesses based on informal observations. Later they may be more specific and more closely tied to a web of theorems. Whenever it occurs, the generation of ideas and hypotheses is a subjective, creative process.

Researchers often try to test specific hypotheses. The advantage of hypothesis testing is that it tends to build knowledge systematically rather than haphazardly. For this reason it is held in high esteem by scientists. Any one investigation rarely proves that a hypothesis is correct or incorrect; instead, it provides evidence for or against the hypothesis. In turn, a hypothesis that is supported serves as evidence for the accuracy and power of the theoretical underpinnings. A failed hypothesis, in contrast, serves to disprove or limit the theory. As Harrison notes:

Thus science progresses through a combination of observations and theories. The observations form the basis of the theories. The theories summarize the observations, and direct researchers' attention to the new observations by making predictions. The new observations test the accuracy of the theories and may require new theories if they disagree with the predictions. (1979, p. 7)

As researchers ask a variety of questions, they employ a variety of subjects, settings, and methods. In all cases, however, observation and measurement, reliability, and validity are always important considerations.

Observation and Measurement

At the heart of scientific endeavors are observation and measurement. The scientific method can thus be applied only to aspects of the world for which these processes can be used. Both observation and measurement are challenging for behavioral scientists. Accurate and reliable observation of overt behavior is not an easy task and thought and emotion, which are intricately entwined with action, present an even more difficult observational challenge.

In the attempt to tap all sources of information, behavioral scientists make many kinds of observations and measurements. They directly observe overt behavior with or without special apparatus; record physiological functioning of the heart, brain, or sense organs; ask people to report or rate their own behavior, feelings, and thoughts; and collect the reports of others about the subject of investigation. Such endeavors may be conducted in the laboratory or in natural settings, and they vary in the confidence and importance given to them.

Reliability

In addition to assuming that knowledge can be gained by observation, the scientific method also assumes that events repeat themselves, given identical or similar conditions. Thus, they can be observed again by others. If the same events are not reported under similar conditions, the original finding is considered unreliable, or inconsistent, and remains questionable. The need for reliability of results places a burden on researchers to clearly and concisely conceptualize, observe, measure, and communicate their findings so that others may replicate and judge their work. Science is a public endeavor that must be open to the scrutiny and evaluations of others.

Validity

While reliability refers to the consistency or repeatability of results, validity directs attention to the correctness, soundness, or appropriateness of scientific findings. Validity of research is a complex matter and in general must be judged in terms of the purpose of the research and how the results are used. The concepts of internal and external validity are especially relevant to the present discussion.

Internal validity refers to the extent to which explanations for phenomena are judged to be correct or sound. Or to put it in another way, it refers to the degree to which alternative explanations can be ruled out (Campbell and Stanley, 1963). The more certain we are that alternative explanations can be ruled out, the more confidence we have in the offered explanation.

Internal validity is closely tied to the notion of control in research. It is maximized by research designs and procedures that build in control over the variables that could affect the findings of the investigation. By controlling the procedures, the researcher is able to speak confidently about the exact conditions experienced by the subjects. By controlling extraneous factors, the researcher optimizes the likelihood of being able to attribute the findings to specific factors. As we shall see, it is only the "true" experiment that approaches such control.

External validity asks the question of generalizability: To what populations and situations can the results of an investigation be generalized (Campbell and Stanley, 1963)? Researchers are virtually always interested in this question and they can take measures to help ensure external validity. Selecting research subjects who are representative of the population of interest is one way to do this. Generalizability cannot simply be assumed, however. It cannot automatically be concluded, for example, that research findings based on a clinic population of children hold for a nonclinic population. Similarly, the results of laboratory studies may or may not generalize to the world outside the laboratory.

The question of generalizability is rarely if ever completely answered, although evidence increases as various populations and settings are tested. It is ironic that attempts to *increase* internal validity may *decrease* external validity because the former requires controls that may create artificial situations. This dilemma is one of several that must be taken into account in the selection of a research method.

BASIC METHODS OF RESEARCH

In the following discussion several basic research strategies are described. As will be obvious, each has strengths and weaknesses and may be more suitable in some situations than others. This makes it virtually impossible to rely on one method to answer all questions.

The Case Study

The case study is commonly used in researching psychopathology. It focuses on an individual, describing the background, life history, and characteristics of the person. The usual aim is to gain knowledge of the nature, course, causes, correlates, and outcomes of behavior problems.

The following is an abbreviated version of a case report of a boy who was considered at risk for a serious disorder, childhood schizophrenia.

Max was a 7-year-old boy when he was first referred for psychiatric evaluation by his school principal. The grade school where he was enrolled could no longer keep him as a student despite his academic superiority. Longstanding problems such as severe rage outbursts, loss of control, aggressive behavior, and paranoid ideation had reached crisis porportions.

Max was the product of an uncomplicated pregnancy and delivery, the only child of a professional couple. There was a history of "mental illness" in the paternal grandmother and two great aunts. Max's early development was characterized by "passivity." "He didn't take a step alone until 16 months; he could play for hours in the middle of the playpen with the same top," his mother stated. He used a bottle until age 3. Verbal development was good; he spoke full sentences at 1 year. Toilet training was reportedly difficult. "He refused to be trained for spite, so I finally took off his diapers at age 3 and told him not to dare do it on my rugs, so he went into my kitchen and did it on the floor." From that time on he was negative and began having temper tantrums when frustrated.

Max was clumsy and had difficulty manipulating toys, his tricycle, and his shoe laces. When he began nursery school, he was constantly in trouble with other children . . . . Max "developed a passion for animals" . . . At age 5 Max acquired an imaginary companion, "Casper—the man in the wall" who was ever present. Max insisted that he could see him, although no one else could. Casper's voice, he said, often told him he was a bad boy.

Max's behavior was so unmanageable during the first and second grade he was rarely able to remain in the classroom . . . . Max described animals fighting and killing people . . . . The psychologists noted a schizoid quality because of the numerous references to people from outer space, ghosts, and martians, as well as the total absence of human subjects. . . . Despite his high intelligence (IQ 130), Max was experiencing the world as hostile and dangerous. The psychologist considered Max to be at great risk for schizophrenia, paranoid type.

On the basis of a psychological examination, Max's parents enrolled him in a school for emotionally disturbed children where he was to have a weekly therapy session. Difficulties with behavior continued, however, and relations with peers deteriorated. He felt that children hated him and that he had to "get even by getting them first." (Cantor and Kestenbaum, 1986, pp. 627–628)

The case study continues to tell of Max's enrollment in another special school and psychotherapy. A major focus of treatment was to reduce Max's anxiety, which was thought to cause his aggression and bizarre behaviors. Parental involvement, rewards for appropriate behavior, and medication were all employed. Despite some quite disturbed behaviors, improvement occurred and Max eventually was able to attend a university engineering program.

The primary goal of this case report was to illustrate a therapeutic approach to treating seriously disturbed children, and to emphasize that treatment must be tailored to each child's needs. The case study can well meet such a goal, for one of its strengths is its power to illustrate. Case reports can richly describe phenomena, even phenomena that are so rare that they would be difficult to study in other ways.

The weaknesses of the case study concern reliability and validity. The descriptions of life events often go back in time, and the accuracy and completeness of such retrospective data are often suspect. Thus, reliability of the data is at question. When case studies go beyond description to interpretations, there are few guidelines to judge the validity of the interpretations. External validity is also weak in the case study method: Since only one person is examined, the findings cannot be generalized confidently to others. There are ways to increase reliability and validity, however (Kazdin, 1981). For example, several case studies demonstrating the same principle can increase generalizability.

Despite these weaknesses, case studies have played a critical role in the development of clinical psychology and psychiatry (Chess, 1988; Wells, 1987). Clinicians consider them "do-able" and relevant to their concerns (Morrow-Bradley and Elliot, 1986). Case reports can work hand in hand with other research methods, to provide hypotheses and clinically examine the findings of results produced by other methods.

Systematic Naturalistic Observation

Systematic naturalistic observation consists of directly observing individuals in their natural environment, in order to describe behavior occurring in the situation and perhaps to answer specific questions.

An example is an investigation by Leach

Direct observation allows the researcher to systematically measure behavior as it is occurring.

(1972) of 18 normal preschoolers and 6 preschoolers who had been diagnosed as having difficulty in separating from their mothers. The purpose of the study was to reveal the social interactions of the children. All the youngsters were observed, with and without their mothers, while at free play in the nursery school. Data were collected on child-child, child-mother, and child-teacher interactions. Observations were recorded with a running commentary that addressed numerous behavioral items (Table 4–1). The observations required a great deal of preparation in defining, recognizing, and accurately recording the behaviors. The investigator was then able to ask an array of questions about the children who had difficulty separating as compared to the normal children. Among the findings was that these youngsters directed less behavior to and were less responsive to other children. Paradoxically, they did not interact more with their mothers, although they did stay with them more. The children apparently were quite deprived of the opportunity to become socially adept.

The Leach investigation is a sophisticated observational study; the techniques had been well worked out in advance, and sta-

TABLE 4–1 Examples of the Behavior Items Recorded from Direct Observations of Normal Children and Those Considered to Have Separation Problems

Approach—The child walks toward a person, or object. (If the child runs towards a person, it is recorded as *run*.)

Avoid (or side-step)—The child is moving in one direction, but is confronted by an object, or person, and steps to the side, and may also bend the body away from obstruction.

Bend over to—This action is most often performed by adults to children. The upper body is inclined towards the child, or overhangs it.

Dress—This is a general term to cover all alterations to the clothing, such as putting on jerseys, tying up shoes. The teacher usually does these things for the children.

Follow—The child *walks* (or *runs*) towards a person who is moving away from it.

Get object—This covers a variety of reaching gestures, to obtain an object.

Give—An object, held in the child's hand or hands, is held out for another person to grasp and is then released, or the object may be placed on the other person's lap (usually mother's).

Grab (or *snatch*)—The child reaches for an object and pulls it abruptly towards itself, often with the body twisted round so that the object is rendered out of reach of another person.

From Leach, 1972. Reprinted by permission of Cambridge University Press.

tistical comparison was possible to ascertain that differences between the two groups of children were not due simply to chance. But even when only one group is involved, direct observation has the benefit of systematically measuring behavior as it is actually occurring. In this regard the method surpasses the clinical case study, which is a retrospective account of global behavior. On the other hand, since direct observation is confined to the particular behaviors selected for study, it sometimes lacks the richness of the case study.

Reliability of measurement in systematic observations is often acceptable because the behavior items have been defined and recording has been practiced prior to the study. The degree to which descriptions can be generalized depends on how subjects are selected and other factors.

Correlational Research

Correlational strategies go beyond simple description, to determine whether a relationship exists between or among variables. The variables may be measured in the natural environment or the laboratory in a variety of ways. Researchers then typically calculate a correlation coefficient, which is a quantitative measure of the existence, direction, and strength of the relationship. Correlational research is extremely helpful in many instances.

It is useful when initial exploration is the goal of research and the investigator first wants to determine whether any relationships exist among variables before specific hypotheses are advanced.

Correlational studies can also be helpful when ethical considerations preclude manipulation. Suppose, for example, that an investigator seeks knowledge about the impact of child abuse, poor nutrition, or family conflict on children's behaviors. It would be ethically impossible to manipulate these factors by exposing children to them. However, some children are exposed to these situations in their natural environments, and correlational research can determine whether these situations are related to children's behavior. Such knowledge can suggest hypotheses. Moreover, when a relationship is revealed, it is possible to predict one variable from another.

In its simplest form the question asked in correlational research is: Are factors X and Y related, and, if so, in what direction are they related, and how strongly? The first step of the research is to select a sample of children that represents the population of interest. Next, two scores must be obtained from each child, one a measure of variable X and the other a measure of variable Y. Statistical analysis of these data must then be performed. In this case the Pearson product-moment coefficient, r, could be computed.

The value of Pearson r,* which always ranges between $+1.00$ and -1.00, indicates the direction and the strength of the relationship. Direction is indicated by the sign of the coefficient. The positive sign $(+)$ means that high scores on the X variable tend to be associated with high scores on the Y variable, and that low scores on X tend to be related to low scores on Y. This is referred to as a *positive*, or direct, correlation. For example, a positive relationship exists between children's age and body weight: Older children usually weigh more. The negative sign $(-)$ indicates that high scores on X tend to be related to low scores on Y, and low scores on X tend to be related to high scores on Y. An example of a *negative* correlation (also called an indirect, or inverse, correlation) is adult age and lung capacity: As adults increase in age, their lung capacity decreases.

The strength or magnitude of a correlation is reflected in the absolute value of the coefficient. Thus a correlation of $+0.55$ is equally as strong as one of -0.55. The

---

* Pearson r is just one of several correlation coefficients that could be calculated, depending on the nature and complexity of the study. The general procedures and interpretations described above apply to these situations.

strongest relationship is expressed by an r of $+1.00$ or -1.00, both of which are considered perfect correlations. As the coefficient value decreases in absolute value, the relationship becomes weaker. A coefficient of 0.00 indicates that no relationship exists at all. In this case the score on one variable tells us nothing about the score on the other variable.

Let us consider a hypothetical example of correlational research. Suppose that an investigator suspected that children's self-concept and performance on a certain achievement test are positively related. After obtaining an appropriate sample of children, the reseacher would obtain two scores for each child—one a measure of self-concept and one a measure of achievement. The hypothetical data might appear as in Table 4–2. Pearson r for these data would be calculated and its value found to equal $+0.82$. How would this finding be interpreted? Obviously, a correlation exists, and the positive sign indicates that children who scored high on the measure of self-concept tend to score high on the achievement test. Moreover, the magnitude of the coefficient indicates that the relationship is quite strong (since $+1.00$ is a perfect positive relationship). Thus, the researcher's hypothesis is supported by the correlational analysis.

The degree to which correlational research is reliable depends mainly on the reliability of the measures used. To the degree to which the study has been appropriately conducted, valid results are obtained about whether relationships exist among variables. However, a common mistake is to draw cause-and-effect conclusions from the results. Casual links cannot automatically be assumed from correlational analyses; two problems of interpretation exist.

Problems of directionality and other variables. One problem is that cause may flow in either direction. The other is that some other variable(s) may be responsible for the revealed correlation. In the hypothetical example above, it is possible that self-concept causes achievement scores or that achievement causes self-concept scores. Or perhaps other variables, such as general intelligence or family dynamics, cause the relationship between self-concept and achievement.

There are, however, a few things that can be done to indicate what causal relationship might exist. For one, the nature of the variables can be examined for a suggestion of cause-and-effect. If a positive correlation were found between the nutritional value of children's diets and school performance in children, for example, it would seem more likely that diet influenced schoolwork than vice versa.

Still, other variables could be responsible for the relationship between diet and school performance—perhaps social-class factors. If there were good reason to suspect some role for social class, a partial correlation statistical procedure could be useful. This method partials out, or removes, the effects of other variables, allowing the investigator to determine whether the two original variables are still correlated. The trouble with partialing, however, is that one can never be sure that all possible causative variables have been examined. That is, perhaps some variable not partialed out contributes to the diet-school relationship (e.g., TV viewing habits).

Other techniques, too complex to discuss

TABLE 4–2 Self-Concept and Achievement Scores

Data from a Hypothetical Study of Children's Self-Concept and Performance on an Achievement Test. The Pearson r value is $+0.82$, which indicates a strong positive relationship between the variables.

Child	Variable X Self-concept Score	Variable Y Achievement Test Score
Daniel	2	5
Nicky	3	4
Sara	4	12
Beth	7	16
Jessica	9	10
Alia	11	22
Brent	13	18

here, also help researchers make inferences about cause-and-effect. Short of these sophisticated techniques, correlations may suggest causation but cannot be assumed to demonstrate it.

This discussion of correlational research has focused on the basics of the method; we shall have further opportunity throughout the text to see how the technique is used in research.

Experimental Research

The true experiment comes closest to meeting the rigorous standards of the scientific method. Regardless of its particular purpose, it is characterized by the following:

1. An explicitly or implicitly stated hypothesis
2. Subjects appropriately selected and assigned to groups that are exposed to conditions or manipulations
3. Two or more conditions or manipulations selected by the investigator (the *independent* variable)
4. Observation and measurement (the *dependent* variable)
5. Control of the procedures by the investigator
6. Comparison of the effects of the manipulations

Control is of utmost importance. The experiences of the subjects are prearranged and meticulously presented, with the different groups being exposed to different conditions. This permits final judgment about the causes of the findings of the study.

To illustrate the experiment, we draw on a study by Ramey and Campbell (1984) who tested the hypothesis that early education prevents intellectual retardation in at-risk children. Based on past research, they believed that such children would benefit from a child-centered, intellectually stimulating environment provided as part of a day-care service.

Potential participants were identified through prenatal clinics and the local social service department. Each family was then surveyed with the High Risk Index to determine parental education, income, presence or absence of father and relatives, children's intellectual performance, and the like. Families meeting a criterion score were considered at risk. Final selection was made

after the mother was interviewed and given an intelligence test. Participants were chosen either before or soon after the birth of the subject child.

Families then were paired according to similarity on the High Risk Index, and the children from each pair were randomly assigned to either the treatment or control group. Such matching and random assignment were crucial to the experiment because it was the method to create groups that were approximately equal in characteristics.

The independent variable in this study was the provision of the educational program. All the children in the treatment group began day care by 3 months of age, and their development was tracked until they reached 54 months. The center operated five full days a week, for 50 weeks of the year. The educational program included language, motor, social, and cognitive components. It varied somewhat, of course, with the child's age. Special emphasis was given to the development of communication skills. Thus, a good deal of attention was paid to verbal exchanges and children were read to each day. Reading, mathematics, and social skills programs were used.

Control-group children did not attend the day-care center and were not exposed to the educational program. Efforts were made to otherwise equate their experiences with those of the treatment group: They were given similar nutritional supplements, pediatric care, and supportive social services.

To assess the possible influence of the independent variable, all children were tested twice annually with standardized developmental or intelligence tests. These measures were the dependent variable. The examiners were randomly assigned to the testing sessions.

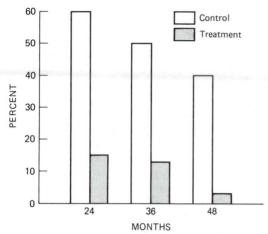

FIGURE 4–1 Percent of Stanford-Binet IQ scores at or below 85 at three ages for treatment and control subjects. From Ramey and Campbell, 1984.

The test results revealed that beginning at 18 months, children in the treatment group scored higher than children in the control group, and the group difference was statistically significant.* Figure 4–1 shows one way of examining the findings. It indicates that at 24, 36, and 48 months the educationally treated children were much less likely to obtain IQ scores at or below 85 than were the control children. The researchers thus concluded that the educational program resulted in intellectual benefits for the treated at-risk youngsters.

Is this conclusion justified? That is, does the study have internal validity? The method by which the subjects were selected and assigned makes it unlikely that the results simply reflect group differences that existed before the study was conducted. Moreover, efforts were made to treat the experimental and control groups similarly

except for the independent variable. To the degree this was accomplished, it can be confidently concluded that the study is internally valid and that the results are due to the treatment. Caution is appropriate, however. When research is conducted in the laboratory, it is relatively easy to control the experiences of the groups. In field experiments such as Ramey and Campbell's, the degree of control and thus internal validity is less clear. An additional issue concerns the actual collection of data. Possible bias of the individual testers was offset by their being randomly assigned to testing sessions. However, it appears that those who gave the standardized tests may have known the group to which each child had been assigned, raising the question of bias in data collection.

What about external validity, or generalizability, of the findings? As mentioned earlier, this matter is rarely completely settled, but validity is enhanced in the Ramey and Campbell study because it was conducted in a setting in which such training might eventually occur. To the extent that other day-care settings would be similar to the original setting, external validity could be expected. Validity would also be anticipated if new subjects would be similar to the original samples. The findings appear to apply to both sexes because no differences were found between girls' and boys' scores.

The Ramey and Campbell experiment is one variation on the experimental method. Other experiments might, for example, be conducted in the laboratory, select subjects in somewhat different ways, include more groups, or collect data at only one point in time. Although specific statistical analyses might also vary, their purpose would be the same: To determine whether group differences go beyond what might be expected by chance. When a significant statistical difference is found and the experiment is rigorously designed and conducted, a causal connection between the independent and dependent variables can be assumed. Thus, the experiment is a powerful tool for explanation.

---

* Statistical significance refers to the statistical probability that a finding is a chance result. As a general rule, a significant finding would occur by chance five times or less were the study to be repeated one hundred times. (This level of probability, the .05 level, is indicated in research by the term $p \leq .05$.) Thus, we are reasonably sure that the result is not a chance finding.

The typical experiment, described in the previous section, is conducted with groups of people, with one or more control groups serving to help rule out alternative explanations of the findings. A strategy akin to the experiment can be conducted with single individuals, provided that some control for alternative explanations is employed. The investigations involve taking many measurements across time periods; thus, they are sometimes referred to as time series studies. With careful control, internal validity is quite possible. External validity is not strong as generalizations from single subjects cannot be made with confidence. However, external validity can be increased by repeating the study with different subjects.

Single-subject designs are frequently used to evaluate the influence of a clinical manipulation on problem behavior. One way to control for alternative explanations is knowns as the ABA' design. The problem behavior is carefully defined and measured across time periods, during which the subject is exposed to different conditions. During the first period (A) measures are taken of the behavior prior to any intervention. This baseline measure serves as a standard against which change can be evaluated. In period B the intervention is carried out while the behavior is measured in the identical way. The intervention is then removed for a period of time known as the reversal period (A').

Figure 4–2 gives a hypothetical example of the ABA' design. Appropriate play behavior occurs at low frequency during the baseline, increases during the treatment phase B, and decreases when the manipulation is removed in the A' phase.

In studies in which behavior improves during intervention, particularly if clinical treatment is the aim, a fourth period (B'), during which the successful intervention is reintroduced, must be added. Typically the relevant behaviors show improvement again.

Nevertheless, the ABA' design is limited in that the intervention may make reversal (A') unlikely. For example, when treatment results in increased academic skill, the child may not display decreases in the skill when intervention is removed. From the standpoint of successful treatment this is a positive outcome; from a research standpoint, it has not been demonstrated that the intervention caused the positive behavior. The ABA' design also has an ethical problem in that the researcher may hesitate to return to baseline condition once a manipulation is associated with positive change. If there is no return to baseline, although the manipulation may appear responsible for the change, a definite demonstration of its effects is lacking.

In some instances in which the ABA' design is inappropriate, alternative designs, such as multiple baselines, may be used. In one multiple baseline design, two behaviors are recorded across time. After baselines are established for both, the intervention is made for only one behavior. During the next phase, intervention is applied to the other behavior as well. For example, a clinician may hypothesize that a child's temper tantrums and object throwing are maintained by adult attention to these behaviors.

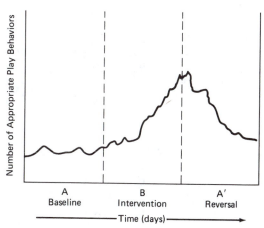

FIGURE 4–2 Hypothetical example of the ABA' design.

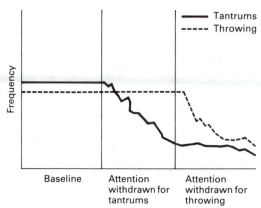

FIGURE 4–3 Frequency of tantrums and throwing across the phases of a hypothetical multiple baseline, single-subject experiment.

Withdrawal of attention would thus reduce the behaviors. Support for the hypothesis can be seen in Figure 4–3, a hypothetical graph of the frequency of both behaviors across time periods. Because behavior change follows the pattern of the treatment procedure, it is likely that withdrawal of attention and not some other variable caused the change.

In another type of multiple baseline design, treatment is given to more than one person, following different time lines. For example, Koegel, O'Dell, and Koegel (1987) evaluated the effects of a new treatment to enhance language development in autistic children. As Figure 4–4 shows, two children began the old treatment (Teaching Method I) at the same time. Child 1 was then put on the new treatment, and child 2 followed several months later. Data were recorded in the clinic for two kinds of verbal imitation. The demonstration of similar patterns of change for both children increases confidence that the treatment actually caused improvement (internal validity). Moreover, external validity is enhanced by the fact that the effect held across two persons.

In addition to reversal and multiple base-

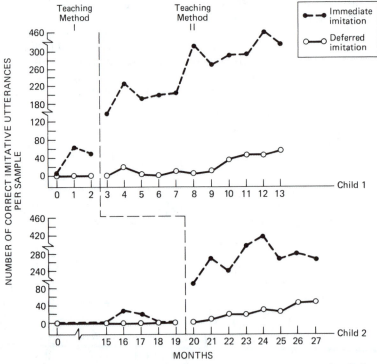

FIGURE 4–4 Number of correct verbal imitations across months during Teaching Methods I and II. From Koegel, O'Dell, and Koegel, 1987.

line procedures, other methods of control have been developed for single subject experiments (Barlow and Hersen, 1984; Hersen, 1990). All these methods permit the researcher-clinician to test hypotheses while working with one (or a few) subjects and, in the case of treatment, focus on the child of immediate concern.

Controlled Observations and Mixed Designs

In studying behavioral disorders researchers frequently select groups of subjects who differ behaviorally, and then compare them on some measured characteristic or behavior. The subjects are selected according to some classification scheme, and the factor on which they are selected is referred to as a *classificatory* factor. The measures are obtained under controlled conditions, and there is no manipulation.

Consider, for example, the investigation of Goldberg and Konstantareas (1981), who were interested in determining that attentional processes are central in children who display hyperactivity. Hyperactive and normal boys were the subjects of this controlled observation. The hyperactive boys had previously been so classified. Their behavior was compared to that of ten boys who were functioning in a typical manner in public school. There were no statistical differences between the groups in age range and intellectual levels.

Each boy was individually tested on a vigilance task. The apparatus consisted of a television-like box and a pair of keys that controlled, in part, the stimuli on the screen. One measure taken was the observing response; that is, the rate at which each boy pressed the left key to bring a clown's face into view. The other measure concerned signal detection. The boys were told that every time the clown's nose lit up (the signal), they were to press the right key. It was hypothesized that due to attentional deficits the hyperactive boys would make fewer observing responses and more errors on the signal detection test. Statistical analysis of the group means supported the hypotheses. It was thus concluded that the hyperactive boys showed deficits in attending to stimuli.

This conclusion was warranted and extended previous similar findings. However, it is problematic in such a study to assume that hyperactivity itself caused the performance differences. There is no clear way to rule out the possibility that factors merely *associated* with hyperactivity produced the results. Perhaps the hyperactive children held lower self-expectations or were overly anxious in the situation due to a history of failure. When classificatory factors are employed to select comparison groups, interpretation of the results must be made cautiously. This is because the classificatory factor is not manipulated and is simply correlated with the observed behavior.

In mixed designs, subject groups are chosen on the basis of classificatory factors and then a manipulation occurs (Davison and Neale, 1990). Take the hypothetical situation in which both hyperactive and normal boys (the classificatory factor) are given a vigilance task under two conditions, one in which they work alone and the other in which they work while observed by another person (the manipulation). Suppose the hyperactive group does better when alone than when observed, but the performance of the normal group is the same under the two conditions. Thus, being observed by another person appeared to disrupt the hyperactive boys in some way. However, the problem of interpretation still exists despite the manipulation: It is not clear that hyperactivity itself rather than some associated feature caused the results.

This is not to say that controlled observations and mixed designs, as described above, are useless. They can demonstrate differences between groups. The problem is that such demonstrations of group differences are limited in what they tell us about disordered behavior, and findings can be misinterpreted.

In addition to the distinctions already made among research methods, investigations can also be categorized as either longitudinal or cross-sectional.

Longitudinal Research

Longitudinal research evaluates the same subjects over time, repeatedly observing or testing them. It "sees" development as it occurs. One of the first such studies was Lewis Terman's investigation of the gifted in which, beginning in 1921, a population was examined several times over many decades (Sears, 1975). Terman's research was followed by other studies that traced the growth of intellectual, social, and physical abilities.

The longitudial strategy is unique in its capacity to answer questions about the nature and course of development. Does an early traumatic event, such as the death of a parent, play a role in the origin of childhood depression? Can preschool intervention for socially disadvantaged children overcome the academic deficits so often found in later childhood? Does aggression in early childhood put children at risk for adulthood aggression? The longitudinal method can be extremely helpful in answering these kinds of questions. (See Box 4.1.)

Still, it has serious drawbacks. Longitudinal studies are extremely expensive and require that investigators commit themselves to a project for several years. Also, it is difficult to retain subjects over many years, and "dropouts" may have certain characteristics. For example, they may be more transient, less psychologically oriented, or less healthy than the subjects who continue. So

---

BOX 4.1 Exploring risk by tracing development

There are several ways to trace children's lives to investigate influences that may put children at risk for behavior disorders.

In *retrospective* designs, groups of children who do or do not display the problem of interest are identified. Then information is collected about their earlier characteristics and life experiences. The purpose of such follow-back studies is to seek hypotheses about the relationship of early variables and the later-observed condition. One obvious weakness of this method concerns the reliability of the data: As with the case study, old records may be inadequate or mistaken and adults' memories of their children's behaviors and lives may be sketchy and biased. Another obvious limitation of the method is that the discovery of a relationship between the past and present does not establish causation. Nevertheless, this kind of study is relatively easy to conduct and it can help form hypotheses about risk factors.

Prospective designs attempt to study risk in a different way. Children already thought to be at risk are followed over time, with observations of several variables being recorded at certain intervals. As time passes, some but not all of the subjects may show problem behaviors. The researcher can then examine the data to determine what variables are linked to the development of the disorder. Prospective studies have the drawback of all longitudinal research (e.g., expense, loss of subjects). In addition, the number of children who eventually develop the disorder may be quite small so that data must be collected on hundreds of children. Also, when researchers begin these demanding investigations, they must select the variables that will be observed along the way. Selection is often based on educated guesses and relevant variables can be left out. Despite these difficulties, though, the prospective design is invaluable in identifying risk factors and is thus commonly employed (Kopp, 1983).

---

subject loss can bias the results. Repeated testing of subjects can also be a problem: They may become test-wise, and efforts to change or improve the testing instruments make it difficult to compare earlier and later findings. Finally, subjects are not the only ones who change over the years; so may society. Thus, for example, if individuals were followed from 1930 to 1950, their development might be different from that of persons of the same age followed from 1970 to 1990, due to historical variables. The 1930 to 1950 group certainly might have had different experiences than the 1970 to 1990 group (e.g., in health care, educational environments). These possible *generational*, or *cohort*, effects must be considered in interpreting longitudinal studies.

Cross-Sectional Research

The cross-sectional strategy focuses on different subjects at one point in time. It tests different groups of people at a particular time. It thus can be thought of as slicing across time rather than following time, as in longitudinal studies.

Although cross-sectional research is often experimental in design, subjects may be described, measured, or differentially treated, depending on the specific goals of the investigation. With this method, the problems of expense, subject loss, repeated measurement, and long-term commitment by researchers are minimized.

On the other hand, tracing developmental change is problematic. This goal is attempted by comparing the performance of different age groups. For example, someone interested in whether the frequency of aggression changes with development may measure aggression in 5-, 10-, and 15-year-olds. If the younger children displayed more aggression, it might be concluded that aggression decreases as children develop. However, this conclusion may not be warranted. *Age difference* is not necessarily *age or development change*. Perhaps specific experiences of the different age groups are responsible for the findings. Younger children might have watched more violent television or received more reinforcement for aggression, due to societal changes over time. Thus the finding may reflect societal change rather than the developmental course for aggression. To make matters more complex, societal changes can influence different age groups differently, making it extremely difficult to interpret cross-sectional data.

Sequential Designs

To overcome some of the weaknesses of the longitudinal and cross-sectional strategies, researchers combine the two approaches in a variety of complex sequential designs (see Achenbach, 1978 for a more complete discussion). One possible design is described here in a hypothetical study in which groups of children of different ages are studied over a relatively short time span. At time I children at ages 3, 6, and 9 years are examined in a cross-sectional study. Similar examination of the same groups occurs again three years later at time II, and again another three years later at time III. Figure 4–5 depicts the study. By reading down the columns of the figure, cross-sectional com-

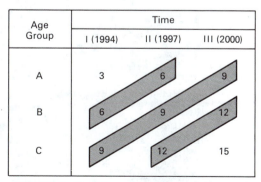

FIGURE 4–5 Schema of a sequential research design in which children of different ages are examined cross-sectionally and longitudinally.

parisons can be made at three different times. In addition, by reading from left to right across the figure, three groups of children (A, B, and C) can be studied longitudinally over a six-year period (1994 to 2000). The age range in the investigation is from 3 to 15 years.

Various comparisons can provide a wealth of information from such a sequential design. To take a simple case, if aggression were found to decrease with age at times I, II, and III (cross-sectional analyses) and also across time for each group of children (the longitudinal analyses), evidence would be strong for developmental change over the entire age range. Moreover, by comparing aggression at age 6, or 9, or 12 (as boxed in the figure), the impact of societal conditions could also be evaluated. It might be found, for example, that aggression at age 9 increased from 1994 to 1997 to 2000. Since only one age is involved, this increase is not developmental and thus indicates a change in societal conditions during the years under investigation.

Thus, sequential designs can be powerful in separating age differences and developmental changes, while taking generational effects into consideration.

ETHICAL ISSUES

Scientific research is enormously beneficial, but it brings some concerns about the welfare and rights of particpants. This is due to both the present emphasis on individual rights and past documented abuse of research subjects. One well-known instance in which the problem of abuse was raised involves a study, begun in 1932, of the

Informed consent by a parent or guardian should be obtained when a child participates in research. What constitutes informed consent by the child is a complex issue. (James Holland/Stock, Boston)

natural course of syphilis. The investigation was continued into the early 1970's, even though the development of antibiotics during that time period could have provided treatment for the subjects long before the 1970's (Kelty, 1981).

Abuse in social science research has probably not been as dramatic as in biomedical research, but ethical issues do exist. In the widely discussed Milgram (1963) study, for example, subjects were deceived into thinking that they were applying electric shocks to another human. The study was designed to evaluate whether subjects would obey a directive to harm others. Many of them did, but they suffered discomfort about their behavior. A postexperimental interview was included to alleviate this stress. Nevertheless, serious questions were raised about the ethics of researchers deceptively setting up a situation that brought guilt, anxiety, and embarrassment to the participants (e.g., Baumrind, 1964; Murray, 1988).

Research with children has sometimes involved procedures in which the participants were made uncomfortable, for example, by waiting alone in a room (Cozby, Warden, and Kee, 1989). Other studies have engaged children in aggressive acts, or have exposed them to aggressive live or filmed models. And children have served as subjects in research on the effects of medications. Clearly, there is potential for harm that must be guarded against.

In general, ethical concerns primarily address the issues of deception, possible harm and discomfort to subjects, and confidentiality. For many years the American Psychological Association has published a manual of ethical guidelines for research. The Society for Research in Child Development publishes similar guidelines, which specifically address research with children. Table 4–3 summarizes these guidelines. Social science research also falls under the guidelines of the National Committee for the Protection of Human Subjects of Biomedical and Behavioral Research. The Committee has demanded that institutions involved in research set up boards to judge the ethics of proposed research before the research is begun. Special considerations have been given to cases involving child subjects, particularly concerning informed consent.

Since the issue of informed consent is more difficult with children than adults, we will look at it further. Informed consent requires that participants be given information, reasonably understand the risks and benefits of the research, and consent to participate (Frankel, 1978; Weithorn, 1987). This includes understanding the purpose of the research, the role of the subjects, procedures, and possible alternatives to participation. Clearly, young children often cannot understand these nuances. Given adequate information, most parents are competent to give informed consent, and they are required to do so because children are not of legal age.

However, unlike in the past, children are now considered as "persons" under the law, whose decisions must be considered (Gaylin, 1982). Thus the question: What constitutes informed consent for children? It is suggested that adolescents be given the same information as adults and be asked to sign consent forms (e.g., Ferguson, 1978; Langer, 1985). The same procedure can be used for the school-age child, but researchers need to convey information in more concrete terms, with personal consequences spelled out. At the very least, children as young as seven years should be asked whether they agree to participate. With infants and toddlers, informed consent is not a reasonable expectation, and parental consent may be sufficient for a child's participation.

Such proxy consent is not without problems, however, because parental and child needs are not always identical. Furthermore, parents may feel coerced by social and economic pressures into permitting their child's participation. For example, if research participation is desired by an agency that offers therapeutic care, the parents of a child needing care may be afraid to refuse permission. These considerations raise doubts about the use of parental consent. In some cases that were brought to the

TABLE 4–3 Ethical Standards for Research with Children

Principle 1: Non-harmful Procedures. No research operation that may physically or psychologically harm the child should be used. The least stressful operation should be used. Doubts about harmfulness should be discussed with consultants.

Principle 2: Informed Consent. The child's consent or assent should be obtained. The child should be informed of features of the research that may affect his or her willingness to participate. In working with infants, parents should be informed. If consent would make the research impossible, it may be ethically conducted under certain circumstances; judgments should be made with institutional review boards.

Principle 3: Parental Consent. Informed consent of parents, guardians, and those acting in loci parentis (e.g., school superintendents) similarly should be obtained, preferably in writing.

Principle 4: Additional Consent. Informed consent should be obtained of persons, such as teachers, whose interaction with the child is the subject of the research.

Principle 5: Incentives. Incentives to participate in the research must be fair and not unduly exceed incentives the child normally experiences.

Principle 6: Deception. If deception or withholding information is considered essential, colleagues must agree with this judgment. Participants should be told later of the reason for the deception. Effort should be made to employ deception methods that have no known negative effects.

Principle 7: Anonymity. Permission should be gained for access to institutional records, and anonymity of information should be preserved.

Principle 8: Mutual Responsibilities. There should be clear agreement as to the responsibilities of all parties in the research. The investigator must honor all promises and commitments.

Principle 9: Jeopardy. When, in the research, information comes to the investigator's attention that may jeopardize the child's welfare, the information must be discussed with parents or guardians and experts who can arrange for assistance to the child.

Principle 10: Unforeseen Consequences. When research procedures result in unforeseen, undesirable consequences for the participant, the consequences should be corrected and the procedures redesigned.

Principle 11: Confidentiality. The identity of subjects and all information about them should be kept confidential. When confidentiality might be threatened, this possibility and methods to prevent it should be explained as part of the procedures of obtaining informed consent.

Principle 12: Informing Participants. Immediately after data collection, any misconceptions that might have arisen should be clarified. General findings should be given the participants, appropriate to their understanding. When scientific or humane reasons justify withholding information, efforts should be made so that withholding has no damaging consequences.

Principle 13: Reporting Results. Investigators' words may carry unintended weight; thus, caution should be used in reporting results, giving advice, making evaluative statements.

Principle 14: Implications of Findings. Investigators should be mindful of the social, political, and human implications of the research, and especially careful in the presentations of findings.

Summarized from the Report from the Committee for Ethical Conduct in Child Development Research, *SRCD Newsletter* (Winter 1990). Society for Research in Child Development, Inc.

---

attention of the courts, guardians were appointed to oversee decisions about the children.

In making judgments about research studies, Institutional Review Boards consider such things as the scientific soundness of the research, the risk/benefit ratio, and protection of privacy (Langer, 1985). In addition, they consider parental legal rights, the child's competence to be informed and make decisions, and the significance of the decision to the child. In some situations, the child's decision may not be binding; for example, when the child refuses to participate in research involving treatment in which risk is minimal and the possible benefits are not otherwise available. Here, parental consent may be sufficient. In other situations, the child's consent may be considered of utmost importance; for example, when risk is greater than minimal and research findings may increase understanding of the child's condition but be of little direct benefit to the child.

In the final analysis, the ethics of research, like other ethical concerns, can never be a completely settled matter. Ongoing discussion and tension are appropriate. The prevailing emphasis on human rights and recognition of past abuse has led to quite stringent surveillance and guidelines. It is important that a balance be maintained, however, so that researchers are not unduly discouraged in their efforts to understand human behavior.

SUMMARY

Knowledge of human behavior is gained by scientific methods that vary with regard to settings, procedures, designs, and purposes. The aim of science is to describe phenomena and offer explanations for them. Explanation is facilitated by information about relationships, especially cause-and-effect relationships.

Theoretical concepts guide all aspects of research, including the hypotheses advanced. Hypothesis testing builds knowledge systematically and is tied to the advancement of theory.

Observation and measurement are at the heart of science. The assumption that events repeat themselves, given the same or similar conditions, places importance on the reliability, or consistency, of findings.

Research must also address validity, the soundness or appropriateness of scientific results. Internal validity refers to the degree to which alternative explanations for results can be confidently ruled out. External validity is the issue of generalizability of findings to populations and settings other than those of the original study.

All the various research methods have strengths and weaknesses. In case studies, the accuracy and completeness of data may be difficult to verify and guidelines for interpretation are weak. Case studies are not readily generalized. Nevertheless, they can provide rich descriptions and generate hypotheses, and they are relevant to clinical concerns.

Systematic naturalistic observations can provide more precise, accurate, and current details of behavior but may lose some of the richness of case studies. Reliability and internal validity depend on measurement and procedures, while judgments about external validity consider the subject population and setting.

Correlational research determines the existence, direction, and strength of relationships between or among variables. It is excellent for initial exploration, the generation of hypotheses, and when experimental manipulation is impossible. Cause-and-effect cannot be definitively established, thus limiting explanations for the findings. Again, reliability rests mainly on the reliability of measurement, internal validity on the degree to which the study has been appropriately conducted, and external validity on consideration of the population and setting.

The experiment is the best tool for determining cause-and-effect. Here the independent variable is manipulated and controlled by the researcher to test its possible effects on the dependent variable. With appropriate design, subject selection, and control of procedures, internal validity can be quite high. As with other methods, generalization must always be considered. One weakness of the experiment is that it requires a degree of control that may make it artificial.

Single-subject (time series) experiments take many measurements across time on a single, or perhaps a few, individuals. There are several specific designs that build control in various ways so that cause-and-effect may be identified. The reversal and multiple baseline procedures are widely known. Internal validity can be readily achieved, but results are not readily generalized from single subjects.

Whenever classificatory factors are used to select the subjects of research, the results are difficult to interpret, limiting internal validity. Mixed designs superficially resemble the experiment, but interpretation is still a problem.

In addition to the distinctions already drawn among research methods, longitudinal and cross-sectional strategies also may be adopted. The longitudinal strategy is superb for tracing development over time, and thus for investigating risk factors. But it is expensive, requires lengthy commitment from researchers, and may suffer from biased subject loss and repeated measurement. Cross-sectional studies, which focus on different people at one point in time, avoid many of these weaknesses while providing useful data, but cannot trace developmental change.

Sequential designs combine the longitudinal and cross-sectional strategies to retain their strengths and overcome some of their weaknesses. They permit examination of developmental change, age differences, and the influence of variables that may be associated historically with the age groups.

Ethical issues in research are currently receiving much attention, and are being addressed by several organizations and committees. Questions about possible harm and discomfort to subjects, deception, confidentiality, informed consent, and coercion are of utmost importance. Children's participation in research raises concerns over and above those expressed for adults. For example, the issues of informed consent requires consideration of the child's ability to understand information, the appropriateness of proxy consent, and the basic rights of children. In the final analysis, the concern for research participants must be weighed with the potential benefits derived from studying human behavior.

5

CLASSIFICATION AND ASSESSMENT

This chapter is concerned with the classification, diagnosis, and assessment of childhood behavior disorders. Although the terms *classification* and *diagnosis* are often used interchangeably here and elsewhere, the former emphasizes description and grouping for scientific study, while the latter involves grouping for clinical purposes. *Assessment* refers to an ongoing process of evaluating the phenomenon that is classified or diagnosed. These entwined processes thus are intricately related to the scientific and clinical aspects of childhood disorders.

CLASSIFICATION AND DIAGNOSIS

A classification system is a systematic arrangement of groups or categories. Biologists have classification systems for living organisms, and physicians classify physical dysfuntion. Similarly, systems exist to classify behavioral disorders. Some systems work better than others, and we may ask: What makes a good system of classification? Before we examine current systems for classifying children's disordered behavior, we need to examine the criteria by which any system will be judged.

First and foremost, the categories of the system must be clearly defined. This means that the criteria for determining if a particular case fits a category must be explicitly stated. Next, it must be demonstrated that the categories exist. This means that features used to describe a category must be observed to occur together regularly—in one or more situations or as measured by one or more methods. A classification system composed of categories that are either poorly defined or that do not exist is doomed to failure.

Classification systems must also be reliable and valid. These terms were applied to research methods in Chapter 4. When applied to classification or diagnosis they retain the general meanings of consistency and correctness but are used in somewhat different ways.

With regard to reliability, *interrater reliability* refers to the consistency with which diagnosticians use the same category to describe a child's behavior. It addresses, for example, the question: Is Billy's behavior called separation anxiety by two or more professionals who observe it? *Test-retest reliability* asks if the use of a category is stable over some reasonable period of time. For example, is Mary's problem again diagnosed as learning disability when she returns for a second evaluation?

A system must also be *valid*. To have validity, diagnoses must be clearly discriminable from one another. Also, a diagnosis must provide us with more information than we had when we originally defined the category. Thus, diagnoses should give us information about the etiology of a disorder, the course of development that the disorder is expected to take, response to treatment, or some additional clinical features of the problem. Does the diagnosis of Conduct Disorder, for example, tell us something about this disorder that is different from other disorders? Does the diagnosis tell us something about what causes this problem? Does it tell what is likely to happen to children who are viewed as having this disorder and what treatments are likely to help? Does it tell us additional things about these children or their backgrounds? The question of validity is thus largely one of whether we know anything we did not already know when we defined the category.

Finally, a classification system is judged by its *clinical utility*; that is, by how complete and useful it is. A diagnostic system that describes all the behavioral disorders that come to the attention of clinicians in a manner that is useful to them is more likely to be employed.

Clinically Derived Classification Systems

Clinically derived classification systems are based on the consensus of clinicians that certain characteristics occur together. Historically the classification of abnormal behavior focused primarily on adult disorders. Until recently there was no extensive classification scheme for childhood behavior disorders.

DSM. The most widely used classification system in the United States is the American Psychiatric Association's Diagnostic and Statistical Manual of Mental Disorders (DSM). There are two other widely recognized clinical systems of classification: that of the Group for the Advancement of Psychiatry (GAP, 1966) and the International Classification of Diseases (ICD) developed by the World Health Organization (WHO, 1978). Since the DSM system has become the dominant system in the United States we will focus our discussion on it.

The DSM classification system is an outgrowth of the original psychiatric taxonomy developed by Kraeplin in 1883, from which children's disorders were omitted. DSM-I contained only two categories of childhood disorders: Adjustment Reaction and Childhood Schizophrenia (American Psychiatric Association, 1952). By the 1960s it had become obvious that a more extensive system was needed. The 1968 revision, DSM-II, added the category of Behavior Disorders of Childhood and Adolescence, which was subdivided into six kinds of disorders (American Psychiatric Association, 1968).

The next two revisions, DSM-III and DSM-III-R, expanded appreciably the number of categories specific to children and involved some changes in the organization of particular categories (American Psychiatric Association, 1980, 1987). As in the past, some adult diagnoses could also be used for children. In addition, it was recommended that each individual be evaluated along five dimensions, or axes, so that a fuller picture would be created. On Axes I and II the clinician indicates any existing mental or developmental disorder. Any condition not attributable to a mental disorder but that, nevertheless, will be focused on in treatment (for example, an academic problem) is also listed. If there are any current physical conditions that are relevant to understanding or treating the child, these are indicated on Axis III. Axes IV and V, respectively, are used to indicate the severity of both recent and enduring psychosocial stressors in the child's life and a global assessment of functioning at present and during the past year. Table 5–1 illustrates how these last two axes might be used in diagnosing a child.

Table 5–2 presents the major DSM-III-R diagnostic categories specific to children. In diagnosing a child a clinician may give a child any of these diagnoses or if an appropriate diagnosis cannot be found, disorders listed elsewhere in DSM-III-R can be considered. Some of the other diagnostic categories that might be employed for children are psychoactive substance-use disorders, schizophrenia, mood disorders, sexual dis-orders, adjustment disorder, and psycho-logical factors affecting physical condition.

The current DSM handling of childhood disorders is considerably more complex and provides more specific categories than did earlier versions. While this was intended to correct the limited attention to childhood problems in earlier versions, the outcome has been controversial. One issue is whether the existence of categories as specific as some of the subcategories is justified by empirical evidence. Another is that the more specific categories may threaten the reliability of the system. For example, in earlier attempts at diagnosing adult disorders, agreement among diagnosticians was considerably lower for subgroups than for larger categories (e.g., Beck et al., 1962). Ward and his colleagues (1962) found that

TABLE 5–1 Guidelines for the Use of Axes IV and V of DSM-III-R

Rating	AXIS IV—SEVERITY OF PSYCHOSOCIAL STRESSORS Examples
1. None	No acute or enduring relevant stressors
2. Mild	Started school; family arguments
3. Moderate	Birth of sibling; chronic illness in parent
4. Severe	Parents divorce; chronic life-threatening parental illness
5. Extreme	Death of parent; recurrent abuse
6. Catastrophic	Death of both parents; chronic life-threatening illness

Rating	AXIS V—GLOBAL ASSESSMENT OF FUNCTIONING Description
90–81	Symptoms absent or minimal; good functioning; generally satisfied
80–71	Symptoms transient and expectable reactions to stressors; no more than minimal impairment of functioning
70–61	Some mild symptoms (e.g., mild insomnia) or some difficulty in functioning (e.g., occasional truancy); has meaningful relationships
60–51	Moderate symptoms (e.g., occasional panic) or difficulty in functioning (e.g., few friends)
50–41	Serious symptoms (e.g., suicidal ideation) or difficulty in functioning (e.g., no friends)
40–31	Some impairment in reality testing or communication or impairment in several areas
30–21	Behavior considerably influenced by delusions or hallucinations or serious impairment in communication or inability to function in almost all areas
20–11	Some danger of hurting self or others or failure to maintain minimal personal hygiene or gross impairment of communication
10–1	Persistent danger of severely hurting self or others or persistent poor minimal hygiene or serious suicidal act

Adapted from and reprinted with permission from the *Diagnostic and Statistical Manual of Mental Disorders, Third Edition Revised.* Copyright 1987, American Psychiatric Association.

Axis I
  Disruptive Behavior Disorders
    Attention-deficit hyperactivity disorder
    Conduct disorder
    Oppositional defiant disorder
  Anxiety Disorders of Childhood or Adolescence
    Separation anxiety disorder
    Avoidant disorder
    Overanxious disorder
  Eating Disorders
    Anorexia nervosa
    Bulimia nervosa
    Pica
    Rumination disorder of infancy
    Eating disorder NOS[a]
  Gender Identity Disorders
    Gender identity disorder of childhood
    Transsexualism
    Gender identity disorder of adolescence or adult-
      hood, nontranssexual type
    Gender identity disorder NOS[a]
  Elimination Disorders
    Functional encopresis
    Functional enuresis
  Speech Disorders Not Elsewhere Classified
    Cluttering
    Stuttering
  Other Disorders of Infancy, Childhood, or
      Adolescence
    Elective mutism
    Identity disorder
    Reactive attachment disorder
    Stereotypy/habit disorder
    Undifferentiated attention-deficit disorder
Axis II—Developmental Disorders
  Mental Retardation
  Pervasive Developmental Disorders
    Autistic disorder
    Pervasive developmental disorder NOS[a]
  Specific Developmental Disorders
    Academic skills disorders
    Language and speech disorders
    Motor skills disorder
  Other Developmental Disorders

[a] The abbreviation NOS stands for not otherwise specified. The term is used to indicate cases that do not fit
well into other specific subcategories.
Reprinted with permission from the *Diagnostic and
Statistical Manual of Mental Disorders, Third Edition Revised*, Copyright 1987, American Psychiatric Association.

two-thirds of these disagreements between
diagnosticians resulted from inadequate criteria for making a diagnosis. Thus efforts
were made in DSM-III and DSM-III-R to

improve this situation by providing operational diagnostic criteria rather than just
general descriptions of disorders.

A study by Werry and his colleagues
(1983) illustrates how the reliability of a
child diagnostic system can be investigated.
A total of 195 admissions to a child psychiatric inpatient unit were diagnosed by two
to four clinicians. The diagnoses were based
on the usual ward-rounds presentation of
the case during the patient's first week of
admission. Therefore, the diagnostic system
was tested under "natural" circumstances.
This approach does, however, also present
a number of problems. Since the clinicians
regularly worked with each other, they may
have unintentionally affected each other's
diagnostic behavior during the case presentations. This could result in higher levels of
agreement than are actually due to characteristics of the diagnostic system itself. On
the other hand, the method used to gather
information for diagnosis in this study was
not very structured nor necessarily consistent across cases. The clinicians heard whatever information was presented for a case,
which varied from case to case. This could
yield less reliable diagnoses. Despite these
potential biases, the results of the Werry et
al. study were similar to findings from several earlier studies (American Psychiatric
Association, 1980; Cantwell et al.,1979; Mattison et al., 1979; Spitzer, Forman, and Nie,
1979; Strober, Green, and Carlson, 1981).
Similar conclusions have also been reached
in a subsequent study with an Hispanic
sample (Canino et al., 1987) and also for
the childhood categories of the World
Health Organization's classification system
(Rutter and Shaffer, 1980).

What, then, were the results obtained by
Werry et al.? The overall reliability across
the categories of the system, 0.71, was satisfactory. A reliability coefficient of 0.70 is
often recommended as the minimum acceptable level. Looking next at reliability
across diagnosticians for the major categories, nine categories proved reliable or came
close, three were moderately unreliable, and
four proved highly unreliable. Thus, for
the most part acceptable levels of reliability

were obtained for a majority of the major categories.

The outcome for the subcategories, however, was quite different. While acceptable levels of interrater reliability were achieved for a small number of subcategories, a much larger number proved to be unreliable. Furthermore, reliability of the subcategories was examined by asking how the reliability of a subcategory compared to the reliability of the larger category in which it was contained. There were one or two instances of good reliability of subcategories, but several instances where no subcategories were as reliable as the larger category. The most frequent pattern by far, however, was where one subcategory achieved levels of reliability comparable to the larger category, with all the other subcategories well behind in reliability. These findings suggest that little may be gained by subcategorization.

There have also been attempts to examine the validity of the DSM approach to classification of children's problems. For example, Last and her colleagues (1987b) found that children meeting the DSM-III diagnostic criteria for the categories of separation anxiety and overanxious disorders differed on a number of characteristics: age, social class, and the presence of another anxiety disorder. This addresses the validity of these diagnostic categories in that knowing whether a child meets the diagnostic criteria for one and not the other category also imparts additional information that did not enter into the diagnostic process: age, social class, and presence of another anxiety disorder. In general, the validity of such differentiation between categories is good for broad categories such as emotional disorder and conduct disorder. But, again, how to subdivide broad groupings validly is less clear. In fact, despite evidence for the validity of some diagnostic categories (cf. Rutter and Gould, 1985), there is still considerable concern regarding the validity of many of the DSM childhood categories, even among those who are in large part sympathetic to the system's approach to classification (e.g., Kazdin, 1985; Rutter and Tuma, 1988).

There is broad agreement that with DSM-III and DSM-III-R many positive directions were taken: the increased use of a structured set of rules for diagnosis, greater comprehensiveness, and the use of a multiaxial system. The system, however, is not without its critics. In addition to concerns of reliability and validity, there are questions raised regarding the appropriateness of the criteria used for some diagnoses (e.g., Quay, 1986a). Concern has also been expressed about the very comprehensiveness of this system. The wisdom of making such a wide variety of children's behaviors classifiable as mental disorders and the motivation behind this decision has been questioned (e.g., Harris, 1979; Schacht and Nathan, 1977).

Some of these critics question the clinical utility of the childhood section (e.g., Bemporad and Schwab, 1986). Others recognize that, despite its acceptance and use, the system is fundamentally inconsistent with some approaches to children's problems (e.g., Kendall, 1987). For example, DSM does not employ situational variability as part of the diagnostic process. This is problematic for a behavioral perspective in which situational factors are presumed to influence behavior. Other criticisms of the system are based on the fundamental question of whether the scientific foundations of the whole approach (e.g., consensus among clinicians) are sound (e.g., Eysenck, 1986).

Empirical Approaches to Classification

The empirical approach to classifying childhood behavior problems is an alternative to the clinical approach. This approach employs statistical techniques to identify patterns of behavior that are interrelated. The general procedure is for the respondent to indicate the presence or absence of specific behaviors in the child. The information from these items is quantified in some way. For example, a "0" is marked if the child does not exhibit a certain characteristic, a "1" is given if a moderate degree of the characteristic is displayed, and a "2" is indicated if the characteristic is clearly present. Such information is obtained for a large number of children. Statistical techniques are then employed to indicate which behaviors tend to occur together. This cluster of behaviors constitutes a *syndrome*. Thus, rather than relying on clinicians' memories and impressions as to what behaviors tend to occur together, empirical and statistical procedures are employed as the basis for developing a classification scheme.

Factor analysis and cluster analysis are the primary statistical techniques employed in these studies. These procedures are based on correlations among items. The correlation of every item with the other items is calculated, and groups of items that tend to occur together are identified. These groups are referred to as factors or clusters.

The similarity of derived syndromes. There have been multiple efforts to develop empirically defined syndromes. This research has involved different instruments, completed by different kinds of adult caregivers, evaluating different populations of children, seen in different settings. The results suggest considerable consistency in the findings obtained (Achenbach, 1985; Quay, 1986b).

Substantial evidence exists for two *broadband*, or general, syndromes. One of these syndromes has been given the various labels of Externalizing, Undercontrolled, or Conduct Disorder. Fighting, temper tantrums, disobedience, and destructiveness are some of the characteristics most frequently associated with this pattern. The second broadband syndrome, variously labeled Internalizing, Overcontrolled, or Anxiety-Withdrawal, has been almost as frequent in its appearance. Anxious, shy, withdrawn, and depressed are some of the characteristics associated with this syndrome.

Syndromes according to age and sex. Among the instruments used to derive the two broad-band syndromes just described is the Child Behavior Checklist (Achenbach and Edelbrock, 1983). Research with this instrument has also found specific subcate-gories, or syndromes, called *narrow-band* factors within the two broad-band categories of Internalizing and Externalizing. Some of the subcategories do not fall clearly within one of the two larger categories and are, therefore, referred to as Mixed. In addition, the subcategories that emerged depended on the age and gender of the child. That is, different subcategories were found for different age-sex groups. Table 5–3 illustrates the different narrow-band factors found for boys and girls in age groups 4 to 5, 6 to 11, and 12 to 16. Thus, it would appear that general Internalizing and Externalizing categories exist for both genders at all ages. However, more specific problems within these syndromes differ, depending upon the age and gender of the child.

Achenback and Edelbrock (1983) suggest that in contrast to describing the multiple characteristics of a single child, the Child Behavior Checklist can be employed to assign children to categories. A profile of scores on the narrow-band syndromes is prepared for each child. By statistically analyzing large samples of profiles of disturbed children and putting them into groups of similar profiles, a typology of profiles can be formed (Achenbach & Edelbrock, 1989). Figure 5–1 illustrates examples of such profile types.

Reliability and validity. Reliability studies of empirically derived systems show an interesting pattern. Test-retest correlations from two ratings by the same informants often range from 0.80 to more than 0.90. Agreement between different raters observing the child in the same situation is also quite good, although somewhat lower than for two evaluations by the same person (Achenbach and Edelbrock, 1983, 1986). For example, interrater reliabilities between two parents who see the child at home (0.59) or between two teachers who observe the child in school (0.64) suggest good levels of agreement. However, agreements are even lower between raters who observe children in distinctly different situations (for example, 0.24 between parents who see the child at home and mental health workers who

TABLE 5-3 Narrow-band Syndromes Found for Boys and Girls of Different Ages

Group	Internalizing Syndromes	Mixed Syndromes	Externalizing Syndromes
Boys 4–5	Social withdrawal Depressed Immature Somatic complaints	Sex problems	Delinquent Aggressive Schizoid
Boys 6–11	Schizoid or anxious Depressed Uncommunicative Obsessive-compulsive Somatic complaints	Social withdrawal	Delinquent Aggressive Hyperactive
Boys 12–16	Somatic complaints Schizoid Uncommunicative Immature Obesessive-compulsive	Hostile withdrawal	Hyperactive Aggressive Delinquent
Girls 4–5	Somatic complaints Depressed Schizoid or anxious Social withdrawal	Obese	Hyperactive Sex problems Aggressive
Girls 6–11	Depressed Social withdrawal Somatic complaints Schizoid-obessive		Cruel Aggressive Delinquent Sex problems Hyperactive
Girls 12–16	Anxious-obessive Somatic complaints Schizoid Depressed withdrawal	Immature Hyperactive	Cruel Aggressive Delinquent

Adapted from Achenbach and Edelbrock, 1983a. Copyright T. M. Achenbach. Reproduced by permission.

observe the child in the clinic). These lower correlations may reveal something about children's behavior, rather than just about the reliability of the approach to classification (Achenbach and Edelbrock, 1989). At the very least, they suggest that behavior can vary considerably across situations. All these findings certainly demand that attention be paid to differences in children's behavior with different individuals and in different situations, as well as to the possible bias of a rater's perspective (Achenbach, McConaughy, and Howell, 1987).

The validity of empirically derived classification systems is indicated by a variety of studies. The findings described above indicating that the same broad-band syndromes have emerged in a variety of studies employing different instruments, different types of raters, and different samples suggest that the categories reflect valid distinctions. Also, Achenbach and Edelbrock (1983a) report studies in which the Child Behavior Checklist and other commonly employed instruments (such as Conners's Parent Questionnaire (1973) and Quay and Peterson's Revised Behavior Problem Checklist (1983)) were administered to the same sample of parents. Correlations were significant for total problem scores, the broad-band syndromes (Internalizing and Externalizing), and for almost all of the comparable narrow-band scales. The correlations tended to be highest for total scores

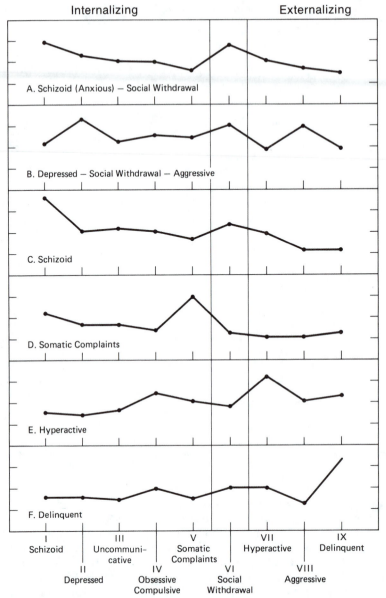

Internalizing Externalizing

A. Schizoid (Anxious) — Social Withdrawal

B. Depressed — Social Withdrawal — Aggressive

C. Schizoid

D. Somatic Complaints

E. Hyperactive

F. Delinquent

| I Schizoid | III Uncommuni-cative | V Somatic Complaints | VII Hyperactive | IX Delinquent |

| II Depressed | IV Obsessive Compulsive | VI Social Withdrawal | VIII Aggressive |

Note: Lettered terms refer to names given to profile types. Numbered terms at bottom of figure are the narrow band syndromes for boys 6–11.

FIGURE 5–1   Child Behavior Profile types found for boys aged 6 to 11. Adapted from Achenbach and Edelbrock, 1983. Copyright by T.M. Achenbach reproduced by permission.

and the broad-band categories. It is important to remember that these significant correlations emerged even though the instruments and their categories often consist of different items. The findings show that the syndromes are valid ones because they emerge under a variety of conditions.

Another way of examining validity is to investigate whether differences in scores relate to other criteria. For example, Achenbach and Edelbrock (1983a) compared a sample of children referred for outpatient mental health services to a sample of non-referred children matched for SES, age, and gender. They found that the clinical sample differed significantly from the non-referred sample on all scores and that this was true for all sex/age groups. Categories based upon empirically derived classifica- tions, particularly the broad-band internal-izer-externalizer distinction, have also been related to differences on a variety of de-mographic, psychological, behavioral and social variables (Achenbach and Edelbrock, 1978, 1989). Thus these categories are valid in that they are related to differences in variables other than those used to define them.

The Dangers of Labeling

As noted in Chapter 3, all people form categories or concepts that help them or-ganize the world. In this way they attempt to deal with and make sense of the variety of experiences that confront them. Thus, forming categories is part of the way people think.

Classification and diagnosis are intended to facilitate understanding and treatment of childhood behavior disorders. As scientists, we can study groups of children to seek common etiologies. As clinicians, we can benefit from previous knowledge in our approach to new cases. However, diagnostic categories, like perspectives, may also limit the information we seek or the interpreta-tions we make of events. This is one reason why applying a category to an individual child and transforming it into a label can be dangerous.

Although classification is intended as a scientific and clinical enterprise, it can be seen as a social process (Rothblum, Solo-mon, and Albee, 1986). The diagnostic label becomes a social status, which carries impli-cations for how children are thought of and treated. If this impact is negative, the label actually detracts from the original purpose of categorizing—helping children.

From the start, formal classification has had the categorization of disorders, not persons, as its stated intent (Rutter and Gould, 1985). Indeed, Cantwell, one of the creators of the current DSM approach, notes: "Any classification system classifies psychiatric *disorders* of childhood; it does *not* classify *children*. Thus it is correct to say, 'Tommy Jones has infantile autism.' It is incorrect to say 'Tommy Jones, the autis- tic'..." (Cantwell, 1980a, p. 350). Often ease of communication is the reason for a particular phrasing. For example, the term "autistic children" may be employed rather than repeating the phrase "children receiv-ing the diagnosis of autism." Thus, it is realistic to expect the use of terms such as "autistic children" or "depressed children", here and elsewhere, despite the intent to avoid misplacement of labels. In light of such practices, it is important to be aware of the potential negative effects of the la-beling process.

One of the dangers inherent in this "mis-placement" of classification, that of only "noticing" information consistent with a label, is illustrated in a study by Foster and Salvia (1977). Teachers were asked to view a videotape of a boy and rate his academic work and social behavior. The tape dis-played age- and grade-appropriate behavior in all cases, but some teachers were told that the boy was learning disabled, while others were told that he was normal. Teachers watching the "learning disabled" boy rated him as less academically able and his behav-ior as more socially undesirable than did teachers watching the "normal" child.

The use of labels invites a number of other difficulties. The danger of overgen-eralization is one concern: It may be as-sumed that all children labeled Attention-Deficit Hyperactivity Disorder, for example, are more alike than they actually are. Such an assumption readily leads to neglect of the *individual* child. It is also possible that if people react to the child as a member of a category, then the child may behave in a manner consistent with the expectations of the label. Critics of labeling also point to the logical fallacy that often results from the use of labels. A label originally used to *describe* a behavioral pattern may then be stated as the *cause* of the same behavior. For example, a clinician who observes a pattern of restlessness, high levels of active behavior, and poor attention may describe this behavior as hyperactivity. In a subsequent conference with the child's parents, the clinician may then state that the child's problem behavior is caused by hyperactivity. Clearly, little is to be gained from this mistake, as it often interferes with the search for better understanding.

Lilly (1979b) and others also suggest that traditional categories ignore the fact that a child's problems "belong" to at least one other person—the one identifying or reporting them. As Algozzine (1977) has noted, the child may not be inherently "disturbed," but is labeled deviant because of the reactions of others to his or her behavior. Algozzine modified the instructions for the Behavior Problem Checklist. Adults were asked "how disturbing" particular items would be in working with children. The responses of adults to this "Disturbing Behavior Checklist" were submitted to a factor analysis. Interestingly, behavior rated as to degree of *disturbingness* seemed to cluster in much the same way as in previous studies of *disturbed* behavior. As we shall see throughout this book, there is much evidence that supports the notion that how a child is described and viewed may reflect as much or more on *who* is doing the describing as it does on the behavior of the child.

Many experts involved in the study and treatment of children express concern regarding the problems inherent in the use of categorical labels and have advocated concerted attempts to reduce the possible harmful effects. Some have recommended that services be provided to children, without inflexible references to categories. It is acknowledged, however, that categorization is embedded in our thinking and problem solving. Completely discarding categorization, even if it were desirable, is probably impossible. Thus, it is both valuable and necessary to be sensitive to social factors inherent in the use of categories, the social status imparted by a label, and the impact of labels on the child and others (Hobbs, 1975; Rutter and Gould, 1985).

ASSESSMENT

Evaluating children's problems is a complex process that most often involves assessing multiple aspects of functioning. The process requires considerable skill and sensitivity. Assessment is best accomplished by a team of clinicians carefully trained in the administration and interpretation of specific procedures and instruments. Because it is usually conducted immediately upon contact with the child or family, it demands special sensitivity to anxiety, fear, shyness, manipulativeness, and the like. If treatment ensues, assessment should be a continuous process, so that new information can be gleaned and the ongoing effects of treatment can be ascertained. In this way the clinician remains open to nuances and can avoid rigid judgments about a multifaceted and complex phenomenon.

Behavior-Personality Assessment

The interview. The general clinical interview is clearly the most common form of assessment. We have included the interview under the category of behavior-personality assessment; however, information on all areas of functioning is obtained, in part, by interviewing the child and various others in the child's social environment. The fact that the child's behavior is likely to vary according to the situation or be viewed differently by various observers argues for interviewing a variety of individuals who have contact with the child (for example, parents, siblings, teachers).

Whether the child will be interviewed alone probably varies with the age of the client. The older child generally is more capable and is more likely to provide valuable information. Nevertheless, clinicians often elect to interview even the very young child in order to obtain their own impressions. Preschool and grade school children can provide valuable information if appropriate developmental considerations are involved in tailoring the interview to the individual child (Bierman and Schwartz, 1986). For example, an adult-like face-to-face interview may be intimidating for a young child. This difficulty may be reduced if the interview is instead modeled after a more familiar play or school task.

Regardless of the theoretical orientation of the clinician or other assessment instruments employed, it is almost certain that an interview will be conducted. The nature of the questions asked and the information sought in the interview, however, might well vary, depending upon the orientation of the clinician. However, most clinicians seek information concerning the nature of the problem, past and recent history, present conditions, feelings and perceptions, attempts to solve the problem, and expectations concerning treatment. The general clinical interview is not used only to determine the nature of the presenting problem and perhaps formulate a diagnosis. It is employed to help gather information that allows the clinician to conceptualize the case and to plan an appropriate therapeutic intervention.

A recent development in the interviewing of children and adolescents is the use of structured interviews (Gutterman, O'Brien, and Young, 1987). The general clinical interview, discussed above, is usually described as open-ended or unstructured. Such interviews are also most often conducted in the context of a therapeutic interaction and are employed along with a variety of other assessment instruments. Thus, it has been difficult to evaluate the reliability and validity of the interview itself.

Structured interviews have arisen in part to create interviews that are likely to be more reliable. They also have been developed for the more limited purpose of deriving a diagnosis based upon a particular classification scheme such as DSM-III-R or for use in screening large populations for the prevalence of childhood disorders. For the latter, a large number of interviewers is likely to be employed and the issue of interrater reliability is of particular concern.

In the unstructured general clinical interview there are no particular questions that the clinician must ask, no designated format, and no stipulated method to record information. That is not to say that there are no guidelines or agreed upon procedures for conducting an effective interview. Indeed, there is an extensive literature on effective interviewing (cf. Cox and Rutter, 1985). However, unstructured interviews are intended to give the clinician great latitude. In contrast, structured interviews are essentially a list of problem behaviors and events that the interviewer must cover. In addition, rules are provided for how the interview is to be conducted and how the data are to be recorded.

Edelbrock and Costello (1988b) suggest that it is useful to distinguish two kinds of structured interviews: highly structured and semistructured. Highly structured interviews seek to minimize the role of clinical judgment and thereby produce higher levels of interrater reliability. This is achieved by specifying the exact wording and sequence of questions and by providing well-defined rules for recording and rating the respondents answers. These interviews are thus likely to yield more objective and quantifiable data. In the semistructured interview, the interviewer is allowed some flexibility in what is asked, how questions are phrased, and how responses are recorded. This allows interviews to appear less stilted and more spontaneous since the clinician can adjust them to the individual client. However, since the interview may be conducted in a slightly different manner by each clinician, the results are more likely to differ as well. At present it is not clear which degree of structure yields better data. The degree of structure most desirable should probably be determined by the purposes and circumstances of the interview.

The investigation of the reliability of interviews must take into account many variables. This is illustrated in a study by Edelbrock and his colleagues (Edelbrock et al., 1985). The Diagnostic Interview for Children, a highly structured interview that covers a broad range of symptoms and behaviors, was administered to 242 children and their parents. The children had been referred for inpatient or outpatient mental health services. Interviews were conducted twice, with both parents and children, approximately nine days apart. Interestingly, the reliability based on the child's reports was lower for younger than for older children, whereas, the reliability based on parents' reports was higher for the younger children. The authors suggest that these findings are related to the cognitive development of the child on the one hand, and to shifts in parents' perceptions and awareness of their child's behavior on the other.

The validity of interviews, like any other assessment instrument, needs to be evaluated as well. One of the questions asked is whether structured interviews discriminate well between vastly different groups. Questions of finer discriminations and other aspects of validity such as the relationship to etiology, prognosis, and response to treatment are required of existing and future structured interviews (Edelbrock and Costello, 1988b). Beyond questions of how to improve structured interviews for diagnostic and research uses, is the question of their potential for more general clinical practice. It is probably too early in the development of these instruments to determine what impact they will have on the practice of the typical clinician (Young et al., 1987).

Psychological tests. At one time the most common form of psychological test employed to assess childhood personality was the projective test. These tests are less commonly used today. This is due, in large part, to a continuing lack of empirical evidence for their reliability and validity, and also to the decreasing popularity of the psychodynamic theories on which they are based (Anastasi, 1982; Benton and Sines, 1985; Gittelman, 1980).

Projective tests were derived from the psychoanalytic notion of projection as a defense mechanism: One of the ways the ego deals with unacceptable impulses is to project them onto some external object. It is assumed that the impulses cannot be expressed directly. Therefore, the child is presented with an ambiguous stimulus, allowing the child to project "unacceptable" thoughts and impulses, as well as other defenses against them onto the stimulus. Projective tests are also used by some clinicians in a manner that involves less psychodynamic inference. This type of analysis examines formal aspects of the test response, for example, whether the child describes the entire stimulus or just part of it. Interpretations are then made based on the response style rather than on the content of the response.

In the Rorschach the child is simply asked what he or she sees in each of ten ink blots (Figure 5–2). Scoring is based on characteristics of the response such as the portion of the blot responded to (location), factors such as color and shading (determinants), and

FIGURE 5–2 Inkblot designs, similar to the one pictured above, are employed in the Rorschach.

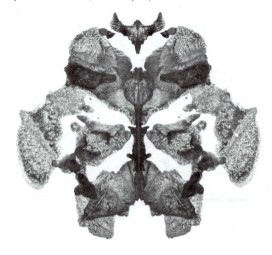

the nature of what is seen in the blot (content). The Human Figure Drawing or Draw-a-Person test (Machover, 1949) requires the child to draw a picture of a person and then a second person of the opposite sex. Typically the clinician then asks questions about the drawings. Murray's (1943) Thematic Apperception Test (TAT) and Bellak's (1971) Children's Apperception Test (CAT) provide the child with pictures for which he or she is asked to make up a story.

Figure 5–3 presents pictures similar to those used in the CAT.

Observational assessment. Early attempts to observe children's behavior made use of diaries or continuous observations and narrations that were deliberately nonselective (Wright, 1960). From this tradition evolved observations of a more limited, pinpointed set of behaviors that could be reliably coded by observers (Bijou et al., 1969). Such ob-

FIGURE 5–3 Drawings similar to those employed in the CAT.

servations are similar or even identical to those done in research studies.

Recent observational methods have come largely from workers with a behavioral/social learning perspective. The observations are most frequently made in the child's natural environment, although sometimes planned situations are created in clinic or laboratory settings. Observations range from single, relatively simple and discrete behaviors of the child, such as the occurrence of toileting, to observations of the child and peers, to complex systems of interactions of family members (e.g., Kolko, 1987; Israel, Pravder, and Knights, 1980; Patterson, 1977). Clearly, ongoing interactions are more difficult to observe and code than are the behaviors of a single individual. Table 5–4 shows some of the behaviors coded in Patterson's work on parent-child interactions in the home.

The first step in any behavioral observation system involves explicitly pinpointing and defining behaviors. Observers who are trained to use the system then note whether a particular behavior occurs during a designated time interval. Most coding systems have been inspected for reliability. Indeed, behavioral/social learning studies commonly report on the reliability of the observations employed, even if a reliability check is not the major purpose of the research.

The aspect of reliability most frequently reported is interrater reliability. Two or more observers independently observe the same behavior, and the degree of agreement is calculated. Research indicates that a number of factors affect reliability as well as validity and clinical utility. For example, the complexity of the observational system and changes over time in the observers' use of the system (observer drift) are two factors known to affect observation. Careful training and periodically monitoring observers' use of the system are usually recommended as means for reducing distortions in the information obtained from direct observation (Foster and Cone, 1986; Hartmann and Wood, 1990).

The issue of reactivity is often cited as the greatest impediment to the utility of direct observation. *Reactivity* refers to whether the knowledge that one is being observed changes one's behavior. Thus, introducing a trained observer into a situation may cause those in the situation to react to this novel stimulus and behave in a different manner than usual. A number of strategies are recommended to help reduce reactivity. One example is the use of persons who are already present in the situation (e.g., parents, teachers, or other staff). Use of such persons as observers is likely to reduce the artificial and novel aspects of observation. Such a strategy may not always be possible or desirable, however. A second approach is to arrange for observers to be present for some period of time prior to data collection,

TABLE 5–4 Some of the 29 Behavioral Categories of Patterson's Behavior Coding System Designed to Evaluate Parent-Child Interactions in the Home[a]

Verbal

CM (Command): This category is used when an immediate and clearly stated request or command is made to another person.

CN (Command Negative): A command that is very different in "attitude" from a reasonable command or request: (1) immediate compliance is demanded; (2) aversive consequences are threatened if compliance is not immediate; (3) a kind of sarcasm or humiliation directed to the receiver.

HU (Humiliate): This category is used when a person makes fun of, shames, or embarrasses another person. Tone of voice is of prime importance for coding HU.

Nonverbal

PP (Physical Positive): When a person caresses or communicates with touch in a friendly or affectionate way.

HR (High-rate): A repetitive behavior *not covered by other categories* that if carried on for a long period of time would be aversive or annoying.

---

[a] Descriptions provided are abbreviated definitions of categories.
Adapted from Maerov et al., 1978.

so that their presence is less artificial and no longer novel.

Behavioral observations are the most direct method of assessment and require the least inference. The difficulty and expense involved in training and maintaining reliable observers is probably the primary obstacle to their common use in nonresearch contexts. Since direct observation is often considered the hallmark of assessment from a behavioral perspective, attempts have been made to create systems that are more amenable to widespread use. Direct observation is, however, just one aspect of a multimethod approach to behavioral assessment that can include self-monitoring of behavior, interviews, ratings and checklists, and self-report instruments (cf. Cone, 1987; Mash and Terdal, 1988).

Problem checklists and dimensional rating scales. Problem checklists and rating scales were mentioned in our discussion of classification (p. 91–95). There is a wide variety of these instruments (Barkley, 1988; Mc-Mahon, 1984). Instruments are available for general use (for example, the Behavior Problem Checklist and the Child Behavior Checklist) and for use with restricted populations (for example, Conners's Teacher Rating Scale, 1969). The considerable empirical literature suggests that these instruments may be valuable tools for clinicians holding a variety of perspectives.

For example, parents of 1,300 children referred for mental health services and 1,300 parents of randomly selected nonreferred children completed the Child Behavior Checklist (Achenbach and Edelbrock, 1981). The checklist clearly discriminated between the clinic and nonreferred children on both behavior problem and social competence scores. Furthermore, referral status accounted for greater differences than did factors such as age, SES, and gender. Figure 5–4 illustrates the differences between clinic and nonreferred children.

A general rating scale may thus help a clinician judge the parent's view of the child's adjustment against norms for re-

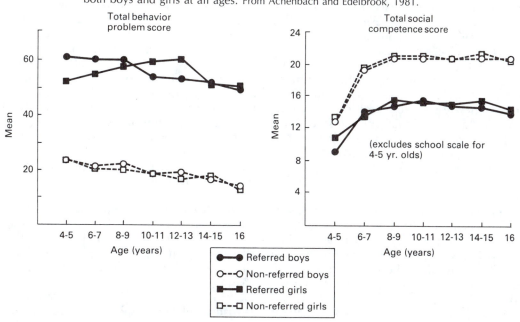

FIGURE 5–4 The behavior problem and social competence scores of clinic-referred and nonreferred children were significantly different for both boys and girls at all ages. From Achenbach and Edelbrook, 1981.

ferred and nonreferred populations. This can help in evaluating the appropriateness of the referral. Furthermore, rating scales completed by different informants may help the clinician gain a fuller appreciation of the clinical picture and of potential situational aspects of the child's problem (Achenbach, McConaughy, and Howell, 1987). Once a particular presenting problem is identified, the use of a more specific rating scale might also be part of the clinician's assessment strategy.

Intellectual-Educational Assessment

The evaluation of a child's intellectual-academic functioning is an important part of almost all clinical assessments. Intellectual functioning is a central defining feature for disorders such as mental retardation and learning disabilities, but it may also contribute to and be affected by a wide variety of behavioral problems. In contrast to most other assessment instruments, tests of intellectual functioning tend to have better established normative data, reliability, and validity. While our present discussion of these instruments is brief, additional information will be presented in later chapters.

Intelligence tests. By far the most commonly employed assessment devices for evaluating intellectual functioning are tests of general intelligence. In fact, they probably constitute the most frequently employed assessment device other than the interview. The Stanford-Binet (Thorndike, Hagen, and Sattler, 1986) and the Wechsler tests—the Wechsler Preschool and Primary Scale of Intelligence (Wechsler, 1967); the Wechsler Intelligence Scale for Children-Revised (Wechsler, 1974)—are some of the intelligence tests widely used in clinical settings. All are individually administered and yield an intelligence quotient score. The average score is 100, and an individual score reflects how far above or below the average person of his or her age an individual has scored.

Intelligence tests have long been the subject of heated controversy. Critics have argued that the use of IQ scores has resulted in intelligence being viewed as a real thing that is measured by these tests, rather than being viewed as a concept. Furthermore, it has led to intelligence being viewed as a rigid and fixed attribute, rather than as something complex and subtle (cf. Wohlwill, 1980). Critics also claim that intelligence tests are culturally biased and have led to social injustice (cf. Kamin, 1974; Kaplan, 1985). Although IQ tests are popular and useful in predicting a variety of outcomes, these criticisms and other considerations demand that they be used cautiously (Berger, 1986; Kaufman and Reynolds, 1984; Weinberg, 1989).

Developmental Scales. Assessment of intellectual functioning in very young children, and particularly in infants, requires a special kind of assessment instrument. Several have been developed: The Gesell Developmental Schedules (Ilg and Ames, 1965), the Cattell Intelligence Tests for Infants and Young Children (Cattell, 1960), and the Bayley Scales of Infant Development (Bayley, 1969). Performance on these tests yields a developmental quotient (DQ) rather than an IQ. Unlike intelligence tests, developmental scales rely heavily on sensorimotor skills and simple social skills rather than on language and abstract reasoning abilities. For example, the Bayley examines the ability to sit, walk, place objects, attend to visual and auditory stimuli, smile, and imitate adults. Perhaps because intelligence tests and developmental scales tap different abilities, there is only a low correlation between performance on them (Sattler, 1988).

Ability and achievement tests. In addition to assessing general intellectual functioning, it is often necessary or helpful to assess functioning in a particular area. A variety of tests has been developed for this purpose (Sattler, 1988). For example, the Frostig Developmental Test of Visual Perception (Frostig, Lefever, and Whittlesey, 1966) and the Illinois Test of Psycholinguistic Abilities (Kirk, McCarthy, and Kirk, 1968) evaluate visual-motor and language ability, respectively. The Wide Range Achievement Test (Jastak and Jastak, 1965) and the Woodcock Reading Mastery Tests (Woodcock, 1973) are administered individually and measure academic achievement. Tests such as the Iowa Test of Basic Skills (Lindquist and Hieronymous, 1955–56) and the Stanford Achievement Test (Kelley et al., 1964) are group-administered achievement tests employed in many school settings. Specific ability and achievement tests are particularly important in working with children with learning and school-related problems.

Assessment of Physical Functioning

Assessment of physical functioning can provide several kinds of information valuable to understanding disordered behavior. Family and child histories and physical examinations may reveal genetic problems that are treatable by environmental manipulation. For example, phenylketonuria is a recessive genetic condition that is affected by dietary treatment. Avoidance of phenylalanine in the child's diet prevents most of the cognitive problems usually associated with the condition. Diseases and defects may be diagnosed that affect important areas of functioning either directly (for example, urinary tract infection causing problems in toilet training) or indirectly (for example, a sickly child being overprotected by parents). Also, signs of atypical or lagging physical development may be an early indication of developmental disorders that eventually influence many aspects of behavior.

The assessment of the nervous system is considered particularly important to understanding a variety of problem behaviors, but especially mental retardation, autism, learning disabilities, and attention-deficit disorders. Brain and other neurological dysfunction is thought to be associated with abnormal physical reflexes, motor coordination problems, and sensory and perceptual deficits, and to be measurable in various ways.

The concept of minimal brain dysfunction (MBD) in describing learning and behavioral problems contributed to interest in the assessment of the brain. It was reasoned that since serious brain damage could result in serious degrees of impairment or death, then lesser degrees of damage—perhaps undetectable by direct biological assessment—could account for lesser behavioral impairments. It was assumed that this minimal dysfunction could be detected through psychological assessment. The notion that behavioral signs can provide a basis for making inferences about nervous system functioning persists, but not without criticism (e.g., Rutter, 1981; Schmidt et al., 1987; Taylor, Fletcher, and Satz, 1984).

Currently, assessment of presumed neurological dysfunction in children usually consists of a combination of direct neurophysiological approaches and indirect neuropsychological assessment. Such assessment requires the coordinated efforts of neurologists, psychologists, and other professional workers.

There are a number of procedures that directly assess the integrity of the nervous system (Solomon, 1985). The computer has revolutionized neurological assessment and new techniques have become the primary mode of evaluation. The electroencephalograph (EEG) is an example of a procedure with a long history (e.g., Kahn and Cohen, 1934) that has been improved by the availability of computers (Kuperman et al., 1990). The EEG consists of electrodes placed on the scalp that record activity of the brain cortex, in general, or while the individual is engaged in a task requiring information processing. New technologies such as brain imaging techniques and diagnostic nuclear medicine have vastly improved our ability to assess and localize damage or abnormalities in brain structure (Fletcher, 1988; Solomon, 1985). For example, computed tomography (CT) allows tens of thousands of readings of minute variations in the density of brain tissue, measured from an X-ray source, to be computer processed and a photographic image of a portion of the brain to be presented. Radioisotope brain scanning makes use of the fact that brain tissue may retain radioisotope compounds. Scanning equipment picks up emissions from these compounds that can be recorded on X-ray film. Other imaging techniques provide information about brain activity. They determine the rate of activity of different parts of the brain by assessing the use of oxygen and glucose, which fuel brain activity. These new assessment tools, along with others, are becoming increasingly important in individual assessment and research (Kuperman et al., 1990).

Neuropsychological assessment. Neuropsychological assessment employs tests that contain learning, sensorimotor, perceptual, verbal, and memory tasks. From the individual's performance on these tasks inferences are made about central nervous system functioning. Neuropsychological assessment is thus an *indirect* means of assessing brain function.

Neuropsychological assessments were originally employed in the hope that they could detect the presence or absence of brain damage. The development of direct methods of assessing the integrity of the central nervous system and the failure to find evidence of brain damage in suspected populations have resulted in a shift of focus. The emphasis is currently more likely to be on distinguishing groups of behavioral and learning disorders that are presumed to have a neurodevelopmental etiology. For example, any test that discriminates learning disabled from normal learners might be considered neuropsychological in this sense (Taylor, 1988b). Interest also exists in assessing changes arising out of alterations in the central nervous system, for example, in evaluating recovery from head injury.

The current interest in neuropsychological assessment is, at least in part, attributable to increased sensitivity to the needs and legal requirements of providing services to children with handicapping conditions—some of whom exhibit problems presumed to have a neurological etiology. Also advances in medicine have resulted in increasing numbers of children who survive known or suspected neurological trauma. The increase in survival rates of infants born prematurely is one example. Children who receive treatment for acute lymphocytic leukemia that includes methotrexate injected directly into the spinal column and radiation to the head are yet another example (Katz, Dolgin, and Varni, 1990).

Two of the most widely used instruments for neuropsychological assessment are the Halstead-Reitan and Luria-Nebraska batteries (Hynd, Snow, and Becker, 1986). The early work of Halstead, begun in the 1930s, and its elaboration by his student Reitan, begun in the 1950s, resulted in two test batteries. The Halstead Neuropsychological Test Battery for Children is used for children between the ages of 9 and 14 (Table 5–5). The Reitan-Indiana Neuropsychological Test Battery is used for children 5-8 years of age. The Luria-Nebraska Neuropsychological Battery-Children's Revision is used for children 8 to 12 years of age.

As the term battery implies, these instruments consist of several subtests or scales, each intended to assess one or more abilities. The use of a broad spectrum of tests, whether it be designated batteries, like the above, or combinations of other existing tests (e.g., the Wechsler Intelligence Scales, achievement tests, the Bender Visual-Motor Gestalt Test) is the usual strategy employed in neuropsychological approaches to assessment (Rourke, 1980; Taylor, 1988a).

In general, research suggests that these test batteries are successful in discriminating normal children from those with independently documented brain damage and, to a lesser degree, these two groups from learning-disabled children. However, the usefulness of neuropsychological tests is still controversial, particularly when they are used to do more than discriminate broad groups. For example, success in localizing dysfunction or predicting recovery rates seems less well supported (e.g., Faust, Hart, and Guilmette, 1988; Fletcher, 1988; Hynd et al., 1986; Morgan and Brown, 1988).

TABLE 5-5 Selected Subtests and Scales of the Halstead Neuropsychological Test Battery for Children

Subtests and Scales	Abilities Assessed
Category Test	Complex concept formation, basic reasoning abilities, intelligence
Tactual Performance Test	Right-left sided sensory perception, sensory recognition, spatial memory, manual dexterity
Seashore Rhythm Test	Sustained auditory attention, perception and matching of auditory rhythmic sequences
Aphasia Screening Test	Letter identification, following directions regarding right-left hands, copying simple shapes, simple arithmetic problems
Trail Making Test	Conceptual set shifting, memory, attention
Lateral Dominance Examination	Right-left sided preference

Note: Other subtests are Speech Sounds Perceptions Test; Finger Oscillation (Finger Tapping); Tactile, Auditory, and Visual Imperception Test; Tactile Finger Recognition Test; Finger-Tip Number Writing Perception Test; Tactile Form Recognition Test; and Grip Strength Test. The WRAT and WISC-R are normally given along with the Halstead.

Adapted from Hynd, Snow, and Becker, 1986. Reprinted by permission from Plenum Publishing Corporation.

FIGURE 5-5 The Bender-Gestalt, a neuropsychological test, consists of designs, similar to those below, which the child is asked to copy.

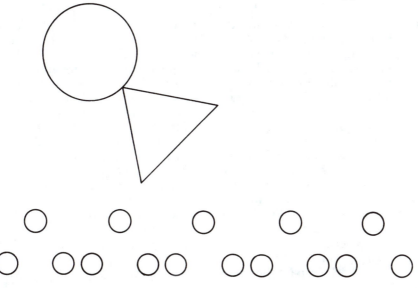

Continued development of instruments that derive from evolving research on cognitive development, neurological development, and brain-behavior relationships is needed. Research evaluating the use of neuropsychological assessment with other populations such as attention deficit disorders and conduct disorders has also been called for (Hahn, 1987; Taylor et al., 1984); as it is, results do not always support such use (e.g., Schaughency et al., 1989).

One other issue that needs to be addressed is the often subtle assumption that the behaviors that are assessed and the neuropsychological assessments themselves are free from social and environmental influences. There is little empirical justification for this assumption (Taylor et al., 1984). For example, brain damage is correlated with social class and family variables that are disadvantageous to social adjustment and physical health (Rutter, Graham, and Yule, 1970; Sameroff and Chandler, 1975). These sociofamilial variables may themselves underlie *both* the brain damage and the observed behavioral or learning problems.

A Comprehensive Assessment

As we indicated in starting our discussion of assessment, evaluating children's problems is a complex process. By the time a child comes to the attention of a clinician, the presenting problem is usually, if not always, multifaceted. Also, since assessment is the first part of any contact, the professional's knowledge of the problem is limited. Both of these factors, as well as common sense and caution, argue for a broad and comprehensive assessment process. Thus, the clinician will likely evaluate multiple areas of functioning and make use of a variety of assessment procedures. The particular device chosen may depend, in part, on the assessor's perspective. However, whatever the clinician's perspective, the best interests of the child are most likely to be served by a comprehensive assessment of multiple facets of the child and his or her environment (cf. Mash, 1987; Mash and Hunsley, 1990).

SUMMARY

Clinically derived classification relies on consensus among clinicians regarding disorders and their definition. The DSM approach is the clinically derived system most likely to be employed in the United States. The recent versions of DSM include an increased number of categories of childhood disorders, provide more highly structured rules for diagnosis, and use a multiaxial system to assess various aspects of functioning. At present limited information exists about the reliability and validity of DSM-III-R. Precise diagnostic rules and structured interviews are likely to increase reliability; the large number of specific categories is likely to work against it.

Empirical approaches to classification rely on behavior checklists and statistical analyses. There is fairly good support for two broad syndromes: an Undercontrolled, Externalizing, Conduct Disorder syndrome and an Overcontrolled, Internalizing, Anxiety-Withdrawal syndrome. There is some support for subcategories within each general syndrome, which probably differ depending on the age and gender of the child.

Critics of diagnostic systems have reminded us that we need to be sensitive to the possible dangers of labeling children. To the extent that such labels reduce our effectiveness as scientists and clinicians, they do not serve the child's best interest.

Conducting a comprehensive assessment is necessary, not only for classification and diagnosis, but also to plan and execute appropriate interventions. The complex process of assessment requires a multifaceted approach. Methods for evaluating the personality-behavioral, intellectual-educational, and the physical functioning of the child are available.

The interview is the most common form of assessment. The development of structured interviews is relatively recent. Many of these interviews are structured to provide information for a DSM diagnosis. Projective tests are probably less widely used than was once the case due to questions concerning their reliability and validity. Observation of behavior is central to the behavioral/social learning approach and is a direct method of assessment. The practicality of implementing current observation systems in general clinical practice is an impediment to their widespread use.

Intellectual-educational assessments are conducted with a wide variety of presenting problems. General intelligence and developmental levels are evaluated, as well as specific abilities and achievement. Intelligence tests are popular, but need to be used cautiously.

Assessment of physical functioning, especially of the nervous system, is important for many childhood behavior problems. Methods include case histories, medical examinations, the EEG, and several new imaging techniques. Much attention has been given to neuropsychological testing of children with known or suspected problems in central nervous system functioning.

Reliability and validity of assessment methods are continuing concerns.

6

INTERNALIZING PROBLEMS:
ANXIETY DISORDERS

With this chapter we begin an examination of specific childhood behavior disorders. The children discussed in this and the next chapter are variously described as anxious, fearful, withdrawn, timid, depressed, and the like. They seem to be very unhappy and to lack self-confidence. These children are often said to have emotional problems which they take out on themselves—thus the term internalizing disorders.

A variety of evidence supports the existence of a broad-band internalizing disorder (see Chapter 5). This cluster of behaviors has variously been designated as an internalizing, overcontrolled, or anxiety-withdrawal dimension or syndrome (Table 6–1).

Historically, the problems now under discussion were referred to as *neuroses*, a term that has become controversial. The labels of phobias, obsessions and compulsions, anxiety disorders, and depression, however, continue to appear in much of the literature on which we will draw and in current clinical practice. Therefore, these next two chapters are organized around these frequently employed terms. It is necessary, however, to first acknowledge two overriding issues, namely whether and how internalizing behaviors can be subcategorized, and the dilemma of identifying such behaviors in children.

The use of specific diagnostic categories, such as the various anxiety and depressive disorders described in the DSM system, for example, is often questioned (cf. Quay and La Greca, 1986). This is based, in part, on the difficulty often encountered in achieving adequate interrater reliability for subcategories (e.g., Mezzich and Mezzich, 1985). On the other hand, information suggesting the possibility of reliable subcategories has come from empirically derived syndromes (Achenbach and Edelbrock, 1983) and some studies reporting high diagnostic reliability for clinically derived subcategories (e.g., Kovacs et al., 1984a,b; Last et al., 1987a).

In addition to the issue of reliability, considerable evidence indicates that a given child or adolescent often meets the criteria for more than one subcategory (e.g., Bernstein and Garfinkel, 1986; Strauss et al., 1988a). In Chapter 3 it was suggested that

TABLE 6–1 Characteristics Associated with the Internalizing, Overcontrolled, or Anxiety-Withdrawal Syndrome

Anxious, fearful, tense
Shy, timid, bashful
Withdrawn, seclusive, friendless
Depressed, sad, disturbed
Hypersensitive, easily hurt
Feels inferior, worthless
Self-conscious, easily embarrassed
Lacks self-confidence
Easily flustered and confused
Cries frequently
Aloof
Worries

Adapted with permission from Quay, H. C. Classification. In H. C. Quay & J. S. Werry (Eds.), *Psychopathological Disorders of Childhood.* Copyright © 1986 by John Wiley & Sons, Inc.

one of the criteria for a good classification system is that categories be distinct and not overlap. Thus, one issue that needs to be addressed for these subcategories is overlapping diagnostic criteria (Shaffer et al., 1989).

The phenomenon of an individual meeting the criteria for more than one disorder is often termed *comorbidity*. The use of this term implies the simultaneous existence of two or more distinct disorders in the same child. Clearly one alternative view is that it is a mistake to conceptualize these disorders in distinct categorical terms. However, even if one accepts the value of retaining distinct categories, there are multiple ways to con-

ceptualize comorbidity (Rutter, 1989b). Perhaps current groupings are misleading in suggesting multiple disorders. It may be, instead, that many disorders have mixed patterns of symptoms. For example, mood disorders may be characterized by a mixture of both depression and anxiety. Another alternative is that comorbidity results from shared risk factors: Some of the same risk factors lead to both disorders. One other alternative is that the presence of one disorder creates an increased risk for developing the other disorder. These are only some of the possible hypotheses to explain comorbidity. At present it is not possible to explain overlap in diagnoses clearly. Examination of these and other hypotheses is needed to clarify the issue.

Before examining particular internalizing disorders, it is worthwhile to note that an additional problem is often encountered in identifying these problems. Diagnosis relies heavily on judgments of emotional discomfort. It may be difficult for adults to reliably identify such discomfort in children. In addition, children may have difficulty in labeling and communicating their subjective feelings. Taken together, this creates a considerable assessment challenge.

With these considerations in mind, let us turn to an examination of internalizing disorders. In this chapter we examine anxiety disorders and in the next we discuss the problems of depression and social withdrawal.

A DESCRIPTION OF ANXIETY DISORDERS

Terms such as fear, clinical fear, avoidance reaction, anxiety, anxiety state, phobia, and phobic reaction all appear in the literature. Attempts have sometimes been made to distinguish among these terms. However, it is often not clear whether or why the various terms are being used to denote distinctive or similar phenomena. Here, as suggested by Barrios and O'Dell (1989), we use the term(s) "fears and anxieties" together or independently.

Despite differences in preference for ter-

minology and classification, there is, however, good consensus on a general definition of the phenomenon of anxiety or fear (e.g., Barrios and O'Dell, 1989; Lang, 1984). Anxiety or fear is defined as a complex pattern of three types of reactions to a perceived threat: motor responses, physiological responses, and subjective responses. Table 6–2 contains examples of each of these types of responses that are characteristic of children's anxieties and fears.

TABLE 6-2 Some of the Motoric, Physiological, and Subjective Responses of Children's Fears and Anxieties

Motoric Responses	Physiological Responses	Subjective Responses
Avoidance	Heart rate	Thoughts of being scared
Gratuitous arm, hand, and leg movements	Basal skin responses	Thoughts of monsters
	Palmar sweat index	Thoughts of being hurt
Trembling voice	Galvanic skin response	Images of monsters
Crying	Muscle tension	Images of wild animals
Foot shuffling	Skin temperature	Thoughts of danger
Screaming	Respiration	Self-deprecatory thoughts
Nail biting	Palpitations	Self-critical thoughts
Thumb sucking	Breathlessness	Thoughts of inadequacy
Rigid posture	Nausea	Thoughts of incompetence
Eyes shut	Pulse volume	Thoughts of bodily injury
Avoidance of eye contact	Headache	Images of bodily injury
Clenched jaw	Stomach upset	
Stuttering	Stomachache	
Physical proximity	Urination	
White knuckles	Defecation	
Trembling lip	Vomiting	

From Barrios and O'Dell, 1989.

Assessment of Anxiety Disorders

In keeping with the above conceptualization, assessment of anxiety disorders must focus on one or more of the three response systems. Our discussion draws on Barrios and Hartmann (1988), who organize available assessment instruments by the three response systems and by methods of measurement (observational, self-report, or mechanical).

Nearly all methods for assessing the motor aspects of children's fears and anxieties make use of direct observation. Behavioral approach tests require the child to perform a series of tasks. Successive steps require the child to approach the feared stimulus situation in a graduated manner. Thus, the child might have to come closer and closer to a feared dog and then increasingly interact with the dog.

Observational systems are also used to evaluate the motor component. Rather than exposing the child to a planned graduated series of steps, observations are made of the child in the natural environment where the fear or anxiety occurs. Trained observers record the child's behavior, in predefined categories, as it is happening. Checklists also make use of the observations of others.

Behavioral approach tests assess the child's anxiety by asking the child to approach the feared stimulus or situation. Each progressive step indicates less fear or anxiety. Initial steps may have the child at a distance observing. Later steps involve interacting with the target stimulus. (Susan Rosenberg)

When using a checklist to assess a child's anxiety, the observer is asked to check off the specific behaviors that the child exhibited. This is usually done a short time after the behavior has occurred. Finally, global ratings of the child's fearful behavior are often obtained. For example, someone is asked to rate on a five-point scale the degree to which the child approached a feared object or situation.

The subjective component of the child's anxiety can be evaluated by a variety of self-report measures. Global self-ratings of degree of anxiety or fear are often obtained. Children may report how anxious they are by choosing from a series of facial expressions, or indicating a number on a drawing of a fear thermometer, or selecting a number on a rating scale. The choice of instrument depends, in part, on the child's developmental level.

There are also questionnaires for a variety of specific fears such as darkness, medical procedures, and test taking. Such questionnaires ask a variety of questions about a single fear or anxiety. A number of general fear questionnaires also exist. They assess the child's reactions to a wide variety of situations, or alternatively assess a wide range of subjective reactions to the child's overall situation. An example of the first category would be the revised version of the Fear Survey Schedule for Children (Ollendick, 1983). Children respond to each of 80 fear items by indicating their level of fear ("none," "some," or "a lot"). The revised Children's Manifest Anxiety Scale (Reynolds and Richmond, 1978) is an example of a questionnaire that assesses the child's overall subjective anxiety. It contains items such as, "I have trouble making up my mind" and "I am afraid of a lot of things."

The physiological component of children's anxiety is assessed by measuring parameters such as heart rate, skin conductance, and palmar sweat. Practical difficulties often inhibit obtaining these measures. The development of portable and inexpensive recording devices has greatly facilitated such recording. However, the physiological aspects of anxiety are less frequently assessed than the other two response systems.

CLASSIFICATION OF ANXIETY DISORDERS

Much like the situation for the larger category of internalizing disorders, there is considerable disagreement as to the value of, and manner in which, anxiety disorders should be subcategorized. It is argued that there is, at present at least, insufficient information to make any particular classification scheme clearly the most valid or useful (e.g., Barrios and Hartmann, 1988).

There is considerable overlap in description, conceptualization, and implications for treatment among potential subcategories, a situation not unlike that for adult disorders (e.g., Barlow, 1988). Nevertheless, before moving to a discussion of particular anxiety problems we need to briefly review the major classification systems employed by researchers and clinicians.

The DSM Approach

The classification system described in DSM-III-R contains three types of anxiety disorders that usually first occur in infancy, childhood, or adolescence. Separation Anxiety Disorder is characterized by the child's excessive distress when separated from persons to whom there is a strong attachment and by the avoidance of situations that require separation. Avoidant Disorder is characterized by marked and persistent avoidance of persons who are unfamiliar, coupled with a clear desire for social involvement with familiar people. Overanxious Disorder describes extreme self-consciousness, unrealistic worry about upcoming events, and a generalized anxiety that is not focused on a specific situation or event.

In addition to these disorders, a child can

be diagnosed with almost any of the adult anxiety disorders including the following. Phobic Disorders are characterized by fear or avoidance of specific objects or situations other than separation or involvement with strangers. Panic Disorder is characterized by sudden attacks of intense anxiety, often in response to unidentifiable stimuli rather than a particular phobic stimulus or threatening situation. Obsessive-Compulsive Disorder is characterized by recurrent thoughts or urges to engage in repetitive and irrational behaviors. Anxiety occurs when these obsessive-compulsive rituals are resisted. Post-Traumatic Stress Disorder describes anxiety that is linked to a catastrophic event (e.g., rape, assault, earthquake, airplane crash). The child persistently reexperiences the event, avoids stimuli associated with the event, and experiences persistent symptoms of increased arousal.

The Empirical Approach

Empirical systems that are based on statistical procedures have also yielded subcategorizations that describe anxiety disorders. Within the broad category of internalizing disorders, for example, Achenbach and Edelbrock (1983) have described subcategories that differ by age and gender. As was illustrated in Table 5–3 (p. 93), a number of these correspond to groupings generally considered anxiety disorders. For example, the obsessive-compulsive syndrome for 12- to 16-year-old boys and the anxious-obsessive syndrome for 12- to 16-year-old girls fit this description.

Although some overlap can be seen in the clinical (DSM) and statistical approaches, they clearly represent different ways of organizing the anxiety disorders (e.g., Edelbrock and Costello, 1988a). Indeed, some large-scale empirical data suggest that this approach yields some rather different groupings and categories than are provided for in the DSM approach (Achenbach et al., 1989). In addition to the DSM and empirically derived classifications, there are systems based on the contents of fears. Some of these are described in the next section.

FEARS AND PHOBIAS

Clinical Description and Classification

Phobias, as distinguished from normal fears, are judged to be excessive, persistent, or unadaptive. Children with phobias try to avoid specific situations or objects they fear. When confronted with the threatening stimulus, they "freeze" and become immobile. In crying out for help, the child may describe feelings of tension, panic, or even fear of death. Nausea, palpitations, and difficulty in breathing may also occur. A reaction may also be judged phobic when the threatening stimulus is benign, and fear is thus inappropriate. Finally, fears that may be appropriate or normal at one age may be judged to be clinically significant if exhibited by an older child.

There is no well-established system of classification for children's fears. At one time it was fashionable to enumerate long lists of phobias including pyrophobia (fear of causing fire), taphephobia (fear of being buried alive), ergasiophobia (fear of activity), and even phobophobia—the fear of phobias (Berecz, 1968). The possibilities were endless, as indeed were the lists generated. This method of classification did not prove useful, and subsequent attempts have tended to group phobias into broader categories.

Miller and his colleagues (1974) proposed a classification system that divided phobic reactions into fears of physical injury, natural events, social anxiety, and miscellaneous. The results of several studies apply-

TABLE 6–3 Factors and Sample Items from the Revised Fear Survey Schedule for Children

Factor 1—Failure and Criticism
My parents criticizing me
Failing a test
Being criticized by others
Having to stay after school

Factor 2—The Unknown
Ghosts or spooky things
Dark rooms or closets
Nightmares
Being alone

Factor 3—Minor Injury and Small Animals
Snakes
Guns
The sight of blood
Rats or mice

Factor 4—Danger and Death
Fire, getting burned
Being hit by a car or truck
Falling from high places
Earthquakes

Factor 5—Medical Fears
Having to go to the hospital
Getting a shot from the nurse or doctor
Going to the dentist
Going to the doctor

Adapted from Ollendick, King, and Frary, 1989.

ing factor analysis to reports of children's fears served as the primary basis for this proposed classification. Conventional wisdom and considerations of treatment and assessment also contributed to the schema. For example, physical injury is subdivided into concrete and abstract objects, since the former, but not the latter, may be more amenable to in vivo treatment. Similar classifications of fears have also been suggested by more recent factor analyses of fear questionnaires such as the revised Fear Survey for Children (FSSC-R). These efforts indicate that fears can be reliably grouped into categories (e.g., Ollendick, King, and Frary, 1989) based on the specific object or situation (Table 6–3).

There is no separate category for childhood phobias in the DSM system. The adult category of Simple Phobia may be applied to children. One problem that exists in employing this diagnosis, especially with younger children, is that the definition presumes that the person is aware that the fear is excessive or unreasonable. It is not clear that all children showing phobic behavior are capable of this perspective.

Developmental Characteristics of Children's Fears

Knowing about the development of normal fears is important for understanding fears that require clinical attention. Many investigators over the last half century have attempted to explore the development of fears, and a number of trends are suggested.

General Incidence. Several classic studies indicate that normal children exhibit a surprisingly large number of fears. Jersild and Holmes (1935) reported that children aged two to six years averaged between four and five fears and exhibited fearful reactions once every 4 1/2 days. MacFarlane, Allen, and Honzik (1954), in their longitudinal study of children from 2 through 14 years old, found that specific fears were reported in 90 percent of their sample. Forty-three percent of the 6- to 12-year-olds studied by Lapouse and Monk (1959) had seven or

more fears. An interesting aspect of the latter study is the suggestion that mothers may underestimate the prevalence of fears in their children. Mothers reported 41 percent fewer fears than indicated by the children's own reports.

Although it appears that fears are quite common among children, the prevalence of intense fears is less clear. In one investigation in the United States, less than 5 percent of mothers indicated that their children exhibited extreme fear, as opposed to normal (5 to 15 percent) or no (84 percent) fear reactions (Miller et al., 1974). This is consistent with Rutter, Tizard, and Whitmore's (1970) Isle of Wight study, in which serious fears were reported in only 7 per 1,000 of the 10- and 11-year-olds studied. In contrast, Ollendick's (1983) sample of children between the ages of 3 and 11 averaged between 9 and 13 extreme fears, and Kirkpatrick's (1984) sample of adolescents 15 through 17 averaged between 2 and 3 intense fears. Other recent epidemiological data also suggest that extreme fears may be quite common (Rutter, 1989b). Thus, the prevalence of intense fears in children remains uncertain.

Sex and Age Differences. Most research suggests that girls exhibit a greater number of fears than boys (e.g., King et al., 1989; Kirkpatrick, 1984; Ollendick, 1983). They are also likely to fear snakes and mice, while boys are more likely to exhibit excessive fear of being criticized (e.g., Lapouse and Monk, 1959; Miller et al., 1974). Some studies suggest a greater fear intensity in girls as well (Graziano et al., 1979). Findings of sex differences should probably be interpreted with caution, since it is quite possible that gender-role expectations influence the displaying and reporting of fear.

It is most commonly reported that the number of fears and anxieties experienced by children declines with age (e.g., MacFarlane et al., 1954; King et al., 1989; Lapouse and Monk, 1959). The data in Figure 6–1, in general, illustrate this pattern. However, there are reports of no such decline (e.g., Angelino, Dollins, and Mech, 1956; Croake and Knox, 1973). The relationship with age may also not be a linear one, since there are reports of an increase at later ages (e.g., Graziano, DeGiovanni, and Garcia, 1979). The data in Figure 6–1, for example, illustrate an increase at 14 and 15 years.

Whatever the trend, certain fears appear to be common at particular ages. For example, fear of strangers at 6 to 9 months, imaginary creatures during the second year, fear of the dark among 4-year-olds, and social fears and fear of failure in older children are common age-related fears (Miller et al., 1974). Most authorities would not classify age-appropriate fears as phobias unless they are exaggerated or continue longer than expected. Table 6–4 illustrates common fears among different age groups

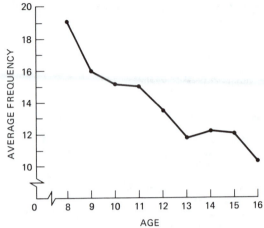

FIGURE 6–1 Frequency of fears across age. With permission from *Journal of Child Psychology and Psychiatry, 30,* N. J. King et al. Fears of children and adolescents: A cross-sectional Australian study using the Revised-Fear Survey Schedule for Children. Copyright © 1989, Pergamon Press plc.

of children completing the revised Fear Survey Schedule for Children.

Research regarding the persistence of childhood fears presents a mixed picture. It was previously widely believed that these problems are short-lived. However, a number of more recent studies has found some children's fears to be more stable. Available research, however, is probably not adequate to appropriately answer the question of persistence (Barrios and Hartmann, 1988; Campbell, 1986).

Should children's fears receive clinical attention? Mild fear reactions and those specific to a developmental period might be expected to dissipate quickly. However, if the fear—even though short-lived—creates sufficient discomfort or interferes with functioning, intervention may be justified.

It is thus quite clear that a developmental perspective is helpful in evaluating children's fears (Campbell, 1986; Marks, 1987). The age-specific and transitory nature of many fears is important in judging the seriousness of this behavior. However, if fears and anxieties disrupt the normal developmental process at sensitive stages this

TABLE 6–4 Percentage of Children Reporting Fears According to Age

8- to 10-year-olds		11- to 13-year-olds		14- to 16-year-olds	
Item description	*Percent Endorsement*	*Item description*	*Percent Endorsement*	*Item description*	*Percent Endorsement*
Nuclear war	68	Nuclear war	80	Nuclear war	69
Being hit by a car	72	Not being able to breathe	62	Not being able to breathe	55
Not being able to breathe	68	Being hit by a car or truck	62	Bombing attacks—being invaded	53
Bombing attacks—being invaded	65	Bombing attacks—being invaded	62	Being hit by a car or truck	50
Earthquakes	62	Earthquakes	51	Fire—getting burned	48
Falling from high places	58	Fire—getting burned	51	Falling from high places	42
A burglar breaking into our house	56	A burglar breaking into our house	47	A burglar breaking into our house	39
Fire—getting burned	52	Falling from high places	46	Snakes	39
Being sent to the principal	47	Snakes	40	Spiders	36
Getting lost in a strange place	46	Death or dead people	39	Earthquakes	35

Adapted and reprinted with permission from King, N. J. et al. Fears of children and adolescents: A cross-sectional Australian study using the Revised-Fear Survey Schedule for Children. *Journal of Child Psychology and Psychiatry, 30.* Copyright (1989), Pergamon Press, plc.

may contribute to their persistence. Developmental changes in children's perception also bear on our understanding of their fears. For example, increasing differentiation of internal reality from objective reality may help explain why younger children fear ghosts and monsters, while older children have more realistic fears of physical danger or injury. Social expectations and the acceptability of expressing certain fears at a particular age must also be considered. Older children, for example, may be socialized to believe that bedtime fears are inappropriate, and they therefore may not express them. Age combined with gender-role expectations may produce similar effects. For example, while equal proportions of younger boys and girls indicate that they have frightening dreams, 10 percent of sixth-grade boys as opposed to 70 percent of same-age girls report this experience (Bauer, 1976).

Etiological Paradigms

As we described earlier, children's fears have played a major historical role in the development of modern theories of behavior (Barrios and Hartmann, 1988). Freud's (1909, 1953) case of Little Hans served as the basis for much of the psychoanalytic conceptualization of phobias. It also marked the beginning of child psychoanalysis and supported several aspects of psychoanalytic theory. Watson's case of Little Albert followed shortly thereafter (Watson and Rayner, 1920). It not only demonstrated the conditioning of fear, but was also one of the early tests of behaviorism. Finally, Jones (1924) provided one of the first interventions based on behavioral principles in her treatment of Peter's fear of white furry objects. Thus the conceptualization of fear played a central role in the development of both the psychoanalytic and behavioral perspectives. Each viewpoint's explanation of the development of phobias is prototypal of its general etiological perspective.

The Psychoanalytic View. To review, in Freud's case study of Little Hans (p. 53), phobias were viewed as arising from unresolved Oedipal conflicts—demonstrated by Hans's desire for his mother and fear of his father and castration. The unacceptable idea of possessing mother and displacing father (and the anxiety associated with it) was repressed. This was followed by projection—Hans believed that his father wanted to be rid of or harm him. The final step, and the essence of the phobia, was displacement. The unconscious anxiety was displaced onto some external object which in some way was related to or symbolic of the unconscious wish. For Hans the horse was related to, among other things, playing horsie with his father, his father's appearance (the horse's muzzle symbolized his father's mustache), and castration (symbolized by the horse's biting). Displacement allowed Hans to avoid the phobic object—the horse—whereas he could not avoid his father. Moreover, displacement eliminated Hans's ambivalent feelings toward his father.

Psychoanalytic theorists have changed and extended Freud's theory, but the basic structure has not been altered. The primary changes allow that affect arising from aggression, separation anxiety, and non-Oedipal sexuality may also serve as the basis for phobia development (cf. Nemiah, 1980).

The psychoanalytic framework for childhood phobias is based almost exclusively on interpretation of case material. Although the clinical detail is rich, generalizations cannot easily be made. Also, the concepts employed are difficult to operationalize and therefore difficult to evaluate or refute.

Behavioral Paradigms. Behavioral theories have taken a number of different forms. Classical conditioning, operant conditioning, and observational learning explanations have all been offered.

CLASSICAL CONDITIONING. Watson and Rayner's (1920) case of Little Albert (described on p. 55) served as the prototype for classical conditioning explanations. A neutral stimulus present during a high-intensity fear response or repeatedly paired with a fear-evoking stimulus comes to evoke anxiety or fear. The acquired response may persist without additional pairings. Moreover, generalization to stimuli perceived as similar to the original phobic stimulus can also occur. Extinction of the fear does not take place since the child avoids the conditioned stimulus and thus never learns that it is no longer followed by the unconditioned stimulus.

OPERANT CONDITIONING. The operant perspective suggests that reinforcement, primarily social reinforcement in the form of attention, is the central etiological mechanism in phobias. According to this viewpoint, children are taught to be afraid by parents or others who selectively attend to and reward fearful behavior, perhaps unintentionally. For example, withdrawal from social situations and accompanying "fearful" behavior may allow the child to stay with the mother, who out of sympathy soothes the child, offers favorite foods, and plays the child's favorite game. Thus, a set of behaviors is maintained by its consequences.

TWO-FACTOR THEORY. As originally proposed by Mowrer (1939), two-factor theory incorporates both classical and operant concepts. Phobias are thought to originate through classical conditioning and to be subsequently maintained through operant conditioning. The pairing of a neutral (conditioned) stimulus with an aversive unconditioned stimulus produces the initial fear or anxiety. Subsequently, avoiding the conditioned phobic stimulus produces a reduction in anxiety or fear—which then maintains the avoidant behavior. A revision of the classical two-factor theory known as approach-withdrawal theory was suggested when research questioned the exclusive relationship of avoidance to fear reduction (cf. Delprato and McGlynn, 1984). Avoidance behavior is not seen as being maintained by fear reduction, but rather by relaxation and relief. Accordingly, the unconditioned stimulus over time has come not to evoke fear, but rather to serve as a cue to approach a nonaversive or safe area. This avoidant response produces relaxation. This represents a shift from emphasis on negative reinforcement (fear avoidance) to positive reinforcement (relaxation).

OBSERVATIONAL LEARNING. Observational learning holds that phobic responses may also be learned when children observe and imitate the phobic responses of others. For example, a little girl who observes her mother's fear of dogs may imitate this reaction. Children can also learn vicariously through another's repeated descriptions. That children often exhibit the same kinds of fears as their parents is consistent with an observational learning explanation (e.g., Bandura and Menlove, 1968).

CRITICISMS AND SUGGESTED MODIFICATIONS. Learning theory explanations have been criticized on a number of grounds. Some attempts to classically condition fears have not been successful (e.g., Bregman, 1934; English, 1929), although the methodological adequacy of these studies has been questioned (cf. Delprato, 1980). Classically conditioned fear responses in humans also seem to extinguish rather quickly (e.g., Bridger and Mandel, 1965). Ethical considerations have restrained researchers from employing highly aversive stimuli in research studies. Nonetheless, rapid extinction in these research studies is not consistent with the observed persistence of actual phobic behavior. Also, clinical reports suggest that a large proportion of phobic cases occur with no evidence of the frightening-traumatic event assumed in the classical conditioning model. For example, snake phobics often report that they cannot recall any frightening experiences with snakes. Similarly, phobic patients often fail to report observations of fearful models. Since both of these are based on retrospective reports, the possibility exists that these experiences did occur and that memory is distorted. On the other hand, people who have traumatic experiences or observe frightening situations do not usually become phobic. Also, some stimuli (for example, snakes) are more likely than others to become conditioned fear stimuli. Some explanation of all these findings is necessary for an adequate understanding of how phobias are acquired.

Criticisms of the operant model have questioned the lack of attention given to thoughts and subjective feelings of fear. Furthermore, critics point out that phobic individuals often suffer considerably as the result of their behavior. They also avoid harmless situations that might provide considerable pleasure. Why do the positive consequences of phobic behavior—attention or anxiety relief—continue, over long periods, to outweigh the negative consequences? While it is possible to argue that the positive rewards are more powerful consequences, this question places some strain on the operant explanation.

Despite these criticisms, some evidence supporting a behavioral conceptualization does exist. It is probably the case that classical conditioning of fear, imitation, and the consequences of avoidant behavior do contribute significantly to the development of phobias. Thus, these explanations may not be so much incorrect as incomplete.

The failure of some attempts to replicate Watson and Rayner's (1920) classical conditioning of fear, along with the observation that phobias seem to develop more readily to some stimuli than others, led some workers to posit an innate basis for fears. Rachman (1977), for example, rather than arguing for a single mechanism, suggested that fears and anxieties can be acquired by a variety of learning mechanisms. In addition he suggested a notion of hereditary determinants of fear to explain why some stimuli are more likely to become fear objects. Similarly, Seligman (1971), following ideas expressed earlier, suggested the notion of *preparedness* to account for the fact that phobias are more likely to occur to some stimuli. It is postulated that organisms are genetically prepared to acquire fear to stimuli that posed threats to their ancestors and were, thus, of evolutionary significance. Thus, fear reactions to these "prepared" stimuli are more easily acquired, severe, persistent, and resistant to treatment.

Caution in drawing conclusions regarding evolutionary preparedness is, however, suggested by a number of criticisms (cf. Delprato, 1980). Methodological criticisms of the research on preparedness have been offered. For example, researchers often ignore the developmental histories of the organisms they study. Individuals may have had neutral, positive, or negative experiences correlated with houses, for example. In contrast, previous associations or references to snakes are likely to have been consistently negative. Deprato (1980) also offers a good example of the logical problems involved in deciding on the preexisting evolutionary potential of stimuli. Mushrooms have been employed as a neutral (nonprepared) stimulus—one to which fear does not easily condition—in these studies. Yet the large variety of poisonous mushrooms that exist suggests that mushrooms have posed a threat to human survival. How does one then determine a priori whether a stimulus should be thought of as biologically prepared? Examination of clinical cases also provides evidence of conflicts with the evolutionary hypothesis. For example, DeSilva, Rachman, and Seligman (1977) retrospectively examined a large number of phobia cases seen over a five-year period and found that acquisition rate and therapeutic outcome were unrelated to the presumed biological preparedness of the phobic stimulus.

Although there may be difficulties with conditioning models of phobias, the innate versus learned dicotomy that is characteristic of much of the literature does not seem necessary. For example, fears need not be innate to be influenced by biology. A child whose autonomic nervous system is very reactive may be more likely to learn phobic behavior. Fear, like any other behavior, can be viewed from a developmental perspective in which a continuing interchange between the organism (upon which genetics has had its impact) and its environment results in particular behaviors at a given point in time (Delprato, 1980). Moreover, with regard to genetic influences, the picture remains unclear. Evidence for a high degree of association between anxiety disorders of children and their parents has been found. However, the extent to which this suggests genetic or environmental influences such as family interaction patterns and styles of information processing remains uncertain (Barrios and O'Dell, 1989; Rutter et al., 1990b; Silverman, Cerny, and Nelles, 1988). Explanations of childhood fears and anxieties are likely to address these variables in the future.

Treatment of Childhood Phobias

A variety of psychoanalytic, pharmacological, and behavioral interventions have been offered to treat childhood phobias. By far the greatest amount of controlled outcome research exists for behavioral treatments.

Behavioral Treatments. A number of different behavioral strategies for treating childhood phobias have been studied. However, before discussing specific treatments, it should be noted that these investigations suffer from a number of limitations (King and Ollendick, 1989; Morris and Kratochwill, 1983). For example, the vast majority deal with the treatment of fears and anxieties of mild to moderate intensity, leaving the effectiveness of treatment of severe problems less well explored. In addition, most studies combine a number of different techniques, making it difficult to evaluate the efficacy of individual procedures.

SYSTEMATIC DESENSITIZATION. One of the most widely used behavioral treatments has been systematic desensitization and its variants. A hierarchy of fear-provoking situations is constructed, and the child is asked to visualize scenes of increasing fearfulness. Actual representations of the feared object or situation, such as a picture or toys, are sometimes used in place of visualization. These visualizations or stimuli are paired with relaxation or some other response that is incompatible with fear. This is done until the most fear-provoking scene can be comfortably visualized. When the actual feared object or situation is employed, treatment is referred to as "in vivo desensitization." Behavioral tests of the ability to approach the feared object (for example, a snake) are usually included in the evaluation of treatment effectiveness.

Systematic desensitization and in vivo desensitization have been shown to be effective in reducing adults' fears, but support for their use with children, while encouraging, is not overwhelming. The evidence may be best for older children and it can be argued that, even here, few methodologically adequate studies exist (Barrios and O'Dell, 1989; Ollendick, 1979).

PROLONGED EXPOSURE. Another procedure to treat childhood fears and anxieties is prolonged exposure. In these treatments the child is asked, from the outset, to confront the "full version" of the feared stimulus. Exposure may be imaginal or in vivo. The child is reinforced for remaining in the presence of the feared stimulus for prolonged periods of time (e.g., Leitenberg and Callahan, 1973). Prolonged exposure treatments have been found to be effective, but there are only a few experimental studies of these procedures.

MODELING. A commonly employed behavioral procedure is modeling. Jones's (1924) treatment of Peter's fear of furry objects is probably the earliest report of the therapeutic use of modeling. The work of Bandura and his colleagues (e.g., Bandura and Menlove, 1968) has served as the impetus for more recent controlled research. In all modeling therapies the child observes another person interacting adaptively with the feared situation. The model can be live or symbolic (e.g., film or slides). Modeling procedures have been demonstrated in numerous experimental studies to be superior to control conditions and to be effective over a fairly wide age range. Observation of a model who is similar to the child (e.g., in age and fear levels) appears to result in better outcomes. *Participant modeling*, in which observation is followed by the fearful child joining the model in making gradual approaches to the feared object, is one of the most potent treatments (Barrios and O'Dell, 1989; Rosenthal and Bandura, 1978).

Lewis's (1974) oft-cited treatment of fear of the water illustrates the use of modeling, and participant modeling in particular. Forty boys between the ages of 5 and 12 were assigned to one of four treatment conditions. Children in the *modeling-plus-participation* condition observed a film of three boys of similar age performing tasks such as those in a swimming test. These coping models initially exhibited fear but gradually increased their competency in dealing with the tasks; eventually they were shown playing together happily in the water. Immediately following observation of the film, the children were taken by a second experimenter to the pool for a ten-minute participation phase. They were encouraged to engage in the activities involved in the swimming test and were given social reinforcements for attempting these activities. Boys in the *modeling only* condition observed the film and then played a game at poolside for ten minutes; those in the *participation only* condition saw a neutral cartoon and then completed the ten-minute participation phase; those in the *control* condition saw the cartoon and played the poolside game. When the behavioral swimming test was repeated the next day, the control group showed no change. Boys who had experienced participation exhibited significant improvement, greater than that provided by modeling alone. The most effective treatment was the combination of modeling and participation. A follow-up evaluation of 25 of the boys five days later suggested that the gains had been maintained and had generalized to a different pool and different swimming instructor. Once again the mod-

Having the child imitate a model is one method for treating children's fears. In participant modeling the child observes the model and then participates with the model in gradually approaching the feared object or situation. (By permission of the New York State Office of Mental Retardation and Developmental Disabilities. Photo by Paul Gerry.)

eling plus participation boys seem to have fared the best.

These findings and others indicate that modeling treatments can be highly effective. However, it is not clear what is responsible for the success of modeling. Treatments such as Lewis's (1974) often involve other components, such as the social reinforcement given to the boys for swimming activities. The mechanism for change is also unclear. Is the child's fear actually being reduced? Or alternatively, are coping skills being improved? Bandura (1977a, 1982), for example, suggests that the child's expectations of personal efficacy may be increased by the modeling and other procedures.

COGNITIVE SELF-MANAGEMENT STRATEGIES. Some investigators have examined the self-management of children's beliefs or cognitions as a treatment strategy. Often teaching of self-managed coping skills is combined with exposure to modeling (e.g., Peterson

and Shigetomi, 1982). Kanfer's cognitive self-control approach is an early example of the use of coping statements (Kanfer, Karoly, and Newman, 1975). Kindergarten children who were afraid of the dark—defined by being unable to remain alone in a dark room for three minutes—experienced one of three conditions. The children were taken individually into a room by a familiar experimenter. The room was equipped with a rheostat that enabled the child to control the illumination and an intercom to call for the return of the experimenter. The experimenter left the room and timed how long the child was able to tolerate the dark. Following this pretest, children in the *competence* condition were taught self-statements, such as, "I am a brave girl (boy). I can take care of myself." Children in the *stimulus* group were taught self-statements intended to reduce the fear-evoking potential of the dark, such as, "The dark is a fun place to be." Those in the *control* condition were taught to use neutral self-statements, such as, "Mary had a little lamb." At a posttest immediately following training, children who learned competence self-statements exhibited the most improvement. All verbalization groups showed improvement, however, and this suggests that some adaptation had occurred from exposure to the feared stimulus. It is also difficult to generalize from these findings to clinical phobias, since the original intensity of the fear was not great; indeed, intensely fearful children were specifically excluded. Finally, children in the study had clear control of the feared stimulus, a situation very different from one in which the child feels helpless and lacking control (Ross, 1981).

Some studies have explored the treatment of fears of a clinical magnitude and have employed cognitive strategies as part of the treatment program. Graziano's home-based program for nighttime fears is one example (e.g., Graziano and Mooney, 1982). Graziano and his associates have combined self-talk with various other elements (relaxation training, pleasant imagery, and contingency management) to successfully treat long-standing fear of the dark.

Like Graziano's approach, many treatments actually combine multiple procedures. Combining one or more of the treatment procedures described above with contingency management—rewarding a child for improvement—is common (Barrios and O'Dell, 1989). It is, therefore, difficult to know which elements are important for which children or for which fears and anxieties.

Other Treatments

There are numerous case studies of psychodynamic treatment of childhood phobias (e.g., Bornstein, 1949; Finell, 1980; Sperling, 1952; Tyson, 1978), but little systematic research. Treatment involves essentially the same goals and methods (e.g., interpretation, transference) employed with adults (Lewis, 1986). Psychoanalytically oriented play therapy is common with younger children.

The literature on pharmacotherapy with anxious children also consists largely of clinical reports and these have numerous methodological difficulties that make conclusions difficult (Gittleman and Koplewicz, 1986). A large number of different pharmacological agents have been used, but there is little support for most of them.

Although the antianxiety agents (e.g., benzodiazepines) would seem to be logical choices, their usefulness with children is not supported. The controlled drug studies with positive outcomes have been those employing tricyclic antidepressants (Gittleman-Klein and Klein, 1980). However, other well-controlled studies employing tricyclics found them to be no more effective than placebos (Berney et al., 1981; Rapoport, Elkins, and Mikkelsen, 1980). Clearly, although drug treatment is recommended by many clinicians, there is little research to support this practice and a great deal more research is obviously needed (Barrios and O'Dell, 1989; Gittleman and Koplewicz, 1986).

SCHOOL REFUSAL

Historically, the term "school phobic" has been employed to describe children who exhibit anxiety regarding school attendance. Severe anxiety and somatic symptoms such as dizziness, stomachaches, and nausea "keep" the child at home. The parents, concerned with the child's health and anx-iety, are often reluctant to force attendance. It is not clear, however, that the child actually fears the school situation in all cases. Thus, some workers question the use of the term school phobia to describe the disorder. Indeed, many cases of school phobia appear to be due to a fear of separation from the mother and home. The theme that avoidance of school may be just one manifestation of the larger fear of separation has long been popular. Thus, some workers suggest the more comprehensive term "school refusal" (e.g., Hersov, 1960a) and we will employ this term. There is, however, still much terminological confusion in the literature.

Classification and Prevalence

The DSM-III-R category of separation anxiety disorder is intended to describe children with excessive anxiety regarding separation from a major attachment figure and/or home. Diagnostic criteria include nine symptoms (Table 6–5), only three of which must be met to receive the diagnosis. Reluctance or refusal to go to school is one of these nine symptoms; however, a child need not exhibit this behavior to receive the di-

Refusing to go to school and/or to be separated from parents is a common reason for referral for psychological services. (Ed Lettau/Photo Researchers, Inc.)

agnosis. Thus, not all children with separation anxiety disorder exhibit school refusal. In addition, not all school refusers need show separation anxiety. Some children, for example, may fear some aspect of the school experience. The latter group might be diagnosed under the adult specific phobia or social phobia categories. Recent studies of clinic-referred children support a distinction between separation-anxious and phobic school refusers (e.g., Last and Strauss, 1990).

It should be made clear that school refusal is differentiated from truancy. Truants are usually absent on an intermittent basis, often without parental knowledge. The school refuser, in contrast, is usually absent for continuous extended periods, during which time the parents are aware of the child's being at home. Also, truants are often described as poor students who exhibit other conduct problems such as stealing and lying.

School refusal is usually estimated to occur in between 0.4 percent and 1.5 percent of the general population (e.g., Granell de Aldaz et al., 1984; Ollendick and Mayer, 1984) and seems less prevalent than other phobias/anxiety disorders. Interestingly, however, some reports suggest that as much as 69 percent of referrals for any kind of child phobia are for school refusal and the problem is seen in approximately 3 to 8 percent of clinic-referred children (Last and Strauss, 1990; Miller et al., 1972; Smith, 1970). Miller and others have suggested that this may be due to the fact that this problem creates the most difficulty for parents and school personnel.

School refusal can be found in children of all ages and intelligence levels. If left untreated, serious long-term consequences seem possible. Prognosis seems best for chil-

TABLE 6–5 Criteria for DSM-III-R Diagnosis of Separation Anxiety Disorder

A. Excessive anxiety concerning separation from those to whom the child is attached, as evidenced by at least three of the following:
1. Unrealistic and persistent worry about possible harm befalling major attachment figures or fear that they will leave and not return
2. Unrealistic and persistent worry that an untoward calamitous event will separate the child from a major attachment figure, e.g., the child will be lost, kidnapped, killed, or be the victim of an accident
3. Persistent reluctance or refusal to go to school in order to stay with major attachment figures or at home
4. Persistent reluctance or refusal to go to sleep without being near a major attachment figure or to go to sleep away from home
5. Persistent avoidance of being alone, including "clinging" to and "shadowing" major attachment figures
6. Repeated nightmares involving the theme of separation
7. Complaints of physical symptoms, e.g., headaches, stomachaches, nausea, or vomiting, on many school days or on other occasions when anticipating separation from major attachment figures
8. Recurrent signs or complaints of excessive distress in anticipation of separation from home or major attachment figures, e.g., temper tantrums or crying, pleading with parents not to leave
9. Recurrent signs of complaints of excessive distress when separated from home or major attachment figures, e.g., wants to return home, needs to call parents when they are absent or when child is away from home

B. Duration of disturbance of at least two weeks

C. Onset before the age of 18

D. Occurrence not exclusively during the course of a Pervasive Developmental Disorder, Schizophrenia, or any other psychotic disorder

Reprinted with permission from the *Diagnostic and Statistical Manual of Mental Disorders, Third Edition Revised,* Copyright 1987, American Psychiatric Association.

dren under the age of 10 years and treatment success seems to be particularly difficult with older children (Berg and Jackson, 1985; Miller et al., 1974). In addition, as adults such individuals may be at risk for a number of problems (Burke and Silverman, 1987).

Etiology

As suggested above it is best not to view all cases of school refusal as having a unitary cause. The most common conceptualization of school refusal attributes the problem to separation anxiety. Psychodynamic explanations describe the child's insistence on remaining at home as satisfying both the child's and mother's dependency needs and conflicts concerning separation. The basic notion is that strong attachment leads the child to fear that something may happen either to the self or to the mother during separation. In the latter instance, such explanations also often describe the possibility of the child's having aggressive wishes toward the parent that the child fears will be fulfilled in his or her absence (e.g., Kessler, 1988). There is little information available about the father's role in this process.

There are problems with the assumption that school refusal is usually accompanied by some anxiety disorder in the mother. The same conflicts have been described in mothers of children with other problems, and it is not known whether some mothers with the same conflicts rear children free of phobias. Moreover, the research has been conducted after the child has already experienced the problem, making cause and effect extremely difficult to separate.

Behavioral explanations of school refusal as separation anxiety presume that the child has learned to avoid school because of some association of school with an existing intense fear of losing the mother. Once avoidance behavior occurs, it may be reinforced by attention and other rewards, such as toys and special foods, that the child receives while at home.

While separation anxiety is the most prevalent explanation for school refusal, some authors have also emphasized a true "fear of school." Leventhal and Sills (1964), for example, offer an interpretation that describes the school phobic as a child with an inflated self-image. When this self-image is threatened in some way in the school situation, the child develops an avoidance pattern, preferring to remain at home where power is not threatened. Thus, some cases of school phobia might be viewed as a fear of failure (Kessler, 1988).

Behavioral explanations, in particular, view many instances as cases of actual fear of school. Indeed, it has been suggested that the term school phobia is appropriate only for these cases (e.g., Last and Francis, 1988). Such explanations are likely to posit that anxiety is conditioned through actual upsetting or traumatic experiences in the school situation. Like behavioral separation anxiety views, an important role is ascribed to the attention the conditioned fear receives. This contributes to the maintenance of the problem.

Treatment

The majority of clinicians of all orientations stress the importance of getting the child back to school (King, Ollendick, and Gullone, 1990). Psychodynamic approaches tend to recommend insight-oriented therapy to strengthen the child's ego. The need for the mother to receive therapy may also be emphasized. Behaviorally oriented treatments emphasize (1) the reduction of anxiety about leaving the mother or about the actual school situation and (2) the alteration of contingencies applied to the avoidant behavior. Anxiety-reduction procedures employed with other phobias, such as systematic desensitization and exposure, have been used with school refusers (e.g., Garvey and Hegreves, 1966). Contingency management involves eliminating the positive consequences of staying at home (for example, attention and access to favorite things) and providing rewards for increased school attendance.

Most workers suggest that the prognosis is quite good for the acute school refuser. Indeed, a frequently cited method used by Kennedy (1965) suggests that successful treatment can be rapid. At an initial meeting the father is instructed to take the child to school the following Monday, and school personnel are instructed to keep the child in school all day. No excuse is to be accepted for altering this plan, and physical complaints are dealt with by after-school visits to the pediatrician. School attendance is praised, even when involuntary. The child is seen briefly by the therapist after school hours. Stories illustrating the transitory nature of fears and the "need to get back on the horse after a fall" are relayed to the child. On Wednesday a party is held to celebrate the child's having overcome the difficulty. Kennedy reports success in 100 percent of the 50 cases treated in this manner. Follow-ups of the subjects of no less than two years and up to eight years later indicate no recurrence of the problem. The absence of controlled comparison studies, however, suggests caution in drawing firm conclusions.

The treatment literature on school refusal contains primarily case studies, and the adequacy or generality of studies with experimental designs is questionable (Burke and Silverman, 1987). It is also suggested that a more prescriptive approach—treatment designed to fit distinctions made among kinds of school refusers—needs to be pursued. Drawing on work with other childhood problems (e.g., Durand and Crimmins, 1988), such efforts have been initiated. Kearney and Silverman (1990) assessed which of four categories of variables maintained school refusal in individual children: specific fearfulness or general overanxiousness related to school, avoidance of aversive social situations, attention-getting or separation anxious behavior that is reinforced, or tangible rewards for not attending school. Successful treatments were designed for each child based on such a *functional analysis* of the school refusal behavior of that child.

THE OVERANXIOUS CHILD

Phobias and school refusal represent relatively focused anxiety disorders. However, anxiety is sometimes experienced in a less focused manner. Children with more extensive anxiety are often described as overanxious.

Description and Diagnosis

Clinicians frequently describe children who worry excessively and exhibit extensive fearful behavior. These disturbances are not focused on any particular object or situation and are not due to a specific recent stress. The children seem excessively concerned with their competence and performance, and they exhibit nervous habits (e.g., nail biting), sleep disturbances, and physical complaints such as stomachaches. DSM-III-R recognizes this clinical entity by providing the diagnosis Overanxious Disorder within the category of Anxiety Disorders of Childhood or Adolescence (Table 6–6).

Current knowledge concerning the overanxious child is based almost entirely on clinical reports, as in the case of the nine-year-old boy described by Anthony (1981).

Like his mother, John had a very low opinion of himself and his abilities . . . and found it difficult to cope with the "scary things" inside himself. His main problem had to do with the numerous fears that he had and the panic attacks that overtook him from time to time. He was afraid of the dark, of ghosts, of monsters, of being abandoned, of being alone, of strangers, of war, of guns, of knives, of loud noises, and of snakes. . . . Like his mother again, he had many psychosomatic complaints involving his bladder, his bowels, his kidneys, his intestines and his blood. . . . He also suffered from insomnia and would not or could not go to sleep until his

---

TABLE 6–6 Criteria for a DSM-III-R Diagnosis of Overanxious Disorder

A. Excessive or unrealistic anxiety or worry, for a period of six months or longer, as indicated by the frequent occurrence of at least four of the following:
1. Excessive or unrealistic worry about future events
2. Excessive or unrealistic concern about the appropriateness of past behavior
3. Excessive or unrealistic concern about competence in one or more areas, e.g., athletic, academic, social
4. Somatic complaints, such as headaches or stomachaches, for which no physical basis can be established
5. Marked self-consciousness
6. Excessive need for reassurance about a variety of concerns
7. Marked feelings of tension or inability to relax

B. If another Axis I disorder is present (e.g., Separation Anxiety Disorder, Phobic Disorder, Obsessive Compulsive Disorder), the focus of the symptoms in A are not limited to it. For example, if Separation Anxiety Disorder is present, the symptoms in A are not exclusively related to anxiety about separation. In addition, the disturbance does not occur only during the course of a psychotic disorder or a Mood Disorder.

C. If 18 or older, does not meet the criteria for Generalized Anxiety Disorder

D. Occurrence not exclusively during the course of a Pervasive Developmental Disorder, Schizophrenia, or any other psychotic disorder

Reprinted with permission from the *Diagnostic and Statistical Manual of Mental Disorders, Third Edition, Revised,* Copyright 1987, American Psychiatric Association.

mother did. . . . He was also afraid to sleep alone or to sleep without a light, and regularly wet and soiled himself. He was often afraid but could not say why and was also fearful of contact with others (pp. 163–64).

Prevalence and Developmental Characteristics

The frequently stated view is that Overanxious Disorder is not common (e.g., DSM-III-R). Clinical reports describe the disorder as being most common among small families, higher socioeconomic groups, eldest children, and families in which there is unusual concern about performance, even when the child is functioning at an adequate or superior level (DSM-III-R, 1987; Werkman, 1980). Recent epidemiological studies of nonclinic samples have reported prevalence rates of between 2.9 percent and 4.6 percent (Costello, 1989). In a sample of children presenting at a clinic for anxiety disorders, however, 52 percent met the DSM-III criteria for Overanxious Disorder (Last, 1989).

Onset is usually described as gradual, and the prognosis is thought to be poor with problems persisting into adulthood. Disagreement exists as to whether the disorder is more common in boys (Last, Strauss, and Francis, 1987) or in girls (Werkman, 1980), or equally represented (DSM-III-R, 1987).

An examination of developmental differences in children and adolescents meeting the DSM diagnostic criteria for Overanxious Disorder (OAD) does provide some interesting information (Strauss et al., 1988b). In this investigation the criteria for OAD were met by 55 of the 106 cases of anxiety disorders examined. In order to examine developmental differences, two groups were formed by dividing children under and over 12 years of age. Strauss and her colleagues found that the two groups did not differ in terms of the prevalence of the OAD diagnosis or sociodemographic characteristics. Both groups also showed similar rates of specific OAD symptoms (as described in Table 6–6). Older children, however, presented with a greater number of symptoms than did younger children and also reported higher levels of anxiety and depression.

The other diagnoses received by the children were particularly interesting. Table 6–7 illustrates the percentage of children in each age group who also met the diagnostic criteria for other disorders. Within the anxiety disorders, young children were significantly more likely to receive a concurrent diagnosis of separation anxiety disorder, and older children a concurrent diagnosis of simple phobia. Older children were also significantly more likely to receive a concurrent diagnosis of major depression and younger children a concurrent diagnosis of attention-deficit disorder. These findings may suggest a developmental difference in how OAD is experienced. However, it should also be noted that many other diagnostic categories were represented in one or both age groups. Also, although the authors do not report the percentage of children receiving one or more diagnoses in addition to OAD, the results presented in Table 6–7 suggest it is quite high. As the authors note, the high degree of additional

TABLE 6–7 Concurrent DSM-III Diagnoses for Younger versus Older Children with Overanxious Disorder

DSM-III Diagnoses	Age Groups	
	<12 years (%)	≥12 years (%)
Anxiety disorders		
Separation anxiety disorder	69.6	21.9*
Avoidant disorder	13.0	25.0
Simple phobia	8.7	40.6*
Social phobia	8.7	9.4
Agoraphobia	0	6.3
Panic disorder	0	15.6
Obsessive-compulsive disorder	4.3	9.4
Major depression	17.4	46.9*
Oppositional disorder	17.4	6.3
Conduct disorder	8.7	0
Attention deficit disorder	34.8	9.4*

* Statistically significant difference.
Adapted from Strauss et al., 1988b. Reprinted by permission of Plenum Publishing Corporation.

diagnoses raises a question addressed earlier in this chapter. Is there justification for distinctions among anxiety or indeed internalizing disorders in children?

OBSESSIVE-COMPULSIVE DISORDER

Obsessions are unwanted, repetitive, intrusive thoughts, while *compulsions* are repetitive, stereotyped behaviors the child feels compelled to perform. The disorder can involve either obsessions or compulsions or, usually, a combination of the two. Rapoport's (1989) description of Sergei illustrates the nature and consequences of the disorder.

Sergei is a 17-year-old former high school student. Only a year or so ago Sergei seemed to be a normal adolescent with many talents and interests. Then, almost overnight he was transformed into a lonely outsider, excluded from social life by his psychological disabilities. Specifically, he was unable to stop washing. Haunted by the notion that he was dirty—in spite of the contrary evidence of his senses—he began to spend more and more of his time cleansing himself of imaginary dirt. At first his ritual ablutions were confined to weekends and evenings and he was able to stay in school while keeping them up, but soon they began to consume all his time, forcing him to drop out of school, a victim of his inability to feel clean enough. (p. 83)

Odd repetitive acts are known to occur in even very young children, and are seen as strange even by the child. Initially the child may have an explanation. For example, seven-year-old Stanley indicated that he had seen a show in which Martians contacted humans by putting strange thoughts in their heads. In this way, Stanley explained his compulsion to do everything in sequences of four, as a sign that he had been picked as the Martians' contact on earth. After two years of no contact Stanley gave up this explanation, but not his ritual (Rapoport, 1989). The child may thus come to recognize that the ideas or behaviors involved are unreasonable but still feel the need to repeat them.

Prevalence

Behavior with obsessive-compulsive qualities occurs in various stages of normal development (Leonard et al., 1990). The feeding and bedtime rituals of very young children are examples; disruption of these routines often leads to distress. Also, young children are often observed to engage in repetitive play and to show a distinct preference for sameness. Benjamin Spock (Spock and Rothenberg, 1985), in his widely read book for parents, notes that mild compulsions—such as stepping over cracks in the sidewalk or touching every third picket in a fence—are quite common in eight-, nine-, and ten-year-olds. Such behaviors, common to the child's peer group, are probably best viewed as games. Only when they dominate the child's life and interfere with normal functioning is there cause for concern. It is not clear at present whether such rituals represent early manifestations of obsessive-compulsive disorder in some children (Leonard et al., 1990).

Obsessive-compulsive disorder is probably not as rare as was once believed. Previous estimates based on records of child clinical agencies reported incidence rates from 0.2 percent to 1 percent (Judd, 1965; Hollingsworth et al., 1980). A prevalence of up to 0.3 percent (depending on how cases were classified) was reported for an unselected general child population (Rutter, Tizard, and Whitmore, 1970). Due to several considerations, including attempts by individuals to hide their difficulties, lack of public awareness, and limited availability of treatment, these figures may be underestimates. More recently, rates of referrals from specific geographic areas to the National Institute of Mental Health (NIMH) have been greater than would be expected based on these earlier estimates (Flament and Rapoport, 1984). Furthermore, an epidemiological study of nonreferred adolescents suggests a prevalence of 1 percent in the general adolescent population (Flament et al., 1988). Most estimates also suggest that boys outnumber girls by about 2:1 or 3:1 (Adams, 1973; Hollingsworth, 1980; Swedo et al., 1989c).

The NIMH Studies

Judith Rapoport and her colleagues at NIMH have conducted a series of studies that have increased attention to obsessive-compulsive behavior in children. Initially, like most clinicians, Rapoport saw few cases of childhood obsessive-compulsive disorder. Indeed, when she began her work she did not know whether or not she would find enough cases to complete the initial research. However, even at this early point, Rapoport was struck by the similarity between child and adult cases of the disorder. For disorders to occur in identical form in children and adults is unusual. From the initial series of cases, the NIMH group was also able to get a sense of obsessions and compulsions that were common in this population (e.g., Swedo et al., 1989c). Table 6–8 indicates the most common obsessions and compulsions among the children and adolescents seen.

As a function of their work with these children, including successful drug treatment trials, these workers came to believe in a biological basis for obsessive-compulsive

Repetitive rituals and keeping things in certain specific locations and order are common among children. It is only when these kinds of behaviors interfere with normal functioning that they should cause concern for clinicians and other adults.

TABLE 6–8 Obsessions and Compulsions Among Children and Adolescents Receiving the Diagnosis of Obsessive-Compulsive Disorder

Obsessions	Percent Reporting Symptom
Concern with dirt germs or environmental toxins	40
Something terrible happening (fire, death or illness of self or loved one)	24
Symmetry, order, or exactness	17
Scrupulosity (religious obsessions)	13
Concern or disgust with bodily wastes or secretions (urine, stool, saliva)	8
Lucky or unlucky numbers	8
Forbidden, aggressive, or perverse sexual thoughts, images, or impulses	4
Fear might harm others or oneself	4
Concern with household items	3
Intrusive nonsense sounds, words, or music	1
Compulsions	
Excessive or ritualized handwashing, showering, bathing, toothbrushing, or grooming	85
Repeating rituals (going in or out of a door, up or down from a chair)	51
Checking (doors, locks, appliances, emergency brake on car, paper route, homework)	46
Rituals to remove contact with contaminants	23
Touching	20
Measures to prevent harm to self or others	16
Ordering or arranging	17
Counting	18
Hoarding or collecting rituals	11
Rituals of cleaning household or inanimate objects	6
Miscellaneous rituals (such as writing, moving, speaking)	26

Note: Percentages total more than 100 percent because many youths had more than one symptom.
Adapted from Rapoport, J. L. The biology of obsessions and compulsions, *Scientific American*, March 1989.

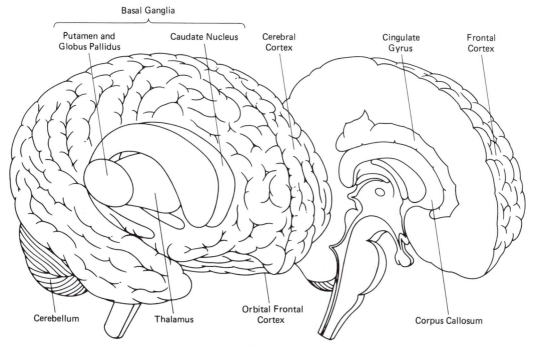

FIGURE 6–2 Neuroanatomy of basal ganglia is shown on a three-dimensional view of the human brain. The basal ganglia consist of several structures, including the caudate nucleus, the putamen and the globus pallidus, that lie under the cerebral cortex. The basal ganglia are connected to the frontal lobe by a variety of pathways, including one that contains tissues in the cingulate gyrus. Rapoport proposes that aberrations in this brain circuitry may underlie the symptoms of obsessive-compulsive disorder. By permission from The biology of obsessions and compulsions by Judith L. Rapoport. Copyright © 1989 by Scientific American, Inc. All rights reserved.

disorder. The disorder was found to be more prevalent among children with a first degree relative (parents or siblings) with obsessive-compulsive behavior than among the general population. This suggested a possible genetic cause (Swedo et al., 1989c). Furthermore, an association between obsessive-compulsive symptoms and certain known neurological disorders suggested that the disorder was linked to the anatomy of the nervous system (e.g., Swedo et al., 1989b). Several lines of evidence implicated the basal ganglia, a group of structures lying under the cerebral cortex (e.g., Luxenberg et al., 1988; Swedo et al., 1989a). These structures and their relationship to other parts of the brain are depicted in Figure 6–2.

Treatment

There are relatively few published reports on the treatment of obsessive-compulsive disorder in children. The follow-up results of Hollingsworth and his colleagues (1980) were not encouraging, at least with respect to insight-oriented psychotherapy. Ten children were followed an average of 6.5 years (range: 1.5 to 14 years). Despite an average

age of 17.7 months of intensive insight-oriented psychotherapy, most of them continued to exhibit some obsessive-compulsive behavior, and all reported serious problems with social life and peer relationships.

The behavioral procedure that has been most successful with obsessions and compulsive behavior in adults is *exposure* to the problem situation combined with *response prevention* (Steketee and Cleere, 1990). Stanley's (1980) clinical report describes response prevention in the treatment of an eight-year-old girl and her family:

Amanda was referred by her G.P. because of her excessive checking behaviour. Three months prior to this referral Amanda's parents became increasingly worried as more and more of her time was involved in carrying out her rituals, e.g., she was taking at least 20 minutes to dress in the morning instead of 5 minutes which had been more than ample previously. The symptoms had first become noticeable 6 months before.

The rituals had begun slowly following the family's move to their present home. This had been the second major move made by the family in three years involving a change of house, school, geographic area and father's job . . . both Amanda and her younger sister had coped reasonably well with the moves, and the parents did not think these had any connection with Amanda's symptomatology. No satisfactory reason for the development of the symptoms was identified. . . .

At interview Amanda presented as an alert, bright eight-year-old whose face fell at the mention of her "fussiness." . . . There was no evidence of obsessional symptoms in her school work and the teacher had not noticed anything unusual in her affect or behaviour.

Amanda was able to talk about her symptomatology as though it were a thing apart from herself. She saw it as an intrusion on her previously happy life and felt depressed by the restrictive elements of her ritual. She found her peer relationships were affected by no longer being able to invite friends home in case they disturbed her ornaments, toys, etc. . . . The family appeared to be functioning very cohesively which may explain how each person had become involved in Amanda's symptomatology.

At the time of referral Amanda's symptoms included the following . . .

1. Every night she closed the curtains, turned down the bed and fluffed up her pillow three times before beginning to undress. Any disruption of this routine caused great distress.

2. The top bedcover had to be placed with the fringes only just touching the floor all around.

3. At night Amanda removed her slippers slowly and carefully, she then banged them on the floor upside-down, and then the right-way-up, three times and nudged them gently and in parallel under the bed.

4. Before going to sleep Amanda had to go to the toilet three times. She often woke up in the middle of the night and carried out the same performance.

5. Before carrying out a ritual Amanda sang:
   "One, two, three,
   Come dance with me
   Tra la la, Tra, la, la."

6. All dressing and undressing had to be done three times. This included pulling up her pants three times after every visit to the toilet.

7. All Amanda's toys had special places which had to be checked and rechecked before leaving the bedroom.

8. The ornaments on top of the piano had special places. These positions were so precise that Amanda's mother found dusting and polishing almost impossible. (pp. 86–87)

The family was instructed not to give Amanda special attention and to treat her as a girl who did not have compulsive urges. The parents were also trained to initiate response prevention procedures. Starting with the least upsetting situation, the parents prevented Amanda from engaging in her rituals. Once she coped with a situation, the next step up the hierarchy was taken. After the first two days in which Amanda experienced considerable anxiety, she gradually began to relax. After two weeks all her symptoms had disappeared. No new or additional problems arose, and Amanda was still symptom free at the one-year follow-up.

Rapoport has also indicated the effectiveness of behavioral procedures for treating compulsions. In addition, the NIMH group has reported evidence for the effectiveness of certain drugs in reducing both obsessions and compulsions. The drug that has been studied most extensively is clomipramine, a drug originally formulated as an antidepressant. The effectiveness of this drug with obsessive compulsive disorders does not, however, appear to be a result of its ability to lift depression. Clomipramine was demonstrated to be effective in treating obsessive and compulsive symptoms while a standard antidepressant was not (Rapoport, 1989).

SUMMARY

A variety of evidence supports the existence of a broadly defined internalizing category of childhood problems. The existence and definition of valid subcategories is, however, far more controversial. This is due in part to findings that children often meet the criteria for more than one of the subcategories or diagnoses. This issue, often termed "comorbidity," represents the challenge of how to conceptualize these problems.

Anxiety or fear is generally defined as a complex pattern of three response systems: motor, physiological, and subjective responses.

DSM-III-R describes three types of anxiety disorders that usually are first evident in infancy, childhood, or adolescence. These are Separation Anxiety Disorder, Avoidant Disorder, and Overanxious Disorder. A child can also receive one of the "adult" anxiety-disorder diagnoses that include Phobic Disorder and Obsessive-Compulsive Disorder.

The empirical approach to classification describes subcategories of internalizing disorders that vary by age and gender. Although there is some overlap with the clinical categories of the DSM system, the two approaches clearly represent different ways of organizing the anxiety disorders.

Phobias, as distinguished from normal fears, are judged to be excessive, persistent, or unadaptive. Fears are quite common in children. However, it is unclear how prevalent intense fears are. There also seem to be variations in numbers and content of fears with age.

The psychoanalytic and behavioral paradigms have been the two dominant explanations regarding the etiology of fears. Within the behavioral perspective, classical conditioning, operant, two-factor, and observational learning explanations are among those that have been offered.

Behavioral treatments of childhood fears have received the greatest amount of research. Systematic desensitization, prolonged exposure, modeling, and cognitive self-management approaches have received attention. Many treatments actually combine two or more of these approaches.

School refusal is preferred to the more common term of school phobia to describe children whose anxieties keep them from school. This term accommodates cases of both separation anxiety and phobias related to aspects of the actual school situation. School refusal is a common reason for referral for treatment. Treatment appears to be most successful if it is begun early, and it probably needs to be tailored to the specific kinds of school refusal exhibited.

Children diagnosed as exhibiting Overanxious Disorder exhibit excessive worry and anxiety that are not focused on any particular object or situation. They exhibit a variety of anxious behaviors. Children meeting the criteria for this diagnosis may be common in clinic samples and the question of overlap with other diagnoses is of concern.

Obsessive-compulsive disorder is characterized by repetitive and intrusive thoughts and behaviors. The problem is probably more common than once thought. Rapoport and her colleagues have begun to see a number of cases in children. They have come to believe that there is a biological basis for the disorder. Treatment combining behavioral procedures and pharmacotherapy is being explored and seems promising.

7

INTERNALIZING PROBLEMS: DEPRESSION AND PEER RELATIONS

In this chapter we examine the problems of childhood depression and peer relations associated with internalizing behaviors. In isolating these categories we confront the same problems of overlap and comorbidity that we found in examining anxiety disorders. For example, children who meet the criteria for a diagnosis of depression are often also given other diagnoses. Similarly, the social withdrawal that one might associate with internalizing problems is part of a more general concern with deficits in peer relations and social skills. Such social deficits are characteristic of children with a number of different disorders. Thus, the isolation of these problems as distinct entities is not without controversy. Nonetheless, examining depression and peer relations in this manner makes sense in terms of how the research and treatment literature are organized.

CHILDHOOD DEPRESSION

Until recently depression in children had not received a great deal of attention. However, interest has clearly increased. This can probably be traced to a number of influences. Certainly promising developments in the identification and treatment of mood disorders in adults has played a role. In addition, developments in diagnostic practices facilitated the application of diagnostic criteria to children and adults. The emergence of a number of measures of depression in children has also allowed researchers to examine the phenomenon in clinic and normal populations. Furthermore, the new perspective of "developmental psychopathology" has focused additional attention on depression in children.

In everyday usage the term *depression* refers to the experience of a pervasive unhappy mood. This subjective experience of sadness, or dysphoria, is also a central feature of the clinical definition of depression. Descriptions of children viewed as depressed suggest that they exhibit a number

Sad affect or dysphoria is the central characteristic of most definitions of depression. (Charles Harbutt/Actuality)

of other problems as well. Loss of the experience of pleasure, social withdrawal, lowered self-esteem, inability to concentrate, poor schoolwork, alterations of biological functions (sleeping, eating, elimination), and somatic complaints are often noted.

Prevalence

In community surveys prevalence rates for major depression in children vary between 2 and 5 percent, depending on age (Anderson et al., 1987; Kashani et al., 1987). In clinical populations estimates typically fall between 10 and 20 percent (e.g., Puig-Antich and Gittelman, 1982). Usually no gender differences are reported for children ages 6 to 12 (e.g., Lefkowitz and Tesiny, 1985; Lobovitz and Handal, 1985). Among adolescents some reports suggest greater prevalence among females, but gender differences are not always found (cf. Kaplan, et al., 1984; Reynolds, 1985).

Estimates of the prevalence of childhood depression, however, vary considerably (Kazdin, 1990a). In addition to variations related to age and gender, there are also other developmental considerations. The difficulty of administering similar measures to children of different ages is one consideration. Factors as simple as the readability of instruments need to be given greater attention in a developmental context (Prout

and Chizik, 1988). Also, widely employed assessment tools such as interviews require from the interviewee introspection, thinking in terms of psychological constructs, and ability to effectively communicate what is remembered. Processes such as these clearly depend on developmental level. Probably most important in estimating prevalence, however, are the different criteria that are employed to define depression.

A study by Carlson and Cantwell (1980) illustrates this point. A sample of 210 children was selected at random from over 1,000 children between the ages of 7 and 17 seen at the UCLA-Neuropsychiatric Institute. At intake the presence of depressive symptoms among the presenting problems was noted. The children were also administered a version of the Children's Depression Inventory. Separate interviews with 102 of the children and their parents were conducted to assess the presence of affective disorder, according to DSM criteria. The use of the presence of depressive symptoms at intake as a criterion led to the largest number of positive diagnoses; the depression inventory led to fewer, and DSM diagnosis led to the least. However, the results also make it clear that this was not simply a matter of using more or less stringent criteria. Rather, there appear to be some differences in definition. For example, not all children designated as depressed by the depression inventory were depressed using the depressive symptom criterion, and not all DSM identified children were depressed using the criterion of the depression inventory score.

These and other findings indicate that different populations will be designated as depressed by different methods (Kaslow and Racusin, 1990). Such variations may be due to differences in method employed (e.g., depression inventory versus DSM diagnostic criteria) or use of different informants. As we have mentioned previously, different informants are likely to give quite different views of children's emotional and behavioral problems (e.g., Achenbach, McConaughy, and Howell, 1987). Researchers may, therefore, need to be aware that selection of different groups may lead to differing conclusions regarding depression.

This is illustrated in a study by Kazdin (1989b). DSM diagnoses of 231 consecutive child admissions to an inpatient psychiatric facility were made based on direct interviews with the children and their parents. This method was compared to criteria based on exceeding a cutoff on the Children's Depression Inventory (CDI). Both the children and parents completed this measure. In addition, children and/or their parents completed a number of other measures to assess attributes reported to be associated with depression. Consistent with the findings of Carlson and Cantwell described above, different groups of children appear to be designated as depressed depending on the criteria employed.

Particularly interesting are the findings regarding the correlates associated with adopting a particular criterion for depression. Some of these results are illustrated in Table 7–1. A comparison of children high and low on depression as defined by self-report on the CDI indicated that depressed children were more hopeless; had lower self-esteem; made more internal (as opposed to external) attributions regarding negative events; and, based on a locus of control (IE) scale, were more likely to believe that control was due to external factors rather than themselves. Depressed and nondepressed children defined by the other two criteria (parent CDI and DSM) did not differ from each other on these characteristics. Employing the parent CDI criterion, children with high depression scores appear to be more problematic across a wide range

TABLE 7–1 Mean Characteristic Scores of Depressed and Nondepressed Children as Designated by Different Criteria

	Criteria					
	Children's Depression Inventory (by Child)		Children's Depression Inventory (by Parent)		DSM Diagnosis	
Measures	High	Low	High	Low	Depressed	Nondepressed
Hopelessness	7.3	3.3	5.3	5.0	5.4	4.8
Self-esteem	22.7	38.9	28.2	30.8	29.2	30.9
Attributions	5.4	6.5	5.8	5.8	6.0	6.0
Locus of Control (IE)	9.8	6.8	8.2	8.7	7.9	8.4
Total behavior problems (CBCL)	75.8	75.3	81.6	69.0	76.5	75.0

Adapted from Kazdin, 1989b. Reprinted by permission from Plenum Publishing Corporation.

of symptoms (as measured by the Child Behavior Checklist) than those with very low depression scores. Depression as designated by the other two criteria did not appear to be associated with this characteristic. These results illustrate that conclusions regarding correlates of depression may be affected by the criterion and informant employed to designate children as depressed.

Description and Classification

While there has always been broad consensus that children can experience sad affect, there has been considerable variation of opinion as to whether or not children experience the full range of affective, somatic, cognitive, and behavioral attributes characteristic of major depression in adults. How then is childhood depression to be described and classified for scientific purposes?

It has been suggested that it is important to make a distinction between the phenomenon (or symptom) of depression and the syndrome (or disorder) called depression (e.g., Rutter, 1986b). The symptom of depression refers to the experience of sadness, the loss of interest or pleasure, the lack of responsiveness, and the like, that are used to describe this negative mood state. The term "symptom" here is used in its colloquial sense (equivalent to terms such as "problem" or "experience of") and does not imply any illness. In contrast, it is suggested that the concept of a depressive *disorder* be reserved for the notion of depression as a syndrome. As a syndrome "depression" refers to a group of attributes that reliably go together. The syndrome consists of the symptom of negative mood state accompanied by certain somatic, cognitive, and behavioral problems. It is sometimes suggested that a further distinction should also be made between a syndrome and a disorder (e.g., Kovacs, 1989). The latter has all the characteristics of a syndrome, but there is also a persistence of the syndrome and social impairment is observed in the child. In addition, it is presumed that more is known about the disorder (e.g., a characteristic family history). Hopefully, careful use of these distinctions in future work will help to clarify some of the confusion regarding childhood depression.

Recent history. A brief look at the recent history of thinking on childhood depression may also help clarify differing viewpoints. As we noted in Chapter 3, the dominant view in child clinical work for many years was the orthodox psychoanalytic perspective. From this perspective depression was viewed as a phenomenon of the superego and of mature ego functioning (Kessler, 1988). It was argued, for example, that in depression the superego acts as a punisher of the ego. Since the child's superego is not sufficiently developed to play this role, it is impossible, within this perspective, for a depressive disorder to occur in children. It is not surprising, therefore, that depression in children received little attention.

A second major perspective on childhood depression added to the controversy regarding the existence of a distinct disorder. The concept of *masked depression* represented an interesting view. This view held that there is a disorder of childhood depression. However, it proposed that there are numerous instances when the dysphoric mood and other features usually considered essential to the diagnosis of depression are not present. It was held that an underlying depressive disorder does exist, but the child's depression is "masked" by other problems (depressive equivalents) such as hyperactivity or delinquency. The "underlying" depression itself is not directly displayed, but is inferred by the clinician. Some workers, indeed, suggested that masked depressions were quite common and may have resulted in childhood depression being underdiagnosed (Cytryn and McKnew, 1974; Malmquist, 1977).

The notion of masked depression is clearly problematic. There is no operational way to decide whether a particular symptom is or is not a sign of depression. Indeed, the symptoms that have been suggested as masking depression have included virtually the full gamut of problem behaviors evident in childhood. The concept of masked depression is, thus, quite controversial. Even some of its early advocates seem to view it as less important than once thought (Cytryn, McKnew, and Bunney, 1980).

The concept of masked depression was, however, important. It clearly recognized depression as an important and prevalent childhood problem. The central notions of the concept of masked depression—that the phenomenon of depression in children does exist and that children may display depression in a variety of age-related forms and in ways that may be different from adult depression—are still widely held. The concept that depression is manifested differently in children and adults contributed, in part, to the evolution of a broader developmental perspective.

A developmental perspective. Childhood depression thus became an important focus for the discussion of the value of normative data and the possible implications of a developmental viewpoint. For example, some workers suggested that behaviors that led to the diagnosis of depression were only transitory developmental phenomena—common among children in certain age groups (e.g., Lefkowitz and Burton, 1978). The classic Berkeley survey, for instance, found that 37 percent of girls and 29 percent of boys at age 6 exhibited insufficient appetite (a problem often thought to be associated with depression). By age 9 these figures had dropped to 9 percent and 6 percent, respectively, and 14 percent of both sexes at age 14 had insufficient appetites (Macfarlane, Allen, and Honzik 1954). Thus, insufficient appetite should probably not be considered a deviant behavior among 6-year-olds. However, if it is present at age 9, especially in boys, it might be considered atypical. Other behaviors, such as "excessive reserve," occur too often in children of all ages to be considered abnormal.

Lefkowitz (1977) also reexamined Werry and Quay's epidemiological study of behavior symptoms in a general population of 1,753 kindergarten through second-grade children. Sixteen of the 55 behaviors surveyed were judged to be those commonly associated with depression. The range of prevalence of these behaviors was 7.2 to 46.3 percent (mean = 22 percent) for boys and 6.4 to 41.4 percent (mean = 18 percent) for girls. This suggests that about 20 percent of the normal population may possess symptoms judged characteristic of depressive disorder in clinical samples.

Thus, it could be held that depression in childhood may not exist as a clinical entity different from common and transient developmental phenomena. Lefkowitz and Burton (1978) suggested that perhaps one of the reasons why clinicians give the diagnosis of childhood depression is the mistaken belief that these behaviors (symptoms) are rare and, therefore, important when manifested.

The distinction between depression as a symptom and depression as a syndrome is important to consider here. One or two "depressive" behaviors of a child might reasonably be viewed as typical of a particular developmental stage. However, it is different to suggest that a cluster of such behaviors is also likely to occur in a large number of children at the same developmental level (Kovacs, 1989). Awareness of normative and developmental patterns, in any case, is clearly important, and might change clinical impressions, leading to changes in diagnostic practices. The developmental perspective has become an important element in the study of childhood depression (Rutter, Izard, and Read, 1986).

Rutter (1986c) examined issues that arise from viewing depression from a developmental perspective. For example, drawing from the Isle of Wight general population study, important changes in depressive features that occur around the time of puberty are highlighted. Among 10- to 11-year old children interviewed, 13 percent showed a depressed mood, 9 percent appeared preoccupied with depressive topics, 17 percent failed to smile, and 15 percent showed poor emotional responsiveness. On parent and teacher questionnaires about 10 to 12 percent were said to be very miserable. When the same children were reassessed at age 14 to 15 years, depressive feelings were considerably more prevalent. For example, 40 percent of the adolescents reported substantial feelings of misery and depression, 20 percent expressed feelings of self-deprecation and 7 to 8 percent reported suicidal feelings.

Particularly interesting are findings regarding these feelings and stage of puberty among the boys. Since boys 14 to 15 included those who ranged from prepubescent to past puberty, it was possible to examine the effects of stage of puberty among boys of the same age. The data in Figure 7–1 illustrate the strong association of depressive *feelings* and puberty. There is little indication of depressive feelings among the prepubertal boys, whereas about one-third of the postpubertal boys do indicate such feelings. Rutter also examined the relationship of depressive *disorders* and puberty. These data (see Figure 7–2) indicate a distinct change in the sex ratio of depressive disorders around the time of puberty. There are also data that suggest a large increase in attempted suicides in the years following puberty (e.g., Hawton and Goldacre, 1982). These findings highlight

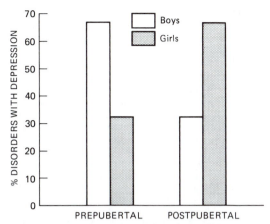

FIGURE 7–2 Sex ratio of disorders with depression before and after puberty. From Rutter, 1986c.

the value of a developmental perspective. However, our understanding of the developmental mechanisms that underly such findings remain incomplete. While much remains to be learned, it seems clear that attempting to answer questions posed by a developmental perspective—such as age differences in prevalence, age-related changes in symptom patterns, and continuities and discontinuities across age periods—will be highly informative.

The DSM perspective. It is not possible at this point to make definitive statements about the "correct" description or classification of childhood depression. A wide range of conceptualizations has been suggested. They range from those that question the existence of a distinct disorder in childhood, to those that perceive childhood depression in terms of the adult classification, to those that subsume most of the important aspects of child psychopathology under the umbrella of this disorder (Petti, 1989). There are potential liabilities in making a priori judgments about what childhood depression *is*. However, it is probably fair to state that the dominant view in the last few years has been that childhood depression is a syndrome or disorder in which the essential features are the same as those manifested in adults.

FIGURE 7–1 Depressive feelings and stage of puberty. From Rutter, 1986c.

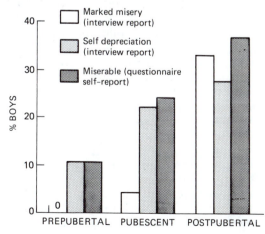

TABLE 7–2   DSM-III-R Criteria for a Major Depressive Syndrome

A. At least five of the following symptoms have been present during the same two-week period and represent a change from previous functioning; at least one of the symptoms is either (1) depressed mood, or (2) loss of interest or pleasure. (Do not include symptoms that are clearly due to a physical condition, mood-incongruent delusions or hallucinations, incoherence, or marked loosening of associations.)

1. Depressed mood (or can be irritable mood in children and adolescents) most of the day, nearly every day, as indicated either by subjective account or observation by others
2. Markedly diminished interest or pleasure in all, or almost all, activities most of the day, nearly every day (as indicated either by subjective account or observation by others of apathy most of the time)
3. Significant weight loss or weight gain when not dieting (e.g., more than 5% of body weight in a month), or decrease or increase in appetite nearly every day (in children, consider failure to make expected weight gains)
4. Insomnia or hypersomnia nearly every day
5. Psychomotor agitation or retardation nearly every day (observable by others, not merely subjective feelings of restlessness or being slowed down)
6. Fatigue or loss of energy nearly every day
7. Feelings of worthlessness or excessive or inapproporiate guilt (which may be delusional) nearly every day (not merely self-reproach or guilt about being sick)
8. Diminished ability to think or concentrate, or indecisiveness, nearly every day (either by subjective account or as observed by others)
9. Recurrent thoughts of death (not just fear of dying), recurrent suicidal ideation without a specific plan, or a suicide attempt or a specific plan for committing suicide

Reprinted with permission from the *Diagnostic and Statistical Manual of Mental Disorders, Third Edition Revised.* Copyright 1987, American Psychiatric Association.

There are probably several factors that have contributed to the dominance of this viewpoint. However, the principal influence has probably been the DSM diagnostic system. The DSM diagnostic criteria for all mood disorders in adulthood, including depression, are applied to children as well. Table 7–2 presents the DSM-III-R criteria for the diagnosis of Major Depression. There are no separate diagnostic categories for mood disorders in children. However, the possibility of different symptoms being evident as a function of age is acknowledged. For example, in prepubertal children mood-congruent hallucinations may occur and in adolescents negativistic and frankly antisocial behavior may be present. The dominance of the DSM system and the findings by several researchers that they could apply adult criteria in unmodified form to diagnose depression in children have contributed to the popularity of this perspective (e.g., Carlson and Cantwell, 1980; Mitchell et al., 1988).

There is also one DSM diagnosis that is specific to childhood and is related to other descriptions of depression. Reactive Attachment Disorder of Infancy or Early Childhood is diagnosed if in response to inadequate caretaking the child exhibits a lack of age-appropriate social responsiveness, apathetic mood, and little or no spontaneity. Onset occurs before five years of age. In infants extreme cases are often referred to as "failure to thrive" or "hospitalism."

In addition to depression, DSM describes mood disorders that include mania. "Mania" refers to abnormally elevated, expansive or irritable mood and excessive activity. Diagnoses may include mania or mania combined with depression (as in Bipolar Depressive Disorder). Manic disorders are thought to be rare in children, diagnosis is thought to be difficult in this age group, and in comparison to depression little information is available (Kovacs, 1989).

The view inherent in the DSM approach, that mood disorders found in children are the same as those found in adults, is supported by some research. Many of the cognitive attributes, biological correlates, and behaviors found in depressed adults are also reported in children (e.g., Kaslow, Rehm, and Siegel, 1984; Kazdin et al., 1985; Puig-Antich, 1983). However, differences have also been found. The gender ratio in prevalence is one example. A greater prevalence among females is characteristic of adults, whereas childhood gender differences are not reported, particularly among preadolescents. In addition, some of the serious concomitants of adult depression are less evident in children and some biological correlates appear to differ as well (Kazdin, 1989b). The need for caution before we "adultomorphise" childhood depression is illustrated in a study by Leon, Kendall, and Garber (1980).

In this investigation third- to sixth-grade depressed children were similar to depressed adults in that they attributed positive events to external causes and negative events to internal causes significantly more than did their nondepressed peers. However, unlike depressed adults, the children did not seem to have motivational deficits or psychomotor retardation.

The study is interesting because it also assessed whether manifestations of depression were present across situations (home and school) and from the perspectives of several individuals (parent, teacher, and the child). There was a significant, but only moderate, consistency between parental and child ratings of depression. Interestingly, children designated by their parents as depressed were also rated by their parents as exhibiting significantly more conduct problems, anxiety, impulsive hyperactivity, learning problems, psychosomatic problems, perfectionism, and muscular tension than children rated as nondepressed. Teachers, however, rated these same depressed children as displaying more inattention-passivity but did not rate the children differently on other behavior problems.

The lack of consistency of behavior across settings is different from the generalized syndrome described for depression in adults. The discrepancy apparent in parent and teacher reports may be due to actual variations in behavior in these different settings, but another interpretation is possible. Perhaps parents who rate their children as depressed are generally inclined to see behavioral problems in their offspring. Alternatively, the variety of behavioral problems displayed at home by depressed children may suggest a more general difficulty rather than a specific depressive syndrome. In contrast, children in this sample who were rated by their parents as hyperactive did not display this same variety of problems.

For several reasons, then, the conceptualization of childhood depression is far from settled. Much developmental information still needs to be obtained and existing information requires explanation (Rutter, 1986c). Also, manifestations of depression in children do seem in some ways to be different from the adult disorder, and the problem of situational specificity must be incorporated into any explanation.

Theories of Depression

Separation-loss. Despite increased interest in recent years, much of the thinking regarding childhood depression is still based on theories and information derived from adults. Probably the most common psychological explanation of depression is separation or loss. Psychoanalytic explanations of depression, following from Freud, emphasize the notion of object loss. The loss may be real (parental death, divorce) or symbolic. Identification with and ambivalent feelings toward the lost love object are thought to result in the person's directing hostile feelings concerning the love object toward the self. Other psychodynamic writers emphasize the loss of self-esteem and feelings of helplessness and minimize the importance of hostility turned inward (Kessler, 1988).

Some behaviorally oriented explanations also involve separation and loss. Both Ferster (1974) and Lewinsohn (1974) emphasize the role of inadequate positive reinforcement in the development of depression. Loss of or separation from a loved one is likely to result in a decrease in the child's sources of positive reinforcement. However,

Separation-loss is a central concept in many theories of depression. The loss may be real or imagined. (Ray Solomon/Monkmeyer Press)

inadequate reinforcement may also result from such factors as not having adequate skills to obtain desired rewards.

Past support for the role of separation in the genesis of depression came from several different sources. For example, a fairly typical sequence of reactions of young children to prolonged separation from their parents was described by a number of investigators (e.g., Bowlby, 1960; Spitz, 1946). In this so-called *anaclitic depression*, the child initially goes through a period of "protest" characterized by crying, asking for the parents, and restlessness. This is followed shortly by a period of depression and withdrawal. Most children begin to recover after several weeks. Evidence of high rates of early parental loss or separation among children referred for treatment of a variety of psychological problems also was cited. Seligman et al. (1974), for example, reported that among 100 consecutive adolescent referrals, 36.4 percent had experienced loss of one or both parents. In contrast, in public school and medical clinic control samples, only 11.7 percent and 16.6 percent, respectively, had experienced such loss. Differences between the treatment and control samples were particularly high for parental loss between 3 to 6 years of age and 12 to 15 years of age. Another comparison, involving depressed and nondepressed children between the ages of 5 and 16, indicated that 50 percent of the depressed group but only 23 percent of the nondepressed group experienced parental separation prior to the age of 8 (Caplan and Douglas, 1969).

The connection between loss and depression has been examined primarily in regard to adult depression. For a long time the widely held view has been that such early loss puts one at high risk for later depression—especially women. More recent examinations of this issue question this view, in part because most studies of the early loss-adult depression relationship were plagued with methodological problems (e.g., Finkelstein, 1988; Tennant, 1988). The more current popular view is that early loss is not in and of itself pathogenic. The link between such loss and later depression is not direct. Rather, it is hypothesized that such loss, as well as other circumstances, can set in motion a chain of adverse circumstances such as lack of care, changes in family structure, and socioeconomic difficulties that put the individual at risk for later disorder (Brown, 1988; Garmezy, 1986; Hetherington, 1989).

Other psychological theories. A learned helplessness explanation of depression (cf. Seligman and Peterson, 1986) suggests that some individuals, due to their learning histories, have come to perceive themselves as having little control of their environment. Seligman's theory thus emphasizes how the person thinks about action and outcome. Learned helplessness is associated with mood and behaviors characteristic of depression. Separation may be a special case of learned helplessness: The child's attempts to bring the parent back may result in the child's thinking that personal action and positive outcome are independent of each other. As indicated above, the concept of helplessness is characteristic of some psychodynamic workers as well.

The role of cognitive factors in depression is the major emphasis of other theorists. Beck (1967), for example, assumes that depression results from the way individuals interpret events—negative views of the self, the world, and the future. Depressed individuals, Beck hypothesizes, have developed certain errors in thinking that result in their distorting even mildly annoying events into opportunities for self-blame and failure.

It is difficult to evaluate at present how applicable theories of helplessness and cognitive distortions are to understanding the etiology of childhood depression. Data suggesting the presence of such phenomena in depressed children (e.g., Asarnow, Carlson, and Guthrie, 1987) and of the promise of interventions derived from these perspectives (e.g., Stark, Reynolds, and Kaslow, 1987) argue for their continued exploration.

Biological theories. Biological views of childhood depression focus on genetic and biochemical influences. They too derive largely from the adult literature since there are relatively little data available on children (Rutter et al., 1990b). There are, for example, some data from linkage analyses in which the family pattern of depression is examined along with another characteristic, a genetic marker, for which the genetics are fully understood. These data support a heritability component to adult depression (Biron et al., 1987; Egeland et al., 1987). Family, twin, and adoption studies also suggest that there is a heritability component in adult depressive disorders, particularly bipolar disorder (e.g., Allen, 1976; Torgersen, 1986; Weissman, Kidd, and Prusoff, 1982; Wender et al., 1986). Furthermore, family studies suggest that the early onset of depression (before age 20) in the identified patient is associated with the early onset of depression among other family members (e.g., Weissman et al., 1988). One possible hypothesis implicated by such findings is that early onset disorders have a strong genetic component (cf. Orvaschel, 1990). At present evidence regarding this point is limited and its application to a broad range of children who are depressed is not warranted (Rutter et al., 1990b).

The data on biochemistry and adult depression have highlighted neurotransmitters: catecholamines such as norepinephrine and indolamines such as serotonin (cf. McNeal and Cimbolic, 1986). For example, the catecholamine hypothesis suggests that low levels of norepinephrine are created by too much reabsorbtion by the neuron releasing it or by too efficient a breakdown by enzymes. This results in too low a level of norepinephrine at the synapse to fire the next neuron. The impetus to study these neurotransmitters came largely from findings that the effectiveness of certain antidepressants was related to levels of these chemicals or receptivity to them. Current research continues to explore the roles of neurotransmitter levels and postsynaptic receptors as well as examine the role of the neuroendocrine system (e.g., the limbic area of the brain and the hypothalamus and pituitary glands) in the etiology of depression (Davison and Neale, 1990).

Research on biological aspects of childhood depression suggests that during the earlier developmental periods of childhood and adolescence the neuroregulatory system is not equivalent to that in adulthood. Thus, while many workers still find support in available data for a neutrotransmitter dysfunction in childhood depression, a simple translation of the adult findings is not sufficient (e.g., Puig-Antich, 1986). For example, EEG patterns during sleep are strong biological markers of major depressive disorders in adults (e.g., Gillen et al., 1979). In contrast, none of the findings reported for adults are characteristic of children diagnosed with major depressive disorders (Puig-Antich, 1986). This might suggest that the child and adult disorders are different. Alternatively, it might be concluded that differences in biological markers represent age-related differences in the same disorder.

Currently a variety of views exists as to what causes childhood depression. There appears to be evidence supportive of a number of perspectives. It is not surprising then that most contemporary reviews of the problem call for a model that integrates multiple causations (e.g., Kazdin, 1989b; Petti, 1989; Rutter, Izard, and Read, 1986).

The development of assessment instruments has contributed considerably to the increased attention to childhood depression. Assessment is likely to involve a number of strategies and to be broadly based in the areas sampled. A general clinical interview and use of a general dimensional scale like the Child Behavior Checklist are common. Interviews intended to yield a DSM diagnosis and a variety of measures that focus more specifically on depression have been developed (Kazdin, 1988). These interviews and assessment devices have also greatly facilitated research on childhood depression.

The Schedule for Affective Disorders and Schizophrenia (K-SADS) for school-age children (Chambers et al., 1985) is one of several interview formats available. It is a semistructured interview of both parents and child that assesses the presence and severity of a broad range of symptoms. Based on the results a DSM diagnosis of mood and other disorders can be made. Several other diagnostic interviews are also available (e.g., Costello, Edelbrock, and Costello, 1985; Herjanic and Reich, 1982; Hodges et al., 1982; Kovacs et al., 1984a).

Of the measures of depression that have been developed, self-report instruments are the most common. They are particularly important given that many of the key problems that characterize depression, such as sadness and feelings of worthlessness, are subjective. The Children's Depression Inventory (CDI) (Kovacs, 1985) is probably the most commonly employed measure. It is an offspring of the Beck Depression Inventory, the most commonly employed inventory with adults. The CDI asks children to choose which of three alternatives best characterizes them during the past two weeks. Twenty-seven items sample affective, behavioral, and cognitive aspects of depression. Research on gender and age differences, reliability, validity, and clinically meaningful cutoff scores has been conducted for the CDI (Kazdin, 1988).

Many self-report measures are also re-phrased so that they can be completed by significant others such as the child's parents. Measures completed by the child and parent often show little or no correlation (e.g., Kazdin et al., 1983). Perhaps information provided by different sources taps different aspects of the child's behavior. For example, children's self-report of depression, but not parents' reports, correlate with hopelessness and suicidal thoughts (e.g., Kazdin, Rodgers, and Colbus, 1986). Parents' reports of depression in their child, on the other hand, correlate with the child's mood-related expression and social behavior (Kazdin et al., 1985).

Instruments may also be completed by other adults such as teachers and clinicians. Ratings by peers can provide a unique perspective. The Peer Nomination Inventory of Depression (Lefkowitz and Tesiny, 1980) asks children to nominate peers who fit certain descriptions. Table 7–3 presents the

TABLE 7–3 Peer Nomination Inventory for Depression Items

Who often plays alone? (D)
Who thinks they are bad? (D)
Who doesn't try again when they lose? (D)
Who often sleeps in class? (D)
Who often looks lonely? (D)
Who often says they don't feel well? (D)
Who says they can't do things? (D)
Who often cries? (D)
Who often looks happy? (H)
Who likes to do a lot of things? (H)
Who worries a lot? (D)
Who doesn't play? (D)
Who often smiles? (H)
Who doesn't take part in things? (D)
Who doesn't have much fun? (D)
Who is often cheerful? (H)
Who thinks others don't like them? (D)
Who often looks sad? (D)
Who would you like to sit next to in class? (P)
Who are the children you would like to have for your best friends? (P)

Note: D = items that are included in depressed score
        H = items in happiness score
        P = items in popularity score

Adapted from Lefkowitz and Tesiny, 1980. Copyright (1980) by American Psychological Association.

characteristics of depression, happiness, and popularity to which the children are asked to respond. A child's score is the sum of the nominations received for all the depression items.

A number of measures of constructs related to depression have also been developed. Measures of attributes such as hopelessness (Kazdin et al., 1986) and self-esteem (e.g., Harter, 1985) have been and are likely to be helpful for both clinical and research purposes.

Treatment of Depression

Relatively little is known regarding the treatment of depression in children and adolescents compared to the sizeable literature regarding interventions for adult depression. That little systematic research exists is not surprising given the recency of attention to the problem of depression in children. Not surprisingly, treatments attempted with depressed children have been adaptations of interventions that seem to be successful for the treatment of depression in adults. Information regarding pharmacotherapy and cognitive-behavioral treatments for childhood depression will be examined briefly.

Pharmacotherapy. Tricyclic antidepressants such as imipramine have been the most widely studied medications for depression in children (Kazdin, 1990a). The use of such medications was for the most part based on uncontrolled clinical reports or poorly designed control-group studies. Better designed studies have begun to appear, but this research does not clearly support the superiority of these drugs over placebo in either prepubertal children or adolescents (Campbell et al., 1989a; Puig-Antich et al., 1987; Ryan et al., 1986). There has been some suggestion that higher levels of imipramine (as assessed in plasma serum levels) are associated with better responses to treatment in prepubertal children (Puig-Antich et al., 1987), but the same is not true for adolescents (Ryan et al., 1986).

It is not clear that antidepressants should be used routinely in the treatment of depression in children and adolescents. In addition to the lack of strong therapeutic findings, there are less well established guidelines for the administration of these drugs than in adults. There is reasonable concern regarding side effects, and reports that a good number of depressed children respond to placebos raise reasonable questions (Campbell et al., 1989a; Kazdin, 1990a).

Cognitive-behavioral treatments. There is far less controlled research regarding psychological interventions than exists for drug treatment. Behavioral case studies of depressed children have emphasized social skills training (Kaslow and Racusin, 1990). Interventions have emphasized the expression and acceptance of feelings and the development of socially appropriate interactions with others. Two control-group intervention outcome studies have evaluated interventions deriving from a cognitive-behavioral perspective.

Butler and her colleagues evaluated the relative effectiveness of role-play, cognitive restructuring, an attention-placebo condition, or no treatment (Butler et al., 1980). Fifth- and sixth-grade children were identified as depressed through self-report measures and teacher referral. Role-play consisted of teaching interpersonal skills as well as problem-solving techniques. Cognitive restructuring focused on altering maladaptive cognitions. The results favored the role-play intervention; however, the differences between groups were not clear-cut.

Stark, Reynolds, and Kaslow (1987) compared self-control, behavioral problem-solving, and a waiting list (no treatment) control in treating nine to twelve year-olds defined as moderately to severely depressed using the Children's Depression Inventory. The self-control treatment focused on teaching the children self-management skills such as self-monitoring, self-evaluation, and self-reinforcement. Behavioral problem-solving emphasized education, self-monitoring of pleasant events, and group problem solving directed toward improving social behavior. Both treatments resulted in improvements in measures of depression and were superior to the control group. The two treatments, however, did not differ from each other.

The literature suggests the promise of treatments derived from the behavioral and cognitive-behavioral perspectives and the success of similar interventions with adults is encouraging. However, it is clear that additional large scale treatment studies with clinically depressed children and adolescents are needed (Kaslow and Racusin, 1990; Kazdin, 1990a).

Maternal Depression as a Risk Factor

A major area of research on childhood depression has been an examination of children of depressed parents. There are several reasons for the proliferation of such research. Because family patterns for mood disorders in adults were known to exist, it was presumed that examining children of parents with mood disorders would result in a population likely to experience childhood depression. Beyond its potential value as a research strategy, such research might provide information on the issue of the continuity between child and adult mood disorders.

Depressive mood states in parents might be presumed to be associated with childhood dysfunction via a variety of mechanisms. For example, parents can influence their child through parent-child interactions, through coaching and teaching practices, and by arranging their child's social environment (Dodge, 1990). Genetic links between parent and child disorders are also clearly a possibility. While a great deal of research on potential genetic contributions to affective disorders in adults is available, rigorous child genetic studies are less available (Cytryn et al., 1986; Rutter et al., 1990b) and therefore hereditary influence is not examined here.

Early reviews of the literature concluded that, indeed, a strong association existed between maternal and child depression (Beardslee et al., 1983; Orvaschel, 1983). Still, many questions remained. For example, was this finding specific to or unique for parental depression or did other forms of parental disorder and distress produce similar outcomes? Was parental depression associated specifically with childhood depression or did parental depression relate to childhood disorder in general? What were the mechanisms underlying the association between parental depression and childhood disorder?

A specific maternal depression-child depression link? Research that examines parents diagnosed as having different disorders helps to answer the question of the specificity of the link between parent and child depression. For example, Weintraub, Winters, and Neale (1986) found that children with a parent with affective disorders did exhibit difficulties along a number of different dimensions as judged by both teachers and peers. This is consistent with other research, as is their finding that there was no singular behavior pattern that characterized these children. In addition, their results indicated that although the children of patient parents differed from normal controls, there were no significant differences between children of parents with mood disorders and children with a parent diagnosed as schizophrenic. Furthermore, children of parents diagnosed as having unipolar and bipolar mood disorders did not differ from each other. This suggests that the child's vulnerability may be related to factors other than the parent's specific diagnosis. Children's difficulties may have more to do with the disruption caused by having a dysfunctional parent (e.g., Goodman and Brumley, 1990).

In a review covering much of the research through 1986, Forehand, McCombs, and Brody (1987) again found support for an association between parental depressive mood states and childhood dysfunction. And again, the association with parental mood state was not limited to any one area of functioning. Rather, the negative impact of parental depression appeared to emerge in multiple areas of child functioning. This association was as likely to occur in studies assessing academic functioning and intelligence, prosocial behaviors and adaptive competencies, externalizing problems, or internalizing problems. This is consistent with suggestions by others that researchers not focus on the presence or absence of diagnostic entities as the main outcome variable in such research, but rather study other dimensions such as adaptive functioning (Beardslee, 1986).

Forehand et al. (1987) examined three types of studies in their review: Studies in which parents were diagnosed as clinically depressed; studies in which children were identified as having some type of behavior problem; and studies in which the children had not been identified as having a behavior problem and the parents were not identified as clinically depressed. A relationship between parental mood state and children's functioning was more likely in studies in which the parent was identified as clinically depressed. This may suggest a relationship between severity of parental depressive mood and child dysfunction. Chronic depression may, for example, lead to disruptions in essential parenting practices and impact on patterns of family interaction (e.g., Breznitz and Friedman, 1988; Hops et al., 1987).

A study by Orvaschel, Walsh-Allis, and Ye (1988) illustrates the type of research and findings available regarding the link between parental depression and childhood disorder. A high-risk group of 61 children was identified from families in which at least one parent was in treatment for recurrent major depression. A low-risk control group consisted of children for whom neither parent met the DSM criteria for any psychiatric disorder. The children ranged in age from 6 to 17 and there were no significant differences between the groups regarding age, gender, or verbal IQ. The families were also matched for social class and income levels.

Childhood disorders were assessed using the Schedule of Affective Disorders and Schizophrenia for School-Age Children-Epidemiologic Version. This semistructured interview designed to obtain information on past and current symptoms of DSM disorders was administered first to mothers and then to their children. The same interviewer conducted both mother and child interviews and interviewers were not blind as to the group membership of families. The authors indicate that this procedure was necessary because of consent procedures. The fact that the interviewer judging the child's disorder knew whether or not the parent was depressed introduces the question of bias. The procedural difficulties encountered in this study, however, serve to illustrate the difficulties faced by researchers investigating sensitive clinical issues. One is often faced with ethical and clinical considerations that make optimal control difficult.

Some of the findings from this study are presented in Table 7–4. The diagnostic findings indicated significantly greater overall rates of disorders for children of depressed parents. Differences in the two groups also emerged for two particular diagnoses—affective disorders and attention-deficit disorders. There also seemed to be

TABLE 7-4 Differences in Children Associated with the Risk of Parental Depression

Childhood Disorder	Percentage of High Risk Children	Percentage of Low Risk Children
Any disorder	41.0	15.2
Affective disorder	21.3	4.3
Anxiety disorder	19.7	8.7
Attention-deficit disorder	19.7	6.5
One diagnosis	18.0	10.9
More than one diagnosis	22.9	4.4
Outpatient treatment	32.8	8.7

Adapted from Orvaschel, Walsh-Allis, and Ye, 1988.

a trend of a similar difference regarding anxiety disorders in these children, but the difference was not significant. Another indication of the difference between the groups was the significant difference in how many children had received outpatient treatment for emotional or behavioral problems. In addition, the low-risk children who were treated had experienced only consultation or brief care. Three children had made suicide attempts and all of these were among the high-risk group. There was no significant association between the depressed parent's gender, the number of parental depressive episodes, or a rating of severity of the parents' depression and any children's diagnostic findings. However, the parent's age of onset for depression was significantly associated with depression in children, but not with any other child disorder. The results of this study, like others, indicate that children of depressed parents are at greater risk. The risk may not be exclusively for depression and many possible explanations, both psychosocial and biological, for this association are still viable. Investigators are attempting to identify risk factors in children of depressed parents that will help explain the association between parental and childhood disorder (Rutter, 1990).

Do effects persist? One of the key questions regarding the association between parental depression and childhood dysfunction has to do with the persistence of the deleterious effects. Do children improve if improvement occurs in the parent's functioning? Answers to this question are best obtained from research that follows families over time. Billings and Moos (1983) compared families with a depressed parent to matched control families with nondepressed parents. They, like others, found substantially higher rates of dysfunction among children of the depressed parents. In addition, they also found that depressed families reported higher levels of social stressors and less cohesive and more disorganized family environments. For both depressed and control families, greater family cohesion

and support were related to better functioning, while severity of family stress was related to children's dysfunction. To add to this information the authors conducted a one-year longitudinal follow-up (Billings and Moos, 1986).

Even over this relatively short period of time such research is often difficult. Of the 133 original families with a depressed parent it was possible to obtain complete data from 120. However, 37 of the families were excluded because their composition had changed due to marital separation (depressed parent no longer residing in household), children leaving home, and so forth. From the remaining families two groups were formed differing in the severity of the parent's depressive symptomatology at follow-up. One group was composed of 34 "remitted" parents who were functioning well at follow-up and receiving no treatment. A second group of 23 "nonremitted" parents met criteria for continued moderate to severe depression. The remaining 26 parents did not meet the criteria for either remission or severe depression and/or were receiving treatment for depression at follow-up. To provide a clear and direct comparison between remitted and nonremitted parents, only differences between the first two groups were examined. Follow-up data were also available on 95 control families who met the same nondepressed criteria as the remitted group.

Children of nonremitted parents exhibited more problems than those of remitted parents and both groups showed significantly more dysfunction at follow-up than children of controls families. Based on parental report and a composite index of disturbance, 52.2 percent of the nonremitted families and 26.5 percent of remitted families had one or more children with substantial dysfunction. In comparison, only 9.5 percent of control families had children with substantial dysfunction. What had happened over the course of the year? Comparisons of children's functioning at the time of the parent's intake and one year later indicated that disturbance increased from 42.9 to 52.5 percent for children in the nonremitted sample and from 21.2 to 26.5 percent for the remitted sample. Both increases were not statistically significant, but suggest that children's dysfunction did not diminish during the year, whether or not their parent's depression was alleviated. Interestingly, at follow-up, the family environments of remitted families did not differ from that of control families. Family environments of nonremitted families, in contrast, were less positive. Even so, stressors and problems other than depression remained for the remitted parents. Changes in the familial/social milieu of the child may change slowly and thereby delay improvements in the child's functioning. Longer term follow-up would be informative, but, at minimum, the findings suggest continued impact from parental depressive episodes.

PROBLEMS IN PEER RELATIONSHIPS

There are several reasons why children's peer relationship problems have been the focus of increasing attention. For example, the increase in numbers of working parents has resulted in increases in the number of children in day care and the amount of time children spend with peers. This provides both an impetus and an opportunity to study children's social relations (cf. Belsky, 1988; Clarke-Stewart, 1989; Scarr, Phillips, and McCartney, 1989).

Peer Relations and Development

Social behavior directed toward peers has been observed as early as 2 to 3 months. At this time the social smile, vocalizations, and head control emerge. Infants can be observed taking long looks at their peers and cooing and smiling. They seem more interested in peers than in their own reflection in a mirror. As development proceeds, changes occur in the quality and extent of social behavior. From 12 months of age through the preschool period, increases in prosocial initiations, a general increase in peer interactions, and a parallel decrease in adult interactions occur (Field, 1981).

The developmental literature indicates the importance of peer relationships. Such relationships provide the opportunity for learning specific skills that may not be available in other social relationships. Some of the ways in which peer interactions may play a unique and essential role include the development of sociability and attachment, the control of aggression, socialization of sexuality and gender roles, moral development, and the development of empathy (Coie, Belding, and Underwood, 1988; Hartup, 1983). Of course, this does not mean that peer social development is independent of child-adult interactions. Indeed, early parent-child socialization seems related to later peer interactions (e.g., Waters, Whippman, and Sroufe, 1980) and both relationships with peers and adults are necessary for optimum growth (Hartup, 1989).

Peer interactions provide a unique and essential opportunity to develop certain skills.

Peer relations and later adjustment. One of the most commonly cited reasons for interest in children's peer relationships is their association with later adjustment. Some early and oft-cited findings report poor peer relations to be associated with high rates of juvenile delinquency (Roff, Sells, and Golden, 1972), dropping out of school (Ullmann, 1957), and bad conduct discharges from the army (Roff, 1961). Cowen and his colleagues found an association with later psychiatric referrals (Cowen et al., 1973). In a series of studies they screened large numbers of children for signs of disturbance. A variety of measures was obtained, including days absent from school, grades, achievement and IQ test scores, child and teacher measures of adjustment, and a sociometric measure of peer acceptance. Of all the measures, low peer status in the third grade was the best predictor of later appearance on a communitywide psychiatric register.

Reviews of available literature generally support the notion that children with poor peer relations are at risk for later difficulties. The evidence is clearest for children with low peer acceptance and those who exhibit aggressiveness towards peers. The link between early shyness/withdrawal and later maladjustment is less clear since this relationship has not been as adequately evaluated (Parker and Asher, 1987). However, recent developmental data suggest that an early shy-withdrawn style may, in some children, be more stable than once thought and have impact on later adjustment (e.g., Kagan, Reznick, and Gibbons, 1989; Moskowitz, Schwartzman, and Ledingham, 1985).

An examination of some archival data from the original Berkley Guidance Study (Macfarlane, Allen, and Honzick, 1954) illustrates this potential developmental stability and long-term impact (Caspi, Elder, and Bem, 1988). Ratings of shyness and excessive reserve when the children were 8 to 10 years old were found to have a significant positive correlation with later pread-olescent ratings by teachers of withdrawal, somberness, and reserve. Also, significant positive correlations were obtained between childhood shyness and an adult shyness index obtained when the participants were about 40. Furthermore, shy boys were more likely to delay entry into marriage, parenthood, and stable careers. They also exhibited less occupational achievement and stability. Those shy boys who were late in establishing stable careers also were more more likely to experience marital instability. In contrast, shy girls were more likely than their peers to follow what the authors term a conventional pattern of marriage, childbearing, and homemaking. These results do not relate early shyness to "pathological" outcomes. However, they do show a pattern of stability of style which may have affected the individual's approach to key life transitions requiring social initiation and interaction. The subjects employed in this study did not exhibit an extreme shyness and were drawn from a relatively homogeneous sample. In a differently defined sample more adverse consequences might have occurred.

TABLE 7-5 DSM-III-R Disorders for Which Social Incompetence Is an Explicit Part of the Diagnostic Criteria

Mental Retardation
Autistic Disorder
Attention Deficit-Hyperactivity Disorder
Conduct Disorder
Oppositional Defiant Disorder
Avoidant Disorder of Childhood or Adolescence
Identity Disorder
Reactive Attachment Disorder of Infancy or Early Childhood
Schizophrenia
Bipolar Disorder, Manic
Social Phobia
Adjustment Disorder
Schizoid Personality Disorder
Schizotypal Personality Disorder
Antisocial Personality Disorder
Borderline Personality Disorder
Avoidant Personality Disorder

Adapted from Dodge, 1989.

Peer relations and childhood problems. Problems with peers are one of the most frequently mentioned problems in referrals to mental health centers. They are reported, depending on age, for 30 to 75 percent of these children (Achenbach and Edelbrock, 1981). Problems in social relationships are also explicitly part of the diagnostic criteria for a wide variety of disorders (Table 7–5). In addition, research has demonstrated that social relationship problems are associated with both externalizing and internalizing disorders in children (Baum, 1989; Strauss, 1988). Successful peer relations, on the other hand, may help insure the development of social competence in the face of multiple adverse factors. They may, thereby, serve a preventive function and reduce the likelihood of disorder (Cicchetti, Toth, and Bush, 1988).

Skills Related to Peer Status and Social Competence

The question of which social skills are related to positive peer status and social competence is a complex one. How best to identify those children who are neglected by their peers, for example, requires continued research (e.g., Dygdon and Conger, 1990). Also, the concept of social competence requires an understanding of the social tasks that are critical to development.

Given the identification of problem children and critical tasks, it would also be necessary to target behaviors for intervention that are problematic for such children and are related to such tasks. When behaviors targeted for treatment improve, it must then be shown that actual changes in the child's peer-related behavior have resulted. In addition, it must be demonstrated that these changes in behavior are related to changes in how others judge the child. A set of relationships such as these is needed to be able to relate peer status to specific skills. As might be expected, all these aspects are rarely analyzed together (Dodge, 1989). However, certain behaviors appear to be associated with positive judgments of social competence.

Responding positively to peers. Global characteristics—friendliness and outgoingness—and certain specific behaviors—giving attention and approval, submitting to another's wishes, giving things to others, and other such prosocial behaviors—have consistently been associated with peer acceptance (Combs and Slaby, 1977; Hartup, Glazer, and Charlesworth, 1967). Interactions with a peer specifically chosen as a friend, as well as general peer acceptance, are characterized by high rates of these positive behaviors. Children who are less popular spend more time daydreaming or "tuned out" (Charlesworth and Hartup, 1967; Gottman, Gonso, and Rasmussen, 1975).

Perspective taking and accurate communication. The ability to judge another's perspective and communicate accurately have been experimentally assessed by asking the child to give appropriate clues in a password-type game or to give descriptions of something from another person's perspective (for example, how a mountain of blocks appears to another person). The child's ability to give helpful clues is assumed to reflect the child's referential communication ability—that is, his or her ability to adopt another person's perspective and communicate accurately from that perspective. This skill is an important aspect of social development (Selman, 1976; Shantz, 1975). Gottman and his colleagues (1975) found that popular children give more good clue words or helpful descriptions. Also, among fifth- and sixth-grade boys in a special class for the emotionally disturbed, social withdrawal was found to be associated with poor perspective-taking ability (Waterman et al., 1981).

Initiating interactions. Popular and unpopular children have also been found to differ when asked to role-play making a friend. Third and fourth graders who were more popular with their peers were more likely to perform certain initiation behaviors—greeting, offering information, extending offers of inclusion, and asking for information (Gottman et al., 1975). Also, analysis of five-year-old children's conversation during friendship formation suggested six patterns that differentiated successful (liked by peers) from unsuccessful outcomes: clear communication; information exchange; establishment of common play activities with peers; exploration of similarities and differences; conflict resolution; self-disclosure (Gottman, 1983). In contrast, Hops and Greenwood (1981) have reported that socially withdrawn children are not as likely to respond to other children's initiation, and when they do respond, most often their responses are nonverbal.

Treatment of the Withdrawn Child

Given this chapter's focus on internalizing disorders, we will emphasize the withdrawn or shy child rather than the aggressive-rejected child in our discussion. It is noteworthy that since 1980 the DSM system has officially recognized the problem of social withdrawal by including the diagnoses of Avoidant Disorder of Childhood or Adolescence and Schizoid Disorder of Childhood or Adolescence. These are distinguished from each other by the nature of the social isolation. The avoidant child is inhibited by anxiety from making friends but enjoys peer relations, once established. The schizoid child is viewed as having no desire for social contact.

Many programs have been designed to improve the social skills of children. A thorough review of this material is beyond the scope of this section. Several reviews provide a good summary and critique of this literature and of interventions with withdrawn children in particular (cf. Combs and Slaby, 1977; Dodge, 1989; Hops, 1983; Ladd and Mize, 1983).

Reinforcing increased peer interaction. Some workers have focused on the antecedents and consequences of low rates of peer interaction. Indeed, the effectiveness of reinforcement in increasing peer contact was the focus of some of the early work on social skills interventions (e.g., Allen et al., 1964; Walker et al., 1979). It was soon realized, however, that reinforcement of high rates of interaction may not always produce positive outcomes. It may also lead to unacceptable rates of aggressive behavior (Kirby and Toler, 1970) and thereby to being unpopular (Conger and Keane, 1981). In addition, there is some disagreement regarding whether rate of interaction is an appropriate treatment target for socially withdrawn children. It has, for example, been argued that little support exists for the notion that overall rate of peer interaction is an indicator of social incompetence or of risk for later difficulties (cf. Dodge, 1989). However, others point out that if children with very low rates of interaction are compared to those showing normal rates, important and valid differences are found (cf. Hops and Greenwood, 1988).

Imitation, coaching, and instruction. Exposure to filmed models has also been demonstrated to positively affect the behavior of preschool isolates (e.g., O'Connor, 1969, 1972). However, a number of methodological concerns with this research have been raised, and it is unclear whether the effects are due to observation of a model or to other variables, such as coaching and instruction (Conger and Keane, 1981).

Several investigators have explicitly employed coaching-instructional techniques. These interventions use a variety of procedures, including instruction in social skills knowledge and concepts, modeling and rehearsal with classmates, and reinforcement and encouragement of generalization (e.g., Bornstein, Bellack, and Hersen, 1977; Gottman, Gonso, and Schuler, 1976; LaGreca and Santogrossi, 1980; Oden and Asher, 1977). For example, Ladd (1981) selected third-grade children low on peer acceptance who were also observed to be deficient in the three areas to be targeted. The latter

A withdrawn or socially isolated child may need assistance in developing appropriate social skills and increasing peer interactions.

criterion is important since it matches specific interventions to pretreatment deficiencies—something often lacking in treatment studies. Children were assigned to either a skill training treatment, attention control, or nontreatment control condition. Training consisted of instructions, guided and self-directed rehearsal, and feedback plus training in self-evaluation. Three verbal skills were targeted: asking questions, leading (offering useful suggestions and directions), and offering support to peers. Differences in both behavioral observations and peer acceptance in favor of the treatment condition were obtained. It seems likely that the finding of improvement in both targeted behavior and actual social acceptance is due to the selection of intervention targets. In this study behaviors that the children were deficient in, rather than general skills, were targeted. Thus, it is likely that these behaviors were related to the children's original unpopular status.

The use of peers in treatment. While most interventions for improving children's social skills are implemented by adults, an interesting approach is the use of peers as helping agents. Peers can provide appropriate models for desired behavior. They are also already present in the setting where the relevant behavior occurs and can provide natural consequences that continue to main-

tain behavior over time. Indeed, a variety of peer-mediated interventions have been demonstrated to improve the social behavior of withdrawn children (Odom and Strain, 1984).

Furman, Rahe, and Hartup's (1979) program employing peers to assist socially withdrawn children is particularly intriguing because of its use of basic research to suggest clinical interventions. A fascinating series of laboratory and naturalistic observations has indicated the importance of peer relations for monkeys. For example, it has been shown that infant monkeys reared by several peers in the absence of a mother show no later disturbances. However, those raised by a mother in the absence of peers show both short- and long-term disturbances in play and affective development (e.g., Harlow and Harlow, 1965). Perhaps most intriguing is the finding that peer "therapists," but not adult monkey "therapists," were effective in getting young monkeys to overcome their social withdrawal (e.g., Suomi and Harlow, 1972).

Drawing on this research, Furman, Rahe, and Hartup identified preschool children who engaged in peer interactions during less than 33 percent of observations and who were at least 10 percentage points below the mean interaction score for their class. Twenty-four such social isolates were assigned to unstructured play sessions with a "therapist" 12 to 18 months younger, to play sessions with a same-age "therapist," or to no treatment. As Figure 7–3 illustrates, exposure to a younger peer was highly effective in increasing the social activity of withdrawn children. Both groups of children exposed to "therapists" showed improvement, while the control group did not. However, seven of the eight isolates exposed to a younger partner increased their social behavior at least 50 percent, while only three of the eight withdrawn youngsters exposed to a same-age partner exhibited comparable increases. The principal effect of the treatments was to increase rates of positive behaviors but not of neutral and punishing acts. The authors hypothesize that the effectiveness of the peer play sessions, particularly with younger children, was due to an increased opportunity to practice initiating and directing social activity successfully.

Additional evidence for the importance of peers in intervention is provided in a treatment that employed the more common adult-directed training. Bierman and Furman (1984) assigned children who were identified as unaccepted by their peers and

deficient in conversational skills to one of four treatment conditions. In the individual condition the child received coaching in conversational skills in the context of making a film. In the group experience condition the child and two nontargeted peers were involved in making the same film, but without any coaching in conversational skills. In a combined coaching and group condition the child and two peers received coaching in the context of making the film. The remainder of the children were assigned to a no treatment control condition. The children were evaluated on their conversational skills and peer acceptance prior to treatment, after ten sessions of 30 minutes each, and again six weeks later. The results in general show a specificity of the impact of interventions. At the end of treatment targeted children who had received skills training, compared to those who had not, had superior conversational skills. Whether training was received in an individual or group context did not significantly affect this outcome. This difference persisted at the follow-up assessment. Thus, skills training, whether done in an individual or group context, produced sustained improvements in conversational skills.

This study's results regarding peer acceptance are also quite interesting. Ratings of peer acceptance were obtained by averaging the ratings given by all the child's same-sex classmates. Children who were involved in group conditions had higher posttreatment acceptance scores than those not involved in group conditions. This difference, however, did not persist at follow-up. Specificity is again suggested in that the presence or absence of skills training did not affect these findings. That is, peer acceptance was affected only by the group experience variable.

For the children involved in the two group conditions a rating of acceptance by the peers actually involved in the training was obtained. Children who received group skills coaching were more liked than those who received only the group experience. This was true at both the end of treatment and at follow-up. Thus, it would appear

FIGURE 7–3 Pre- and posttreatment rates of peer interaction in the classroom. From Furman, Rahe, and Hartup (1979) *Child Development, 50,* 915–922. Copyright © The Society for Research in Child Development, Inc. By permission.

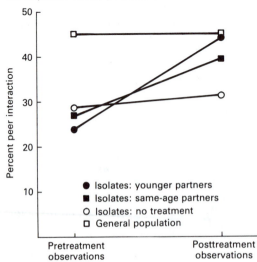

that group involvement can improve peer status, but this effect may be short-lived. Sustained peer acceptance may require more than a structured group experience.

Skills training that involves relevant peers may be an essential component of long-term success.

SUMMARY

Childhood depression has only recently received concentrated attention. Estimates of the prevalence of childhood depression vary considerably. This is due to a number of considerations, most importantly the use of differing criteria and measures.

The psychoanalytic theory of depression suggested that the problem could not exist in children. The concept of masked depression, although problematic, resulted in greater attention to the problem and highlighted developmental issues. Data supporting the importance of a developmental perspective in understanding issues such as prevalence and symptom patterns are emerging.

The view that childhood depression is a disorder with the same essential features as its adult counterpart is probably the dominant view at present. This is the approach taken by the DSM system. Research findings suggest both similarities and differences with the adult disorder.

Much of the theorizing about the etiology of childhood depression is based on theories or information derived from adults. Separation-loss has been a major theme in many theories of depression. Another view, learned helplessness, suggests that a learned perception of lack of control leads to behavior characteristic of depression. Cognitive theories such as Beck's emphasize the role of distorted thinking. The applicability of adult theories to childhood depression, while promising in many cases, is still unclear.

Biological hypotheses such as those regarding the role of neurotransmitters, are also largely based on adult findings. Differences between children and adults regarding biological markers of depression leave the issue of the similarity of the two disorders unresolved.

Assessment of depression has been facilitated by the development of interviews that are designed to yield specific DSM diagnoses including depression. In addition, a number of self-report measures such as the Children's Depression Inventory has received considerable research attention. Information from various informants does not always agree. It may be that different aspects of the child's behavior are being assessed. Thus, obtaining information from a variety of informants and with a variety of measures seems important. Instruments to assess attributes associated with depression (e.g., hopelessness) help make assessments more thorough.

The impact of maternal depression and its relationship to childhood depression have received considerable attention. Maternal depression does appear to be related to childhood dysfunction, but this relationship does not seem to be specific to childhood depression.

Peer relationships provide the opportunity for learning certain skills that may not be available in other social relationships. Also poor peer relations have been of interest because of their oft-cited association with later adjustment difficulties. While the link between shyness/withdrawal and later adjustment is less clear than it is for peer rejection, emerging evidence suggests a potential link to later adjustment.

Having problems with peers is one of the most frequently mentioned reasons for referrals for psychological services. Successful peer relations, on the other hand, may protect the child from the impact of other adverse factors and thereby decrease the likelihood of disorder.

The definition and measurement of peer status and social competence requires continued attention. How to best identify a particular peer status (e.g., the neglected child) remains unclear. Also, while several behaviors related to peer acceptance have been identified, identification of appropriate target behaviors is an ongoing task.

Many programs have been designed to improve the social skills of children. Reinforcing increased rates of peer interactions; interventions combining imitation, coaching, and instruction; and the use of peers in treatment have all been demonstrated to contribute to successful interventions.

8

CONDUCT DISORDERS

Clinicians commonly hear complaints of a child's aggressive and antisocial behavior. Such concerns come from parents, teachers, other adults, and peers. These same behaviors are problematic for parents and teachers of children who are not seen in clinical or legal settings. Most parents at some time or another have problems with a child's fighting, lying, destroying property, or repeatedly failing to follow directions.

In addition to the fact that these problems are common, the degree of disturbance and destruction that extreme and persistent forms of these behaviors cause makes them a concern for the family, the school, and society at large. It is also the seeming persistence of these behaviors over time—perhaps from early childhood through adult life—that highlights their importance.

The case description of Doug illustrates many of the features that characterize children who exhibit persistent aggressive and antisocial behavior. This chapter deals with those children to whom the labels of Conduct Disorder or Juvenile Delinquency are often applied.

Doug is an eight-year-old white male who was brought for treatment by his mother because of his unmanageable behavior at home. The specific concern was with Doug's aggressive behavior, especially aggression toward his 18-month-old brother. When Doug is angry he chokes and hits his younger brother and constantly makes verbal threats of physical aggression. In the months immediately before his referral to treatment, Doug's behavior became more out of control, and his mother felt she was unable to cope. Apart from his aggression in the home, Doug has played with matches and set fires over the last three years. These episodes have included igniting fireworks in the kitchen of his home, setting fires in trash dumpsters in the neighborhood, and starting a fire in his bedroom, which the local fire department had to extinguish.

At school his behavior has been disruptive over the last few years. His intellectual performance is within the normal range (WISC-R full scale IQ = 96) and his academic performance is barely passing. His aggressive behavior against peers and disruption of class activities have led to his placement in a special class for emotionally disturbed children. Even so, his behavior is not well controlled. The school has threatened expulsion if treatment is not initiated.

Doug currently lives with his mother and two brothers. He is second born. For the first few years of Doug's life, there was considerable disruption in the home. Doug's father frequently abused alcohol. When drunk, he would beat his wife and children. The mother and father separated on a number of occasions and eventually were divorced when Doug was five years old. After the divorce, the mother and children moved in with the maternal grandfather who also drank excessively and physically abused the children. Less than two years ago, the mother had another child by her former husband. With the stress of the new child, the death of her father with whom she was living, and Doug's continuing problems, the mother became depressed and began to drink. Although she is not employed, she spends much of her time away from the home. She leaves the children unsupervised for extended periods with a phone number of a neighbor for the children to call if any problems arise with the baby. (Kazdin, 1985, pp. 3–4).

PREVALENCE

The exact prevalence of conduct disorders is difficult to establish. Differences in definition as well as socioeconomic and familial factors influence the number and kinds of problems reported. Nonetheless, aggression—as well as antisocial, oppositional, and similar behaviors— certainly are among the most common childhood problems. In their review of prevalence studies Wells and Forehand (1985) note that 33 to 75 percent of clinic referrals were for conduct-disordered behavior. Studies of the prevalence of conduct disorders in the general population often report rates of around 4 to 6 percent (e.g., Anderson et al., 1987; Offord, Adler, and Boyle, 1986; Rutter, Tizard, and Whitmore, 1970). Disobedience, tantrums, demandingness, and whining are also among the most common concerns expressed by parents in private pediatric settings (Mesibov, Schroeder, and Wesson, 1977; Schroeder, 1979). Many of these behaviors are also reported by parents of children not referred for problems (Achenbach and Edelbrock, 1983). Boys show more of the behaviors associated with conduct disorders than do girls. In most cases the reported ratio is at least 2:1 or 3:1 (Quay, 1986c).

CLASSIFICATION

Empirically Derived Syndromes

Empirically derived syndromes involving aggressive, oppositional, destructive, and antisocial behavior have been identified in a wide variety of studies (cf. Achenbach and Edelbrock, 1989; Quay, 1986b). These broad-band syndromes have been designated as Undercontrolled, Externalizing, or Conduct Disorder. It would appear that the conduct-disorder category is a robust one in that it emerges when a variety of measures, reporting agents, and settings are involved (Patterson, 1986).

There is also the suggestion that two distinct syndromes of conduct disorders exist: undersocialized-aggressive and socialized-aggressive (e.g., Quay, 1986b). Similar

TABLE 8–1 Some Behaviors Characteristic of Conduct Disorder

Undersocialized-Aggressive Syndrome
Fights, hits
Disobedient, defiant
Temper tantrums
Destructive
Impertinent, impudent
Uncooperative, resistant

Socialized-Aggressive Syndrome
Has "bad" companions
Truant from school
Absent from home
Steals with peers
Loyal to delinquent friends
Belonging to a gang

Adapted from Quay, 1986b.

distinctions are sometimes found as narrow-band syndromes within the broader conduct disorder syndrome (e.g., Achenbach and Edelbrock, 1983). Some of the behaviors characteristic of these syndromes are listed in Table 8–1. Achenbach and Edelbrock (1983) noted that conduct disorders, although a stable syndrome over time, are manifested by different patterns of behavior in different age-gender groups.

The DSM Approach

According to DSM-III-R, the essential feature of the diagnosis of Conduct Disorder is a persistent pattern of behavior that violates the basic rights of others and major age-appropriate societal norms. Conduct disorders are part of the larger category of Disruptive Behavior Disorders that also includes Attention-Deficit Hyperactivity Disorder and Oppositional-Defiant Disorder. The list of symptoms that are intended to describe the various manifestations of Conduct Disorder are presented in Table 8–2. The diagnosis of Conduct Disorder requires a period of six months or more during which at least three of these behaviors are present.

Three subtypes of Conduct Disorder are described in DSM-III-R. Physical or verbal aggression that is not part of a group activity is the basis for diagnosing the *aggressive* subtype. The description of this subtype also suggests that the individual usually does not attempt to conceal antisocial behavior and is often socially isolated. The *group delinquent* subtype is characterized by antisocial or aggressive behavior mainly as part of a group of friends with similar problems. A third subcategory is provided for children and adolescents with patterns of conduct disorder that do not fit easily into either of the other two categories.

This system of subcategories is a shift

TABLE 8–2 DSM-III-R Diagnostic Criteria for Conduct Disorder

At least three of the following are present as part of a conduct disturbance lasting at least six months.
1. Steals without confronting the victim
2. Runs away from home overnight at least twice
3. Often lies
4. Deliberately sets fires
5. Often truant from school (absent from work)
6. Breaks into a house or car
7. Deliberately destroys another's property
8. Physically cruel to animals
9. Forces someone into sexual activity
10. Uses a weapon in more than one fight
11. Often initiates physical fights
12. Steals with confrontation of victim
13. Physically cruel to people

Adapted and reprinted with permission from the *Diagnostic and Statistical Manual of Mental Disorders, Third Edition, Revised.* Copyright 1987, American Psychiatric Association.

from the DSM-III approach. Previously four categories (socialized-aggressive, socialized-nonaggressive, unsocialized-aggressive, and unsocialized-nonaggressive) were defined. The basis for and utility of the current system for subtyping conduct disorders is controversial, some seeing it as more consistent with empirical data, while others question the justification for the change (e.g., Cantwell and Baker, 1988; Kazdin, 1990b).

Other Approaches

Dimensions or categories other than those described by the empirical and DSM approaches have been suggested. For example, the pending ICD-10 has subcategories for disorders confined to a family context, and the socialized versus unsocialized distinction (Rutter, 1989a). Two other approaches have been described as the *salient symptom* approach and the *overt-covert dimension* (Kazdin, 1989a). Distinguishing antisocial children whose primary problem is aggression from those whose primary problem is stealing is an example of the first approach. The validity of this distinction is supported by findings that these two groups differ in other characteristics of the child, parental behavior, and response to treatment (e.g., Patterson, 1982). The salient symptom approach, thus, suggests subcategorizing conduct disorders based on the primary behavior problem displayed by the child. Expansion of this distinction suggested a broader distinction between overt confrontational antisocial behaviors (e.g., arguing, fighting, temper tantrums) and covert or concealed antisocial behaviors (e.g., fire setting, lying, stealing, truancy). In this approach subcategorization is based on a group of related behaviors rather than on a single problem. The reliability and validity of the overt-covert distinction is supported by evidence that problem behaviors do tend to cluster together in these groupings and that different outcomes are associated with such clusters (Loeber and Schmaling, 1985). Systems to subcategorize conduct disordered behavior are still controversial (Cantwell and Baker, 1988; Kazdin, 1989a).

DEVELOPMENTAL COURSE

Much attention has been given to the developmental aspects of conduct disorders (e.g., Farrington, 1986; Loeber, 1990; Patterson, DeBaryshe, and Ramsey, 1989; Robins, 1978). There may be different developmental courses in the way that conduct-disordered behavior develops. Loeber (1988) proposed a classification of conduct problems based on developmental progressions. The model suggests that individuals pass through different stages of increasingly serious antisocial acts, but only a few individuals progress through all the stages. Progression is characterized by increasing diversification of antisocial behaviors: Variety increases rather than decreases over time, and previous behaviors are retained rather than replaced. Individuals differ in their rate of progression—or innovation rate—defined as the number of novel categories of antisocial behavior during a time period.

Loeber hypothesizes three developmental paths. In the *aggressive/versatile path* youngsters initially develop aggressive behaviors. A proportion of these youngsters later become exclusive violent offenders. Another group, however, early in life, adopts nonaggressive acts as well. These latter individuals also become, over time, involved in property and nonviolent forms of delinquency and may or may not engage in substance use or abuse. Individuals in the *nonaggressive antisocial path* show early nonaggressive antisocial behavior and develop into exclusively nonaggressive offenders. They engage in property crimes

with or without drug offenses. The final path is an *exclusive substance abuse path*. Individuals in this path appear not to exhibit serious conduct problems early in life. Table 8–3 indicates some of the characteristics

TABLE 8–3 Characteristics During Juvenile Years of Aggressive/Versatile Path, Nonaggressive Antisocial Path, and Exclusive Substance Use Path

---

The Aggressive/Versatile Path
Onset of conduct problems in preschool years
Aggressive and concealing conduct problem behaviors
Hyperactive/impulsive/attention problems
Educational problems
Poor social skills
Poor relationships with peers and adults
High innovation rate
Low remission rate
More boys than girls

The Nonaggressive Antisocial Path
Onset in late childhood or early to middle adolescence
Mostly nonaggressive conduct problems
No appreciable hyperactive/impulsive/attention problems
Capable of social skills
Association with deviant peers
Low innovation rate
Higher remission rate, at least for delinquency
Higher proportion of girls than in aggressive/versatile path

The Exclusive Substance Abuse Path
Onset in middle to late adolescence
No appreciable antecedent conduct problems
Possibly antecedent internalizing problems

From Loeber, 1988. Reprinted by permission from Plenum Publishing Corporation.

thought to be associated with each of the three paths. One aspect of conduct problems that is highlighted by the concept of developmental paths is the frequent stability of conduct disorders.

The Stability of Conduct Disorders

Perhaps the most disturbing aspect of conduct problems is their reported stability over time (e.g., Loeber, 1982; Moskowitz, Schwartzman, and Ledingham, 1985; Olweus, 1979; Rutter et al., 1976; Spivack, Marcus, and Swift, 1986). Early evidence of conduct disordered behavior appears to be related to later aggressive and antisocial behavior and to a range of psychological and social-emotional difficulties later in life (Caspi, Elder, and Bem, 1987; Hafner, Quast, and Shea, 1975; Parker and Asher, 1987; Robins et al., 1971).

This persistence of aggressive and antisocial behavior has been noted repeatedly by both clinicians and researchers. To help understand how the question of continuity of behavior can be approached from a research perspective, let us examine one study in detail. Roff and Wirt (1984) were interested in being able to contribute to developing a causal model for delinquency. Based on available information they selected aggressive behavior in childhood, peer status, socioeconomic status, degree of family disturbance, predelinquent behavior, and school achievement as variables for investigation. In the early 1960s they began by gathering peer status information for approximately 17,000 third- through sixth-grade children. Based on the ratings of same-sex classmates, a child's peer status was determined by the difference between the number of liked-most and liked-least choices the child received. The investigators then interviewed all teachers regarding five children in their classroom—the least and most popular boy and girl and a child of middle popularity. Through the use of records the investigators were able to follow into the young adult period 2,453 of the children for whom they had interviews. They found that the rates of delinquent behavior were much higher for the low peer status group than for children who were of middle or high popularity.

The authors decided to undertake further analyses for the low-peer status group (1,127 children). Socioeconomic status was examined. Analysis of the teacher interviews for the types of problem behaviors exhibited by these children at the time of the interview was also undertaken. Coding and factor analyses of this information indicated four areas of problems. These were aggressiveness-rebelliousness, anxiety expressed as excitability and restlessness, poor school achievement, and a motivational deficit primarily involving apathy and indifference toward classroom activities. A measure of predelinquent behavior was also derived from the teacher interview. This index was based on six variables: stealing in school, stealing in the community, trouble with the law, running away from home, lying, and truancy. A global rating of severity of family disturbance was also abstracted from the teacher interview.

Thus SES, the four behavior problem scores, the predelinquent index, and family disturbance were the variables assessed for these 8- to 11-year-old children. By searching later juvenile records each of the children was rated as either delinquent or nondelinquent as an adolescent. Delinquency was defined as the opening of a formal juvenile record indicating juvenile court referral. State Bureau of Investigation records indicated which of the subjects had committed adult criminal offenses between the ages of 18 and 24 to 27. A statistical procedure known as path analysis was employed to define the joint effects of all the measures taken when the children were 8 to 11 years old and to suggest a causal model for later delinquent and adult criminal behavior.

Figure 8–1 illustrates the model as it

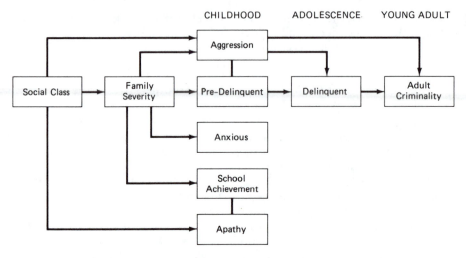

CHILDHOOD   ADOLESCENCE   YOUNG ADULT

Note: The arrows indicate which paths between variables were statistically significant.

FIGURE 8–1 A model of antecedents of delinquency and criminal behavior for low peer-status boys. Adapted from Roff and Wirt, 1984. Reprinted by permission from Plenum Publishing Corporation.

applies to boys. Separate models were derived for each gender since the rate of delinquent and criminal behavior was much lower for females. Aggression and predelinquent behavior appeared to be directly related to later delinquency for the low peer status males. Social class and severity of family disturbance contributed to these two childhood problem behaviors as well as to the other problems during childhood. However, they did not appear to be directly linked to delinquent outcome. In addition to there being a significant path from delinquency in adolescence to young adult criminal behavior, aggressiveness during childhood appeared to have a direct link to this adult behavior, as well. These results suggest a stable pattern of behavior over time for boys of low peer status, linking early aggres-

sion with later delinquency and criminal behavior.

The model for girls was different. There did not appear to be a direct path between early aggression and later antisocial behavior. Indeed, for girls, severity of family disturbance during childhood emerged as the best predictor of delinquency in adolescence. The frequency of adult criminal behavior among females was too low to permit an analysis into adulthood. These findings regarding girls are consistent with the interesting suggestion by others that early conduct problems in girls may be associated with a range of social-emotional difficulties later in life rather than primarily criminal outcome (Caspi, Elder, and Bem, 1987; Rutter, 1989c).

CAUSES AND CORRELATES OF CONDUCT DISORDERS

Family Influences

There is widespread agreement that family influences play an important role in the genesis of conduct-disordered behavior. A

high incidence of deviant or criminal behavior has been reported in families of delinquents and young children with conduct problems (Kazdin, 1985; Rutter and Giller, 1984; West, 1982). Longitudinal studies in fact suggest that such behavior is stable across generations (Glueck and Glueck, 1968; Huesmann et al., 1984). Furthermore, programs emphasizing improved parenting practices or effective family problem-solving and coping techniques report decreases in antisocial behavior and recidivism (repeat offenses) rates in untreated siblings (e.g., Gordon and Arbuthnot, 1987; Horne and Van Dyke, 1983). It seems, then, that conduct-disordered children may be part of a deviant family system. In fact, several family variables have been implicated in the genesis of aggressive and antisocial behavior (Hetherington and Martin, 1986; Kazdin, 1990b).

Parent-child interactions. The manner in which parents interact with their children contributes to the genesis of conduct-disordered behavior. The characteristics of parents who raise well-adjusted children have received extensive attention in the developmental literature (Robinson, 1985). Parental warmth, frequent use of reasoning, firm control, and demands that go slightly beyond the child's current level of maturity have been implicated in positive outcomes. One approach to the study of conduct problem children is to hypothesize that their parents do not behave in the manner suggested by this developmental literature. Some empirical support for this notion can be found for the variables of control and warmth (e.g., Baumrind, 1967; Olweus, 1980).

It has also been shown that parents of children with conduct disorders apply inappropriate reinforcement contingencies: They reinforce antisocial behavior and ignore and punish appropriate behavior (Patterson, 1982). The nature and number of commands given by these parents have also been shown to differ from those given by parents of nonclinic children (e.g., Williams and Forehand, 1984). Inconsistency in following up on commands and in providing consequences for behavior also seem to characterize these parent-child interactions

(e.g., Gardner, 1989). Indeed, it has been suggested that in such families the parents' behavior becomes more predictable during aversive interactions and this is reinforcing to the child. The child prefers this predictability to the inconsistency that he or she finds aversive (Wahler and Dumas, 1986).

It is appropriate to remember that much of this research is only descriptive of group differences and is correlational in nature. It is often assumed that parental behavior causes childhood conduct disorders. The relationship, however, may be at least reciprocal. Anderson, Lytton, and Romney (1986) found that mothers of conduct-problem boys and mothers of normal boys both interacted more negatively with conduct-problem boys than with normal boys. They suggested that the child's behavior is the influence in these interactions, not the mother's. In addition, it may be inappropriate to assume that fundamental deficiencies in parenting skills account for conduct problems in children. It may be that a high level of environmental stress experienced by the parents, and not always the absence of parenting skills, accounts for observed parenting difficulties (McLoyd, 1990; Wahler and Dumas, 1989).

Marital discord. There appears to be a clear association between marital discord and parental perceptions of behavior problems in their children (O'Leary and Emery, 1985). Indeed, the combination of marital dissatisfaction and high levels of child disruptive behavior is more likely than either factor alone to produce perceptions of behavior problems (Forehand, Brody, and Smith, 1986).

Interparental conflict has frequently been cited in homes of delinquents and children with conduct disorders (Kazdin 1985; Rutter and Giller 1984). Also, divorce and father absence have been associated with conduct disorders, particularly for boys (e.g., Guidubaldi and Perry, 1985; Hetherington, Cox, and Cox, 1982). It would appear that the conflict leading to and surrounding the divorce are principal influences in this relationship. Less conflict

Children's observations of parental interactions clearly influence behavior. If these interactions are hostile, they may contribute to the development of aggression and other aversive behaviors in the child. (Mimi Forsyth/Monkmeyer Press)

and greater cooperation are associated with fewer problems in children (Hetherington, Stanley-Hagan, and Anderson, 1989). The relationship between family conflict and conduct disorders is found more often for boys than for girls (Emery, 1982; Reid and Crisafulli, 1990). If aggression between the parents is also present, childhood disorder seems even more likely than would be expected based on marital discord alone (Jouriles, Murphy, and O'Leary, 1989).

The relationship between marital conflict and conduct disorders can be explained in a number of ways. For example, parents who engage in a great deal of marital conflict or aggression may serve as models for their children. It may be the case that such parents direct higher than usual rates of conflictual and aggressive behavior at others as well, including the child. The stress of marital discord and the adjustment of the single parent to divorce may also interfere with parenting practices and the ability of the parent to monitor the child's behavior. The relationship between discord and conduct problems may also operate in the opposite causal direction. The child's disruptive behavior may contribute to marital discord.

Social-Cognitive Influences

Moral development. Since many of the behaviors characteristic of conduct disorders violate societal rules or norms, some workers have related the process of moral development in children to conduct problems. Research over the last several decades has documented the role of parents, schools, peers, sex-role socialization, television, guilt, empathy, and cognitive development in moral development (Ellis, 1982; Hoffman, 1979; Rest, 1983).

The development of morality, like most developmental tasks, is a complex process. It is clear, however, that the kinds of action, feeling, and thought one can expect is related to the child's level of development. For example, a five-year-old is likely to act and judge others' behavior by objective standards. Breaking five dishes is worse than breaking one. Accident versus intention are not considered. Also, for a child of this developmental level the source of moral rules is some authority—"My father said . . ."—and consequences are assumed to be imminent. Both the rules and the consequences are outside the child. As children get older they can consider relative factors such as an individual's intention and the "social contract" nature of rules. Also self-direction and self-imposed consequences presumably shape their actions and reasoning.

Much of the attention to the development of moral reasoning has centered around Kohlberg's (1964, 1976) extension and revision of Piaget's original account. His stage theory, like Piaget's, is based on the assumption that each stage represents hierarchically more complex and abstract levels of reasoning. Children are assumed to pass through the stages in a fixed order. Movement to the next stage occurs only after the reasoning of the earlier stage is mastered. It is also assumed that an individual's level of moral development may stop at any point. Thus, a person may be below the level characteristic of most same-age individuals. Indeed, findings of low levels of moral reasoning among delinquents have been the basis of much of the speculation in this area (Nelson, Smith, and Dodd, 1990). Low levels of moral reasoning have also been reported to be associated with conduct problems in younger children (Baer and Richards, 1981; Nucci and Herman, 1982). It can not, however, clearly be said that all conduct-disordered youth have lower levels of moral reasoning. Considerable individual variability in moral reasoning may exist among samples of such youth (Blasi, 1980; Jurkovic, 1980; Nelson et al., 1990).

Kohlberg's conceptualization has generated a great deal of research and commentary, and also a great deal of controversy. The method for assessing moral reasoning (Table 8–4) has been criticized. Also some research suggests that children may possess age-appropriate moral concepts, but not reveal that understanding in every situation (e.g., Shultz, Wright, and Schleifer, 1986). Issues of potential bias and sex-role influences and of cultural relativity have also been raised (Baumrind, 1986; Gilligan, 1982; Snarey, 1985; Walker, 1984, 1986).

The contribution of moral thought to the development of conduct-disordered behavior has been examined by other approaches

---

TABLE 8–4 Kohlberg's Method of Assessing Moral Reasoning

An individual child's level of moral reasoning is assessed through administration of hypothetical dilemmas such as the following:

Bill saved up $10 for a catcher's mitt. When he arrives at the store, he sees the sales clerk going down the stairs to the cellar. The clerk doesn't see Bill. Bill looks at the gloves, and just as he sees one he likes, he reaches for his money. It's gone, he realizes he has lost it. He feels awful. It occurs to Bill that the mitt would just fit under his jacket. He hides the mitt and walks out of the store. Now you finish the story. (Kohlberg, 1964, p. 410)

The child's verbal response to this and other dilemmas are scored to provide an index of moral stage and moral maturity.

---

as well. For example, it may be that parents of children with conduct problems are less likely to provide reasons along with their disciplinary actions. If explanations are provided, they may rest on power rather than concepts such as fairness. The developmental literature suggests that such strategies are less likely to result in the child's developing internalized standards (e.g., Hoffman, 1979). In this and other ways these children may not have had the experiences required to create cognitive schemes necessary for appropriate social behavior.

In addition numerous other skills may be involved in what we call moral judgment. These may include empathy and the ability to take another's perspective, both of which have been found to differ among delinquent groups (e.g., Ellis, 1982; Jurkovic and Prentice, 1977). Lee and Prentice (1988) studied several such variables. Adolescent delinquent boys in a state juvenile correctional facility and matched nondelinquents were given two individually administered measures of empathy. They also completed tasks to assess the stage of their role-taking development; that is, the ability to take another's perspective. Two measures to assess Piagetian level of cognitive development and two of Kohlberg's structured moral dilemmas were also administered. Delinquents displayed more immature modes of role-taking, and less formal operational thinking than did nondelinquents. Delinquents also displayed lower levels of moral reasoning than nondelinquents. The groups did not differ, however, on either measure of empathy. An attempt to find differences between subcategories of delinquents in this study also failed.

The question of if and how deficits in moral development contribute to conduct disorders and delinquency remains controversial and in need of continued investigation. Some investigators have, however, demonstrated that sociomoral training programs for conduct-disordered and delinquent youths can produce changes in the levels of moral development exhibited. Furthermore, such changes are associated with changes in relevant conduct and academic measures (e.g., Arbuthnot and Gordon, 1986; Chandler, 1973).

Interpersonal relations. Difficulties in interpersonal relations have repeatedly been found among conduct disordered youth (Baum, 1989). The interpersonal difficulties described in this section are most often thought to be associated with aggressive and unsocialized conduct disorders.

Research indicates that aggressive children are frequently rejected by their peers (Coie, Belding, and Underwood, 1988). These rejected children not only suffer the immediate social consequences, but are also at risk for negative long-term outcomes such as delinquency, adult criminality, educational failure, and a vareity of indices of adult psychological maladjustment (Parker and Asher, 1987).

The importance of peer relations for normal development has been recognized for a long time and has received considerable research attention (Hartup, 1989). Although identification of the specific attributes that differentiate rejected children from their peers is a topic of continuing investigation, a number of interesting attributes have been identified (Baum, 1989; Dodge, 1989).

For example, aggressive children and adolescents who are rejected by their peers have been found to exhibit deficits in social information processing and interpersonal problem-solving skills. They may generate fewer alternative solutions to social problems, seek less information, define problems in hostile ways, and anticipate fewer consequences for aggression (e.g., Spivack and Shure, 1974; Slaby and Guerra, 1988). Aggression also seems to be related to a belief system that supports its use. Thus, aggression may be held as a legitimate response—"It's OK to hit someone if you don't like him or her." Aggression may also be supported by its expected positive outcomes—reduced aversive behavior by others, tangible rewards, increased self-esteem, and avoidance of negative judgements by others (Bandura, 1986; Perry, Perry, and Rasmussen, 1986; Slaby and Guerra, 1988).

Dodge and Somberg's (1987) examination of attributional biases among aggressive boys is an example of how such social-cognitive influences may operate. Previous research established that following provocation by a peer, the interpretation of the peer's intent affected the child's subsequent response. If the peer's intent was perceived to be hostile, aggressive retaliation was viewed as justified. In contrast, if the peer's intent was perceived as benign, the child was likely to refrain from aggression. Children who were themselves both aggressive and socially rejected were more likely to attribute hostile intent to a peer's behavior in ambiguous circumstances. Dodge and Somberg were interested in investigating whether this hostile attributional bias was exacerbated under conditions of threat.

Aggressive-rejected and nonaggressive-adjusted boys, eight- to ten-years old, viewed videorecorded scenes involving different pairs of boys in play activity. In each vignette one boy engaged in a behavior that led to a negative outcome for the second youngster. The intention of the boy varied across

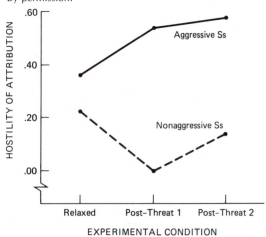

FIGURE 8–2 Attributions of hostility to ambiguous provocations by aggressive and nonaggressive boys under relaxed and threatening conditions. From Dodge and Somberg (1987), *Child Development, 58,* 213–224. Copyright © The Society for Research in Child Development, Inc. By permission.

the scenes (either hostile, accidental, pro-social, or ambiguous). Subjects answered two questions about each vignette: Which of the four intents did the boy have and how would they respond if the provocation happened to them (get mad, tell the teacher, ask the peer why it happened, forget it and keep playing). Each subject saw scenes and responded under two circumstances—a relaxed and, twice, in a threat condition. (The threat condition was created by leading the subjects to believe they would have to work with another child who disliked both them and the experimenter and that this child would likely get into a conflict with the subject.) The results showed that, as expected, aggressive subjects were more likely to attribute hostile intent to the boys in the vignettes. They were also more likely to indicate aggressive responses to perceived hostility. The hypothesis that the bias toward hostile attribution would be exaggerated under conditions of threat was also supported. These findings are illustrated in Figure 8–2.

Biological Influences

The idea that antisocial and criminal behavior has strong biological roots has a long history. As early as the late nineteenth century, the Italian physician Lombroso wrote of the "stigmata of degeneration." Law violators were described as a distinct physical type at birth with distinct physical features such as long ear lobes, fleshy and protruding lips, and abundant wrinkles. Females were said to commit fewer crimes because their lesser intelligence and sexual coldness overcame their naturally jealous and vengeful nature (cited in Empey, 1978). This conceptualization had extensive impact on criminology and social policy for over a third of a century, but current-day scientists have accumulated sufficient evidence to reject it.

Genetics. Contemporary versions of genetic contributions to antisocial behavior do, however, exist. Research findings are based primarily on adult samples. For example, by examining the extensive social records available in Denmark, Mednick and his colleagues evaluated rates of criminal behavior in the biological and adoptive relatives of adopted individuals with criminal records (Mednick, Gabrielli, and Hutchings, 1984). Higher rates of criminal behavior were found in biological relatives. Contemporary research also generally appreciates that the interactions between biological and environmental factors are so complex that any biology-conduct disorder linkages will be nowhere as direct as implied in earlier theories. For example, in examining adoptees, it has been found that alcoholic criminals tended to commit violent offenses. Criminal behavior in these individuals was related to their alcoholism but not to any criminal behavior in the biological parents. A link to criminal behavior in biological parents was, however, found for nonalcoholic criminals. Placement history prior to adoption, however, was also a factor. These nonalcoholic individuals tended to commit petty rather than violent crimes (Bohman et. al., 1982; Cloninger et. al., 1982).

There is little or no direct evidence regarding genetic contributions to childhood conduct problems. There is limited evidence regarding the role of genetics in adolescent delinquency. The findings that are available suggest a lesser genetic component for adolescent delinquency than for adult criminal behavior. How might this difference be explained? Conduct-disordered and delinquent behavior are quite common and in many cases these behaviors do not persist into adulthood. It might, therefore, be reasonable to hypothesize an increased genetic component in antisocial behavior that persists from childhood into adult life (Rutter, 1990b). This hypothesis may be addressed by future research.

However, even conclusions regarding the nature of genetic contributions to adult antisocial behavior need to be made with caution. Rosenthal's (1975) hypothesis that certain inherited characteristics (for example, body build, sensitivity to alcohol) make an individual prone to criminal behavior in response to environmental pressures seems reasonable. Most reviewers seem to agree that while biological influences may play some role, they inevitably interact in complex ways with environmental influences such as social conditions, family variables, and certain social learning experiences that are major factors in determining etiology (e.g., Rutter et al., 1990b).

Psychophysiology. Psychophysiological variables have also frequently been hypothesized to be related to antisocial behavior. A physiologically based need for stimulation has been hypothesized to account, in part, for antisocial personality and criminality. On the basis of the hypothesis that there is an optimal level of arousal for all human beings, it is reasoned that a person will seek to adjust his or her arousal level when it is either too high or too low. The antisocial personality is viewed as an individual with chronic underarousal who is thus motivated to provide additional arousal. Some support for these notions came from studies that found that the performances of delinquents and younger conduct-disordered children were affected by the novelty and complexity of tasks (e.g., DeMyer-Gapin and Scott, 1977; Orris, 1969; Skrzypek, 1969; Whitehill, DeMyer-Gapin, and Scott, 1976). However, interpretation of these results as stimulation seeking is controversial (e.g., Rutter and Giller, 1984).

Findings of differences in heart rate and electrodermal responding [skin conductance responses (SCRs)] also seem consistent with the hypothesis of low arousability. Raine and Venables's (1984) review of the literature found support for the existence of lower resting heart rate among antisocial youths. These findings are difficult to interpret, however, because of the relationship of resting heart rate with other variables such as SES, physical fitness, and larger body size. Differences between antisocial/conduct-disordered youths and non-antisocial controls in the SCRs to stimulation have been reported in both adolescent and younger samples (e.g., Borkovec, 1970; Delamater and Lahey, 1983; Schmidt, Solanto, and Bridger, 1985). Quay (1986c) suggests that the combination of heart rate and SCR findings can provide a more specific hypothesis than general arousability. He suggests that an overactive reward system (reflected in heart rate) combined with an underactive behavioral inhibition system (reflected in skin conductance) may be implicated in the genesis of undersocialized conduct disorders.

Central nervous system functioning. Some research has examined central nervous system functioning through the use of electro-encephalograms (EEGs) and suggests an immature underaroused nervous system in criminals. For example, Gabrielli and Mednick (1983) reported that the EEG patterns of boys when they were 11 to 13 years old discriminated 9 years later between non-delinquent, one-time delinquent, and recidivist-delinquent groups. There are also indications of differences in the metabolites (products of metabolism) of neurotransmitters, such as serotonin and norepinephrine, that are related to the presence of antisocial and aggressive behavior (e.g., Rogeness et al., 1989). Conclusions regarding the importance of these findings to understanding the causes of conduct disorders are presently limited by concerns regarding methodology, interpretation of results, and generalizability to noncriminal conduct problems (Baum, 1989).

Conduct-disorders involve an array of problematic behaviors—and psychologists have studied several of them extensively. We will now discuss some of these specific behaviors. The problems of youths labeled as juvenile delinquents will also be explored.

CONDUCT-DISORDERED BEHAVIORS AND TREATMENTS

Aggression

Aggression as a learned behavior. Children clearly may learn to be aggressive by being rewarded for such behavior (Patterson, 1976b). For example, Patterson, Littman, and Bricker (1967) found that among nursery school children aggressive acts that were followed by "positive" consequences (for example, passivity or crying by the victim) were likely to be repeated, while "negative" responses (for example, retaliation or telling the teacher) resulted in the aggressor switching either behaviors or victims. Another interesting finding emerged from this study. Children who were initially passive and unassertive were frequently victimized. However, they eventually exhibited aggressive behaviors, were reinforced by positive consequences, and increased their frequency of such behavior. While illustrating the importance of reinforcement for aggression, this study also suggests another

source of learning—imitation of aggressive models.

A great deal of attention has been focused on how children learn through imitation of aggressive models. Bandura's (1965) study with nursery school children, described earlier (p. 57), demonstrated that children imitated an aggressive, filmed model and that the consequences experienced by the model affected the performance, but not the acquisition, of imitative aggression. It has also been demonstrated that children may not only learn new and novel responses following observation of an aggressive model, but that aggressive responses that were previously in the child's repertoire are more likely to occur—disinhibition of aggression.

Children certainly have ample opportunity to observe aggressive models. Parents who physically punish their children serve as models for aggressive behavior. In fact,

The viewing of aggression on TV and in movies contributes to the development of aggression and antisocial behavior.

children exhibiting excessive aggressive or antisocial behaviors are likely to have siblings, fathers, and even grandparents with records of aggressive and criminal behavior (Farrington, 1987; Huesman et al., 1984; West, 1982) and to have observed especially high rates of aggressive behavior in their homes (Patterson, 1976b; Patterson, De-Baryshe, and Ramsey, 1989). Exposure to aggression is also ubiquitous on television and in other media.

Cognitive aspects of the acquisition and persistence of aggression have also been addressed by the social learning approach. For example, Perry, Perry, and Rasmussen (1986) explored two types of cognitions: children's perceptions of their ability to behave aggressively (perceptions of self-efficacy) and their beliefs about expected outcomes of aggressive behavior. Aggressive and nonaggressive boys and girls from fourth through seventh grades completed questionnaires designed to measure the two classes of cognitions. Aggressive children reported greater confidence in their ability to be aggressive, more difficulty in inhibiting aggression, and greater expectation that aggression would produce tangible rewards and reduce aversive treatment by others. While there were negligible sex differences in perceptions of self-efficacy, there were differences in expected consequences. Girls were more likely than boys to expect aggression to cause more suffering for others and to expect more disapproval from peers and themselves. Other research has confirmed that the gender of both the aggressor and the target of aggression affect the consequences that children anticipate for aggression (Perry, Perry, and Weiss, 1989). These and other findings highlight the role of children's perceptions and expectations regarding aggression.

The work of Patterson and his colleagues.
Gerald Patterson and his colleagues have developed an intervention program for families with aggressive children based on a social learning perspective (Patterson et al., 1975; Patterson, 1986). Patterson developed what he referred to as *coercion theory* to explain how a problematic pattern of behavior develops in children labeled aggressive. Observations of referred families suggested that acts of physical aggression were not isolated behaviors. On the contrary, they tended to occur along with a wide range of noxious behaviors that were used to control family members in a process labeled coercion. How and why does this process of coercion develop?

One factor is parents who lack adequate family management skills (Kazdin, 1985; Loeber and Dishion, 1983; Patterson, 1986). According to Patterson (1976, 1980), parental deficits in child management lead to an increasingly coercive interaction within the family. Central to this viewpoint are the notions of *negative reinforcement* and the "*reinforcement trap*." For example, a mother gives into her child's tantrum in the supermarket and buys him a candy bar. The short-term consequence is that things are more pleasant for both parties. The child has used an aversive event (tantrum) to achieve the desired goal (candy bar), and the mother's giving in has terminated an aversive event (tantrum and embarrassment) for her. Short-term gains, however, are paid for in long-term consequences. The mother, though receiving some immediate relief, has increased the probability that her child will employ tantrums in the future. She has also been provided with negative reinforcement that increases the likelihood that she will give in to future tantrums. In addition to this negative reinforcement trap, coercive behavior by children may also be increased by direct positive reinforcement. Aggressive behavior, especially in boys, may meet with social approval. However, escape conditioning provides the most important set of contingencies. The child uses aversive behaviors to terminate aversive intrusions by other family members (Patterson, 1982).

This concept of *reciprocity* adds to our understanding of how aggression may be learned and sustained. As indicated earlier, children as young as nursery school age can learn in a short time that attacking another in response to some intrusion can terminate that intrusion. In addition, the victim of the attack learns from the experience and is more likely to initiate attacks in the future (Devine, 1971; Patterson, Littman, and Bricker, 1967). The eventual victim of escalating coercion also provides a negative reinforcer by giving in. This also increases the likelihood that the "winner" will start future coercions at higher levels of intensity and thereby get the victim to give in more quickly.

This process is exacerbated by the ineffectiveness of punishment. The finding that in problem families punishment does not suppress coercive behavior but may serve

Even at an early age children can learn that attacking another may result in the termination of an aversive intrusion. (S. Sheridan/Monkmeyer Press)

to increase it has been referred to as "*punishment acceleration.*" The ineffectiveness of punishment may be due to the strong reinforcement history for coercive behavior and to inconsistent use of punishment in these families (Patterson, 1982).

The description of a coercive process and ineffective parenting has served as the basis for an ongoing project and a continually evolving developmental model (Patterson, 1986; Patterson et al., 1989). This model also addresses the contextual variables that influence the family interaction process. In addition to describing the "training" of antisocial behavior in the home, Patterson has described a relationship between antisocial behavior in boys and poor peer relationships, academic incompetence, and poor self-esteem. It is thought that the coercive, noncompliant core of antisocial behavior, produced by ineffective parenting, produces these other disruptions. Furthermore, it is hypothesized that each of these outcomes serves as a percursor to subsequent drift into deviant peer groups. (See Figure 8–3.) Patterson himself is cautious concerning statements of causation based on correlational data. Ongoing longitudinal research and experimental studies are expected to clarify the proposed relationships.

The question of why some families and not others exhibit inept management practices has received some attention. Patterson (1986) points to two sets of variables that may account for changes over time in family management skills: stressors and parental substance abuse. Heavy drinking by parents may be associated with inept monitoring of the child and less parental involvement (West and Prinz, 1987). Patterson's own findings and those of other investigators (e.g., Wahler and Dumas, 1989) support the relationship between extrafamilial stressors and parenting practices. The literature on the impact of divorce is also consistent with a model that emphasizes disruption of parenting practices (Hetherington, Stanley-Hagan, and Anderson, 1989). In addition, handing down faulty parenting practices from one generation to the next, social disadvantage, and early child difficulty of

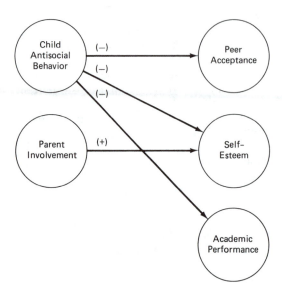

Note: (−) indicates that high levels of antisocial behavior were associated with less of the other variables.
(+) higher levels of parental involvement are associated with greater self-esteem.

FIGURE 8–3 Peer acceptance, self-esteem, and academic performance as products of antisocial behavior. Adapted from Patterson, 1986. Copyright (1986) by American Psychological Association.

temperament are seen as contributing to early onset of antisocial child behavior. Figure 8–4 illustrates how a variety of influences may lead to disruption of effective parenting.

The importance of parenting skills in Patterson's formulation led to the development of a treatment program that focused on improving these skills (cf. Patterson et al., 1975). Indeed, a variety of parent training programs have been proposed and implemented by other workers as well. Studies evaluating the outcome of these interventions indicate that parent training is among the most successful in reducing the problem behaviors of children labeled as antisocial and aggressive (Dumas, 1989; Kazdin, 1990). Also, group treatments and other cost-effective procedures can be introduced and be effective (e.g., Webster-Stratton, Hollinsworth, and Kolpacoff, 1989). It does, indeed, seem that modification of problematic parenting skills can serve as the primary mechanism for change in these families. It should be noted, however, that even those who acknowledge the success of such interventions do not necessarily agree on the mechanisms that account for dysfunctional family processes (cf. Robinson, 1985; Wah-

FIGURE 8–4 Disruptors of Effective Parenting. From Patterson, DeBaryshe, and Ramsey, 1989. Copyright (1989) by American Psychological Association.

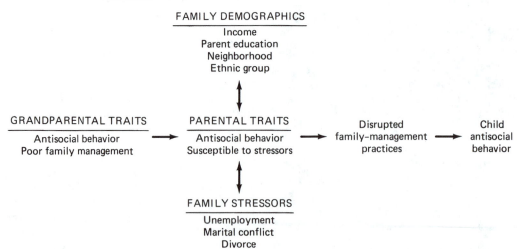

BOX 8.1   A parent-training approach to treatment

Patterson's program can serve to illustrate the social-learning-based parent training approach. The program teaches parents to pinpoint problems, to observe and record behavior, to use social and nonsocial reinforcers more effectively for appropriate or prosocial behavior, and to withdraw reinforcers more effectively for undesirable behavior. Families are introduced to these procedures by studying a programmed text (Patterson, 1975, 1976a). Each family also attends clinic and home sessions and has regular phone contact with a therapist who helps develop interventions for particular targeted behaviors and who models desired parenting skills. Problematic behaviors in the school setting are also targeted, and interventions involve both the parents and school personnel. Active treatment is terminated when both the therapist and family believe that a sufficient number of problematic behaviors has ceased, appropriate behavior has stabilized, overall family functioning has become more positive, and the parents are able to handle additional problems with little, if any, assistance. Treatment might be expected to average about 17 hours for a family (Patterson, Chamberlain, and Reid, 1982).

A study by Fleischman (1981) illustrates the program's success in changing deviant behavior and parental attitudes. The results also suggest that improvements are maintained. Observations of 20 families by trained observers indicated significant reductions in total aversive behavior. These behaviors did not increase during the one-year period following termination. Furthermore, although initial baseline levels of aversive behavior were greater than in a sample of normal children, the treatment sample was not more deviant than the normal group one year later. Decreases in problem behavior were also obtained for the parents' direct observations and their reports. Parents' opinions regarding the target child also improved. Encouragingly, for the two attitudes most centrally related to treatment objectives (opinions of whether less aggression and fewer conduct problems existed), positive changes were maintained a year later according to both parents.

Other programs that involve training of parenting skills have also been successful in working with families of conduct-disordered children. However, treatment is not always effective (Dumas, 1989). Families who are socioeconomically disadvantaged and isolated appear to do less well. Parents in these families who show significant improvement in parenting skills may have difficulty in maintaining them in the face of multiple problems and stresses. Parental personal (e.g., depression) and marital difficulties may also interfere with the successful completion of treatment. It would appear that the effectiveness of parent training can also be enhanced by providing parents with help for their personal or marital difficulties (Dadds, Schwartz, and Sanders, 1987; Griest et al., 1982).

---

ler and Dumas, 1989). It is important to remember that the success of a particular treatment does not prove the theory that served to generate it.

Oppositional-Noncompliant Behavior

Noncompliance is clearly a common problem. It is prevalent among nonclinic children (Johnson et al., 1973) and one of the most frequently reported problems of children referred to clinics (Christophersen et al., 1976; Patterson, 1976b). Reports indicate that clinic-referred children are more noncompliant than nonreferred children (e.g., Griest et al., 1980).

Noncompliance seems to be part of the

problematic behavior exhibited by children exhibiting other conduct problems and antisocial behavior (Baum, 1989; McMahon and Forehand, 1988). However, DSM-III-R also includes a separate category of Oppositional-Defiant Disorder in which a noncompliant style is central. Table 8–5 presents the diagnostic criteria for this disorder. It is unclear if this distinction as a separate category is valid (Kazdin, 1989a; McMahon and Forehand, 1988). Whatever the issues of classification/diagnosis are, noncompliance represents a practical problem for parents, teachers, and clinicians.

Given that noncompliance occurs in both clinic and nonclinic families, what factors might account for the greater rate of noncompliance in some families? One possible factor is suggested by evidence that parents of clinic and nonclinic children differ in both the number and types of commands they give. Parents of clinic-referred children issue more commands, questions, and criticisms and also issue commands in a more angry, humiliating, or nagging manner (Delfini et al., 1976; Forehand et al., 1975; Lobitz and Johnson, 1975). Such parental behavior has been shown to be associated with deviant child behavior (Griest et al., 1980).

Two types of commands have also been distinguished. *Alpha commands* are those to

TABLE 8–5 DSM-III-R Diagnostic Criteria for Oppositional Defiant Disorder

Disturbance of at least six months during which at least five of the following are present more frequently than expected for a person of the same mental age.
1. Loses temper
2. Argues with adults
3. Defies or refuses adult requests or rules
4. Deliberately annoys others
5. Blames others for own mistakes
6. Touchy—easily annoyed by others
7. Angry and resentful
8. Spiteful and vindictive
9. Swears or uses obsenities

Adapted and reprinted with permission from the *Diagnostic and Statistical Manual of Mental Disorders, Third Edition, Revised.* Copyright 1987, American Psychiatric Association.

which a motoric response is appropriate and feasible. *Beta commands* are vague, interrupted, or carried out by the parent, and thus the child has no opportunity to demonstrate compliance. Parents who give more alpha commands and few beta commands are likely to achieve greater child compliance. Consequences that parents deliver also affect the child's noncompliant behavior. A combination of negative consequences (ignoring and verbal reprimands) for noncompliant behavior and rewards and attention for appropriate behavior seems to be related to increased levels of compliance (Forehand and McMahon, 1981).

On the basis of these findings and an earlier program described by Hanf (1972, cited by Forehand 1977), Forehand and his colleagues developed a treatment program for noncompliant children (four to seven years old) and their families (Forehand and McMahon, 1981). Parents are taught to give direct, concise commands, allow the child sufficient time to comply (alpha commands), to reward compliance with contingent attention, and to apply negative contingencies to noncompliance.

The effectiveness of this program has been investigated in a number of studies and targeted program changes have been shown to occur (McMahon and Wells, 1989). Forehand and his colleagues have also demonstrated successful generalization. For example, Forehand, Wells, and Griest (1980) compared 15 clinic-referred children and their mothers to an equal number of nonclinic child-mother pairs. Of particular interest is the finding that although the parents of clinic children initially perceived their offspring as less well adjusted than did parents of nonclinic children, this was not true at two-month follow-up. These findings indicate that the success achieved is not only statistically significant but clinically and socially relevant as well. This conclusion is given further support by a sample of treated children who were followed into adolescence. When this group was compared on a variety of measures to a matched sample of "normal" adolescents who had never had any contact with a mental health professional, few differences were found between the groups (Forehand and Long, 1986, cited by McMahon and Wells, 1989). Successful treatment of noncompliance also seems to result in significant reductions in other deviant behaviors such as tantrums, aggression, and crying (Wells, Forehand, and Griest, 1980). Untreated siblings also increase their compliance, and it seems likely that this is due, at least in part, to the mother's use of her improved skills with the other children (Humphreys et al., 1978).

It should be noted that there are ethical issues involved in reducing noncompliance in children (Forehand, 1977). Compliance is not always a positive trait, and the ability to say "no" to certain requests is something that seems desirable to either train or retain. In this regard it is important to ensure that parents do not expect 100 percent compliance. This is neither the norm nor desirable in our society. A quiet, docile child should not be the treatment goal.

Firesetting

Ample documentation exists that juvenile firesetting produces serious damage in terms of loss of life, injury, and property damage. It is also associated with serious difficulties for the child, family, and community (Kolko, 1985). Although firesetting by young people has come to the attention of clinicians and fire officials for a considerable period of time, it is only recently that this problem has received systematic attention.

Kolko and Kazdin (1986) have proposed a tentative model of firesetting behavior. Their conceptualization focuses on risk factors that make firesetting likely to occur. These risks are divided into three domains: learning experiences and cues, personal repertoires, and parent and family influences and stressors. This tentative model is presented in Table 8–6. The relative importance and stability of each of these factors and their relationship to one another are as yet unknown. The issue of the sequencing of these influences also remains to be clarifed. Finally, these factors may not encompass all of the possible influences on firesetting. What the model does provide is a basis for organizing what we do know and suggestions for future investigation.

Support for some aspects of the model was obtained through development of the Firesetting Risk Inventory (FRI) (Kolko and Kazdin, 1989). Parents of firesetters and nonfiresetters from three samples (nonpatients, outpatients, and inpatients) completed the interview. The FRI tapped di-

mensions specific to fire and dimensions not specific to fire. Firesetters were described as showing more curiosity about fire and involvement in fire-related activities, being exposed more to peers and family members who are involved with fire, and eliciting more complaints about the child's firesetting behavior. Firesetters also were viewed as exhibiting higher levels of negative social behaviors, more frequently exposed to harsh discipline, and seemed less affected by mild punishment for general misbehavior.

What information is available about the

TABLE 8–6 A Proposed Model of Risk Factors of Fireplay and Fire Setting

---

1. Learning experiences and cues
   a. Early modeling (vicarious) experiences
   b. Early interest and direct experiences
   c. Availability of adult models and incendiary materials
2. Personal repertoire
   a. Cognitive components
      (1) Limited fire-awareness and fire-safety skills
   b. Behavioral components
      (1) Interpersonal ineffectiveness/skills deficits
      (2) Covert antisocial behavior excesses
   c. Motivational components
3. Parent and family influences and stressors
   a. Limited supervision and monitoring
   b. Parental distance and uninvolvement
   c. Parental pathology and limitations
   d. Stressful external events

From Kolko and Kazdin, 1986. Reprinted by permission from Plenum Publishing Corporation.

emergence of firesetting suggests that fireplay is probably a part of normal development for many children as well as those who become firesetters (Kolko, 1985). It seems likely that interest in fire is almost universal and fireplay occurs in a very large proportion of preschool children. However, this early interest along with the early presence of models to imitate may then be followed by additional later models and/or easy access to materials. This provides a possible context and the beginnings for the firesetting problem.

What other factors may distinguish those children who actually set fires? One frequently cited factor based on clinical experience is the lack of social competence and difficulties in interpersonal situations. Indeed, a comparison of inpatient firesetters and other children hospitalized for a psychological disorder indicated that the firesetters possessed poorer social skills (Kolko, Kazdin, and Meyer, 1985). Some workers view this deficiency as resulting in an inability to express anger effectively. Indeed,

Fascination with fire is common among children. It may be that this initial interest, combined with the presence of other influences, sets the stage for the problem of firesetting. (Michael Weisbrot/Stock, Boston)

subcategories of firesetters based on the presence or absence of anger have been suggested. This relates to the issue of the motivation for firesetting. The distinction is often made between those who set fires as a form of aggression and those who set fires without an awareness of the consequences (e.g., curiosity, retardation). Thus, some children may actually become firesetters due to a lack of awareness of the consequences of firesetting.

It has also been suggested that firesetting is part of a cluster of *covert* antisocial behaviors. These concealed or unobserved behaviors include destruction of property, stealing, lying, and truancy. In a controlled study with inpatients, it was found that firesetters engaged in more of these kinds of behaviors than did nonfiresetters. In contrast, the two groups were not different in aggressive behaviors (Kuhnley, Hendren, and Quinlan, 1982). This is consistent with Loeber and Schmaling's (1985) suggestion that there are two separate clusters of antisocial behavior, one covert and the other overtly confrontative.

The family influences that have been suggested as being related to firesetting resemble those that have been suggested for conduct disorders in general (Kolko, 1989). They include limited supervision and lack of parental involvement, parental pathology, and the presence of stressful life events involving disruptions to the family system. While much of this is based on clinical cases and descriptive reports, controlled research has begun to confirm and clarify aspects of this description.

In examining a sample of severely disturbed children, ages 6 to 12, Kazdin and Kolko (1986) found differences in parental psychological adjustment and marital satisfaction associated with the presence of firesetting. In this sample 20 of the 27 firesetters received a primary or secondary diagnosis of conduct disorder, compared to only 11 of 27 nonfiresetters. The authors were able to compare firesetters and nonfiresetters who either did or did not receive a diagnosis of conduct disorder. They found significantly higher scores of overall psychological difficulties, and depression in particular, among the mothers of firesetters than among the mothers of nonfiresetters. No such difference existed based on the presence or absence of a conduct disorder diagnosis or the combinations of conduct disorder and firesetting. Similarly, when the marital relationships of these children's parents were evaluated, it was only the presence or absence of firesetting that appeared to be the differentiating factor. Consensus between the parents, expression of affection in the marital relationship, and total marital adjustment were significantly superior in the families of nonfiresetters. Thus, even in families that have a severely disturbed child (both conduct disorder and nonconduct disorder), families of firesetters appear to differ from those of nonfiresetters.

Many of these and similar findings have led some workers to suggest a particular conceptualization of many firesetting children. In this conceptualization, firesetting represents a later stage in the progression of antisocial symptoms to behaviors that are more extreme, may occur at a low rate, and be covert (cf. Kolko and Kazdin, 1986; Patterson, 1982). Indeed, this view is consistent with the more general conceptualizations of an orderly progression of antisocial behavior from higher to lower rate symptoms, from less to more extreme forms of behavior, and from more overt to more covert expressions (e.g., Kazdin, 1985; Patterson, 1982).

Juvenile Delinquency

The problem of definition. The term *delinquency* is a legal rather than a psychological one. It refers to a juvenile (usually under 18) who has committed an index crime or a status offense. An index crime is an act that would be illegal for adults as well (e.g., theft, aggravated assault, rape, or murder). A status offense is an act that is illegal only for juveniles (e.g., truancy, association with "immoral" persons, violation of curfews, or incorrigibility). There is little doubt that juvenile crime is a serious problem. It is important, however, to make a distinction between delinquent behavior and what might be called official delinquency.

This distinction is important because some behaviors described as delinquent are quite common. Surveys based on adolescent self-reports show that as many as 80 to 90 percent of youths report involvement in delinquent activity before reaching the age of 18. In contrast, if one examines official records (e.g., police, courts) a much lower rate of delinquency is suggested—15 to 35 percent for males and 2 to 14 percent for females. The estimate of rate varies with the stringency of the definition of "official record" (Moore and Arthur, 1989).

Thus, it appears that delinquent behavior that is relatively minor and does not persist over time is common (e.g., White, Moffitt, and Silva, 1989). Such behavior is not usually considered by professionals as an indication of persistent psychological or social difficulties, but is more likely to be thought of as within the normal range of adolescent experimentation. Indeed, it would appear that approximately half of official delinquents commit only one offense. The probability of future delinquent acts rises dramatically, however, with each additional adjudicated offense, continuing into adulthood, and these recidivists account for a vast majority of juvenile offenses (Moore and Arthur, 1989). These chronic delinquents appear to start their career early. For example, Tolan (1987) reported that commiting a first juvenile offense before the age of 12 was the single best predictor of the seriousness, number, and variety of future offenses.

It is important to recognize that whether an act by a juvenile is classified as official delinquency may depend as much on the actions of others as it does on the youth's behavior. The norm violation must, of course, be noticed by someone and be reported to a law-enforcement official. A police officer can then arrest the youth or merely issue a warning. If the youth is arrested, he or she may or may not be brought to court. Once in juvenile court, only some individuals receive the legal designation of delinquent; others may be warned or released in the custody of their parents. Various definitions of delinquency can be used anywhere in this process. And then of course many individuals apparently commit offenses but don't get caught.

Causes and correlates of delinquency. The issues of definition and methodology can readily be seen when one examines the research on correlates of delinquency. The relationship between variables such as social class, race, and gender to delinquency provides a good example. Comparisons based on official records often indicate greater delinquency among lower-class and minority youths and boys. However, self-report delinquency surveys that rely on confidential reports of behaviors by the youths themselves are less likely to find these differences (Moore and Arthur, 1989). This set of findings has led some to conclude that reported differences based on social class, race, gender, and other variables such as having a family member with a criminal record were due to selection of certain groups for prosecution and not to real delinquency-related differences. Subsequent reviews, however, suggest that such bias is not as strong as originally proposed (e.g., Moore and Arthur, 1989; Rutter and Giller, 1984; West, 1985). Self-report studies may have given too much weight to minor and occasional misbehavior that may be quite widespread. However, if one compares youths who admit to more serious and frequent misconduct to those who are convicted delinquents, the populations emerge as alike on the variables studied. Indeed, youths who have high scores on self-reports of offenses are also likely to have official conviction records. For example, West (1982) found that almost half of the 16-year-old boys with high self-report scores had a juvenile conviction record compared to only 11 percent of boys with lower scores. Furthermore, 44 percent of the boys

with higher scores and only 15 percent of others had a criminal record in later years.

These findings suggest that while it is likely that certain advantaged youngsters probably do avoid the legal designation of delinquent, this in and of itself is probably not sufficient to explain differences in delinquency among certain social groups. Real associations between delinquency and social class, for example, probably do exist. They are, however, probably more moderate than once contended and it still largely remains to be explained what it is about lower social status that makes such youths prone to delinquency (Rutter and Giller, 1984).

What else do we know about the correlates of serious delinquency? They seem to be much the same as those described earlier in the chapter as related to conduct disorders in younger children. Indeed, as we have already seen, early evidence of antisocial and aggressive behavior is one of the best predictors of the later delinquency. This continuity of antisocial behavior, at least as defined by convictions for legal offenses, seems to reach its peak in adolescence and early adulthood and then to rapidly decrease between the ages of 20 to 25. However, for a minority of delinquents this criminal pattern does continue into adulthood. Indeed, individuals with adult criminal records, but no history of juvenile offenses, are rare. The identification of this persistent antisocial subgroup is of obvious importance. A number of studies suggest that the earlier existence of the cluster of aggressive and antisocial behaviors described for conduct-disordered children coupled with parental criminality, ineffective supervision, and living in a "delinquent" neighborhood are predictive of belonging to this subgroup. West (1982), for example, found that being judged by teachers as part of the worst 10 percent of the school population in terms of behavior coupled with criminality in the family allowed the identification of 10-year-old boys who had an even chance of persisting in criminal offenses into adulthood.

While the majority of efforts have focused on identifying influences associated with later delinquency and criminality, another perspective is possible. Not all individuals high on these risk factors become delinquents. This has led some to search for protective factors. Rutter and Giller's (1984) review suggests several protective influences: peer groups, employment, marriage, changed environmental circumstances, one good relationship, compensatory good experiences, and the existence of coping mechanisms. Protection can also be conceptualized in terms of stressors. It may take a number of stressors to achieve a negative outcome or the impact of a particular stressor may be greater if others are present. Perhaps, then, the absence of certain combinations of stressors serves as a protective factor.

Subtypes of delinquency. Clinicians and researchers tend to agree that delinquents are a heterogeneous group. However, disagreements exist on whether subclassification is useful, and if so, how to do it. As mentioned above, the seriousness of the delinquency, defined by such considerations as frequency and the seriousness and range of offenses, seems to be an important dimension. It is not clear at present, however, that specific subcategories based on this dimension can be created.

A distinction that has received a great deal of attention is that between the socialized and unsocialized delinquent. This distinction is based on the results of factor analytic studies that have distinguished such dimensions, other research, and on clinical observations (Quay, 1986c; Rutter and Giller, 1984). The socialized or subcultural subgroup describes youths who associate with a delinquent subgroup and accept the values of that subculture. This category is defined by such characteristics as (1) has bad companions, (2) steals in company with others, (3) belongs to a gang, or (4) stays away from home and school. These individuals are also described as not experiencing much distress or psychopathology and as not having difficulty relating to peers.

Lower socioeconomic status is frequently suggested as contributing to this form of delinquency. It is presumed that atypical values and norms are supported among lower-class youth. In addition to peer support for antisocial behavior, the real economic, social, and educational problems associated with poor neighborhoods are presumed to encourage antisocial behavior. Yet not all youths from high delinquency areas become delinquent. Subcultural factors, therefore, cannot provide a complete explanation. In an oft-cited series of studies, Glueck and Glueck (1970) compared delinquent and nondelinquent boys from high-crime neighborhoods. A number of factors were more common among the delinquent boys: muscular (mesomorphic) body build, lower verbal IQs than performance IQs, unstable and disorganized homes, and parents with psychological and physical problems.

Other studies support the notion that these youths are disadvantaged in a number of ways. For example, longitudinal studies of Danish boys by Mednick and his colleagues suggest that the relationship between SES and later delinquent and criminal behavior may be mediated by poor educational performance (McGarvey et al., 1981; Moffitt et al., 1981). They hypothesize that SES predicts verbal ability and educational performance. Poor language skills and educational performance in turn lead to criminal activity. This explanation is consistent with a frequently cited association between specific reading difficulties and antisocial behavior. It seems clear that the relationship to reading difficulty is strong and important for prognosis (e.g., Maughan, Gray, and Rutter, 1985). However, the specific mechanisms responsible for the association remain unclear (Rutter, 1989b).

The second dimension identified, unsocialized-psychopathic, is described as applying to delinquents who do not seem to be part of a delinquent subgroup. Furthermore, this subcategory is part of a distinction made for delinquency in which emotional disturbance is present. Delinquent behavior in this unsocialized category is thought to result from disturbances characterized by the conduct-disorder—externalizing dimension described earlier.

Finally, another subgroup of disturbed delinquents has also been described by some workers. Delinquency in this disturbed-neurotic group is thought to be related to the anxiety-withdrawal—internalizing dimension of behavior problems.

Again, some argue that it is not clear whether the socialized-unsocialized distinc- tion constitutes distinct subgroups or is better considered a dimension on which extreme groups clearly differ (e.g., Rutter and Giller, 1984). Neither is it clear that this distinction rests on clusters of behaviors as defined in the factor analytic studies. A single feature such as the presence or absence of enduring peer relationships may be the essential distinction.

BOX 8.2   The use of alcohol and other drugs

The use of illicit substances, once considered an adult problem, is now common among adolescents and preadolescents. In addition to concern about illegal drugs such as marijuana, cocaine/"crack," hallucinogens (e.g., LSD), and heroine, there is concern about abuse of "legal" substances. The use of alcohol, nicotine, psychoactive medications (e.g., stimulants, sedatives), over-the-counter medications (e.g., sleep and weight reductions aids), and inhalants (e.g., glue, paint thinner) are of concern because of their accessibility and negative effects. They may also play a role in starting a young person on a course of long-term and increased substance abuse (Bailey, 1989).

Alcohol is the most commonly used drug among all age groups, including the young. Available reports suggest that the use of other drugs occurs together with the use of alcohol. Indeed, multiple drug use appears to be characteristic of the majority of substance-using adolescents (Clayton, 1986). Thus, much of the information that we have concerning substance abuse by youngsters reports on both alcohol and other drugs.

What constitutes misuse or abuse of alcohol? One extreme would be to view any use of alcohol by a minor as abuse since it is illegal. Less extreme and more prevalent definitions address drinking patterns and related negative consequences (e.g., difficulties with school, legal authorities, peers, or family).

A variety of theories have been offered to explain the origins and maintenance of alcohol abuse (Holden, Moncher, and Schinke, 1990; Maisto and Carey, 1985). No one explanation has received clear acceptance; however, the kinds of influences that these theories highlight are among those that most workers in the field believe may contribute to alcohol abuse by youngsters.

One variety of explanation views adolescence as a period of transition (e.g., Jessor and Jessor, 1977). Certain behaviors mark this transition. For example, use of alcohol is a behavior that may be deemed appropriate for adults but inappropriate for adolescents. A variety of individual differences and environmental and behavioral variables are assumed to affect an individual's rate of transition and thereby the age of onset of these behaviors. This transition notion is consistent with findings that problem drinking in adolescence is not necessarily related to abuse of alcohol as an adult.

Social learning explanations of alcohol or other substance abuse emphasize the variables of exposure and consequences. Exposure to drinking or abstaining models is assumed to provide not only an impetus toward certain behaviors, but also to influence attitudes toward drinking. The child at greatest risk is the child of an alcoholic or other substance abuser (Bailey, 1989). The anticipation of positive or negative consequences for drinking is also a central aspect of such explanations.

A cross-sectional study of students in grades 7 to 12 illustrates the importance of these influences (Akers et al., 1979). Re-

BOX 8.2   The use of alcohol and other drugs

sponses of these students to questionnaires indicated that differential association (involvement in groups that also use alcohol) was the best predictor of alcohol *use*. Attitudes toward alcohol, social and nonsocial reinforcement, and imitation also predicted use. Alcohol *abuse* was also best predicted by differential association, with the next best predictor being the reinforcement variables (drug effects and social reinforcement). Similar conclusions also seem to apply to high school age students. Drug use among eleventh and twelfth graders was highly correlated with whether the youth had friends who used drugs and encouraged drug use. Emotional distress variables were related to drug use (using drugs to alleviate emotional distress) to a much lesser degree (Swaim et al., 1989).

Kandel (1982), who also emphasizes socialization influences, draws on longitudinal studies to posit a developmental sequence. The use of legal drugs such as alcohol and tobacco precede the use of illicit drugs. It is virtually never the case that a nonuser goes directly to the use of illegal drugs. At least four distinct developmental stages in adolescent drug use have been identified: (1) beer or wine; (2) cigarettes or hard liquor, (3) marijuana, and (4) other illicit drugs. It has been suggested that problem drinking may be a fifth stage that occurs between marijuana use and the use of other illicit drugs.

Participation in one stage does not necessarily mean that the young person will progress to the next stage. Only a subgroup at each stage progresses to the next level of use. However, it does appear that the earlier a youngster begins one stage, the greater the likelihood of other drug use (e.g., Windle, 1990). Thus, the earlier legal drugs are used, the greater the likelihood of illicit drug use. Also, heavier use at any stage seems to be associated with "progress" to the next stage.

There is no single factor that can easily explain which youths start or stay on this path. Explanations must include a variety of variables—biological, psychological, and social—that affect development over time (Morrison and Smith, 1987; Newcomb et al., 1986). Prevention and treatment programs for substance abuse need to address these multiple influences and be aware of developmental issues.

Treatment of delinquency. As some observers have noted, interventions with youthful offenders probably depend as much or more on prevailing social and political attitudes as they do on research evidence. Sheldrick (1985) has traced the history of approaches to the problem in Britain. Until the middle 1800s child and adult offenders were treated equivalently under British law. Children were hanged for theft in the eighteenth century. Those who were not dealt with in this manner served sentences in harsh and brutal prisons or were sent to Australia. It was not until the 1900s that children were treated separately from adults and the concept of punishment was supplemented with the notion of reform. Parallel developments took place in the United States.

Beginning in the 1970s attitudes seem to have changed again with the questioning of the value of a treatment orientation. The relative value of treatment versus punishment remains an issue of much debate. The current ambiguity as to whether delinquency is a homogeneous phenomenon, or how to classify it into different types, along with the recognition that only a small proportion of offenders will continue on a delinquent/criminal path, make the issues even more complex.

Reviewers of the treatment research literature agree that conclusions about effectiveness are difficult to draw due to the

Association with a peer group that supports the use of alcohol and other drugs is clearly a contributing influence to the development of substance use and abuse. (Joseph Szabo/Photo Researchers)

and his colleagues (Alexander and Parsons, 1982; Morris, Alexander, and Waldron, 1988). This program seems to integrate behavioral-social learning, cognitive-behavioral, and family systems perspectives. The problem behavior of the child is assumed to serve a function. It is the only way that some of the interpersonal functions of the family can be met. Treatment focuses on the interpersonal processes of the family system. The goals of therapy are to improve the communication skills of families; modify cognitive sets, expectations, attitudes, and affective reactions; and establish new interpretations and meanings of behavior. Evidence supporting this approach has been reported (Alexander, 1973; Alexander and Parsons, 1973; Alexander et al., 1976; Alexander et al., 1989).

Therapists employ a variety of techniques: modeling, prompting, shaping and rehearsing effective communication skills, and feedback and reinforcement for positive changes. In addition, contracting is used to establish reciprocal patterns of positive reinforcement that may have broken down or that rarely existed in these families. For example, a contract regarding a privilege for a certain family member also specifies that person's responsibilities for securing those privileges and provides bonuses for all parties for compliance with the contract.

The program has been demonstrated to improve significantly the interactions of families of status offenders who had been arrested for running away or possessing alcohol. In addition to improved interactions, significantly lower rates of recidivism were also obtained 6 to 18 months following treatment (Alexander and Parsons, 1973; Parsons and Alexander, 1973). Klein, Alexander, and Parsons (1977) also demonstrated a preventive impact for the treatment program. Examination of juvenile court records for siblings of initially referred delinquents indicated that after 2 1/2 to 3 1/2 years siblings from this behavioral-family systems treatment had significantly lower rates of court referrals than siblings from other treatment groups, or nontreated controls. Although this treatment has been

limited availability of methodologically adequate research and a lack of consistent findings (e.g., Kazdin, 1987; Rutter and Giller, 1984; Sheldrick, 1985). However, several approaches are viewed as promising and directions are suggested as potentially fruitful. The problem of reducing juvenile delinquency includes many facets. Alterations in the operation of the legal and policing system are certainly part of such efforts. We will concentrate on those interventions that are likely to involve psychologists, psychiatrists, teachers, and similar professionals.

Family interventions. In general the kinds of interventions such as parent training that have been described as successful with younger conduct-disordered children have been far less successful with adolescents and chronic juvenile delinquents (McMahon and Wells, 1989). In part it may be that these interventions call for families who are willing and able to participate in a demanding and time consuming change process. Many chronic delinquents may not have such families.

A treatment program for delinquents and their families, called functional family therapy, has been developed by Alexander primarily applied to families of status offenders, one report has replicated positive outcomes with families of youths who have committed more serious and repeated offenses (Barton et al., 1985).

The rationale for this approach and the treatment results described suggest that functional family therapy holds some promise. However, as reviewers have indicated, there is considerably less evidence than for other approaches, such as the parent training/family approaches described earlier, and replications of these findings by other groups would be desirable (Dumas, 1989; Kazdin, 1990b). In addition, for more seriously delinquent youths, the question of the availability and ability of families to engage in this process of change can again be questioned.

Institutional and community-based programs. Institutionalization might be considered a traditional and perhaps obvious approach to intervention with delinquents. Reform schools, training schools, and detention centers may include therapeutic, educational, or rehabilitative programming or may only provide custodial care. Evidence that incarceration reduces recidivism is not encouraging (Gibbons, 1976; Griffin and Griffin, 1978). It is likely that persistence of appropriate behavior upon release has as much or more to do with the environment to which the youth returns as it does with the nature of institutional programming. Furthermore, placing youths in institutions may expose them to a pervasive and sophisticated delinquent subculture in which deviant behaviors may be learned and reinforced. This and other concerns have led to attempts to deal with delinquency outside of institutionally based programs.

One approach to this problem has been labeled diversion (Lemert, 1971). The goal is to divert youthful offenders away from the juvenile justice system and to provide services for them through a variety of different agencies (for example, education, job training). It is hoped that by providing adequate skills and avoiding stigmatization

and labeling, recidivism would be reduced. Some have argued that the original intent of these programs has not been fulfilled. Some workers suggest that such programs have increased the numbers of youths involved in legal processing and a number of intended diversion programs seem to have been preempted or co-opted by law enforcement agencies (Lemert, 1981; Rutter and Giller, 1984).

However, such an approach seems promising and indeed minimal and community-based intervention seems appropriate. Given that a large number of delinquents are not destined for careers of crime, even less intensive interventions would appear to be the best strategy for first or minor offenses. However, it must be recognized that some portion of youthful offenders will require additional intervention. In such cases community-based programs that remove the youth from the juvenile justice system seem recommended.

Davidson and his colleagues' examination of treatment alternatives is an example of findings that support such a conclusion (Davidson and Basta, 1988). In one investigation one of several different forms of intervention was provided to 213 male juvenile offenders averaging 14.2 years of age. Youths were randomly assigned to treatments that differed in content; however, all had a college student volunteer who worked with the youth six to eight hours per week in the community. In one of these treatment conditions volunteers were trained in the same setting; however, their weekly supervision was provided by a juvenile court staff member rather than at the university and supervision took place in the court worker's office. The various treatment conditions that took place *entirely* outside the juvenile justice system did not differ from each other. The treatments located outside the juvenile justice system resulted in lower rates of recidivism than for a control group of youths not given treatment but routinely processed by the court. Treatment with a juvenile justice system component, however, did not result in lower recidivism than for this nontreated control group. The results of this intervention program have been replicated in other locations and using other kinds of volunteers and paid staff (Davidson and Basta, 1989). For example, Figure 8–5 illustrates the lower rates of recidivism achieved by youths working with paid project staff in the Adolescent Diversion Project as compared to those processed through juvenile court and those who were simply released to their parents.

Achievement Place is an oft-cited example of a community-based program for delinquent youth, and an example of the many behaviorally based (largely operant) interventions. Achievement Place is a home-style residential treatment program begun in 1967 by the faculty and students of the Department of Human Development at the University of Kansas (Fixsen, Wolf, and Phillips, 1973; Phillips, 1968). It is currently known as the "Teaching-Family Model" (TFM). Adolescents who have legally been declared delinquent or dependent-neglect cases live in a house with two trained teaching-parents. The youths attend school during the day and also have regular work responsibilities. The academic problems, aggression, and other norm-violating behaviors exhibited by these adolescents are viewed as an expression of failures of past environments to teach appropriate behaviors. Accordingly, these deficits are corrected through modeling, practice, instruction, and feedback. The program centers on a token economy in which points and praise are gained for appropriate behaviors and lost for inappropriate behaviors. Points can be used to purchase a variety of privileges that are otherwise unavailable. If a resident meets a certain level of performance, the right to go on a merit system and thus avoid the point system may be purchased. This is seen as providing a transition to usual sources of natural reinforcement and feedback, such as praise, status, and satisfaction. The goal is to gradually transfer a youngster who is able to perform adequately on merit to his or her natural home. Teaching-parents help the natural parents or guardians structure a program to maintain gains made at Achievement Place.

One of the outstanding features of the TFM approach is the large quantity of research the program has produced (cf. Willner et al., 1978). Numerous single-subject design experiments have evaluated the components of the program, thereby suggesting cause-and-effect relationships. The effectiveness of TFM also has been evaluated by its developers and independent investigators (Kirigin et al., 1982; Weinrott, Jones, and Howard, 1982). These evaluations suggest that the TFM approach is more effective than comparison programs while the adolescents are involved in the group-home setting. However, once they leave this setting those differences disappear.

Difficulties in transitions back to the youths' own families and long-term effectiveness are, in general, characteristic of all interventions with this population. The developers of TFM have thus suggested a "long-term supportive family model" in which specially trained foster parents would provide care for a single adolescent into early adulthood (Wolf, Braukman, and Ramp, 1987). Findings from Patterson's group also offer preliminary support for

FIGURE 8–5 Percentage of adolescents having one or more new juvenile court appearances during the treatment period and one-year follow-up for each intervention. Adapted from Davidson and Basta, 1989.

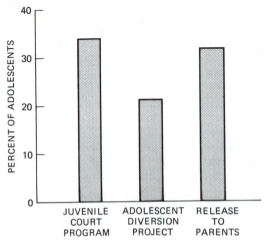

such an approach (Chamberlain 1987, cited in McMahon and Wells 1989).

The difficulties and lack of success achieved in treating conduct-disordered adolescents have led some to suggest a change in the way in which conduct disorders are conceptualized. The suggestion is that the disorder be viewed as "social disability" (Wolf et al., 1987) or as analogous to a chronic physical disease such as diabetes (Kazdin, 1987). These kinds of models suggest not single and short-term treatments, but multiple interventions throughout the child's life—perhaps into early adulthood.

SUMMARY

Aggressive and antisocial behavior are common, and in extreme form, of great concern to families, schools, and society as a whole. These behaviors are more prevalent in boys and are the most common reason for referrals to clinics.

A syndrome designated as Undercontrolled, Externalizing, or Conduct Disorder has been repeatedly identified in empirical approaches to classification. DSM-III-R includes Conduct Disorder within the category of Disruptive Behavior Disorders. Other approaches to classification emphasize the predominant behavior problem and make a distinction between overt and covert behaviors. Distinct developmental paths have also been suggested for different types of conduct disorders.

Conduct-disordered behavior appears to be highly stable. Early conduct-disordered behavior and rejection by peers appears to be related to later antisocial behavior and other negative outcomes.

Family patterns of interacting, parenting skills, and family discord seem to be prominent factors in the development of conduct disorders. Social-cognitive influences and biological influences have also been documented.

The existence of a coercive family environment as an arena for learning aggression has received support from the work of Patterson and others. Disruption of parenting skills is seen as an important factor, and programs that improve parenting skills have proved effective.

Oppositional and noncompliant behavior is a common problem in children. These behaviors are particularly common among children exhibiting other conduct and antisocial behaviors. Interventions based on changing parenting behaviors and focusing on family variables have been successful in reducing noncompliance.

Firesetting has only recently received systematic attention. A variety of risk factors is proposed to account for the emergence of this behavior. It has been suggested that firesetting may represent a later stage in the developmental progression of antisocial behaviors.

Juvenile delinquency is a legal term. Many behaviors described as delinquent are quite common, but official delinquency is much less common. Chronic delinquents account for the majority of offenses and their "careers" are likely to persist into adulthood. The correlates of delinquency are much like those suggested for conduct disorders. Delinquents are a heterogeneous group, however, and controversy exists as to how to best subcategorize the problem. While considerable effort has been directed at the treatment of delinquent behavior, the problem has been difficult to address.

Substance use and abuse, particularly alcohol, are prevalent among adolescents. There appears to be a progression from the use of legal to illegal substances. While there are multiple influences on the use and abuse of drugs, association with peers who use drugs certainly is an important factor.

9

ATTENTION-DEFICIT HYPERACTIVITY DISORDER

He never sits still; he's always into something.

She won't pay attention for one minute.

He doesn't think before he acts.

In school, he's up and out of his seat in a flash.

She just doesn't get along well with others.

He's not doing well in school, and he's two grades behind his age-mates.

These kinds of complaints, commonly voiced by parents and teachers, are the main presenting problems for children who receive the diagnosis of Attention-Deficit Hyperactivity Disorder (ADHD), more commonly known as hyperactivity.

Few disorders of childhood receive as much public interest and controversy as hyperactivity. It was first described in 1845 by the German physician Henrich Hoffman (Cantwell, 1975). In the early twentieth century hyperactivity was variously associated with brain damage, but it was not widely studied until the 1950s. At that time concern was increasing for children with behavior and learning problems (Safer and Allen, 1976). The widespread introduction of pharmacological treatment for hyperactivity in the late 1960s brought additional interest and controversy, which still exist today.

As with other childhood disturbances, recent years have brought shifts in how this disorder is conceptualized and classified. One shift had to do with the specific behaviors emphasized; as these changed so did the name given to the disorder. The second shift had to do with causation. Our discussion will start with a brief history of how the behavioral manifestations of ADHD have been reconceptualized.

CRITERIA FOR ATTENTION-DEFICIT HYPERACTIVITY DISORDER

Early conceptualizations of ADHD emphasized overactivity or motor restlessness, and the terms *hyperkinesis*, *hyperkinetic reaction*, and *hyperkinetic syndrome* were variously ap-

184

plied (Barkley, 1989). However, several other behavioral problems were associated with hyperactivity. By the 1970s the importance of attention deficits and impulsivity was widely recognized. In fact, hyperactivity in itself was downgraded in importance. Moreover, the nature of the activity problem was no longer seen as general motor excess but as a deficit in regulating motor activity in specific situations.

The shift in conceptualization was so important that the category of Attention Deficit Disorder (ADD) appeared in DSM-III (1980), with a subcategory of ADD with Hyperactivity and a subcategory of ADD without hyperactivity. Clearly, attention problems had become central. To receive the diagnosis of ADD with hyperactivity a child had to display attention deficits, impulsive behavior, and hyperactivity.

In DSM-III-R (1987), further change occurred. The disorder was relabeled Attention-Deficit Hyperactivity Disorder (ADHD). The new label echoes the past by giving increased recognition to hyperactivity.

The criteria for ADHD are given in Table 9–1. The diagnosis demands onset before age seven, and the display of symptoms for at least six months. The behavioral manifestations of ADHD reflect difficulties in motor activity, attention, and impulsivity. However, since only 8 of 14 behaviors must be present, diagnosed children may differ in the degree to which they display each of these behavior classes. It is assumed that these difficulties may appear to some degree in normal children and may vary with developmental level. Thus, the diagnosis of ADHD is given only when the behaviors are greater than they would be for normal children of the same developmental age.

In the following section we examine the

TABLE 9–1 DSM-III-R Criteria for Attention-Deficit Hyperactivity Disorder

A. A disturbance of at least six months during which at least eight of the following are present:
1. Often fidgets with hands or feet or squirms in seat (in adolescents, may be limited to subjective feelings of restlessness)
2. Has difficulty remaining seated when required to do so
3. Is easily distracted by extraneous stimuli
4. Has difficulty awaiting turn in game or group situations
5. Often blurts out answers to questions before they have been completed
6. Has difficulty following through on instructions from others (not due to oppositional behavior or failure of comprehension), e.g., fails to finish chores
7. Has difficulty sustaining attention in tasks or play activities
8. Often shifts from one uncompleted activity to another
9. Has difficulty playing quietly
10. Often talks excessively
11. Often interrupts or intrudes on others, e.g., butts into other children's games
12. Often does not seem to listen to what is being said to him or her
13. Often loses things necessary for tasks or activities at school or at home (e.g., toys, pencils, books, assignments)
14. Often engages in physically dangerous activities without considering possible consequences (not for purpose of thrill-seeking), e.g., runs into street without looking

B. Onset before the age of seven

C. Does not meet the criteria for a Pervasive Developmental Disorder

Adapted from DSM-III-R. Reprinted with permission from the *Diagnostic and Statistical Manual of Mental Disorders, Third Edition, Revised.* Washington, DC, American Psychiatric Association, 1987.

three primary manifestations of ADHD and then look at other difficulties often experienced by children who acquire the ADHD label.

PRIMARY BEHAVIOR PROBLEMS

Activity Problems

ADHD children often are described as always on the run, restless, fidgety, and unable to sit still. These children squirm, wiggle, tap their fingers, and elbow their classmates

(Whalen, 1989). All too often they have minor mishaps, such as spilling drinks and knocking over objects, as well as more serious accidents that result in bodily harm. The quality of the motion often seems different from ordinary activity by being excessively energetic, haphazard, disorganized, and lacking in goals. ADHD children appear to have difficulty in regulating their actions according to the wishes of others or the demands of the particular situations.

Much of the information about activity problems comes from parent and teacher reports, although these ratings might reflect the difficulty adults have in managing ADHD children more than hyperactivity itself (Whalen, 1989). More objective assessment can be made with direct observations, and with "wiggle'" cushions and small devices (actometers, pedometers) worn by the child that measure movement. These methods have weaknesses too; for example, they do not distinguish task-related from nontask-related movement (Cammann and Miehlke, 1989). When multiple measures are taken, they correlate with each other only modestly, indicating that hyperactivity has several dimensions. In any event though, considerable individual variation exists in activity level. Moreover, hyperactivity depends on the situation at hand.

The latter was shown in a study that used a special recording device to monitor motor activity continuously over days (Porrino et al., 1983). Hyperactive boys were more active than controls when reading and doing

Many children are highly active. The term "hyperactivity" is applied only when activity level goes beyond what is considered age-appropriate and has a restless, fidgety quality.

math in school, playing on the weekends, and sleeping. They were not more active during school physical education, and lunch/recess. Another investigation showed that control children were less active in regular compared to open-structure classrooms, but hyperactive children did not modulate their actions according to room structure (Jacob, O'Leary, and Rosenblad, 1978). In general, motor excess is more likely in highly structured situations than in relaxed settings with fewer external demands. And the high intensity and inappropriateness of motor activity may be more problematic than its frequency and duration (Whalen 1989).

Attention Deficits

The attention problems of ADHD children show up in various ways. Parents report that, compared to most of their peers, these children skip rapidly from one activity to another and do not pay attention to what they say. Teachers complain of lack of attention to directions, poor concentration, and "off-task" behavior.

Attention has multiple dimensions, however, and so efforts have been made to understand what specific attentional processes might be disordered. One hypothesis suggests a deficit in *selective attention*; that is, in the ability to attend to relevant environmental stimuli or ignore irrelevant stimuli. Some studies indicate that the introduction of irrelevant stimuli does disrupt ADHD children. Others indicate little disruption or that in any event performance is no more impeded in ADHD children than in normal children (Whalen, 1989). Certain conditions may especially elicit distractibility; for example, boring, distasteful, difficult tasks and salient or novel distractors (Douglas, 1983). Nevertheless, the research evidence does not, on balance, strongly support the selective attention hypothesis (Barkley, 1989; Douglas, 1983; Whalen, 1989). Moreover, attempts to help ADHD children by placing them in simple environments that restrict irrelevant stimuli do not appear effective. In some cases, irrelevant stimuli even enhance performance (van der Meere and Sergeant, 1988b).

Perhaps the most widely accepted hypothesis about attention is that *sustained attention* is deficient. Sustained attention refers to the child's maintaining attention to a task over a period of time. Off-task behavior in school and at home could reflect

such a deficit. In the laboratory, sustained attention has often been tested with the Continuous Performance Test (CPT). The child is presented with a series of stimuli, such as letters, and must press a button upon the appearance of one of the letters that has been specified as the target or signal. Errors can be made by not reacting to the target, which shows lack of attention or vigilance, and by reacting to nontarget stimuli, which may show inattention or impulsivity. ADHD children have often been shown to make more of both errors and to be slower on the CPT than normal children and children with other diagnoses (Douglas, 1983; Barkley, 1988a).

However it is questionable that this is sufficient evidence for a deficit in sustained attention per se. Since ADHD is a classificatory variable (p. 79), perhaps group differences result from differences in motivation, cooperation, and the like. Some researchers also argue that a better test of sustained attention would evaluate performance over time. A true deficit would lead to a worsening of performance as the length of the task increased. When comparisons are made in this situation, the results are mixed. Sometimes ADHD children do less well over time than controls, but in other studies their performances are not worse (Prior et al., 1985; van der Meere and Sergeant, 1988a). Perhaps this inconsistency is due to research confounds, but it does raise questions about sustained attention in ADHD (Seidel and Joschko, 1990).

Another issue is whether the monotonous and artificial tasks of the CPT actually relate to the everyday demands put on children. This concern has been lessened by the finding that ADHD children react similarly on the CPT and in the classroom (Whalen, 1989). Overall, the hypothesis about sustained attention has some support, and it is widely recognized that ADHD children have difficulty in maintaining attention during routine activities.

Impulsivity

The third componenet of ADHD is impulsivity. The essence of impulsivity is a deficiency in inhibiting behavior, which appears as "acting without thinking." The child may jump in and try to fix something before figuring out the first step, or run out into a busy street without first looking for traffic. In the classroom, impulsivity may be displayed by calling out, interrupting others, and cutting in front of others in line. Such behavior is not hostile in intent; rather, the child seems unable to hold back or control behavior.

In the laboratory, the main task for measuring impulsivity is the Matching Familiar Figures Test (MFFT). Children are presented with a set of pictures that vary slightly and are asked to select the one that best matches a standard picture. Relatively fast selection and errors in matching across different sets of pictures are taken as indicators of impulsivity. Both measures have been found to discriminate ADHD and normal children at various ages, and to correlate with playroom measures of activity level (Barkley, 1988a; Douglas, 1983). Nevertheless, limitations of this test have been noted. Whalen (1989) reports that the MFFT "more than rarely" fails to discriminate ADHD and may even show superior performance for ADHD children. Questions also have been raised about just what the MFFT measures. Correct matching, for example, may tap more general cognitive functioning rather than impulsivity.

Thus, as with activity and attention deficits, impulsivity has several dimensions and there is some difficulty in conceptualizing and measuring it. Nevertheless, ADHD children show a range of behaviors that are captured—perhaps imperfectly—by the term impulsivity.

SECONDARY BEHAVIOR PROBLEMS

The behaviors we have just discussed are central in ADHD, but as a group ADHD children experience several additional difficulties, including more than their share of motor incoordination, enuresis, encopresis, language problems, chronic health problems, depression, and low self-esteem (Dulcan, 1989). More consistently found than these, however, are academic and conduct/social difficulties.

Academic Performance

Evidence about the performance of ADHD children on general intelligence tests suggests that many fall into the normal range but that deficits exist for others, perhaps especially when there is nervous system dysfunction or learning problems (August and Garfinkel, 1989; Weiss and Hechtman, 1986). Academic failure, however, is common as indicated by achievement test scores, school grades, failure to get promoted in school, and placement in special education classes (Dulcan, 1989). In one sample of U.S. boys, about 75 percent were underachieving in reading, spelling, and mathematics (Cantwell, 1986). More than one-third were performing a full grade level below their expected level in at least two academic subjects. A large study of New Zealand children similarly indicated that 80 percent had various learning problems, with

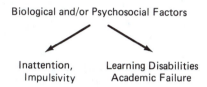

FIGURE 9-1 Possible initial causal links between ADHD and academic failure.

about one-half having difficulties in at least two areas (McGee and Share, 1988). It has been reported that by the time hyperactive children reach adolescence, 50 to 60 percent have repeated one grade, and some have repeated two or more (Milich and Loney, 1979).

Due to academic failure and because many ADHD children perform less well than would be predicted from their general intelligence, many are said to display learning disabilities. Estimates of the percentage of ADHD children who have learning disabilities vary greatly—from 9 to 92 percent depending no doubt on actual differences among the samples as well as on varying criteria for the two disorders (Shaywitz and Shaywitz, 1988; Whalen, 1989).

Although the relationship between ADHD and academic failure is well established, the reasons for the link are not (McGee and Share, 1988). Several possibilities exist, and causation may vary from child to child (Figure 9–1). In some cases, core deficits in attention and impulsivity may interfere with learning. In others, learning difficulties may create an array of behavioral problems: inattention/inpulsivity, low motivation and self-concept, aggression and other externalizing actions. Or perhaps behavioral and learning deficits occur simultaneously but more or less independently, due to common biological or environmental factors. In all of these models, once initial causation gets underway a more complex causal chain might operate, with all factors influencing others.

Investigations are being conducted to find out more about cognitive functioning in ADHD that might help explain academic difficulties. Children have been evaluated on a broad array of tasks (Benezra and Douglas, 1988; Douglas, 1983). Although some deficits have been found, results are inconsistent and incomplete. There is reason to suspect deficits in the processing of information when the task is difficult and requires sophisticated strategies. But we are far from understanding cognition in ADHD. The degree to which any such deficits overlap with academic failure or uniquely define ADHD remains to be discovered (McGee and Share, 1988).

Conduct and Social Problems

Misconduct and social problems are reported in high percentages of ADHD children, often in the 80 percent range (Safer and Allen, 1976; Whalen and Henker, 1985). Such troublesome behavior may lead adults to seek professional help even more than the primary problems of the disorder.

How do ADHD children actually behave

to upset others? Whalen and Henker (1985) describe their behavior as falling into four categories.

First, ADHD children are bothersome, intractable, and socially awkward. In the classroom, they are disruptive and noncompliant; at home and in play, they tend to be disagreeable, noncompliant, and involved in other negative social interactions. Some social situations are difficult for many children at certain developmental levels (e.g., sitting through adults' conversations). But ADHD youngsters seem unable to meet even the ordinary demands of living, such as going to a shopping mall or playing with acquaintances. The annoying and inappropriate quality of their actions often seems unintentional, and the negative reactions of others sometimes take the child by surprise. Indeed, the child's intent may be altruistic, as in the case of a ten-year-old who, in trying to help a man in a wheelchair while balancing a carton of milk, succeeded in dribbling more and more milk on the man. Such an isolated incident would not in itself be disastrous, but ADHD children all too often get in "trouble" in situations that they ought to be able to handle.

Second, ADHD children are socially busy—perhaps more than their age-mates. They often are talkative and they often initiate social exchanges. Some interactions are clearly prosocial. Nevertheless, perhaps high social activity puts them at risk for negative interpersonal experiences. And it is likely that their social behavior falls short in subtle ways with regard to style, content, and appropriateness.

Third, many ADHD youngsters also are highly aggressive, both verbally and physically. This puts them at risk for being disliked and excluded, thereby missing opportunities for social learning.

Fourth, ADHD children are socially salient and intense. They tend to be louder, faster, and more forceful than peers. Their high level of vigor and intensity frequently is out of keeping with the social situation, social expectations, and the needs of others. By no means is this style continuous or unaffected by environmental changes. As with other kinds of behaviors, ADHD children show a good deal of variation.

Nevertheless, social problems are sufficiently pervasive to be reflected in the ways that others judge and behave with these children. Other youngsters view ADHD children as troublesome, noisy, sad, and unhappy; they tend to dislike and reject them (Flicek and Landau, 1985; Pope, Bierman, and Mumma, 1987). Moreover, sibling pairs that contain a hyperactive child show much more negative behavior than pairs without a hyperactive child (Mash and Johnston, 1983). And teachers and parents tend to be more directive, controlling, and intrusive with ADHD children compared to normal children (Barkley, 1988a; Whalen and Henker, 1985).

Several mechanisms have been proposed to explain the social problems of ADHD children, including deficits in social information processing and reasoning, deviant social goals, and the expectations of others (Whalen, Henker, and Granger, 1990). So far little is understood, however.

In looking at all of the behaviors that characterize ADHD, the disorder is increasingly conceptualized as a deficiency in the regulation of behavior by its consequences (Barkley, 1989). Perhaps there is a greater need for arousal, a higher threshold for reinforcement, or underactivity in the inhibitory system. Such deficits could interfere with the regulation of behavior by reinforcement and punishment. For example, the child may require greater reinforcement to maintain responses or greater punishment to inhibit action. Regulatory problems may then adversely affect academic learning, rule adherence, and social interactions and relationships.

ISSUES IN CLASSIFICATION

Problems concerning classification of ADHD have plagued researchers and clinicians for a long time and continue to do so. We will deal here with two important issues: (1) the problem of overlap with other diagnostic categories and (2) the distinction between pervasive and situational ADHD.

ADHD and Other Diagnostic Categories

Given the previous discussion, it should come as no surprise that distinguishing ADHD from learning disabilities and conduct disorders has been troublesome. Chapter 11 further addresses the overlap with learning disabilities; in this section we continue to examine the overlap with conduct disorders.

One of the most confusing issues in classification is whether ADHD can be reasonably distinguished from Conduct Disorder (Quay, Routh, and Shapiro, 1987). That the two disorders are similar is reflected in DSM-III-R by both being listed as Disruptive Behavior Disorders. There is no doubt that a portion of ADHD children display conduct disorder/aggression, and that some conduct disordered children show ADHD behaviors (Szatmari, Boyle, and Offord, 1989). Depending on the sample, 30 to 90 percent of children in one category will also be classified in the other (Hinshaw, 1987). Some researchers argue that the behavioral manifestations, etiology, and outcomes are so similar that a distinction between the disorders is unwarranted (Prior and Sanson, 1986; Whalen, 1989).

A large number of investigations have now compared children diagnosed as ADHD or conduct disordered (CD). Despite methodological weakness and some inconsistent results, the findings appear to show sufficient differences to validate the categories (Loney and Milich, 1982; Szatmari, Boyle, and Offord, 1989; Whalen, 1989). For example, ADHD is more likely to be associated with cognitive impairment and neurodevelopmental abnormalities. Conduct disorder appears more strongly related to adverse family factors and psychosocial disadvantage.

Some investigations have subgrouped ADHD children on the basis of whether or not they also display conduct disorder/aggression. The behaviors that differentiate the subgroups are hostile and defiant actions, such as temper outbursts, argumentativeness, and unpredictable explosive behaviors (Barkley, et al., 1989). The subgroups have been compared to each other and in some cases to a "pure" conduct disordered group. Differences are evident in several social, academic, and family factors (Hinshaw, 1987). For example, children showing conduct problems are more likely to have poorer peer relationships and family dysfunction (Barkley et al., 1989). Findings are not completely consistent, though, and more research is needed. The potential importance of this research can be seen in the following study.

Schachar and Wachsmuth (1990) found that ADHD + CD and CD boys showed a stronger history of parental psychopathology than ADHD boys without CD and normal control children. The latter two groups did not differ from each other. Differences did exist between the ADHD + CD and CD groups in, for example, types of parental psychopathology. This suggests that CD that goes with ADHD develops under different circumstances. The study also underlines the importance of distinguishing ADHD children who do and do not display conduct disordered behaviors. Results of other research shows that ADHD with conduct disorder may put children at greater risk for certain problems in adulthood than ADHD with no conduct problems (Hinshaw, 1987).

Overall, then, this research appears to holds promise for better understanding the overlap between ADHD and Conduct Disorder and recognizing differences that may exist in subgroups of ADHD children.

Situational and Pervasive ADHD

As previously mentioned, the primary behavioral manifestations of ADHD depend somewhat on the settings in which they are measured. ADHD children are more like normal children in low-demand situations, are less disruptive and more compliant with fathers than mothers, display fewer behavior problems in novel and unfamiliar settings, and have fewer attention deficits when task behavior is immediately reinforced and noncompliance punished (Barkley, 1989).

Related to these findings, the hypothesis has been put forth that some children are pervasively inattentive, hyperactive, and impulsive; that is, display problems in many different situations, with teachers, peers, and parents. In contrast, other children are said to show disturbed behavior in relatively few situations, with teachers, peers, or parents but not all three. Such a distinction could be important were it to relate to other characteristics of the children or predict degree of disturbance, outcome, or treatment effects.

Attempts to categorize ADHD children on this basis and to find important correlates show mixed results (Barkley, 1988a). Some evidence exists that pervasive ADHD is linked with cognitive deficits and stability over time (Gillberg and Gillberg, 1988; Rutter, 1989b). British workers in particular look for pervasive symptoms, as well as cognitive deficits, when diagnosing ADHD (Hinshaw, 1987). Short of finding them, they tend to use the diagnosis of Conduct Disorder. This diagnostic difference probably accounts for the fact that ADHD is reported less often in Britain than in the United States; in fact, a twentyfold discrepancy exists in the rate of ADHD in these countries (Taylor, 1988).

PREVALENCE

The prevalence of ADHD is frequently estimated at about 3 percent of the school-age population (DSM-III-R, 1987). However, the data have shown much variation, reaching as high as 20 percent (August and Garfinkel, 1989; Trites et al., 1979). Variation can be accounted for by differences in criteria, raters, measuring instruments, and cutoff points on any one instrument.

More boys than girls consistently receive the diagnosis of ADHD, with the ratio of perhaps six to nine boys to one girl in clinic samples. In the general population the ratio is much smaller, perhaps 3:1 (DSM-III-R, 1987; James and Taylor, 1990).

There is some evidence that ADHD is associated with low social class or psychosocial adversity (Rutter, 1989b). Cross-cultural variation also has been noted (O'Leary, Vivian, and Nisi, 1985), but differences in diagnostic practices make interpretation difficult.

ETIOLOGY

The search for causes of ADHD implicates several variables, many of which are biological or thought to affect biological functioning. Much of the research is correlational and causation often is not determined. It is worthwhile to remember that most ADHD children are normal with respect to any variable that has been implicated (Whalen, 1989). Conversely, many children who are positive for the variable, do not display ADHD behaviors.

Biological Functioning

Brain damage. Brain damage or injury was once seen as a primary cause of ADHD behaviors. The hypothesis stemmed from the links between brain damage in adults and behavioral deficits, such as language loss or behavioral rigidity and disorganization (Bryan and Bryan, 1975). Research with children who had suffered from an epidemic of encephalitis after World War I showed various behavioral problems, including inattention and hyperactivity (Kessler, 1980).

Soon investigators attributed these and other behavioral disturbances to brain damage without evidence that damage actually existed. For example, Kahn and Cohen (1934) attributed school problems (hyperactivity, distractibility, impulsivity, poor attention) to brain stem lesions (Satz and Fletcher, 1980). Laufer and Denhoff (1957) defined the hyperkinetic impulse disorder and presumed brain dysfunction, while Strauss and Lechtinen (1947) suggested that distractibility or hyperactivity was the fundamental sign of brain injury (Kessler, 1988).

When it became evident that brain damage could not be identified in most children who showed these difficulties, minimal brain damage was assumed. This approach was eventually criticized on the basis of its being circular: Brain dysfunction can lead to certain signs, so the presence of these signs means the existence of brain dysfunction (Satz and Fletcher, 1980). Such circularity can be misleading. Moreover, it appears that although brain damage can lead to ADHD-like behaviors it is not a major cause of ADHD (Anastopoulos and Barkley, 1988).

CNS dysfunction. Recent advances in studying the central nervous system do suggest, however, that some kind of brain dysfunction may exist in ADHD. Various parts of the brain have been studied (Anastopoulos and Barkley, 1988; Zametkin and Rapoport, 1986). There is particular interest in the frontal and frontal-limbic areas. ADHD children have been found to have both decreased blood flow and decreased EEG activation in the frontal lobes, and parents of ADHD children who themselves displayed ADHD behaviors had lowered metabolism in the frontal area.

For some time it has been hypothesized that the arousal-inhibitory processes of the brain are abnormal (Ferguson and Pappas, 1979). Intuitively, it seems that these pro-

cesses might go hand in hand with excessive activity and inattention. Furthermore, drugs that are beneficial in some cases of ADHD appear related to these processes. Interestingly, both overarousal and underarousal have been proposed as underlying ADHD. Research testing the hypotheses has had methodological problems, and the findings are mixed. Nevertheless, the weight of the evidence favors the idea that ADHD children are underaroused or underreactive to stimulation (Anastopoulos and Barkley, 1988; Whalen, 1989; Zemetkin and Rapoport, 1986). This fits nicely with the theoretical notion that all organisms seek optimal stimulation and that ADHD children are excessively active in order to obtain stimulation (Zentall and Meyer, 1987). All of these findings are indeed exciting, but a word of caution is appropriate: The findings are extremely complex and at best preliminary (e.g., Jacobvitz et al., 1990).

Biochemistry. Unsurprisingly, recent investigations have tried to identify abnormalities in central nervous system neurotransmitters. Most emphasis has been given to norepinephrine, dopamine, and serotonin (Shaywitz et al., 1983).

Typical of this kind of research, one approach has examined the biochemistry of urine, plasma, blood, platelets, and cerebrospinal fluid (Zemetkin and Rapoport, 1987). Consistent differences between ADHD children and controls have not been found for these measures.

Another approach has examined the behavioral effects of certain drugs known or thought to influence the suspected neurotransmitters. The best evidence implicates the neurotransmitters norepinephrine and dopamine. However, the evidence does not fit into a neat package and is not strong (Zemetkin and Rapoport, 1986). Still, given that these neurotransmitters are considered important in the functioning of the frontal-limbic areas of the brain, the finding is consistent with other evidence implicating these brain areas (Anastopoulos and Barkley, 1988).

Many difficulties are inherent in biochemical research, not the least of which are the intricacies of the neurotransmitter systems. And establishing a link between ADHD and neurotransmitter abnormalities would still leave the question of cause and effect unanswered (Whalen, 1989). Neurotransmitters must somehow affect behavior, but the opposite also may occur.

Neurological immaturity. Another hypothesis is that the nervous system functions normally but its development is delayed (Anastopoulos and Barkley, 1988). This idea does not necessarily imply that ADHD children will catch up with their peers. Support for the hypothesis comes from studies sug-

gesting that ADHD children function in ways that are similar to younger normal children. The data include measures of attention, impulsiveness, activity level, social interaction, and brain wave activity. The presence of neurological soft signs—clumsiness, poor balance and coordination, abnormal reflexes—can also be considered a sign of immaturity. Several studies have shown high rates of soft signs (Whalen, 1989). However, such deficits are not consistently found, and their interpretation is questioned. The idea of neurological immaturity has some preliminary support, but awaits further evaluation.

Genetics

Not infrequently parents with high-activity children come into clinics expressing the belief that such disturbance runs in families. For example, a client of one of the authors claimed that many of her hyperactive child's cousins behaved like her child. This mother suspected hereditary transmission. Although her observation may indeed have been accurate, research has only slowly provided some support for this idea.

To begin with, activity level appears to have a constitutional basis in the general child population (e.g., Buss and Plomin, 1986). This suggests that the range of activity level in nonclinic children may be genetically influenced.

There is evidence that the parents and siblings of ADHD children show higher

than would be expected rates of the disorder (Barkley, 1989; Biederman et al., 1986). A limited number of adoption studies point to some genetic transmission (Heffron, Martin, and Welsh, 1984). In one study, for example, over 20 percent of the biological parents but only 4 percent of the adoptive parents of ADHD children had histories of ADHD (Deutsh, 1979, cited by Barkley, 1989). Twin comparisons, although few in number, support the genetic hypothesis by showing greater concordance in identical pairs (Goodman and Stevenson, 1989; Lopez, 1965; Heffron et al., 1984). Nevertheless, it is difficult to draw conclusions about the role of heredity in ADHD due to limitations in the research (Rutter et al., 1990b).

Pregnancy and Birth Complications

The popular idea that ADHD is traceable to pregnancy and birth complications has not received strong support (Anastopoulos and Barkley, 1988; Goodman and Stevenson, 1989; Whalen, 1989). Perhaps this is unsurprising, in light of the evidence that environmental conditions can moderate the potential adversities of pregnancy and birth complications (p. 32).

There is reason to suspect, however, that maternal alcohol consumption may be related to increased rates of ADHD (cf. Streiss-

guth et al., 1984, 1989). In an extensive study that followed 1,500 women from pregnancy to the time their children were seven years old, alcohol use was linked to activity level, attention deficits, and difficulties in organizing tasks.

ADHD children also show a higher than usual incidence of minor physical abnormalities (MPAs). Over 35 of these abnormalities have been identified by researchers; examples are asymmetrical or low-seated ears and a wide gap between the first and second toes (Whalen, 1989). Most of the abnormalities are frequently found in the general population, with perhaps two to four occurring in persons with no known physiological or psychological disorders. Higher numbers are found in a variety of disturbances, such as autism and Down's Syndrome. As MPAs develop during the first three months of pregnancy, they suggest prenatal or genetic causation (Anastopoulos and Barkley, 1988).

Diet

Two aspects of diet have especially been considered: (1) food additives and salicylates and (2) sugar.

In 1975, Feingold, a physician researcher interested in allergies, published a book *Why Your Child is Hyperactive* that inspired both controversy and investigation into dietary effects on hyperactivity. Feingold asserted that food containing artificial dyes and flavors, certain preservatives, and naturally occurring salicylates (for example, in apricots, prunes, tomatoes, cucumbers) was related to hyperactivity. He claimed that 25 to 50 percent of hyperactive–learning-disabled children responded favorably to diets that eliminated these substances (Harley and Matthews, 1980; Tryphonas, 1979). On the other hand, it was claimed that when children on the diet ingested a prohibited food, hyperactivity occurred dramatically and persisted for two to three days. Feingold's position received pervasive media coverage and was rapidly espoused by many parents, who reported impressive anecdotes about behavioral improvement in their children on Feingold's diet. Some of the fanfare undoubtedly was due to the fact that Feingold advocated the diet for mental retardation, delinquency, learning problems, and autism as well as for hyperactivity. Evaluation by skeptical committees called for well designed research to examine the efficacy of the Feingold diet.

Conners and his colleagues were among the first to examine hyperactive children while they were on a special diet and while they were on a control diet. Teachers, but not parents, found the diet more effective, as measured by the Conners rating scale. Subsequently, three "challenge" studies were run in which children who were on the Feingold diet and had shown improvement were "challenged" by a cookie with food dyes or a cookie with no dyes. The results were ambiguous but for the most part did not support Feingold's claims (Conners, 1980). Other research is consistent with this finding (Gross, et al., 1987; Harley and Matthews, 1980; Spring, Chiodo, and Bowen, 1987).

Nevertheless, some researchers point to evidence that a small number of hyperactive children benefit from special diets (Marshall, 1989; Weiss, 1982). Furthermore, some data indicate that these children have higher than usual rates of allergies and that allergies other than food allergies could be involved (e.g., pollen, mold). Marshall (1989) suggests that severe allergies combined with stressors might play a role in the etiology of a subgroup of ADHD.

Anecdotal reports of the effects of sugar are commonly made. Many parents of hyperactive and normal children say that sugar intake causes their offspring to become hyperactive and disorganized. A limited number of correlational studies shows a link between sugar consumption and restless and destructive-aggressive behavior in hyperactive children (e.g., Prinz, Roberts, and Hantman, 1980). A study by Prinz and Riddle (1986) showed that nondisturbed boys who consumed high levels of sugar had deficits on the Continuous Performance Test similar to hyperactive children's. It is difficult to interpret these correlations. Perhaps sugar intake affects behavior, but alternative explanations can be offered; for example, perhaps high activity and consumption of excess sugar are both due to a high metabolic rate (Spring et al., 1987).

In contrast to correlational studies, most experimental studies suggest that sugar has no effect. In two experiments, for example, hyperactive boys on a sucrose-free diet received a challenge beverage with either sucrose or the sugar substitute, aspartane (Wolraich et al., 1985). No significant differences were found for the groups on measures of physical activity, attention, impulsivity, and learning. The effects of sugar on performance of clinic and nonclinic samples have been looked at in other studies, with mixed results (Kaplan et al., 1989; Roshon and Hagen, 1989; Spring et al., 1987).

It should be noted that research into dietary influence is difficult. Correlational studies can be misleading, and well-controlled experiments are not easy to conduct. It is hard to manage what people eat and to select appropriate control diets. Given these considerations, the evidence suggests that diet does not play a strong role in the etiology of hyperactivity but may affect a small number of children.

Environmental Lead

That lead exposure can lead to coma, seizure, mental retardation, and death is not in dispute (Hansen, Belmont, and Stein, 1980). In addition, animals experimentally exposed to lead and children exposed to undue levels of lead in early development have been shown to display atypical motor activity, irritability, learning difficulties, and the like (Henker and Whalen, 1980). Could low levels of exposure over long periods of time also adversely affect children?

A number of correlational studies have examined lead levels and attention and activity levels. Lead levels of the blood most typically have been looked at, and occasionally the amount of lead in the dentine of children's deciduous ("baby") teeth. Some studies have shown a relationship to behavior; others have not (Lansdown, 1986; Fergusson et al., 1988a). Serious methodological problems exist in the research, including inadequate measurement of lead and of behavior.

Investigators are attempting to improve the quality of the studies. Three recent studies that were sensitive to methodological weaknesses found small links between lead levels and problems of attention and activity (Fergusson et al., 1988b; Silva, et al., 1988; Thomson et al., 1989). The possible effects of other variables (such as SES, family-social environment, the child's prenatal history, and school experience) were controlled for in some of this work. However, the relationships found were very small. Moreover, it may be that variations in children's behavior cause variations in lead levels.

Given the weak correlations found in these studies, decreases in environmental lead would probably not substantially impact the prevalence of ADHD. Nevertheless, any high technology society concerned about children's development should acknowledge the possible benefits from control of lead paint, lead emissions from factories and autos, and the like.

Psychosocial Factors

Although psychosocial variables are typically not considered as critical in etiology as biological factors, they do appear to play some role in ADHD.

For example, Campbell and colleagues (1986) studied parental ratings of ADHD behaviors in their three-year-olds when the children were referred for help. Children whose families were lower in social status and experienced relatively more family stress and disruption were more likely to be rated high on ADHD behaviors. This link was evident when the children were six years of age. Of course, these data do not reveal causal paths.

In a population study of twins, Goodman and Stevenson (1989) found an association of ADHD behaviors with seven adverse family variables, including parental problems, marital discord, coldness to the child, and criticism of the child. Importantly, assessment of ADHD behaviors was accomplished by objective measures and teacher ratings, as well as parental ratings.

The link with family adversity and social class has been found in other studies (e.g., Rutter, 1989b). Nevertheless, it does not appear to be very strong. Furthermore, these correlational analyses can be interpreted in several ways. Perhaps psychosocial factors directly or indirectly cause ADHD, perhaps they only help maintain ADHD over time, or perhaps they are a consequence of the condition.

It is not unreasonable to speculate that for at least some children ADHD results from being born with a predisposition for the relevant behaviors that interacts with psychosocial variables. A burdened or chaotic home, regardless of social status, may fail to foster attentive and reflective behavior. Organized and regular mealtimes, being read to, quiet games, exposure to rules under appropriate adult supervision, and so forth may indeed be important (Eisenberg, 1979). Also, teacher behaviors could well play a role in shaping attention and reflection. How a classroom is organized and how activities are structured can influence academic achievement and perhaps especially for children predisposed to ADHD behaviors (Whalen, 1989). As with parents, teacher perception and tolerance of student behavior may influence daily social interactions.

Summary

It is quite striking that after much research the etiology of ADHD remains uncertain. A leading view is that biological dysfunction involving the frontal-limbic parts of the brain and the arousal-inhibitory system interferes with behavioral regulation that, in turn, impacts the learning and social domains. Several causal factors, or their combinations, are involved. Whereas biological variables seem more strongly implicated, psychosocial variables are not precluded and may at least be involved in shaping and maintaining ADHD behaviors.

DEVELOPMENTAL COURSE AND PROGNOSIS

It is believed that ADHD often begins in infancy or early childhood, but that three to four years of age is the more commonly reported age of onset (Barkley, 1989; Campbell, 1985). Apparently many of the parents become distressed in trying to manage the inattention and noncompliance of their toddlers. Still, most referrals for assessment do not occur until the early school years (Weiss and Hechtman, 1986). In general, the primary manifestations of ADHD are then quite evident and conduct problems may begin, if they have not already.

The negative consequences of ADHD may increase with age for at least some children (Massman, Nussbaum, and Bigler, 1988). These include falling more and more behind in school. Negative feedback about school performance and other behaviors can accumulate to adversely affect self-concept and motivation.

In adolescence, the primary deficits of ADHD may lessen (Weiss and Hechtman, 1986). In fact, perhaps 25 percent of all cases can be considered recovered in this regard. Even for these individuals, however, other difficulties remain, including poor school performance. Up to one-third of adolescents may drop out of school, and few go to college (Barkley, 1989). Social relationships are problematic, and many ADHD adolescents have poorer social skills, lower self-esteem, and impulsive styles of behaving compared to controls (Weiss and Hechtman, 1986).

Studies that follow ADHD children into adulthood indicate that one-third to one-half are no different than normal adults.

The remainder variously show the primary deficits and/or impaired social relationships, depression, low self-concept, antisocial behavior, and drug use (Weiss and Hechtman, 1986). Serious drug problems and alcoholism do not appear common, however. Typically, these individuals are employed and economically independent, although work history is somewhat unstable and job status is on the low end.

Adolescent and adult outcomes are related to several earlier-occurring variables, especially aggression, intelligence, social status, and family adversities (Dulcan, 1989; Whalen and Henker, 1985).

In a particularly interesting prospective study, Lambert (1988) examined several variables with respect to adolescent outcome. She concluded that different outcomes were linked to different early factors, as follows.

1. Early biological variables (measured by pre-, peri-, and postnatal conditions), early temperament, and early health were linked to the adolescent mental health problems of depression and conduct disorder.
2. With regard to adverse educational outcome, these early variables contributed much less. Rather, family, social, and cognitive variables present during the children's elementary school years were more important.
3. Other outcomes, such as substance abuse and delinquency, were explained equally by the early and later occurring variables.

Lambert points to the importance of better understanding the pathways of risk—and protection. So far little beyond general knowledge is known about what protects children from acquiring the label of ADHD. Clearly, the better we understand developmental paths, the more guidelines we have for the assessment and treatment of ADHD.

IDENTIFYING THE ADHD CHILD

Considerable effort has gone into identifying ADHD. Due to its long association with brain dysfunction, assessment has often included methods to assess biological dysfunction, particularly the neurological examination, the EEG, medical history, and neuropsychological testing. Nevertheless, these methods have limited value in differentiating ADHD children from normals and children with other disorders and in guiding treatment (Kenny, 1980). They can be useful when biological factors are highly suspect, particularly since a subgroup of ADHD children may have brain dysfunction.

Intellectual assessment may also be warranted, since academic difficulties are so common. In all cases, however, procedures to assess specific behaviors and social interactions of the child are of utmost importance.

Barkley's (1981, 1988a) recommendations for assessing ADHD can serve as a model for this approach. Interviews with the child, parents, and teachers—along with rating scales and direct observation—are the major components. Laboratory measures also are considered.

Interviews

The nature and length of the child interview depends on the age and ability of the youth. With young children the interview may simply be a time for getting acquainted and observing appearance and behavior. With older children, inquiry may be made into the child's views of his or her functioning, family dynamics, school performance, peer relationships, and the like. Barkley has res-

ervations about the reliability of information obtained from children under 12 years of age. However, he believes that establishing rapport and detailing the child's characteristics are beneficial.

The parent and teacher interviews are alike in their emphasis on social interaction. Nine questions about several situations are asked of parents, as shown in Table 9–2.

TABLE 9–2 Interview Format Suggested by Barkley

Questions	Situations
1. Is this a problem area?	Overall interactions
2. What does the child do in this situation?	Play alone
3. What is your response?	Play with others
4. What will the child do next?	Mealtimes
5. If the problem continues, what will you do next?	Dressing in morning
6. What is usually the outcome of this interaction?	Washing and bathing
7. How often do these problems occur in this situation?	Parent on telephone
8. How do you feel about these problems?	During television
9. On a scale of 0 to 10 (0 = no problem, 10 = severe problem), how severe is this problem to you?	Visitors at home
	Visiting others' homes
	In public places
	While mother is occupied
	Father at home
	Chores
	Bedtime
	Other situations

An illustration of the question format is presented in Table 9–3. The situation being explored is how the child acts when visitors are in the home. Note that noncompliance is quite evident and that the chain of interaction is increasingly aversive. This is a common pattern in child-parent exchanges.

Rating Scales

Somewhere in the process of speaking with parents and teachers, behavior rating scales are completed. These scales can help determine whether the child's behavior is deviant from the norm and different from behaviors displayed by other diagnostic groups. Several of them suggest cutoff scores to identify ADHD, and are reasonably reliable and valid.

The Conners Scales are among the most widely used. They are easy to use and there is good evidence for their validity (Edelbrock and Roncurello, 1985). The Conners Parent Rating Scale consists of 48 items that yield scores on 5 factors: impulsive-hyperactive, learning problems (attention), conduct problems, psychosomatic problems, and anxiety (Goyette, Conners, and Ulrich, 1978). The original Conners Teacher Rating Scale has 39 items, while the revised form has 28; the factors they yield are similar to the parent-scale factors (Conners, 1969; Goyette et al., 1978). Table 9–4 shows a few of the behaviors examined. On all the Conners scales children are rated on whether they display each behavior (0) not at all, (1) just a little, (2) pretty much, or (3) very much.

The Werry-Weiss-Peters Activity Rating Scale consists of 31 items rated by parents across seven situations: mealtime, television, homework, play, sleep, public places, and school. For each setting the child is rated on a few items concerning activity level (Werry, 1968).

The Home Situations Questionnaire and the School Situations Questionnaire evaluate specifically where problem behaviors

TABLE 9–3   Illustration of Interview Format Suggested by Barkley

Examiner: How does your child generally behave when there are visitors at your home?
Mother: Terrible! He embarrasses me tremendously.

E: Can you give me some idea of what he does specifically that is bothersome in this situation?

M: Well, he won't let me talk with the visitors without interrupting our conversation, tugging on me for attention, or annoying the guests by running back and forth in front of us as we talk.

E: Yes? And what else is he likely to do?

M: Many times, he will fight with his sister or get into something he shouldn't in the kitchen.

E: How will you usually respond to him when these things happen?

M: At first I usually try to ignore him. When this doesn't work, I try to reason with him, promise I'll spend time with him after the visitors leave, or try to distract him with something he usually likes to do just to calm him down so I can talk to my guests.

E: How successfully does that work for you?

M: Not very well. He may slow down for a few moments, but then he's right back pestering us or his sister, or getting into mischief in the kitchen. I get so frustrated with him by this time. I know what my visitors must be thinking of me not being able to handle my own child.

E: Yes, I can imagine it's quite distressing. What will you do at this point to handle the situation?

M: I usually find myself telling him over and over again to stop what he is doing, until I get very angry with him and threaten him with punishment. By now, my visitors are making excuses to leave and I'm trying to talk with them while yelling at my son.

E: And then what happens?

M: Well, I know I shouldn't, but I'll usually grab him and hold him just to slow him down. More often, though, I may threaten to spank him or send him to his room. He usually doesn't listen to me though until I make a move to grab him.

E: How often does this usually happen when visitors are at your home?

M: Practically every time; it's frustrating.

E: I see. How do you feel about your child creating such problems in front of visitors?

M: I find myself really hating him at times (*cries*); I know I'm his mother and I shouldn't feel that way, but I'm so angry with him, and nothing seems to work for me. Many of our friends have stopped coming to visit us, and we can't find a babysitter who will stay with him so we can go out. I resent having to sacrifice what little social life we have. I'm likely to be angry with him the rest of the day.

occur (Barkley and Edelbrock, 1987). The former asks about behavior in 16 home situations and public places, while the latter asks about behaviors in 12 school situations such as in hallways, bathrooms, and small group work. Ratings of severity are also obtained for each situation.

TABLE 9–4   A Few of the Items on the Conners Teacher Rating Scale

Restless or overactive	Oversensitive
Excitable	Temper outbursts
Sits fiddling with small objects	Disturbs other children
Difficulty in concentrating	Destructive
Inattentive	Appears to be unaccepted by group

From Conners, 1969.

Direct Observation

Barkley recommends direct observation whenever it can reasonably be accomplished. In the home, compliance and stimulus-consequence patterns are important. In the school, such patterns are equally important, along with behaviors such as "out of seat," aggression, disruption, and inattention. Several observational coding procedures for ADHD behaviors exist, for example, for the structured classroom and clinic playroom (Jacob, O'Leary, and Rosenblad, 1978; Milich, Loney, and Roberts, 1986).

Laboratory Measures

The final assessment component recommended is the use of laboratory measures. The Continuous Performance Task (CPT), the Matching Familiar Figures Test (MFFT), and actometers/pedometers, all described earlier, are among the most well-known measures. However, laboratory procedures are still being developed, and the lack of normative data and standardized procedures is problematic. Moreover, the need for equipment means that these measures are not always feasible in the clinic and private practice. In fact, it appears that many clinical and school psychologists rarely use them, and also rely less on rating scales than researchers (Rosenberg and Beck, 1986). Perhaps further development of laboratory measures will make them more useful and feasible.

TREATMENT

A variety of treatments have been applied to Attention-Deficit Hyperactivity Disorder. Traditional psychotherapy and play therapy are not considered especially helpful (Barkley, 1989). Medication with stimulants, behavioral techniques, and cognitive behavioral methods are of greatest interest today.

Pharmacologic Treatment

In 1937 Bradley first reported the treatment of behavior disordered children with stimulant medication (Zemetkin and Rapoport, 1987). Since then over 20 pharmacological agents have been used with ADHD children, but none as successfully as stimulants. In fact, stimulant medication is the most popular treatment in the United States for ADHD (Vyse and Rapport, 1989). The most commonly employed stimulants are methylphenidate (Ritalin), dextroamphetamine (Dexedrine), and pemoline (Cylert). These medications have been extensively researched with methylphenidate, the most used, being the most studied.

Although controversy surrounds the use of stimulants, it is not, in the view of professionals, due to their failure to alleviate the primary deficits of ADHD. An impressive amount of data indicates that about 75 percent of medicated ADHD children show increased attention and reduced impulsivity and activity level, especially in the structured, demanding situations that elicit ADHD behaviors (Dulcan, 1986; Tannock et al., 1989). Stimulants also decrease children's disruptive, noncompliant, oppositional behaviors (Dulcan, 1986; Hinshaw et al., 1989; Whalen, Henker, and Granger, 1990). Figure 9–2 exemplifies these findings.

Only since it became evident that many children do not "outgrow" ADHD have adolescents been treated with medications. Reductions in inattention/impulsivity and noncompliance and enhancement of cog-

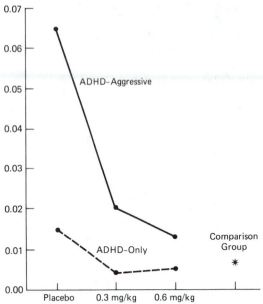

FIGURE 9–2 Mean proportion of aggression for ADHD-aggressive, ADHD only, and untreated normal boys. All treated boys received a placebo, and methylphenidate in two dosages (in varying orders). Decreases in aggression occurred in the majority of subjects with methylphenidate. All boys were in a program that awarded tokens for cooperative behavior. From Hinshaw et al., 1989. Copyright 1989 by the American Psychological Association.

are commonly given two or three times a day. Slow release medications that can be taken less often are also available (e.g., Birmaher et al., 1989). Because individual children respond differently to medications and dosage effects, each child must be monitored.

On the surface, it once seemed strange that stimulants, which induce arousal, would benefit ADHD. The effects were thus said to be *paradoxical*, implying that it was puzzling that ADHD children would be calmed. This notion enjoyed considerable popularity for some time (Peloquin and Klorman, 1986). But is has now been shown that stimulants influence ADHD individuals, as well as normal children and adults, by focusing attention and the like.

Despite the positive effects, however, several concerns have been expressed about treatment with stimulants. One, of course, is that not all children benefit from them. (Antidepressant drugs may be an alternative for some.) It is worth noting, too, that stimulant use is not recommended for children under three years of age, and that gains are probably small for children between three and five years (Barkley, 1989).

A second concern about stimulant medication is the confusing data regarding academic improvement. Since stimulants decrease the core deficits of ADHD and performance on many laboratory learning tasks is also enhanced, academic improvement might well be expected (e.g., Richardson et al., 1988). In fact, some early studies sometimes demonstrated improvement on the amount of work completed in the classroom and on standardized measures of achievement. However, the weight of the evidence did not support significant academic improvement (Barkley, 1989; Gadow, 1985). Many investigators recognized weaknesses in the research (Douglas et al., 1986). For example, it was argued that dosage of medication confounded the results and that achievement tests often did not contain enough items to detect short-term changes. Furthermore, if ADHD children were already behind in certain skills, medication could hardly improve performance unless

nitive functioning have been demonstrated in this population (Coons, Klorman, and Borgstedt 1987; Klorman, Coons, and Borgstedt 1987).

It is quite understandable that parents and teachers interact more positively and use fewer controlling behaviors with hyperactive children who are benefiting from medication (Barkley, 1988c; Whalen, Henker, and Dotemoto, 1980). There is evidence, too, that ADHD children are rated more positively by peers following medically related improvement (Whalen et al., 1989). These findings indicate that pharmacologic treatment may not only benefit children directly, but also through improved social relationships.

The effects of most stimulants are rapid but wear off within a few hours; thus, they remedial training was also given. More recently, the evidence for short-term improvement on complex cognitive and academic tasks seems stronger, perhaps due to improved research (Douglas et al., 1986; Pelham, 1986; Richardson et al. 1988). Still, long-term effects have not been established (Abikoff et al., 1988; Jacobvitz et al., 1990).

A third concern about treatment with stimulants is possible adverse biological side effects. Most common are insomnia, anorexia, weight loss, irritability, and abdominal pain (Dulcan, 1986). They often diminish in two or three weeks or after a reduction in dosage. Suppression of growth is reported, but it too is often temporary or growth rebounds with drug withdrawal. The question of possible long-term effects on heartrate and blood pressure has been raised, and motor or vocal tics occur in 1 to 2 percent of treated children. To minimize side effects, medications may be avoided on weekends or over summer vacation from school. Overall, stimulants are considered relatively safe drugs, but adverse side effects preclude their use with some children.

Finally, various concerns focus on broad issues of using medication with children. Parents and professionals alike have expressed fear, sometimes in emotionally charged ways, over the misuse of medication. Several complaints have found their way into the courts (Williams, 1988). It is argued that children have been misdiagnosed and then prescribed medication that cannot help them and could harm them. A related complaint is that ADHD is being overdiagnosed, which leads to the overuse of medication. There is evidence that the amount of Ritalin being sold has gone up considerably in the last few years. The reasons for this are disputed and could include the increased treatment of adolescents. Concerns are expressed, too, that medication is overused because it is a "quick fix" for the schools or for some parents. Reliance on medication can preclude the use of other beneficial treatments that avoid the weaknesses of stimulant treatment. And reliance on medication might especially interefere with children's developing a sense of internal control over their behavior (see Box 9.1). Certainly, many professionals who recognize the benefits of stimulants point to the limitations and weaknesses of these drugs and warn against their misuse or overuse.

Behavior Modification

The rationale for behavior modification is that, regardless of etiology, behavioral manipulations might decrease both the primary and secondary manifestations of ADHD. It is believed that changes in child management by parents and teachers at the very least will reduce interpersonal stress and improve the child's social relationships.

Behavior modification programs are conducted in the home and school, and training of parents and teachers is critical. The approach emphasizes the importance of reinforcement and punishment in controlling inattention, impulsivity, rule adherence, academic effort, and social interaction. Reinforcers typically include tangible rewards, especially tokens or points that can be traded for a variety of rewards, and also social consequences such as praise. There is some evidence that reinforcement alone is insufficient, for example, in controlling behavior in the classroom (Pfiffner and O'Leary, 1987). Punishment is often given in the form of time-out or response cost; that is, the child loses opportunity for reinforcers or must give up a portion of the tokens or points previously earned.

A parent training program. Barkley (1989) has proposed a parent training program that emphasizes the management of noncompliance and defiance in 2- to 11-year old ADHD children. It is consistent with his view that ADHD involves a deficit in rule-governed behavior and with the data that ADHD overlaps with conduct disorders. The program consists of ten steps that are dealt with in weekly parent training

BOX 9.1   The implicit messages of medication

Whalen, Henker, and Hinshaw point out that all treatments carry unintentional, implicit messages to the treated and the people around them. These researchers have studied such "emanative effects" by listening to ADHD children treated with medication (Whalen, 1989; Whalen, Henker, and Hinshaw, 1985).

Children are strikingly ambivalent about medication. On the one hand, they describe improvements in their behavior. On the other hand, they worry about becoming addicts, other children teasing them, displeasing their parents by taking medication, losing strength or speed, or becoming "hyper" when medication wears off. The daily intake of pills can clearly influence children's beliefs about themselves, how their bodies work, and what controls their actions.

Medication use goes hand in hand with attributing behavioral problems to biological causes. This can alleviate family members' blaming themselves or others, including the child, for deliberate misbehavior. However, it also can result in unrealistic expectations that biological maturation will solve the difficulties or unrealistic beliefs in the power of medicines.

Here is what 11-year-old Lisa said about the influence of medication.

INTERVIEWER: This is an "imagination" question. Let's say you stopped taking Ritalin altogether.

CHILD: Oh wow, I'd stay home from school!

INTERVIEWER: How come?

CHILD: Because I know what would be happening if I didn't. I wouldn't get my work done at all.

INTERVIEWER: How about your friends?

CHILD: Nobody would like me then, if I didn't take it. They'd think in their minds, "Gosh, she doesn't even want to play. What a baby!"

INTERVIEWER: Pretend that a friend of yours was about to start taking Ritalin and she asked you what you thought.

CHILD: They'd ask me, like, "What does it do?" I'd just tell them, "Well, it helps you concentrate, get more friends, and you want to join in the games more. And you'd be invited more places." (Whalen, 1989, p. 158)

In other interviews children have reported that taking pills keeps them from being mean to pets, allows them to lend things to friends, makes the teacher like them, reduces fighting, helps them like themselves, and prevents them from breaking things, killing frogs, and acting crazy. Fogetting to take medications has been cited as the cause of poor grades, tantrums, breaking others' toys, and unrolling toilet paper down the stairs while parents were entertaining!

Whereas some of these attributions may be realistic, there is reason to believe that not all are. In one case study, when nine-year-old Tom was suddenly taken off medication, his behavior deteriorated and he was heard to comment that the pills helped him complete his work and control his temper (Rosen, O'Leary, and Conway, 1985, cited by Whalen et al., 1985). Tom's behavior improved when he was put back on pills, along with the teacher's emphasizing his control of his own behavior. Unknown to Tom, the pills were a placebo. Giving too much credit to medication may thus work against children's believing they have control.

The researchers note, however, that attributions about medication are not necessarily detrimental. For example, when behavior improves, children might gain feelings of competence. The point is that the cognitions that emanate from use of medication need to be harnessed during treatment. Medication is best conceptualized as a temporary aid while the child and family are actively working and mastering problems. A reasonable hypothesis is that children who develop a sense of control are more likely to have a positive outcome than those who believe they are controlled by medicine and biology.

sessions. The steps are briefly described here.

1. Information on the nature, course, prognosis, and etiology of ADHD is provided to parents by direct instruction, readings, and tapes.

2. The causes of oppositional/defiant behavior are discussed, particularly in terms of child characteristics, parent characteristics, situational consequences, and stressful family events.

3. Parents are trained in effective ways to attend to their children to enhance the value of parental attention. For example, they are advised to increase attention to prosocial behavior and ignore inappropriate behavior. Underlying this step is the assumption that parental reinforcement has been too weak to adequately shape behavior.

4. Parents are next trained in methods of giving commands to optimize compliance in their children. For example, they are taught to reduce question-like commands (such as "Why don't you pick up your toys now?") and to reduce task complexity. They are asked to use brief commands at home and to reinforce complaince.

5. Parents are asked to set up a home token economy for reinforcing the child's completing home responsibilities. This involves the child's earning tokens that can be exchanged for a variety of reinforcers.

6. Next, parents are trained to use response cost for noncompliance and time-out for two behaviors that they believe are serious forms of defiance.

7. Problems in the use of time-out are reviewed and parents are told to extend time-out to other problem behaviors if needed.

8. Parents are next taught to generalize the home management procedures to noncompliance in public places such as stores and restaurants. They are told to use a "think aloud—think ahead" procedure: Before entering the public place they review with the child rules for conduct, reinforcers available, and punishments for inappropriate behavior. They follow the rules and procedures once they enter the public place.

9. Parents have by now acquired effective management techniques. Discussion is held about how they will use these skills in the future if other forms of noncompliance arise.

10. One month later a review session is held that includes discussion of problems parents had in managing their child. Additional sessions are sometimes needed, but the ten sessions appear adequate for most families.

Parents' success in acquiring the skills targeted in the program seem to be affected by several factors. Maternal depression and isolation, marital discord, and parental psychopathology appear to interefere with success.

Classroom management. Much research has been devoted to the classroom management of ADHD children. Improvement has been found in attention, disruptive behavior, and academic performance. Cooperation between parents and teachers can be beneficial. In one early study, for example, ten-year-olds were treated with a home-based reinforcement program for meeting academic and social goals in the classroom (O'Leary et al., 1976). The specific goals and reinforcers were individually set for each child. Teachers completed a daily checklist, which the child carried home. Reinforcers could be earned daily as well as at the end of the week. They consisted of an array of enticing items: special dessert, play time with parents, dinner at a fast-food restaurant, and the like. Compared to a no-treatment control group, children treated for ten weeks showed improvement on two rating scales.

Reinforcement of on-task, attentive behaviors in the classroom does not necessarily improve academic performance. Thus, specific academic behaviors need to be pinpointed. Interestingly, this may also improve behaviors that interefere with learning. For example, Ayllon, Layman, and Kandel (1975) worked with three children in a learning disabilities classroom. When these children discontinued taking Ritalin, inappropriate behavior initially increased. However, a token program that rewarded math and reading performance not only resulted in academic improvement but also in control of hyperactivity (Figure 9–3). These children apparently had the requisite

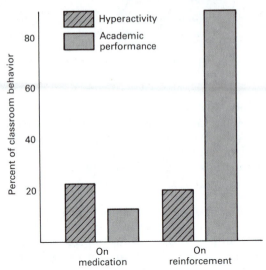

FIGURE 9-3 Average percentage of hyperactivity and academic performance for three children when they were on medication and off medication with reinforcement for academic tasks. From Ayllon, Layman, and Kandel, 1975.

academic skills, and reinforcement acted as a motivator.

Laboratory research suggests that stimulus control techniques might benefit learning in ADHD children (Barkley, 1989). Increasing stimulation within the task—for example, by the use of color and shape—might increase attention to the task (Zentall, 1985). So might a teaching style that is active and enthusiastic and engages the child. Keeping the length of the task within the child's attention span and using timers to pace performance might be of benefit. Rules that are written and displayed may also help guide the child. Research is needed to better understand how stimulus control techniques might enhance learning.

There seems little doubt that behavioral methods can help many ADHD children in the short run. However, the question remains about whether training in one situation carries over to other situations. Moreover, most children benefiting from behavior modification have not been followed over time to determine the durability of effects. For the most part, generalization of behavioral treatment over situations and time cannot be automatically assumed. Techniques to foster children's self-regulation, which often include cognitive-behavioral methods, have evolved in hopes of rectifying this shortcoming.

Self-Regulation and Cognitive-Behavioral Intervention

Self-regulation would seem a natural target in treating ADHD children, since it appears inadequate in these children. Moreover, if a child's behavior could be brought under self-control, generalization and maintenance might increase because the behavior would not solely depend on cues and contingencies in the new situations.

Three techniques are commonly employed to enhance self-regulation (Kendall and Braswell, 1985). *Self-monitoring* involves children's learning to observe and record their own behaviors. For example, they may record the frequency of on-task behavior that is the goal of intervention. Self-monitoring often is part of a broader intervention involving the evaluation and *self-reinforcement* for desired behavior. Typically chil-dren award themselves points that can be exchanged for reinforcers. As an example of this approach, Bowers et al. (1985) compared teacher-reinforcement and self-reinforcement in the classroom. While performing in a reading workbook, 8- to 11-year-olds were assigned points either by the teacher or by themselves for being on-task. The points could be exchanged weekly for money. Both conditions improved attention to and accuracy of the work, but self-reinforcement was the more effective for attention. In fact, several studies demonstrate the efficacy of these techniques on ADHD behaviors (Abikoff, 1985; Barkley, 1989).

The third technique, *self-instruction*, is a popular cognitive-behavioral strategy (p. 59). It involves children's being trained to make statements to themselves to help focus and guide their behaviors on a task. The self-statements may include questions that help clarify the task, answers to the questions, and self-guidance (e.g., "slow down", "the next step is . . ."). The verbalizations usually are combined with modeling, reinforcement, and other procedures, making it difficult to evaluate the effectiveness of the self-statements. Nevertheless, it appears that self-instruction reduces the primary deficits of ADHD only modestly and inconsistently (Dush, Hirt, and Schroeder 1989; Whalen, Henker, and Hinshaw, 1985).

Overall, cognitive-behavioral interventions have had mixed results. Improvements have been found in attention and cognitive performance more than in academic and social performance. Little evidence exists for the generalization of improvement. And when follow-up research has been conducted, little maintenance over time has been seen. This is disappointing since the cognitive-behavioral approach was specifically aimed at improving generalization and maintenance. Despite this picture, however, interest still exists in determining whether children might benefit in some ways depending on age, task, and specific techniques.

Comparing Treatments and Combining Treatments

Since different treatment approaches show some success, it is reasonable to ask whether one approach is more effective than another. In addition, since no one approach "cures" ADHD, children have been treated with various combinations of approaches, and the combinations have been compared to single approach interventions.

As we have seen, stimulant medication and contingency management alone can improve some ADHD behaviors. Comparisons of these approaches show mixed results. For example, Abikoff and Gittelman (1984) and Gittelman and colleagues (1980) demonstrated greater effectiveness for medication over parent and teacher contingency in reducing ADHD deviant behavior. Gadow (1985) reviewed several studies and concluded that various behavioral methods benefited academic performance more than pharmacologic treatment, and that stimulants did not markedly enhance the effectiveness of behavioral interventions. It appears that when behavioral approaches are superior, it is in the academic domain (Barkley, 1989). And interestingly, a general finding is that the combination of drug and behavioral methods is not more powerful than either approach alone.

The results of comparisons of cognitive-behavioral and pharmacologic approaches alone and combined seem even more mixed (Barkley, 1989; Brown et al., 1986; Hinshaw, Henker, and Whalen, 1984). Thus, no clear picture has emerged.

Overall, it appears that many variables influence the outcome of the different interventions, including the behaviors targeted, the specific techniques used, and the age of the children. It is thus difficult to predict what intervention might best serve any one child at any particular time. Some clinicians prefer trying behavioral techniques initially, to see whether medications might be avoided. Others believe that a combination of treatments might be the best approach for many children, since different treatments might address different deficits. In addition, parental management of their ADHD youngsters is important when children need to "vacation" from medications to control possible side effects. Moreover, when ADHD children are still having difficulties into adolescence, training in self-regulation might be highly appropriate. What does seem apparent is that treatment is best tailored to suit each child's needs, even as these needs change over time. Given that problems associated with ADHD do not simply disappear, even with treatment, continued research is needed.

SUMMARY

Attention-Deficit Hyperactivity Disorder has often been in the public eye. Commonly known as hyperactivity, conceptualizations of ADHD have changed somewhat over the years. Hyperactivity was initially the focus of concern, then attention deficits were considered central, and presently both deficits are recognized as primary manifestations, along with impulsiveness.

Activity problems are defined in terms of restless, excessive, disorganized, and inappropriate behaviors. Different measures of activity do not correlate highly with each other, and there is considerable variation from child to child. In general, though, activity problems are more likely to show up in structured environments.

Considerable research has been conducted to ascertain the specific attention mechanisms involved. The research does not well support the hypothesis that ADHD children have deficits in selective attention. There is stronger support for deficiencies in sustained attention.

It is also widely reported that ADHD children act impulsively without thinking. Laboratory measurement of impulsivity has been only partly satisfactory. In fact, conceptualizing and measuring all of the primary manifestations of ADHD have been problematic.

Although ADHD children show intelligence that approaches the normal range, they experience much academic failure and a noticeable percentage are learning disabled. The link between ADHD and academic/learning failure is not well understood. ADHD children also display an array of conduct disordered and otherwise socially disturbing behaviors. Research comparing children diagnosed as ADHD or conduct disordered supports the distinction between these categories. Differences also have been noted between ADHD children with or without conduct disorder.

A distinction is made between situational and pervasive ADHD. Perhaps the latter is more strongly associated with cognitive deficits and persistance of symptoms. British workers look for pervasive ADHD before using the label, probably accounting for lower rates of ADHD in Britain than in the United States.

About 3 percent of the school population is estimated to show ADHD, although there is much variation in the data. Boys are diagnosed more frequently than girls, with a ratio of 6:1 to 9:1.

Many biological factors are implicated in etiology. Brain damage has been outruled as central, but some brain dysfunction is considered likely. There is special interest in the frontal-limbic area of the brain, and in the neurotransmitters norepinephrine and dopamine. However, the complexity of the brain and the difficulties inherent in conducting brain research make the present findings preliminary at best.

Some evidence exists that inheritance may play a role in etiology, and the hypothesis of neurological immaturity has limited support. The popular idea that pregnancy, prenatal adversities, and birth complications cause ADHD has received only weak support.

Diet and environmental lead appear to have small influence. Like other research, investigations are mostly correlational and so causation is difficult to determine.

Associations have been revealed between ADHD and family and social class factors. Characteristics of the home and school environment might elicit and shape ADHD behaviors. Overall, the etiology of ADHD remains elusive and it is likely that ADHD can result from various factors or their combinations. A leading hypothesis implicates brain dysfunction that impairs behavioral regulation.

ADHD is often noticed by age three or four, and the early school years are a common time for referrals. Perhaps 25 percent of cases see major reductions in primary symptoms by adolescence, but academic and social difficulties often persist. In adulthood, up to one-half of the cases are recovered. Early aggression, intelligence, social status, and family factors are related to outcome.

Identification of ADHD may include medical and intellectual assessment, and the evaluation of specific behaviors and social interactions is necessary. To accomplish the latter, Barkley's (1981, 1988a) comprehensive model includes interviews with the children, parents, and teachers; the use of standardized rating scales; direct observation; and perhaps laboratory measures.

Stimulant medication is widely used in treating ADHD. Stimulants appear to alleviate the primary and many secondary manifestations in a sizable proportion of children. There are many concerns about medication: its failure to help some children, questionable effectiveness for academic difficulties, adverse biological side effects, misuse and overuse, and possible detrimental lessons about self-control.

Behavior modification, also a popular intervention for ADHD, emphasizes reinforcement and punishment for attention, rule adherence, academic effort, socially appropriate behaviors, and the like. Parent and teacher training are widely employed, and cooperation between parents and teachers has been shown to be helpful. Stimulus control techniques might enhance classroom learning, but more research is needed in this area.

Lack of generalization and maintenance of the gains made in behavioral treatment led to an interest in training ADHD children to regulate their own behavior. Self-monitoring and self-reinforcement have proven somewhat effective. The efficacy of self-instruction is modest.

Comparisons of the effectiveness of the different treatment approaches provide some useful information as a guideline for treatment selection. For example, stimulant medications have been shown as more effective in some situations than behavior modification, and behavior modification may be especially helpful in ameliorating academic deficits. Nevertheless, the effectiveness of intervention depends on many variables and treatment must be individualized to serve each child.

10

MENTAL RETARDATION

The saga of the "Wild Boy of Aveyron," otherwise known as Victor, began around 1800. It was to have far-reaching implications for the conceptualization and treatment of mental retardation.

Victor was first seen running naked through the woods in France, searching for roots and acorns to eat. He escaped more than once before his final capture and assignment to a medical officer, Jean M. Itard, at the National Institute for the Deaf and Dumb in Paris. Expectations were rampant: The wild boy would be astonished at the sights of Paris; he would soon be educated; he would describe his fascinating existence in the forest. When he arrived in Paris, however, Victor was a dirty child who suffered from convulsions, swayed back and forth, bit and scratched, and showed no affection for those who attended him (Itard, cited in Harrison and McDermott, 1972).

Victor's senses were underdeveloped; his memory, attention, judgment, and reasoning deficient; and his ability to communicate almost nil.

Some people drew a parallel between Victor and children considered incurably afflicted with "idiocy." Itard believed that Victor had existed alone in the woods from at least age four or five and he attributed the boy's deficiencies to lack of contact with civilized people. But Itard's attempt to treat the Wild Boy of Aveyron was largely unsuccessful, and Victor lived in custodial care until his death. Nevertheless, the efforts to treat Victor did much to stimulate interest in the "feebleminded" or "retarded" (Rie, 1971).

Since that time, progress has been made and many changes have occurred in the definition, labeling, diagnosis, and treatment of mental deficiency.

HOW IS MENTAL RETARDATION DEFINED?

From the beginning of history, even in simple societies, some individuals have probably been considered intellectually disabled and socially incompetent (Clarke and Clarke, 1985). Different labels have been used to describe individuals so identified.

The terms *idiot*, from the Greek meaning "ignorant person," and *imbecile*, from the Latin meaning "weakness," were long used in medical writings (Potter, 1972). *Feeble-minded* was commonly used in the late 1800s. During the 1920s, *mental deficiency* became the more popular label, but it was replaced in the 1950s by the term *mental retardation*. At least in part, these changes were an attempt to substitute labels that had become negative with more acceptable ones. The current trend to use *mental handicap* continues this effort.

The most widely accepted definition of mental retardation is given by the American Association on Mental Deficiency (AAMD):

Mental retardation refers to significantly subaverage general intellectual functioning existing concurrently with deficits in adaptive behavior and manifested during the developmental period (Grossman, 1983, p. 1). *General intellectual functioning* is defined as performance on individually administered general tests of intelligence, such as the Stanford-Binet and the Wechsler scales. *Subaverage* refers to an IQ of approximately 70 or below. *Adaptive behavior* is the degree to which individuals meet the standards of personal independence and social responsibility for their age and social group. It may be measured by scales designed for this purpose. *Developmental period* is the time between birth and the eighteenth birthday.

DSM-III-R has adopted AAMD's definition and ICD-9 criteria are very similar. All three systems recognize degrees of retardation, and also that retardation may occur with other psychological disorders. However, DSM-III-R codes mental retardation on Axis II, as it does other developmental disorders that are expected to persist in a stable form into adulthood. AAMD, on the other hand, specifically avoids the assumption that the condition, especially when less severe, is chronic and irreversible.

The criteria for mental retardation (MR) reflect many gradual changes in how the condition has been viewed and identified. At first primarily considered a medical disorder, diagnosis of MR was based on physical examinations and global, ill-defined judgments of competence. The construction of more objective general tests of intelligence, along with greater recognition of nonmedical factors, resulted in an emphasis on intelligence test performance. Perceived limitations and abuse of these tests, in turn, resulted in greater attention to adaptive behavior. Thus, according to AAMD, individuals who fall into the retarded range on intelligence tests but otherwise get along adequately at home, school, or work are not judged as mentally retarded. Deficits in adaptive behavior without poor performance on intelligence tests also do not warrant the diagnosis of retardation.

The present view of retardation is also developmental, tying the beginnings of the condition to the early years. Older persons who display mental deficits for the first time thus receive other diagnoses. The developmental approach demands, of course, that assessment of intelligence and adaptive behavior be based on age norms.

THE NATURE AND MEASUREMENT OF INTELLIGENCE

Since performance on intelligence tests is critical for diagnosing mental retardation, an understanding of these tests is essential. As with all psychological tests, one must examine the issues of reliability and validity. These issues, in turn, relate directly to how intelligence is conceptualized.

Most of us have an intuitive idea about the general nature of intelligence and would be willing to identify individuals we believe are "very smart" or "not so smart." We might agree, as have theorists, that intelligence involves the knowledge possessed by a person, the ability to learn, or the capacity to adapt to new situations. Beyond these general definitions, we might run into disagreements. Indeed, theorists themselves are unsure of the precise nature of intelligence. It is sometimes said that "intelligence is whatever is measured on intelligence tests"—a definition that sheds little light on the matter. However, because measured intelligence has been intricately tied to the definition of MR, we will examine the most widely used individually given tests of intelligence.

The Binet Scales

Credit for the first successful intelligence tests is given to Alfred Binet and Theophile Simon, who were asked by the Minister of Public Instruction in Paris to find a way to better identify children who needed special educational experiences (Tuddenham, 1963). Binet and Simon approached their task in a practical way—by selecting and testing children on brief tasks that had direct relevance to the classroom. Their original 1905 scale consisted of 30 tasks of diverse content that gradually became more difficult. In the 1908 revision the scale was ordered according to age, that is, all the tasks passed by normal five-year-olds were placed together, as were those passed by normal six-year-olds, and so on. Such age-ordering reflected the belief that mental development increases with age throughout childhood. On the basis of their performance, children were assigned a mental age (MA), the age corresponding to the chronological age (CA) of children whose performance they equaled. Thus, a seven-year-old who passed the tests that the average seven-year-old passed was assigned a MA of seven; a seven-year-old who passed the tests that the average six-year-old passed obtained a MA of six.

In 1911, just prior to his death, Binet published another revision of the scale, adding and refining specific tasks. All this work reflected concern for scientific integrity. Efforts were made to check reliability by testing groups of children and then retesting them at a later time. Validity was established by comparing children's tests scores with other judgments of their ability, such as teachers' ratings and actual school performance.

Although Binet was interested in theories of intelligence, his aim was largely humanitarian: To identify children who might benefit from special education. He feared that children could be inaccurately identi-

fied and argued that carefully constructed and standardized tests were absolutely necessary to minimize this outcome. According to Binet, his scales assessed intellectual processes by sampling performance on different tasks. No claims were made about the causes of retardation. Nor did Binet see intelligence as unchangeable. In fact, he and his colleagues devised methods to raise the intellectual functioning of retarded children, and they recommended that educational programs be fitted to each child's special needs.

The Stanford-Binet. The testing movement began in the United States when Henry Goddard translated the Binet scales for use with retarded residents of the Vine-

Alfred Binet (1856–1911), a French psychologist, helped develop the first intelligence tests. (New York Public Library Picture Collection)

land Training School in New Jersey (Cushna, 1980). Goddard directed early research on mental retardation and he distributed thousands of copies of this test (Achenbach, 1982). Then, in 1916, Lewis Terman, working at Stanford University, revised the early scales into the Stanford-Binet (S-B). He adapted the items to the new population and tested a relatively large number of American children with them. Terman and his associates also adopted the idea of the intelligence quotient (IQ), which is the ratio of an individual's mental age to chronological age, multiplied by 100 to avoid decimals. The ratio IQ enabled direct comparison of the performance of children of different ages. Today, IQ is calculated statistically and is no longer a quotient but it still denotes age comparisons.

Goddard and Terman brought several assumptions to intelligence testing that were markedly different than those of Binet's. Both espoused belief and interest in the inheritance of intelligence and the need for *eugenics*, the improvement of the human species by control of inheritance (Gould, 1981). Both assumed that standardized tests measured inherited intelligence that would remain stable over the life of the individual. These assumptions eventually caused serious conflicts about the meaning of "intelligence" and the use of intelligence tests.

Not all who used the Stanford-Binet adhered to hereditary assumptions, of course, and the test has been further revised and updated, independent of this issue. On the current S-B, items are no longer grouped into age levels; instead, similar items make up subtests (e.g., vocabulary, copying, memory for objects). The 15 subtests focus on four cognitive areas: verbal reasoning, abstract/visual reasoning, quantitative reasoning, and short-term memory (Anastasi, 1988; Thorndike, Hagen, and Sattler, 1986). Some subtests span the entire age range of 2 to 18 years, while others span a restricted age range, and no individual takes all 15 subtests. Each person's performance is converted to Standard Age Scores (SASs), which are compared with those of the standard norm group of the same chronological age. SASs are calculated for the four cognitive areas and the entire scale. The average SAS is set at 100 by statistical procedures. Thus, an obtained SAS higher than 100 means that the person has performed better than average for his or her age; an obtained SAS less than 100 means a less-than-average performance. These SASs are what most people call "IQ," or more correctly "deviation IQ." (Table 10–1 summarizes the various measures to test intelligence discussed in this section.)

TABLE 10–1 Measures Relevant to Tests of Intelligence

CA	Chronological Age.
MA	Mental Age. The age score corresponding to the chronological age of children whose performance the examinee equals. For the average child, MA = CA.
IQ (ratio)	The ratio of mental age to chronological age multiplied by 100. IQ = MA/CA × 100.
IQ (deviation)	A standard score derived from statistical procedures that reflects the direction and degree to which an individual's performance deviates from the average score of the age group.

The Wechsler Scales

Based on the work of David Wechsler, these scales originated in 1939 with the Wechsler-Bellevue test. Three instruments designed for different ages now exist. The Wechsler Adult Intelligence Scale and its revision (WAIS and WAIS-R) evaluate adults; the Wechsler Intelligence Scale for Children and its revision (WISC and WISC-R) assess children from 6 to 16 years of age. The Wechsler Preschool and Primary Scale of Intelligence (WPPSI) evaluates functioning in the 4 to 6 year range.

All the Wechsler scales follow the same format. They consist of different kinds of subtests—such as vocabulary, puzzles, and arithmetic problems—each of which becomes gradually more difficult. Each examinee works at each subtest completing as many items as possible before moving on to the next. In general, older children are able to complete more of each subtest than younger children. The subtests are designated as either verbal or performance tasks. The former emphasize verbal skills, knowledge of the environment, and social understanding. Performance subtests emphasize perceptual motor skills, speed, and nonverbal abstraction. The Wechsler scales permit the calculation of three deviation IQs: a verbal IQ, a performance IQ, and a Full Scale IQ that combines verbal and performance scores. As with the S-B, performance is compared with the norm group of similar age, and the average performance is 100.

Infant Tests of Intelligence

Because it is believed that early identification of mental deficiency is beneficial, efforts have been made to evaluate very young children. Several individually administered scales exist. Performance on them is usually termed developmental quotient (DQ).

As noted in Chapter 5, infant tests of intelligence differ from those designed for older children in that they give greater emphasis to sensorimotor functioning and less emphasis to language and abstraction. This may partly account for the fact that performance on infant tests does not correlate highly with later IQ. Other factors may also underlie such discontinuity. Perhaps insufficient time has elapsed for infants to develop individual differences relevant to later intelligence, or perhaps mental processes lack stability so early in life.

Whatever the reason, tests administered during the first few years of life cannot be relied upon to predict later intellectual performance for most children. However, predictions of mental deficiency are more accurate than predictions of average and superior performance, especially when deficits are severe and when histories and clinical impressions are also considered (Illingworth, 1971). Thus, if an infant's test performance falls substantially behind that of its age-mates and, for example, the infant had suffered perinatal damage, a diagnostician might strongly suspect mental retardation. Nevertheless, miscalculation often occurs and there is a need to develop more useful instruments for early identification (Berger and Yule, 1985; Fagan et al., 1986). In the meantime, the most reasonable course of action is to provide infants who have below average DQs with regular follow-up examinations and enriched environments.

Interpretation of IQ Tests

The use of intelligence tests for nonretarded and retarded persons alike raises a host of important questions. What do these tests actually measure? Do tests produce reliable measures? Do IQ scores predict later intellectual performance? These concerns are both theoretical and practical.

Validity: What IQ tests measure. Perhaps the most central issue is the question of what an IQ score tells us about a person. Recall that Binet and Simon sought to measure academic ability, and produced some evidence for the validity of their scale. Indeed, if intelligence is defined as ability that relates to, or is taught in, school, evidence exists for validity. Most IQ tests emphasize verbal abilities, which are important in academics (Matarazzo, 1972; Robinson and Robinson, 1976). After age five, the correlations of IQ with school grades and reading, spelling, and mathematics achievement scores are generally in the range of 0.40 to 0.75 (Achenbach, 1982; Berger and Yule, 1985). Moreover, the relationship between IQ and academic performance appears even stronger for individuals whose IQ scores fall into the below average range. Thus, intelligence tests can help predict school performance.

However, correlations with out-of-school achievement are relatively low (Baumeister, 1987). In discussing his own tests, Wechsler (1974) pointed out that IQ tests were not designed to evaluate attitudes, persistence, and the like, which may contribute to general intelligence. Scarr (1982) notes that intellectual performance includes noncognitive aspects such as cooperation, ability to sit still, and social responsiveness. She suggests the term "intellectual competence" to refer to the combination of cognitive, motivational, and adjustment variables involved in human intelligence. Similarly, Zigler and Balla (1982) recognize motivational variables, such as expectancy for success and failure, which influence intellectual behavior. It stands to reason that noncognitive factors affect everyday intellectual performance and may influence test scores, but this influence is not well discriminated on intelligence tests.

Finally, it is important to note that intelligence tests are given in highly controlled situations and that the questions are highly structured. IQ performance may thus be an inadequate reflection of the everyday world where individuals are called on to adopt various strategies to solve problems in various situations (Frederiksen, 1986). IQ scores thus can be expected to be more valid in some situations than in others. Furthermore, validity can be different for groups of people to the extent that these groups function in different situations (Garcia, 1981).

Are IQ scores stable or changing? The stability of IQ scores has been a much-argued issue. The question can be examined by studying people longitudinally, comparing their earlier IQ scores to later IQ scores. When measurement is made after infancy, IQ scores are relatively stable for groups of normal-functioning individuals. In general, over a ten-year interval the correlations between two sets of scores is about 0.5, perhaps slightly higher (Berger and Yule, 1985). And, in general, correlations between sets of scores are stronger when the time between testings is briefer.

It is important to note, however, that correlational analyses compare the rankings of scores. To determine whether the scores of individual children actually change, we must look at the values of the scores.

Earlier in this century it was widely held that IQ scores could not change. But information gradually emerged to challenge this view. McCall, Applebaum, and Hogarty (1973), for example, concluded from their own and other data that IQ changes of 30 and 40 points occur fairly often, that boys' scores are more likely than girls' to increase, that the scores of children of low SES are less likely to change, and that personality variables are associated with the direction of shift. Transient conditions such as illness, fatigue, change in the family situation, educational opportunity, social adjustment, and mental health have all been associated with change in individual IQ (Robinson and Robinson, 1976).

Do these findings apply to mentally retarded individuals? In general, the IQs of the mentally handicapped are more stable than those of persons with average and superior scores, and the lower the scores the greater the stability (Berger and Yule, 1985). But, again, change can occur. For example, Silverstein (1982) tested mildly retarded children for four consecutive years, starting when they averaged about 11 years of age. Almost 12 percent of the children showed 10 to 12 points change in either direction. More dramatic change has been documented when the social environment has been deliberately improved (Clarke and Clarke, 1984). Caution is necessary, then, in interpreting measured intelligence and using it to label a child mentally retarded. IQ scores are relatively stable—which means that they provide a relatively reliable way to assess children—but they are not cast in stone and can change for some children. Indeed, given what is known about IQ tests, their use as a primary tool for identifying retardation and making decisions about education and placement is discouraged (Weinberg, 1989). Scores should be interpreted within the broad context of the child's life, including how the child functions in the various environments encountered.

ADAPTIVE BEHAVIOR

Numerous instruments exist to measure adaptive behavior. These scales center on the domain of everyday life—on current ability to cope with environmental demands. Some evaluate broad populations while others are restricted, for example, to assess only severely retarded persons (Grossman, 1983). Adaptive behavior scales may be employed for diagnosis or to provide specific information for intervention. Most of the scales depend heavily on interviews with parents and other caregivers. In the next sections we look at two of the most popular scales.

Vineland Adaptive Behavior Scales

Working for many years at the Vineland Training School, Edgar Doll emphasized the importance of social adequacy and the ability of the retarded to manage their lives. In 1935 he published a scale to measure social competency, which he assumed grew with chronological age (Myers, Nihira, and Zetlin, 1979). Doll believed that social competency could be quantified by summing performance across eight domains of behavior: self-help general, self-help eating, self-help dressing, self-direction, occupation, communication, locomotion, and socialization (Doll, 1965). A social age (SA) and a social quotient (SQ) were calculated, analogous to MA and IQ, to reflect the examinee's standing as compared to nonhandicapped individuals.

The Vineland was revised and expanded in 1984 by Sparrow, Balla, and Cicchetti.

The abillity to perform everyday adaptive behaviors has become an important criterion in evaluating mental retardation. (New York State Office of Mental Retardation)

Three versions now exist. Two versions are semistructured interviews for parents and other caretakers, which can be used from birth to 18 years of age and with low-functioning adults. The third version consists of questions to be completed by teachers of 3- to 12-year-old children. All the versions cover four major behavioral domains: Communication, Daily Living Skills, Socialization, Motor Skills. Scores from the separate domains can be compared to scores earned by a large, normal standardization group and also to the performance of smaller special groups such as mentally retarded, emotionally disturbed, and hearing-impaired persons.

AAMD's Adaptive Behavior Scales

The AAMD Adaptive Behavior Scale (ABS) and the ABS-Public School Version are based on the performance of mentally retarded, emotionally disturbed, learning disabled, and normal children (Myers et al., 1979). They include a wide range of behaviors and can be used for persons between three years and adulthood. Table 10–2 lists the several areas of behavior for which separate scores are calculated. Part I of the ABS consists of 10 areas of self-care and socialization. Part II rates 14 areas of maladaptive behaviors, including violent, withdrawn, and stereotyped behaviors.

Assessment of maladaptive behavior is especially important because such behavior is related to institutional placement of retarded children (MacDonald and Barton, 1986). This kind of evaluation can also be useful in treatment. However, Part II of the ABS considers only the frequency of behavior, not the severity. A person who displays many mildly inappropriate behaviors can thus obtain a higher score than a person who displays a few seriously inappropriate behaviors. To correct this, researchers have offered alternative scoring methods (Clements et al., 1980; MacDonald and Barton, 1986).

TABLE 10–2 Areas of Competence and Maladaptive Behavior Assessed by AAMD's Adaptive Behavior Scale

Part I	Part II
Competence	*Maladaptive Behavior*
Independent functioning	Violent and destructive behavior
Physical development	Antisocial behavior
Economic activity	Rebellious behavior
Language development	Untrustworthy
Numbers and time concepts	Withdrawal
Domestic activity	Stereotyped behavior, odd mannerisms
Vocational ability	Inappropriate interpersonal manners
Self-direction	Unacceptable vocal habits
Responsibility	Unacceptable or eccentric habits
Socialization	Self-abusive behavior
	Hyperactive tendencies
	Sexually aberrant behavior
	Psychological disturbances
	Use of medication

From Nihira, Foster, Shellhaus, and Leland, 1974.

AAMD Adaptive Behavior Scale, Manual, pp. 6–7. Copyright, 1975, the American Association on Mental Deficiency.

Strengths and Weaknesses of Adaptive Behavior Scales

The construction of adaptive behavior scales lags behind that of intelligence tests and less is known about their adequacy and how to interpret them. While some lack adequate standardization and evidence for reliability and validity, research on others is going forward. For example, test-retest and inter-rater reliabilities are reported as adequate in the manual of the revised Vineland (Sparrow, Balla, and Cicchetti, 1984). As with intelligence tests, individual scores must be examined before conclusions can be reached about stability and change for individuals.

If adaptive behavior scales are to be useful at all, they must accurately reflect at least current functioning. Whether they do or not depends partly on the accuracy of reports from parents and caregivers. Ratings of specific questions are more likely to be accurate than ratings of general and vague questions (e.g., can the child count to ten versus can the child count). Even so, reports may suffer from caretakers' being insensitive, lacking opportunities for observation, or holding idiosyncratic standards.

One way to examine the validity of adaptive behavior scales is to determine their relationship to IQ scores. We would expect IQ scores, which reflect intellectual development, to correlate with how individuals can care for themselves, act independently, and relate to others in daily living. In fact, several studies show a moderately strong correlation between IQ and adaptive behavior. With an emphasis on everyday coping, adaptive behavior overlaps with intelligence but also taps factors other than the mental processes tapped by IQ tests. Thus, an IQ of 70 or below does no more than put individuals at risk for social maladaption, but the lower the IQ, the greater the risk (Clarke and Clarke, 1985; Grossman, 1983).

Although the concept of adaptiveness is generally looked upon with favor, investigators also note that it is a vague, elusive concept that varies in different places, at different times, and within different social classes (Clarke and Clarke, 1985; Zigler, Balla, and Hodapp, 1984). For this reason, Zigler and his colleagues argue that it should not be used to classify individuals as mentally retarded. To make their point, they give a hypothetical example of a child with an IQ of 65 who fails in school. This child might easily be classified as mentally retarded. Yet with added resources, perhaps just special help from a caring teacher, the child might perform adequately in school (i.e., adapt) and no longer meet the criteria for retardation. The child's intellectual processes would probably not have changed; what changed was the social environment.

But even these investigators do not suggest that adaptive behavior is unimportant in understanding retardation. Evaluating adaptive behavior makes it possible to relate it to intelligence, gain knowledge of other variables that might influence the ability to succeed in life, and plan and assess specific goals of treatment for retarded individuals.

LEVELS OF RETARDATION

Great variability exists in the capabilities and behaviors of mentally retarded people. Thus, levels of retardation are set according to severity of retardation by all major classification systems. Table 10–3 indicates how AAMD associates IQ scores with four levels of functioning: mild, moderate, severe, profound. (The DSM and ICD set similar levels.)

AAMD also recognizes adaptive behavior levels according to degree of impairment, from mild to profound. However, these levels are used less often than those based on IQ, and they do not rely on adaptive behavior scales. Instead, AAMD provides descriptions of general patterns of skills and levels for specified ages. Table 10–4 illustrates two of the standard descriptions. Assignments to levels require that the highest level of routine functioning of the individual first be matched as well as possible to a description. Next, using the left-hand column, age is matched and the level is assigned. Since all ages are not included, it is necessary to estimate levels for some ages.

Levels of retardation set by educators correspond closely to those set by AAMD and are judgments of the learning ability of the retarded person. Three categories have

TABLE 10–3 Levels of Retardation According to Performance on Intelligence Tests

Level	IQ Range for Level
Mild	50–55 to approximately 70
Moderate	35–40 to 50–55
Severe	20–25 to 35–40
Profound	Below 20 or 25

From Grossman, 1983.

TABLE 10–4 Illustrations of Adaptive Behavior Levels According to AAMD

Age and Level	Highest Level of Adaptive Behavior Functioning
Age 3 years: **Severe** Age 6 years and above: **Profound**	**Independent Functioning:** Feeds self finger food; "cooperates" with dressing, bathing, and with toilet training; may remove clothing (e.g., socks) but not necessarily as act of undressing as for bath or bed. **Physical:** Stands alone or may walk unsteadily or with help; coordinates eye-hand movements. **Communication:** One or two words (e.g., Mama, ball) but predominantly communicates through vocalization or simple gestures. **Social:** May respond to others in predictable fashion; communicates by gestures and noises or pointing; plays "patty-cake" or plays imitatively with little interaction; or occupies self alone with "toys" few minutes.
Age 3 years: **Moderate** Age 6 years: **Severe** Age 9 years and above: **Profound**	**Independent Functioning:** Tries to feed self with spoon; considerable spilling; removes socks, pants; "cooperates" in bathing; may indicate wet pants; "cooperates" at toilet. **Physical:** Walks alone steadily; can pass ball or objects to others; may run and climb steps with help. **Communication:** May use four to six words; may communicate many needs with gestures (e.g., pointing). **Social:** Plays with others for short periods, often as parallel play or under direction; recognizes others and may show preference for some persons over others.

From Grossman, 1983.

traditionally been recognized. Educable mentally retarded persons (EMR) have IQs above 50 and are viewed as being able to learn some academic skills. The trainable mentally retarded (TMR) have IQs roughly between 25 and 50. They can learn basic self-help and vocational skills. Children labeled as custodial mentally retarded have IQs below 25; they require much help, even in caring for themselves, and are frequently institutionalized. There is some tendency today for educators to avoid these traditional labels, and especially to combine EMR and other learning-disabled children under a more general rubric, such as educationally handicapped.

PREVALENCE

Mental retardation is often estimated at about 3 percent of the population, but the figure has varied from about 1 to 16 percent. This is not surprising because the criteria for MR have varied.

One common way to arrive at prevalence for this disorder is to estimate it from the theoretical distribution of IQ scores. Intelligence, it is assumed, is normally distributed. Figure 10–1 depicts the theoretical normal curve, showing that an IQ of 100 is the mean. It is obvious that as scores increasingly differ from the mean they decrease in frequency. This relationship is measured by statistical units called standard deviations, which are related to the percentage of scores under the curve and to specific IQ scores. IQs of 70 or less fall two or more standard deviations below the mean, and they make up about 2.27 percent of all the scores. Thus, about 2.27 percent of the population is defined as retarded according to the current IQ criterion.

FIGURE 10–1 Theoretical normal distribution of IQ scores.

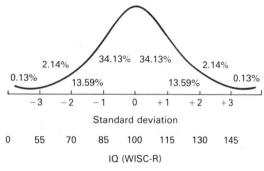

As a demonstration of how the definition of MR has influenced prevalence, consider that AAMD had previously taken the IQ of approximately 84 as the cutoff for retardation. This meant that almost 16 percent of the population theoretically fulfilled the IQ criterion. Those whose IQ fell between approximately 70 and 84 were categorized as borderline retarded. Many of the children in this category were of low socioeconomic class or minority ethnic/racial background. Concern about group bias and the labeling of such a large percentage of the population as retarded influenced AAMD to change its criterion.

So far nothing has been said about prevalence when mental retardation is defined by both IQ and adaptive behavior. This is because IQ scores are so heavily relied upon to define mental retardation. Some evidence exists, however, that prevalence is about 1 percent when a count is made of cases that were diagnosed using the dual criteria (Mercer, 1973; Szymanski and Crocker, 1985).

Prevalence data for MR is especially interesting when age and severity are inspected. Figure 10–2 demonstrates the general finding that the greatest number of cases is found in school-age and adolescent persons. Preschool youngsters are only rarely identified, and there are fewer and fewer adult mentally retarded individuals with advancing age.

Figure 10–2 also shows that extremely low IQ is rare, and mild retardation is by far the most common. When preschoolers are identified, they most often have IQs below 50, apparently because the more severe cases are obvious and elicit attention. But a dramatic shift occurs when children enter school; then they are identified when even mildly retarded, probably because they are unable to meet the new demands in this situation. The decline in moderate and mild retardation in adulthood is probably due to several factors. Death may account for some decline, as well as unavailability for assessment. Also, with the intellectual demands of school gone, essentially unchanged individuals may successfully undertake unskilled jobs and function adequately in society (Clarke and Clarke, 1985). Other individuals may continue to learn and mature into adulthood, so that they are increasingly able to meet various demands.

Other variables are important when prevalence is examined (Crnic, 1988). Low socioeconomic groups account for a disproportionate number of cases, especially of mild retardation. MR is also more prevalent in some minority groups. And it appears more among males than females. Males may be at greater biological risk, but high social expectations may play a role: If cultural standards are higher for males than for females, the risk of being labeled retarded might also be higher.

The epidemiology of mental retardation

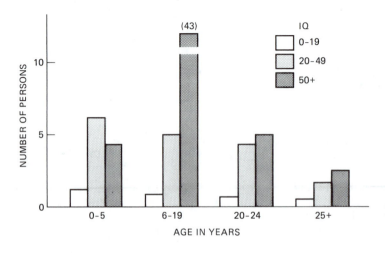

FIGURE 10–2 Estimated number of retarded persons in a community of 100,000. From Tarjan, Wright, Eyman, and Keeran, 1973.

clearly indicates that different environments use different criteria for identifying the condition or vary in sensitivity to retardation (Baumeister, 1987).

ETIOLOGY

There are many known and suspected etiologies of MR, but the specific causes of most cases remain undetermined (Deitz and Repp, 1989).

Although IQ scores are said to be normally distributed in the general population, it has been noted that they fall into a distribution that resembles the normal curve except for a "bump" at the low end. The excess of low scores, it is suggested, is accounted for by individuals who have suffered some major biological impairment (Zigler, Balla, and Hodapp, 1984). Major organic factors are known and believed to be the primary cause in about 25 percent of the cases of retardation (Scott and Carran, 1987). Moreover, although known organic factors are associated with all levels of mental deficiency, they are especially associated with the more severe levels. (See Table 10–5 for one analysis.)

But the vast number of cases, most of which fall into the mild/moderate range, are not easily explained. Subtle, unknown organic abnormalities may be primary in some of these cases. Perhaps a large majority of them reflect normal variation of intelligence in the population, or less-than-optimal environmental input, or the interaction of such influences. In this section we examine some of the causes of MR, beginning with known chromosome abnormalities.

TABLE 10–5 Percentage of cases of milder and more severe retardation accounted for by nervous system pathology

	IQ below 50	IQ 50–69
white 7-year-olds	72	14
black 7-year-olds	54	6

From Nichols, 1984.

Chromosome Abnormalities

Aberrations in the number and structure of the chromosomes are associated with specific syndromes of mental retardation. For the most part, the exact way in which these abnormalities cause lowered intelligence and other problems is not understood. A few of these conditions are described next.

Down's syndrome. Down's syndrome was described in 1866 by Langdon Down, a British physician. For several years it was noted that older mothers in particular had babies with the syndrome and that concordance in monozygotic twins approached 100 percent (Rainer, 1980). The latter fact, especially, made genetic causation suspect. In 1959, only three years after human chromosomes were fully described, Lejeune and others discovered trisomy 21 in persons with Down's syndrome. As shown in Figure 10–3, the #21 chromosome appears in a triplet instead of a pair.

Down's syndrome is the most common single chromosome abnormality in infants. Incidence increases with maternal age. At age 20 incidence is 1 per 2000 live births; at age 35 it is 1 per 500; at age 45 it is 1 per 18 (Evans and Hammerton, 1985). It is believed that advancing maternal age is related to failure of the chromosome pairs to divide in meiosis, with trisomy 21 being one result. However, other genetic mechanisms are also involved and the extra chromosome has been traced to fathers in about 15 to 25 percent of the cases. Whatever the mechanism, a woman who has had a Down's syndrome baby has a 1 percent risk of having another such child.

Down's syndrome children are born with a variety of physical abnormalities that make them look strikingly alike. Most characteristic is the epicanthal folds at the corners of the eyes and the upward slant of the eyes, which gave rise to the now outdated name

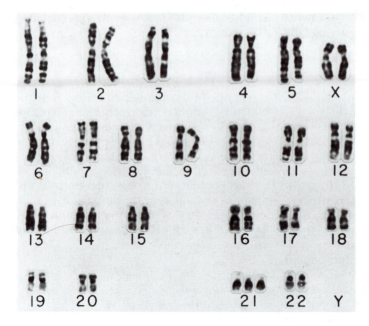

FIGURE 10–3 The chromosome complement of a female with #21 trisomy. Courtesy of the March of Dimes Birth Defects Foundation.

"mongolism." The face also tends to have a flat nose, small square-shaped ears, and a small mouth with a short roof that makes the tongue protrude (Robinson and Robinson, 1976). Surgical reconstruction of parts of the faces of these children has been done, in the hope for greater social acceptance, but this is a complex matter that needs to be dealt with sensitively (Turkington, 1987; Szymanski and Crocker, 1985). Down's syndrome children also are at risk for serious health problems, such as heart defects and hearing impairment. These children have the reputation for being content, friendly, affectionate and lovable, and while this profile may be accurate in part, it is too limited (Gunn and Berry, 1985). In fact, Down's syndrome infants are perceived by their mothers as showing considerable variations in behavior.

Developmental deficits are usually evident during the first few years of life. Tested intelligence ranges from mild to profound retardation, with an average IQ of about 40 (Evans and Hammerton, 1985). Evidence is also accumulating for unique behavioral patterns; for example, in the Strange Situation (p. 35) these babies are emotionally subdued compared to normal babies (Thompson et al., 1985). As with all children, the home environment is important in development. Mother-child interaction may be subtly different than normal as early as the first year (Landry and Chapieski, 1989). Smith and Hagen (1984) found that the home environments of Down's syndrome babies had become different from those of nonretarded babies by the time the infants were 17 months of age. Specifically, mothers of the retarded children encouraged their babies more with smiles and physical stimulation while the other mothers used speech to a greater extent. Furthermore, Down's syndrome babies who showed the least decline from 6 to 24 months had mothers who spoke to them frequently with reference to the environment. It is likely that maternal behavior was shaped in part by the babies' behavior and needs. Further study of environmental influences might well lead to helpful interventions. Given the large differences among individuals with Down's syndrome and their capacity for mental growth into adulthood (Berry et al., 1984), efforts toward optimal intervention are certainly worthwhile.

Fragile X anomaly. The fragile X condition derives its name from the tendency of the X chromosome to break. Although discovered relatively recently, it is second to Down's syndrome as a known cause of MR (Rutter et al., 1990b). At first the fragile X condition was reported as being inherited in the X-linked, recessive pattern, and more males than females were reported as mentally retarded. Now it appears that transmission may be more complex, and that females may be affected more than previously thought. In any event, even carriers of the defective chromosome seem to have delayed mental development, or perhaps less severe mental deficiency. All levels of MR are associated with the fragile X. The males tend to have long faces, large ears, and oversized testicles (Szymanski and Crocker, 1985).

Other sex chromosome abnormalities. Other abnormalities of the sex chromosomes are associated with mild levels of retardation, poor academic performance, physical defects, and in some cases, behavioral problems. Klinefelter's syndrome occurs in phenotypic males, who usually have an extra X chromosome but can have several additional Xs. The sex organs are under-developed, sperm is lacking, and a tendency toward increased height is seen. Some Klinefelter boys show below average intelligence and auditory, perceptual, and language deficiencies (Evans and Hammerton, 1985). They also tend to be introverted, passive, timid, lacking in self-confidence, and disinterested in sex (Bancroft, Axworthy, and Ratcliffe, 1982). Treatment with male sex hormones is helpful to varying degrees, promoting deeper voice, hair growth, and enlargement of the penis.

Turner's syndrome is found in phenotypic females, who have only one X chromosome or a structurally abnormal X chromosome. The girls lack ovarian tissue and do not develop normal secondary sexual characteristics. They are short and stocky, and may have webbed necks and abnormalities of the elbows, knees, aorta, and kidneys. Although mild levels of MR are reported, cognitive deficits in space-form perception, perhaps including problems in interpreting facial expression, are more typical (McCauley et al., 1987; Skuse, 1987). Social relationships also tend to be inadequate. Nevertheless, treatment with female sex hormones can bring on secondary sex characteristics and adjustment may be satisfactory.

Mendelian Inheritance

A number of specific syndromes associated with mental retardation are inherited in Mendelian patterns. Many of the syndromes involve defective metabolism in which handicaps gradually worsen. Recessive genes are often implicated, although sex-linked and dominant gene patterns are also found. Although they account for a small proportion of mental deficiency, further research may establish metabolic errors in perhaps ten percent of all cases (Cytryn and Lourie, 1980). This prospect is exciting because the identification of specific syndromes holds promise for specific treatments or preventions. Treatment often involves diet control to reduce the biochemical substance that is not appropriately metabolized or to add a missing biochemical. Table 10–6 describes a few of the metabolic defects known to be associated with mental retardation.

Prenatal, Birth, Postnatal Damage

Prenatal exposure to disease, chemicals, drugs, radiation, poor nutrition, and Rh incompatibility may jeopardize the intellectual development of the child. Birth injury and anoxia, too, may take their toll. Low birth weight and prematurity are associated with neurological and intellectual deficits. Mental retardation may also be caused postnatally by seizures, malnutrition, diseases such as encephalitis and meningitis, head

TABLE 10–6   Some Inherited Metabolic Disorders Associated with Mental Retardation

Disorder and Mechanism	Metabolic Disturbance	Manifestation	Treatment
Phenylketonia recessive inheritance	Inability to convert the amino acid phenylalanine due to deficient liver enzyme.	Retardation, hyperactivity, unpredictable behavior, convulsions, eczema.	Diet low in phenylalanine, if begun early, can prevent or reduce retardation.
Maple Syrup Urine Disease (named after characteristic odor of urine) recessive inheritance	Abnormal metabolism of amino acids—leucine, isoleucine, valine	Infants develop rigidity, seizures, respiratory irregularities, hypoglycemia. Most die in few months if untreated or are severely retarded.	Diet low in leucine, isoleucine, valine
Hartnup Disease (named after family in which it was detected) recessive inheritance	Defective transport of amino acid, tryptophan	Symptoms vary. Mental deficiency; photosensitive skin rash; coordination problems. Personality change and psychoses may be only symptoms. Mild cases not detected until late childhood or adolescence.	Nicotinic acid and antibodies may relieve rash, but retardation is not relieved
Niemann-Pick Disease recessive inheritance	Abnormal metabolism and storage of fats in neurons, liver, spleen	Early mental regression and developmental arrest. Abdominal enlargement; anemia; emaciation; occasionally a red spot in retina.	No known treatment; death usually occurs before age 4
Schilder's Disease sex-linked inheritance	Decrease in fats in CNS resulting in demyelination of cerebral white matter	Onset more common in older children and adults. Personality and behavioral changes. Paresis, cortical blindness and deafness; convulsions; dementia.	No established treatment; may respond to steroids
Galactosemia recessive inheritance	Inability to convert galactose (carbohydrate) to glucose	After few days of milk intake, jaundice; vomiting; diarrhea; failure to thrive. Leads to rapid death or mental retardation; cataracts; liver insufficiency; occasional hypoglycemia convulsions.	Early galactose-free diet permits normality

Based on Cytryn and Lourie, 1980.

injuries from household and auto accidents, and child abuse. All these factors can interfere with nervous system functioning and development.

Cultural-Familial Retardation

Family and psychosocial variables have been examined especially with regard to what is called cultural-familial retardation, which comprises about 75 percent of all retarded children (Crnic, 1988). In the past, the labels "garden variety" and "undifferentiated" were also used, reflecting the large number of cases of MR that were not readily distinguished from one another. Individuals assigned the label of cultural-familial retardation have no identifiable organic etiology and usually appear physically normal. Their IQ scores range from about 50 to 70, and they possess relatively good adaptive skills. They are often identified as retarded when they enter the educational system and upon reaching maturity they frequently blend into the larger population. Cultural familial retardation does "run in families." In one study twenty percent of the siblings of mildly retarded children were retarded and the average IQ score was 85 (Nichols, 1984, cited in Plomin, 1989). This contrasted with the siblings of severely retarded children, none of whom was retarded and whose average IQ was 103.

The following description of six-year-old Johnny, who was in the second year of kindergarten in a middle-class school, exemplifies cultural-familial retardation.

He was fifth of eight children of a rather pleasant, quiet mother who had seemed not at all upset when the teacher informed her that Johnny would not be promoted. His father, a cloth man in a textile mill, provided the family living by loading finished bolts of material from weaving machines onto carts to be taken elsewhere in the mill. Johnny's mother occasionally worked in the mill while the grandmother took care of the younger children. Three of Johnny's four older brothers and sisters were in the slowest groups in their schoolrooms.

Johnny was not able to master the reading-readiness materials of the kindergarten. He had difficulty in wielding a pencil, folding paper, coloring within lines, and differentiating one symbol from another. He usually had a pleasant smile and often seemed to be listening carefully to what the teacher told him, but half the time he was unable to repeat her instructions. His attention span was considerably shorter than that of his classmates. Johnny liked the other children, but they paid him little attention and usually left him out of their play at recess. At best, he was

allowed to be one of the firemen who held the ladder while the others put out the fire.

The school psychologist administered a Stanford-Binet to Johnny, who gave a rather even, cooperative performance and attained an IQ of 67 (a mental age of 4 years, 9 months). On the Goodenough Draw-a-Man Test, his drawing, a large head with arms and legs extending from it, earned an IQ of 73.

Johnny's parents, their children, and the maternal grandmother lived in a four-room house situated on the edge of town, near a middle class apartment development. The family kept a cow and several chickens. Johnny shared a bed with three older brothers; three sisters were in another bed. The house was untidy and run-down. Meals were cooked somewhat erratically, and the children often ate their meals cold while walking about the house.

His mother reported that Johnny was a very good child who played outdoors much of the day and seldom cried. His health was mediocre; he usually had a runny nose and coughed throughout the winter. She was somewhat surprised by the teacher's interest in Johnny's "special" problem, since he seemed so much like her other children and had never given her any trouble. (Robinson and Robinson, 1976, pp. 167–68)

The etiology of cultural-familial retardation is controversial. It is often assumed that the IQ scores simply reflect the somewhat lower end of the normal distribution of intelligence in the population. This view suggests to some a polygenic inheritance that "runs" in families (Clarke, 1985; Nichols, 1986). But, of course, family similarity in intellectual performance can also be explained by the sharing of environmental input.

Heredity and environment. Family patterns of intelligence have long been observed. In his influential study of the Kallikak family, Goddard (1912) traced the quite distinct genealogical lines of Martin Kallikak. One of them originated from Kallikak's liason with a barmaid; the second from his latter marriage to a woman of a "better stock." From information on several hundred of Kallikak's descendants, Goddard found a pronounced difference in the two families; namely, that the first liason had resulted in more mental deficiency, criminality, alcoholism, and immorality. Obvious weaknesses existed in this study, most notably the questionable accuracy of the data. Moreover, the results were taken as evidence that mental deficiency was inherited, although family environment could just as well have played a role.

Current understanding of hereditary influence on tested intelligence is based more firmly on research with twins and adopted children. In fact, more behavior genetic data exist for IQ than for any other behavioral characteristic (Plomin, 1989). Performance of identical twins is overall more similar than performance of fraternal twins (Segal, 1985; Scarr and Kidd, 1983). This holds even on specific intellectual tasks. Greater similarity of the environments of identical twins might explain these results, but evidence exists that identical twins reared apart still tend to be similar to each other (Bouchard, 1983). Moreover, developmental patterns of intelligence are more similar for identical than fraternal twins (Wilson, 1983). Still, less than perfect correlations for identical twins implicate effects from the environment.

Several well-controlled studies of adopted children are now underway. One finding is that intelligence test scores of adopted children tend to correlate more highly with scores of their biological parents than with scores of their adoptive parents (Scarr and Kidd, 1983; Horn, 1983). However, when actual scores are examined, the mean IQs of adopted children fall between the mean IQs of their biological and adoptive parents. Since the adoptive parents tend to have higher scores than the biological parents, it appears that the children benefit from their advantaged adoptive homes. Adopted children whose biological parents have relatively high intelligence seem to profit more than adopted children whose biological parents have relatively low intelligence.

Taken together, the behavior genetic data indicate that heritability for IQ performance is about 0.50 (Plomin, 1989). That is, genetic influence accounts for about half of the variation of IQ scores in populations. This means, of course, that environmental influences are also substantial. Genetic factors may play a role in cultural-familial retardation, but environmental factors cannot be ruled out.

Because cultural-familial retardation occurs disproportionately in families of lower socioeconomic class, the influence of poverty and class may be critical. Prenatal adversity, prematurity, postnatal malnutrition, some diseases, and lack of medical attention are relatively high among poor families.

Of importance, too, is the quality of the social-cultural environment, including family relationships (Grossman, 1983). Severe social isolation can result in serious retardation, but even a milder lack of stimulation might lead to intellectual deficits. Specific associations have been demonstrated between home environment variables and children's intellectual development. For example, maternal involvement with the child and provision of play material have been found to be related to increases in functioning for children from 6 to 36 months of age (Caldwell, Bradley, and Elardo, 1975). Inadequate organization of the home environment has been associated with decreases in functioning. Educationally and economically deprived parents may lack skills and knowledge to stimulate children's language and cognitive development. And like parents of any social class who are stressed and without social support, they may find it difficult to provide their families with consistent expectation and motivation for intellectual achievements.

Although few believe that the environment has no effect on intellectual growth, it is difficult to pinpoint any one variable as crucial. Indeed, something as complex as intelligence undoubtedly is the result of many factors that add and interact (Deitz and Repp, 1989).

BOX 10.1   Mild retardation: are intelligence tests biased?

It is especially when we speak of mild retardation and family/cultural influences that the issue of bias in intelligence tests is raised. Are these tests constructed and administered in such ways that they disadvantage certain groups of people, namely those of low SES and certain racial/ethnic background? In fact, it is established that children of poor families and minority families (e.g., black, Hispanic, and native American) do not do as well on the tests, on average, as children of majority, middle-class families. In interpreting this fact it must be recognized that social class is confounded with racial/ethnic background. Even so, the question of bias remains.

These group differences have resulted in serious concerns about intelligence testing, especially since the 1950s (Cronbach, 1975). One concern has been that minority students have been disproportionately labeled mildly retarded (EMR) and placed into special education classes in the public schools. Many people believe that group differences on test performance (and subsequent school placements) reflect test bias rather than true differences in intelligence. Confrontations with the educational system, some of which reached the courts, have ensued over a variety of test practices and test fairness issues (MacMillan, Keogh, and Jones, 1986).

For example, based on verbal IQ scales, some bilingual students were classified as mentally retarded and placed into special education (Reschly, 1981). Perhaps they were penalized for lack of knowledge of the English language. In other cases, poorly trained personnel and questionable short-form and group-administered tests were used to classify students. Another issue revolves around minority students, who are exposed to nonstandard English in their subcultures, being handicapped by the verbal components of intelligence tests and by certain items that relate poorly to their cultural experiences (Bersoff, 1981).

Legal outcomes often, but not always, have favored plaintiffs for the minority groups. For instance, the *Larry P.* v. *Riles* case, a class action suit in which the plaintiffs were blacks, resulted in severe restrictions of intelligence tests for identifying and placing black children into special education programs in California. On the other hand, the California ruling in *PASE* v. *Hamilton* judged that Wechsler and Stanford-Binet items were not biased against black children when these tests were used with other criteria for placement. Overall though, educational systems have been forced to stringently monitor the use and administration of intelligence tests.

School placement is only one area of controversy in a long line of concerns about bias in intelligence testing. Historical accounts describe how IQ tests played an important role in establishing immigration quotas for people of southern European background and laws for the sterilization of mentally deficient individuals (e.g., Gould, 1981; Kamin, 1974). Inherent in such uses and abuses of tests was the assumption that measured intelligence is a stable, inherent, biologically-programmed characteristic of individuals.

Many people now believe that intelligence tests sample important behaviors that result from the interaction of heredity and environment, which at least to some degree can be changed throughout life by environmental impact. Moreover, strong argument exists that standard intelligence tests are bound to create group differences when they are applied to culturally diverse groups with little consideration for obvious group differences in practice and motivation (Garcia, 1981). At the very least, these enlightened views must guide the use of all tests.

Efforts to understand mental retardation rest heavily on the search for the learning and cognitive processes that underlie deficient intellect. Investigators motivated by a variety of theoretical and practical concerns are interested in several questions. What exactly are the capabilities of the retarded? Does intelligence in retarded persons develop the same way as it does in others but just more slowly, or do qualitative differences exist? Can training overcome intellectual deficits and if so, to what extent and what kind of training?

Investigations of learning and cognition have producd a wealth of information since the 1950s. Before we look at some of the findings, it is worthwhile to acknowledge the difficulties in researching this area. One is the selection of appropriate comparison groups in judging the performance of retarded persons. Groups of the same chronological age can be employed; for example, ten-year-old retarded and nonretarded children can be compared. If the retarded children show deficits, an important difference has been demonstrated, but it is unclear whether the deficit simply reflects

slower growth. To help rule out this possibility, comparisons can be made between retarded and average children of the same *mental*, not chronological, age. A significant group difference favoring the nonretarded would suggest a "real" deficit in the retarded rather than just a developmental lag. No group difference would suggest that retarded children are able to perform like average children but develop more slowly.

Another research problem is that investigations of mental retardation seem especially vulnerable to confounds. The retarded frequently have language and communication problems, which can interfere with their understanding the experimental instructions and communicating answers (Justice, 1985). They may also have had different learning experiences with regard to experimental tasks and materials. Differences in motivation may also influence experimental results. Although all of these factors are of interest in themselves, they can confound the interpretations of the research designed to identify intellectual deficits.

Studies of Conditioning

Early investigations of classical and operant conditioning aimed at showing that learning is indeed possible in mentally deficient individuals (Haywood, Meyers, and Switsky, 1982). Both kinds of learning were demonstrated at even the severe and profound levels of MR.

Over the years, operant conditioning has been of special interest. It is now known that some differences in operant learning exist between retarded and nonretarded persons. For example, mildly and moderately retarded children appear less responsive to nontangible reinforcers than average, middle-class children (Zigler and Balla,

1982). And conditioning can be difficult to achieve in severely and profoundly retarded individuals. When behavioral repertoires are limited and response rates are low, extensive shaping is required. Also, reinforcement effects can be inconsistent and extinction can easily occur.

In general, though, operant conditioning principles apply quite well to the retarded. New behaviors can be shaped by successsive approximations, desirable behaviors can be maintained by reinforcers, and undesirable behaviors can be weakened by punishment. Thus, behavior modification is an effective approach to intervention.

Piagetian Theory

According to Piagetian theory, the mind of the child qualitatively changes as adaptation

to the environment occurs through assimilation and accommodation (p. 22). Growth takes place in the capacity of the mind to integrate information, as seen in the child's increasing ability to solve complex problems. This developmental framework suggests ways in which the mental apparatus might go awry.

Piagetians proposed that retarded children follow the same universal sequence of stages as other children, but that they advance more slowly and stop short of full mental growth. Piaget's colleague, Inhelder, was the first to study retardation from this perspective (Woodward, 1979). She found evidence that the profoundly retarded progress no further than the sensorimotor stage; the severely retarded no further than the beginning of preoperations; the moderately retarded no further than preoperations; the mildly retarded no further than concrete operations. Formal operations are regarded as beyond the reach of the mentally deficient. Other studies have tended to corroborate these findings (Robinson and Robinson, 1976).

One application of Piagetian theory is the construction of new intelligence tests. Traditional intelligence tests are empirically based: The items are ordered according to level of difficulty revealed in actual performance. Piagetian tasks, in contrast, can be arranged according to theory. Uzgiris and Hunt's test (1975; Uzgiris, 1976) emphasizes early developmental tasks, and is especially useful with retarded children of four to ten years. For example, it has been employed to study the cognitive growth of Down's Syndrome children (Mervis and Cardoso-Martins, 1984). Humphreys, Rich, and Davey (1985) have constructed a Piagetian scale that correlates with Wechsler IQs and adds information about children's performances. Overall, Piagetians-inspired tests hold promise in work with the retarded.

Information Processing

Cognition, or the so-called higher thinking functions, are often conceptualized within an information processing framework. This approach analyzes cognitive processes employed in gathering information and using it to solve problems and acquire knowledge (Weinberg, 1989).

In general, the information processing system is viewed as consisting of three structures (Figure 10–4). The sensory register receives information through the senses and rapidly passes it to short-term memory, with some possible loss of information. Short-term memory can deal with a limited amount of information for a limited time; some of it moves on rapidly and automatically and some might be lost. However, short-term memory, sometimes referred to

FIGURE 10–4 A general model of information processing. Adapted from Atkinson and Shiffrin, 1968, and Swanson, 1987.

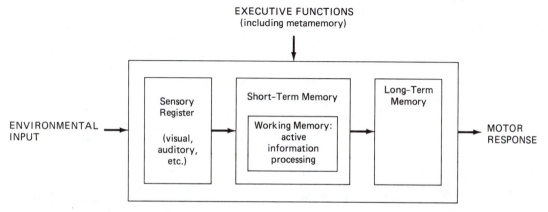

as working memory, can also keep information somewhat longer when it is actively processing it to prepare it for long-term memory. It is long-term memory that permanently stores information, which can be retrieved with varying degrees of ease.

The sensory register, short-term memory, and long-term memory are likened to the hardware of computer analysis; that is, to the computer itself, which cannot be modified. The mental processes themselves, including attention and the strategies used by working memory to prepare information, are viewed as the controls in the system—that is the software, or program. These can be modified.

Theorists also acknowledge what they call the *executive functions* of the information processing system. Executive functions involve the abilities to select, monitor, evaluate, and revise information processing strategies depending on the situation (Butterfield and Belmont, 1977). Part of the executive functions is *metamemory*, the understanding of one's own memory system and how it works with specific information processing tasks (Haywood et al., 1982).

Applying this model to retardation, it is reasonable to assume that cognition may go awry at any point. Unmodifiable structural deficits might exist, particularly when organic syndromes are present. For example, a structural deficit in short-term memory could result in atypically slow processing, causing unusually large loss of information. Deficits may also exist in the modifiable mental processes. Research has focused on these processes in mildly and moderately retarded individuals.

Attention is one such process, as it is believed to be crucial in all effortful information processing. It has been studied in various ways. The study of discrimination learning has contributed to knowledge about attention. Typically the individual is presented with sets of stimulus figures over several trials and must learn which stimulus has been preselected as "correct." Learning is possible on the basis of information given in each trial. Zeaman and House (1979) found that retarded children performed

more poorly than average children, that higher IQ was related to better performance, and that performance depended on *attention* to stimuli. Retarded children had a low probability of attending. Once they attended, they rapidly solved the problems.

Vigilance tasks have also been used to study attention (p. 187). There is some evidence that sustained attention in retarded children increases with age, just as in average children, but at a slower rate (Warm and Berch, 1985). The studies involved relatively simple monitoring tasks. It appears that feedback can help performance of retarded adolescents, and that by late adolescence the retarded behave much like their chronological-age peers on simple vigilance tasks.

Much research is being conducted on the information processing strategies that prepare information for long-term memory. Successful strategies include rehearsing material, organizing and clustering it, and elaborating and transforming it so that it fits with what is already stored. Some of these strategies obviously demand complex thinking.

Overall, retarded persons frequently fail to employ effective strategies or use them ineffectively (Borkowski and Cavanaugh, 1979; Borkowski, Johnston, and Reid, 1987; MacMillan et al., 1986). In some cases, performance improves when retarded children are taught effective strategies and/or instructed to use them. For example, in paired associate learning, a pair of stimuli (usually words or pictures) is first presented and then the subject is given one of the stimuli and asked to give the other. By age five or six most children are able to produce and employ mediators that help them associate the paired stimuli. They may, for instance, connect the stimuli "snow" and "ice cream" by thinking the word "cold" or imagining mounds of a white substance. This strategy of elaboration improves throughout childhood in normal children. However, retarded children do not easily generate and use mediators in paired associate learning. When they are provided mediators by experimenters or instructed to use mediators, they often improve performance (Borkowski and Cavanaugh, 1979).

To some extent retarded subjects can even continue to use acquired strategies later on with tasks identical to the training tasks. However, they do not readily generalize strategies to new tasks, thus seriously limiting training effects (Borkowski et al., 1987; Glidden, 1985). Such failure appears related to deficits in executive functions and metamemory. That is, retarded children inadequately select strategies, monitor how well a strategy is working, and understand their own memory functioning (MacMillan et al, 1986).

The extent to which training in generalization might be helpful is being evaluated. Turnure (1985) notes that the average child's ability to generalize is not taken for granted. Rather, adults teach children by pointing to task similarities, monitoring errors and showing how to correct them, and otherwise coordinating cognitive strategies. Such teaching would be all the more important for retarded children. But the best way to teach, and the degree to which teaching is effective at the different levels of retardation, remain to be established. There is some agreement on the importance of what Turnure calls "functional cognition," thinking about and understanding real-life tasks.

The Developmental-Difference Controversy

No discussion of learning and cognition in retarded individuals would be complete without mention of the developmental-difference controversy. This dispute goes to the very nature of mental deficiency, but it applies only to retardation in which clear organic factors are absent.

The *developmental* position holds that retarded persons grow more slowly in cognitive skills and reach lower limits, but that they reason in ways essentially the same as others do (Weisz, Yeates, and Zigler, 1982). In contrast, the *difference* hypothesis holds that even when retarded and nonretarded persons are matched on intellectual level (MA), they exhibit different cognitive processes.

The controversy was initially tested with Piagetian tasks. The developmental position made two proposals. One was that retarded persons progress through the same sequences of stages as the nonretarded. In their review of the research, Weisz and Zigler (1979) found the same sequence in the two populations. The second proposal was that basic reasoning processes are also alike. Weisz and Yeates (1981) evaluated

this by reviewing 30 studies comparing retarded and nonretarded subjects matched on MA. They concluded that the developmental position had been largely supported, but they noted the need to study cognition and learning processes outside of Piagetian theory.

Weiss, Weisz, and Bromfield (1986) followed this suggestion by conducting a meta-analysis. They reviewed and statistically summed the results of investigations of discrimination learning, attention, memory, and the like. They found that on a variety of tasks the retarded showed significantly inferior performance compared to normal subjects matched on MA. This suggests that retardation is more than just slow development. Despite possible alternative explanations (e.g., differences in motivation), Weiss et al. allow that at least for some tasks mental retardation in which no organic factor is evident may involve different ways of reasoning. Whatever the final outcome of this controversy, it might well lead to more complete understanding of the cognitive functioning of retarded individuals.

SOCIAL DEFICITS AND BEHAVIOR PROBLEMS

A considerable amount of study has been devoted to the social and behavioral problems of retarded individuals, especially of the mildly and moderately retarded. Intellectual deficits may directly interfere with the development of social behavior. Or perhaps being mentally retarded makes it more likely that children will have experiences that hinder social growth or lead to maladaptive behavior.

Interpersonal Skills

The mentally retarded often show deficits in the social skills crucial to personal relationships. These include:

Motor skills, such as facial expressions and body contact

Verbal behaviors, such as asking questions, greeting, and making "small talk"

Affective behaviors, such as responding with empathy

Social cognitive skills, such as role taking and understanding social cues and norms (Davies and Rogers, 1985).

For the mentally retarded child, social competence may be even more important than it is for normal children. Nonretarded children hold negative attitudes about their retarded peers and reject them, but social competence in retarded children may lessen these negative attitudes. In a study that tested this hypothesis, fourth- through sixth-graders were asked to express their attitudes towards nonretarded and retarded peers depicted on videotapes and in stories as socially competent, aggressive, or withdrawn (Siperstein and Bak, 1985). Importantly, the school children described the retarded, competent targets as helpful, kind, and friendly and said they would be willing to interact with them in school. This study does not show what would happen in an actual school setting, but from what is known about peer interaction in general we would expect retarded children to benefit from social skills training. In fact, programs exist to train skills in everyday conversation, work settings, sexual-social situations, and other interpersonal circumstances (Foxx et al., 1984).

Behavior Problems

Mentally deficient children are more likely to display behavior problems than the general child population (Crnic and Reid, 1989; Levine, 1985; Reid, 1985). Retardation is associated with autism, hyperactivity, self-injury, and stereotyped behavior. Stereotypies such as purposeless hand flapping and body rocking have been reported in up to 40 percent of severely retarded children (Corbett, 1985). Irritability, tantrums, conduct disturbance, anxiety, and depression are also noted. Behavior disorders appear more frequently in severe retardation, perhaps in one-third to one-half of all cases.

Brain pathology no doubt accounts in part for disturbed behavior, especially at the lower levels of retardation. But social factors also come into play. Social isolation can curtail exposure to appropriate behavioral models; educational failure and the stigma of labeling can lead to feelings of incompetence. Certain kinds of institutional care and even the use of medication may also be associated with behavior problems. And unsurprisingly, the home environment is important. For example, degree of stability in the home (parents in the home, parental work and health histories, changes in caregiving) was found to be related to behavior disturbance in mildly retarded young adults (Richardson, Koller, and Katz, 1985).

FAMILY REACTIONS AND INFLUENCES

The birth of a handicapped child is likely to be one of the most traumatic events experienced by a family. Most parents expect that their children will be attractive, smart, graceful, athletic, and loving. Parents of a handicapped child not only mourn the loss of unfulfilled expectations but often face enormous strain on their psychological and economic resources.

Parental reactions to having a handicapped child have been studied by questioning and observing parents. Many common themes emerge from the data, and some researchers suggest that family reaction/adjustment occurs in three stages (Blacher, 1984). Upon first being informed of their child's condition, parents only partly perceive the reality of the situation. Shock and denial are frequently experienced. Looking back on this event, parents believe that families benefit by being told as early as possible and by being told the truth (Carr, 1985). Some "shop around" for other professional opinions; this behavior may reflect denial or a reasonable search for the best medical judgment. When malformations are not visible, families are more apt to deny the diagnosis for longer periods of time.

When the diagnosis is confirmed and better accepted, and further information is gathered, the child's special needs become recognized. Parents then enter the second stage, which is characterized by emotional disorganization. Chronic sadness, low self-esteem, hopelessness, guilt, disappointment, and anger are reported. Parent-child attachment may be delayed due to emotional upheavals, and also to the delay of reciprocal eye-to-eye contact, smiling, and other social interactions. This does not mean, of course, that attachment never develops; indeed, some parents become uniquely attached to their handicapped child.

Eventually a third stage is usually reached, in which emotional reorganization, adjustment, and acceptance occur. Parents reconstruct the needs of the entire family, and become more comfortable with their situation. They actively seek services and may even become advocates for the handicapped.

It should be noted that some researchers are suspicious of a stage model of parental reactions. They are wary of weaknesses in the research and clinical impressions. Although parents do report common experiences, it seems reasonable that families may be required to continually adjust and readjust in a more complex pattern than stages would predict. Also, families vary greatly in their capacity to adapt to the retarded child and in how they are affected by the situation (Hagamen, 1980). For example, shaky marriages may be at risk (Harris, 1984). And whereas normal siblings are not generally seriously affected (Carr, 1985), older sisters may be especially stressed. At the same time, many children with disabled siblings appear more considerate and kind to those siblings, which could be a forerunner of altruism and humanistic concerns in adulthood (Dunn, 1988).

Unsurprisingly, families of retarded children experience relatively high rates of stress (Crnic, 1988). A number of factors can influence reaction and adjustment, including the severity of the retardation. Moderate and severe levels require planning for a lifetime of extensive care and supervision. Family adaptation is also influenced by the availability and quality of professional services, marital interaction, religious beliefs, attitudes, family size and structure, SES, and intellectual functioning of the parents. A high level of intelligence and education does not guarantee good adjustment, of course, but it is believed that the capacity to clearly understand what is wrong and what resources exist facilitates coping. Yet, it is just such knowledge that may be lacking in many families (e.g., Kornblatt and Heinrich, 1985).

Family adjustment is likely to result from a complex of variables, and may vary over time. Such adjustment is critical in determining how the child is to develop and be cared for. Essential to the growth of the intellect of all children are mental, sensory, and verbal stimulation and the mediation of experience by significant adults (Grossman, 1983). The medical and child-management needs of retarded children also demand special parent involvement. Adequate intervention requires not only that parents be knowledgeable but also that they be motivated to work with their child.

Fortunately, greater recognition is now being given to family needs. These include economic assistance, medical care, general child psychological counseling, child management training, and training of parents as teachers for their handicapped children. Behavioral family therapy, marital therapy, and individual intervention can all be of help (Harris, 1984). They are always of immense importance but especially when the philosophy of treatment encourages home care for retarded individuals.

PLACEMENT, TREATMENT, AND EDUCATION

Although MR can be viewed as a psychological, medical, or educational handicap, in the final anaysis it is a social concern (Cytryn and Lourie, 1980). Attitudes about mental deficiency have reflected the general feelings of the times. Ancient Roman laws permitted exterminations of retarded persons; medieval Europe looked upon them as jesters or creatures of the devil. Modern history is marked by three distinct periods of heightened interest and creative thinking about MR. These periods were associated with social upheaval and liberal, democratic attitudes toward the less fortunate members of society.

The first modern period coincided with the French and American revolutions of the late 1700s. This was the time of Itard and an increased concern for the mentally disturbed. The second period followed the revolutions in Europe in the mid-1800s; among other things it was characterized by a favorable climate toward special education. Itard's student, Sequin, was a leader in this movement, which spread rapidly to the United States. Residential schools opened to educate retarded children and then return them to the community (Szymanski and Crocker, 1985). This enlightened view, marked in 1876 by the formation of the forerunner of AAMD, was gradually overwhelmed, however, by several events. Increased interest in biology as a cause of MR, developments in genetics and eugenics, the rise of psychoanalysis, and misuse or misunderstanding of IQ tests all strengthened the view that mental deficiency was incurable and that retarded persons were a detriment if not a danger to society. This led to widespread institutionalization, with institutions growing in number and size throughout the first half of this century. Custodial care rather than actual treatment became commonplace.

Soon after the mid-1900s, the third period began (Cytryn and Lourie, 1980). Improved medical care had led to longer lifespans for the retarded and better diagnosis and treatment for certain conditions. Follow-up studies of retarded persons who had been released to the community showed that many had done quite well. And the 1960s brought renewed interest in the rights of the poor, handicapped, and minority children. The concept of normalization, first popularized in Scandinavia, became the backbone of attitudes toward mental retardation.

Normalization is a philosphy about the goal of treatment and how the goal is to be reached. Its main idea is that treatment should aim at producing behaviors that are as normative as possible and should accomplish this goal by methods as culturally normative as possible (Szymanski and Crocker, 1985; Wolfensberger, 1980). Each person is seen as having the right to living arrangements, treatment, and education that are most suitable, most normal, and least restrictive as possible.

Living Arrangements

Normalization played a role in the movement to deinstutitionalize retarded persons. Observers put forth convincing arguments against public institutions, many of which were large and poorly staffed. They argued that the residents did not receive individualized training and medical care, much less human interaction. In fact, it was believed that residents often learned damaging behaviors, such as excessive dependency. Such arguments combined with concern over the costs of institutions to produce change.

In the United States the number of retarded persons in public institutions declined in the late 1960s (Craig and McCarver, 1984), as did the number of institutions (Braddock and Heller, 1985a). Moreover, individuals were placed at older chronological ages, and fewer mildly/moderately retarded persons were institutionalized (Epple, Jacobson, and Janicki, 1985; Scheerenberger, 1982).

Along with these changes has come the rise of community settings that serve as alternatives for traditional institutional living (Bruininks, Hauber, and Kudla, 1980; Emerson, 1985). These include small regional centers, small group homes, and foster homes, which provide a more homelike atmosphere and greater opportunity for privacy, independence, and interface with the larger community. Such placements can fall short of ideal, of course. When relocation from a traditional to a community setting occurs, it can be traumatic to mentally retarded persons and their families, who worry that the retarded will be forced into an unprotective environment (Braddock and Heller, 1985b). And some researchers warn that alternative settings too often have the weaknesses of traditional institutions: Social isolation, stigmatization, dependency and regimentation, and lack of power of the residents (Emerson, 1985). Still, others speak of a higher quality of life for clients, including progress in what they can do and greater happiness. Placement outcome can be expected to depend on the match between the retarded person's needs and the living arrangement. Large institution size does not always mean negative outcome; indeed, retarded children often continue to develop in traditional institutions (Hodapp and Zigler, 1985). But smaller regional centers are veiwed as more optimal for children. What is unfortunate is that placement decisions may not rest on the needs of the individual.

Regardless of the increase in alternative residential settings, most retarded youngsters remain with their families throughout childhood. Family members need some freedom to pursue their interests without the burden of supervising the retarded child (Hagamen, 1980; Joyce, Singer, and Isralowitz, 1983). They also require relief in times of increased stress. Respite care programs are designed to provide such support in a variety of ways. In-home care involves trained caregivers coming to the home on a part time schedule to care for the handicapped youngsters. Out-of-home programs entail the handicapped child's traveling to some other place for care; for example, the child may live at home during the week and stay at a hospital or foster home on weekends. Mothers receiving respite care have reported that they do feel relieved, have more time for other family members, enjoy leisure activities, and relate in a more positive way to their disabled children (Joyce et al., 1983).

Treatment

Treatment for retarded children must take into account not only intellectual deficits but also medical, social, and behavioral problems. The family is an important consideration (Crnic and Reid, 1989). Medical procedures, individual and family therapy, and behavior modification are commonly employed.

Medications are not known to enhance intellectual functioning in the retarded (Szymanski and Crocker, 1985). However, they may be used to alleviate anxiety, overactivity, aggression, self-abuse, and psychotic behavior. Inappropriate use of drugs and overdosage have been documented in the care of the institutionalized (Rivinus, 1980). Specific rules have been developed in most states to deal with pharmacologic treatment.

Special Olympics is an example of community programs that attempt to normalize the lives of retarded persons and to provide them with success experiences and a sense of self-worth. (Alan Carey/The Image Works)

Many require only the usual medical standards, such as adequate indications for the use of a drug and periodic review. Some states call for more stringent procedures, such as seeking legal permission when the person is considered incompetent for informed consent.

It is often assumed that cognitive and language deficits preclude individual "talking" therapies for the retarded. Of course, psychotherapeutic techniques must be adapted to the developmental level of the client. Among other guidelines, Szymanski (1980) suggests that therapists be directive and set specific goals and limits. Language must be concrete and clear, and nonverbal techniques need to be used in the face of communication difficulties (e.g., play or other activities). Contact with parents and caregivers may be important in helping

them adjust to the handicapped child's condition.

Group therapy with retarded persons has been reported (Szymanski and Rosefsky, 1980; Szymanski and Crocker, 1985). With children, the focus may be on activities or family interactions. Multiple family groups can provide opportunities for families to learn from each other, improve communication, share feelings, and encourage independence in retarded youngsters. Evaluation of such therapy indicates that it can be helpful.

The single most important innovation in treatment for the retarded has been the application of behavioral techniques. Fuller's 1949 demonstration of operant conditioning in a profoundly retarded 18-year-old was a landmark in the use of behavior modification. Widespread application in institutions took another decade or so but helped tranform custodial care into active treatment (Birnbrauer, 1976). Learning principles, especially operant procedures, currently are used to teach self-help, imitation, academic and work skills, social skills, and language. They also help reduce inappropriate behaviors such as aggression, self-stimulation, self-injury, and tantrums (Kiernan, 1985).

Even the simplest skills can be beneficial. For example, the ability to dress, feed, bathe, and otherwise care for one's basic physical needs enhances integration of the retarded with others. Children who cannot perform these behaviors may be limited from participating in educational and social activities. Thus, self-help programs have targeted the gamut of behaviors: Eating with utensils, dressing, washing and combing the hair, toothbrushing, and the like (e.g., Doleys, Stacy, and Knowles, 1981; Matson, Ollendick, and Adkins, 1980).

Consistent with the behavioral approach, efforts have been made to train caregivers. Teaching packages and courses have been developed to disseminate information. Evaluation of outcome has been conducted, with attempts to establish the value of programs to the everyday activities of the child (Kiernan, 1985). Overall, there has been considerable success in serving the retarded child, who so often had been viewed as unable to learn. This is not to say that the application of behavioral techniques is simple; it requires skill, effort, and perseverance. Enormous gains have been made, but more is yet to be accomplished. One of the greatest needs is to disseminate the more advanced techniques and thinking.

Education

If Itard's efforts to train the Wild Boy of Aveyon marked the beginning of endeavors to educate the retarded, only in the present century did wide-scale and improved methods of individualized education come into their own. In the United States there was a dramatic expansion of special education for the mildly retarded from around 1925 to 1960 (Lilly, 1979c). But the public schools were not compelled to admit more severely retarded children, nor were parents given public assistance for the education of these youngsters.

In the late 1950s, lack of education for handicapped children and reported abuses of intelligence testing were closely examined. Growing commitment to the idea that all handicapped children have a right to appropriate education resulted in a sweeping legal reform: Public Law 94–142, the Education for all Handicapped Children Act of 1975.

The purpose of this law is to assure that all handicapped children obtain a free public education designed to meet their unique needs; to assure the rights of the handicapped and their parents and guardians; to assist states and localities in providing education; and to assess and assure the effectiveness of educational efforts. P.L. 94–142 specifies that:

1. All children, between the ages of 3 and 21, are entitled to a free appropriate public education, no matter what their handicap.
2. All children receiving special educational services must be fairly and accurately evaluated. More than one type of assessment procedure must be used, tests must be free of racial/cultural bias, and tests must be administered by trained personnel.
3. An individualized educational program (IEP) must be constructed for each student receiving special education. It must consider the child's present functioning, educational objectives, long-term goals, educational services to be given, expected length of services, and procedures for evaluations. IEPs must be reviewed annually by a committee and the child's parents.
4. Handicapped children must be educated with nonhandicapped children, to the maximum extent that is appropriate; that is, they must be placed in the least restrictive environment and be placed close to home.
5. Parents' and students' rights must be protected throughout the special education process. Parents have the right to participate in decisions, review records, present complaints about educational plans, and call for hearings if disputes cannot be resolved. Procedures must be established to ensure these rights. (Haring, 1986)

There is no doubt that P.L. 94–142 has brought about many changes in educating MR children. In particular it has strengthened individualized programming, increased parental participation, and encouraged maintenance of the retarded in the community and regular classroom. Let us look more closely at this last issue.

Historically, special education for the mentally handicapped typically meant assigning them to special classes or schools, thus drastically limiting contact with normal children. This policy, especially as it applied to EMR students, was attacked in several ways (Corman and Gottlieb, 1978; MacMillan et al., 1986). It was argued that minority group students were disproportionately labeled EMR largely on the basis of biased IQ tests. Second, special education did not seem to benefit the children. Third, there was no reason that individualized programming could not be accomplished within the regular classroom.

P.L. 94–142 endorsed this position, and

thousands of mildly retarded children have been transferred from segregated classrooms and "mainstreamed" in the educational system. They may spend the entire day in regular classrooms or divide the day between regular and special programming. How is this policy affecting mentally handicapped children? More specifically, has mainstreaming facilitated academic progress and social acceptance?

To date, there is no convincing evidence that the children do any better academically. However, it is difficult to control research in the natural school setting, and the findings are somewhat mixed (MacMillan et al., 1986). Perhaps the influential variables are not being examined. Academic progress can be expected to depend on the specific ways in which children are handled and on the quality of teacher training and motivation

(Szymanski and Crocker, 1985). Both regular and special classrooms vary a great deal in these respects, but it is difficult to measure the variations and their effects.

Mainstreaming also has not brought social acceptance. Mainstreamed handicapped children have inferior social status; they are less well known and less accepted by other children (MacMillan et al., 1986). Advocates of mainstreaming had hoped that familiarity would lead to increased acceptance, but this does not appear to be the case. The picture is not entirely bleak because interventions can improve social status. Also, mainstreaming has enhanced the self-concepts of some retarded children.

It is important to remember that the least restrictive environment clause of P.L. 94–142 does not require mainstreaming into regular classrooms for all children. Rather,

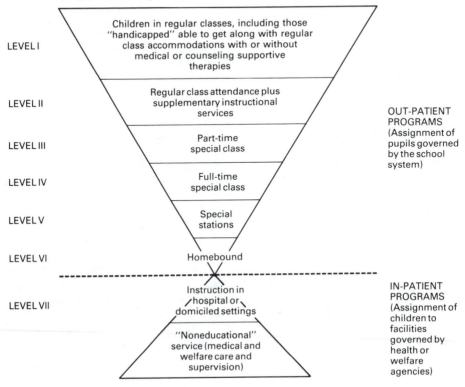

FIGURE 10–5 Deno's model for special education services that incorporates the philosophy of the least restrictive environment. The tapering indicates the differences in number of children at different levels. From Deno, 1970.

LEVEL I — Children in regular classes, including those "handicapped" able to get along with regular class accommodations with or without medical or counseling supportive therapies

LEVEL II — Regular class attendance plus supplementary instructional services

LEVEL III — Part-time special class

LEVEL IV — Full-time special class

LEVEL V — Special stations

LEVEL VI — Homebound

OUT-PATIENT PROGRAMS (Assignment of pupils governed by the school system)

LEVEL VII — Instruction in hospital or domiciled settings

"Noneducational" service (medical and welfare care and supervision)

IN-PATIENT PROGRAMS (Assignment of children to facilities governed by health or welfare agencies)

a continuum of placements is called for, ranging from the regular classroom to residential settings. As shown in Figure 10–5, most children would be assigned to the regular classroom, but many alternatives exist. The overriding goal is to place each child, to the extent feasible, in the situation that is most similar to the environments of the nonhandicapped, and encourage the most normative learning and social interaction. In other words, the philosophy of normalization underlies P.L. 94–142.

SUMMARY

Mental retardation is defined by AAMD as subaverage intellectual functioning and deficient adaptive behavior that are manifested by the eighteenth birthday. Subaverage intellectual functioning refers to performance of about 70 or less on individual standardized tests of intelligence. The criterion for adaptive behavior is not as stringently set and in practice adaptive behavior is less important in the definition.

Modern intelligence testing began in the early 1900s, with Binet's test to identify children in need of special education. Goddard and Terman were instrumental in applying this work in the United States but, unlike Binet, they assumed that intelligence is an individual, inherent, and stable characteristic.

The Stanford-Binet and Wechsler tests are widely used to identify MR. They consist of a variety of intellectual tasks, and performance is judged in comparison to age-norms. These tests correlate reasonably well with academic performance, but less so with other achievements. They also are reasonably reliable over time for groups of people, but changes in individual scores are often observed. Many psychologists have noted several limitations in IQ tests.

Infant tests of intelligence, which yield a DQ, do not correlate highly with IQ tests. However, they can be helpful in screening infants for MR when used with clinical information.

Adaptive behavior scales assess domains of everyday behavior, and rely on reports of adults who come into contact with the client. They vary in reliability, and in general correlate moderately well with intelligence test scores. The Vineland Adaptive Behavior Scales and AAMD's scales are widely used.

Levels of MR, from mild to profound, are recognized according to IQ scores and, to a lesser extent, adaptive behavior. Prevalence data show that mild retardation is by far the most common. The data also indicate that MR is most prevalent in persons of school age, low SES, and male gender. Social expectations play some role in creating this epidemiologic profile.

The causes of MR vary, and include chromosome abnormalities, metabolic defects inherited in Mendelian patterns, prenatal and birth variables, and an array of postnatal factors such as disease, diet, and disadvantaged social/intellectual environment. Known biological factors are more closely associated with severe levels than with less severe levels of MR.

Much discussion has ensued over cultural-familial retardation, in which the child is mildly retarded and shows no obvious biological etiology. A family pattern is observed, which could be accounted for by genetic or environmental factors or their combination. Twin and adoption studies indicate some genetic influence on measured intelligence, but along with other kinds of investigations they also indicate a role for the environment.

Mild retardation especially has been discussed with regard to the cultural bias of IQ tests. Legal decisions have forced the stringent monitoring of intelligence testing in the public schools.

Research into learning and cognition has shown that operant learning principles apply to the retarded, although learning is more difficult to achieve with lower levels of retardation. Retarded children appear to develop in Piagetian stages but develop more slowly and do not reach the most advanced stages. They also show deficits in information processing (e.g., some attention processes, strategy use, generalization), including the executive functions. Some cognitive deficits appear as developmental lags but others appear to be true differences from normal processes.

Retarded children show social skill disabilities and greater than average behavior problems. Biological causation may operate, especially for behavior problems, but social factors also are likely causes.

Family adjustment to having a retarded child has been described as occurring in three stages, but may be more complex than this. Many variables are involved in adjustment, and families are receiving more support than in the past.

Attitudes about MR reflect society's general attitudes, and three periods of progress marked the last three centuries, most recently in the 1960s. The philosophy of *normalization* has served as a backdrop for recent changes in placement, therapy, and education of the mentally handicapped. Deinstitutionalization went hand in hand with an increase in community living arrangements. Individual and group psychotherapy, which often include the family, can be helpful when the special needs of mentally handicapped persons are considered. Behavioral programs have brought dramatic improvement, changing treatment from custodial care to actual treatment. P.L. 94–142 has brought similarly dramatic changes to the educational system, including the mandate to provide the most appropriate education in the least restrictive environment.

11

LEARNING DISABILITIES

This chapter is about children whose failure to learn in school is viewed as a *primary specific* learning disability that is discrepant with their general intellectual ability. Concern over academic failure is far from new, of course. However, particularly in industrialized societies, successful negotiation through the educational system is increasingly important to occupational and social success. Thus, specific learning problems that interfere with academic success are of increasing interest.

Until the 1960s children whose school performance was below their general ability were often referred to as "underachievers" (Kessler, 1988). Much attention was given to their psychosocial behavior, motivation, anxiety, and family functioning. It was also recognized that some of these children had specific learning problems, such as in reading and arithmetic, and some were said to have "minimal brain damage." Parents and professionals alike were concerned that the needs of these children were not being met, and they encouraged the creation of the category of learning disabilities.

DEFINITION

In 1963 representatives from several organizations met at a symposium sponsored by the Fund for Perceptually Handicapped Children. In his address to the conferees, Samuel Kirk (1963) noted that their concern was for children usually labeled according to two criteria. One criterion was etiological: It was assumed that the children had some kind of neurological or brain dysfunction. The other criterion was behavioral: The children exhibited a variety of deficiencies, especially learning difficulties, perceptual problems, and hyperactivity. Kirk suggested that the term *learning disability* would be suitable for all of the children and would also avoid the need to establish nervous system dysfunction. Importantly, he thought that the term could encourage and guide the assessment and educational remediation so needed by the children.

Learning disabilities (LD) was not a new term, but Kirk's presentation marked the creation of a new field (Hallahan and Kauffman, 1978; Taylor, 1988b). The term gradually became widely accepted by professional groups and parents, and a field of study grew around it. Parents whose children might otherwise have been labeled mentally retarded were given hope that the problem was limited and could be treated. Teachers were relieved of the suspicion that they were to blame for the failure of certain students. School administrators and other concerned professionals were provided with a label that could make children eligible for special services. Thus, from the beginning *learning disabilities* not only referred to a heterogeneous group of children, but also simplified the complex social issues for labeling these children (Senf, 1986).

The definition of learning disabilities given by Kirk's group became especially important because an adaptation of it was later employed by the federal government in mandating special education for learning disabled children. The definition used by the government states:

"Specific learning disability" means a disorder in one or more of the basic psychological processes involved in understanding or in using language, spoken or written, which may manifest itself in imperfect ability to listen, think, speak, read, write, spell, or to do mathematical calculations. The term includes such conditions as perceptual handicaps, brain injury, minimal brain dysfunction, dyslexia, developmental aphasia. The term does not include children who have learning problems which are primarily the result of visual, hearing, or motor handicaps, or mental retardation, or emotional disturbance, or of environmental, cultural, or economic disadvantage. (U.S. Office of Education, 1977, p. 65083)

This is not to say, however, that there is complete satisfaction with this definition. To the contrary, dissatisfaction has been expressed about several theoretical, social, and practical issues, especially about how to operationalize the definition, the exclusionary criteria, and the lack of a statement about neurological etiology.

Specific Criteria For LD

The federal government's definition of LD (and other similar ones) is conceptual and lacks specific guidelines to identify a learning disability. Is it necessary to determine dysfunction in basic psychological processes? If so, how is this to be done, and what criteria should be used, especially since these basic processes are not well established? And what criteria are to be used to decide that performance in listening, reading, writing, arithmetic, and other such skills are disordered? These questions have not been easy to answer. Two basic methods, nevertheless, have been generated to identify learning disabilities (Morris, 1988). They grew from criteria set by the Office of Education and, interestingly, neither of them targets the psychological processes assumed to be deficient (Haring and McCormick, 1986).

One method defines LD by a discrepancy between intellectual ability and achievement level. It is assumed that LD children have at least average general intellectual ability (IQ) but below average functioning

(achievement) in some academic area. Comparisons are thus made between IQ and achievement tests scores. Various procedures and formulas are used to accomplish this, and dissatisfaction with them has been expressed. In addition, there is no scientifically established guideline for selecting how large a discrepancy should define learning disability. In fact, this criterion may be varied to control the number of children eligible for special education services.

Still other problems exist with the IQ-achievement discrepancy approach. It is assumed that IQ and achievement performances are independent and that a learning disability will not affect IQ (Siegel, 1989, 1990). However, IQ tests measure many of the abilities considered deficient in LD children, such as language expression and knowledge of specific facts. Indeed, IQ may decrease due to a learning disability (Stanovich, 1986). This poses a problem, since LD children are supposed to have about average intellectual potential. As it is, for most groups of LD children, the average

IQ is about 90, or low average (Taylor, 1988b). Moreover, children with somewhat lower IQ scores can be disqualified from special education services, although they otherwise appear learning disabled.

A second way to operationalize LD is by performance below expected grade or age level in at least one academic area. Variations occur in the specific criteria, although they often are set from two years to one-half year. Thus, with the two-year criterion, a sixth grader who is achieving at the fourth-grade level in arithmetic can be labeled as learning disabled, providing that certain other factors do not account for the performance. One obvious problem in this approach is that a large discrepancy would seem more serious for a younger child than for an older child. For example, being two years behind is more serious for a third grader than for a sixth grader. This problem can be reduced by setting the criterion according to grade, for example, at one year deficiency for younger children and two for older children. Of course, judgments still must be made as to when the criterion should change.

Exclusionary Criteria

Another widely expressed concern about the definition of LD has to do with the exclusion of children with certain sensory and motor handicaps, emotional disturbances, or disadvantaged environmental background. Although it is fairly easy to measure sensory and motor handicaps, the degree of handicap required for exclusion is arguable. And it is not always easy to determine whether emotional disturbance caused learning problems or resulted from them. The exclusion of children who are environmentally disadvantaged has been of special concern. Of course, these children can be classified as learning disabled as long as deficits in psychological processes are considered primary. However, it is difficult to make this distinction, and for that matter to distinguish some cases of LD from underachievement due to other causes, for example, to lack of motivation (Stanovich, 1986).

Other Dissatisfactions

Other dissatisfactions with the definition have been expressed. Thus, for example, the National Joint Committee for Learning Disabilities (now the Learning Disabilities Association of America) recommended a definition that deletes any reference to "basic psychological processes," the criteria for which had never been spelled out by the federal guidelines (Hammill, 1990). Further, the NJCLD definition states that learning disabilities are presumed to be due to central nervous system dysfunction. To give another example, DSM-III-R recognizes the disorders as Specific Developmental Disorders and has its own way of classifying them (Table 11–1).

Overall, some of the disagreements over the definition of LD reflect basic controversy about how to conceptualize learning problems. Others reflect concern about the practical and social implications of the definition, for example, about the number of

TABLE 11–1 Specific Developmental Disorders, DSM-III-R*

Academic Skills Disorders
Arithmetic (dyscalculia)
Expressive writing
Reading (dyslexia)
Language and Speech Disorders
Articulation
Expressive language
Receptive language
Motor Skills Disorder
Coordination disorder

* These disorders are coded on Axis II, as are other developmental disorders. They are diagnosed when performance is below what is expected on standardized tests or developmental norms. They are not due to known physical or neurological disorders, Mental Retardation, Pervasive Development Disorder, or deficient educational opportunities. All are associated with academic impairment. The child may function at a level that is normal for younger children, but there is no assumption that the child will catch up.

children requiring special education and who will be excluded from special education. Over the years, different definitions and criteria have been used by different groups and have led to difficulties in establishing prevalence, inconsistency in assigning children to special education, and incomparability of research groups. Still, to put the issue in broad perspective, it can be argued that despite the shortcomings of defining LD, the creation of the category has called attention to a real problem (Taylor, 1988b). Considerable effort is being made to describe and identify learning-disabled children, to understand their functioning, and to maximize their achievements.

PREVALENCE

A widely accepted estimate of the prevalence of learning disabilities among U.S. school-age children is 5 to 15 percent (Taylor, 1989). But estimates have varied enormously (Hallahan and Kauffman, 1978). Boys are more often identified than girls, perhaps two to five times as often (DSM-III-R, 1987; Taylor, 1988b).

Prevalence rates are extremely difficult to establish for LD. Not only are there differences in definitions and criteria, but prevalence is related to demands on the school system, which often provides the data. Thus, for example, between 1977 and 1987, the number of learning-disabled children served by special education just about doubled (Kirk and Gallagher, 1989). It is debatable whether actual prevalence increased or whether more children were being placed into the LD category.

Prevalence rates regarding social class and cultural groups are also related to school placement and sociopolitical issues (Kessler, 1988). It appears that initially white middle-class children compared to black children were disproportionately placed in learning disabilities classes, and black children disproportionately placed into classes for the educably mentally retarded. Indeed, learning disabilities were said to be middle-class disorders (Senf, 1986). However, in 1984 learning disabilities classrooms reflected proportionate numbers of blacks, whites, and Hispanics (Chinn and Hughes, 1987). This change probably reflected pressure to recognize standardized tests as discriminatory towards certain groups, to avoid the stigma of mental retardation, and to obtain school placements that would optimize learning.

ACADEMIC PERFORMANCE

LD children most commonly show deficits in reading, written expression and spelling, and mathematics (Taylor, 1989). The vast majority are reading disabled. In the classroom, teachers report that LD children fail in simple arithmetic computation, confuse one word with another, rapidly forget too much of what they have learned, or struggle to write neatly (Figures 11–1 and 11–2).

Deficits may exist in only one or two academic areas, so that the child shows an uneven profile of skills. However, deficits often occur in several areas. Also, although some children show quite isolated deficiencies within an area, the deficits tend to be pervasive. In spelling, for example, deficits may exist in only some or all of the required skills for associating sounds with symbols, recognizing and remembering written words, and using spelling for writing. In arithmetic, deficits may exist in only some or all of the needed computational, visual-spatial, memory, and mathematical reasoning skills. Thus, academic failure is best viewed in terms of the different components of reading, writing, spelling, and arithmetic.

Older LD children and adolescents have increasing academic demands made upon

a)

$$9\overline{)4527}$$

$62.04
-5.30
————
11774

b)

$82.04
-5.30
————
5634

75
+8
———
163

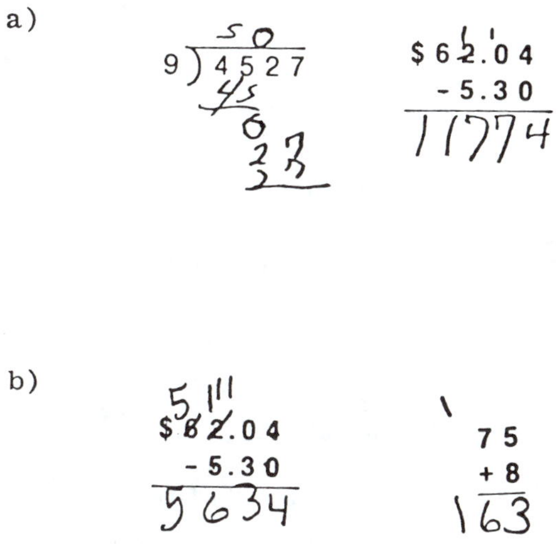

FIGURE 11–1 Arithmetic computation errors made by (top) a 12-year-old boy and (bottom) a 10-year-old girl. From Taylor, 1988. Permission to reprint by Guilford Press. Copyright 1988 by Guilford Press.

them, which they often cannot meet. These include complex language demands and performance in areas such as science and social studies (Lerner, 1989; Schumaker, Deshler, and Ellis, 1986). Overall, there are deficits in knowledge, as the handicapped youngsters have not learned as many facts and concepts as nondisabled children (Taylor, 1989). This becomes more obvious as they proceed through grade levels. In turn, the lack of networks of knowledge makes new learning more difficult. LD children thus may be increasingly handicapped by what they have failed to learn in the past.

Some evidence exists that older LD children do not use the most effective strategies for learning. In the typical course of development, children gradually acquire increasingly effective skills in listening, note taking, and study habits. This developmental course may go awry in LD children. Deficits in basic cognitive processes may certainly underlie ineffective study, but loss of motivation and interest may also be involved.

COGNITIVE DEFICITS

It is agreed that learning-disabled children show a wide variety of cognitive deficits and also that much individual variation exists in the specific deficiencies displayed. The following discussion highlights the general findings about these deficits.

Attention Deficits

An association between learning problems and attention deficits has long been recognized. The overlap of learning disorders and Attention-Deficit Hyperactivity Disorder is well documented and was detailed earlier in this text (pp. 188–189). Indeed, research samples have often contained an unknown mix of LD, ADHD, and LD-ADHD subjects, so that is has been difficult to draw firm conclusions about LD children. In fact, a complete picture of attention deficits has not emerged (e.g., Ackerman et al., 1986; Felton and Wood, 1989).

Krupski (1986) has concluded that learning disabled children are among those who have impairments in sustained attention. For example, non-ADHD learning disabled youngsters appear to show deficits on vigilance tasks, which require sustained attention.

Distractibility (selective attention deficits) is frequently mentioned as part of learning disabilities. LD children are said to be overly sensitive to a variety of environmental stimuli and thus respond to stimulation that is irrelevant to the task at hand. However, Kruspki notes that the children are distracted by some but not all irrelevant stimuli. Distal distractors, which occur at some distance and are easily distinguished from the task, have no adverse affect. Examples are background classroom noise and intermittent flashing of lights on the ceiling. On the other hand, task performance can be im-

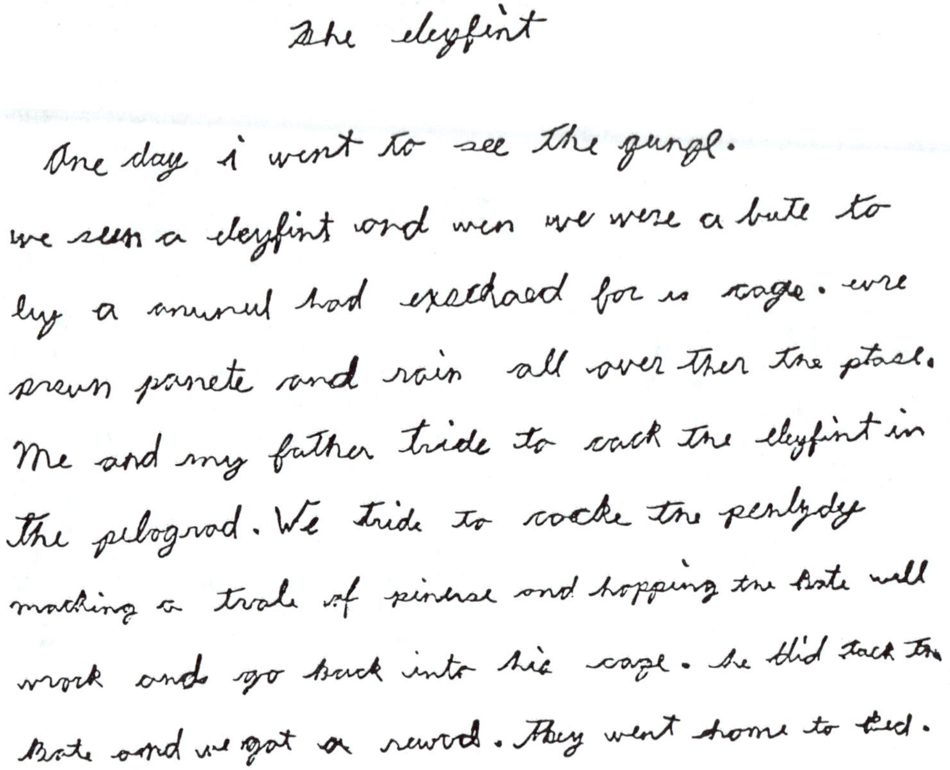

the elyfint

*One day i went to see the gungl.
we seen a elyfint ond wen we were a bute to
ly a anumul had exethaed for is cage. evre
prown panete and rain all over ther the ptasl.
Me and my father tride to cack the elyfint in
the pilogrod. We tride to rocke the penlyjdy
maching a trale of pinese ond hopping the Bate will
work onds go back into hie cage. he thid tack the
Bate and we got a rewrd. They went home to bed.*

The Elephant
One day I went to see the jungle. We seen a elephant and when we
were about to leave an animal escaped from his cage. Every person
panicked and ran all over the place. Me and my father tried to catch the
elephant in the playground. We tried to catch the elephant by making a
trail of peanuts and hoping the bait would work and he would go back
into his cage. He did take the bait and we got a reward. Then we went
home to bed.

FIGURE 11–2 The writing of an 11-year-old boy and the probable
translation. The writing shows imagination, a rich vocabulary, and a
basic grasp of story telling. There also are misspellings of common and
uncommon words, added and missing words in sentences, poorly
formed letters, and retracing of letters that suggests difficulty in the
mechanics of writing. From Taylor, 1988. Permission to reprint by Guilford
Press. Copyright 1988 by Guilford Press.

paired by distractors that are embedded in the task. An example of a task would be asking the child to sort cards with or without a drawing of a flower. Some of the cards would also have a distractor such as the drawing of a square. In general, the tasks themselves appear to make greater cognitive demands than those used with distal distractors. This at least raises the question of whether performance reflects a cognitive deficiency broader than attention.

Overall though, the research pinpoints sustained attention as problematic for LD children, and shows that selective attention especially depends on the situation. In this regard, attention deficits of LD appear similar to those of ADHD. It is probably the case that in some studies these two groups were not clearly differentiated. Further research with carefully defined learning-disabled groups is needed for a more complete description of attention deficits.

Perceptual and Perceptual-Motor Problems

Perceptual and perceptual-motor deficits also have long been implicated in learning disabilities. Perceptual problems are associated with brain dysfunction and motor coordination problems, which are seen in some LD children. In addition, it appears quite reasonable that perceptual processing deficits might interfere with learning, for example, by limiting the ability to distinguish the sound of one word from another or perceive differences between written letters such as *b* and *d*.

By far, hearing and vision are the perceptual modes most studied. Auditory information processing consists of numerous functions such as discriminating, sequencing, and comprehending sounds, assigning meaning to sounds and remembering them (Bryan and Bryan, 1986). Visual processing encompasses the same functions with regard to visual material. In either case, it is assumed that difficulty with one perceptual function interferes with others, and affects academic performance.

Perceptual processing is usually evaluated by standardized tests or laboratory tasks. When compared to nonhandicapped subjects, LD children have shown a variety of deficits in both the auditory and visual modalities. For example, they may respond more slowly to visual stimuli, and show deficits in short-term memory for auditorily presented letters, words, and named objects (Mann, 1986).

However, interpreting the findings as perceptual impairments has become suspect. The results could be due to factors other than perceptual deficits, such as differences in attention, language skills, learning strategies, following instructions, or motivation. Moreover, even when perception is implicated, the direction of causation can be questioned: Perhaps learning disabilities cause perceptual problems rather than the other way around.

At the present time, there is a tendency to downplay the importance of perception in learning disabilities (Bryan and Bryan, 1986; Haring and McCormick, 1986). However, Taylor (1988b) notes that nonverbal (motor-perceptual) skills are related to academic performance. It can probably be said that some LD children have some perceptual deficiencies, and that such deficits play some role in LD. It is important that research continue in this area.

Memory, Cognitive Strategies, Executive Functions

There is evidence for memory deficits in learning disabilities. For example, memory impairment is correlated with reading disability (Stanovich, 1986). Poor readers typically recall fewer items from lists of linguistic material than good readers (Mann and Brady, 1988). This finding holds for lists of letters, words, nonsense syllables, sentences, digits, and nameable objects—and whether they are heard or seen. Different explanations are offered for the memory deficits displayed by poor readers. One is that disabled readers fail to remember the sounds connected to words (Mann, 1986). Another popular explanation emphasizes deficiencies in using memory strategies.

Poor readers do use fewer strategies that promote memory such as rehearsal, clustering, and elaboration (Stanovich, 1986). They also use them less often and less efficiently.

For example, in learning lists of words, rehearsal is used less and so is organization of the words by meaning (Pressley and Levin, 1987). In more complex tasks, such as the learning of prose, poor readers do not elaborate, or add context to help learning, and do not as efficiently select cues from the text that would aid the retrieval of information from memory.

Executive skills also show deficits (Torgesen, 1986). LD children fail to adapt to learning tasks. They lack knowledge about when, why, and how to use the strategies they possess (Pressley and Levin, 1987). They fail to notice what a specific task requires, and to monitor how well they are doing. Perhaps even more disturbing, when they realize that they are having difficulty, they give up instead of switching strategies and trying harder, as efficient learners do. Whereas giving up has to do with motivation, it is clear that executive functions, including metamemory (p. 230), are inadequate in some LD children.

Language Deficits

Language problems are viewed as central to learning disabilities, as most definitions of LD make clear. Speech and language deficits are clearly tied to reading disability, and language obviously is part of the "basics" of writing and spelling. But arithmetic also requires linguistic ability for understanding mathematical terms, signs, and word problems. Moreover, language is intricately tied to thinking and information processing.

Language disorders are referred to as *aphasia* or *developmental aphasia*, terms that are not quite accurate as they mean loss of language that was already acquired. *Dysphasia*, meaning that the functions never developed, is also used (Baker and Cantwell, 1989).

As we saw in Chapter 2, basic language skills develop rapidly in sequence so that most six-year-old children are amazingly adept in language. Table 11–2 defines basic

components of language that must be mastered. As complex as language is, there are many ways in which development can go awry.

In discussing language disorders, we will follow the DSM-III-R approach, which considers problems in articulation and expressive and receptive functions. Table 11–3 provides summary descriptions of these disorders. *Articulation* disorder has to do with the misproduction of speech sounds. The child makes errors, distortions, substitutions, and omissions in producing speech. For example, incorrect sounds may be used in the place of more difficult ones, as in the use of *wabbit* for *rabbit*. Or difficult phonemes may be omitted, as when *bu* is used instead of *blue*. Most children make some misarticulations as they acquire speech, and articulation disorder is diagnosed according to developmental norms. In general, articulation disorders have less serious consequences for the child than other language disorders.

Expressive language disorder involves inadequacies in the production of speech with regard to vocabulary, sentence structure, and other rules of language. Thus, for example, the child may have a limited vocabulary and speak in short, simple sentences. However, the child does understand speech and age-appropriate concepts and obeys simple commands, uses objects correctly, and points to objects when they are named. *Receptive language disorder*, which is the more serious, refers to difficulties in

TABLE 11–2 Basic Components of Language

Phonology	Sounds of a language and rules for combining them
Articulation	Actual production of speech sounds
Morphology	Formation of words, including the use of prefixes and suffixes (e.g., un, ed, s) to give meaning
Syntax	Organization of words into phrases and sentences
Semantics	Meanings in language
Pragmatics	Use of language in social contexts

TABLE 11–3 Developmental Language Disorders, DSM-III-R Language and Speech Disorders

Articulation	Severe cases apparent by 3 years; others by age 6	Speech sounds incorrectly made at developmentally appropriate age; some sounds omitted or some substituted by other sounds
Expressive Language	Severe cases apparent before 3 years; less severe may become apparent as late as adolescence	Impairment in expressed language: small vocabulary, vocabulary errors, short sentences, simplified grammar, unusual word order, slow rate of language development, etc.
Receptive Language	Typically apparent before age 4; less severe cases not until 7 or older	Impaired language comprehension; in mild cases, difficulty with meaning of particular kinds of words (e.g., spatial) or statements (e.g., if-then); in severe cases, inability to understand basic vocabulary and simple sentences

comprehending another's communication. The child may fail to respond to speech, seem deaf, and be uninterested in television. Language production occurs only gradually.

Developmental language disorders appear to be present in large numbers of LD children. One recent report found language dysfunctions in 90 percent of the sample (Gibbs and Cooper, 1989). The disorders are more common in boys than in girls, and expressive aphasia may be more common than the receptive type (Baker and Cantwell, 1989).

Language disorders are often evident prior to the child's going to school, but milder impairments may become evident when school work places greater cognitive demands on the child. Children may display one type of language disorder or combinations of them. Hearing is normal, and nonverbal intelligence and nonverbal communication can generally be described as normal (Baker and Cantwell, 1989). In fact, these children seem to want to communicate: They maintain eye contact, enjoy games such as pat-a-cake, and relate to others (Baker and Cantwell, 1980). Many of the problems seem to be delays in normal language. However, abnormal features such as the use of jargon may be present, especially in receptive disorder.

BOX 11.1 The role of language in reading: shifting hypotheses

Reading disabilities, or *dyslexia*, not only cause school failure and limit occupational opportunities; they also hinder everyday activities like reading a newspaper, vicariously traveling the world with *National Geographic*, and delighting in poetry. No wonder, then, the often asked question: What makes a poor reader a poor reader? (Mann, Cowin, and Schoenheimer, 1989).

In his influential theory of reading, Samuel Orton (1937) put visual deficits at the heart of the problem and this hypothesis remained central for many years. Orton noted that among other difficulties, visual deficits caused dyslexic children to reverse letters

(*d* for *b*; *saw* for *was*) and even write in mirror images (Vellutino, 1979). Other theorists suggested that dyslexia was caused by eye defects that led to impairments in scanning or tracking visual stimuli or by deficits in the processing of form, pattern, and spatial organization in visual stimuli. These theories implied defects at the early sensory stage of visual processing, which distorted visual stimuli. Such deficits were inferred from children's matching stimuli, drawing figures, and the like.

Despite its popularity, however, evidence for the visual-perceptual hypothesis was gradually called into question. In fact, it appears that few cases of reading disabilities stem from visual processing (Mann and Brady, 1988). Rather, dyslexia, it is argued, is a complex language deficiency. In one demonstration of this point, Vellutino (1987) asked poor readers in the second through sixth grades to copy words and other stimuli after a brief visual presentation. They were then requested to name the word stimuli. Poor readers had difficulties in naming words they had correctly copied. For instance, they copied *was* correctly but then called it "saw." Even then they correctly named the letters of the words (e.g., *w, a, s*). Thus, calling *was* "saw" appeared to be a problem in memory for language rather than a visual defect.

A relationship between reading disabilities and language deficits is suggested by other data and arguments. First, reading problems are more common in children who have language delays (Mann and Brady, 1988). Second, poor readers do worse than excellent readers on many language tasks but not on nonverbal tasks. Third, by definition, reading involves the recoding of language and the child who is weak in phonology, syntax, and semantics could be expected to be at risk for reading disabilities (Vellutino, 1979).

Considerable research now shows the importance of phonology in reading, and especially in learning to read (Mann and Brady, 1988; Mann et al., 1989; Torgesen and Morgan, 1990). Young children who are aware of the sounds (phonemes) of their native language and can map sounds to letters become the better readers. And training in phonological awareness can improve disabled reading. There also is some evidence that phonological deficits underlie the problems of disabled readers in naming objects and recalling verbal material.

Thus, there is a notable shift in hypotheses about the processes underlying dyslexia. Although vision obviously is involved in reading, language abilities are now seen as critically important. Emphasis is now placed on later stages of information processing rather than on early sensory processing. Reading is, of course, enormously complex and much theoretical and empirical work is needed to further test the newer hypotheses mentioned here as well as to delineate the roles of attention, syntax, and semantics.

SOCIAL AND MOTIVATIONAL FACTORS

Although intellectual functioning has been the main concern of LD research, the role of social and motivational variables is increasingly recognized (Bryan and Bryan, 1990). Current ideas and interest in children's social and emotional life are being applied to learning disabilities, even though most major definitions of LD hardly mention socioemotional functioning. Much is being learned about social status, social behavior, and academic motivation.

Social Status

Numerous studies provide evidence that peers, teachers, and parents hold negative attitudes about at least some portion of LD children and tend to reject them (Gresham and Elliott, 1989; Margalit, 1989; Rourke, 1988).

Several investigators requested children to rate classmates or to nominate classmates who, for example, would make a good president or would not be welcomed at their birthday party (Pearl, Donahue, and Bryan, 1986). LD children were often rated less

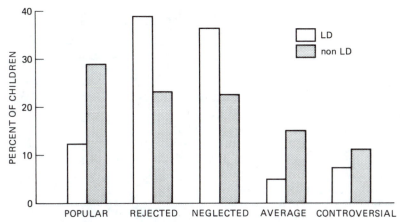

FIGURE 11–3 Percentage of disabled learners and nondisabled learners selected by classmates into each social category. All children were in regular fourth- through sixth-grade classrooms. Data from Stone and LaGreca, 1990.

popular than nondisabled peers, and they were more frequently rejected or neglected. Figure 11–3 represents this general finding.

Similar negative attitudes have been shown by teachers. They believe some LD children possess a variety of annoying and otherwise problematic characteristics. Among these are conduct and personal problems, anxiety, immaturity, disruptiveness, and hyperactivity (e.g., Heavey et al., 1989). LD children have received lower ratings than nondisabled youngsters on cooperation, organization, coping, tactfulness,

responsibility, and other such attributes. Parents not only recognize their handicapped children's academic problems, but they also note deficiencies in impulse control, anxiety, and less ability to structure the environment.

In reviewing the research, Pearl et al. (1986) noted that LD youngsters seem not particularly appealing as playmates or students, and they are not seen as easy to live with. They may even make a less favorable impression on strangers than other children (Taylor, 1988b).

Social Competence, Behavior Problems

Actual observations of the behavior of learning-disabled children are limited. However, research suggests that they are less socially competent than non-LD peers, as measured by inventories and laboratory tasks (Pearl et al., 1986; Ritter, 1989; Toro et al., 1990). This is manifested in a variety of ways: difficulty in identifying the emotional expression of others, misreading of social situations, errors in guessing how other children feel in particular situations, and deficits in social problem solving. In addition, LD children may display atypical conversational behavior with peers, either more

passive and deferential or more hostile (Pearl et al., 1986). They may also be less skillful in maintaining conversation.

It is important to note that not all of the children show social deficits (Gresham and Elliott, 1989). Indeed, they often do not appear different from other students in the classroom. Moreover, situational influences may be quite strong in determining whether a child behaves competently or not.

Many hypotheses have been put forth to explain how social skill deficits are linked to LD. The proposals tend to focus on some cognitive or perceptual deficit. For example, linguistic disability is said to lead to poor interpersonal communication, and perceptual disability to lead to failure to accurately interpret the emotions of others (Rourke, 1988). It has also been suggested that a *primary* deficit in social skills be included in the definition of learning disabilities (Gresham and Elliott, 1989). The argument holds that social skill deficits result from neurological dysfunction, just as academic difficulties do. Presently there is little evidence supporting this view. Other hypotheses emphasize that social skill deficits indirectly stem from academic deficiencies, probably acting through peer rejection. Although LD children frequently interact with their peers (Pearl et al., 1986), some may lack opportunity to acquire social skills, perform them, and be reinforced for them. To date, no one hypothesis satisfactorily explains the social skills deficits of LD children.

Research into the behavior problems of learning-disabled children is still limited and it is difficult to draw firm conclusions. There is some evidence for higher than average risk for various kinds of disturbances, including internalizing problems (Rourke, Young, and Leenaars, 1989; Thompson and Kronenberger, 1990).

A link has been noted between LD and juvenile delinquency. One investigation found that 36 percent of incarcerated juveniles had a learning disability and that learning-disabled youth were more than twice as likely as nondisabled youth to commit a delinquent act (Dunviant, 1982, cited by Brier, 1989). Drawing on research findings, Brier proposes that a child with LD is more likely to become delinquent if he or she shows, among others factors, ADHD/aggressive behaviors, relatively low IQ, social problems, language problems, and frustration over school achievement. Research is needed to test this proposal, which suggests that the risk of an LD child's becoming

The study of social interaction becomes increasingly important as psychologists realize its role in the development of learning difficulties. (Ken Karp)

delinquent increases with the number of these factors and the degree to which they are present.

In any event, though, most learning disabled children are *not* delinquents, not all are viewed by others as having social or behavioral problems, and considerable individual differences are shown in social behavior (Rourke, 1988). When Porter and Rourke (1985) analyzed profiles on the Personality Inventory for Children, they were able to classify 77 of the 100 LD subjects into four behavioral subtypes. About 50 percent of the classified children were rated as well adjusted. About 25 percent showed a profile suggesting internalizing disturbance, that is, depression, withdrawal, and anxiety. About 15 percent fell into an externalizing, hyperactivity profile. The remaining 10 percent of the children showed somatic complaints but otherwise normal socioemotional functioning.

Motivation

There is considerable interest in the motivational behavior of LD children, since it is believed that effort is essential for their academic success. Contrary to this need, many of the children appear to enter a vicious cycle of academic failure and low motivation that works against them (Licht and Kistner, 1986). Based on academic failure the children come to doubt their intellectual abilities and believe that efforts to achieve are futile. This results in their being frustrated and giving up easily in the face of difficulty. In turn, further failure is experienced, which reinforces the belief in lack of ability. At this point, any achievement is attributed to luck, the ease of the task, help from a teacher, or some other source external to the self (Figure 11–4). Thus, success gives little satisfaction and is unlikely to boost confidence.

There is evidence that this cycle operates. Studies show that LD children tend to have lower expectations for success than other children. They also are less likely to credit successes to their ability, and more likely to attribute failure to inadequate ability. In addition, learning handicapped children tend to believe that their efforts will not improve the situation since control is viewed as external (e.g., Tarnowski and Nay, 1989). Although these beliefs may have some reasonable basis, they also tend to contribute to the difficulties.

Nevertheless, individual differences in response to failure is seen, with some children being more adaptive than others. Licht and Kistner (1986) note several factors that play a role in creating these differences. Unsurprisingly, one factor is the degree of failure experienced: Less failure is associated with more adaptive motivation. For example, one study showed that LD children who were doing somewhat better academically than others were more likely to attribute failure to insufficient effort on their part. This internal attribution implies that effort could pay off. Even so, some relatively successful youngsters have little confidence in their ability, while some who fail continue to believe that they will succeed sooner or later.

A child's developmental level may help explain this. In the normal course of events, perceptions of ability change in several ways. Younger children tend to judge their ability independently of others' abilities, and believe that the more you try, the more you learn and the greater is your ability. Subsequently, social comparison becomes more important and by age ten most children also view ability as quite stable and less influenced by effort. Older children may thus be more susceptible to negative feedback about their failure. Indeed, research shows that children under age seven generally have high opinions of their abilities and even when they do not, motivational problems may not appear. But this protection gradually disappears for many, although not all, children.

Teacher feedback also can influence children's self-perceptions. Although feedback can be highly critical, teachers also try to encourage lower achieving students by giving less criticism and more praise. In fact, praise may be given following quite poor

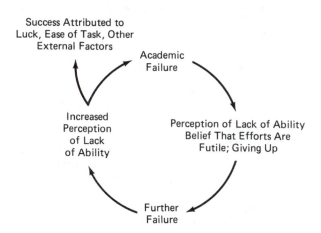

FIGURE 11–4 Learning disabled children may experience a vicious cycle of academic failure and low motivation.

performance. There is some evidence that feedback depends in part on the child's behavior. High criticism and low praise are more likely to be given to defiant children who are hard to manage; low criticism and high praise are more likely when the child is viewed as low in ability and high in effort. How children interpret these consequences is complex. Nevertheless, praise for performing easy tasks that require little effort probably does not help LD children in the long run, when they must persist in the face of difficulty (Licht and Kistner, 1986). To be effective, praise should depend on effortful work and should provide specific information as to how the child might further improve performance.

Parents certainly can be expected to play a role in determining children's self-perceptions and motivation. Some parents appear to attribute their LD children's success more to luck and failure more to lack of ability (Pearl et al., 1986). They also tend to hold lower expectations for their children. While parental denial of learning problems could hardly be helpful, encouragement of internal locus of control and high effort can be supportive. Parents (as well as teachers) are also in the position to build confidence in areas in which the child may have some confidence, which can contribute to general positive self-regard (cf. Grolnick and Ryan, 1990).

ETIOLOGY

As we have already seen, the assumption that neurological damage or dysfunction underlies LD has been a dominant hypothesis. This perspective was obvious among early theorists. Orton, Strauss, Werner, Lehtinen, and Kephart, among others, linked brain disorder to children of average intelligence who displayed learning, perceptual, language, and behavioral problems such as hyperactivity (e.g., Strauss and Kephart, 1955; Strauss and Lehtinen, 1947).

How has the hypothesis of biological etiology fared? Connections between known brain damage and learning handicaps certainly exist (Bigler, 1987). There are learning disabled children with histories of neurological disorders, such as cerebral palsy, epilepsy, nervous system infections, and head injury (Taylor, 1988). Links between LD and maternal alcohol use, neurological

delays, and neurological soft signs are also evident although they are not strong (e.g., Taylor, 1989; VanDyke and Fox, 1990). These relationships at least suggest that nervous system dysfunction underlies learning difficulties.

Considerable effort has been made to examine genetic influence and to find abnormal structure and functioning in the brain. Recent studies benefit from advances in genetic research, better knowledge of brain-behavior relationships, and methods to study the brain. The latter have included neuropsychological testing of persons with known brain damage, EEGs taken during various tasks, techniques to evaluate the functioning of the brain hemispheres, and brain scans of subjects with learning disabilities.

Genetic Influence

Although genetic influence on learning disabilities was suspected for some time, the more recent sophisticated genetic techniques are beginning to shed more light on this possibility. Pennington and Smith (1983, 1988) and Smith et al. (1990) have

reviewed the work on reading (and spelling) disabilities, the area most extensively examined. Reading disabilities "run in families"; that is, children of affected parents have a greater chance of reading problems than children of unaffected parents. Twin comparisons indicate that genetic transmission is involved (DeFries, Fulker, and La-Buda, 1987).

Some progress is being made in identifying the specific mechanisms that might be responsible. Polygenic and oliogenic (causation by a few major genes) mechanisms are suspected. Chromosome 15 may be implicated in some cases. Evidence is growing that reading disabilities are transmitted through several different genetic mechanisms. Since the disabilities themselves may vary, it is tempting to speculate that different genetic mechanisms underlie different reading disabilities. However, Smith et al. (1990) warn against jumping to conclusions, since no such relationship is yet established. It is also too early to draw definite conclusions about the strength of genetic influences, but so far it seems modest (Rutter et al., 1990b).

Brain Abnormalities in Dyslexia

Some of the more interesting studies of etiology concern brain abnormalities in dyslexia. In 1937 Orton proposed that visual information is processed by both hemispheres of the brain but that the right hemisphere holds visual stimuli in reversed form and order (Vellutino, 1979). For most children this was not seen as a problem because the left hemisphere became dominant over the right. In dyslexia, left hemisphere dominance was considered flawed so that the right hemisphere gained some control and its reversed patterns were expressed in a variety of ways.

Since Orton's time, interest in the hemispheres has continued, based largely on evidence that the left hemisphere is specialized for processing language and the right for processing spatial information. Current hypotheses include the possibilities that hemisphere specialization is inadequate or does not follow the usual pattern, or that the hemispheres do not properly communicate with each other (e.g., Gladstone, Best, and Davidson, 1989). Interest also exists, of course, in other aspects of brain functioning.

There is much inconsistency in the research findings about the brains of reading-disabled persons. However, Hynd and Semrud-Clikeman (1989a, b) have looked at findings from brain scan, EEG, and post-mortem (examination of the brain after death) studies. They conclude that a small but growing body of findings points to brain abnormalities. One of the findings is that the left side of certain areas of the brains of dyslexics is not larger than the right, as it is in nondisabled people. Another is poorly organized EEG activity in the areas of the brain thought important in fluent reading. Dyslexics also show abnormal cell structure in certain brain areas, which the investigators believe was probably present during the first six months of prenatal development. Nevertheless, they point out that some of the overall findings are inconsistent with theories about brain-language relationships and thus call for further theorizing.

Furthermore, given the many years of investigation, it can be argued that relatively little has been learned about the neurological basis of LD. Interesting work is ongoing but for most learning handicapped children, definitive biological causation has not been established.

Environmental Factors

Although biological variables may be critical causes in LD, environmental influences also operate. In fact, the importance of psychosocial and motivational effects on learning is well recognized by professionals and parents. It is reasonable to speculate that even in the presence of neurological dysfunction a potential learning disability may be moderated or precluded by an advantaged social environment. Taylor (1988b) notes several variables known to influence learning that might well act on the learning handicapped child: SES, cultural values, family interactions, parental attitudes toward learning, child management practices, child characteristics such as motivation and temperament, and the matching of expectations for the child to the child's ability. We might easily elaborate on this list by noting the importance of the school in setting expectations and providing educational experiences.

Although most conceptualizations of learning disabilities assign environmental causation a back seat to biological etiology, not everyone agrees with this view. In 1987, Gerald Coles wrote *The Learning Mystique: A Critical Look at "Learning Disabilities"* in which he argued that only a very small percentage of the children identified as LD have neurological dysfunction that may interfere with learning and academic achievement (Coles, 1989). He proposed that learning disabilities can best be explained by *interactivity*, that is, the numerous and complex activities and interactions involved in creating, maintaining, remediating, and preventing learning disabilities. Part of interactivity are individual *differences* (not disorders) in biological functioning. But it is assumed that social, cultural, political, and economic influences are fundamental in creating and preventing LD. Thus, for instance, when a child fails to learn in school, the cause of failure must be explored by examining the child-teacher interaction, and also by looking at broader factors, such as how the school's structure and attitudes might be causing failure. Even more, it is important to identify social, economic, and political variables that affect the child, teacher, and school. In effect, Coles has called for a broadening of causal hypotheses about learning disabilities.

His position has been greeted with strong reactions, perhaps partly because of his challenging style, but also for many other reasons. He has been criticized for having a sociopolitical agenda (that LD is socially determined), insulting many of the researchers in the field, ignoring the very real fact that some children display learning problems even when provided good opportunity to learn, ignoring evidence for a brain-LD link, and broadening the definition of LD to include poor achievers not ordinarily labeled as LD (Galaburda, 1989; Rourke, 1989; Stanovich, 1989). At the same time, some researchers welcome Coles's challenge as a chance for broad discussion (e.g., Miller, 1990). And others agree with Coles that some learning handicaps can best be viewed as originating from both neurological and environmental variables (e.g., Adelman, 1989). Interactional approaches emphasize the importance of knowing more about environmental factors, including instructional methods, that might influence whether and how learning handicaps might occur or be maintained.

DEVELOPMENTAL COURSE AND OUTCOME

Much is yet to be learned about the developmental course and outcome of the different learning disabilities. Some disabilities may reflect a developmental lag that may disappear, and early interventions with at-risk preschoolers can prevent potential learning failure (Lerner, 1989). The prognosis is not always that positive, however.

Receptive language disorders do not easily remit. Depending on the severity of the deficits, many children eventually acquire language comprehension but only after traveling a long and difficult path (Baker and Cantwell, 1989). Some may never develop completely normal comprehension of language. The course of expressive language disorders is less clear but prognosis is better. Certain aspects of language appear sometimes to be merely delayed and the child "catches up." Other aspects may be deviant from the norm, but even so most children, although not all, acquire substantially normal language expression.

The outcome for deficient readers is

poor, although there is much individual variation (Yule and Rutter, 1985). It appears that outcome is best when the child has achieved high IQ and comes from a socially advantaged background. Since reading failure is so prevalent among LD children, learning handicap persists for many children. In fact, basic academic skills are also reported to reach a plateau during the high school years (Schumaker et al., 1986).

Overall, there appears to be growing recognition that learning-disabled children all too often become learning-disabled adolescents and adults (Silver, 1989). At least for some, LD is a chronic condition. In a review of follow-up studies, Spreen (1988) noted that the evidence to date suggests that outcome depends on the severity of the disorder during childhood, the SES of parents, and the presence or absence of neurological problems.

ASSESSING THE LEARNING DISABLED CHILD

Identification and assessment of learning handicaps most often occur in the educational system, and follow procedures set up for compliance with the Education For All Handicapped Children Act of 1975. Teachers typically have the critical role of seeking consultation for the child, most likely having already spoken to the parents about the child's problems. School psychologists do much of the actual assessment; they gather information from the teacher and often are the persons who observe the child in the classroom, as mandated by P.L. 94–142 (Bryan and Bryan, 1986). In some cases, the child may be evaluated in mental health settings, and the school will subsequently do an assessment and then arrange a meeting among school professionals, parents, and other relevant persons to discuss the evaluation and plan for intervention.

Adequate assessment demands an interview with the parents and seeks information about the child's prenatal, developmental, and medical history; the child's behavioral and social functioning; family background; and family functioning and concerns. Parents have complained that they were not always adequately considered by the educational system, and this was probably the case. At the same time, all parents are not equally concerned or willing to participate in assessments, which they may even believe are unnecessary. Clearly, it is to everyone's advantage to cooperate as a working team and, fortunately, this is frequently the case.

Of obvious importance in identifying learning disabilities are batteries of tests that help establish the child's academic achievement, general intelligence, and specific cognitive/perceptual/motor skills. A large number of tests are available for this purpose (Bryan and Bryan, 1986). Selection of tests should, of course, take into consideration reliability and validity, as well as cultural bias.

The focus of academic achievement usually is reading, spelling, and arithmetic, although tests are available to examine other areas such as social studies. Commonly employed are the Wide Range Achievement Test (Jastak and Wilkinson, 1984), the Peabody Individual Achievement Test (Dunn and Markwardt, 1970), and the Woodcock-Johnson PsychoEducational Battery (Woodcock and Johnson, 1978). In addition to a standardized general test of intelligence, such as the Wechsler test, the child may be given tests that evaluate specific visual, auditory, motor, language, and thinking skills. Examples are the Illinois Test of Psycholinquisitic Abilities (Kirk, McCarthy, and Kirk, 1968) and the Frostig Developmental Tests of Visual Perception (Frostig et al., 1968). These tests are neuropsychological in that they presume neurological dysfunction. Their function, however, is not to test neurological hypotheses but to assess strengths and weaknesses. Indeed, it is important that the child's learning difficulties be described in detail, as they can take several forms and involve several cognitive components (Taylor, 1988).

In working with the child, the evaluator also has the opportunity to discuss the child's

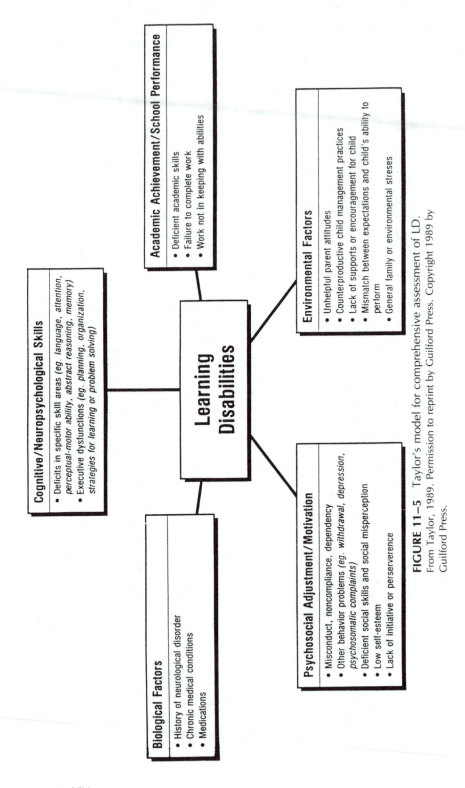

Cognitive/Neuropsychological Skills

- Deficits in specific skill areas (eg. language, attention, perceptual-motor ability, abstract reasoning, memory)
- Executive dysfunctions (eg. planning, organization, strategies for learning or problem solving)

Academic Achievement/School Performance

- Deficient academic skills
- Failure to complete work
- Work not in keeping with abilities

Learning Disabilities

Biological Factors

- History of neurological disorder
- Chronic medical conditions
- Medications

Psychosocial Adjustment/Motivation

- Misconduct, noncompliance, dependency
- Other behavior problems (eg. withdrawal, depression, psychosomatic complaints)
- Deficient social skills and social misperception
- Low self-esteem
- Lack of initiative or perserverence

Environmental Factors

- Unhelpful parent attitudes
- Counterproductive child management practices
- Lack of supports or encouragement for child
- Mismatch between expectations and child's ability to perform
- General family or environmental streses

FIGURE 11–5 Taylor's model for comprehensive assessment of LD.
From Taylor, 1989. Permission to reprint by Guilford Press. Copyright 1989 by Guilford Press.

study habits, motivations, self-esteem, and broad concerns. Because LD is essentially defined in terms of achievement and cognitive abilities, there is probably a tendency to inadequately assess the behavioral, social, and motivational contexts in which the child is operating. Figure 11–5 presents Taylor's schema for all of the areas that a complete evaluation would encompass. Psychosocial and environmental factors, including the match between the child's abilities and expectations of the social-educational environment, are important aspects of assessment.

It is also the case that identification and assessment are often not done as early as they should be (Satz and Fletcher, 1988). Most LD children are not referred until about ten years of age, after they have experienced several years of academic failure.

TREATMENT APPROACHES

Although learning disabilities have primarily been viewed as an educational problem, they have been addressed by several disciplines and approaches. The following discussion roughly organizes these approaches from the biological to the more cognitive and behavioral.

Medical Treatments

Despite the assumption that biological abnormality causes learning handicaps, direct medical intervention plays only a small role in treatment for most LD children. The medical condition of the child should especially be considered when there is a history of neurological dysfunction or damage (Taylor, 1989). The brain injured child may require medical treatment for continuing physical difficulties, such as seizures.

Another instance in which medical treatment may be appropriate is in the presence of Attention-Deficit Hyperactivity Disorder. Stimulant medications may be considered. As discussed in Chapter 9 stimulants appear helpful to many of these children in that they increase attention, and decrease activity, social problems, impulsivity, and disruptive noncompliant behaviors (Barkley, 1989; Dulcan, 1986). The degree to which these medications improve academic difficulties is still questioned. Evidence exists for an increase in classroom productivity and short-term academic improvement, but long-term improvement has not been firmly established.

Other biological approaches are viewed with more skepticism by researchers and clinicians. For example, various recommendations have been made about the diets of learning-disabled children, including the need for massive doses of vitamins and specific elements such as copper and zinc, reduced refined sugar, and the Feingold diet that reduces food additives and preservatives (Silver, 1987). Some of these proposals go hand in hand with recommendations for decreasing ADHD (e.g., the Feingold diet). Overall, there is little evidence that diet modification helps learning-disabled children, although behavioral improvement may occur in a very small percentage of ADHD-learning disabled children.

Treating Underlying Perceptual-Motor Deficits

Historically a popular treatment approach rested on the belief that neurological dysfunction is reflected in disordered sensory or perceptual and motor systems, which affect the child's learning.

Doman and Delacato (1968) attributed learning disabilities to failure in the normal early developmental sequence of movement, language, and sensory functions. They called for motor and sensory experiences that were extremely demanding of the time and resources of the family. In 1983 the American Academy of Pediatrics concluded that this approach had not proven effective (Silver, 1987). Another approach that is currently controversial at best is visual or visual-motor training directed by optometrists who believe that visual problems are a central cause of learning handicaps. Improvement after visual-motor training has not been established.

Perceptual-motor training has been incorporated into several other treatment efforts. One example is the work of Kephart (1960, 1971), who proposed that children develop through six stages, from the motor through the perceptual to the conceptual-perceptual. This progression was assumed to have broken down, and treatment aimed at producing normal developmental outcomes. Kephart advocated individual assessment and emphasized early motor-perceptual abilities. Various activities were suggested to establish a "perceptual-motor match," in which children receive information from their own movements that allows them to monitor the correctness of their perceptions and motor actions (Kirk, 1972). These activities included (1) the use of walking boards, trampolines, and games to teach movement, (2) chalkborad exercises to develop the matching of movement and visual perception, and (3) form perception exercises such as peg boards and puzzles. Still another method is Frostig's visual-perception method that trains children in eye-hand

Although visual motor activities like working with blocks and puzzles have been emphasized in treating learning disabilities, they are now given less importance.

coordination, shape constancy, spatial relationships, and the like (Frostig and Horne, 1964).

Perceptual training progams offered by some of the best educational specialists, such as Kephart and Frostig, were widely accepted and respected for several decades. However, research did not prove them successful in boosting academic performance or remediating the proposed underlying perceptual-motor deficits (Taylor, 1989).

Sensory Modality and Language Approaches

All of these approaches emphasize that instruction is best conceptualized in terms of sensory modalities or the ways in which language is received and expressed (Bryan and Bryan, 1986). Fernald's multisensory method, for example, presents academic material by way of sight, touch, hearing, and kinesthetic (muscle) cues; it assumes that learning is facilitated by multisensory experiences. Other programs identify the modality strengths and weaknesses of the learning handicapped child and teach to the strengths. Thus, a child who learns more effectively with visually presented material is encouraged to learn by seeing; the child who cannot write well is given oral tests. Within this general framework, some of these approaches emphasize language development.

Several of the modality approaches have been well received by learning disabilities professionals. However, they have often not been adequately evaluated or strong evidence is lacking for their efficacy. Indeed, the lack of support for both the perceptual-motor and sensory-modality approaches has suggested that efforts to remediate underlying cognitive processes might be fruitless. However, the more recent research into information processing has created interest in enhancing functions such as metacognition and attention. In addition, emphasis has been given to the direct training of deficient academic tasks.

Enhancing Metacognition and Executive Functions

This approach focuses on remediation of metacognition and the executive functions in information processing. That is, students are taught to better understand their own cognitive processes and to regulate cognitive activity (Palincsar and Brown, 1986). They are encouraged to be active problem solvers. Instruction emphasizes increased awareness of task demands, the use of appropriate strategies, monitoring the success of the strategies, and switching to another strategy when necessary. The approach has been applied to reading comprehension, mathematics, written expression, memory skills, and study skills (Lyon and Moats, 1988).

As an example, we take the work of Schumaker and Deshler and their colleagues, which aimed at improving reading comprehension in junior- and senior-high-school LD students (Palincsar and Brown, 1987; Schumaker et al., 1984). The students were initially evaluated as to how they were dealing with a reading task. Then failure to use strategies to comprehend the material was discussed. Specific strategies were next proposed and used by the teacher. They consisted of surveying the material for the main ideas, examining the questions at the end of the readings, and re-reading the material while constructing questions about the main points. Students then practiced using these strategies and were able to apply them successfully to school work. In another study, Ellis, Deshler, and Schumaker (1989) successfully trained some LD adolescents to generate strategies for novel problems more independently and use them in the classroom.

This research and other studies indicate that the metacognitive and executive functions of learning-handicapped children can be enhanced. Of course, successful training depends on several variables; for example, the teacher's knowledge of the subject matter and ability to teach strategy use, as well as the student's past learning experiences and motivation. So far the evidence suggests that such training is indeed worthwhile and that further research will be helpful.

Behavioral Treatment

In contrast to the approaches already described, the behavioral approach makes few assumptions about underlying biology or process deficits (Lyon and Moats, 1988). It aims at identifying academic skill and social deficits and modifying them through modeling, direct instruction, feedback, and contingency management, which may be used together (Koorland, 1986). For example, the goal may be to increase the number of correct arithmetic problems or words read, comprehension of written material, or legibility of handwriting. Or it may be to increase on-task behavior or cooperation. Reinforcement has included verbal praise and preselected activities available during free time; tokens, usually points, are commonly employed. The effectiveness of such treatments has been demonstrated through single subject studies that employed the ABA' and multiple baseline designs.

Behavioral techniques are effective in enhancing the academic and social behaviors of learning-disabled children. Many of them are part and parcel of effective teaching strategies. As is often the case, there is concern about inadequate generalization across tasks and time. The cost-effectiveness of this approach also is being examined.

EDUCATIONAL EFFORTS AND POLICY

Consistent with P.L. 94–142's mandate for the least restrictive placement, several educational options are available. About 15 percent of LD children are in regular classrooms, 62 percent in a combination of the regular classroom and the resource room, and 21 percent in self-contained special classrooms (Lerner, 1989).

If the regular classroom teacher has no training in learning disabilities, a special education teacher may act as a consultant, provide materials, or actually teach the child in that setting. The teacher in the resource room typically has special education training and teaching is conducted in small groups. It is important, of course, that experiences in the resource room be integrated with those of the regular classrooom. Self-contained special classrooms usually serve the most severely handicapped students. Teachers typically have special training and class size is small so that instruction can be individualized. Some students do not do well even in small groups, but can profit from one-to-one instruction.

As with school placements for the mildly retarded, which placement is best is debatable and undoubtedly depends on teacher, child, instructional, and other situational factors. It is somewhat disconcerting that more is not known about the effectiveness of different placements and approaches. At the same time, there is growing evidence for the general efficacy of several principles of instruction, including the following (Taylor, 1989):

1. Academic competence is related to the amount of time devoted to students' being actively engaged in academic work. Research shows that much class time is not spent on academics.

2. Academic competence is also related to the teacher's actively instructing, modeling, directing, and guiding learning. Learning-handicapped children do not benefit from discovery learning; they require structure and feedback.

3. Some degree of individualized instruction is helpful. This principle is related to the idea of mastery learning; that is, that a specific

level of achievement be set and the child provided with instruction and practice to reach that level.

4. Generalization of learning across tasks and time usually has to be built into instruction. For example, after a child learns a particular arithmetic technique, practice in using the technique on slightly different problems can be given.

5. Incentives are usually helpful and they should be tied to specific goals, such as number of words spelled correctly.

6. Training is best aimed at remediating all deficiencies rather than focusing on a single one, because improvement in one skill is often not related to improvement in another (e.g., accuracy in reading and comprehension in reading). In addition, mastery of lower-order skills and knowledge is necessary for higher-order abilities.

These principles are likely to enhance learning in a variety of settings and in children with various academic difficulties, but the degree to which they can remediate LD is unclear. Nonetheless, teachers in regular classrooms will serve LD children if the Regular Education Initiative (REI) is adopted. REI proposes that all learning handicapped children be educated in regular classrooms (Carnine and Kameenui, 1990). Its advocates fault current practices for diminishing the role of the regular classroom teacher, fragmenting services, stigmatizing LD children, and weakening any true partnership between schools and parents. Moreover, the assumption is made that learning difficulties reside in the educational environment, which must be adapted for children's needs (Chalfant, 1989). The proposal is controversial (e.g., Kauffman, Gerber, and Semmel, 1988; Keogh, 1988). Concern is expressed, for example, that teachers in regular classrooms are not adequately trained, will not receive adequate support, and do not desire to teach students who vary so widely in performance.

FUNDAMENTAL ISSUES ABOUT LD

This chapter ends by raising issues that are being widely discussed by those in the learning disabilities field. Transitions in thinking about LD are apparent today and some of them focus on the fundamental assumptions about LD: that learning disabilities are caused by neurological abnormalities and are manifested in specific cognitive impairments (e.g., Torgesen, 1986). These assumptions are criticized for not adequately serving as guidelines for diagnosis and treatment. Moreover, it is argued that the assumptions are not sufficiently supported by research.

As we saw previously, the hypothesis of neurological causality has some support but many years of research have not established firm support. Direct biological evidence has been difficult to demonstrate; some indirect support comes from genetic studies, neuropsychological testing, and biological indicators such as the association of LD with neurological soft signs. On the other hand, increasing recognition is being given to the possible role of broad social factors and the importance of psychosocial and educational contexts.

The assumption that learning disabilities are specific rather than general cognitive impairments is reflected in the widely accepted definition of LD as a discrepancy between normal IQ and achievement in specific academic areas. There is evidence for the existence of specific psychological deficits not measured by general tests of intelligence. For example, phonological deficits in reading disabilities (see Box 11.1) may be a specific dysfunction that is relatively independent of general intelligence (Stanovich, 1989).

Nevertheless, the assumption of specificity is being challenged by certain findings (Stanovich, 1986; Torgesen, 1986). The problems that some LD children have in using cognitive strategies and executive functions appear very similar to those described for mildly retarded children. From their study of memory in learning disabled children, Ceci and Baker (1989, 1990) have come to question the old views about impairments. They propose that LD is best seen as the interplay of a poorly developed knowledge base in an area, biologically determined mental processes, and the demands of the task. Although we cannot do justice here to this conceptualization, it is important to note their suggestion that the model holds for all children and that LD children are not qualitatively or specifically different from others. Much more research is needed to address the question of specific versus general cognitive deficits.

Intricately involved in discussions of the nature of LD is the heterogeneity of students who acquire the label. As we previously saw, learning handicapped children display great variation in both academic-cognitive and social-motivational functioning. Such heterogeneity, but especially in academic-cognitive behaviors, raises questions about the adequacy and usefulness of the category of learning disabilities. Attempts have been made to better understand such heterogeneity by identifying subtypes of LD children that differ from each other on characteristics considered critical in learning disabilities (Forness, 1990).

For example, Rourke and his colleagues identified three subtypes based on academic achievement and showed that the groups also differed on cognitive skills (Rourke and Finlayson, 1978; Ozols and Rourke, 1988). McKinney (1986) identified subtypes based on teacher ratings of behavior and related them to later academic problems. However, substantial weaknesses and limitations of subtyping have been noted (e.g., Taylor, 1988), and its eventual contribution is debatable.

It is nevertheless useful to examine Weller and Strawser's summary of five subtypes that they believe have been widely identified by researchers (cited by Forness, 1990). Described in terms of cognitive deficiencies, these are: (1) global disorders involving multiple processing deficits, (2) visual-spatial, motor deficits, (3) language deficits, (4) inefficient cognitive strategies, and (5) a non-LD pattern. Forness points out that these subtypes reflect some of the long-standing views and issues in the learning disabilities field. Subtype 1 reflects the view of LD as a complex of deficiencies; subtype 2 recalls the original emphasis on perceptual-motor functioning; subtype 3 reflects the importance given to language. Subtype 4, which possibly involves inattention and hyperactivity, might reflect the comorbidity of LD and ADHD. Subtype 5 is especially interesting: It is characterized by a discrepancy from grade level but not from IQ level. Thus it seems to reflect children who underachieve for reasons other than specific learning disabilities, given current assessment methods. This subtype is estimated to encompass from one-fourth to more than one-third of all learning disabled children.

Children in subtype 5 appear to be the focus of differing opinions about the LD category. The question has been raised whether the category should remain under P.L. 94–142 (Chalant, 1989). In the past few years children labeled as LD have made up 40 percent or more of all those receiving special education, and it is argued that many would not have previously been labeled LD. It is suggested that the LD category has broadened from children with neurological problems to children whose only similarity to each other is academic difficulties. Some professionals thus believe that it is not useful to maintain the LD category, especially because identifying neurological disorder is so difficult (Algozzine and Ysseldyke, 1986). A better strategy, they argue, would be to serve all youngsters who display learning handicaps. Others believe, however, that further effort should be made to identify "true" learning disabled students and evaluate what specific programs can best help them (Chalant, 1989). The resolution of this controversy remains to be seen. However, with regard to research on learning disabilities, it appears essential that participants be more carefully selected on theoretical assumptions rather than on the varying criteria employed by schools (Torgesen, 1986).

SUMMARY

Concern for learning-handicapped children culminated in 1963 in the creation of the category *learning disabilities.* Children assigned the label were considered to be of at least average intelligence and to have neurological dysfunctions that were manifested in perceptual, motor, and hyperactive behaviors.

The definition used by the Office of Education is widely employed. Specific learning disability refers to a deficit in psychological processes underlying language that is not due to physical (sensory or motor) handicaps, mental retardation, emotional disturbance, or environmental disadvantage. Children are usually identified on the basis of academic achievement being lower than general intelligence. Several dissatisfactions are expressed with this definition.

Estimates of prevalence among school children range from 5 to 15 percent with boys identified more than girls. Prevalence data have fluctuated due to varying definitions and demands made on schools to serve children with academic difficulties.

Academic deficits are displayed in writing, spelling, mathematics, and especially reading. Deficits may be isolated but often exist in several areas. Older LD children especially show deficits in knowledge and learning strategies.

An array of cognitive deficiencies has been shown including attention, perceptual, perceptual-motor, memory, cognitive strategies, executive function, and language problems. Less emphasis is now given to perceptual deficits, although perceptual-motor problems do exist. Hypotheses about reading have notably shifted from an emphasis on visual deficits to language and related high-level auditory processing deficits.

Research indicates that peers, teachers, and parents have negative attitudes and expectations for at least some LD children. Some of the children show deficits in social competence, and several hypotheses have been proposed to explain this. There also appears to be risk for internalizing and externalizing disorders.

LD children may enter a negative motivational cycle that can interfere with their progress. It includes frustration, giving up, and external locus of control.

General indications of neurological dysfunction exist for LD children; for example, a link with neurological soft signs and maternal alcohol use. Evidence is growing for genetic transmisstion of reading disability, but the mechanisms remain unknown. Direct evidence of brain dysfunction in dyslexia (e.g., EEG, hemisphere, and cell abnormalities) is small but growing. Overall, though, the evidence for neurological disorder is far from overwhelming.

Environmental factors that influence learning undoubtedly act on the LD child, for example, SES and parental attitudes. Coles suggests that most learning problems can best be explained by the interaction of individual differences and broad social influences. His position is controversial.

Although much is to be learned about the course and outcome of LD, it appears that some disabilities are seen in adulthood. Severity of the disorders, SES, and neurological problems are linked with outcome.

Identification and assessment of LD most often occurs in the educational system, as part of P.L. 94–142's mandate. The teacher and school psychologist play critical roles, as do tests of academic achievement, intelligence, and cognitive processes. Broad assessment is ideal, as is early identification.

Treatment of LD has included several approaches. Medical care is appropriate in known cases of neurological dysfunction and perhaps when ADHD is present. Doman and Delacato's and the optometric approaches are not generally held in high esteem and other perceptual-motor training programs have also not proven effective. Sensory modality and language approaches are more popular but require further evaluation. On the other hand, training in metacognition and executive function appears promising, and success has been shown for behavioral training in specific academic and social behaviors.

In the schools, most LD children are served by a combination of the regular classroom and the resource room. Not enough is known about the effectiveness of one placement over another, and several factors can influence effectiveness. Principles of good instruction have emerged, however, and can be applied in various settings.

The basic assumptions that learning disabilities are caused by neurological abnormalities and manifested as specific psychological deficits are being attacked. The evidence is debatable, and there is dissatisfaction that the assumptions have not led to better diagnosis and treatment. Heterogeneity in LD populations raises questions about the adequacy and usefulness of the LD category. Some professionals argue for better identification of LD but others prefer to eliminate the category with regard to P.L. 94–142.

12

AUTISM AND CHILDHOOD SCHIZOPHRENIA

Some of the most distressing behaviors are displayed by children who are given the labels of autism or childhood schizophrenia. These conditions affect the broad range of social, emotional, cognitive, and perceptual motor behaviors. Fundamental functions are affected in such a way that the children often appear qualitatively different from other youngsters.

THE PROBLEM OF DEFINITION

Despite long recognition of the disorders we are about to discuss, description and classification have been marked by confusion and disagreement (Newsom, Hovanitz, and Rincover, 1988). Historically the disorders have been tied to adult psychoses; that is, to severely disruptive adult disturbances implying "insanity," and the need for supervision and protection (Prior and Werry, 1986).

Adult psychotic disturbances were noted in early twentieth-century classifications of mental disorders (Goldfarb, 1970). Kraepelin, who set the basis for classification, used the term *dementia praecox* and attributed psychoses to biological factors. *Dementia* reflected his belief that progressive deterioration occurred; *praecox* indicated that the

disorders began early, usually in young adulthood or adolescence. Bleuler later applied the term *schizophrenias* to the disorders. He argued that deterioration was not inevitable, that psychological factors might play some role, and that time of origin was more varied. In fact, both Kraepelin and Bleuler noted a small number of cases that had begun in childhood (Cantor, 1988).

These ideas about adult disturbances were soon extended to children. An array of diagnostic terms was applied, including *dementia infantilis*, *disintegrative psychosis*, *childhood schizophrenia*, and *childhood psychosis*. Beginning around 1930 and for several years afterward, childhood schizophrenia served as a general label, while a confusing number of subcategories were generated

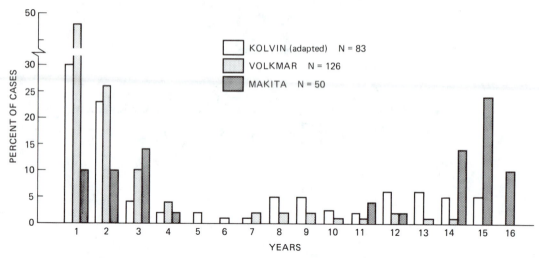

FIGURE 12–1 Age of recognition of childhood "psychosis" in three studies. From Volkmar and Cohen, 1988. Reprinted by permission of Plenum Publishing Corporation.

(Volkmar, 1987; Rutter and Schopler, 1987). In 1943, Leo Kanner described what he called *infantile autism*, arguing that it was different from other cases of severe disturbance. Kanner's work reflected the effort to better understand childhood psychosis and whether it was one disorder or several.

Since Kanner's initial work the effort has been influenced by data indicating that the disturbances seem to fall into an age-related bimodal frequency distribution. Information from several countries shows a large number of cases in infancy and a smaller peak in late childhood and early adolescence (Kolvin, 1971; Rutter, 1978). It is striking that very few cases occur in the age range from four to seven years, even though the severity of the disorders makes it unlikely that they go unreported (Figure 12–1). This pattern suggests that different syndromes underlie the earlier and later peaks.

Part and parcel of the task of understand-

ing the disorders have been two major questions (Volkmar and Cohen, 1988). One is: What constitutes the core problem? That is, does a perceptual, cognitive, or socioemotional deficit lead to distorted development? The other is the question of etiology, particularly whether organic or psychosocial factors underlie the conditions.

All these issues have led to changing conceptions of the disorders, which have been reflected in both formal diagnosis and clinical practice. The categories of disorders that have been most seriously considered and researched are infantile autism and childhood schizophrenia, both of which have been recognized by the major classification systems. This chapter focuses on these syndromes, with emphasis on autism. Other more minor diagnostic categories exist for children who show related disturbances, but there is less agreement about them.

AUTISM

The following case description was taken from 1 of the original 11 cases presented by Kanner (1943). The child had been re-

ferred at age five for suspected intellectual deficiency.

Paul was a slender, well built, attractive child, whose face looked intelligent and animated. He had good manual dexterity. He rarely responded to any form of address, even to the calling of his name. . . . He was obviously so remote that the remarks did not reach him. He was always vivaciously occupied with something and seemed to be highly satisfied, unless someone made a persistent attempt to interfere with his self-chosen actions. Then he first tried impatiently to get out of the way and, when this met with no success, screamed and kicked in a full-fledged tantrum.

There was a marked contrast between his relations to people and to objects. Upon entering the room, he instantly went after objects and used them correctly. He was not destructive and treated the objects with care and even affection. . . . He got hold of a pair of scissors and patiently and skillfully cut a sheet of paper into

Leo Kanner offered the first description of infantile autism and is considered a pioneer in the study of childhood psychoses. (The Johns Hopkins Medical Institutions)

small bits, singing the phrase "cutting paper," many times. He helped himself to a toy engine, ran around the room holding it up high, singing over and over again, "The engine is flying." While these utterances, made always with the same inflection, were clearly connected with his actions, he ejaculated others that could not be linked up with immediate situations. . . . However, some of those exclamations could be definitely traced to previous experiences. He was in the habit of saying almost every day, "Don't throw the dog off the balcony." His mother recalled that she had said those words to him about a toy dog while they were still in England. . . .

None of these remarks was meant to have communicative value. There was, on his side, no affective tie to people. He behaved as if people as such did not matter or even exist. It made no difference whether one spoke to him in a friendly or a harsh way. He never looked up at people's faces. When he had any dealings with persons at all, he treated them, or rather parts of them, as if they were objects. . . .

His enunciation was clear and he had a good vocabulary. His sentence structure was satisfactory, with one significant exception. He never used the pronoun of the first person, nor did he refer to himself as Paul. All statements pertaining to himself were made in the second person. . . . He would express his desire for candy by saying, "You want candy." . . . Occasionally there were parrot-like repetitions of things said to him.

Formal testing could not be carried out, but he certainly could not be regarded as feeble-minded in the ordinary sense. After hearing his boarding mother say grace three times, he repeated it without a flaw and has retained it since then. He could count and name colors. He learned quickly to identify his favorite victrola records from a large stack and knew how to mount and play them.

His boarding mother reported a number of observations that indicated compulsive behavior. He often masturbated with complete abandon. He ran around in circles emitting phrases in an ecstatic-like fashion. He took a small blanket and kept shaking it, delightedly shouting, "Ee! Ee!" He could continue in this manner for a long time and showed great irritation when he was interfered with. All these and many other things were not only repetitions but recurred day after day with almost photographic sameness. (Kanner, 1943, reprinted in Kanner, 1973, pp. 14–15).

On the basis of the 11 cases, Kanner

pinpointed communication problems, obsessiveness, fascination with inanimate objects, and good but atypical cognitive potential. He emphasized, however, that the fundamental disturbance was an inability to relate to people and situations from the beginning of life. He quoted parents as referring to their disturbed children as "self-sufficient," "like in a shell," "happiest when left alone," and "acting as if people weren't there" (1973, p. 33). To this extreme disturbance in emotional contact with others Kanner applied the term *autistic*, which means an absorption in the self or subjective mental activity.

Classification

Most of the characteristics originally described by Kanner were subsequently observed by others. Autism was gradually recognized by the major classification systems as a distinct syndrome, accounting for many cases of severe disturbance in infancy or very early life. In 1980 DSM-III recognized the condition as Infantile Autism, under the more general category of Pervasive Developmental Disorders. One of the criteria was that the disorder be present by the time the child was 30 months of age. Infantile Autism encompassed serious problems in social interaction, communication, and reactions to the environment. It was viewed as different from schizophrenia, with an absence of delusions, hallucinations, and thought disorder.

The category was revised in DSM-III-R. Autistic Disorder, as it is now called, is still classified as a pervasive developmental disorder, and the behavioral criteria still have the same focus. However, to better operationalize autism and to recognize the great variability among autistic children, many specific behaviors are noted. These are listed under three domains (Table 12-1). The age criterion no longer holds, though.

TABLE 12-1 Summary of DSM-III-R Criteria for Autistic Disorder

At least eight of the following must be present, including at least two from A, one from B, and one from C.

A. Impairment in reciprocal social interaction shown by:
 1. marked lack of awareness of the existence or feelings of others
 2. no or abnormal seeking of comfort at times of stress
 3. no or impaired imitation
 4. no or abnormal social play
 5. gross impairment in ability to make peer friendships

B. Impairment in communication and imaginative play shown by:
 1. no mode of communication
 2. markedly abnormal nonverbal communication
 3. absence of imaginative activity
 4. marked abnormalities in producing speech
 5. marked abnormalities in the form or content of speech (e.g., echolalia, pronoun reversal)
 6. marked impairment in ability to initiate or sustain conversation despite adequate speech

C. Restricted repertoire of activities/interests shown by:
 1. stereotyped body movements
 2. persistent preoccupation with parts of objects (e.g., spinning wheels of cars) or attachment to unusual objects
 3. marked distress over trivial environmental changes
 4. unreasonable insistence on following routines
 5. markedly restricted range of interests and preoccupation with one narrow interest

D. Onset during infancy or childhood. Specify if after 36 months.

Adapted from DSM-III-R. Reprinted with permission from the *Diagnostic and Statistical Manual of Mental Disorders, Third Edition, Revised*. Washington, DC, American Psychiatric Association, 1987.

Although autism usually is identified in early life, the term can be applied to later identified cases.

DSM-III's Infantile Autism had received reasonably high marks on reliability but more mixed evaluations on validity (Prior and Werry, 1986). Only research can determine whether the revised category is an improvement. It must also be noted that autism can be diagnosed by other than DSM criteria. Agreement is quite high across the various classification systems but research samples have been somewhat differently defined.

Prevalence

Lotter's (1966) pioneering population study showed the frequency of autism to be 4.5 per 10,000 children. Since then several investigations in different countries have reported fewer than 5 cases per 10,000 (Gillberg, 1988; Tanoue et al., 1988; Volkmar and Cohen 1988).

Some recent studies, however, show the rate as high as 20 per 10,000 (Bryson, Clark, and Smith, 1988; Cialdella and Mamelle, 1989; Tanoue et al., 1988). It appears that different criteria are employed (Vicker and Monahan, 1988). The lower rates seem to apply to criteria similar to those used by Kanner. Discrepancy in rates may also be due to misdiagnosis and the varying ages of the children studied.

Boys quite consistently display autism more than girls, with the ratio of 3 or 4 boys to 1 girl widely reported (DSM-III-R, 1987; Gillberg, 1988). Interestingly, there is some evidence that autistic females are more impaired than the males (Campbell and Green, 1985).

Kanner's (1943) early description noted that autism typically occurs in the upper social classes. However, several recent large scale studies indicate no social class bias (Gillberg, 1990).

Psychological and Behavioral Functioning

Relative to its frequency, autism is of enormous interest to professionals and lay people alike. One reason undoubtedly is its severity; another is the unusual and even bizarre behavior displayed. In this section, behavioral and psychological functioning will be detailed. It is important to remember, though, that despite commonalities, children labeled autistic show great variation.

Obsession and stereotypies. Many atypical and bizarre behaviors of autism are described as obsessive fascinations, stereotypies, and resistance to change. The child may seem obsessed with spinning tops, bus schedules, numbers, or letters (Newsom et al., 1988). Scraps of paper or bits of string may be hoarded, as if there were an attachment to them. Play may be rigid and lacking in imitation and imagination, with the child simply repeating over and over such behaviors as lining up items (Rutter, 1985a). Any change in the environment, such as rearrangement of furniture or schedules, may be reacted to with considerable upset. These strange behaviors may be related to the language problems of autism (Dadds et al., 1988), and they may lessen in the presence of others.

Perception. Although most autistic children have intact sensation—that is, they can see, hear, and the like—perceptual disturbances exist (Ornitz, 1985; Prior, 1986). Difficulties have been observed in the visual, auditory, touch, smell, balance, and pain systems. Perception of sound seems particularly imparied, so that parents often report their children as deaf (Prior and Werry, 1986). Deficits may show up very early in life and decrease somewhat over time.

Both over- and undersensitivity are reported. Oversensitivity is reflected in the child being disturbed by moderate stimulation. Undersensitivity is more likely and is reflected in many ways. Children may fail to show the startle response or to otherwise respond to verbal communications and sounds, not react to the sight of others, walk into objects, or let objects fall from their hands. Perhaps undersensitivity is the reason they seem to seek stimulation by scratching surfaces, flapping their hands, whirling, and rocking (Adrien et al., 1987). And perhaps hitting, pinching, and otherwise injuring themselves are related to sensory disturbance.

Ornitz and Ritvo have proposed that a defect in the regulation and integration of sensory input is central to autism (Ornitz and Ritvo, 1968; Ornitz, 1985). They suggest that the child is unable to construct a stable representation of the world, which prevents normal development. Although this hypothesis receives less attention than others (e.g., Rutter 1985a), perceptual deficits are a part of the clinical picture of autism and may be an early sign that something is wrong (Gillberg, 1990).

Intelligence, learning, cognition. Kanner originally described children displaying autism as of average or better intelligence, perhaps with special abilities. Some do fall into this range and some display quite remarkable abilities (Box 12.1). But intelligence test scores vary from superior to severely retarded, with 75 percent of all cases showing some intellectual deficits and many falling into the retarded range (Rutter and Schopler, 1987). Lower scores are related to poorer communication skills, a higher chance of seizures, and poorer prognosis. For this reason, some researchers suggest that autism should be subgrouped according to high and low functioning.

Because so many autistic children obtain low intelligence scores, it is necessary to show that their behavioral deficits are not due simply to mental retardation. This requires comparisons with nonautistic retarded persons of comparable intelligence.

In fact, autistic people perform differently on intelligence tests than mentally retarded people of comparable mental age. They show more peaks and valleys compared to the fairly uniform deficits dis-

played by the mentally retarded (Newsom et al., 1988). And they show greater deficits in abstraction, language, and social development.

Intelligence test scores operate much the same way for children displaying autism as they do for others (Rutter, 1985a; Lord and Schopler, 1989). They are moderately stable over time and predict academic achievement, occupation, and social status. To this extent they are useful. However, to better understand intellectual functioning, researchers also examine specific learning and cognitive processes.

Deficits appear even in basic learning skills. *Overselectivity* is often apparent; that is, the child selectively attends to a particular stimulus while ignoring other relevant ones (Lovaas, Koegel, and Schreibman, 1979). Since much basic learning depends on the association of various cues, when children "hook" onto an irrelevant stimulus, learning can be impeded. Autistic children also show deficits in generalizing what they have learned in one setting to another setting. Thus, they often require special environments to learn what most children accomplish in average environments (Lovaas and Smith, 1988). However, many of these learning problems exist in retarded children and so they do not uniquely define autism.

The picture regarding memory ability in autism is unclear and incomplete. Memory in savants can be extraordinary and autistic youngsters are well known for recalling phrases and songs. Especially in relatively higher functioning children, some memory skills can be at least adequate. Boucher and Lewis (1989) described certain deficits, though, such as for free recall of recent events and of spoken instructions after a distraction. In their study, which confirmed earlier results, comparison was made with a nonautistic group of similar age and mental ability. Nevertheless, much more research is needed to clarify memory functioning in autism (Prior and Werry, 1986).

There is evidence for information processing deficits; that is, deficiencies in coding, categorization, abstracting, sequencing, and using concepts, rules, and meaning

Box 12.1   Islands of mental ability in a sea of mental handicaps

The title of this box is taken from Treffert's (1988) review of the functioning of *savants*, people with severe mental handicaps who display contrasting, even spectacular, islands of abilities or knowledge.

Descriptions of savants were provided in the 1800s, but most cases have been studied in this centry (O'Conner and Hermelin, 1988). Recently, the film *Rainman* depicted a savant autistic man; although fiction, it drew on descriptions of actual persons.

With the exception of a few experimental studies, only case reports have been presented. From one review of cases, general intelligence could be estimated at about 54 (O'Conner and Hermelin, 1988). Although it is difficult to procure data, savant behaviors are found in perhaps 6 to 10 percent of those displaying autism or autisticlike symptoms. This compares to less than 1 percent found in nonautistic mentally handicapped people.

Savant abilities mostly involve memory, mathematics and calendar calculations, extraordinary word knowledge known as hyperplexia, and muscial, graphic art, and mechanical talents. Some are quite spectacular. One savant needed only 1.5 minutes to calculate the number of seconds in 70 years, 17 days, and 12 hours, considering the effects of leap years (Treffert, 1988). And one five-year-old, despite limited language and daily living skills, had perfect music pitch, a classical piano repertoire, and the ability to improvise music. Such abilities often emerge early, without training, and without obvious inheritance.

What psychological functioning might underlie savant abilities? Several suggestions have been made. Rote "unconscious" memory has been cited for unusual knowledge and calendar calculation. Extraordinary visual imagery also might play a role in calendar calculation, so that the savant choses an answer from the image of a huge scroll of the calendar (Treffert, 1988). Excessively concrete and limited thinking have also been postulated (O'Connor and Hermelin, 1988). That is, the savant is seen as lacking in abstraction skills and as overspecializing in the talent—which is consistent with the obsessional tendencies of autistic people. Still, none of these suggestions seems to hold for all cases. And some savants do abstract and use rules (Hermelin, O'Connor, and Lee, 1987; O'Connor and Hermelin, 1987).

Biological explanations have been proposed. Many of the abilities shown by savants tend to be associated with right hemisphere brain function. Perhaps, then, there is left hemisphere damage, which the brain compensates for by over development of the right hemisphere. Or perhaps atypical brain circuits or genetic factors operate. Social reinforcement for unusual skills also might have influence, and could be especially powerful for the mentally handicapped.

Interestingly, savant behaviors challenge the idea of generalized intelligence as some of the abilities appear to be independent of IQ (O'Connor and Hermelin, 1987, 1990).

(Fine et al., 1986; Hermelin and O'Conner, 1970; Ohta, 1987, Rutter, 1985a). For example, play and imitation tend to be concrete and restricted rather than symbolic and imaginative. Failure to use meaning in reading has been shown, as well as deficits in verbal abstraction.

Deficits also exist in *theory of mind*: the ability to infer mental states in one's own self and in others (Perner et al., 1989). This involves assuming that mental states (knowledge, beliefs) exist, and are connected to action. For example, if we observe another being exposed to a situation, we assume that the other holds in his or her mind knowledge of the situation that may then determine behavior. Having a theory of mind enhances relating to others and predicting the social world.

Theory of mind develops gradually. Inferring that another knows something because he or she has seen it is acquired by two years of age (Perner et al., 1989). Understanding that another holds a false belief develops somewhat later. And being able to think about another's thinking about a third person's thoughts is not present until about age seven. In autism, theory of mind may fail to develop or seem severely delayed (Baron-Cohen, 1989). General retardation or specific language problems do not seem responsible for this deficiency.

Communication. Disturbed communication is pervasive in autism. Both nonverbal and verbal communication are affected.

Overall, autistic children use fewer nonverbal signals, and may project an expressionless "woodenness" (Attwood, Frith, and Hermelin, 1988). The absence of eye contact, the social smile, and facial expression has been widely noted. Some children lack the relatively simple gesture of pointing; others may use simple gestures but not more complex ones. Deficits can be seen even in adolescence (Figure 12–2). In one sample, gestures that expressed feelings were not used, although pointing and instrumental gestures meaning "come here," and "be quiet" were. Expressive gesturing may require an awareness of the other person's state of mind and the possibility of influencing that state; that is, a theory of mind.

Recent research emphasizes the importance of *joint attention* interactions; that is, gestures such as pointing and showing that focus the child's and caretaker's attention on an object (Landry and Loveland, 1988). Autistic children show deficiencies in this area compared to nonautistic children who have developmental language problems and are matched on IQ.

In addition to expressive difficulties, the comprehension of nonverbal signals is also atypical and slow to develop. Hobson (1986), for example, demonstrated deficits in matching facial emotional empressions with

EXAMPLES OF EXPRESSIVE GESTURES

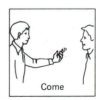

EXAMPLES OF INSTRUMENTAL GESTURES

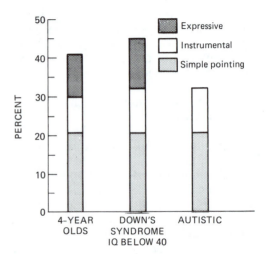

FIGURE 12–2 Percentage of types of interpersonal gestures (per interaction) in three groups of adolescents. Adapted from Attwood, Frith, and Hermelin, 1988. Reprinted by permission of Plenum Publishing Corporation.

gestures, vocalizations, and situations. Autistic subjects were asked to select faces that "went with" different bodily postures/gestures, sounds such as a moan, and settings such as receiving a birthday cake. They seemed to understand the task and were able to match nonhuman objects such as a car or bird. But compared to control children, they had difficulties in comprehending human facial expressions.

As with nonverbal communication, both expression and comprehension of speech is problematic (Rutter, 1985a; Schopler and Mesibov, 1985). Some children remain mute or never say more than words or simple phrases. About half do not develop useful speech. Babbling and later verbalizations often are abnormal in tone, pitch, and rhythm. Grammar and meaning fall short of normal. And specific deviances are notable, such as echolalia and pronoun reversals.

In *echolalia* the person echoes back what another has said, immediately or at a future time, sometimes with modification (Roberts, 1989). Echolalia is seen in aphasia and schizophrenia, and it is probably a passing feature of normal development. In autism, it is related to poor language comprehension, and it lessens as comprehension increases (McEvoy, Loveland, and Landry, 1988). Why echolalia occurs is not known. It is sensitive to the environment; for example, it occurs more frequently with unfamiliar tasks and persons (Charlop, 1986). It may be an automatic response but it may also be an attempt to communicate, perhaps the best communication the child can manage (Wetherby, 1986).

Errors in *pronoun reversal* are quite common. The child may refer to others as "I" or "me," and to the self as "he," "she," or "them." Perhaps this deviance stems from echolalia, inadequate comprehension, or failure to attend to how pronouns are used (Oshima-Takane and Benaroya, 1989).

The language deficits of autism have been increasingly conceptualized as problems in *pragmatics*, that is, using speech and gesture in a communicative way, considering the social context (Baron-Cohen, 1988). Pragmatic skills typically begin early in life and normal preschoolers have reasonably good ability to adapt their communications to listeners and situations. In contrast, children with autism show a variety of pragmatic difficulties (Baron-Cohen, 1988; Tager-Flusberg, 1981, 1985). They ask embarrassing questions, fail to use greetings such as "hello," maintain an inappropriately formal style of speech, interrupt or do not

signal for turn taking, persevere on a topic, fail to use speech for joint attention interaction, and fail to otherwise adapt to listeners' knowledge and needs.

In summary, autistic children show language delay and language deviance. Compared to children with similar mental age and nonautistic language disabled children, they differ especially in (Cantwell et al., 1989, Rutter, 1985a):

The use and understanding of gesture

Abnormal features such as echolalia, repetitions and made-up words that have no meaning for others

Fewer spontaneous verbalizations

Greater comprehension deficits

Failure in pragmatics

Perhaps less progress over time.

Social impairments. Disturbed social interaction is a criterion for autism in all major classification systems (Baron-Cohen, 1988). Social deficits may change in form with development but they remain into adulthood (Rumsey, Rapoport and Sceery, 1985; Rutter, 1985a).

DSM-III-R (1987) provides examples of deficient social interactions in a rough developmental sequence. Early parental attachment may be disturbed and toddlers may fail to follow their parents around, greet them when they return, or seek comfort and affection from them (Rutter, 1985a). This interaction is very different from other attachment problems, for example, from the indiscriminate attention seeking by some children reared in institutions. After age five or so, the more blatant impairments may lessen and family relationships may appear more normal. However, difficulties can continue in cooperative play and other peer interactions. There may be failure to form friendships and perhaps inappropriate social actions. Autistic people rarely marry.

It is important to recognize, however, that not only do some autistic children have greater social skills than others, but also that their social skills are not equally impaired. For example, simple gestures are used and attachment behaviors that approximate normal appear in some of the children (Sigman and Ungerer, 1984; Sigman and Mundy, 1989). Finally, social impairment is not unique to autism. One epidemiological study found social deficits in 21 of every 10,000 handicapped children but only a small portion of these children showed autistic behaviors (Wing and Gould, 1979).

Summary: What is the deficit? It is clear that autistic children display many problems in many areas of functioning. Individual variation exists, and a high functioning subgroup can be identified. Furthermore, some of the deficits of autism are observed in other syndromes, such as mental retardation and developmental language disorder. Researchers are continuing to try to identify deficits that are unique to autism and to understand the primary, or core, dysfunction.

The primary deficit is considered either affective or cognitive (Fine et al., 1986). Kanner's original paper referred to the disturbance as one of "affective contact," and this position continues to have many proponents. On the other hand, Rutter (1985a) has represented the popular argument for the primacy of cognitive deficits.

Let us look at two models described by Baron-Cohen (1988) that exemplify these different views. Both focus on the social and communication deficiencies shown in autism (Figure 12–3). Hobson's (1989) model assumes that the primary deficit is affective. He proposes that humans have an innate ability to acquire and comprehend information about the emotions of others. Through this they develop reciprocal social relationships, which are necessary to establish the social world. It is from relationships with others that children come to know how people conceive the world, which, in turn, enables them to develop abstract and symbolic thinking. According to Hobson, autistic children lack the innate ability to interact affectively, thereby blocking subsequent growth. Impairments show up especially in abstract and symbolic thinking, theory of mind, pragmatic language, imaginative

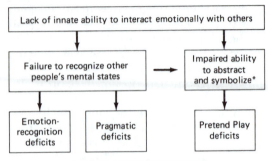

HOBSON'S AFFECTIVE THEORY

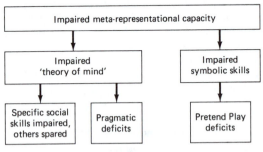

BARON-COHEN, LESLIE, AND FRITH'S COGNITIVE THEORY

FIGURE 12–3 Two conceptualizations of autism. From Baron-Cohen, 1988. Reprinted by permission of Plenum Publishing Corporation.

play, and recognizing emotions. Hobson's own work showing deficits in matching facial expressions with posture, sound and events supports his model.

Baron-Cohen, Leslie, and Frith (1985) have offered a cognitive model, in which the basic deficit is seen as a failure in meta-representation. The distinction is made between the child's own representation of the world, called primary representation, and the child's beliefs about others' representations of the world, called meta-representations. Failure of meta-representation results in an impaired theory of mind and related social skills, such as pragmatic communications. It also results in imparied symbolic skills.

Although our brief discussion of these models can hardly do justice to them, it does indicate how researchers can use the clinical picture of autism to draw different conclusions about the primary deficit of autism. Baron-Cohen believes that affective theory makes better sense of autistic children's difficulties in recognizing emotional behaviors, while cognitive theory does a particularly good job in accounting for pragmatic language problems and select social skill deficits. Perhaps partly because of this, he raises the possibility that the two theories can be integrated.

Goodman's (1989) analysis of autism is consistent with this idea. He argues that the search for a single core psychological deficit may be misleading, that multiple primary deficits may be involved. The coexistence of several primary deficits results in the distinct syndrome of autism. These core deficits would, of course, have to account for autism's language, social-emotional, general intellectual, perceptual, and motor difficulties. Goodman further suggests that the primary deficits rely on different neural systems, but that these systems share vulnerability to dysfunction. He thus relates psychological deficiencies to underlying biological dysfunctions. Goodman's model, as well as others, provides a framework for further testing.

The Causes of Autism: Psychological Theories

The etiology of autism is unknown, but is being vigorously pursued. Psychological theories have largely emphasized the role of parents.

Kanner originally described the families of autistic children as highly intelligent and professionally accomplished. He noted that they were preoccupied with scientific, literary, and artistic concerns, and treated their offspring in a cold mechanical way. Although Kanner did not believe that "refrigerator" parenting sufficiently explained autism (Kanner, 1943; Kanner and Eisenberg, 1956), the idea grew that inadequate parenting caused the condition. In part, this was due to the *zeitgeist*, which from about 1945 to 1965 emphasized the psychoanalytical view that childhood problems might be rooted in parental behavior (Schopler, 1978).

Bettleheim's (1967a, b) theory exemplified this approach. He hypothesized that autism results from early unsatisfactory and threatening experiences. Accordingingly, normal personality depends on the child's acting successfully on the environment to fulfill needs and communicate with others. When mutual interaction develops, the infant's cries, smiles, and other signals are validated by responses from others. The child continues to act on the world and a sense of self grows. However, when the early environment is not appropriately responsive, the child may perceive the world as threatening and destructive and may withdraw. The will to act and to learn is left behind, and the child retreats to an "empty fortress."

Another psychogenic explanation focused on operant learning. Ferster (1961, 1966) proposed that the parents of autistic children failed to properly shape the behavior of their offspring through reinforcement and punishment. The children thus lacked support for a normal behavioral repertoire. Further, self-stimulation and other primitive actions were strengthened by the reinforcements children received. Unresponsive parents were seen as the most likely to fail their offspring, due to their preoccupation with other activities, rejection of the child, depression, and the like. Thus, although Ferster's and Bettleheim's approaches were clearly different, they shared the view that early parenting plays a central role in bringing autism about.

As interesting as psychological theories are, their influence is not strong today. One reason for their decline is the very nature of autism. Parental interaction hardly seems adequate to explain the severity and bizarreness of the behaviors—displayed so early in life. A more decisive reason is the lack of empirical support (Koegel et al., 1983; McAdoo and DeMyer, 1978). With some exception (e.g., Wolff, Narayan, and Moyes,

1988), the parents do not appear different in personality and adaptive behaviors, nor in intelligence and social class, from parents of normal children or children with other behavioral difficulties.

The Causes of Autism: Biological Factors

As the evidence for psychogenesis has weakened, evidence for biological causation has grown. Autism is associated with various biological factors.

Genetic factors. Gross chromosome abnormalities are linked to autism (Mariner et al., 1986; Payton et al., 1989). An association with the fragile X chromosome has been reported by several investigators and may be involved in 5 to 16 percent of all cases (Gillberg, 1988). The data vary a good deal, however, perhaps because of variation in the diagnosis of autism and in identification of fragile X (Folstein and Rutter, 1988). Perhaps the link may show up more for boys than girls, and especially in mentally retarded autistic children.

Tuberose sclerosis, which is transmitted by a dominant gene, is also linked to autism, perhaps in about 5 percent of all cases (Gillberg, 1988). And there is some relationship with recessively-transmitted PKU. Both these conditions are associated with mental retardation as well.

Family and twin studies shed more light on the question of inheritance. About 2 percent of families have two autistic offspring, many more times what would be expected by chance—even with conservative estimates (Folstein and Rutter, 1988). And a small number of families have three or four autistic offspring, for which researchers found no shared medical reason (Ritvo et al., 1987). Evidence also exists that disproportionate numbers of parents and siblings of autistic children show language and cognitive deficits ("Genetic Evidence", 1989; Folstein and Rutter, 1988).

Data from twin studies provide more definitive evidence than data from family studies. In Folstein and Rutter's (1978) well-known investigation, 21 pairs of same-sex twins were identified in which one twin met stringent criteria for autism. The results showed that 36 percent of the identical and none of the fraternal pairs were concordant for autism. Interestingly, 82 percent of the identical and only 10 percent of the fraternal twins were concordant for various cognitive/lingusitic problems. The data also indicated that biological hazard, mostly prenatal in origin, had some role. The researchers thus concluded that while inheritance may be sufficient to cause autism, brain injury alone or in combination with inherited abnormalities may also be sufficient. Subsequent studies have confirmed that concordance for autism is higher for identical than fraternal twins, although the specific data vary somewhat (Ritvo et al., 1985; Steffenburg et al., 1989).

Prenatal and birth complications. Many prenatal and birth complications have been identified for persons displaying autism (Bryson, Smith, and Eastwood, 1988; Levy, Zoltak, and Saelens, 1988; Mason-Brothers et al., 1987). Prenatal rubella and influenza could account for a small percentage of cases (Rutter, 1985a). Other variables identified include low birth weight and prematurity, older age of mothers, breech delivery, respiratory distress, and maternal bleeding. However, findings from study to study are inconsistent, and significant results are often obtained only when several complications occur together. Overall, and despite weaknesses in the investigations, it is widely believed that prenatal variables may play a role in etiology but this role is yet to be clarified.

Nervous system dysfunction. Autistic children have high rates of seizures, which appear to increase at puberty, and some show neurological soft signs such as motor clumsiness. EEG abnormalities are frequently found (Campbell and Green, 1985). Brain scans suggest that abnormalities and tissue damage are relatively common (Gillberg, 1988, 1990). Of particular interest have been the temporal lobe, hemispheres, cerebellum, and brainstem, with the latter most implicated.

Biochemical analyses include studies of the immune system, endorphins, peptides, varied metabolic pathways, and especially serotonin and dopamine systems (Le Couteur et al., 1988; Warren et al., 1986; Weizman et al., 1988). A quite consistent finding is that autistic persons have higher than normal blood levels of the neurotransmitter serotonin (Geller et al., 1988; Kuperman et al., 1987; Launay et al., 1987). Evidence also exists for high levels of dopamine and related neurotransmitters (Garnier, 1986; Minderaa, 1989). Still, findings about the nervous system are incredibly complex and in many cases, inconsistent.

As is obvious, despite informative research, no one biological cause for autism has been identified. Chromosomal disorders, infection, prenatal insult, heredity and other factors may work alone or together to adversely affect the nervous system and basic psychological functions.

Developmental Aspects and Prognosis

Only recently have data been brought to bear on the developmental aspects of autism.

One aspect concerns the question of whether autistic behaviors are qualitatively deviant, that is, have no counterpart in normal children. This may be so for some behaviors and some children. For example, severely autistic children display minimal expressiveness, indifference to social demands, and bizarre behaviors unlike normal youngsters (Wenar et al., 1986). However, less disturbed autistic children may follow a developmental sequence that is similar to the normal path, although the rate of growth may differ.

Another aspect of interest concerns the rate of growth of behavior over time (Snow, Hertzig, and Shapiro, 1987). Some investigators have found slow stable growth; others describe an erratic course with spurts and lags, perhaps with sudden loss of skills. Clearly much is yet to be discovered about the development of autistic behaviors.

Nevertheless, research has established that although behavioral problems tend to decline with age, eventual outcome is usually not favorable (Mesibov et al., 1989; Prior and Werry, 1986). Kanner (1973) revealed that only 11 of the 96 children he examined were maintaining themselves in the second and third decades of life. The 11 were doing moderately well: Several had achieved a college education; their jobs included bank teller, accountant, and trucking supervisor; they had hobbies; but most were living alone with few friends or romantic involvements. Lotter's (1974) review of three independent studies concluded that 61 to 74 percent of cases were judged as having poor or very poor status by adolescence. More recent studies confirm that the vast majority of autistic children continue to have difficulties into adolescence and adulthood in communication, social relationships, ritualistic behavior, and independent living skills (Cantwell et al, 1989; Rumsey et al., 1985). Despite the methodological weaknesses of many of the investigations (Cantwell et al., 1989; Lotter, 1978), it is difficult to be optimistic about outcome.

Still, quite a bit of variability is found and close to normal functioning can be seen at adolescence and young adulthood (Szatmari, Bartolucci, et al., 1989). The variables that best predict outcome are intelligence test scores, language development, and degree of initial problems (e.g., Rutter, 1985a).

Helping the Autistic Child through Assessment

Medical evaluation is valuable, especially for research into the causes of autism and treatment of associated medical conditions such as seizures. It is psychological assessment, however, that primarily identifies autism and guides treatment. This discussion is a brief introduction to various approaches to psychological assessment, which rely on reports of parents and other significant adults, standardized tests, and behavioral observations.

Diagnostic checklists. The several checklists that have been developed focus on the child's behavior and some also inquire into prenatal, family, and other variables. Ratings are based on actual observation of the child, impressions of the child's past or present behavior, or records. Diagnostic checklists vary in the degree to which reliability and validity have been established, and further research is needed in this area (Newsom et al., 1988; Parks, 1983). Here, we only briefly describe two widely known checklists.

The Childhood Autism Rating Scale (CARS) consists of 15 scales covering many areas of functioning, including emotional response, imitation, social relations, communication, perception, and intelligence (Schopler et al., 1980; Schopler, Reichler, and Renner, 1988). Based on total score, children are considered severely autistic, mildly to moderately autistic, or nonautistic. Although the validity of CARS to distinguish autism has been questioned (Newsom et al., 1988), this instrument seems useful in screening children and older persons with autism (Mesibov et. al., 1989).

The Autism Behavior Checklist (ABC) has 57 items placed in five categories: sensory, relating, body and object use, language, social and self-help skills (Krug, Arick, and Almond, 1978). It is part of a larger assessment instrument aimed at educational planning (Newsom et al., 1988; Volkmar et al., 1988). Each yes/no item is assigned a weight from 1 to 4 according to how well it predicts autism. For example, "has no social smile" is rated 2; "has pronoun reversal" is rated 3. Children are rated on the basis of how well each item describes them. The ABC appears most useful in screening individuals for whom the diagnosis of autism is unclear, but like other checklists it cannot take the place of broad clinical assessment (Volkmar et al., 1988).

Standardized intelligence and adaptive behavior tests. The use of intelligence tests in autism can be problematic since they emphasize language and require cooperation and motivation. But they are worthwhile, for example, in helping to determine classroom placement for higher functioning children and the effects of treatment (Newsom et al., 1988). In addition, several of these tests rely less on verbal and more on performance tasks (e.g., the Leiter International Performance Scale).

AAMD's Adaptive Behavior Scale and the Vineland Adaptive Behavior Scales (p. 216) are among the most widely used to examine adaptive functioning. Recent studies of the Vineland pinpoint social deficits in autistic compared to other developmentally disabled children (Freeman et al., 1988; Volkmar et al., 1987). The deficits are greater than would be expected from IQ scores, and are especially noticeable in social relations, coping skills, and communication. Thus, the scale can help differentiate autistim and also provide information critical to treatment planning.

Behavioral and skill analysis. Behavioral and skill analysis focuses on assessment of the individual's behavior in particular environmental settings. It seeks to understand how children do or do not meet specific environmental demands, and how they might better do so. Behavioral observation, task analyses, and checklists are major techniques.

Table 12–2 provides a general guideline for evaluating environmental expectations and further examining the specific skills required for each task. In addition, it is usually necessary to assess behaviors that interfere with productive action, such as self-stimulation, self-injury, and high activity level. Another critical component is evaluation of the stimuli that are guiding a behavior and the consequences that are reinforcing or weakening it.

This approach is commonly used by those working daily with developmentally disabled persons and is especially valued by

TABLE 12–2 Guidelines to Assessment in Natural Environments

Steps to Evaluate the Environment
1. Determine important environments in which the child functions (e.g., home, restaurant, supermarket)
2. Divide these environments into subenvironments (e.g., home into kitchen, bedroom, etc.)
3. Identify the most important activities in each subenvironment (e.g., cooking, washing dishes)
4. Identify specific skills needed for child's partial or full participation in the activities (e.g., cutting potatoes, stacking dishes)

Steps to Evaluate Specific Skills Needed by an Activity
1. Analyze skills used by normal persons in the activity
2. Determine the skills the child can perform by observing the child in the environment or a simulated environment
3. Compare the child's performance with that of normal person's to identify missing skills
4. Consider possible adaptations of skills, materials, rules, etc. (e.g., teach a mute child to order restaurant foods with pictures)

Adapted from Newsom, Hovanitz, and Rincover, 1988.

behaviorally oriented professionals. It is time consuming and requires meticulous observation and implementation, but it can be enormously useful for targeting and monitoring treatment.

Family assessment. Now that families are no longer blamed for causing autism, emphasis is on understanding family interaction and stress (Newsom et al., 1988). One aim of assessment is the alleviation of stress for humanitarian reasons. Another is the enhancement of family participation in the management and treatment of autism. Child management practices and parental ability to follow through in home interventions can be evaluated. Warnings of potential diffi-culties include marital conflict, financial or work-related burdens, and emphasis only on medical approaches that require little of parents.

Family assessment depends mostly on interviews and questionnaires. However, ob-servational assessment has been done in treatment programs involving parents as therapists. Here, parental teaching and management skills have been assessed be-fore and after parent training (e.g., Harris, 1986; Schreibman et al., 1984). Although family assessment is nowhere as advanced as that of disabled offspring, it appears to be receiving more attention than it did in the past.

Traditional Psychotherapeutic Treatment

Historically, traditional psychotherapies have been employed with children variously labeled autistic and psychotic. The focus is intrapsychic processes, such as the devel-opmental task of separation from parents and ego growth.

Bettleheim's residential program at the Orthogenic School in Chicago is an example of the psychoanalytic framework in combi-nation with milieu therapy (Bettleheim, 1967a; Ekstein, Friedman, and Carruth, 1972). As we already saw, Bettleheim attrib-uted autism to failed parenting that involves outright rejection or lack of mutual inter-action. Treatment consists of creating an environment away from parents in which the child can develop as an autonomous person. The therapist serves as a steady object around which the new personality forms. The environment must permit the child to explore freely and safely, to exper-iment with letting go of autistic defenses. In doing so, the child gives up the world of fantasy and achieves more normal affective relationships.

Bettleheim (1967a) claimed that treat-ment success was related to the child's orig-inal language ability and that reasoning, mastering reality, and reading comprehension often never reached normal developmental levels. Still, he reported that 79 percent of treated cases showed good or fair progress. This unusually high rate raised questions about the definition of success (Werry, 1979b). Today's more popular treatments aim at (1) changing biological functioning with medications or (2) creating special structured environments in which development and learning are fostered (Lovaas and Smith, 1988).

Medical Treatment

The use of medication for severely disturbed children has gradually increased since the early 1930s (Conners, 1978). Many kinds of medications have been tried including stimulants, antidepressants, antipsychotics, hallucinogens, and megavitamins. Adequate evaluation is lacking for many drugs, or results indicate little benefit and even a worsening of behaviors (Campbell, 1988; Campbell, Geller, and Cohen, 1977; Conners and Werry, 1979).

Haloperidol is one of the more systematically studied medications (Campbell, 1988). This antipsychotic drug is potent in reducing dopamine. Clinically it decreases hyperactivity, withdrawal, stereotypies, and negativism, and may facilitate laboratory learning (Anderson et al., 1989). Improvements are maintained when haloperidol is given over several months, but negative side effects also can appear. Side effects can be minimized by discontinuing the drug from time to time.

Much current interest exists in fenfluramine, which is antagonistic to serotonin. Since about one-third of autistic children show high blood serotonin—and those with the higher levels show greater intellectual and stereotypic disturbance—it is reasonable that reduction of serotonin could be beneficial. Some studies, especially preliminary ones, reported improvement in cognitive and social functions with serotonin reduction and no serious side effects (Geller et al, 1982; Ritvo et al., 1983). Other investigations are not as positive, however (Aman and Kern, 1989; Campbell, 1988; du Verglas, Banks, and Guyer 1988; Reiss et al., 1988). Fenfluramine's place in treatment is unresolved.

Initial study of naltrexone has begun (Campbell et al., 1989b). This medication is antagonistic to the opioids (endorphins), which may relate to withdawal, insensitivity to pain, self-mutilation, attention deficits, and other behavioral problems (e.g., Sahley and Panksepp, 1987). Evidence of benefits with only mild behavioral side effects calls for further research.

A Broad Educational Treatment: TEACCH

TEACCH is a statewide program that began as a research project at the University of North Carolina (Schopler, Mesibov, and Baker, 1982). Today it operates 5 regional centers and directs 62 public classrooms (Schopler, 1987).

TEACCH, which stands for Treatment and Education of Autistic and related Communication handicapped CHildren, is committed to a structured learning environment in which behavioral tasks are embedded. It encourages and organizes cooperation among teachers, parents, and therapists.

At the regional centers children are individually assessed as the basis for treatment. Classroom activities are tailored to meet the child's needs. Parents are instructed by teachers on how to conduct a home teaching program, and they also are trained as co-therapists for their children. Efforts are made to strengthen and support families and to encourage community involvement.

Over the years and 4,000 or more students, TEACCH has been evaluated in various ways. The effectiveness of specific techniques was examined by comparing highly structured operant learning sessions with nondirective and psychoanalytic play therapy. The structured approach more effectively produced change in attention, affect, language, and bizarre behavior. Parental teaching skills were evaluated by rating mother-child interaction before training and two months later. Improvement occurred on all measures, including organization of materials, teaching pace, language use, behavior management, and atmosphere of enjoyment. Outcome was examined by comparing the rate of institutionalization as the students became adults with rates reported in other follow-up studies (Schopler, 1987). The 8 percent rate was considerably lower. Another outcome measure, parental perception of the program a few years after participation, indicated extremely positive attitudes.

In fact, the program is also well received by children, staff, student trainees, the general public, and the research community. Schopler (1987) has summarized the factors that he believes garner positive attitudes. Among them are interpreting the cause of autism as biological rather than parental, supportive parent-therapist partnerships, giving top priority to service, and social advocacy.

Behavioral Intervention

Ferster's conceptualization of autism (p. 277) heralded behavioral treatment for the disorder. He emphasized operant conditioning and discrimination learning, and offered evidence that autistic children could learn simple tasks (Lovaas and Smith, 1988). Operant conditioning, along with observational learning, became a cornerstone for some of the most successful treatments.

The behavioral approach has been applied successfully to teaching, among other things, language, social interaction, and self-care. Success also has been attained in reducing stereotypic, self-stimulating, and other maladaptive behaviors. Reinforcement, punishment, extinction, shaping, fading, and generalization techniques are the primary tools in this effort. There is a strong thrust to train parents and teachers in behavioral techniques. The following discussion focuses on language, maladaptive behavior, and intensive behavioral training.

Language and communication. Lovaas and his colleagues at the University of California at Los Angeles were among the first to teach speech to autistic children. Language acquisition was conceptualized as the learning of two basic events (Lovaas, Young, and Newsom, 1978). First, children must acquire verbal responses of increasing complexity: basic speech sounds (phonemes), words and parts of words (morphemes), and the arrangement of words into phrases and sentences (syntax). Second, they must acquire skills to use language meaningfully and in a social way.

It is often necessary to prepare children for language learning, especially to suppress behaviors that may interfere with learning and to establish generalized imitation. Autistic children show deficits in observational learning, but can be taught imitation skills. For example, the therapist may at first clap the hands and reinforce the child for copying this action. When consistent imitation is established, the therapist can then switch to another motor behavior—perhaps opening the mouth—and eventually to uttering a sound. The child is reinforced in turn for each of these imitations and gradually copies the therapist's novel actions. Imitation of language is then possible.

The acquisition of verbal responses can be seen as a four-step process (Lovaas and Newsom, 1976). First, the child is rewarded with food for any verbalizations. In step 2 reward is given only when the response immediately follows the therapist's prompt. In step 3, reward is given for closer and closer approximations to the verbalization of the therapist, until the child matches the verbalization. In step 4, the therapist introduces other, dissimilar sounds and reinforces only correct responses. Speech sounds, words, and phrases are painstakingly programmed so that the child gradually acquires a repertoire of language through modeling and reinforcement.

The ability to use language in a meaningful way involves both expressive and receptive discriminations. Expressive discrimination occurs when the child is presented with a nonverbal stimulus and verbally describes or names it. For example, a cup is presented and the child labels it *cup*. Such labeling is taught as soon as possible. Receptive discrimination occurs when a verbalization is presented and the child makes a nonverbal response, as when the command "touch the cup" is given and the child does so. As expressive and receptive discriminations are acquired, new ones are presented that are based on the ones already learned. With progress, language itself becomes reinforcing and external rewards and prompts are faded. More abstract terms (pronouns, adjectives, verb tenses) are gradually added.

Immense time and effort are required, but some children can learn to generate sentences and respond to an array of verbalizations. One weakness of this approach is that children often do not use acquired speech when they leave the training setting.

Imitation and reinforcement are critical in language training with autistic children. (Alan Carey/The Image Works)

This problem can be reduced when training is done in different settings and different situations, and by different teachers (Durand and Carr, 1988). Another difficulty is that children may respond to someone's comment but fail to initiate communication. There is some evidence that this can be overcome when teaching is done in everyday environments, with reinforcers of spontaneous speech being natural to the environments.

Even so, some children hardly benefit from speech training. For a portion of them, an alternative is to learn sign language or the combination of speech and sign language.

Reducing maladaptive behavior. Self-stimulation, bizarre speech, tantrums, aggression, and self-injury are among the behaviors that interfere with social relationships, learning, and educational placement, and even directly harm autistic children. Several techniques have been employed in treatment, and success has been documented with single-subject research designs. Nevertheless, success has not been inevitable. This is exemplified with regard to self-injurious behavior (SIB), which results in damage to the person's own body.

Common forms of SIB are head banging, biting, scratching, pinching, and gouging. SIB tends to be chronic and repetitious, varying from a few times a day to several times a second. Damage is usually quite minor, but can be life threatening, due to concussion or to recurrent infection (Russo, Carr, and Lovaas, 1980). SIB occurs among normal children, but usually disappears by age five (Schroeder, Mulick, and Rojahn, 1980). It occurs in perhaps 15 percent of developmentally disabled youngsters (Durant and Carr, 1985).

Several hypotheses have been put forth to explain self-injury (Carr, 1977; Durand and Carr, 1985). Organic etiology is possible; indeed, SIB is associated with the genetic Lesch-Nyhan syndrome and with middle ear infection. Even so, SIB can be analyzed as an operant behavior that responds to environmental consequences. One of these consequences is attention from others. It is only natural for caretakers to comfort, distract, or verbally persuade a child engaging in self-injury. Such attention can actually increase SIB, whereas withholding attention can reduce it (Lovaas and Simmons 1969; Russo, Carr, and Lovaas, 1980). Tangibles such as food, toys, and activities can also reinforce self-injury (Durand and Carr, 1985). Yet another positive reinforcer may be the sensory feed-back inherent in SIB; for example, scratching the arm provides sensation that may strengthen scratching.

In other instances SIB appears to be negatively reinforced. Carr, Newsom, and Binkoff (1976) noted that when one eight-year-old was alone self-injury was negligible. When an adult made demands, the rate of slapping and punching himself immediately rose. It is easy to understand that when confronted by such a situation, caretakers might readily cease to make demands, thereby negatively reinforcing SIB.

Analysis of SIB as an operant suggests many ways in which reinforcement contingencies might be rearranged to reduce the behavior. Attention and sensory feed-back can be eliminated when they are serving as reinforcers. In some cases, it is helpful to assure that SIB does not result in the child's escaping demands. Furthermore, there are procedures to decrease the chance that SIB will occur at all. One involves the reinforcement of other behaviors (DRO) that are incompatible with SIB or that distract the child from self-injury.

Nevertheless, these treatments have not always been effective and some have built-in drawbacks. For example, withdrawal of attention can be a lengthy procedure, and it commonly results in an increase of self-injury before an eventual decrease. These difficulties have sometimes led to reliance on physical and other punishments to manage SIB.

Much debate has centered on treatment that involves the application of a noxious but harmless electrical stimulus that may be paired with a verbal reprimand such as "No." This procedure is often effective in immediately suppressing SIB, but it is crit-icized on the grounds that the result tends not to generalize to other situations. Just as important, electric shock and other punishment raise serious ethical questions, which have been widely debated for some time. The recent marketing of an electrical shock device, the Self-Injurious Behavior Inhibiting System, has sparked particular concern ("Public Interest," 1989). This device has dramatically decreased severe, chronic SIB in several cases (Linscheid et al., 1990). Nevertheless, advocacy groups, government representatives, parents, and professionals have lined up on both sides of the ethical argument. (see photo p. 286)

Those in opposition to the use of aversive treatment see it as inhumane, painful, and potentially the cause of physical side-effects, stress, and death. They have organized into various groups to gain support for their position, such as the Committee for Non-Aversive Behavioral Intervention of the Association for Persons with Severe Handicaps. Supporters of aversive treatment argue that it ought to be a last resort for persons who engage in extreme, unmanageable self-abuse. They view such treatment as brief and effective, no worse than commonly used aversive medical treatments that bring about long-term gain. Supporters of aversive treatment have formed the International Association for the Right to Effective Treatment. It is not likely that the issue will be readily or rapidly settled, as it elicits strong opinions and emotions.

Meanwhile less aversive operant treatment is being sought. Durand and Carr (1985) point to the importance of careful analysis of the motivation for maladaptive behaviors. For example, when the bizarre speech of a nine-year-old boy was "punished" with time-out, it increased. In fact, the bizarre speech was functioning to remove the child from task demands—which was accomplished by the time-out that served as a reinforcer (Durand and Crimmins, 1987). One way to assess what motivates behavior is to expose the person to different conditions and observe whether the behavior increases or decreases. Durand and Crimmins (1988) also have developed

The Self-Injurious Behavior Inhibiting System delivers mild shock to the leg or arm in response to head banging. Aversive treatment is controversial, even among parents. While some parents voice strong opposition, others express appreciation that this apparatus rapidly controlled self injurious behavior. By permission of Johns Hopkins University Laboratory. Courtesy of Mr. & Mrs. Garry Potter.

the Motivation Assessment Scale, a teacher rating scale to determine the influence of attention, tangibles, escape, and sensory feedback on SIB.

Carr and Durand (1985; Durand, 1986) conceptualize their approach to treatment as Functional Communication Training (FCT). They view SIB and other maladaptive behaviors as intentional communication by the child. Assessment of the behavior's function is followed by training appropriate verbal alternatives to the behavior. For example, if SIB is motivated by social attention of the teacher, the child might be taught to obtain attention by asking, "Is my work good?" Preliminary results indicate that this procedure holds promise.

An intensive behavioral program. So far we have looked at efforts that targeted specific behavioral domains for change. Now we turn to a more comprehensive

behavioral program. In 1970 Lovaas and his colleagues began a program to maximize the benefits of behavior modification by providing full-time treatment (Lovaas, 1987; Lovaas and Smith, 1988). Very young children were chosen because it was assumed that they would not strongly discriminate environments and thus they would generalize learning across environments. Also, it was believed that school mainstreaming, which was considered desirable, would be more easily accomplished in preschools than with older children in elementary schools.

To be accepted into the study children had to (1) have been independently diagnosed as autistic, (2) be less than 46 months of age, and (3) have a specified mental age. Nineteen subjects were assigned to intensive training (group I) and 19 to a minimal training control condition (group II). Comparison was also made with group III, an outside group of autistic children that re-

TABLE 12–3 Educational Placement and Average IQ Score at Follow-up in the Lovaas Intensive Treatment Program

	Percent of children completing regular first grade		Percent of children in language handicapped and LD class		Percent of children in first grade for autistic-retarded	
Group I	47	IQ: 107	42	IQ: 70	11	IQ: 30
Group II	0		42	IQ: 74	58	IQ: 36
Group III	5	IQ: 99	48	IQ: 67	48	IQ: 44

Adapted from Lovaas, 1987.

ceived no training in the project. All three groups were very similar.

Treatment lasted for two or more years. Children in group I worked with student therapists and with their parents for more than 40 hours of one-to-one treatment per week. Operant techniques were the basis of training. Behavioral deficits were targeted for improvement. Aggression and self-stimulation were treated by ignoring them, time-out, shaping more acceptable alternatives, and as a last resort by a loud "no" or a slap on the thigh. During the first year treatment focused on reducing maladaptive behaviors, compliance to simple verbal commands, imitation, appropriate play, and extending training in the family. The second year emphasized language growth, interactive play, and teaching children to function in the preschool. The third year emphasized emotional expression, preacademic skills, and learning by observation of other children. Effort was made to place children in normal preschools where teachers would help in training. Children in group II received almost the same treatment but with less than 10 hours of one-to-one interaction per week.

At follow-up the experimental children had significantly higher educational placement and IQ than the control groups, which did not differ from each other. Table 12–3 shows the percent of children in different educational placements and their average IQ scores. Prior to the study only 2 of the experimental children had scored in the normal range of IQ while 11 had scored in the severely retarded range; 7 had been echolalic and 11 mute. Furthermore, a later investigation when the children averaged 13 years of age showed that 8 of the 19 experimental children were indistinguishable on several measures from age-matched normal children (Lovaas, Smith, and McEachin, 1989).

The Lovaas study has its critics (Schopler, Short, and Mesibov, 1989) and replication would be helpful. Also, the subjects were limited to the very young and even so, around-the-clock treatment did not benefit some of them. But the success rate must be judged in light of previous failures to help autistic children. In fact, the success of the program is consistent with the high marks that behavioral treatment often receives, and it raises hopes that intensive programs may make a difference to at least some autistic youngsters.

CHILDHOOD SCHIZOPHRENIA

As noted early in this chapter, both Kraepelin and Bleuler identified a small percentage of cases of schizophrenia in which onset occurred in childhood. By the 1930s, the first descriptive, high-risk, and epidemiological studies of childhood schizophrenia had appeared (Cantor, 1988). During the next two and more decades, many efforts were made to conceptualize the nature of the condition. Although just attention cannot be paid to all of this work, a few efforts are mentioned here.

In a now-classic paper, Potter (1933) emphasized differences between childhood and adult schizophrenia. Beginning in 1935 Bender (1947) worked for many years at New York City's Bellevue Hospital, describing, treating, and following the progress of severely disturbed children she labeled schizophrenic. Some of her observations are questioned today, but her influence was great and her approach continues. Despert (1940) and Bradley (1947) also offered rich descriptions and conceptualizations of schizophrenia in children.

It is ironic that despite the many lines of investigations, concise knowledge about childhood schizophrenia is still limited (Volkmar and Cohen, 1988). This is because of historical changes in, and disagreements about, the nature and classification of schizophrenia in childhood. The struggle for better understanding goes on, with many of the major questions asked by early workers still being researched.

DSM-III-R Criteria

Neither DSM-III nor DSM-III-R recognize schizophrenia as a specific childhood disorder. Rather, children can be classified schizophrenic if they meet the criteria for the adult disorder. DSM-III-R criteria are summarized in Table 12–4. The hallmarks of schizophrenia are delusions, hallucinations, thought disorders such as loose associations, inappropriate emotions, and markedly rigid or flexible posture (catatonia). The disturbed child must previously have shown a higher level of functioning, and may not achieve normal social development.

These criteria are more explicit and narrower than those previously used for childhood schizophrenia, and thus may produce more homogenous samples (Asarnow, Sherman, and Strandburg, 1986). However, they make it unlikely that very young children would be diagnosed as schizophrenic, since early developmental level limits the display of the psychotic symptoms noted in section A of Table 12–4. This is a serious problem for researchers who propose that the schizophrenic process can begin very early, perhaps in the second or third year (e.g., Cantor, 1988). They argue that the early manifestations of schizophrenia are not taken into account.

DSM-III-R and other classification systems include subcategories of schizophrenia, such as disorganized and paranoid schizophrenia. However, reliability for the subcategories is questionable and their usefulness for children is not established.

TABLE 12–4 A Summary of DSM-III-R Criteria for Schizophrenia

A. Presence of psychotic symptoms in the active phase: either 1, 2, or 3 for at least one week.
   1. Two of the following: delusions, hallucinations, incoherence or loosening of associations, catatonic behavior, flat or inappropriate affect
   2. Bizarre delusions
   3. Prominent hallucinations of a voice with content unrelated to depression or elation, or commenting on the behavior or thoughts of the person, or two or more voices conversing with each other

B. Functioning markedly below previous highest level. With onset in childhood or adolescence, failure to achieve expected social development.

C. Related disorders have been ruled out

D. Continuous disturbance for at least six months, which includes an active phase of at least one week with symptoms in A. May or may not include a prodromal phase (prior to the active phase) or a residual phase (after the active phase) marked by isolation, role impairment, peculiar behavior, etc.

E. If a history of autism, diagnosis of schizophrenia is made only if delusions or hallucinations are present.

Adapted from DSM-III-R. Reprinted with permission from the *Diagnostic and Statistical Manual of Mental Disorders, Third Edition, Revised.* Washington, DC, American Psychiatric Association, 1987.

Prevalence

Epidemiological data are scant and of poor quality, due to low frequency of the disorder and the many problems of classification and diagnosis (Prior and Werry, 1986.) Probably the best that can be said is that prevalence is thought to be lower than for autism (Tanguay and Cantor, 1986). Frequency is thought to be extremely low before age 6, to increase somewhat and be relatively stable for ages 7 to 12, and then to rapidly rise.

The condition is more frequent in males than females. However, this sex difference seems to disappear at puberty (Green et al., 1984; Prior and Werry, 1986). There is evidence that childhood schizophrenia is disproportionately high in the lower social classes. This is one of several ways in which it is believed to differ from autism.

Psychological and Behavioral Functioning

Schizophrenic children display many problem behaviors, although there is variation from child to child. This discussion focuses first on the primary psychotic features of the disorder and then looks at other characteristics. (Also see the case study, p. 70.)

Hallucinations. Hallucinations are perceptions that occur in the absence of identifiable stimuli. They thus reflect a perceptual disturbance. Table 12–5 shows some of the data presented by Russell et al. (1989) from their own and two other major studies of schizophrenic children. The occurrence of hallucinations was high and remarkably consistent across these investigations. Auditory hallucinations were by far the most common. Visual hallucinations were reported fairly often, while those involving

touch and smell were quite rare. These findings are consistent with other studies of child and adult schizophrenia (Kemph, 1987; Davison and Neale, 1990).

Table 12–6 shows the variety of hallucinations reported in the Russel et al. study, which examined children in the Los Angeles area. The table also gives the percentage of subjects who experienced each type. It was not uncommon for a single child to report several kinds, but nonauditory hallucinations never occurred in this sample without auditory hallucinations. The following examples give some sense of the children's reports of their experiences.

Auditory (unrelated to affective state): One child reported the kitchen light saying to do things and "to shut up."

TABLE 12–5 Characteristics of Schizophrenic Children in Three Studies

	Kolvin et al., 1971	*Green et al., 1984*	*Russell et al., 1989*
Number	33	24	35
Mean age	11.1 (estimated)	9.96	9.54
Male:Female	2.66:1	1.67:1	2.2:1
Lower social classes	47%	83%	14%
Mean IQ	86	89	94
Percent Showing Symptoms			
Auditory hallucinations	82	79	80
Visual hallucinations	30	46	37
Delusions	58	54	63
Thought disorder	60	100	40

Adapted from A. T. Russell, L. Bott, and C. Sammons, The phenomenology of schizophrenia occurring in childhood, Journal of the American Academy of Child and Adolescent Psychiatry, 28(3), 399–407, 1989. © by Am. Acad. of Child and Adolescent Psychiatry.

TABLE 12–6 Percentage of Children with Hallucinations and Delusions

Types of Hallucinations	Percent
Nonaffective auditory	80
Command	69
Visual	37
Conversing voices	34
Religious	34
Persecutory	26
Commenting voices	23
Tactile	17
Olfactory	6
Somatic	6

Types of Delusions	Percent
Persecutory	20
Somatic	20
Bizarre	17
Reference	14
Grandiose	11
Thought insertion	11
Control/influence	9
Mind reading	9
Thought broadcasting	6
Thought control	3
Religious	3

From A. T. Russell, L. Bott, and C. Sammons, The phenomenology of schizophrenia occurring in childhood, Journal of the American Academy of Child and Adolescent Psychiatry, 28(3), 399–407, 1989. © by the Am. Acad. of Child and Adolescent Psychiatry.

Command: A man's voice said, "Murder your stepfather" and "Go play outside."

Visual: A ghost with a red, burned and scarred face was seen several times in different places.

Conversing voices: Various animals talked softly with each other about the child.

Religious: God said, "Sorry D., but I can't help you now, I'm helping someone else."

Persecutory: Monsters said child is "stupid" and that they will hurt him.

Tactile: Feelings of snakes and spiders on the back

Delusions. Delusions are false beliefs that are maintained even in the face of realistic contradiction. They occurred relatively frequently and with consistency across the sam-

ples summarized in Table 12–5. There are many kinds of delusions, as reflected in data from the Russell et al. investigation (Table 12–6). Again, some children reported several types. The following are some examples.

Persecutory: A child believed his father had escaped from jail and was coming to kill him.

Somatic: One child believed that a boy and a girl spirit lived inside his head.

Bizarre: A boy was convinced he was a dog and growing fur. One time he refused to leave the veterinarian's office unless he got a shot.

Reference: A girl believed that people outside her house were staring and pointing at her to send her a message.

Grandiose: A boy had the firm belief that he was different and able to kill people. He felt that when God "zoomed" through him he became very strong.

Thought disorder. Delusions are a disturbance in the content of thought but the form of thinking also can be disordered. The child may display loose associations, which show up in jumping from topic to topic with no obvious connection between them and without awareness of the problem. Speech may lack logic and be quite incoherent and incomprehensible to others. It may be impoverished, that is, adequate in amount but conveying little information because it is vague, too abstract or concrete, or repetitive. Some of these features are demonstrated in the following excerpt from an interview with a seven-year-old boy.

I used to have a Mexican dream. I was watching TV in the family room. I disappeared outside of this world and then I was in a closet. Sounds like a vacuum dream. It's a Mexican dream. When I was close to that dream earth I was turning upside down. I don't like to turn upside down. Sometimes I have Mexican dreams and vacuum dreams. It's real hard to scream in dreams. (Russell et al., 1989, p. 404)

Table 12–5 shows high percentages of thought disorder in the three studies, but also variations across the samples (that is, 60, 100, 40 percent). Although these differences may indeed be real, they may also be the result of different interpretations of thought disorder and difficulty in reliably identifying it (Russell et al., 1989).

Intellectual/cognitive/language functioning. Intellectual functioning as evaluated on IQ tests is somewhat deficient in childhood schizophrenia but not nearly as much as in autism (Prior and Werry, 1986). Many of the children score at the borderline to average levels. There are few studies of IQ subtest performance, but schizophrenic children may have difficulties on tasks requiring short-term information processing (Asarnow et al., 1987).

Other research also suggests disturbance of information processing, especially in attention. For example, schizophrenic children responded to auditory stimuli with abnormal brain waves, which were similar to those of adult schizophrenics (Erwin et al., 1986). From a series of laboratory studies Asarnow and his colleagues concluded that schizophrenic children fail to develop certain attentional mechanisms, which also are deficient in adult schizophrenics (Asarnow et al., 1986). The researchers reason that such attention deficits could show up in vague, digressive speech because the child is unable to keep up with the short-term processing demanded by normal conversation. Similarly, inability to attend to various cues at any one moment in social interaction could cause the social ineptness that is seen in schizophrenic children.

Impaired language development has been reported (Cantor, 1988; Watkins et al., 1988), and would be expected with low IQ or very early onset that interferes with general development. Speech obviously can reflect thought disorder, and atypical features such as echolalia occur. Nevertheless, basic language skills do not seem as deficient as in autism (Prior and Werry, 1986).

Other deficits. Schizophrenic children often show little emotion or they laugh, cry, or show anger when the situation does not warrant such a response. Other emotional disturbances have been reported—such as coldness, moodiness, anxiety, and depression—but their extent and nature need further documentation (Eggers, 1978; Prior and Werry, 1986).

Although there is little systematic study of social behavior, a variety of difficulties has been reported (Bettes and Walker, 1987; Kydd and Werry, 1982; Watkins et al., 1988). These include social withdrawal and isolation, inability to initiate social interactions, ineptness, and social anxiety.

Finally, motor deficiencies often are reported. They include awkwardness, delayed milestones, poor coordination, and peculiar posture (Bender, 1972; Cantor, 1988; Eggers, 1978; Watkins, Asarnow, and Tanguay, 1988).

Developmental Course

Information is beginning to accumulate about the course of schizophrenia in childhood. Onset can be acute, gradual, or show short episodes of disturbance before a full-blown episode (Prior and Werry, 1986). Children with schizophrenia appear to resemble adults with schizophrenia in that some have a chronic condition, others have recurrent episodes, and still others have only a single episode.

A developmental trend is seen in the content and nature of hallucinations and delusions (Eggers, 1978; Russell et al., 1989). The themes of childhood, such as animals and monsters, make their way into reports of children's psychotic experiences. When delusions first appear they are quite simple (e.g., a monster wants to kill me), but they gradually become more elaborate, complex, abstract, and systematized. These changes are in keeping with cognitive and socioemotional development.

In a recent comprehensive study of 18 schizophrenic children, symptom development was charted from birth to 12 years of age (Watkins et al., 1988). Data were collected from school records, reports of referral agencies, parents, physical examinations, intelligence tests, and interviews with the children. Onset in some of the children had occurred by 2.5 years, and all had been identified by age 10. Many different kinds of behaviors were noted, and the symptoms tended to change with age. For example, language problems, motor delay, bizarre responses to the environment, and lack of social responsiveness were first seen in infancy. During early childhood, mood shifts, inappropriate clinging, rage reactions, and hyperactivity appeared. After 6 years of age, thought disorder and inappropriate affect emerged. Then, usually after age 9, hallucinations and delusions appeared.

One must be cautious not to overgeneralize from this small sample, but it is clear, in the words of the researchers, that the early histories of some of the children were "far from benign." Other studies, too, suggest that early adjustment may be poor for many schizophrenic children—perhaps poorer than for adult schizophrenics (Asarnow and Ben-Meir, 1988; Cantor et al., 1982; Fish, 1986).

Causation

Biological factors. It is highly likely that biological dysfunction plays a role in childhood schizophrenia, but the evidence is piecemeal and not always consistent. The most direct evidence comes from the study of schizophrenic children, but more of the research has been conducted on adult schizophrenia.

Biological disorder is inferred from some of the characteristics of schizophrenic children, especially motor delay and coordination problems, perceptual deviations, and delayed language. Thus, Goldfarb (1970) identified a subgroup of children showing neurological signs, for whom he assumed biological etiology. Bender (1947) described uneven and slow development in every area of nervous system functioning (including sleeping, eating, timing of puberty), and argued for a core biological deficit. So did Fish (1984) and Cantor (1988). It should be noted that all these investigators argued that schizophrenia can begin very early in life, and that the behavioral manifestations differ with developmental level.

A variety of findings gives support to the biological hypothesis (Asarnow et al., 1986; Davison and Neale, 1990; Neuchterlein, 1986; Rieder, Broman, and Rosenthal, 1977). For example, a high incidence of abnormal EEG activity has been found in child and adult schizophrenia. Abnormalities are also indicated by brain scans and biochemical analyses. Prenatal and birth complications also appear linked to childhood schizophrenia, although by no means are they inevitable (Cantor, 1988).

It is generally believed that hereditary influence operates. Schizophrenia is present in the families of schizophrenic children and adults more than would be expected by chance (Fish and Ritvo, 1979; Cantor, 1988). Overall, the closer the genetic relationship is to a schizophrenic person, the greater is the chance of the diagnosis. Twin studies show greater concordance for identical than fraternal twins (44 percent vs. 12 percent), and adoption studies also support hereditary transmission (Davison and Neale, 1990).

Although inheritance apparently is involved, the mode of transmission is not established. Further, other factors must be considered. Concordance for identical twins is far from perfect, and there is evidence that stress has a role in etiology.

Psychogenesis. The hypothesis that family characteristics and interactions cause schizophrenia has a long history. Various processes have been hypothesized, including identification with abnormal parents, pathological role taking, reaction to pathological family dynamics, and inability of the child to separate from the mother (Alanen, 1960; Mahler, 1952). Mothers sometimes were depicted as psychotic and emotionally immature; fathers as too passive to counteract the destructive impact of mothers (Rank, 1955; Goldfarb, 1970).

The work of Goldfarb and his colleagues stands as an early effort to evaluate the families of psychotic children. They found that parents of schizophrenic children tended to score lower than an adult clinic group and higher than adult nonpatients on measures of psychopathology (Goldfarb, Spitzer, and Endicott, 1976). However, it was not possible to conclude that parental psychopathology had caused schizophrenia in the offspring.

Running parallel to the early child studies were investigations to identify deviant interactional patterns in families with an adult schizophrenic (e.g., Bateson et al., 1956; Mishler and Waxler, 1965). It was unclear whether any deviant interactional patterns had preceded and caused mental disorder or had developed as a family response to having a disordered member. Moreover, it was difficult to replicate findings due to differences in criteria for selecting samples, methods, and coding systems (Goldstein, 1988). In any event, no specific family pattern was reliably identified, and enthusiasm for this line of research waned.

Today there is renewed interest in the area, with an emphasis on the interactional model of development. A recent study, for example, compared families of children diagnosed as schizophrenic (or having a related condition) with families of children showing depression (or a related condition). The rates of communication deviance (CD) were higher for the schizophrenia group; that is, verbal communication was more vague, unfocused, and distorted (Asarnow, Goldstein, and Ben-Meir, 1988). Children in the high CD families also were the most impaired and showed the poorest attentional functioning. The researchers suggested that vulnerability to attention deficits together with exposure to CD might bring about attentional dysfunction and psychosocial impairment. Replication and extension of this work would be helpful.

High-risk research is also providing new data about family climate (Goldstein, 1988). This strategy has the potential to identify causal factors prior to the onset of schizophrenia. In the Finnish Adoption Study, most adopted children who eventually became schizophrenic had schizophrenic mothers. However, in all cases, these adoptees had been reared in families rated as having disturbed relationships. Moreover, adopted offspring of schizophrenics with healthy rearing environments had rates of schizophrenia only at or about the general population rates (Goldstein, 1988).

High parental expression of emotions of a hostile, critical nature has also been associated with the eventual diagnosis of schizophrenia or schizophrenia-related disorder in high-risk adolescents (Valone, Goldstein, and Norton, 1984). In a study that examined the patterns of interaction between high EE parents and their at risk nonschizophrenic offspring, the parents who had expressed excessive criticism during family discussion and their offspring were more physiologically aroused during family discussion than low-EE families.

Overall, the research suggests that at risk children who experience certain family interactions are especially stressed (aroused), and that this combination of variables increases the risk for schizophrenia or related disturbances. A wait-and-see attitude is probably appropriate, however. The research studies are often complex, correlational, and difficult to compare. Furthermore, most subjects in the high-risk studies do not break down until adolescence or adulthood, so we do not know whether the findings apply directly to childhood schizophrenia. (Box 12.3 contains other results of high-risk research.)

Vulnerability-stress model. Both biological and environmental factors appear to be involved in the etiology of schizophrenia, and neither set of factors explains the condition adequately. Thus, the diathesis-stress model is endorsed by many professionals. This model assumes that schizophrenia results from organismic vulnerability (diathesis) interacting with stress, much of which originates in the environment. A leading candidate for stress is family dynamics, but other stressors also are likely.

In the final analysis, as with autism, schizophrenia may be one or more related disorders that have diverse and often complex etiological pathways.

BOX 12.2   Precursors of adult schizophrenia

The first high-risk study of adult schizophrenia was begun by Mednick and Schulsinger and their colleagues (Mednick and Schulsinger, 1968). The adolescent subjects were selected on the basis of their having a schizophrenic parent, by far the most popular method of identifying risk for schizophrenia. The 207 subjects, who were functioning normally, were matched with low-risk individuals on age, sex, residence, and the like. Comparisons between the two groups were drawn from information from midwives, teachers, and psychological tests. Follow-up evaluations have continued over the years, with special emphasis given to the subjects who developed behavioral problems.

Many other similar investigations are now underway (Erlenmyer-Kimling et al., 1984; Weintraub and Neale, 1984). They commonly compare children with schizophrenic parents to children of normal parents and parents with other mental disturbances. This potentially permits the identification of factors specific to schizophrenia, as opposed to factors associated with behavioral disorders in general.

The findings from these studies continue to come in, although so far relatively few individuals have broken down. The following summary describes the major findings

(Asarnow and Goldstein, 1986; Neuchterlein, 1986).

1. Evidence is quite good that high-risk children and adolescents show some attentional and cognitive deficits.
2. Some evidence exists for overresponsivity of the autonomic nervous system, but the findings are so mixed that it is unlikely that a simple relationship to risk will be established.
3. The evidence is good that high-risk youth show neurological soft signs such as poor motor coordination, motor delays, and sensory-perception deficits.
4. High risk is associated with negative peer and teacher evaluation, aggression, irritability, low social competence, and the like. However, children of nonschizophrenic, mentally disturbed parents are very similar in this regard. Thus, early social problems are unlikely to predict later schizophrenia.

In fact, more research is needed to ascertain what childhood variables, if any, are specifically related to later development of schizophrenia. Nevertheless, the variables implicated so far appear similar to the characteristics or premorbid descriptions of childhood schizophrenia. This supports the idea that schizophrenia in childhood and adulthood are the same syndrome, the view taken in DSM-III-R.

Prognosis

Reliable outcome studies of childhood schizophrenia are scarce because it is difficult to find large pools of subjects who have been identified by the same criteria. Eggers's (1978) study of 57 children, ages 7 to 13, is one of the more notable ones; it followed subjects 16 years on average. Half of the children showed improvement, with 20 percent appearing recovered. About one-third showed very poor status, and the remainder fair to poor status. Eggers found that the children who had become psychotic before age 10 had the poorer outcome. Above average intelligence was associated with fa-

vorable outcome. So was good premorbid personality: Children had a better chance of recovery if they had once been well-adapted, kind, warm-hearted, capable of making friends, and interested in things. Less favorable outcome was seen in those who had been insecure, inhibited, and shy. In this study family climate and mental disorders did not predict outcome.

Other investigations generally support these findings (Kydd and Werry, 1982; Prior and Werry, 1986). Good premorbid personality, symptoms that can be easily distinguished, acute onset, and identifiable precipitants are related to better outcome. Age of onset is a strong predictor, the later the onset the better the outcome. This may be confounded with how the condition first appears, however, as late onset tends to be acute.

Treatment

Treatment of schizophrenic children depends on the severity of the case, opportunity for treatment, community/family support, and the perspective of the therapist. Some severely disturbed children remain at home and attend special schools; others are placed in residential settings for periods of time. Treatment methods run the gamut of medical and pscyhotherapeutic approaches.

Medical treatment. Electroconvulsive shock and medication are the best-known medical treatments for childhood psychosis. Shock treatment was recommended by Bender (1947), who claimed it was effective with at least some of her patients. Nevertheless, it is not widely accepted today.

The medical treatment of choice is the antipsychotic medications (i.e., phenothiazines, butyrophenones, thioxantheses). In adults, such medications can lessen thought disturbance, emotional disturbance, withdrawal, hallucinations and other symptoms. Nevertheless, there has been little systematic, controlled research of medication with children and adolescents (Campbell and Spencer, 1988; Tanguay and Cantor, 1986). Very limited research suggests that the antipsychotics may be effective in prepubertal cases but less effective than in adult cases, perhaps because the condition has a more pervasive effect on functions that are still developing in the young. These drugs can cause excessive sedation.

Many other medications have been discussed and tried (Campbell, Geller, and Cohen, 1977; Conners and Werry, 1979). The efficacy of antidepressants, hallucinogens, lithium, megavitamins, and stimulants is not established and stimulants actually appear to worsen the condition.

Traditional psychotherapy. Psychoanalytic therapy has focused on the child's being dominated by id impulses, having poor ego function, and being unable to separate from the mother.

The role of the therapist, depending somewhat on the child's age, is to help the child establish a separate self, interpret the world, distinguish reality from fantasy, develop a sense of mastery, and find more adaptive defenses (Cantor and Kestenbaum, 1986; Ekstein et al., 1972). An intense, warm, and trusting relationship is critical.

Ekstein, Friedman, and Caruth's (1972) approach can serve as an example of analytic treatment. They view psychotic children as suffering from a fragmented and disassociated personality, which originated in a failure to progress from normal mother-child connectedness. Due to this basic flaw, development is abnormal and thinking is fixated at a primitive level (primary process). Psychotic children are thus unable to distinguish reality; they are driven by instinctual impulses; they lack knowledge and trust in the future. Ego functions that control, integrate, and synthesize do not develop. The therapist's task is to aid in the development of a stable ego. The tools employed are the usual psychoanalytic tools of the therapeutic relationship (transference) and interpretation. Success is marked by the child's developing the capacity to master reality.

Other approaches. Treatment is often a mix of milieu, educational, and behavioral methods. Milieu therapy aims at providing a completely supportive environment in which the child can grow socially, emotionally, and cognitively. Educational approaches emphasize the teaching of specific skills, within a schoollike setting (Achenbach, 1982). Behavioral interventions focus on shaping adaptive responses and weakening maladaptive ones, as they do with autism. All of these approaches are compatible with each other, and can also be combined with psychoanalytic methods (although the differing assumptions of behavior modification and psychoanalysis make their combination less likely). No matter what the approach, however, there is consensus that more needs to be done to help children who exhibit schizophrenic behaviors.

SUMMARY

Severe childhood disorders similar to adult psychoses have long been recognized, but have been difficult to conceptualize and classify. Age-related frequency distributions argue for a distinction between early onset and later onset syndromes. Autism and childhood schizophrenia are two disorders recognized by the major classification systems.

Kanner's idea that autism is a distinct early onset syndrome is widely accepted today. DSM-III-R contains the category of Autistic Disorder as a childhood developmental disorder. The criteria center on impaired social interaction, impaired communication, and preoccupations and stereotypies.

As a group, autistic children display bizarre stereotypies and obsessions, and over- and undersensitivity to perceptual stimulation. About 75 percent show intellectual deficits and many are retarded. Puzzling "savant" abilities are also shown by a small percentage of autistic persons.

Disturbed communication is pervasive among autistic children. Deficits are seen in expressing and understanding gestural communication, such as in joint attention interaction, and especially with regard to emotional-social messages. The expression and comprehension of spoken language also are deficient, with some children remaining mute and others showing various degrees of difficulty.

The lack of social-emotional responsiveness of autistic individuals is well noted. Although social problems may decrease into middle childhood, they often are chronic. As with other characteristics of autism, considerable individual differences are observed.

Both cognitive and affective problems have been seen as the primary deficits in autism; it is possible, though, that several deficits are primary.

Psychological theories of autism are nowhere as popular as they once were. These theories focused on child-parent interaction and parental pathology and research data do not support them. There is much evidence for biological causations including hereditary transmission, prenatal and birth complications, neurological soft signs, and brain abnormalities. Nevertheless, no one process has been definitively identified and it is likely that various factors or their combination can give rise to autism.

Although much is yet to be discovered about the developmental course of autism, about two-thrids to three-quarters of all cases have poor outcome. Intelligence level and language ability predict outcome.

Many assessment methods are used to identify autism. Traditional psychotherapeutic treatment generally is not considered effective. Medications have given mixed results. TEACCH, a broad educational program with behavioral components, and Lovaas's intensive behavioral program report some of the best outcomes. Operant methods can facilitate language and other skills and reduce undesirable behaviors. The use of aversive treatments, especially to control self-injurious behavior, has raised ethical concerns; Functional Communication Training may be an alternative in some cases.

Schizophrenia in childhood is diagnosed in DSM-III-R with the same criteria used for adults. The hallmarks of schizophrenia are hallucinations, delusions, and thought disorder. Dysfunctions have also been noted in attention, language, social, emotion, and motor behaviors.

The onset of schizophrenia can be acute or gradual, and the condition can be chronic but is not always so. Hallucinations and delusions are more likely as middle childhood is reached and their content shows developmental trends.

Biological etiology is inferred from, among other things, motor and language delay, reports of slow and uneven nervous system development, abnormal EEGs, prenatal and birth complications, and hereditary studies of twins and families. Supportive evidence is given by studies of adult schizophrenia, to the degree to which it is assumed that childhood and adulthood schizophrenia are related.

Family causation has long been suspected but early studies produced no definitive findings. More recent studies have found correlations with deviances in family communication, disturbed rearing environments, and high parental emotional expression. Some of the research consists of high-risk studies, and the assumption is made that at risk children who experience certain family interactions may be more likely to display schizophrenia. Further research is needed to test this hypothesis. The possibility exists that schizophrenia is actually several related disorders that have complex etiology.

The prognosis for schizophrenia is not as well established as for autism, but seems somewhat more favorable. Above average intelligence, good premorbid personality, acute onset, and late onset are related to more favorable outcome.

Medical treatment of schizophrenia consists of antipsychotic drugs, which may be less helpful than for adulthood schizophrenia. Traditional psychoanalytic therapy has advocates, as do milieu, educational, and behavioral treatments. The effectiveness of treatments is not well established.

13

DISORDERS OF BASIC PHYSICAL FUNCTIONS

Problems of physical functioning and health are discussed in this chapter and the next. In many ways these problems represent the interface between psychology and pediatrics. The term *pediatric psychology* is often applied to this field of research and practice. For many of the problems discussed, parents first turn to their pediatrician for help (Roberts and Lyman, 1990). For example, early problems with feeding of infants and toddlers, initiating and managing toilet training, and difficulties in getting children to sleep are among the problems brought to pediatricians (Gross and Drabman, 1990). Also, the problems discussed here involve issues of physical functioning that require collaboration between psychologists and physicians. The life-threatening starvation of anorexic adolescents and the problem of enlarged colons in encopretic children are two examples.

It is common for children to exhibit some difficulty in acquiring appropriate habits of eating, elimination, and sleep. The child's ability to master these tasks, and the parents' ability to train the child, are important to the immediate well-being of both. Beyond the immediate effects, how these tasks are handled can set the foundation for later difficulties. Problems may occur in the same area (for example, the later eating disorder of anorexia nervosa) or in more general ways (for example, problems with authority figures). While parents solve many early difficulties themselves, professional assistance is also frequently sought (Routh, Schroeder, and Koocher, 1983). In this chapter attention is given to some commonly encountered difficulties that are part of normal development. The principal focus, however, is on problems that are serious enough to make them of clinical concern.

DISORDERS OF EATING

A wide range of problems having to do with eating and feeding are commonly reported (Hertzler 1983a, b). These include under-

eating, selective eating, overeating, problems in chewing and swallowing, bizarre eating habits, annoying mealtime behaviors,

Young children often exhibit feeding and eating problems. This may result in disruption and cause their parents considerable distress. (Jean-Claude Lejeune/ Stock, Boston)

and delays in self-feeding. Many of these problems can cause considerable concern for parents and appreciable disruption of family life. For example, children's refusing to eat certain foods or vary their diets is a common complaint made by parents. Adequate nutrition and growth are clearly a concern, but restricted eating is also often accompanied by other behavioral problems such as tantrums, spitting, and gagging. Severe cases of food refusal may be associated with even more difficult social and

psychological problems and result in medical complaints and malnourishment. Indeed, some cases of failure to thrive (life-threatening weight loss or failure to gain) can be conceptualized as a special case of food refusal (Kelly and Heffer, 1990). Thus, some eating problems may actually endanger the physical health of the child. The clinical disorders discussed in the next sections are some that have attracted attention from researchers and clinicians.

Rumination

Rumination (or mercyism), first described in 1687, is a syndrome with a long history (Kanner, 1972). It is characterized by the voluntary regurgitation of food or liquid and usually appears during the first year of life. When infants ruminate, they appear to deliberately initiate regurgitation. The head is thrown back and chewing and swallowing movements are made until food is brought up. In many instances the infant initiates rumination by placing his or her fingers down the throat or by chewing on objects. The child exhibits little distress; rather, pleasure appears to result from the activity. If rumination continues, serious medical complications can result, with death being

the outcome in extreme cases (Halmi, 1985). Rumination is said to either occur equally in both sexes or be more prevalent in males (DSM-III-R; Linscheid, 1978; Mayes et al., 1988).

Etiology and treatment. Rumination is usually attributed to a disturbance in the mother-infant relationship (Mayes et al., 1988). The mother is either described as having psychological difficulties of her own that prevent her from providing the infant with a nurturant relationship or as experiencing significant life-stress that interferes with her ability to attend to the infant. Rumination is sometimes seen as the infant's attempt to provide this missing gratification (e.g., Halmi, 1985). Alternatively, others view the act as habitual in nature. The pattern may start, for example, with the normal occurrence of spitting up by the infant. The rumination is then reinforced by a combination of pleasurable self-stimulation and increased attention from adults (e.g., Kanner, 1972; Linscheid, 1978).

A wide variety of treatments have been suggested (Halmi, 1985; Lavigne, Burns, and Cotter, 1981). Restraining the infant and providing thick feedings (for example, thickened farina) are often recommended. Aversive procedures have also been demonstrated to be successful (e.g., Lang and Melamed, 1969; Sajwaj, Libet, and Agras, 1974; Sisson, Egan, and Van Hasselt, 1988). A mild shock or unpleasant tasting substance is administered contingent on the child's initiating behaviors that lead to rumination. However, both professionals and parents are reluctant to apply aversive procedures to infants and prefer to find nonaversive alternatives. Treatments emphasizing contingent use of social attention have been reported to be successful (Lavigne et al., 1981). These procedures also have the advantage of being easily implemented by the parents in the home and being made acceptable to them. However, in general, sufficiently controlled evaluations of interventions are lacking.

Pica

Pica is the Latin term for magpie, a bird known for the diversity of objects it eats. This disorder is characterized by the habitual eating of substances usually considered inedible, such as paint, dirt, papers, fabric, hair, and bugs.

During the first year of life, most infants put a variety of objects into their mouths, partly as a way of exploring the environment. Within the next year they typically learn to explore in other ways, and come to discriminate between edible and inedible materials (Doll, 1965). The diagnosis of pica is therefore usually made when there is a persistent eating of inedibles beyond this age, and pica is most common in two- and three-year-olds.

Pica has been observed in children from all backgrounds, but the problem may be more common among low-income and black populations (Halmi, 1985; Millican and Lourie, 1970). The prevalence of pica is also reported to be particularly high among mentally retarded individuals (e.g., McAlpine and Singh, 1986). Pica can lead to a variety of damage, including parasitic infection and intestinal obstruction due to the accumulation of hair and other materials. It also appears related to accidental poisoning (Halmi, 1985).

Etiology and treatment. A number of causes for pica have been postulated. Because youngsters have been observed eating strange substances when food is unavailable, it has been suggested that pica is an attempt to satisfy nutritional deficits. Parental inattention, lack of supervision, and lack of adequate stimulation have also been suggested. Several findings also suggest cultural influences (Fultz and Rojahn, 1988; Halmi, 1985; Kanner, 1972; Millican and Lourie, 1970).

Millican and Lourie (1970) found, for the black children they studied, that most of the families had migrated from the southeastern United States, where eating earth containing clay and laundry starch is a frequent custom among pregnant women (Halmi, 1985). Certain superstitions are reported to govern this behavior. Eating clay and other nonfood substances is believed to prevent a curse on the fetus, reduce the side effects of pregnancy, produce good blood in the unborn child, and eliminate the possibility of syphilis. Interestingly, the mothers of children with pica were found to have a higher frequency of the behavior than mothers of children without pica. And young black children, who might be strongly affected by cultural acceptance of pica, exhibited a lower rate of psychological difficulties than did older and white children displaying pica.

Educational approaches aimed at informing mothers of the dangers of pica and encouraging them to discourage the behavior may be somewhat successful. However, even reports of successful programs indicate a need to supplement the interventions with more intensive therapeutic endeavors in some cases. Behavioral interventions such as the use of aversive procedures to stop the inappropriate eating and reinforcement programs for appropriate behavior that also increase the attention given to the child are suggested (Finney, Russo, and Cataldo, 1982; Halmi, 1985; Millican and Lourie, 1970).

Obesity

Childhood obesity is a common and important health problem whose prevalence increases with age (Aristimuno et al., 1984; Garn and Clark, 1976; Huse et al., 1982). Also, the older the obese child the greater is the likelihood that he or she will become an obese adult (Garn et al., 1986; Rolland-Cachera et al., 1987). What is perhaps most striking are reports that the prevalence of childhood obesity is increasing (Gortmaker et al., 1987; Raymond, 1986). Dietz (1988), comparing national health survey data over a 15-year period beginning in the mid-1960s, found that obesity increased 54 percent among 6- to 11-year-old children and 39 percent among 12- to 17-year-old adolescents.

Overweight parents are more likely to have overweight children (e.g., Garn, 1986). This relationship does not seem attributable to genetic factors alone, since it appears to hold for adoptive children as well (Garn, Cole, and Baily, 1976). And interestingly, Mason (1970) reported that when dog owners have normal physique, the incidence of obesity in their pets is 25 percent while for owners who are obese the incidence rises to 45 percent! These data certainly argue for the importance of environmental factors.

Accumulating evidence suggests that obesity in childhood is associated with numerous health problems (Aristimuno et al., 1984; LeBow, 1984). In addition, there are social and psychological consequences (e.g., Israel and Stolmaker 1980). Indeed, a National Institutes of Health panel concluded that "Obesity creates an enormous psychological burden. In fact, in terms of suffering, this burden may be the greatest adverse effect of obesity" (NIH, 1985, p. 4).

An example of research supporting such concern is a study by Israel and Shapiro (1985). Parents of overweight children enrolled in a weight-loss program completed Achenbach's Child Behavior Checklist prior to treatment. The behavior problem scores of children in this study were significantly higher than the norms for the general population. However, they were significantly lower than the norms reported for children referred to clinics for psychological services. These findings are illustrated in Figure 13–1. Thus, it would appear that overweight children attending a weight-loss program experience psychological difficulties to a greater extent than members of the "general" population, but that their problems are not as severe in most areas as those exhibited by children receiving psychological assistance for other behavioral problems. Clearly, it cannot be determined from this study whether these problems contribute to or result from being overweight.

The obese child's social interactions are likely to be adversely affected by negative evaluations. For example, when children were asked to rank pictures of other children in terms of their likeability, obese children were ranked as less liked than those with recognized physical handicaps (Maddox, Back, and Liederman, 1968). While findings on such stigmatization are methodologically controversial, they clearly deserve clinical and research attention (Jarvie et al., 1983; Woody, 1986). Furthermore, the reduction of activity and dexterity that

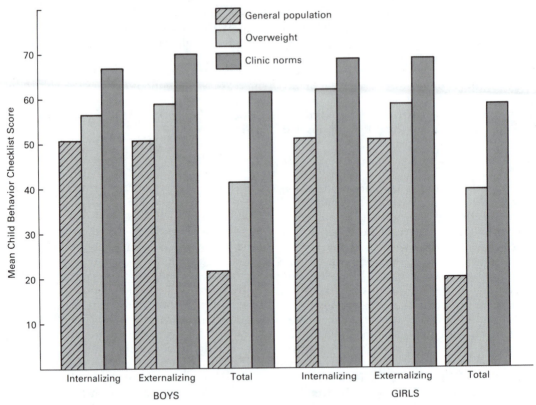

Legend:
- ▨ General population
- ▨ Overweight
- ▨ Clinic norms

(Y-axis: Mean Child Behavior Checklist Score, from 10 to 70)

X-axis categories: Internalizing, Externalizing, Total (BOYS); Internalizing, Externalizing, Total (GIRLS)

FIGURE 13–1 Mean Internalizing, Externalizing, and total behavior problem scores for overweight children, clinic norms and general population norms. Adapted from Israel and Shapiro, 1985.

often accompanies obesity makes social isolation and rejection even more likely. It thus seems likely, but not inevitable, that obese children may experience significant psychological difficulty.

The etiology of obesity. The causes of obesity are certainly multiple and complex. Any explanation must include biological, psychological, and social/cultural influences (Krasnegor, Grave, and Kretchmer, 1988).

Biological influences include genetic factors (cf. Epstein and Cluss, 1986; Siervagel, 1988) and the metabolic effects of dieting (e.g., Dietz, 1988). One prominent biological theory is known as set-point theory. There is some evidence that humans have a point at which body weight is set. Changes away from this set point result in psychological

and metabolic changes intended to defend the "ideal" body weight (Bennet and Gurin, 1982; Nisbett, 1972). It is presumed that obese individuals have a high set point. Of course, these biological influences are not independent of environmental influences; rather these influences interact. For example, early feeding behavior has been shown to be related to adiposity (body fat) in infants (Agras, 1988).

The significant influence of psychosocial factors on the development of obesity is acknowledged by most major workers in the field. Social learning theory, probably the most influential of the psychosocial theories, recognizes biological influence but focuses on social/psychological factors. Both logic and research suggest that obese children have food intake and activity behaviors that are in need of change (cf. Klesges and Hanson, 1988). Problematic food intake and inactivity are presumed to be learned in the same manner as any other behavior. Children, for example, observe and imitate the eating behavior of their parents and others around them and are reinforced for engaging in that style of eating (e.g., Klesges et al., 1986; Rozin, Fallon, and Mandell, 1984). Eating and inactivity may also become strongly associated with physical and social stimuli, so that they become almost automatic in some circumstances. Moreover, some people learn to use food to overcome negative mood states such as boredom and anxiety. The treatment of obesity developed from a social learning perspective seeks to break these learned patterns and develop more adaptive ones.

Society's view of obesity is an important cultural influence (cf. Rozin, 1988). Television provides a striking example of how the larger society might contribute to the development of weight problems in children (Jeffrey and Krauss, 1981). American children watch a great deal of television, on average about two to three hours each day (Scarr, Weinberg, and Levine, 1986). In addition to the negative effects of inactivity associated with television watching, children's diets are probably adversely influenced (Jeffrey et al., 1979). Indeed, a significant association between time spent watching television and the prevalence of obesity has been reported (Dietz and Gortmaker, 1985).

Behavioral treatment. Multifaceted behavioral programs have been the most effective treatments for childhood obesity (Epstein and Wing, 1987). The work of Israel and his colleagues (Israel and Solotar, 1988; Israel et al., 1984) illustrates the general approach. Children and parents attend meetings, during which four areas are regularly addressed: *intake*, which includes nutritional information, caloric restriction, and changes in actual eating and food preparation behaviors; *activity*, which includes both specific exercise programs and increasing the energy expended in daily activities,

for example, walking to a friend's house rather than being driven; *cues*, which identifies the external and internal stimuli associated with excessive eating or inactivity; and *rewards*, which provides positive consequences for progress by both the child and parent. Homework assignments are employed to encourage the families to change their environments and to practice more appropriate behavior. The frequency of contact is gradually reduced over time. Phone contact and periodic visits assist the family in problem solving.

Research supports the effectiveness of the behavioral approach to children's weight reduction (Epstein and Wing, 1987; Israel, 1990; Israel and Zimand, 1989). The importance of positively reinforcing changes in the child's behavior and of including parental behavioral changes have both been emphasized (e.g., Aragona, Cassady, and Drabman, 1975; Israel et al., 1984). Israel, Stolmaker, and Andrain (1985) investigated the contribution of training in general parenting skills. Parents were given a three-week course in the general principles of child management. They then participated with their children in a behavioral weight-reduction program. Throughout these sessions the application of the general parenting skills to weight reduction was emphasized. Another group of parents and children received only the behavioral weight-reduction program. At the end of treatment both groups achieved a significantly greater weight loss than control children not receiving treatment. A measure of change in eating habits also indicated changes for treated children but not for controls. Parents who received child-management training scored higher on a test of knowledge of behavior change principles than did parents who participated in the behavioral weight-reduction-only group. One year following treatment, children whose parents had received separate child-management training maintained their weight losses better than did other treated children (see Figure 13–2).

These results and others indicate the importance of providing parents with the

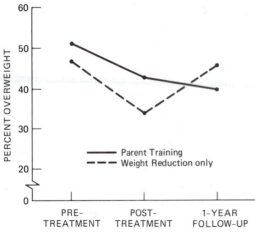

FIGURE 13–2 The effect of adding parent training to a children's weight reduction program. Adapted from Israel, Stolmaker, and Andrian, 1985.

Establishing family lifestyles that include healthy eating habits and regular activity are important in managing childhood obesity. (Swiss National Tourist Office)

skills necessary to maintain appropriate behavior once the treatment program has ended (Graves, Meyers, and Clark, 1988; Israel, 1988). This is a particularly important issue in light of repeated evidence that individuals frequently regain the weight they have lost. In addition to parenting skills, the importance of adherence to treatment assignments, the need for exercise prescriptions that are part of the family's life style, and various family factors have been shown to be related to treatment outcome (Epstein et al., 1985; Israel, Silverman, and Solotar, 1986, 1987, 1988). Treatments have been more successful than no intervention; however, there is still a need for improved interventions that produce greater, more consistent, and more long-lasting weight loss.

Anorexia Nervosa and Bulimia

Anorexia and bulimia are two eating disorders that have received increasing attention. This is due in part to a dramatic increases in the number of young people exhibiting these problems. Until recently both disorders were considered quite rare. Also, revelations or suggestions regarding anorexic and bulimic behavior among celebrities such as Karen Carpenter, Jane Fonda, and Princess Diana have increased popular interest.

Anorexia nervosa refers to a persistent refusal to eat which results in a body weight that is well below expected levels. Bulimia refers to a pattern of repeated binge eating followed by purging (e.g., self-induced vomiting or the use of laxatives and diuretics). There has been considerable debate regarding the definitions of these two disorders and whether bulimia is a separate syndrome or only a manifestation of anorexia nervosa.

One avenue that has been pursued is to identify two subtypes of anorexics. *Binging* anorexics exhibit a persistent pattern of binge eating and purging. In contrast, *restricting* anorexics achieve their weight loss by fasting and do not binge. These subgroups have been found in large clinical samples and the two groups do differ on a number of preexisting and family characteristics (Foreyt and McGavin, 1988; Humphrey, 1989; Strober and Humphrey, 1987).

Grammy award singer Karen Carpenter, who died at age 32 of heart failure, had suffered from the effects of anorexia nervosa for many years. (Schiffmann/Gamma-Liaison)

has been reported that 10 to 15 percent of untreated cases end in death (Schwartz and Thompson, 1981). The seriousness of extreme weight loss is also ilustrated by Bruch's (1979) description of one of her clients:

... she looked like a walking skeleton, with her legs sticking out like broomsticks, every rib showing, and her shoulder blades standing up like little wings. Her mother mentioned, "When I put my arms around her I feel nothing but bones, like a frightened little bird." Alma's arms and legs were covered with soft hair, her complexion had a yellowish tint, and her dry hair hung down in strings. Most striking was the face—hollow like that of a shriveled-up old woman with a wasting disease, ... Alma insisted that she looked fine and that there was nothing wrong with her being so skinny. "I enjoy having this disease and I want it." (pp. 2–3).

The DSM-III-R criteria for the diagnosis of Anorexia Nervosa are presented in Table 13–1. Other definitions have stressed that extreme dieting and weight loss are not enough to distinguish anorexia nervosa. Rather, psychological variables such as a sense of personal inadequacy are considered central and necessary (e.g., Bruch, 1973, 1986; Yates, 1989). Research comparing nonclinical, but extremely weight preoccupied individuals, to anorexics is supportive of this perspective (e.g., Garner et al., 1984).

The distinction is also supported by findings that bulimics who had never met the weight loss criteria for anorexia were more similar to binging anorexics than either was to restricting anorexics (Garner, Garfinkel, and O'Shaughnessy, 1985). While the restricter versus bulimic distinction appears to be an important one, the relationship between anorexia and bulimia remains to be resolved (Yates, 1989).

Description and diagnostic criteria. It is generally agreed that a drive for extreme thinness and a fear of gaining weight are characteristics of anorexia nervosa. The extremeness of weight loss is indicated by the life threatening nature of the disorder. It

TABLE 13–1 DSM-III-R Diagnostic Criteria for Anorexia Nervosa

A. Refusal to gain or maintain body weight over a minimal normal weight (15 percent below expected weight for height and age)

B. Intense fear of gaining weight or being fat, although underweight

C. Disturbance in the way in which one's body weight, shape, or size is experienced (e.g., feels fat even when emaciated)

D. Absence of at least three consecutive expected menstrual periods (amenorrhea)

Adapted from and reprinted with permission from the *Diagnostic and Statistical Manual of Mental Disorders, Third Edition, Revised.* Copyright 1987 American Psychiatric Association.

The DSM-III-R criteria for the diagnosis of bulimia are presented in Table 13–2. One of the issues faced in diagnosing bulimia as a disorder is the frequency of bulimic behavior reported in the general population of late adolescents and young adults. This fact and the newness of bulimia as a diagnosible disorder make it difficult to estimate its prevalence (Mitchell and Eckert, 1987).

Predisposing variables. Deliberate self-starvation is clearly a puzzling and bizarre phenomenon and binging and purging have become alarmingly common. In an attempt to understand anorexia nervosa and bulimia, researchers and clinicians have sought to identify preexisting conditions and personality patterns. A typical clinical report of a child diagnosed as anorexic describes a good student, who is well-behaved, introverted, and conscientious. A number of different preexisting personality patterns have been described for bulimics. No distinct preexisting causal pattern, however, has been demonstrated to exist in either group of individuals.

Clinical reports and some research findings indicate early feeding difficulties for adolescents exhibiting eating disorders (Marchi and Cohen, 1990). Much debated is the idea that self-starvation begins as an attempt to control genuine obesity. Comments that the young girl is "getting plump"

may stimulate normal dieting, which evolves into anorexic refusal to eat. The frequency of dieting among adolescent girls, however, raises the question of why some girls who begin this common social ritual persist well beyond the point of socially desired slimness. Faust's (1987) study of girls, ages 11 to 14, who had never been treated for either eating disorder or parent-child conflict suggests two factors that may be important. Greater dissatisfaction with one's body and an inability to accurately read internal hunger cues were important predictors of a drive for thinness.

Numerous clinical reports suggest that anorexia nervosa is a response to levels of stress for which existing skills seem inadequate. Since eating disorders generally begin during the adolescent years, stresses associated with this period, such as the onset of puberty, expectations of greater autonomy and responsibility, and increased social demands are implicated (Bruch, 1973; Foreyt and McGavin, 1989). Research findings also lend some support to the idea of negative sexual attitudes and a poor self-evaluation of their social skills among anorexic girls (Coovert, Kinder, and Thompson, 1989; Leon et al., 1985).

Etiology and treatment. A variety of causal mechanisms have been proposed to explain the development of anorexia nervosa (Yates, 1989). However, no definitive explanation exists. Indeed, it is not necessary to presume that there is a single causal explanation. It may be that the behaviors that we see as anorexia nervosa may result from a variety of different patterns of causal factors (Strober, 1986). In fact, it is most likely that both anorexia and bulimia are multidetermined disorders; that is, no single cause is sufficient to explain their development.

BIOLOGICAL VIEW. Several types of biological influences have been suggested. Explanations describing faulty hormonal regulation are suggested by the nature of some of the symptoms associated with anorexia (e.g., amenorrhea) and the fact that onset is frequently around puberty (cf. Russell, 1985). However, many of the hormonal abnor-

TABLE 13–2 DSM-III-R Diagnostic Criteria for Bulimia Nervosa

A. Recurrent episodes of binge eating

B. A feeling of lack of control over eating during binges

C. Regular self-induced vomiting, use of laxatives or diuretics, strict dieting or fasting, or vigorous exercise to prevent weight gain

D. Minimum of an average two binges a week for at least three months

E. Persistent concern with body shape and weight

Adapted from and reprinted with permission from the *Diagnostic and Statistical Manual of Mental Disorders, Third Edition, Revised.* Copyright 1987 American Psychiatric Association.

malities that have been found in anorexics seem to result from starvation rather than cause it. For example, the abnormalities are also found in nonanorexic individuals who have reached starvation weight and hormonal indicators return to normal when adequate weight is gained (Barbosa-Saldivar and Van Itallie, 1979; Kaplan and Woodside, 1987).

Genetic models have also been suggested. Some genetic explanations of both anorexia and bulimia link them to family patterns of depression. Episodes of depression have been reported in individuals diagnosed as anorexic and bulimic. Also, unusually high incidences of major mood disorders are reported in relatives. Response by bulimics to medications employed with mood disorders are also seen as supportive of such a view (e.g., Hudson et al., 1983; Pope et al., 1983). Some workers, however, do not view the data on family patterns of depression in eating disorder patients as indicating a shared genetic etiology (Strober and Katz, 1987; Rutter et al., 1990b).

Case reports have suggested that a number of different drugs treatments can be successful with eating-disordered patients. However, there is no single medication that has proven to be successful and caution regarding side effects with individuals who are already physiologically at risk is indicated (Yates, 1990). Controlled trials of the use of medications with anorexia nervosa in general have yielded negative or equivocal results. Antidepressant medication may be effective for some bulimic patients, but not all individuals respond to these drugs.

PSYCHODYNAMIC TRADITION. The psychodynamic perspective on anorexia nervosa has its origins in the early psychoanalytic proposition that equated eating behavior with sexual instinct (S. Freud, 1918/1959). It was suggested that the adolescent is unable to meet the demands of mature genitality, and anorexia is a symbolic expression of the rejection of sexuality and specifically of oral impregnation fantasies. This interpretation of anorexia nervosa can be criticized on a number of grounds including exclusive reliance on case reports, lack of support for basic assumptions, and data that question the symbolic significance of symptoms (cf. Bemis, 1978). Bruch, whose training had led her to initially adopt this treatment perspective, found that it did not fit her patients and that classical psychoanalysis was not effective in treating them (Bruch, 1986).

Bruch and many other clinicians working within the psychodynamic tradition have shifted their focus from oral drives to disorders of the mother-child relationship (Bruch, 1973). Anorexia is viewed as a deficit in ego development that arises out of disturbances in mother-child interactions. The resulting ego deficiencies are manifested in disturbances in body image, a failure to accurately recognize hunger and appetite, and a severe and pervasive sense of personal ineffectiveness (Bruch, 1986). From this perspective, the anorexic is viewed as poorly prepared to face adulthood and as rejecting food (the maternal substitute) and the feminine role. Some suggest that it is not rejection of the feminine role, but rather low self-esteem in the face of a desire to accomplish many roles (Yates, 1989).

Bruch (1979) also described the anorexic girl as the object of much family attention and control who is trapped by a need to please. Anorexia is seen as a desperate attempt by the child to express an individual identity.

She enjoyed being home but missed the fuss they had made about her in the past, when everybody was acutely concerned about her. . . . Even as a child Ida had considered herself not worthy of all the privileges and benefits that her family offered her, because she felt she was not brilliant enough. An image came to her, that she was like a sparrow in a golden cage, too plain and simple for the luxuries of her home, but also deprived of the freedom of doing what she truly wanted to do. (pp. 23–24)

Bruch (1973) has presented information on the long-term outcome of a number of cases she has treated. However, it is difficult to attribute various outcomes to specific therapeutic procedures. Length of contact varied from brief consultation to long-term psychotherapy, and the mode and length of treatment in each case are not sufficiently detailed. Thus, conclusions regarding the efficacy of psychodynamically oriented treatments also appear to rest heavily on clinical observation and inference.

COGNITIVE-BEHAVIORAL VIEW. Many workers from a cognitive-behavioral perspective view anorexia as an avoidance response. This is consistent with the view that the anorexic's fear of weight gain is related to concerns about psychosexual maturity (Crisp, 1984). Stringent dieting prevents the appearance of a mature body and also results in menstruation being avoided or reversed. Thus, such behavior is negatively reinforced since it allows the young girl to avoid negative thoughts, feelings, and fears. This behavior is also positively reinforced. The young woman may feel a sense of mastery, self-control, or virtue while avoiding certain intra- and interpersonal demands of adolescence (Garner and Bemis, 1985).

Treatment of anorexia can be conceptualized as consisting of two phases: intervention to restore body weight and save the patient's life, and subsequent extended intervention to ameliorate long-standing adjustment difficulties and maintain normal weight (Garner and Rosen, 1990). Behavioral interventions had tended to focus on the first phase and to rely almost exclusively on operant learning principles. One of the strengths of this approach was relatively precise experimental control. These interventions successfully employed positive and negative consequences contingent on weight change to produce weight gain in a relatively brief period of time (Agras and Kraemer, 1984). Most interventions focused on treating hospitalized patients at a fairly critical point in their illness, and their effectiveness at this life-threatening point is an obvious contribution. However, there was less success regarding long-term maintenance of these weight gains and the social-emotional adjustment of patients after they left the hospital was not addressed. Behavioral investigators themselves (e.g., Foreyt and Kondo, 1985; Garner, 1988; O'Leary and Wilson, 1987) called for the development of more broadly based cognitive-behavioral strategies that addressed both phases of treatment and introduced such multimodal treatments (e.g., Fundudis, 1986; Garner, 1988).

Bulimia has been viewed in several ways within a cognitive-behavioral perspective. These explanations, rather than being conflicting, emphasize different aspects of multifaceted cognitive-behavioral treatment programs (Hawkins, Fremouw, and Clement, 1984; Wilson, 1986). One hypothesized mechanism is that bulimic behavior develops as a faulty weight-control method among individuals who have had poor self-control patterns modeled for them (Orleans and Barnett, 1984). Another, primarily cognitive, view described individuals who have abnormal attitudes and beliefs about weight regulation, who evaluate their self-worth in terms of their body shape, and who thus become preoccupied with weight control. These unrealistic cognitive standards are part of what has been described as *dietary restraint* (Polivy and Herman, 1985). A continuum is defined between restrained eaters, who constantly worry about their eating and struggle to diet, and unrestrained eaters who eat as the desire arises. Research has demonstrated that when disruptions in self-control occur, restrained eaters overeat—"I broke my diet, I may as well continue to eat." This disinhibition has been demonstrated to occur in response to stress and depressed mood (Polivy, Herman, Olmstead and Jazwinski, 1984; Ruderman, 1986).

Several authors describe multifaceted cognitive-behavioral treatment programs that serve as examples of interventions that might arise from such a perspective (e.g., Fairburn, 1984; Garner and Rosen, 1990). Behavioral techniques are first employed to establish control over eating. These are supplemented with cognitive restructuring techniques targeting inappropriate weight-gain concerns and training in self-control strategies. Further cognitively oriented in-

terventions then address inappropriate beliefs concerning food, eating, weight, and
body image. A maintenance strategy to sustain improvements is also included.

Bulimia has also been viewed as similar
to an obsessive-compulsive disorder (Leitenberg et al., 1984). A typical pattern might
be as follows. A young person binges. The
overeating is due largely to feeling quite
anxious or depressed. The immediate effect
is that the negative emotion is reduced.
However, the person starts feeling distressed about the binge and fears weight
gain. Vomiting reduces this fear and the
physical discomfort of feeling full. The vomiting can thus be viewed as a negative reinforcement situation. It is like compulsive
handwashing that relieves the fear of con-
tamination and is thereby maintained. From
this perspective, treatments shown to be
successful with anxiety disorders (e.g.,
obsessive-compulsive behaviors) such as
exposure and response prevention are
suggested. Thus, treatments would be recommended that required the bulimic individual to eat the foods they binge on
(exposure) without allowing vomiting afterward (response prevention). Including such
an active exposure/prevention component
in a cognitive-behavioral treatment program
has been reported to either enhance or
detract from treatment (Agras et al., 1989;
Leitenberg et al., 1988; Wilson et al., 1986).
The success of interventions involving exposure and prevention of vomiting does not
mean, of course, that the two-factor anxiety
reduction explanation, described above, is
correct. Indeed, explanations of the success
of such intervention that rest more heavily
on cognitive-social learning principles have
been offered (Wilson, 1989).

FAMILY VIEWS. The family dynamics of
anorexics have also received a great deal of
attention. It is difficult, however, to determine whether any pattern observed in a
family subsequent to the onset of a disturbance is a cause or effect. This is especially
the case in anorexia, in which family observations have frequently followed the offspring's life-threatening refusal to eat. Re-

views of research on family characteristics
do suggest that family patterns are associated with eating disorders; however, there
is no single pathway of influence. Such
families tended to have a higher incidence
of weight problems, physical illness, affective disorder, and alcoholism in relatives. In
addition, the families could be described as
exhibiting controlling interdependent family relationships together with parental discord (Kog and Vandereycken, 1985; Strober
and Humpfrey, 1987). How and when such
family variables come into play is difficult
to determine. Faust (1987), for example,
did not find such variables to be related to
a drive for thinness among her young nonclinic sample of girls.

Family therapy for eating disorders derives from the observation by clinicians of
varying persuasions that the families are
intimately involved in the *maintenance* of this
behavior. The family systems approach,
represented by Minuchin and his colleagues, views the family context as central
to many disorders involving somatic symptoms, including anorexia nervosa (Minuchin, Rosman, and Baker, 1978). These
investigators criticize other perspectives for
continuing to view the locus of pathology
as within the individual and for emphasizing
the past. Minuchin does employ behavioral
procedures to produce weight gain during
brief hospitalization or on an outpatient
basis.

The families of anorexics, according to
Minuchin, can be described as enmeshed.
The members of the family do not have
distinct identities. Rather, there are diffuse
boundaries among family members. They
are highly involved in each others' lives and
exhibit a high degree of communication and
concern. In this kind of family the child
learns to subordinate the self (individuality)
to family loyalty. In turn, the child is protected by the family, and this further weak-
ens the child's autonomy. This highly enmeshed family is a tightly woven system in
which questioning of the system is not permitted. Even the usual kind of individual
life change threatens the family's equilib-
rium. Adolescence may produce a particu-

larly difficult crisis in such a family. The child's overinvolvement with the family prevents the individualization that is necessary at this time of life; the view of one's self as independent of the family is blurred at best, and peer experience is lacking.

The anorexic's family also has always had a special concern with eating, diet, and rituals pertaining to food. The anorexic adolescent begins to challenge the family system, and rebellion is exhibited through refusal to eat. The family comes to the "protection" of the child—and maintains its stability—by making the child a sick, incompetent person who requires care. The sick role is reinforced, and the child is both protected and scapegoated.

It follows from this conceptualization that the entire family system must be treated. The specific techniques employed vary with the age of the identified patient and the structural characteristics of the family. Although controlled research is lacking, Minuchin and his colleagues (1978) report that 86 percent of the 53 cases they treated recovered from both the anorexia and its psychosocial components. There is also empirical support for the existence of hypothesized differences in anorexic families (e.g., Humphrey, 1989; Leon et al., 1985), and the logic of family systems therapy seems compelling.

CULTURAL INFLUENCES. Any explanation offered for the development of anorexia and bulimia must keep cultural influences in mind. Our society's emphasis and valuing of slim and young bodies likely contributes to the development and prevalence of such disorders. Some authors remind us, however, that these eating styles are not only recent phenomena. An appreciation of history may cause us to examine carefully our conceptualization of these eating disorders.

There were, for example, a group of women living in the High Middle Ages (thirteenth through sixteenth centuries) who exhibited extreme eating restrictions and what might be viewed as bizarre and pervasive behaviors and images regarding eating and food (Bell, 1985; Brumberg, 1986). Descriptions of these women bear a remarkable similarity to contemporary eating disorders. The most interesting "twist" to this tale, however, is that these women were later canonized as saints. Bell (1985) chose the term "holy anorexia" to describe these women and call attention to the cultural dimension that is often lost in current diagnostic efforts. Questions such as why a set of behaviors at one time is viewed as pious and at another as a disease force us to address important issues. To say that anorexia merely went undiagnosed in the past fails to appreciate that behaviors that appear similar may have very different origins and meanings. This is just one of the many complexities presented when one includes a cultural perspective into thinking about eating or other disorders.

The eating disorders of anorexia and bulimia have proven to be complex and difficult to treat. It is generally agreed that they are complex problems that derive from and are maintained by a variety of influences (Mitchell and Eckert, 1987; Strober and Humphrey, 1987; Yates, 1989). Indeed, there is probably considerable heterogeneity among individuals exhibiting these eating disorders. There are not, at present, treatments that are effective for all individuals, nor can we predict which treatments will work for particular individuals. Treatments that address multiple influences thus seem most likely to be effective (Foreyt and McGavin, 1989; Johnson, Connors, and Tobin, 1987; Wilson, 1989; Yates, 1990).

DISORDERS OF ELIMINATION

Toilet training is something about which many parents express concern and a task that is likely to cause at least some difficulty.

For example, in a survey of parental responses to 22 categories of preschool problems, parents rated difficulties in toilet training second in importance (Mesibov, Schroeder, and Wesson, 1977). The usual sequence of acquisition of control over elimination is nighttime bowel control, daytime bowel control, daytime bladder control, and finally, nighttime bladder control. While there is considerable variation in children's developmental readiness, training usually is completed between the ages of 18 and 30 months.

Parents vary as to the age at which they feel it is appropriate to begin daytime training. Many child care manuals suggest two years as the appropriate age to begin training. Much of this decision is related to cultural values, attitudes, and real-life pressures on the parent (e.g., day-care requirements, other siblings). An example of how day-to-day considerations probably affect this decision is illustrated by the disposable diaper. Ready availability of disposable diapers changed many parents' attitudes toward the desirability of starting training early and perhaps facing difficulty.

Several factors no doubt contribute to successful training. Judging that the child is developmentally ready to begin training is certainly of importance. Also correctly judging when the child has to go to the toilet can lead to important early success experiences. Adequate preparation, such as having a child size potty seat available, is also helpful. Finally, the common practice of providing praise and positive reinforcement (e.g., stickers, raisins) for appropriate toileting behavior, and doing so in a relaxed manner, has been demonstrated to be effective (O'Leary and Wilson, 1987).

Enuresis

The term *enuresis* comes from the Greek word meaning "I make water" and refers to the involuntary voiding of urine, after an age at which toilet training is expected to have been completed. About 50 percent of two-year-olds in the United States display daytime bladder control; this figure rises to 90 percent for four-year-olds. Nighttime bladder control is achieved more slowly. It is achieved by approximately 70 percent of three-year-olds and 90 percent of eight-year-olds (Erikson, 1987). The comparison between daytime and nighttime control is shown in Figure 13–3.

Disagreement exists as to the precise definition of enuresis. The most obvious question is the *age* at which lack of urinary control should be diagnosed as enuresis. Recommendations usually vary between three and five years of age, but it is rare for children under the age of five to be treated for enuresis (Doleys, 1989). A second issue is the *frequency of lack of control* necessary for diagnosis. Often cited criteria range from at least two such events per month to a more stringent standard, requiring regular wetting an average of three or more times a week. Clearly, the criterion for frequency is likely to be tied to age, with less frequent wetting required for the diagnosis of enuresis in older children.

Enuresis is often classified into subtypes. One distinction is that between the more common nocturnal enuresis (nighttime bed wetting) and diurnal (daytime) enuresis. A second distinction exists between primary enuresis, in which the child has never dem-

FIGURE 13–3 Percentage of children of various ages achieving daytime and nighttime bladder control. From Robert M. Liebert, Rita Wicks-Nelson, *Developmental Psychology*: 3rd ed., © 1981, p. 481. Reprinted by permission of Prentice-Hall, Inc., Englewood Cliffs, NJ.

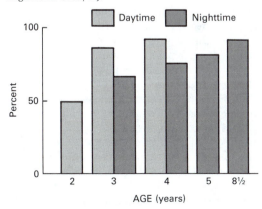

onstrated bladder control, and secondary enuresis in which the problem is preceded by a period of urinary continence. About 85 percent of all cases of enuresis are of the primary type (Walker, Kenning, and Fault-Campanile, 1989).

The causes of enuresis. At one time the view that enuresis was the result of emotional or psychiatric disturbance was widely held (e.g., Gerald, 1939). The evidence, however, did not support this position (Baker, 1969; Rutter, Yule, and Graham, 1973; Schaffer, 1973). This conclusion seems to be consistent with more recent empirical results (e.g., Wagner, Smith and Norris, 1988). When emotional difficulties are also present in a child with enuresis, they are likely to be a consequence rather than a cause. Enuretic children, especially as they become older, are very likely to experience difficulties with peers and other family members. It would not be surprising if the child's self-image suffered (e.g., Wagner et al., 1988). Support for the importance of such consequences comes from a finding that greater success in treatment was found for children who reported being teased by siblings (Butler, Brewin, and Forsythe, 1988).

It is frequently suggested that differences in sleep and arousal contribute to the development of enuresis. Many parents and professionals, for example, assume that nocturnal enuresis occurs because the child is an unusually deep sleeper. Indeed, parents often spontaneously report difficulty in arousing their enuretic children during the night. However, research regarding the role of sleep and arousal is inconsistent (Doleys, 1989). It appears that wetting can occur in any of the stages of sleep, not just in "deep sleep." This and other evidence raises doubts about viewing enuresis as a disorder of sleep arousal (Walker et al., 1989).

It is a common observation that the family histories of enuretics frequently reveal a number of relatives with the same problem. Also in a study of Israeli kibbutz children there was a markedly greater incidence of bed wetting among the siblings of enuretic children than among siblings of dry children, even though each sibling had been toilet trained by a separate caretaker in a different communal house (Kaffman and Elizur, 1977). Comparisons of monozygotic and dizygotic twins also suggest a genetic component (e.g., Bakwin, 1971). While the results can be interpreted in terms of family attitudes and child-rearing practices rather than family genes, they strongly suggest that at least some portion of enuretic children may have an organic predisposition toward enuresis. This, as yet unspecified, risk factor may or may not result in the development of enuresis, depending upon various experiential factors, such as parental attitude and training procedures.

The central tenet of behavioral theories of enuresis is that wetting results from a failure to learn control over reflexive wetting. This failure can result from either faulty training itself or other environmental influences that interfere with learning. Many behavioral theories incorporate some physical difficulty (for example, arousal deficit) into their explanation.

Treatment approaches. Although a variety of drugs have been used in the treatment of enuresis, imipramine hydrochloride (Tofranil), a tricyclic antidepressant, is probably the most commonly employed. The specific mechanisms responsible for imipramine's action are not well understood (Doleys, 1989). Although a number of studies have demonstrated that imipramine is superior to placebos, the effect seems to rely on the child's continuing to take the drug and it appears that it is not as successful as the urine-alarm procedure, which is described below (Werry, 1986). Moreover, there is reason for concern regarding possible side effects (Pierce, 1985b; Walker et al., 1989).

Behavioral treatments for nocturnal enuresis have received considerable research attention (Doleys, 1989; Walker et al., 1989). The most popular of these methods is the urine-alarm system. This procedure was originally introduced by the German pediatrician Pflaunder in 1904 and was adapted and systematically applied by Mowrer and Mowrer (1938). Since then the device and the procedures have been refined by a number of investigators. The basic device consists of an absorbent bed sheet between two foil pads (Figure 13–4). When urine is absorbed by the sheet, an electric circuit is completed that activates an alarm. The awakened child is taught to turn off the alarm and go to the bathroom to finish voiding. The bedding is then changed, and the child returns to sleep. Usually records of dry and wet nights are kept, and after 14 consecutive nights of dryness, the device is removed. According to the Mowrers, the procedure is based upon classical conditioning. Tension of the full bladder (the conditioned stimulus) is paired with the alarm (unconditioned stimulus) to produce awakening (the conditioned response) and inhibition of urination. Eventually the child wakens in response to a full bladder prior to wetting and setting off the alarm. Lovibond (1964) proposed an alternative theoretical explanation—avoidance learning. He suggested that the child learns to inhibit urination in order to avoid the aversive consequences of being awakened by the alarm.

Research conducted on the urine-alarm system indicates that it is successful in 70 to 90 percent of the cases, with treatment durations of between 5 and 12 weeks. The urine-alarm system also proved to be superior to placebo, no-treatment, and verbal psychotherapy groups, and to achieve success rates greater than those reported for imipramine (Doleys, 1989).

Two modifications of the standard urine-alarm procedures have been found to reduce relapses (Walker et al., 1989). In the *intermittent alarm procedure* the alarm sounds subsequent to some percentage of wettings rather than to each wetting (continuous alarm procedure). With *overlearning*, once the initial criterion for dryness is met, the child's intake of liquids prior to bedtime is increased, and the urine-alarm procedure is continued for some period of time.

Azrin and his co-workers combined a number of procedures for nighttime treatment into a program referred to as *dry-bed training* (Azrin, Sneed, and Foxx, 1974). These procedures, derived from an operant perspective, stress the attention to the consequences of wetting. The procedures employed include positive practice (practicing the appropriate series of toileting behaviors), praise for a dry bed, and cleanliness training that consists of the child changing his or her bed and nightclothes. In general dry-bed training has been shown to be an effective technique; however, other researchers have not always reported the same degree of success as Azrin and his co-workers. While dry-bed training is a viable alternative to the urine-alarm, it is demanding on the parents' and child's time (Doleys, 1989).

A multifaceted and low-cost treatment developed by Houts, Liebert, and Padawer (1983) illustrates the way in which behavioral interventions have been combined in the treatment of nocturnal enuresis. Full Spectrum Home Training was designed to build upon the success of behavioral treat-

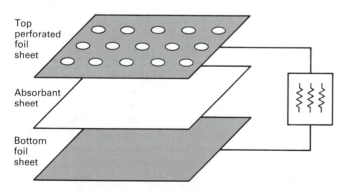

Top perforated foil sheet

Absorbant sheet

Bottom foil sheet

FIGURE 13–4 The urine-alarm apparatus has become one of the most popular methods for treating enuresis.

TABLE 13–3 Results of Treating Enuresis with Components of Full Spectrum Home Training

Group/Assessment time	Success Percent	Failure Percent	Dropout Percent	Relapse Percent
Group 1				
End of treatment	60	20	20	
Three-month follow-up				44
Group 2				
End of treatment	87	0	13	
Three-month follow-up				62
Group 3				
End of treatment	60	27	13	
Three-month follow-up				11

Adapted from Houts, Peterson, and Whelan, 1986. Copyright (1986) by the Association for Advancement of Behavior Therapy. Reprinted by permission of the publisher and the author.

ments such as the urine alarm in achieving initial treatment success. It was also designed to reduce relapse and decrease the rate at which families dropped out of treatment. The procedure is also cost effective. It is a manual-guided treatment package that includes bell-and-pad, cleanliness training, a procedure to increase bladder capacity known as retention control training, and overlearning. The training program is delivered in a single one-hour group session and a contract is completed by parents and children to complete the training at home with regular calls from the treatment staff as the only additional contact.

A study by Houts, Peterson, and Whalen (1986) illustrates the program's success and examines the contribution of the components to reducing relapse. Participating families received one of three treatment combinations: Group 1 received bell-and-pad plus cleanliness training (BP), Group 2 these two components plus retention control training (BP-RCT), and Group 3 these three components plus overlearning (BP-RCT-OL)—the full package. A control group of children was followed over an eight-week period. No spontaneous remission of wetting occurred and they were then randomly assigned to one of the three treatment conditions.

The findings of this study are illustrated in Table 13–3. While the proportion of success versus failure plus dropouts was slightly greater in the BP-RCT condition, these differences were not statistically significant. The three conditions were also equivalent in terms of the number of dry nights during training. At three-month follow-up relapse was significantly less in the BP-RCT-OL group than in the other two conditions. These results suggest the importance of overlearning in preventing relapse.

Encopresis

Functional encopresis refers to the passage of feces into the clothing or other unacceptable area, in the absence of any organic pathology. As with enuresis, there is some disagreement as to the age at which encopresis should be diagnosed. The generally agreed upon age is four (DSM-III-R). The significance of deciding when to acknowledge the problem and intervene lies primarily in the fact that in retentive encopresis (described below) the longer one waits to intervene, the more distended the child's colon becomes.

Several subcategories of encopresis are usually suggested. The *primary-secondary* distinction, similar to the distinction made for enuresis, refers to whether or not the child exhibited a previous period of bowel control. The other major distinction is between *retentive and nonretentive* encopresis. Encopretic children who produce normal stools, which are passed into clothing or some other inappropriate place, are described as non-retentive. The retentive type refers to the child who retains feces in the bowel, resulting in the rectum and colon being distended by hard feces. The bowel then becomes incapable of responding with a defecation reflex when filled with normal amounts of fecal matter. Children exhibiting retentive encopresis may demonstrate overflow incontinence, the leakage of fecal matter around the impacted material. Retentive encopresis is usually viewed as more common, accounting for approximately 80 percent of all cases (Walker et al., 1989).

Less writing and research have been done concerning encopresis than concerning enuresis. Estimates of the prevalence of encopresis range from 0.3 to 8 percent of children. Percentages appear to decrease with age, being very low by adolescence, and the problem occurs more frequently in males (Doleys, 1989). Pediatricians, who are likely to see unselected populations of children, argue that the majority of encopretics have no associated psychopathology, a position supported by other workers. To the extent that associated psychological difficulties do exist, the question of whether they are etiological or secondary to this socially distressing problem needs careful consideration (Walker et al., 1989; Werry, 1986).

The causes of encopresis. Most theories acknowledge the possibility that different types of encopresis may result from different causative mechanisms. Medical perspectives on the problem tend to take a neuro-developmental approach (Doleys, 1989). Encopresis is viewed as resulting from developmental inadequacies in the structure and functioning of the physiological and anatomical mechanisms required for bowel control. These organic inadequacies are viewed as temporary.

As is the case in enuresis, psychodynamically oriented theorists tend to view encopresis as a sign of some deeper conflict. Recent psychodynamic explanations tend to place more emphasis on family and social context, particularly disruptions in the mother-child relationship (Bemporad, 1978; Pierce, 1985a).

The behavioral perspective on encopresis stresses faulty toilet training procedures. Primary encopresis is largely explained by a failure to apply appropriate training methods consistently. Secondary encopresis is accounted for through avoidance conditioning principles; that is, pain or fear avoidance reinforces retention. Positive consequences may also maintain soiling, and inadequate reinforcement may be given for appropriate toileting (Doleys, 1989). These various learning explanations are not incompatible with physiological explanations. For example, insufficient physiological-neurological mechanisms may be compounded by poor parental training.

Treatment approaches. The treatment of encopresis has also received less research attention than enuresis. Medical treatments tend to rely on laxatives and enemas, usually combined with manipulation of diet. Davidson, Kugler, and Bauer (1963) describe a successful three-phase program employed with 119 encopretics. The first phase consisted of the use of enemas to eliminate fecal impactions and mineral oil to induce regular bowel movements. The second phase was begun after one month and consisted of the gradual removal of laxatives to develop regular nonlaxative bowel movements. This phase lasted three months. The final phase consisted of parental counseling and maintaining and monitoring the habits established during the program. Doleys (1989) suggests that a careful examination of the procedures indicates that these later psychological interventions are employed throughout along with the laxatives and enemas.

The use of psychoanalysis or some other form of verbal psychotherapy has often been advocated. However, most information is based on clinical case reports, treatment procedures are only vaguely described, and controlled studies comparing these interventions to other procedures are lacking (Doleys, 1989). Furthermore, reported success rates fall below those for other methods. This may, in part, be due to highly selected, more severe samples (Werry, 1986).

Most current behavioral reports advocate a combination of both medical and behavioral procedures (e.g., Doleys, 1988; Houts, Mellon, and Whelan, 1988). One such program is described by Walker and Wright (Walker, Milling, and Bonner, 1988; Wright and Walker, 1976). Positive reinforcement is delivered for both appropriate toileting behavior and having clean pants. Loss of privileges, fines, and the like are given as punishments for soiling. Enemas and suppositories are used to induce defecation on days when it does not occur, but these artificially induced bowel movements are not reinforced. The program is withdrawn gradually and discontinued following one week of continence. Research suggests that the program is highly effective, with success rates up to 100 percent and low relapse rates. As we might expect, program success and duration were related to parental consistency in carrying out the program (Walker et al., 1980). Although reports of comprehensive behavioral programs suggest good success rates, there is a clear need for well-controlled group studies and attention to the relationship between treatment success and individual case characteristics.

SLEEP DISORDERS

Parents commonly complain of sleep problems in their children. During the first year of life, the most frequent complaint is that the child does not sleep through the night. A reluctance to go to sleep and nightmares often occur during the second year, and the three- to five-year old presents a variety of problems, including difficulty in going to sleep, nighttime wakenings, and nightmares. Complaints to pediatricians and others regarding children's sleep are common. However, parents usually seek psychological assistance only when these problems become severe or chronic. Beyond concern for the disruption and worry these problems cause for families, one question often raised is whether sleep difficulties indicate more extensive disturbance, perhaps excessive fear of separation from the parents.

The classification of sleep disorders by the Association of Sleep Disorders Centers and the Association for the Psychophysiological Study of Sleep (ASDC & APSS, 1979) groups these problems into two major categories: Dysfunctions of Initiating and Maintaining Sleep (DIMS), commonly also referred to as insomnias, and Dysfunctions Associated with Sleep, Sleep Stages, or Partial Arousals (Parasomnias).

Difficulties in Initiating and Maintaining Sleep

The problems that parents commonly report of difficulty in getting children to sleep and having them sleep through the night, if severe and chronic enough, would fall into the DIMS category. Such problems are frequently viewed as manifestations of the child's neurophysiological development and therefore expected to eventually clear up. However, parental and environmental factors do seem to play a role in a substantial number of cases. These difficulties may persist over many years, and they can result in considerable distress to the families (Richman et al., 1985).

It is often difficult to discriminate between "true" cases of insomnia and attention seeking. Does the child call to the parent— "I can't sleep" or "I woke up"—to get parental attention or is he or she experiencing genuine sleep difficulties? Perhaps some genuine sleep problems go unreported because they are dealt with as "attention needs" or in contrast perhaps what are viewed as sleep problems are not really that. The child's level of cognitive development is also a factor. In order for children to recognize a sleep problem they must be able to conceptualize difficulties in initiating and

Establishing a predictable bedtime routine is helpful in reducing children's sleep problems. (Ken Karp)

maintaining sleep as such (Wilson and Haynes, 1985). In older children sleep problems may also be associated with reports of worrisome cognitions—concerns about school or peers, ruminating about past or anticipated experiences, or fears.

Drugs have been among the most widely used treatments; however, support for their effectiveness is not strong and there is concern regarding negative side effects (e.g., Richman, 1985). Behavioral approaches to the problems of initiating and maintaining children's sleep have included the use of relaxation, but especially for young children, have focused on the consequences applied to the child's behaviors and techniques of stimulus control (Wilson and Haynes, 1985; Bootzin and Chambers, 1990). So, for example, attention given to the child after saying goodnight can be withdrawn, praise and/or star charts for desired behavior can be given, and a distinct bedtime routine that makes the signs for going to sleep clear can be developed (Durand and Mindell, 1990; Richman, et al., 1985).

Dysfunctions Associated with Sleep, Sleep Stages, or Partial Arousal

Several of the childhood sleep disorders that cause concern for parents fall in the second category of parasomnias. These include sleepwalking, sleep terrors, and nightmares.

Sleepwalking. Sleepwalking (somnambulism) begins with the child sitting upright in bed. The eyes are open but appear "unseeing." Usually the child leaves the bed and walks around, but the episode may end before the walking stage is reached. An episode may last for a few seconds or 30 minutes or longer. There is usually no later memory of the episode. It was once believed that the sleepwalking child was exceptionally well coordinated and safe. This has proven to be a myth, and, although physical injury is rare, it is one danger of the disorder.

Approximately 15 percent of children between the ages of 5 and 12 have isolated experiences of walking in their sleep. Sleepwalking disorder, that is, persistent sleepwalking, is estimated to occur in 1 to 6 percent of the population and to be more frequent in boys than in girls (Anders and Weinstein, 1972). Somnambulism usually persists for a number of years but then disappears by adolescence.

The vast majority of sleepwalking episodes occur in the first one to three hours following sleep onset during stages of non-REM sleep (deep sleep). This appears to invalidate the idea that sleepwalking is the acting out of a dream. A characteristic EEG pattern has been found to precede each episode. The pattern exists in 85 percent of children during the first year of life but is present in only 3 percent of seven- to nine-year-olds. Thus it has been suggested that central nervous system immaturity is of significance in sleepwalking disorder and knowledge that the disorder is usually outgrown is consistent with the conceptualization (cf. Anders, 1982). This does not, however, rule out psychological or environmental factors. Frequency of sleepwalking has been reported to be influenced by the specific setting, stress, fatigue, and physical illness (Ablon and Mack, 1979; Anders and Weinstein, 1972). Greater concordance rates for sleepwalking among monozygotic twins than among dizygotic twins and family patterns of sleepwalking have also been reported, leading some to propose a genetic component to the disorder (Anders and Weinstein, 1972; Bakwin and Bakwin, 1972). Unlike adults, the presence of sleepwalking in children has not be found to be associated with any psychological disturbance (Dollinger, 1986).

Nightmares and night terrors. Both nightmares and night terrors are fright reactions that occur during sleep. Night terrors are officially labeled as Sleep Terror Disorder. It is estimated that from 1 to 4 percent of children experience this disorder and it is more common in males. Night terrors typically occur between the ages of 4 and 12.

Nightmares and night terrors are often confused, but they differ in a number of ways (see Table 13–4).

Night terror is quite striking in that the still-sleeping child suddenly sits upright in bed and screams. The face shows obvious distress, and there are signs of autonomic arousal, such as rapid breathing and dilated pupils. In addition, repetitive movements may occur, and the child appears disoriented and confused. Attempts to comfort the child are largely unsuccessful. Later recall of the episode or its contents is lacking. The conceptualization of the causes of night terrors is similar to that described above for sleepwalking (cf. Wilson and Haynes, 1985), and, indeed, night terrors occur in the same part of the sleep cycle.

In many cases of sleepwalking and night terrors treatment may not be indicated since the episodes usually disappear spontaneously. However, a number of treatments have been suggested. These include re-

TABLE 13–4 Characteristics Differentiating Nightmares and Night Terrors

Nightmares	*Night Terrors*
Occur during REM sleep	Occur during Non-REM sleep
During middle and latter portions of the night	During first third of night
Verbalizations, if any, are subdued	Child wakes with cry or scream and verbalizations usually present
Only moderate physiological arousal	Intense physiological arousal (increased heart rate, profuse sweating, pupils dilated)
Slight or no movements	Extreme motor activity
Easy to arouse and responsive to environment	Difficult to arouse and unresponsive to environment
Episodes frequently remembered	Very limited or no memory of the episode
Quite common	Somewhat rare (1 to 4 percent)

Adapted from Wilson and Haynes, 1985.

sponse interruption, contingency management, instructional procedures, and anxiety reduction procedures (Dollinger, 1986; Wilson and Haynes, 1985). Since the literature consists of case studies one cannot say whether these treatments were responsible for reported changes. Drug treatments of both disorders have also been reported; however, the medications may actually produce effects that set the stage for recurrences of the disorders (Wilson and Haynes, 1985).

The other fright reaction that occurs during sleep, nightmares, has also been termed sleep anxiety dreams, dream anxiety attacks, and Dream Anxiety Disorder . It is frequently thought that dreams are a direct manifestation of anxieties that the child faces. It has been suggested that children typically extinguish their fears by gradually exposing themselves to the feared stimulus (Kellerman, 1980). Some events, such as parental protectiveness, however, might restrict such exposure and thus exacerbate the anxieties and associated nightmares. No single theoretical framework has proven successful in explaining the development of nightmares and explanations allowing for multiple causality (e.g., developmental, physiological, and environmental factors) are more likely to have the greatest utility (Wilson and Haynes, 1985). Consistent with anxiety being viewed as the basis for nightmares, the majority of treatments have involved anxiety reduction techniques. However, no treatment strategy can be stated as most effective, nor are the active components of the various treatments known.

SUMMARY

Several eating disorders have received attention from researchers and clinicians. Of these, obesity and anorexia/bulimia have probably generated the most interest. Behavioral and biological explanations of the etiology of obesity have probably received the greatest support. The learning of eating and activity patterns are the basis of behavioral treatment programs. This approach to treatment is probably the most successful; however, greater weight loss and better maintenance results still need to be achieved.

The appropriate way to classify and conceptualize the eating disorders of anorexia and bulimia has received considerable attention. The distinction between restricting and bulimic anorexics has received support.

Anorexia nervosa is a serious, life-threatening disorder characterized by extreme weight loss. A number of other physical and psychological problems are present as well. Biological, psychodynamic, cognitive-behavioral, and family systems theorists have all offered explanations for this puzzling phenomenon. An explanation that incorporates multiple influences is most likely, but no particular explanation is clearly supported. The treatment of anorexia has been conceptualized as a two-phase process: resumption of eating with associated weight gain, and maintenance of improvement and treatment of associated problems.

Bulimia refers to a repeated pattern of binge eating followed by purging. Similarities have been noted between bulimics and bulimic anorexics. One of the difficulties faced in diagnosing bulimia is the frequency of bulimic behavior among late adolescents and young adults. Among the various explanations of bulimia, several cognitive-behavioral viewpoints have received considerable attention and multifaceted cognitive-behavioral treatments have been developed.

Enuresis and encopresis are disorders of elimination that seem best explained by a combination of biological predisposition and failure to train (learn). The use of imipramine is the most popular and best-supported medically oriented procedure for treating enuresis. Behavioral interventions based on classical conditioning and operant learning theories have reported high success rates and low rates of remission and seem to be the treatments of choice at present. Encopresis, which has received considerably less attention, is probably best dealt with through a combination of medical (for example, enemas) and behavioral (for example, reinforcement) procedures.

Difficulties in initiating and maintaining sleep are most effectively dealt with by establishing bedtime routines and the appropriate cues for sleep. Sleep disorders such as sleepwalking and night terrors are probably best conceptualized as resulting from a combination of nervous system immaturity and environmental factors. At present the effectiveness of various treatments remains unclear.

14

PSYCHOLOGICAL FACTORS AFFECTING PHYSICAL CONDITIONS

This chapter continues the discussion of the problems of physical conditions and health. In the past the topics we will examine would have come under the heading of psychosomatic disorders. The main focus of interest was on actual physical conditions such as asthma, headaches, ulcers and nausea. These were known or presumed to be affected by psychological factors. The terminology for describing these disorders has undergone a number of changes in the last few decades. The term *Psychosomatic Disorders* was replaced in DSM-II by *Psychophysiological Disorders*; DSM-III and DSM-III-R selected the term *Psychological Factors Affecting Physical Conditions*.

A CHANGING PERSPECTIVE

The uncertainty over terminology reflects a longstanding controversy over the nature of the relationship between mind and body, the psyche and the soma. One of the most influential statements concerning the mind-body problem is found in the writing of René Descartes, the early seventeenth-century French philosopher. Descartes, influenced by strong religious beliefs, viewed human beings as part divine and as possessing a soul (mind) that somehow must affect the mechanics of the body. The point of contact between the two systems was presumed to be the pineal gland, located in the midbrain. This version of mind-body dualism was part of a long history of shifting opinion about whether or how spiritual or psychological factors affected bodily conditions.

During the twentieth century interest in the impact of psychological processes on the body resulted in development of the field of psychosomatic medicine. Early workers began to accumulate evidence and develop theories of how psychological factors played a causative role in specific physical disorders (e.g., Alexander, 1950; Grace and Graham, 1952; Selye, 1956). As this field developed, several trends emerged. An increasing number of physical disorders were seen to be related to psychological factors. Even the common cold was thought to be affected by emotional factors. The question therefore arose as to whether it was fruitful to identify a specific group of psychosomatic disorders or whether psychological factors were operating in all physical conditions. In addition, the focus began to shift from psychogenesis, that is psychological cause, to multicausality, the idea that social and psychological (as well as biological) factors all contribute to both health and illness at multiple points. The latter view is holistic, assuming a continuous transaction among influences.

With this shift in thinking, the field began to expand considerably. The ongoing role of social and psychological factors in physical conditions; the social, psychological and developmental consequences of physical conditions; the role of psychological treatments for physical disorders; social and psychological aspects of medical treatments; and the role of social and psychological variables in prevention and health maintenance all began to receive increased attention (cf. Drotar, 1981; Routh et al., 1983). Indeed, the concept of psychosomatic disorders as physical conditions caused by emotional factors became inadequate to encompass this expanded perspective (Tuma, 1982b). Writers began to suggest other definitions (cf. Wright, 1977), and various other terms came into existence, such as *behavioral medicine*, *health psychology*, and the term most commonly used in reference to children, *pediatric psychology*.

This chapter is in keeping with these changes. However, it is clearly not possible to survey this rapidly expanding field completely. Whole volumes have been dedicated to this topic or segments of it (e.g., Routh, 1988; Tuma, 1982a; Varni, 1983) and several scientific journals have emerged to deal exclusively with research in this area (e.g., *Journal of Pediatric Psychology, Behavioral Medicine, Health Psychology*). In this chapter we examine some of the specific medical problems of children that have received the attention of psychologists. This will allow us to describe the current status of information regarding these problems. It will also provide the opportunity to illustrate the manner in which ideas and knowledge in this area have evolved. We also present some other selected topics of interest, which will allow us to illustrate the current status and diversity of this field.

ASTHMA: PSYCHOLOGICAL CAUSES AND THE ROLE OF FAMILY

In this section we look at information on asthma in children. We will see how thinking about the role of psychological variables in physical illness has changed and expanded. Asthma is an example of a disorder for which the early focus was on psychological causation. One of the primary interests was and continues to be the role of the family in asthma. Thus, this section will also illustrate one of the interests of contemporary pediatric psychology, the role of the family in the child's illness.

Before beginning our discussion it would also be wise to remember that interest is not limited to a particular issue and a single disorder. For example, the involvement of family in the child's illness is clearly relevant to disorders other than asthma. Relatedly, in thinking about any disorder, it is likely that many issues will be relevant. Thus, other issues that are dealt with elsewhere in the chapter, for example compliance to treatment, are relevant to asthma as well. It is important to keep this overlap and complexity in mind and to understand that a simple one-to-one matching of disorders and issues is not a reality. Rather the grouping of issues and disorders is a convenience employed to organize information.

Description of Asthma

Asthma is a disorder of the respiratory system. Hyperresponsiveness of the trachea, bronchi, and bronchioles to various stimuli occurs with the result that the air passages are narrowed and air exchange is impaired, particularly during expiration. For the child this produces intermittent episodes of wheezing and shortness of breath (dyspnea). It is generally agreed that in any description of asthma three characteristics need to be acknowledged: intermittence, variability, and reversibility (e.g., Creer, Harm, and Marion, 1988). That is, attacks occur on an aperiodic and perhaps irregular basis. Within the same individual as well as across individuals attacks may vary in severity. And finally, with treatment, or perhaps spontaneously, the condition can reverse to normality. Thus asthma is an illness that is quite unpredictable, a problem for both research and management of the disorder.

Unpredictability is one of the challenges faced in treating the asthmatic child. Severe attacks, known as *status asthmaticus*, which are life threatening and require emergency medical treatment, are another. The fear of not being able to breathe and the danger of severe attacks are likely to create appreciable anxiety in the child and family members.

Prevalence and Prognosis

Asthma is probably the most common chronic disease in children occurring in perhaps 38 per 1,000 children (e.g., Gortmaker and Sappenfield, 1984). The impact of the disease on the asthmatic child is considerable. In addition to the psychological difficulties experienced by many children, asthma has been estimated to account for 25 percent of school days lost due to all chronic diseases combined (Purcell, 1975).

Clearly, the greatest threat is loss of life, and all measures used to treat the physical symptoms of asthma—daily medication to prevent wheezing, environmental control of potential irritants, desensitization to allergens, avoidance of infection, and emergency treatment to stop wheezing—are geared to prevent death. Fortunately, with appropriate treatment asthma tends to get better with age. Approximately 70 percent of asthmatics are reported to be considerably improved or free of attacks 20 years after the onset of symptoms, and the fatality rate appears to be less than 1 percent (Bronheim, 1978; Purcell, 1975).

Causation

The causes of asthma are complex, and there is a considerable history of controversy concerning etiology. To help clarify the problem of etiology, Figure 14–1 presents a simplified schematic description of the asthmatic process. Some cause or variety of causes produces a hypersensitivity of the air passages. Once established, this hypersensitivity results in the child's responding to a variety of irritants more easily than a non-asthmatic individual. The resulting wheezing and shortness of breath may have additional psychological consequences. Anxiety and fear may occur in anticipation of attacks or during them. This in itself may be a contributing irritant that increases the probability or intensity of attacks. A second class of possible psychological consequences is dependency, isolation from peers, and other behavior problems that may result from the management of the asthmatic child's physical symptoms.

Whatever its etiology, individuals with highly sensitive and labile respiratory tracts are potentially exposed to a second set of factors that influence whether or not asthmatic attacks occur. This second set of influences has come to be thought of as trigger

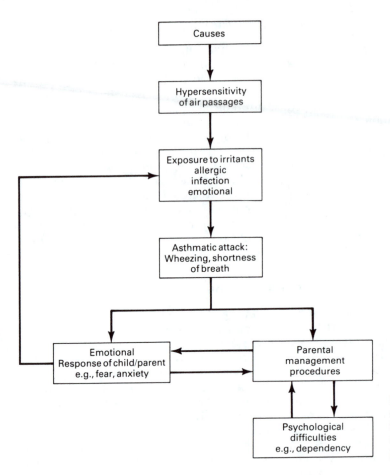

```
                    ┌─────────────┐
                    │   Causes    │
                    └─────────────┘
                           │
                           ▼
                 ┌───────────────────┐
                 │  Hypersensitivity  │
                 │  of air passages   │
                 └───────────────────┘
                           │
                           ▼
                 ┌───────────────────┐
                 │ Exposure to irritants│
                 │      allergic      │
                 │     infection      │
                 │     emotional      │
                 └───────────────────┘
                           │
                           ▼
                 ┌───────────────────┐
                 │  Asthmatic attack:  │
                 │ Wheezing, shortness │
                 │     of breath       │
                 └───────────────────┘
```

FIGURE 14–1   Schematic diagram of a general model for the development of asthma and its concomitant psychosocial effects.

mechanisms or irritants rather than as causes of asthma. It is widely held that a variety of agents can trigger wheezing in different individuals or on different occasions for the same individual (Creer and Reynolds, 1990).

Repeated respiratory infection may play a role in the development of asthma and respiratory viral infections can set off or worsen the severity of an attack. It has been recognized that viral infections are transmitted through some type of close contact; for example, from the nasal mucosa to the hand and then to the hand of another. The fact that such infections are likely transmitted to individuals via modifiable behaviors has led some investigators to develop behavioral interventions designed to directly modify such behaviors (e.g., Corley et al., 1987).

Allergies may also be related to the development and occurrence of asthmatic attacks. Allergies may exist to inhaled substances such as dust, the dander of a pet, or pollen, or to ingested substances such as milk, wheat, or chocolate. Physical factors such as cold temperatures, tobacco smoke, pungent odors, and exercise and rapid breathing may also contribute to wheezing. Further, psychological stimuli and emotional upset are often considered important triggers of asthma attacks (Creer and Reynolds, 1990).

Indeed, it is virtually impossible to analyze asthma without recognizing psychosocial factors. This is powerfully shown in

Alexander's brief description of the young asthmatic patient:

The early-onset asthma patient and his or her family face some very severe hardships. These youngsters tend to grow up watching the other children play from the livingroom side of the front window. Most have poor self-concepts. Often both academic and social development suffer greatly because of the amount of time lost from school and the restricted and specialized contacts with agemates. They face both peers and adults who are variously overindulgent, or lacking in understanding of their difficulties. Often these children react with shame and embarrassment, and/or demandingness to the extreme. At home their asthma may become the sole focus around which all family activities and concerns come to revolve. Their parents may feel responsible, guilty, and helpless; and at other times resentful and angry. Certainly, an asthma sufferer can learn to manipulate others with the disorder, or use it to avoid unpleasant activities or situations. It is also often difficult for the patient to sort out clearly what he or she can really do, from what is accomplished in the face of asthma. Many maladaptive and inappropriate behavior patterns can develop, as patient and family struggle with the ravages of this disorder. Such patterns can severely cripple family life and retard the social and psychological development of the child. Often, the undesirable behavior patterns affect the course of the disorder substantially. Asthma is, of course, potentially life-threatening, and many patients have experienced bouts of status asthmaticus, which on occasion may have brought them close to death. Such experiences often generate enduring anxiety responses which can manifest themselves in fears of death, hospitals, and treatment. Some patients

Parental concern over precipitating a symptomatic attack often leads children with chronic illnesses, such as asthma, to spend appreciable time isolated from their peers. (By permission of U.S. Department of Health and Human Services—Public Health Service (ADM, 77-497)

develop conditioned fear responses, which can begin at even the first signs of wheezing. The frantic, worried behavior of parents and those treating the patient can exacerbate the young patient's fear. . . . (Alexander 1980, p. 274)

In much of the early literature asthma was viewed primarily as a disease with psy-chological causes. This traditional psycho-somatic approach appeared reasonable: For many years those working with asthmatic children had observed psychological and emotional disturbances even as they lacked adequate physiological models. The distur-bances were attributed to the family.

Role of the Family

Probably the earliest and most widely known psychosomatic explanation of asthma was the psychoanalytic explanation originally of-fered by French and Alexander (1941). Asthma was hypothesized to arise from an excessive, unresolved dependence on the mother and a resultant fear of separation. The symptoms of wheezing and shortness of breath were viewed as "a suppressed cry for the mother," brought on because crying, and the desire for the mother it represents, become intolerable to the parent. French and Alexander were clearly influenced by their psychoanalytic training and much of the support for this theory came from other psychoanalysts and from individual case studies. Research studies designed to evalu-ate the hypothesis often suffered from se-rious methodological flaws (Freeman et al., 1964) or failed to demonstrate the hypoth-esized relationships (e.g., McLean and Ching, 1973). It is probably important to examine the specifics of this hypothesis and its validity, however. As Creer (1982) has pointed out, French and Alexander's ideas about psychological factors and asthma had as much impact as anything written. More-over, these ideas were applied to other disorders.

Renne and Creer (1985) have summa-rized the basic aspects of the explanation and the information concerning its validity. The four major conclusions offered by French and Alexander are (a) that a uni-versal conflict exists in asthmatic patients between an infantile dependent attachment to their mothers and other emotions (par-ticularly sexual wishes) that are incompati-ble with this dependent attitude; (b) asthma attacks are related to an inhibited sup-pressed cry for the mother; (c) there is a unique personality pattern characteristic of asthmatic patients; (d) psychoanalysis will alleviate the asthmatic symptoms. Recent reviews of research conducted since the publication of the original monograph by French and Alexander suggest that there is little if any support for their conclusions (e.g., Renne and Creer, 1985). No unique relationship appears to exist between asth-matic children and their mothers. To the extent that asthmatic children cry less, this is more likely due to the realization that crying may trigger an attack. Furthermore, there is no evidence for a personality pattern unique to asthma, and asthmatic patients would seem to be as psychologically healthy as other people. Finally, psychotherapy has not been effective in alleviating the disorder.

All in all, there is little, if any convincing evidence that the above explanation, or any other psychological factors play a significant role in the genesis of the reduced respira-tory capacity found in asthma. However, there is evidence that psychological factors may play an important role in *precipitating* asthmatic attacks in at-risk children. Family variables are among those that receive most frequent attention.

Psychological irritants. Like many inves-tigators, Purcell and his colleagues—work-ing at the Children's Asthma Research In-stitute and Hospital (CARIH) in Denver—observed that some children became symp-tom free fairly soon after being sent away from their parents for treatment. Indeed, in the 1950s "parentectomy" was suggested as the treatment of choice for some children (Peshkin, 1959). Were these effects due to changes in the emotional environment or physical environment? What other variables accounted for this reaction?

An interesting study on separation suggested some answers to these questions (Purcell et al., 1969). Prior to the beginning of the study, parents of asthmatic children were interviewed and asked about the degree to which emotions precipitated asthmatic attacks. Children for whom emotions were important precipitants were expected to respond positively to separation from their parents (predicted positive), while children for whom emotions played less of a role were not expected to show improvement. Twenty-five asthmatic children participated in four two-week periods labeled (1) qualification, (2) preseparation, (3) separation, and (4) reunion. During the qualification period the families were aware that the project involved a careful evaluation of asthma in children but were unaware of possible separation. During the second phase, preseparation, the idea of separation was introduced. The third phase was a two-week period during which the children had no contact with their families but continued their normal daily routines at home under the care of substitute parents. In the fourth phase the children were reunited with their families. A postreunion evaluation was also conducted.

For the predicted positive group all measures of asthma improved during the separation period. Figure 14–2 illustrates this finding for the peak expiratory flow rate (PEFR) measure. This is a measure of the maximum expiration of air possible. The children who were not predicted to respond to separation exhibited no differences across phases on any measure.

The findings of this research study, and others like it, led investigators to view changes in the psychological atmosphere as

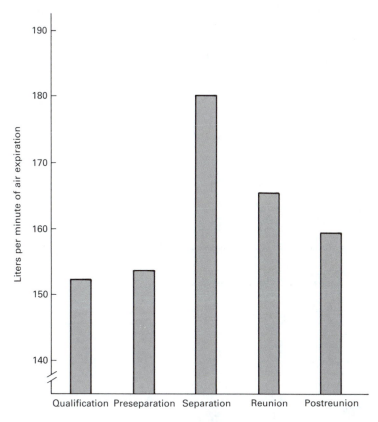

FIGURE 14–2 Mean daily peak expiratory flow rate for predicted positive group during each period of study. Reprinted by permission of the publisher from article by K. Purcell et al., *Psychosematic Medicine, 31,* 144–164. Copyright © 1969 by the American Psychosomatic Society, Inc.

the basis for improvement in asthmatic symptoms. However, over time the investigators at CARIH and others came to view such findings somewhat differently. It was recognized that the magnitude of changes reported might be statistically significant, but were not clinically significant. Obtained changes might have been due to increased compliance with prescribed medical regimens when the surrogate parents moved in and the children's parents lived in a hotel. While high percentages of children treated at CARIH in the early years exhibited rapid remission of their symptoms, this percentage decreased rapidly over the years. This is probably due to several factors. With increasing information and improved medications available, milder cases of asthma came to be treated by the home physician (cf. Ellis, 1988). Thus, only more severe cases were sent to the facility. Indeed, it may be the case that in the later years of the program children were sent because of severe behavior problems, their asthma playing only a minor role in the decision. Such children were dismissed from the program that was not designed to manage such

problems. The population at the facility also changed in terms of the demographics of the families. For example, more residents came from broken homes. Finally, the diagnostic criteria used to confirm asthma shifted over time. In fact, it is questionable that children diagnosed as asthmatic with current diagnostic procedures would exhibit a remission of symptoms as a result of being separated from their parents (Renne and Creer, 1985).

This, of course, does not mean that family functioning plays no role in asthma. It would appear, however, that the primary impact is more indirect than originally suggested. Psychological variables appear to influence behaviors related to the management of asthma. McNabb, Wilson-Pessano, and Jacobs (1986) identified critical self-management competencies that asthmatic children must acquire. These are summarized in Table 14–1. It is clear from looking at these that family functioning would play a major role in teaching the child how to meet these needs and also be central to maintaining the appropriate behaviors and environment. Later in the chapter we will

---

TABLE 14–1   Self-Management Competencies for Children with Asthma

Prevention
  Avoids allergens (e.g., foods, pollen, animal dander)
  Avoids irritants and other precipitants (e.g., extreme air temperature, dampness, smoke, exercise)
  Controls or avoids emotional triggers
  Takes action on exposure to minimize attacks
  Takes preventive medicine (routine and anticipatory)
  Ensures that medications for symptoms are accessible
  Cooperates in treatment of upper respiratory infection

Intervention
  Takes corrective action when attack starts (e.g., "leaves" precipitating situation, takes medication, controls breathing, drinks fluids, rests)
  Practices a variety of strategies dependent on progression/severity of symptoms (e.g., tries alternative treatment, seeks specific assistance from another person, seeks medical assistance)
  Develops or requests individually adaptive intervention
  Uses medicine correctly (dosage, side effects)

Compensatory Behavior
  Discusses asthma with peers, seeks acceptance/support
  Accepts primary responsibility for management
  Tries to overcome limitations or expand capabilities
  Accepts/cooperates with treatment regimen even if painful or restrictive
  Avoids using asthma to manipulate or get attention

Adapted from McNabb, Wilson-Pessano, and Jacobs, 1985.

---

discuss one aspect of this, the importance of psychological influences on compliance with medical routines.

There seems little doubt that psychological factors play a role in the occurrence and exacerbation of asthma. The anxiety created in the child and the family can affect not only the actual asthmatic attack but the entire lifestyle of the family. Behavioral problems that result from the asthma can interfere with successful medical management. Also, the creation of problematic parent-child interactions and the family's handling of the physical disorder can threaten all aspects of the child's social and emotional development. It is therefore not surprising that psychological interventions in childhood asthma have focused on these precipitants and consequences (Creer et al., 1988; Creer and Reynolds, 1990).

PSYCHOLOGICAL CONSEQUENCES OF CHRONIC ILLNESS

We now turn to a more extended discussion of how illness may effect the development of the child and the adjustment of the child and other family members. The effects of any chronic illness are likely to be pervasive, particularly if the illness is life threatening. Stress and anxiety experienced by the child are likely to be substantial, and limitations due to illness often place obstacles in the way of normal developmental processes. For example, contact with peers may be limited, adversely affecting socialization experiences and social skill development (e.g., Noll et al., 1990).

Of course, the family will need to cope with the illness, its treatment, and its effects over long periods of time. Such long-term demands are bound to be difficult and the consistency required by treatment regimens is stressful in its own right. Thus, the entire family may experience considerable anxiety and have appreciable stress placed on its daily routines. It is also important to remember that families with an ill child are not immune to the other considerable stresses experienced by all families.

Kalnins, Churchill, and Terry (1980) followed 45 families of children with leukemia over a 20-month period following diagnosis. In addition to the stress of caring for the leukemic child, the vast majority of these families also had to cope with a variety of other problems (Table 14–2). These accumulated stresses impact on the adjustment of the other family members themselves. This, in turn, affects the family's behavior and its interactions with the ill child. Dependency and manipulativeness by the child may be consequences of parental styles of coping.

Exactly what chronically ill children and their families experience may vary with the

TABLE 14–2 Concurrent Problems Experienced by Families of Leukemic Children

Categories of Events	Frequency of Occurrence	Percentage of Families Who Experienced Event
Major complications related to the child's leukemia	12	27
Death of another leukemic child	17	35
Death of a family member or friend	9	13
Concurrent illness in a family member requiring hospitalization, surgery, or regular medical care	35	44
Occupation changes	12	22
Financial problems	6	13
Miscellaneous events: moving, purchase or sale of home, postponement of major trip or a marriage, automobile accidents	25	40

Adapted from Kalnins, Churchill, and Terry, 1980. Reprinted by permission of Plenum Publishing Corporation.

nature of the illness. Nevertheless, one frequent question is: Does chronic illness lead to poor adjustment? The answer would appear to be not necessarily, but these illnesses and related life experiences probably place the child at increased risk for such difficulties (Pless, 1984). For example, children with diabetes are frequently described by parents and teachers as having difficulty in school. Controlled investigations in which these children are compared to their nondiabetic siblings on measures of intelligence or school achievement, however, usually find no differences (Johnson, 1988b). However diabetes onset before age five may be associated with poorer school achievement and intellectual performance (e.g., Ryan, Vega, and Drash, 1985).

The same kind of findings seems to apply to social and emotional adjustment. For example, Wertlieb, Hauser, and Jacobson (1986) found no differences between Child Behavior Checklist scores of a group of diabetic children and a comparison group of children with acute illnesses that were neither trivial nor life threatening. In another investigation Child Behavior Checklists completed by mothers of children with a variety of chronic illnesses indicated that these children's behavior problem and social competence scores were, respectively, higher and lower, than the norms for children in general. However, the ill children's scores were better than the norms for children referred to mental health clinics (Wallander et al., 1988). Adjustment that is on average poorer than the general population but better than that of children specifically referred for psychological treatment is similar to the adjustment of obese children in a weight reduction program (p. 301).

In addition to comparing chronically ill children to controls, it may be informative to compare them to their healthy siblings. One such investigation compared the adjustment of 93 juvenile rheumatic disease patients to that of their healthy siblings as well as to demographically matched healthy controls (Daniels et al., 1987). The patients and their siblings had more adjustment problems than did the controls, but they did not differ from each other. This suggests that adjustment difficulties are not necessarily a direct result of having a chronic disease. It is possible, however, that having a child with a chronic disease creates stress in the family environment. The stress placed on some families may affect the adjustment of both the patient and other children.

While some children with chronic illnesses and their families experience adjustment difficulties, not all do. It is useful to obtain information on variables that may help predict such outcomes. Available research suggests that disease status and family functioning are two such variables (Johnson, 1988a).

Disease Status and Adjustment

The type of disease, the severity of the illness, and the degree of impairment of functioning produced by the illness have been examined as variables linking disease status to psychological adjustment. Of course, it is not always possible to analyze these dimensions separately. For example, certain illnesses are more severe than others and severity is likely related to greater restrictions in normal functioning. However, each of these variables seems to be of importance. Steinhausen (1988), for example, found poorer adjustment in youngsters with cystic fibrosis than those with asthma, both diseases affecting the lungs. In addition, poorer adjustment was associated with more severe illness in both of these groups as well as in groups of children with Chron's disease and ulcerative colitis (both affecting the colon). Similarly, children suffereing from severe forms of arthritis had more behavior problems than healthy children, but children with milder or inactive forms of the disease did not (Billings et al., 1987). However, more severe forms of a disorder are not always associated with poorer adjustment (e.g., Wallender, Feldman, and Varni, 1989).

Other investigators found that adjustment was associated with the degree of functional limitation (for example, the number of absences from school) caused by the condition (e.g., Fowler, Johnson, and Atkinson, 1985). The degree to which the illness is controlled also appears to be important. For example, more emotional and behavioral problems are found when diabetes is poorly controlled (e.g., Mazze, Lucido, and Shannon, 1984). While these results suggest that anxiety, depression, and the like are outcomes of poor control, investigators acknowledge that causation is not clearly established. Emotional conditions can also contribute to problems in metabolic control. Ethically, we cannot manipulate emotional conditions or illness severity, nor can we randomly assign children to diseases. Thus, research and interpretation of data on causality and the dimensions of illness are inevitably difficult. However, research suggests that it may be that multiple aspects of chronic illness contribute to the psychosocial stress experienced by the child and thereby adjustment (e.g., Hurtig, Koepke, and Park, 1989).

Family Functioning and Adjustment

As we have seen in previous chapters, family functioning has frequently been linked to children's adjustment. It is, therefore, not surprising that family functioning is related to the psychological adjustment of chronically ill children as well.

In fact an early study suggested that poor functioning in families might be especially detrimental to a chronically ill child. Comparison of large samples of chronically ill children and healthy controls indicated that both family dysfunction and chronic illness were associated with more adjustment problems. However, youngsters with chronic illnesses who lived in poorly functioning families had the highest incidence of problems (Pless, Roghmann, and Haggerty, 1972). Steinhausen suggests that this relationship may vary depending on the nature of the child's illness. It is argued that the severity of some illnesses (such as cystic fibrosis) are so influential on the child's adjustment that family functioning is less influential than it is in milder illnesses such as asthma (Steinhausen, Schindler, and Stephan, 1983). This is an interesting hypothesis worthy of further exploration. Findings that family functioning was somewhat more important to the adjustment of healthy siblings and control children than it was for rheumatic disease patients is at least consistent with this thinking (Daniels et al., 1987).

Researchers have questioned whether specific aspects of family functioning are differentially related to adjustment in healthy children and those with chronic illnesses. Again the answer is likely to be a complex one. Daniels et al. (1987) found few significant differences between rheumatic disease patients, their healthy siblings, and healthy controls in family variables that related to child functioning. This suggests similar patterns of family dysfunction are related to behavior problems in each of these groups. In contrast, Wertlieb, Hauser, and Jacobson (1986) in their comparison of diabetic youngsters and matched controls with acute illnesses found that while overt expression of family conflict was related to greater problem behavior in both groups, other factors differentiated the groups. For example, low family cohesion was related to problems in the acutely ill children, but not in the diabetic sample. On the other hand, family emphasis on morality and religion was associated with more internalizing problems in the diabetic, but not the acutely ill group.

One particularly interesting finding emerged with respect to differences in attempts to control and maintain the family system. A greater control orientation in the family was strongly and positively related to behavior problems for the acutely ill children. In contrast, low levels of family organization were associated with high levels of behavior problems among the diabetic children. Families with a diabetic child have appreciable demands placed on them to organize daily routines involved in the management of the child's illness. Successful management of the child's diabetes probably requires appreciable organization as well as overtly dealing with issues of control. These data suggest that families who do not emphasize organization are families more likely to have a child who exhibits behavior problems. Family emphasis on rules and control may be related to behavior problems in nondiabetic adolescents, but a different relationship seems optimal in families with a diabetic adolescent.

It seems likely that issues of organization and control that are part of maintaining the family system are central in dealing with a chronically ill child. Indeed, issues such as the balance of parental and child control would seem to apply to most, if not all, chronic illnesses (e.g., Allen et al., 1983). Other hypotheses generated from available information also seem worthy of investigation. For example, does a pattern of consistency-inflexibility by one parent and flexibility by the other help children cope with chronic illness? (Johnson, 1988a).

PSYCHOLOGICAL INFLUENCES ON MEDICAL TREATMENT

Attempts to provide psychological treatment that would improve a patient's medical condition have long been one of the aspects of the interface between psychology/psychiatry and medicine. The vast majority of early attempts sought to provide the patient with psychotherapy as a means of reducing physical symptoms or curing illness. Such assaults on illness through psychotherapy proved to be largely ineffective (Werry, 1986). More recent efforts have sought alternative methods of psychological intervention that might affect physical functioning. For example, relaxation training has been employed to attempt to improve respiratory functioning in asthmatic children (e.g., Alexander, Cropp, and Chai, 1979). A somewhat different approach to integrating a psychological perspective into the treatment of physical problems is to facilitate the delivery of medical services. While a comprehensive review of these efforts is beyond the scope of the present chapter, a few important illustrations follow.

Diabetes Mellitus: Adherence to Medical Regimens

The terms "adherence" and "compliance" are most commonly used to describe how well a child or family follows recommended medical treatments. Diabetes, because of the complex and difficult tasks required in its management, provides an excellent opportunity to illustrate the way psychologists have addressed the problem of adherence.

The role that psychologists have taken in the management of diabetes in children illustrates an important trend in the area of pediatric psychology. As with asthma, there has been a shift away from tasks such as identifying the diabetic personality and family. Psychologists have increasingly attended to understanding the complex tasks encountered by familes facing chronic childhood disorders.

Description of diabetes mellitus. Diabetes is the most common endocrine disorder in children, affecting approximately 1.8 children per 1,000 (Gortmaker and Sappenfield, 1984). It is a chronic, lifelong disorder that results from the pancreas producing insufficient insulin. Type I, also known as insulin-dependent diabetes mellitus (IDDM), requires daily replacement of insulin by injection due to the complete failure of the pancreas. As the onset of IDDM typically occurs in childhood, this form of diabetes is often referred to as childhood or juvenile diabetes. In Type II, non-insulin-dependent diabetes mellitus (NIDDM), some insulin is produced by the pancreas. NIDDM is an adult-onset disorder and weight reduction and careful diet can often control this form of diabetes.

Diagnosis of IDDM most often occurs during two age periods, 5- to 6- and 11- to 13-years of age. However, the onset of the disease can occur at any time from infancy to early adulthood. A combination of genetic, immunologic, and viral factors appears to be involved in the etiology of childhood diabetes. Theory currently suggests that diabetes may be an autoimmune disease in which the body attacks its own pancreatic cells (Johnson, 1988a, c).

Diabetes is characterized by free fatty acids (ketones) in the blood as well as increased sugar in the blood (hyperglycemia) and urine (glycosuria). Overt symptoms include excessive thirst, increased urination, weight loss, and fatigue. If the disorder is not controlled, a condition known as ketosis or ketoacidosis may occur. This very serious condition can lead to coma and death (Johnson, 1988b).

The child and family face a complex treatment regimen (see Table 14–3), including dietary restrictions, daily injections of insulin, monitoring of urine, and testing of blood glucose levels using small samples of blood obtained from a finger stick. On the basis of the daily tests for the level of sugar and consideration of factors such as timing of meals, diet, exercise, physical health, and emotional state, the daily dosages of insulin must be adjusted. This is a complex therapeutic regimen, and under the best of circumstances "insulin reactions" occur often. Thus, the child must be sensitive to the signs and symptoms of hyperglycemia (excessively high levels of blood glucose) and hypoglycemia (excessively low blood glucose). These reactions involve irritability, headache, shaking, and—if not detected early enough—unconsciousness and seizures. The task of identifying these states is complicated by the fact that subjective symptoms are different for different children.

TABLE 14–3 Some Activities Required of Diabetic Children and Families

Inject insulin regularly
Test blood regularly
Exercise regularly
Avoid sugar
Check for symptoms—low
Check for symptoms—high
Careful when sick
Shower regularly
Wear diabetes ID
Watch weight
Eat meals regularly
Adjust diet to exercise
Carry sugar
Test blood as shown
Change injection site
Inject insulin as shown
Watch dietary fat
Take care of injuries
Eat regular snacks
Control emotions
Inspect feet

Adapted from Karoly and Bay, 1990.

Thus, it is possible for families to be misinformed about such reactions. Parents and child are, therefore, faced with a difficult, often unpredictable, and emotion-laden therapeutic program. Management of the regimen and its integration into daily life presents a considerable challenge (Delamater, 1986; Johnson, 1988b).

Management of the diabetic condition. The first task in treatment is for the team of professionals to gain and maintain control of the diabetic condition. As this is achieved, insulin requirements often decrease and the initial fears and concerns of the child and family are often reduced. This has come to be known as the "honeymoon period." This period of partial remission will terminate gradually and usually ends about one to two years after initial diagnosis. This is but one example of the fact that diabetes is not a static disease. Adolescence is another time period during which management of diabetes often deteriorates (Johnson, 1989; LaGreca, 1987). Transferring control for management of the disease from the professional to the family and child, and requiring maintenance of such control over long periods of time, is one of the challenges of working with chronic childhood illnesses. It is also one of the areas that has clearly benefited from the interface of psychological and medical perspectives.

Adherence to the diabetic regimen. The concept of adherence is multifaceted (Dunbar and Waszak, 1990; LaGreca, 1988). Probably the initial step addressed in most programs is to educate the child and family about the disease. While such efforts are regularly made it is also a common observation that adequate knowledge cannot be assumed (Delamater, 1986). Therefore, efforts have been made toward developing methods to assess knowledge. Behavioral observational methods have been employed to assess whether the child knows how to execute necessary skills such as urine and blood glucose testing (e.g., Harkavy et al., 1983). Questionnaires are frequently used to measure cognitive knowledge of the disease and the application of that knowledge in different situations (e.g., the role insulin, and adjusting diet based on blood sugar readings). An example of such an instrument is the Test of Diabetes Knowledge: General Information and Problem Solving (Johnson, 1984). Examples of some of the items included in this test are presented in Table 14–4. Even these few examples illustrate the difficulty and complexity of the information required of children and families. However, adherence is not just a matter of accurate information and knowledge. The child and family must acutally carry out the prescribed tasks accurately and consistently.

There are a number of reasons why it is important to know whether such adherence to prescribed regimens occurs. For the clinician working with a particular child, effective treatment relies on the patient's actually completing the necessary tasks. In a larger sense, it is impossible to assess the effectiveness of treatments without such information. Interventions conducted outside

TABLE 14–4 Sample Items from Test of Diabetes Knowledge and Problem Solving

GENERAL INFORMATION

When giving insulin injections, you should:
  (a) Inject into the same area.
  (b) Inject into different areas every time.
  (c) Inject only in the leg.
  (d) I don't know.
Insulin:
  (a) Lowers the blood sugar level.
  (b) Raises the blood sugar level.
  (c) Increases sugar in the urine.
  (d) I don't know.
Ketones in the urine of a person with diabetes are:
  (a) A warning sign of an insulin reaction.
  (b) A warning sign of acidosis.
  (c) A warning sign of hypoglycemia.
  (d) I don't know.

PROBLEM SOLVING

You are at a school football game and begin to feel dizzy, shaky, and faint. You should:
  (a) Leave the game right away and go straight home.
  (b) Buy a coke and a hot dog and eat them.
  (c) Lie down, until you feel better.
  (d) I don't know.
You are trying out for your school's swimming team and practice is midafternoon. Your urine tests are usually negative before lunch and in midafternoon. Your blood sugar is usually 80–180. You should:
  (a) Not take your insulin the days you practice.
  (b) Eat a big lunch that day and keep a snack handy.
  (c) Increase your insulin to give you more energy that day.
  (d) I don't know.
You take 30 units of NPH insulin each morning. One day your blood sugar at 10:00 A.M. is 300. Your urine sugar is 5% with large ketones. In this situation you should:
  (a) Eat less today.
  (b) Eat more to counteract the ketones.
  (c) Drink extra fluids and check your blood again in 15 to 30 minutes, or if you check your urine, test again in an hour or two.
  (d) I don't know.

Adapted from Suzanne Bennett Johnson (1984) Test of Diabetes Knowledge, Revised-2. Gainesville: University of Florida, Department of Psychiatry.

the hospital or doctor's office cannot be evaluated unless we know if patients are adhering to recommendations. Is a treatment ineffective in controlling diabetes or was it not followed adequately?

Adherence to diabetes treatment recommendations is, as indicated above, a complex task. A study by Johnson and her colleagues (1986) provides a way of looking at the aspects of daily management faced by the child and family. This study also provides interesting information about adherence to these management tasks. Interviews were conducted with 168 diabetic children and their parents concerning their diabetes-relevant behavior during the previous 24 hours. These interviews, structured to allow recording of details of behavior, were conducted on three occasions for each family. A factor analysis of the 13 behaviors indicated that they grouped into 5 categories. Table 14–5 presents these categories and behaviors.

The adherence of the child in one diabetes management area did not predict the adherence of that same child in other areas. This suggests that adherence cannot be viewed as a global concept. Each aspect of the child's and family's compliance may need to be separately evaluated and addressed if programming is to be effective.

Other research supports this conclusion. For example, youngsters with diabetes were found to have distinct conceptualizations for "told to do" versus "want to do" health-related goals. Furthermore, these dimensions were differentially related to metabolic control (Karoly and Bay, 1990).

Turning again to the Johnson et al. (1986) study, it was possible to look at the relationship between the reports of children and their mothers. In general, correlations were statistically significant and moderate to strong (0.42 to 0.78). However, the age of the child seemed to affect mother-child agreement. On measures involving time (e.g., injection-meal timing, exercise duration) correlations were poorer for younger children. The young child's lesser sophistication regarding time is probably responsible. Children in the 9 to 12 and 13 to 15 age groupings had the most consistent parent-child agreement across the 13 behaviors. Older adolescents (16 to 19 years) had highly variable correlations across behaviors. For example, the correlation for injection interval was quite high (0.91), whereas agreement on injection regularity was extremely low (−0.04). Older patients are likely to be less frequently monitored by parents and this also suggests different treatment challenges. These findings and others point to the importance of considering the child's level of cognitive development in treatment planning (cf. Band, 1990).

It is not possible to examine all of the aspects of the multifaceted concept of adherence in this chapter. However, reviews of the contribution of a psychological perspective on diabetes highlight several important variables (Johnson, 1988a, b, c; Stark, Dahlquist, and Collins, 1987). One major concern is the accuracy of the child's adherence efforts. For example, it has often been observed that children may be inaccurate in reading their glucose level tests (Gross, 1990). The majority of such errors are likely errors of knowledge or skill, but actual faking of results, to avoid restrictions or the need for additional treatment, must also be considered. Interventions need to be planned to address both forms of inaccuracy.

TABLE 14–5 Factor Analysis of 13 Diabetic Adherence Behaviors

Factor I	Exercise
	Time spent exercising
	Strenuousness of the exercise
	Exercise frequency
Factor II	Injection
	Injection regularity
	Injection-meal timing
	Regularity of injection-meal timing
Factor III	Diet (type)
	Percent calories: Fat
	Percent calories: Carbohydrates
Factor IV	Testing/Eating Frequency
	Number of meals and snacks eaten each day
	Number of glucose or ketone tests per day
Factor V	Diet (amount)
	Calories consumed
	Quantity of concentrated sweets ingested

Adapted from Johnson et al., 1986.

Developmental level is an important variable affecting adherence (Johnson et al., 1986; LaGreca, 1988). In general, knowledge and skills seem to increase with age. For example, current findings suggest that children under 9 years may have difficulty accurately measuring and injecting insulin. Also, it is probably best to avoid giving primary responsibility for glucose testing to children under 12 (Johnson 1988c). Children's attributions as to the cause of their diabetes would also appear to be related to the diabetic control achieved (e.g., Tennen et al., 1984). Adolescence appears to be a period of adherence difficulties. Social and emotional issues such as acceptance and greater participation in peer activities as well as conflicts over independence with parents are present. These most likely combine with actual physical changes, like those associated with puberty, and increase management and compliance difficulties (e.g., Amiel et al., 1986; Gross et al., 1983; LaGreca, 1987).

Attention to the role of the primary health care provider (pediatrician, nurse) has also been examined as an important aspect of the adherence process. This work also highlights the interdisciplinary benefits achieved through the emergence of pediatric psychology. Available literature indicates that there is a considerable discrepancy between what primary providers have recommended and what is recalled by patients and their families (e.g., Page et al., 1981). It also seems that health care providers are not aware enough of the child's level of cognitive development, treating youngsters of varying ages as essentially the same. Thus, younger children's understanding is likely to be overestimated while the cognitive abilities of older children are underestimated (e.g., Perrin and Perrin, 1983).

Although it is frequently presumed that treatment failure is a problem of patient compliance, this is only part of the issue. The communication gap between health care provider and patient/family seems larger than is often realized and other problems also seem to exist. Doctors and patients may not share the same goals for treatment.

This is illustrated by a comparison of the goals of physicians treating children with diabetes and those of the children's parents. Significant differences were found. Parents' goals were more focused on the short-term consequences of diabetes (e.g., hypoglycemia) and physicians' on more long-term threats (complications). Children's diabetic control was more related to the parents' goals (Marteau et al., 1987).

Also, from the perspective of the physician, adherence may be defined as 100 percent compliance with medical recommendations. Such a perspective may fail to appreciate the ability of parent and child to adjust treatment regimens—this might be termed "adaptive noncompliance" (Deaton and Olbrisch, 1987). For one, not all interventions may be highly effective for all individuals. Families and patients may respond to these variations. Also, families may be more likely than physicians to adjust regimens based on consideration of the psychological and social impact of treatment. Taken together, these factors suggest that an important focus of adherence efforts needs to be on the behavior of the health care provider.

It is clear that many other problems regarding adherence are worthy of continued attention. For example, it is important to anticipate environmental obstacles to compliance. Creating interventions that help adolescents deal with peers concerning their diabetes, for instance, may greatly facilitate compliance with recommendations (e.g., Gross et al., 1983). Realization that the immediate consequences of diabetes management are often negative and, therefore, more consistent with nonadherence than with adherence, may also help to anticipate difficulties. For example, the immediate consequence of injections is discomfort and the effects of skipping injections is not immediate. Thus, interventions that reduce the negative effects of compliance are likely to be of value (e.g., Schafer, Glasgow, and McCaul, 1982).

An oft-cited study illustrates two other ways in which behavioral interventions have been employed to increase adherence—

cueing and reinforcement. These procedures recognize the difficulty of the diabetic management task. Reminders may be necessary and providing positive consequences may be important in the context of naturally occurring unpleasant outcomes. Lowe and Lutzker (1979) conducted a single-subject experiment on the use of written instructions ("memo") and a point system to increase compliance by Amy, a nine-year-old diabetic girl. Observations were made of three behaviors: dieting, urine testing, and foot care required to detect sores and prevent gangrene. Following a baseline period, memos regarding foot care were given to Amy and posted in the home. In order to demonstrate that changes were the result of planned interventions, memos were in-

FIGURE 14–3 Percentage compliance to foot care, urine testing, and diet. From Lowe, K. and Lutzker, J. R., *Behavior Therapy, 10, 57–64.* Copyright © 1978 by the Association for Advancement of Behavior Therapy. Reprinted by permission of the publisher and the author.

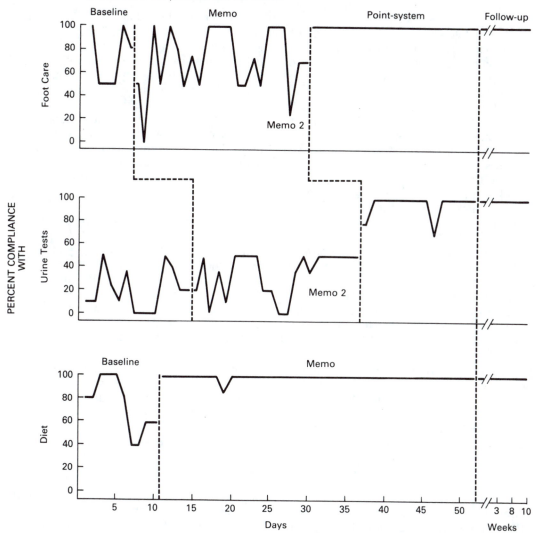

BOX 14.1   Type-A behavior

There has been a great deal of recent interest in examining behavior patterns that may be related to physical health. Do certain lifestyles prevent people from becoming ill or at least reduce the risk of certain serious and life-threatening diseases?

One of the most intensively studied topics is what has come to be known as the Type-A behavior pattern, which was first described by Friedman and Rosenman (1974). The Type-A behavior pattern is characterized by extreme competitiveness and achievement striving, hostility, aggressiveness, and a sense of time urgency. It has been studied extensively as a risk factor for coronary heart disease in adults. Available research does suggest that these behaviors are predictive of the development of coronary heart disease, although there are some controversy and confusion as to what the critical behaviors are and how they may relate to etiology (e.g., Dimsdale, 1988; Friedman and Booth-Kewley, 1988; Matthews, 1988; Wright, 1988).

To better understand the origins of such behavior, researchers have also examined the Type-A pattern in children. The Type-A pattern, similar to that described in adults, can be reliably assessed in children (Saab and Matthews, 1986). One question that has been examined is the relationship between parent and child behavior patterns. Parental socialization practices that may lead to the development of Type-A behavior (e.g., parental attitudes toward achievement in competitive situations) are one focus of interest. Parents may selectively encourage or reinforce particular styles of behavior or children may be imitating parental models (e.g., Vega-Lahr and Field, 1986). It has been found, for example, that father's goal setting was significantly related to Type-A behavior in sons (Kliewer and Weidner, 1987). Also significant positive correlations have been found between measures of Type-A behavior in fathers and both their adolescent and young sons (Weidner et al., 1988).

Another question that has been asked concerns the stability of the Type-A behavior pattern. Some research suggests that the behavior pattern is stable even during childhood, while other findings indicate that the pattern is not stable until adolescence (e.g., Steinberg, 1986; Visintainer and Matthews, 1987). It is possible that Type-A behavior actually consists of different behavior patterns during different stages of development. In order to study continuity, Type-A profiles at different ages need to be established.

While it seems that children with Type-A patterns can be identified, it is important to know if they necessarily grow to be Type-A adults. Also, what if any link exists between these early behavior patterns and later coronary heart disease? This information and programs geared at modifying detrimental behavior patterns may have great preventive potential.

troduced at different points in time for the other two behaviors. A point system was introduced next, also at different points in time for the different behaviors. Points earned for following the regimen could be exchanged for daily and weekly reinforcers. Compliance with diet regimen increased to a consistently high level using the memo alone. The point system achieved similar success for foot care and urine testing (see Figure 14–3). Improvements were maintained at a ten-week follow-up.

Psychological Modification of Physical Functions

The Eastern mystic who walks on hot coals, voluntarily slows the heart, and by the power of the mind closes a wound has always fascinated inhabitants of the Western world. Fascinating too are the primitive shaman's cures by removal of evil spirits; the miracles of faith healers; and cures of medical ailments by inert placebos (cf. Ullmann and Krasner, 1975). These phenomena dramatically highlight the possible role of psychological interventions in the treatment of medical disorders. Each suggests that psychological procedures can directly affect physical functioning. The systematic and scientific study of how psychology can be used to treat physical symptoms directly has become part of the shifting emphasis in understanding mind-body relationships.

Experimental research has demonstrated that responses of the autonomic nervous system can be modified by classical and operant conditiong (e.g., Bleeker and Engle, 1973; Kotses et. al., 1976; Miller, 1969; Shapiro, Schwartz, and Tursky, 1972). This suggested that procedures such as relaxation and biofeedback could be employed to train a person to control systems that are overreactive in a particular physical disorder. Indeed, a variety of psychological interventions has been applied to children's physical disorders. The research is promising but also limited and strong conclusions regarding effectiveness cannot be drawn (Andrasik and Attanasio, 1985; Williamson et al., 1987).

The use of relaxation and biofeedback to treat children's headaches is one example of attempts to directly modify physical functioning through psychological interventions. Headaches are usually classified as migrane, tension, or a combination of the two. *Migraine* headaches are presumed to be a vascular disorder: Vasoconstriction and vasodilation (narrowing and expansion) of the blood vessels in the head produce pounding and throbbing. *Tension* headaches, as the name implies, are presumed to result from muscular/psychological tension (Williamson, Davis, and Kelly, 1989). Although migraines are less common, their treatment has received more research attention (Andrasik, Blake, and McCarran, 1986; Williamson et al., 1987). These headaches

produce very intense pain and often are accompanied by nausea and vomiting. This suffering and the desire to avoid potential negative aspects of drug treatment have led to the exploration of nonpharmacological approaches (Andrasik et al., 1986; Masek and Hoag, 1990).

Biofeedback refers to a procedure in which some device provides immediate feedback to the person about a particular biological function. Feedback is usually provided by a signal such as a light or tone or by some graphic display. Such feedback to teach children to warm the temperature of their hands has been employed to treat children's migraines. The mechanism whereby controlling hand temperature affects vasodilation is not clear. However, a number of uses of this procedure in combination with other techniques such as relaxation seem to be promising in producing clinically meaningful levels of improvement in children's headaches (Andrasik et al., 1986).

Although procedures such as biofeedback and relaxation have been employed to directly modify physical functioning, available findings suggest cautious expectations. Some areas in which early results suggested success as well as some more recent efforts indicate that the levels and persistence of change may not always be sufficient enough to be viewed as clinically meaningful (Ewart et al., 1987; Williamson et al., 1987). This has led to the suggestion that rather than always emphasizing such procedures as primary interventions, exploration of psychological interventions as adjuncts to medical treatment should be considered (e.g., Masek, Fentress, and Spirito, 1984). Such endeavors are another part of the impact of psychology on the treatment of medical problems. Indeed, compared to direct psychological intervention, even greater attention has been given to the ways in which psychological variables can facilitate the delivery of medical treatment.

Facilitating Medical Treatment

Psychological factors also influence the effective delivery of medical treatments for physical disorders. Developing psychologically based procedures for enhancing the effectiveness of medical treatment is another important and growing area of interest. Procedures for dealing with pain and discomfort and for preparing for hospitalization illustrate this potentially important contribution.

Pain and distress. Despite its seeming simplicity pain is a complex phenomenon that is difficult to assess. It is difficult, for example, to separate the pain or discomfort the child is suffering from the anxiety the child is experiencing while undergoing a painful medical procedure. This has led some to use the term distress to encompass both pain and anxiety (Jay, 1988). Whatever term is employed, three different response systems need to be assessed: behavioral, physiological, and cognitive-affective. Self-report measures of the cognitive-affective component of pain are the most frequently employed measures. This is probably an intentional choice. Pain is a subjective experience and thus assessing the child's experience of pain is important. In addition, the greater accessibility of this component and the relative ease of measurement are certainly factors as well. However, measurement of this component is not without its difficulties. For example, the child's developmental level will play a large role in selecting a self-report measure. Older children may be able to describe pain in semantic terms, but younger children need to rely on concrete and visual methods. The use of a pain thermometer that visually represents degrees of pain in numerical terms is one procedure that has been employed (see Figure 14–4). In very young children who may not have the number concepts and discriminations required by this method, different measures can be employed. Thus, faces with expressions from broad smiles to severe frowns and colors to indicate intensity of pain may be useful (Dolgin and Jay, 1989b).

The behavioral component of children's distress (for example, behaviors that require the child to be physically restrained) can often interfere with effective medical treatment. Observational methods are often used

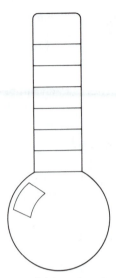

FIGURE 14–4 A child's subjective pain experience must be assessed in a developmentally appropriate manner. A pain thermometer like the one pictured is one way of concretizing differences in pain experience for young children.

to assess children's distress behaviors. Structured behavioral observations employing a system of defined behaviors and trained observers have been employed in a variety of contexts. Table 14–6 describes the categories of behavior included in the Observational Scale of Behavioral Distress developed by Elliot, Jay, and Woody (1987). Because such procedures can be expensive and time consuming, global ratings of distress by parents or nurses are often used to assess the behavioral component.

Assessment of the physiological aspect of children's pain is far less common. Melamed and Siegel's (1975) measurement of palmar sweat before and after children underwent elective surgery is one of the earliest reports using physiological measures along with self-report and behavioral observation. However, the sophisticated equipment necessary and the difficulty involved in reliably obtaining measures such as heart rate, blood pressure, and skin conductance result in such measures typically not being employed.

Measurement difficulty is but one aspect of the complexity of evaluating pain. Find-

TABLE 14–6 Categories for the Observation Scale of Behavioral Distress

Category	Definition
Information seeking	Any question regarding medical procedure
Cry	Onset of tears and/or low-pitched nonword sounds of more than one second duration
Scream	Loud, nonword, shrill vocal expressions at high pitch intensity
Physical restraint	Child is physically restrained with noticeable pressure
Verbal resistance	Any intelligible verbal expressions of delay, termination or resistance
Seeks emotional support	Verbal or nonverbal solicitation of hugs, physical or verbal comfort from parents or staff
Verbal pain	Any words, phrases, or statements that refer to pain or discomfort
Flail	Random gross movements of arms, legs, or whole body

Adapted from Elliot, Jay, and Woody, 1987. Reprinted by permission from Susan M. Jay, University of Southern California School of Medicine.

ings that the three response systems are far from perfectly correlated obviously cause difficulties. It is also the case that different measures within a single response system often show less than desirable levels of correlation. To further complicate the issue, developmental level may affect the relationship between the different response systems (Jay, 1988). Developmental issues may also interact with aspects of the pain situation. It has been suggested, for example, that younger—more cognitively concrete—children may exhibit greater distress when experiencing a more obvious but relatively minor injury (e.g., a small cut) than when they are subject to internal pain related to a more serious condition such as arthritic joint pain (Johnson, 1988a).

As a means of organizing work on pediatric pain, Varni, Katz, and Dash (1982) delineated four categories: (1) pain associated with a disease state; (2) pain associated with an observable injury; (3) pain not associated with a well-defined or specific disease or injury (e.g., recurrent abdominal pain, headache); (4) pain associated with medical or dental procedures. We will examine some of the research related to this fourth category to illustrate how procedures derived from a psychological perspective have been employed to assist children experiencing medically related pain.

Helping the child cope. Many of the medical procedures used to assess and treat children with chronic disorders are aversive. It is commonly agreed that preparation of the child for an aversive procedure is the first step in helping the child cope and in reducing distress (cf. Peterson and Mori, 1988). The basic rationale behind providing preparatory information is that unexpected stress is worse than predictable stress. From the simple statement that preparation is good follows the complex question of how this is best achieved for each child. Research

Fears of medical procedures are common among children, particularly for children who must undergo frequent treatment. Techniques that reduce fearful behavior can facilitate good medical care. (Alan Carey/The Image Works)

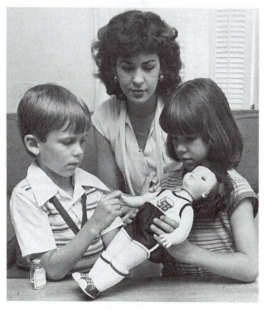

provides some guidelines and suggests certain procedures. However, it is also clear that more information is still needed and that different types and timing of procedures will need to be matched to individual children (Peterson and Mori, 1988; Ross and Ross, 1988).

Some general recommendations have been made, in part based on suggestions made by children themselves (Ross, 1988). Many of these suggestions cluster around the concept of being in control, and many involve the child's controlling the environment during the aversive treatment procedure. The following comment by a ten-year-old boy undergoing emergency room burn treatment illustrates this well.

I said, "How about a hurting break?" and he (intern) said, "Hey, man, are you serious?" And I said, "Sure. Even when ladies are having babies they get a little rest between the bad pains." And they (the pediatric emergency room personnel) all laughed and he said, "OK, you get a 60-second break whenever you need it" and then it was *much, much better*, like you wouldn't believe it. (Ross, 1988, p.5)

While children may be capable of generating their own strategies for coping with pain and distress, procedures for teaching effective stress management/coping skills have also received considerable attention (Ludwick-Rosenthal and Neufeld, 1988; Peterson and Mori, 1988; Jay, 1988; Varni, Walco, and Wilcox, 1990). Much of the work has derived from behavioral and cognitive-behavioral perspectives (Kendall and Braswell, 1986; Peterson and Harbeck, 1990). Most current interventions consist of several procedures derived from this perspective.

The work of Jay and her colleagues on reducing the stress of children undergoing bone marrow aspirations is a good example of such efforts (e.g., Jay et al., 1985, 1987a). Bone marrow aspirations (BMA) need to be routinely conducted for children with leukemia in order to examine the marrow for evidence of cancer cells. A large needle is inserted into the child's hip bone and the marrow is suctioned out. This is a very painful procedure. An injection of Lidocaine is given to anesthetize the skin surface and bone, but it does not lessen the excruciating pain that is experienced with the suctioning of the marrow. The use of general anesthesia is avoided due to medical risks and expense. Intramuscular injections of sedatives are relatively unpopular as well, since they are painful and there is concern regarding substantial side effects.

The intervention package developed by Jay and her colleagues consists of five major components: filmed modeling, positive incentive, breathing exercises, emotive imagery/distraction, and behavioral rehearsal. The intervention package is administered on the day of the scheduled BMA, about 30 to 45 minutes prior to the procedure.

In the first step children are shown an 11-minute film of a same age model. While undergoing the BMA, the model, on a voice overlay, narrates the steps involved in the procedure as well as his or her thoughts and feelings at crucial points. The model also exhibits positive coping behaviors and self-statements. The film is based on a coping rather than mastery model. The child in the film exhibits a realistic amount of anxiety, but copes with it rather than having exhibited no anxiety and distress at all.

Next, the children are taught simple breathing exercises. These are intended as active attention distractors, but may also promote some relaxation.

The children are then taught imagery/distraction techniques. Emotive imagery (Lazarus and Abramavitz, 1962) is a technique in which images are used to inhibit anxiety. A child's hero images are ascertained in a discussion with the child. They are then woven into a story that elicits positive affect that is presumed to be incompatible with anxiety, that transforms the meaning of the pain, and encourages mastery rather than avoidance of pain. One girl's emotive imagery resembled the following story.

She pretended that Wonderwoman had come to her house and asked her to be the newest member of her Superpower Team. Wonderwoman had given her special powers. These special powers made her very strong and tough so that she could stand almost anything. Wonderwoman asked her to take some tests to try out these superpowers. The tests were called bone marrow aspirations and spinal taps. These tests hurt, but with her new superpowers, she could take deep breaths and lie very still. Wonderwoman was very proud when she found out that her superpowers worked, and she made the Superpower team. (Jay et al., 1985, p. 516)

Another imagery distraction technique involves teaching the child to form a pleasant image that is incompatible with the experience of pain (e.g., a day at the beach). The child chooses either the emotive or incompatible strategy and is given guidance during the bone marrow procedure to help in forming the images.

Positive incentive consists of a trophy presented as a symbol of mastery and courage. The child is told she can win the trophy if she does "the best that she can possibly do." The situation is structured so that every child can be successful in getting the trophy.

During the behavioral rehearsal phase younger children "play doctor" with a doll, while older children are guided in conducting a "demonstration." The children are instructed step by step in the administration of the BMA. As the child goes through the procedure the doll is instructed to lie still and do the breathing exercises and imagery.

Jay et al. (1987a) compared this cognitive behavioral package to a low-risk pharmacological intervention (oral Valium) and a minimal treatment-attention control condition. Each child experienced each of these interventions during three different BMAs. Which of the six possible orders of these interventions a child received was randomly determined. When in the cognitive-behavioral intervention condition, children had significantly lower behavioral distress (evaluated using trained observers employing the observational system described in Table 14–6), lower pain ratings, and lower pulse rates than when they were in the control condition. When children were in the Valium condition they showed no significant differences from the control condition ex-

cept that they had lower blood pressure scores. The findings of this study represent one example of a promising early step in developing interventions that will help children and families cope with the distress associated with certain medical procedures. Such interventions hold the promise of making delivery of effective medical treatment more likely.

Hospitalization. Children suffering from chronic illnesses often require periodic hospitalization to stabilize their functioning. Normal children, too, often need to enter the hospital for minor surgery, such as tonsillectomy. In the mid-1950s the importance of the child's psychological reaction to early hospitalization and surgery began to be recognized. Researchers noted that a majority of children experienced mild to extreme stress reactions during and following hospitalization and that many demonstrated behavioral problems following surgery (e.g., Prugh et al., 1953). Vernon et al., (1966) described five potential negative consequences of hospitalization: general anxiety and regression, separation anxiety, sleep-related anxiety, eating disturbances, and aggression. A particularly impactful finding was Douglas's (1975) examination of the long-term effects of early hospitalization. Follow-ups were conducted on a sample consisting of one out of every four children born in Great Britain during a particular week. Approximately 20 percent of the children who were later hospitalized before the age of five seemed to experience some immediate adverse effect. Adolescent conduct disorders and reading difficulties seemed to occur more frequently among some small proportion of those children who had experienced early hospitalization. Early research seemed to indicate that at least some aspects of hospitalization could be damaging to children.

Improvements certainly have occurred since the 1950s and 1960s when much of this research was conducted. For example, in 1954 most New York hospitals allowed parental contact only during 2 visiting hours per week. By 1974, 83 percent of children's

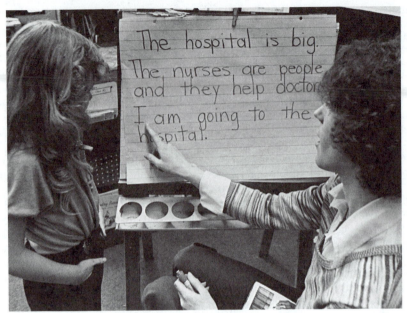

Preparation of children for hospitalization and the procedures they will undergo not only help reduce the children's distress, but also help in delivering effective treatment. (Teri Stratford/Photo Researchers)

hospitals allowed parents to be with children 24 hours a day (Hardgrove 1980).

The majority of pediatric hospitals now also offer prehospital preparation for both the child and parents (Peterson and Ridley-Johnson, 1980). The issue is now not whether to prepare children for hospitalization, but how best to do it. While most facilities offer some form of preparation, procedures used are not always those best supported by research (Peterson and Mori, 1988). One well-supported method of preparation involves the use of models who, although apprehensive, cope with the hospitalization stresses. Melamed and Siegel's (1975) film *Ethan Has an Operation* showed a seven-year-old boy prior to, during, and

after surgery. It has been shown to be an effective prevention vehicle (e.g., Melamed and Siegel, 1980; Peterson et al., 1984). This is but one example of the use of modeling. Other films and the use of puppets have been shown to be effective as well (e.g., Peterson et al., 1984). Current efforts are directed at preparation procedures that are cost-effective and, therefore, likely to be used. Attention is also being given to developing procedures that are matched to such individual characteristics as developmental level, the child's existing coping dispositions, and previous medical experience. Additional attention to parental and family roles is also evident (Peterson and Mori, 1988; Peterson et al., 1990).

THE DYING CHILD

Clearly, one of the most distressing aspects of working with severely ill children is the prospect of death. Several important questions are raised. What is the child's understanding of death? How can we best prepare

the child and the family? How do we prepare people for death while sustaining their motivation for treatment? Can we help the family begin to accept the child's impending death but yet prevent it from premature distancing from the child? What do we do after the child dies? How is the helper affected by working with the dying child? These are difficult questions.

It does appear that children's conceptions of death are influenced by their parents' views and change during development (e.g., Candy-Gibbs, Sharp, and Petrun, 1985). Young children may think of death simply as being less alive and assume it to be reversible. At about 5 years of age, an appreciation of the finality of death may be present, but death still does not seem inevitable. An understanding of death as final and inevitable and of personal mortality emerges at about age 9 or 10. Cognitive development plays a role in the evolving conceptualization of death (Ferrari, 1990). Koocher (1973), employing a Piagetian framework, evaluated 75 healthy children ranging in age from 6 to 15 years to determine their primary level of cognitive functioning. In addition, they were asked four questions: "What makes things die? How can you make dead things come back to life? When will you die? What will happen then?" The children's understanding became more realistic and reflected higher levels of cognitive organization as their levels of cognitive functioning progressed from preoperational, to concrete-operational, to formal operational. Fatally ill children's concepts of death do not appear to be more advanced than physically well children's (Jay et al., 1987b).

While developmental differences in cognitive understanding exist, it must also be appreciated that children may be aware of death and worried about their fatal illness even if they do not have a fully developed concept of death.

What of family members? Certainly, they too must be made aware of the seriousness of the child's illness. However, an appropriate balance between acceptance of death and hope for life is probably adaptive. It is a genuine challenge to prepare the parents for the death of the child yet enable them to help their child emotionally and assist with the treatment regimen. It requires mental health staff who are knowledgeable

and sensitive. As our ability to lengthen survival—and perhaps raise hopes of some future cure—increases, the problem will become even more difficult. Integration of support services into the total treatment program and immediate availability and access are important in delivering needed help. Moreover, the family should not be abandoned after the child's death (Rando, 1983). Provisions for continued assistance and support should be conceptualized as part of the total treatment.

Caregivers, too, are not immune to the effects of seeing a child dying. Koocher (1980) suggests that efforts must be made to reduce the high cost of helping: the inevitable stress and feelings of helplessness and the likelihood of burnout. These are not trivial matters. The helpers' adjustment and efficiency are not the only concern. The potential impact of their behavior on the family and child is also significant. In "Who's Afraid of Death on a Leukemia Ward?" Vernick and Karon (1965) offer poignant anecdotes to this effect. One describes the impact of a helper's behavior on a nine-year-old patient who, after taking a turn for the worse, received some medical treatment and began to show improvement.

One day while she was having breakfast I commented that she seemed to have gotten her old appetite back. She smiled and agreed. . . . I mentioned that it looked as if she had been through the worse of this particular siege. She nodded in agreement. I went on to say that it must have been very discouraging to feel so sick that all she could do was worry—worry about dying. She nodded affirmatively. I recognized that the whole episode must have been very frightening and that I knew it was a load off her mind to be feeling better. She let out a loud, "Whew," and went on to say that except for me, nobody really talked with her. "It was like they were getting ready for me to die." (p. 395)

Certainly, one of the most difficult decisions is what to tell the dying child. A "protective" approach or "benign lying" was once advocated. The child was not to be burdened, and a sense of normalcy and optimism was to be maintained. Many workers now feel that this approach is not helpful and probably is doomed to failure anyway. The stress on the family of maintaining this deception is great, and the likelihood that the child will believe the deception is questionable. Some balance must be struck that takes into consideration the child's developmental level, past experiences, timing, and an understanding of the family's belief system (Dolgin and Jay, 1989a). An example of such a balance is illustrated in the following excerpt:

A child with a life-threatening illness should be told the name of the condition, given an accurate explanation of the nature of the illness (up to the limit of his ability to comprehend), and told that it is a serious illness of which people some-times die. At the same time, however, the child and family can be told about treatment options and enlisted as allies to fight the disease. An atmosphere must be established in which all concerned have the opportunity to ask questions, relate fantasies, and express concerns, no matter how scary or far fetched they may seem.

When the patient is feeling sick, weak, and dying, there is no need to [be reminded] of the prognosis. If a family and patient know a prognosis is poor but persist in clinging to hope, one has no right to wrest that from them. The truth, humanely tempered, is important, but we must be mindful of the patient and how [the patient's] needs are served. To tell the "whole truth" or a "white lie" for the benefit of the teller serves no one in the end. (Koocher and Sallan, 1978, p. 300)

SUMMARY

Determining the role of psychological factors in physical disorders is part of a long tradition of trying to understand the relationship between mind and body. The current view that psychological factors are relevant to physical disorders in a number of different ways is a shift from the earlier (psychosomatic) view that physical diseases are caused by emotional factors.

Current conceptualizations of the role of psychological factors in asthma illustrate many of the changes that have occurred regarding causation. For example, a distinction is made between the causes of the asthmatic disorder and the mechanisms that trigger an asthmatic attack. Psychological influences are one of a variety of possible trigger mechanisms that can bring on an asthmatic episode. There is, however, little support for the idea that psychological factors play a role in causing reduced respiratory capacity. For asthma, as well as for other disorders, there has been a shift from exploring the role of emotional factors in the genesis of the physical condition to examining the multiple ways that psychological factors affect children with the condition.

The appreciable social and emotional consequences of chronic illness have received increasing attention. For juvenile di-abetes (and other chronic illnesses) considerable individual variability in how children and families cope is likely. The first task for the professional is to achieve and maintain control of the diabetic condition. Child and family acceptance of the disorder and attitude toward its control are crucial in successful treatment. Shifting of responsibility from the professional to the family, and ultimately to the child, is required if control of the condition is to be maintained. The impact of the disease on the child's overall development and the family's functioning is likely to be substantial, and this needs to be incorporated into any comprehensive treatment program.

Psychology can contribute to effective treatment of medical conditions in a number of ways. Medical treatment is often rendered ineffective due to failure of the patient and family to adhere to the prescribed treatment regimens. Researchers have demonstrated how behavioral interventions can increase adherence.

Psychological treatments (for example, relaxation and biofeedback) may be able to modify physical functioning directly. Initial successes with disorders such as migraine headache suggest a cautious optimism regarding their potential.

Psychology may also facilitate the delivery

of medical interventions. By reducing the anxiety felt by children undergoing medical procedures, not only do psychologists make the child more comfortable, but they also make the task of medical personnel easier.

The prospect of death is one of the most distressing aspects of working with physically ill children. A psychological approach that considers the child's conception of death and the child's and family's mechanisms of coping can aid effective and caring treatment. Facilitation of coping in professionals working with these children is important in enhancing treatment and in the well-being of the professionals themselves.

15

EVOLVING CONCERNS FOR THE CHILD

Every society depends on its children for its future. Nevertheless, the welfare of the young fluctuates with social, political, and economic conditions. From the earliest days of its existence, the United States has shown concern for its children (Kopp and Kaler, 1989), and solicitude is apparent today. However, actual practice and policy do not consistently reflect this concern. Although much is being done for children, much more needs to be done.

Some of today's concerns for children go back to the immediate past, to the 1960s and 1970s, when emphasis was placed on the care and rights of groups of individuals deemed disadvantaged and powerless in society. But in addition, the more recent years have seen sociopolitical change that has brought new concerns. Children's lives are shaped by a broad spectrum of influences and are impacted by what is happening in the personal lives of their parents, the value assigned to the young, the priorities given to health care and education, the economics of their nations, and a host of other factors. Sensitive and caring adults are looking at these influences with an eye toward better care for the young.

Progress in understanding the development of children has also stimulated efforts toward optimizing the potential of the young. Although no one would deny that knowledge about development is incomplete, we have come far from simply viewing children as little adults. Their unique needs are better known; the general course of physical, intellectual, and social growth is well on the way to being mapped; and developmental influences, including risk factors, are increasingly understood. Child specialists and others are enthusiastic about using this knowledge to enhance children's development and lives.

In this final chapter we turn to some of the evolving concerns for children and the ways in which they are manifested in programs and policies. Due to the enormous number of possibilities, it is necessary to limit discussion. One topic we will consider is prevention and early treatment of childhood difficulties. Discussion begins with a framework for conceptualizing prevention and early treatment, and specific risk areas are highlighted: low birth weight, socioeconomic disadvantage, and school maladjustment. The critical role of the family is apparent early in the chapter, and becomes central as we examine how the family is changing and the stresses brought by this transition. In the last section of the chapter, we look at additional current and future challenges to children's welfare.

IMPORTANCE OF PREVENTION AND EARLY INTERVENTION

There is considerable interest today in the prevention of maladaptive or disordered behavior. Few would dispute the proposition that, at least in the abstract, prevention is superior to treating conditions that already exist. From a humanitarian point of view, prevention clearly is more desirable. Practical considerations also argue for prevention. Treatment can scarely keep up with demands. And treatment often is costly and largely unavailable or ineffective with diverse groups of needy people. Moreover, it is difficult to undo certain kinds of damage once they set in.

Much current thinking about prevention has evolved from Caplan's work *Principles of Preventive Psychiatry* (1964). This public health approach seeks to reduce the prevalence of mental problems in the population by prevention rather than treatment. Caplan suggested a three-prong attack consisting of primary, secondary, and tertiary prevention.

Primary prevention attempts to stave off disorders in the first place. It can be accomplished by provision of the physical, psychosocial, and cultural resources considered necessary for healthy development, and by special support during developmental and accidental crises. *Secondary prevention* is usually defined as the effort to shorten the duration of existing cases through early referral, diagnosis, and treatment. It frequently focuses on populations at high risk for a disorder, and is a "nipping in the bud" strategy. *Tertiary prevention* aims to reduce problems that are residual to disorders. Thus, it might seek to minimize the negative impact of a learning disabled child's being labeled in school. Although tertiary efforts certainly may reduce the prevalence of problems, primary and secondary programs are what come to mind when the term prevention is used. Of these two, secondary

prevention that intervenes with high-risk populations is the more common.

Some behavioral conditions are preventable in large measure; they often involve a known etiological agent. The American Public Health Association noted six categories of disorders it considered preventable: those caused by poisoning, infectious agents, genetic processes, nutritional deficits, injuries, and systemic abnormalities (Bloom, 1981). Most of these disorders result from chronic brain syndromes. It is also possible, however, to prevent disorders in the absence of known etiology. The general model calls for the study of people identified as showing the disorder so that hypotheses can be constructed about its path of development. Interventions to disrupt the path can then be mounted and evaluated. This approach shows associations between behavioral disorders and (1) psychologically damaging infant and childhood experiences, (2) poverty and degrading experiences, (3) powerlessness and low self-esteem, and (4) loneliness, social isolation, and social marginality (Albee, 1986). Thus, there is a base for preventive efforts when etiology is undetermined, although it is a very general one.

Prevention programs for the young vary tremendously in focus and setting (e.g., Levine and Perkins, 1987). They include genetic screening that aims to decrease the number of infants born with hereditary disorders. Infant high-risk interventions help overcome the adverse affects associated with infant low birth weight and with motherhood in single, disadvantaged adolescents. Early screening of general intelligence, reading deficits, attention deficits, school maladjustment, and other problems is seen as crucial for an array of secondary prevention programs. Still another approach is the alleviation of stress and potential crisis, such as when the child enters school or experiences parental divorce. Efforts are also made to develop child competence on the assumption that competence goes hand in hand with good decision making, social support, and coping with stress. Other programs aim at fostering positive lifestyles, such as developing an unfavorable attitute toward drug abuse.

Let us take a look at a few of these efforts, sampling their great diversity as well as focusing on areas that are of great concern.

The Mother-Infant Transaction Program

The short-term purpose of the Mother-Infant Transaction Program (MITP) was to assist mothers in adjusting to the birth and care of their low birth weight infants (Rauh et al., 1988). The long-term goal was to enhance the infants' development. The MITP is one of many such interventions, which have an interesting history.

Six to seven percent of all births in the United States are of low birth weight (Kopp and Kaler, 1989). The association of low birth weight with a variety of adverse outcomes was reported many years ago, but it took several years of research to clearly demonstrate that infant outcome depends in part on the care that infants receive. Except for cases of extreme physical damage, adverse effects can be overcome by a high quality of care, which appears related to parents' attitudes and skills, family resources, and social support (e.g., Werner and Smith, 1982; Greenberg and Crnic, 1988). The transactional model of development has frequently been used to explain this finding. Complex, ongoing interactions among the child, parents, and larger social environment produce different developmental paths which differentially affect infant growth. Thus, although low birth weight babies now receive extraordinary medical intervention immediately after birth, interest still exists in enhancing parental care.

A fundamental assumption of the Mother-Infant Transactional Program was that confident, knowledgeable, and effective parenting would reduce the probability of infant developmental problems. Each mother worked with a supportive, specially trained nurse for three months, during which time she was guided toward (1) appreciating her infant's unique characteristics, (2) recognizing the infant's signals, particularly those of distress and readiness for interaction, and (3) appropriately responding to the signals to facilitate mutually satisfying interactions. Such training was expected to improve maternal adaptation.

The infants weighed below 2,250 grams at birth, their gestational age was under 37 weeks, and they had been in the hospital's intensive care nursery for at least ten days. They were randomly assigned to the intervention or a no-treatment control condition. A group of normal weight, full-term infants served as a second control. Intervention occurred over 11 sessions, the first 7 of which took place in the hospital prior to the infants' going home. Mothers, infants, the nurse, and fathers when possible spent an

FIGURE 15–1 Developmental test scores at different ages for the MITP infants, the low birthweight controls, and full-term controls. From Rauh et al., 1988.

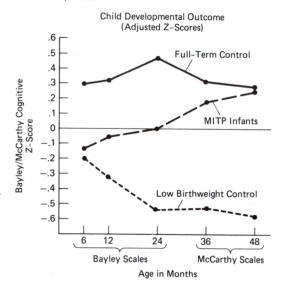

Child Developmental Outcome
(Adjusted Z-Scores)

hour together in each session. Techniques included direct instruction, demonstration, modeling, and practical experience in handling the infant. The nurse encouraged parental feelings of comfort and confidence. Sessions 8 through 11, which were conducted in the home during the next three months, focused on encouragement, building interaction skills, and recognition of the infant's changing behavior.

Both mother and infant measures were taken in this program. It was demonstrated that for the most part mothers in the intervention group expressed more self-confidence and satisfaction with the mothering role, and perceived their infants as less difficult temperamentally. Infant develop-

mental status was measured at 6, 12, 24, 36, and 48 months. As Figure 15–1 shows, treated infants became progressively different from the low birthweight control and more similar to the full-term control infants.

The investigators believe that the enhanced cognitive growth of the MITP infants is sufficiently large to make a difference in school, although this awaits further study. The success of the program is consistent with other studies that show environmental impact on low birth weight babies (e.g., Barrera, Rosenbaum, and Cunningham, 1986). Clearly this is an area in which preventive efforts are feasible and worthwhile.

Head Start and Preschool Intervention

The War on Poverty was formally initiated in 1964 by the Economic Opportunity Act. Head Start was earmarked by this legislation and began in the summer of 1965. A central assumption was that poor youngsters are at risk for low academic achievement which, in turn, works against their attaining decent jobs and healthy, fulfilling lives. It was also assumed that early experience is especially important for later growth and that intervention during the preschool years would put the children on the road to achievement. From the beginning, Head Start was conceptualized as a comprehensive developmental program with four major components (U.S. Department of Health and Human Services, 1980).

1. *Education.* The educational component places children into classes that have a high teacher-student ratio and that try to meet each child's needs. The ethnic and cultural characteristics of the community are considered in structuring the educational experience. For example, when a majority of the children are bilingual, there is a mandate for some of the staff to speak the native language.

2. *Health.* Physical and mental health are emphasized. Meals are served that meet at least one-third of daily minimal nutritional needs of the students. Parents are offered educa-

tion in nutrition. Medical examinations including hearing, vision, and dental checkups are conducted; follow-up medical treatment is provided when appropriate. A mental health professional is available to evaluate special needs and to provide training in child development for staff and parents.

3. *Parent Involvement.* Community involvement is fundamental to Head Start. Parents participate in decision making about planning and managing the program, and about the day-to-day operation of activities. Many serve as volunteers or employees. They also particiapte in workshops on various topics related to the welfare of their children or the family.

4. *Social Services.* Head Start families often have needs for other services; it is the task of the Head Start social service coordinator to help obtain these services. The object is to strengthen the family unit so that it may do the best job possible in rearing children and supporting its adult members.

In addition to the typical program just described, Head Start has had several special projects designed to evaluate new ways of helping children and families. For example, *Home Start* focused on training mothers in their homes. It was based on the premises that the mother-child relationship should not be disrupted by removing the child from the home, and that maternal training would generalize to all children in the home (e.g., Bronfenbrenner, 1974; Levenstein, 1974). However, the out-of-home intervention has remained the cornerstone of Head Start and it has served thousands of children. Evaluations of the program have been extensive and have played a role in Head Start's being continuously funded by the federal government.

Head Start barely got off the ground when it was concluded that it did not result in intellectual advancement for preschoolers (e.g., Jensen, 1969; Cronbach, 1975). However, not all agreed with this assessment (e.g., Bereiter, 1972; Palmer and Semlear, 1977; Zigler and Trickett, 1978). The test of time favors the conclusion that Head Start can be beneficial. The evidence comes from two sources. First, based on data from actual Head Start programs, it appeared that Head Start children improved in cognition, school readiness, and school achievement, and that these improvements could be observed three years afterward (Harrell, 1983). Gains also were made with regard to socioemotional growth and health status (Woodhead, 1988). As important as these conclusions are, methodolgical weaknesses of the studies are recognized.

The second source of evidence is evaluations of 11 independent well-planned and well-researched preschool interventions for the disadvantaged (Lazar et al., 1982; Haskins, 1989; Woodhead, 1988; U.S. Department of Health and Human Services, 1979). These were published between 1977 and 1983 by the Consortium of Longitudinal Studies. Additional data about some of the projects also are available. Taken as a whole, the evaluations show that preschool participants did better academically as they proceeded through school than control children. They were less likely to have been retained at grade level and less likely to have been assigned to special education classes. Fifteen percent more completed high school. In addition, one of the programs, the Perry Pre-School Project, found benefits even later in life. Participants were more successful in obtaining jobs and rates of juvenile delinquency and teenage pregnancy were lower. Whereas care must be taken not to overstate benefits based on this exceptionally good program, there is general consensus that preschool interventions can be helpful. For this reason and because it is believed that Head Start supports families in a variety of ways, it is likely to continue to be funded.

To the extent that educational benefits accrue, the intriguing question is, Why? There is a little evidence that any permanent change in tested intellectual functioning accounts for the most firmly established finding, which is that participants make their way through the school system more successfully (Woodhead, 1988). Initial gains in tested intelligence are not maintained. Rather, benefits appear to occur by indirect paths. First, upon entering the public schools, the children were more able to do the work, had more positive attitudes, and adapted more easily to school. There is evidence that teachers viewed them as competent and treated them as such. Positive attitudes and motivation for school were thus reinforced, and this chain of success continued. Second, indirect effects likely operated through the home. Head Start parents have overwhelmingly reported the program a success (e.g., Zigler, 1978). Among other things, they have noted improved understanding of children, increased opportunity for education and employment, increased aspirations, and increased commitment to the community. In the words of two mothers:

. . . Parents are invited to be in the classroom as volunteers. I feel this is good for us because a lot of times we can see a more positive way to handle our children . . .

. . . The best has come out of the changes in myself. I started out as "just a depressed housewife," but my experience made me feel that I was not stupid and my confidence began to grow. For me, the most important change is in the way I can work with the system—the public schools, hospitals, and other agencies. (O'Keefe, 1979, pp. 22, 24)

In examining the process of the long-term effectiveness of Head Start, Woodhead

A critical component of Head Start is preschool experience that offers multiple activities and a high teacher-child ratio. (Elizabeth Crews/Stock, Boston)

(1988) suggests that it is like a relay race: The burst of cognitive and school readiness fades, but not before the baton has been given to other runners on the team—teacher expectations, self-confidence, school promotions, avoidance of special education, parental aspirations, and so forth. In fact, the process may be more complex; for example, parental effects may operate as early as the decision to enroll the child in Head Start. No matter what the specific factors, though, it is clear that the intervention operates in a broad social context that helps write the script for success or failure.

The Rochester Primary Mental Health Project

The Rochester Primary Mental Health Project (PMHP), initiated in 1957 by Cowen, Zax, and their colleagues, took the school as its focus for preventive efforts (Cowen et al., 1975; Zax and Cowen, 1967). The school was selected not only because it is the setting for much socialization and learning but also because children were experiencing school maladjustment. Teachers were complaining that several children demanded excessive amounts of time and energy. These students were not being well served, the rest of the class was being disrupted, and teacher morale was suffering. Mental health services for these children were either unavailable or it had been assumed that the troubles would disappear with time. They had not (e.g., Cowen et al., 1966).

Although PMHP has evolved over the years, its continuing thrust has been systematic early identification and prompt preventive intervention for school maladjustment. The program's focus is secondary intervention; the term "primary" in the title refers to the primary grades. What follows is a brief description of the principal aspects of the program. More extensive descriptions are available elsewhere (e.g., Cowen and Hightower, 1989a).

One of the innovative aspects of PMHP is mass screening of youngsters soon after they begin first grade. Screening methods have consisted of parental interviews, psychological testing, teacher reports, and direct observations. Diverse kinds of data are collected concerning developmental and health history, school behavior problems and competencies, and factors in the children's life situations that may relate to school adjustment.

Children identified by PMHP as already manifesting maladjustment, or as likely to do so in the future, become the recipients of special treatment by nonprofessional child-aides. Conversation, books, games, and media provide a framework for interaction with the child. The child is encouraged to access problem areas and feelings, and enhancement of self-esteem is considered important. Specific activities depend on the needs of the individual child. Aides are supervised by school mental health professionals, and they exchange information with the teachers. The utilization of minimally paid nonprofessionals as "therapists" is a noteworthy dimension of PMHP. Many of the child-aides are mothers with relatively modest formal education. They receive some training at the project, but personal qualities are considered a potent treatment resource. Although the use of nonprofessional child-aides was initially justified on the basis of professional shortages and financial austerity, the child-aides are now seen as an asset to the program rather than a compromise (Cowen and Hightower, 1989b).

The general model of PMHP has thus been characterized by (1) its focus on young children; (2) use of active, systematic screening for early school maladjustment; (3) expansion of services through the use of nonprofessional aides; and (4) the use of professionals in activities such as training, supervision, consultation, and research/program evaluation. The program has been flexibly applied to meet the demands of particular situations.

Research has been an essential component of PMHP; from the start it was designed to improve the program and to demonstrate possible benefit. Research has been conducted, for example, on assessment instruments to initially screen children and to evaluate their progress (e.g., Gesten, 1976; Hightower et al., 1987). Evaluation of the program's effectiveness has been extensive. Examination of several hundred children who participated in PMHP at some time during 1974–1981 indicated reductions in acting out, shyness, and learning problems, as well as gains in sociability, assertiveness, and tolerance of frustration (Weissberg et al., 1983). However, the raters knew that the children were PMHP participants, and the study had no control group.

While constraints of doing research in schools has often limited the rigor of the studies, the large number of program evaluations over the years suggests that PMHP has been effective. And importantly, research findings have been fed back into the program to structure improvements (Cowen and Hightower, 1989b). For example, some data indicated that those most helped were the shy-anxious children, and greater efforts then were made to facilitate the aides' effectiveness with acting out and learning-disabled students (Cowen, Gesten, and Wilson, 1979; Lorion, Cowen, and Caldwell, 1974).

PMHP began as a single demonstration project and by 1983 twenty PMHP projects were operating in the Rochester, New York, area. Since 1982 four states (New York, California, Washington, and Connecticut) have been actively and continuously involved in the program. They have established programs in more than 300 schools in 182 school districts (Cowen et al., 1989). The program has also been adopted elsewhere and the project staff estimates that there are 350 implementing school districts around the world (Cowen and Hightower, 1989b).

Issues In Prevention

Although the benefits of prevention seem indisputable, preventive efforts have been resisted and criticized on a number of grounds. Society's commitment to treatment rather than prevention has a long history and remains strong. Professionals are trained for treatment (Goldston, 1986), and are financially rewarded for treatment. Since adequate resources are lacking to meet the needs of those already displaying problems, there is a reluctance to divert funds into prevention (Bloom, 1981). Serious questions have also been raised about ethical issues in prevention and about effectiveness. Let us look at these two issues in more detail.

Ethics. Ethical questions easily come to the fore when human behavior is examined or modified (e.g., Bond, 1989). They become especially compelling when large segments of the population are involved—which is precisely the stated intent of the preventive ideology (Seidman, 1987). Among the major concerns is the relationship of the professional and the client population, and the question of who is to have the power to select goals. To illustrate, we return to the topic of preschool intervention for socially disadvantaged children.

The goals of Head Start and related programs seem simple enough: to provide educational input, health services, and community support to disadvantaged families. But initially these programs were often based on the *deficit model*, which suggested that poor (frequently black) children were disadvantaged by inferior genetic endowment, subculture, or both (Ginsburg, 1972; Rappaport, 1977). According to this model, intervention required an injection of middle-class culture, the earlier the better. This raises the fundamental question about differential value being placed on the behaviors of one social class or ethnic group over the behaviors of others.

In fact, another model, the *difference model*, argues that poor children are not deficient: They learn, think, and operate successfully in their home environments. Professionals who endorse the difference model insist that programs must build on what children already possess and that programs recognize the richness of the environments of the poor and culturally differ-ent. The difference model may suggest, for example, the valuing and use of nonstandard language, with middle-class language and customs gradually being presented as a necessary alternative. Only in this way, it is argued, can the young develop with self-respect and motivation. This controversy, often heard in the earlier days of Head Start, is akin to concerns about "top-down" approaches in which the "experts" fail to acknowledge the unique strengths and diversities of the communities they seek to help (Gesten and Jason, 1987). In so doing, they fail to enhance people's sense of control and to understand what approach might be most effective. Some of the pitfalls of the "top-down" approach may have been avoided in Head Start by placing some control in the hands of the community. In addition, the input of professionals whose cultural backgrounds are other than "mainstream" has increasingly helped avoid the deficit model (Rogoff and Morelli, 1989).

Efficacy. Concerns about the effectiveness of secondary prevention probably are lessening as the knowledge base for prevention grows and as evaluations of programs show the efficacy of some. However, doubt and controversy about primary prevention are considerable (e.g., Marlowe and Weinberg, 1985). It has been difficult to conceptualize how to prevent psychological disorder in those who show no disturbance at all. The issue was addressed by Lamb and Zusman (1981), who claimed that in only a few areas is primary prevention reasonable. These include genetic counseling, prenatal care, and control of environmental toxins. However, since the etiology of most behavioral disorders is elusive and multidetermined, guidelines for primary prevention are lacking. Lamb and Zusman argued, as others still do, that prevention be limited to "diagnosable mental illness." They rejected the idea that prevention can reasonably deal with everyday problems in living, improve the quality of life for everyone, or eliminate basic social problems such as poverty.

Opposing viewpoints have been set forth by writers such as Cowen and Albee, who support broad preventive programs. Cowen (1980) accepts the goal of "psychological adjustment, effectiveness, happiness, and coping skills of large numbers of individuals" (p. 264). He views primary prevention as intentional mental health building or harm avoiding that can be attained through education, modification of social systems, competence training, stress reduction, enhancement of coping, and support networks. Albee (1982) adamantly argues that reduction of emotional stress and of problems such as shyness and reading deficits, whether one calls them "mental illness" or "problems in living," are a legitimate focus of prevention. For Albee (1986), the causal connection between emotional disturbance and poverty, sexism, and racism is clear. He thus argues for broad social change and competence building, noting that his position is threatening to those who hold that certain groups (e.g., blacks, women, southern Europeans) are defective due to organic factors.

Many of the issues surrounding prevention make clear the close connection between children's welfare and broad social, political issues. We shall see more of this relationship as we proceed.

FAMILIES IN TRANSITION

The importance of family influences on children's development has been evident throughout this book. Families will no doubt be an issue of continuing interest and concern. In this section we will highlight three family topics that are not necessarily linked to any particular childhood disorder. Rather, they illustrate how contemporary change in the family is a part of evolving concerns for the child.

The current state of the family and its future is a common topic in the media and of conversations at social events, over the dinner table, in shopping malls, and, indeed, wherever people meet. It is also a politically salient issue (e.g., Bennett, 1987; Schroeder, 1989). While it is often assumed that the issue is the decline of the traditional family, it need not, and indeed should not, be articulated in this way. Scholars who have studied the history of the American family have argued that we are suffering from the "mystique of the traditional family." Bahr (1988), for example, challenges the idea that the family has decayed from some past idyllic form: well-ordered, agreeably run, psychologically supportive of its members, and superior to today's families. Undoubtedly stable, warm, and supportive families with "traditional" structures did, and do, exist. But they have probably been atypical in all times and places. In fact, Bahr suggests that the family is as strong as ever, and that perhaps our notions of family are more varied and adaptable than before.

Several influences have caused us to rethink our definitions of family. Among these are recognition of the increasing number of children raised in single-parent homes and the new family relationships created by remarriages (Bureau of the Census, 1985; Hetherington, 1989; Schroeder, 1989). The number of women working outside of the home also is a salient influence on contemporary conceptualizations of family.

Maternal Employment

Social and economic influences have resulted in the majority of mothers being employed outside the home. Among two-parent families with school-aged children the rate of maternal employment is approximately 71 percent (Hoffman, 1989). In their examination of women's changing work roles, Matthews and Rodin (1989) review a number of trends. The increase in maternal employment over time is illustrated in Table 15–1. Although increases occurred for mothers with children of all ages, the increase was most dramatic for mothers of younger children. This can be

TABLE 15–1 Percentage of Women in the Workforce, According to Age of Youngest Child

| Children's Ages | Wives with Husband Present | | | | Women Maintaining Families Alone |
	1970	1975	1980	1986	1986
0–1	24.0	30.8	39.0	49.8	44.7
0–3	25.8	32.6	41.5	51.0	50.9
3–5	36.9	42.2	51.7	58.5	64.5
6–17	49.2	52.4	62.0	68.5	76.8
0–18	39.8	44.9	54.3	61.4	69.5

Matthews and Rodin, 1989. Copyright 1989 by the American Psychological Association.

further illustrated by taking the child as the referent point. Among children under the age of six years, 28.5 percent had mothers in the labor force in 1960. By 1986, however, the figure was 50.4 percent or almost 10 million children. The comparable figures for children 6 to 17 years were 43.2 percent and 62.2 percent (Matthews and Rodin, 1989). In 1970, 24 percent of married mothers with children age one and under were in the labor force compared to 53 percent in 1987 (Hoffman, 1989).

Considerable attention has been given to the impact of maternal employment on the women themselves, marital relations, and of course on the development of their children (Hoffman, 1989; Scarr, Phillips, and McCartney, 1989). For example, concern has been expressed regarding the relationship between maternal employment during the first year of the child's life and the development of a secure mother-infant attachment. The majority of research suggests that full-time employment does not affect attachment (Hoffman, 1989). However, some researchers conclude that although most babies are securely attached to their full-time employed mothers, these women are more likely than part-time employed and nonemployed mothers to have insecurely attached infants (Belsky, 1988). Another body of research that has examined effects of employment on older children suggests benefits to daughters in particular (Hoffman, 1989).

In general, the influences of maternal employment on children are likely to be indirect. That is, the impact depends on parental attitudes, family structure, and other psychological, social, and economic variables that affect family environment and child care arrangements (Gottfried and Gottfried, 1988; Hoffman, 1989; Scarr et al., 1989).

Clearly, increased maternal employment has focused attention on the need for adequate child care and evaluation of the impact of care arrangements on the child (Clarke-Stewart, 1989; Schroeder, 1989; Stipek and McCroskey, 1989). Concern is expressed not only for very young but also for the older so-called "latchkey" children, who must use a key to let themselves into their empty homes after school. Less value-laden terms, such as "children in self-care" have increasingly been advocated to describe this situation. Although an accurate estimate is hard to come by, estimates of the number of children in self-care range from 7.2 percent to 15 to 20 percent of early elementary and 45 percent of late elementary school age children (Peterson and Magrab, 1989).

Attention to self-care arrangements is relatively recent and the developmental implications for children are uncertain (Peterson and Magrab, 1989). Of course, the impact will not be the same for all children. The amount of time in self-care, parental attitudes, the child's developmental level, other family influences, and available social supports are likely to influence an individual child's reaction.

One question regarding self-care focuses

Many children return to empty homes after school. The impact of such "self-care" requires further study.

problems between latchkey and nonlatchkey children. There were, of course, differences in adjustment among the latchkey children. Adjustment was related to both background variables (e.g., age, race, sex, life stress) and situational latchkey variables, such as length of time and hours per week in self-care and whether other children were present when the child was in self-care. Among the latch-key situations, being with other children, in particular, seemed to be associated with greater anxiety.

TABLE 15–2 Guidelines for a Safe Home Environment

A. Safety from Strangers
1. Deadbolt locks on doors, locks on all windows, a window or peephole for a visual check of anyone at the door.
2. Children do not open the door.
3. Children have access to both adult contact (e.g., parent at work or neighbor) and an emergency number (e.g., 911).

B. Safety from Burns
1. Water thermostat set for 125°F.
2. Smoke alarms with active batteries.
3. Matches and chemicals stored safely.
4. No frayed electrical wires.
5. Children know how to treat burns (put in cold water, contact an adult).
6. Children know how to escape fire (crawl to exit checking doors for heat, call fire department from outside of home).

C. Safety from Falls
1. Child gates on stairs with toddlers or infants.
2. Windows locked or with window guards on upper floors.
3. Children do not climb bookcases, kitchen cabinets, or ladders.

D. Safety from Poisons
1. Poisons, cleaners, drugs, and alcohol out of reach of children.
2. Poisonous plants are out of reach of children.
3. Poison control telephone number posted near telephone.

E. Safety from Severe Weather
1. Children in mobile homes should have a designated shelter.
2. At first warning, children should exit to basement or interior room with fewest windows.
3. No one should pause to open windows, etc.

By permission of Lizette Peterson, Ph.D., Department of Psychology, University of Missouri-Columbia.

on its potential impact in the cognitive and academic domain. Does the child miss one-to-one after school interactions with an adult that enhance development of cognitive and social problem solving skills? And does adult monitoring and assisting in homework completion suffer? Perhaps these needs are met later in the evening, amidst completion of household chores (Peterson and Magrab, 1989). There is evidence to suggest that working parents do spend nonwork time in child-centered activities and that this is achieved by less attention to homemaking chores (Scarr et al., 1989).

Much has been written about the possibility that self-care has negative emotional effects on children. There is little empirical, carefully conducted research, however, to support the hypothesis of adjustment difficulties among latchkey children (Lovko and Ullman, 1989). In their own research these authors found no differences in anxiety, self-perceived social ability, or behavior

It may be that self-care, even if not ideal, is an alternative child-care arrangement for some children. Additional research is needed to help guide this decision. When self-care is chosen it is necessary to ensure that the child is adequately prepared. Peterson (1989) suggests that three major areas need to be considered in preparation: injury risk, emotional difficulties, and selection of activities. Preparation has several components, including discussion with the child and arranging for a contact person if the child feels help is needed. It is also essential that the child have a safe and secure environment. Table 15–2 presents some of Peterson's recommendations for environmental safety.

The Impact of Divorce

That many marriages end in divorce is well documented. The divorce rate more than doubled between 1970 and 1981 (Guidubaldi and Perry, 1985). Although this has leveled off and perhaps declined in recent years, large numbers of children will experience parental divorce (Bureau of the Census; 1985; Hernandez, 1988). In 1983 alone 1,179,000 divorces were granted in the United States. In 1984 nearly 23 percent of the children in the United States lived in one-parent families (Bureau of the Census, 1985).

As compelling as they are, these statistics underestimate the actual number of children who have experienced divorce and its impact. Children whose parents have remarried are not considered in these totals. Divorce rates are higher in remarriages than in first marriages. Also periodic separation and discord are experienced by children in families where divorce petitions are filed and withdrawn. Thus divorce and remarriage are not static events, but a series of family transitions that modify the lives of children (Guidubaldi and Perry, 1985; Hetherington, Stanley-Hagan, and Anderson, 1989).

The impact of divorce is probably best conceptualized as a highly stressful life event calling for a variety of competencies and coping strategies on the part of the child and family. Divorce frequently has a negative impact on children. Research studies and literature reviews repeatedly show that in the first few years following divorce children experience more behavior problems than children from intact families (Emery, 1982; Guidubaldi and Perry, 1985; Hetherington and Camara, 1984; Wallerstein and Kelly, 1980). Such findings have emerged from a variety of methodologies, including clinical studies, research studies using samples that were convenient (but nonrepresentative), and large-scale surveys.

One of the most consistent findings is that children frequently react to divorce with aggressive, antisocial, impulsive, and noncompliant behaviors. Several factors appear to affect the expression and intensity of the reactions. Boys appear to suffer greater reactions than girls (Guidubaldi and Perry, 1985; Hetherington, Cox, and Cox, 1982). Age would also appear to affect the expression of the child's reaction. Young children have been reported to demonstrate irritability and tantrums, whereas sexual acting-out has been reported in adolescent females. In fact, reported gender differences may partly be due to the ages of the samples studied in many of the major investigations. The impact of the child's age at the time of divorce can be indirect. Stolberg and Bush (1985) studied 82 mother-child pairs from divorced homes. Externalizing problems in the children were related to two background variables. There was a direct link between a history of marital hostility and the presence of these problems in the child following divorce. The second background variable was the age of the child. Younger children had more externalizing problems but they also reported more life changes. More life changes were in turn related to greater externalizing problems.

Research on the impact of divorce has been very helpful in guiding clinicians, who counsel an increasing number of divorced families. However, the early findings of greater problems for boys and more frequent externalizing problems were based largely on the immediate or short-term impact of divorce. Several major longitudinal studies are now reporting some longer-term findings as well (Guidubaldi and Perry, 1985; Hetherington, 1989; Wallerstein, 1984, 1985; Wallerstein and Blakeslee, 1989).

Long-term results are available from Wallerstein's California Children of Divorce Study. The original project that began in 1971 was designed to explore the divorce experience in a nonclinic population in 60 California families with 131 children between the ages of 2 and 18 at the time of the marital separation (cf. Wallerstein and Kelly, 1980). The primary method of assessment was in-depth clinical interviews with parents and children during and after the divorce. It is important to keep in mind that generalizations based on this work are limited by the restricted sample of middle-class families from Marin County, California. Moreover, despite growing up in a failing marriage, all of the children who were originally included in the study had reached appropriate developmental milestones, were performing at appropriate levels in school, and had never been referred for psychological treatment. As Wallerstein (1985) suggests, these children were "probably skewed in the direction of psychological health."

Wallerstein has reported on two age groups of children. One sample was between 2.5 and 6 years at the time of parental divorce (Wallerstein, 1984). Interviews were conducted with 30 children, by then in their teens, and 40 parents. While this was the age group most affected by the crisis at the time, few memories of the intact family or the marital rupture appeared to remain. These children had spent a great portion of their lives in divorced or remarried households and most were performing well in school. Many did express sorrow at the emotional and economic deprivations they felt they had suffered. They spoke wistfully of the better life they imagined in intact families, and half had fantasies of parental reconciliation. While relationships with the custodial mother reflected closeness and concern for her difficulties, a need to establish relationships with absent fathers was heightened as the children approached adolescence. This seemed to be especially true for girls. Interestingly, the children looked forward to marriage and family and expected to avoid the unhappiness they associated with their parents' divorce.

Wallerstein's other sample of children was 9 years old or older at the time of their parents' separation (Wallerstein, 1985). Ten years later these young men and women ranged in age from 19 to 29. They appeared more adversely affected then the offspring who experienced divorce earlier in life. In contrast to the younger group, a significant number were burdened by memories of marital strife and breakup. Most were committed to a lasting marriage and a conservative morality, but they were concerned about repeating their parents' unhappy marriage. About one-third of the young women seemed to have problems about commitment and seemed caught in a series of short-term sexual relationships. While the majority of these young people were law abiding and either full-time students or self-supporting, a significant number, especially women, seemed to be troubled and drifting. Of particular interest was the finding that 68 percent had engaged in mild to serious illegal activity, including underage alcohol consumption and recreational drug use, and to a lesser extent assault, burglary, arson, drug dealing, theft, and serious traffic violations. The young men were far more likely than the women to have been involved in the more serious violations. The lack of an appropriate comparison group and objective measures, however, suggests caution in interpreting these findings.

Guidubaldi and Perry (1985) have reported on a two-year longitudinal follow-up of the National Association of School Psychologists study. This research, among other strengths, employed a more random and nationwide sample than previous studies. A national sample of school psychologists collected a variety of assessments from randomly selected children from single-parent divorced families and intact families. Of the original sample of 699 children, data were available for 122 two years later. The two samples did not differ on demographic and descriptive characteristics. At the second assessment the average length of time since divorce for the 40 children from divorced families was 6.41 years. Consistent with the original findings, children from divorced families performed more poorly than those from intact families on several measures and boys exhibited more adverse effects than girls. One particularly interesting finding was that SES appeared to account for a substantial amount of the difference between the adjustment of children from divorced and intact families. In this particular sample, at least, the socioeconomic stress produced by the divorce seems to have been a major influence on the child's adjustment. However, this factor does not easily account for the differences between the boys and girls in these divorced families.

Hetherington and her colleagues also have conducted longitudinal research on the impact of divorce (Hetherington, 1989a, b). As in Wallerstein's study, the research relied on a restricted sample. The original sample consisted of 144 well-educated, middle-class, white families, half mother-custody divorced families and the other half nondivorced families (Hetherington et al., 1982). In this research, however, comparison samples were included and multiple methods of assessment (interviews, rating scales, and observations) from multiple sources (parent, child, teachers, peers) and settings (school and home) were employed.

The data reported by Hetherington, Cox, and Cox (1985) were collected six years following the divorce, when the children averaged 10 years of age. In addition to the original families for whom complete information was obtained at follow-up, a new cohort of families was added. This allowed the investigators to expand the size of the three groups they examined to 30 boys and 30 girls. These groups were remarried mother/stepfather families, mother-custody nonremarried families, and nondivorced families. The original sample allowed longitudinal analyses of the impact of divorce and cross-sectional analyses were conducted with the total (expanded) sample.

By examining the correlations between the measures of adjustment during the first two years following divorce (sometimes termed the crisis period) and the six-year follow-up measures, the stability of behavior problems was addressed. Among other findings was that externalizing behavior was more stable for boys and internalizing behavior was more stable for girls. However, the importance of earlier levels of externalizing behavior was clear for both sexes: Early externalizing behavior was significantly correlated with later internalizing behavior for both boys and girls. Hetherington et al. (1985) also found that negative life events since divorce were related to children's behavior at the six-year follow-up. The relationships were greater with externalizing problems for boys and internalizing problems for girls.

By examining the six-year follow-up measures for each of the kinds of families, the long-term outcome of divorce and remarriage was assessed. It would appear, based on this sample and this age group, that divorce has more long-term adverse effects on boys and remarriage is more disruptive for girls. If one examines divorced families in which the mother has not remarried, a difference in the long-term adjustment of girls and boys emerges. Daughters in these families are similar in their adjustment to those from nondivorced families. In contrast, sons are clearly still exhibiting more externalizing problems and based on some measures more internalizing problems and less social competence.

If, however, one looks at families in which remarriage has occurred, the findings are quite different. The length of remarriage appears important as well. In general, when the remarriage had occurred less than two years earlier, both boys and girls exhibited more problems than children from nondivorced families, perhaps because they were adapting to another life transition. In families in which the remarriage had occurred more than two years earlier, daughters but not sons exhibited more problems. These girls do, however, appear to adapt to the remarriage over time.

The long-term results of Hetherington's research indicate that while many children do indeed suffer negative outcomes related to divorce and remarriage, many also do quite well. Indeed, for some, coping with these life transitions can have developmental benefits. Increased understanding of the protective variables and resiliencies of these children can contribute to interventions to reduce or eliminate the potential negative impact of divorce.

Several kinds of interventions seem promising (Stolberg, 1988). Divorce mediation involves bringing together divorcing adults to discuss with an impartial party the resolution of disputes. With respect to children, the intent is to develop cooperative co-parenting and to lay the groundwork for resolving future conflicts. Other prevention programs intervene with single parents. By improving parenting skills and parent-child interactions, they can enhance child adjustment (e.g., Stolberg and Garrison, 1985). School-based intervention programs have the advantage of working with children in a natural setting with similar peers. The Children of Divorce Intervention Project is an example of such a program that has proven successful (cf. Alpert-Gillis, Pedro-Carroll, and Cowen, 1989). Children experiencing separation or divorce meet in groups that provide support, explore feelings, and examine perceptions of divorce.

Child Maltreatment

Increased numbers of child maltreatment cases have been reported to child protective agencies (Wolfe and St. Pierre, 1989). Since the late 1970s the problem has become a major public concern. For example, in 1976 only 10 percent of the population thought abuse was a serious problem compared to over 90 percent in 1983 (Magnuson, 1983). The American Humane Association reported that between 1976 and 1984 the rate of official maltreatment reports rose at the rate of 10 percent each year (AHA, 1984). Such reports raise the question of whether we are "uncovering" a larger proportion of existing cases or whether actual maltreatment is increasing.

Nonetheless, there is agreement that child abuse and neglect are a serious and prevalent problem. What is not as clear is an agreed-upon definition of what constitutes abuse or neglect and therefore what the real prevalence of the problem is. This obviously creates difficulties for research, interventions, and legal practice as well.

When most people hear the widely used term "child abuse," they assume that it refers to physical assault and serious injury. But workers in the field have a broader conceptualization of the problem (e.g., Emory, 1989; Wolfe, 1988). The general legal definition of child abuse that evolved over several decades includes nonaccidental injuries that result from acts of commission (physical assault) and acts of ommission (failure to protect) as well (NIMH, 1977). Thus, neglect is addressed along with physical assault.

A profile of reported maltreatment between 1976 and 1982 indicated that 62 percent of the children experienced "deprivation of necessities," such as inadequate provision of nourishment, clothing, shelter, or supervision (American Humane Association, 1984). An additional 25 percent experienced either major physical injuries (e.g., skull or bone fracture, internal injuries, burns) or minor injuries (e.g., minor cuts, welts, or bruises). Most of the physical abuse involved minor injuries. Thus, two-thirds of the total maltreated population experienced neglect and the majority of physical injuries were minor. As Wolfe and St. Pierre (1989) indicate, this contrasts with the public's image of child maltreatment as mainly involving severe physical injury.

In addition to physical abuse and neglect, two other aspects of child maltreatment have received increasing attention—sexual and psychological abuse. In general, sexual abuse refers to sexual experiences that occur between children and older persons or the sexual exploitation of children (e.g., pornographic photography). The extent of the problem is difficult to estimate. Most experts agree that sexual abuse is underreported. This is suggested by adults' descriptions of their childhood experiences and by a 500 percent increase since 1976 in the reporting of sexual abuse in both the United States and Canada (Miller-Perrin and Wurtele, 1988; Wolfe and Wolfe, 1988).

Psychological maltreatment is probably even more difficult to define and estimate. Hart and Brassard (1987) indicate that attempts to define psychological maltreatment have concentrated on broad categories that encompass verbal and emotional assault; inattention to needs; and interference with the development of self-esteem, interpersonal skills, personal autonomy, and other positive characteristics. They suggest that psychological maltreatment includes acts of rejecting, terrorizing, isolating, exploiting, mis-socializing, degrading, corrupting, and denying emotional responsiveness. It is clear that this covers broad ground. Indeed, one of the controversial issues is the relative advantages of broad or narrow definitions (Hart and Brassard, 1987). But in any event, psychological maltreatment is increasingly seen as an inherent part of all child abuse and neglect (Brassard, Germain, and Hart, 1987; Garbarino and Vondra, 1987).

The study of child abuse and neglect has focused on the factors that cause abusive relationships and the consequences for the child. The majority of research addresses causation of physical abuse (Emery, 1989; Wolfe and St. Pierre, 1989).

The possible causal factors that have been studied can be grouped into three general categories: social-cultural influences (economic hardship, stress, societal tolerance for violence), characteristics of the abusing parents, and parent-child interaction patterns (e.g., ineffective parental discipline for child misbehavior, limited knowledge about child-rearing). It is impossible to even enumerate all of the influences that have been examined. However, contemporary explanations of abuse recognize complex and multiple determinants (Azar and Wolfe, 1989; Belsky, 1980; Cicchetti and Rizley, 1981; Parke and Lewis, 1981; Wolfe, 1985). Further research is needed to better understand how different forms of maltreatment may be influenced by various combinations of factors (Finkelhor, 1986; Rosenberg, 1987; Wolfe and St. Pierre, 1989). Here we highlight only some of the key findings from reviews of the child abuse literature (cf. Emery, 1989; Wolfe, 1988).

A strong relationship has consistently emerged between socioeconomic disadvantage and abuse and neglect. While it is hard to isolate the specific causal factors, reduced resources, stress, and other problems that are associated with socioeconomic disadvantage put the child at increased risk. It has been suggested that neglect, in particular, is related to low SES (Wolock and Horowitz, 1984). However, it is important to recognize that the majority of families who experience chronic deprivation *do not* maltreat their children.

For the most part, parents are the perpetrators of abuse. The age of the child plays a role in abuse: Victims are on the average younger. Two age groups seem at special risk for physical injury, the very young and adolescents. These ages may be associated with periods of particular kinds of parenting difficulties.

The overwhelming majority of abusive parents are not psychiatrically disturbed. Parents who began their families at a younger age, many in their teens, are most typical. However, the average age of the parent at the time of the report is 32. In general, more female than male caregivers are reported as abusers. However, more male caregivers are reported for physical injury and more females for neglect. This finding probably reflects differences in social, cultural, and economic influences on men and women.

Several other characteristics of abusive parents have been noted including social isolation from family and friends, more emotional symptoms and mood changes, more physical health problems, inadequate parenting skills, limited childrearing knowledge, inappropriate expectations regarding children's behavior, lower tolerance for common demands such as infant crying, and misattributions of the child's motivation for misbehaving. None of these characteristics is limited to abusive parents, but all are part of the complex influences that contribute to the development of abusive and neglectful situations.

Finally, in looking at the development of abuse and neglect it is important to address intergenerational patterns of maltreatment. Although parents who were themselves maltreated as children are at greater risk for abusing and neglecting their offspring, the risk is probably not as clear as is widely believed. In a review of the intergenerational abuse literature, Kaufman and Zigler (1987) found that abuse is more common in the backgrounds of abusing parents. However, they also found that many parents who had not been abused became abusive and some who had been abused did not. They estimate that based on all forms of maltreatment approximately 30 percent of maltreated children repeat the cycle as adults. It is generally agreed that the majority of maltreated children do not perpetuate the intergenerational cycle. A number of positive influences, including the development of later supportive relationships, can help break the cycle (Egeland, Jacobvitz, and Sroufe, 1988; Wolfe and St. Pierre, 1989).

We have noted that less attention has been given to the consequences of maltreatment for the child. What is known, however, suggests that there is no single pattern of emotional or behavioral difficulties that characterizes all maltreated children. The outcomes of maltreatment are diverse (Emery, 1989; Wolfe and St. Pierre, 1989). Difficulties include increased aggression, poor peer relationships, insecure attachments, impaired social-cognitive abilities, lack of empathy and social sensitivity, depression, lower IQ scores, speech and language deficiencies, and poor grades and achievement test scores. Given these numerous and diverse outcomes, the impact of abuse probably is best viewed in terms of disruptions in normal developmental processes, such as child-caregiver attachment and other interpersonal relationships (cf. Sroufe and Fleeson, 1986; Wolfe and St. Pierre, 1989).

Information on interventions is consistent with the fact that most research has focused on the causes rather than the consequences of maltreatment and on abuse more than neglect. More attention has been directed to parent and family-centered interventions than to child-centered approaches. And the problem of neglect has been given lower priority, perhaps because there is less consensus about society's right to intervene when parental behavior is not overtly offensive (Melton and Davidson, 1987). The low priority given neglect might also be related to the greater association of neglect with poverty (Wolock and Horowitz, 1984). It is not possible to describe examples of all the different kinds of intervention programs that have been attempted. Table 15–3, however, provides an overview of approaches to early intervention and treatment of child maltreatment. Given the combinations of factors that contribute to the development of child maltreatment, it seems clear that effective treatment must include multiple components. Furthermore, as the different forms of maltreatment become better defined and differentiated, treatment can be better shaped to specific cases.

Educational efforts are part of the preventive approach to the problem of maltreatment. In addition to promoting public awareness, these efforts seek to decrease the rates of child maltreatment. Also, attention to social influences such as poverty, stress, and social isolation would be expected to reduce the risk of abusive relationships continuing or perhaps developing in the first place.

Earlier we noted that the incidence of maltreatment reports had been rising and the question was raised as to whether this represents an actual increase in maltreatment or a greater sensitivity to and aware-

TABLE 15–3 Approaches to Child-Abuse Early Intervention and Treatment

Method	Target Population	Timing of Program	Target Behaviors	Examples of Content
Parent and Family-centered Approaches				
Child management training	Parents who have serious conflict with the child; parents requiring concrete demonstration and rehearsal	Early childhood; on referral to clinic	Effective parenting skills, (e.g., positive reinforcement, attending, commands, affect and voice tone); nonviolent discipline methods	Therapist demonstrates for parent how to use social and tangible rewards for positive child behavior.
Parent education and support groups	Socially isolated parents in need of group support, information, and sharing of feelings	Transition to parenthood; following crises or self-referral	Understanding of parental responsibilities and different approaches to child rearing; self-esteem; social skills and competence	Community resource person speaks to group about services for small children.
Anger and stress management	Self- and court-referred parents demonstrating anger control problems	On recognition or admission of a problem	Excessive anger, arousal, impulse control problems; inappropriate coping reactions	Parent is taught to use positive imagery or relaxation while dealing with difficult child
Treatment of antecedent conditions in the family	Any family member(s) with major psychological or health-related problems	On recognition or admission of a problem	Stress-related health problems; marital problems or violence; financial problems related to job skills, etc.	Paraprofessionals or therapists conduct marital counseling, relating to issues that affect parenting.
Child-centered Approaches				
Developmental stimulation	Children showing delays in major developmental areas; parents who give inadequate stimulation	Infancy, toddlerhood, and early childhood	Expressive and receptive language; compliance; sensorimotor development, attachment	Therapist demonstrates visual, auditory, and tactile activities with child; parent imitates.
Consultation with school, day-care, or foster-care personnel	Children who may present problems across different settings and placements	On recognition; at start of new placements	Aggression, social isolation; peer problems; academic delays	Professional meets with teacher and others to suggest ways of improving child's behavior.

From D. A. Wolfe (1987). *Child Abuse: Implications for Child Development and Psychopathology.* Copyright 1987 by Sage Publications. Reprinted by permission of Sage Publications, Inc.

ness of the problem. It would be encouraging if the latter were the case, and there is some suggestion that this is so (e.g., Gelles and Straus, 1987). Perhaps educational efforts have increased public awareness and rejection of abusive behavior. Cultural values such as tolerance for violence and neglect and a rigid reluctance to intrude on family autonomy are part of the context in which abusive and neglectful relationships develop. To the extent that families are being harmed by these values, change is appropriate.

CURRENT AND FUTURE CHALLENGES

So far in this chapter we have conceptualized prevention, examined some specific prevention programs, and taken the family as a particular focus of concerns about children. In conjunction with what has already been said, we now overview current and future challenges that must be met for the optimal growth of children. Although the picture is by no means completely bleak, many children are in jeopardy as we approach the twenty-first century and several challenges are apparent (Kopp, 1989).

Poverty

Quite shocking is the number of children living in poverty in the United States. As Figure 15–2 indicates, approximately one-fifth of all children are living below the federal guidelines for poverty. Poverty is disproportionately high among children of minority groups. Moreover, the poverty rate for children has been higher than for other age groups since 1975. Of course, it is well known that poverty puts children at risk with regard to diet, health, teenage pregnancy, exposure to drugs, family stress, and educational and occupational opportunity. A complex of factors has created increasing poverty among children, but it is nevertheless appalling given the wealth of our country.

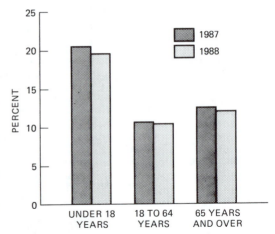

FIGURE 15–2 Percentage of people living in poverty, according to age group. From *Money Income and Poverty Status in the United States: 1988*, Series P-60, no. 166, U.S. Government Printing Office.

Families

Although it is not easy to predict the future, the family is not expected to return to traditional structure. Single-parent households and households with an employed mother are expected to increase (Gesten and Jason, 1987). Clearly, this has implications for social policy. The United States has not been in the forefront of dealing with changes in the family. For example, unlike many industrialized countries, the United States lacks a national policy that allows a parent to take extended leave from a job to care for a new child in the family. Similarly, the enormous need for quality day-care programs, especially for preschoolers, has been resisted on philosophical and economic grounds. Only recently has limited support been given to the idea of national preschools for both middle-class children as well as the 80 percent of disadvantaged children who are not attending Head Start (Scarr and Weinberg, 1986; Zigler, 1987).

Related to family needs is the issue of foster care. Approximately 270,000 children are in foster care in the child welfare system, and their numbers have been increasing (Tuma, 1989). Such placement occurs when families voluntarily participate or when children are involuntarily removed from their homes due to abuse, neglect, abandonment, or some emergency. In some cases, foster care could be avoided if day care, crisis intervention, emergency housing, or other alternatives were more available (Knitzer, 1981). In too many cases, the quality of foster care is inadequately monitored, children are moved from placement to placement, and children remain in care for long periods of time. Foster care is intended as temporary, but 66 percent of children and 88 percent of adolescents have been found to remain until they reach the legal age to be on their own (Tuma, 1989). Such "foster care drift," as this situation is called, can be alleviated by prompt, decisive action to either support children in their family homes or locate permanent placement for them. The federal government encourages this strategy through the Adoption Assistance and Child Welfare Act.

With regard to families, there is a clear need for stronger support, whatever family structure exists. Historical accounts and cross-cultural descriptions of the family tell us that a variety of structures can work if they are supported by the larger culture in which they are embedded.

Physical and Mental Health

The medical needs of children are not being adequately met, nor are their needs for psychological and behavioral health. To say that health care costs have sky rocketed is probably an understatement. Middle-class families have been impacted by this and the poor even more so. Federal health programs do provide some relief, but have not lived up to the demands.

One of the most ambitious attempts to improve the health of poor children was the Early and Periodic Screening, Diagnosis, and Treatment Program (EPSDT). An attempt at liberal social reform, this program originated as part of the Social Security Act of 1967 (Meisels, 1984). It called for prevention and treatment as early in life as possible and periodic follow-ups. Early screening—for example, for PKU, deafness, early symptoms of contagious disease, and developmental problems—was conceptualized as secondary, if not primary, prevention. Individuals with positive or suspicious findings were then further examined and diagnosed; treatment followed. Screening for developmental problems was to focus on early identification of intellectual and behavioral difficulties. Although the EPSDT program undoubtedly helped children, it failed to meet the high hopes with which it was instituted. There were several reasons for this, including administrative vagueness, misjudgment of costs, difficulties in linking risk with later health problems, and perhaps resistance to such social programs.

Over the years, many studies of children's mental health services have been conducted. They fundamentally agree that resources have been inadequate. It is currently estimated that anywhere from 11 to 19 percent of children display a mental health problem in need of treatment (Saxe, Cross, and Silverman, 1988; Tuma, 1989; Inouye, 1988). This means anywhere from 6 to almost 12 million children.

Funding for mental health services comes from state and federal governments, "third party" (insurance) companies, and clients themselves. State governments carry the burden more than the federal government. The services are delivered in various settings including mental health clinics, hospitals and residential centers, private professional practices, child welfare and juvenile agencies, and the schools. However, there is a particular lack of community-based services (Saxe et al., 1988). The educational system has a stronger role than it previously had due to P.L. 94–142. An amendment to this law, P.L. 99–457, has extended its mandate to all children, necessitating the evaluation and care of children from birth to three years of age. The ultimate effects of this law are yet to be seen.

Analyses of children's mental health services typically recognize both the complexity of children's care and the fragmentation of services. Because childhood disorders stem from the interaction of multiple factors, services must often have several components. To take a relatively uncomplicated hypothetical case, a child displaying attention-deficit hyperactivity disorder may require a psychologist to plan and monitor a behavior modification program, school personnel to coordinate an academic program, and a psychiatrist for medication evaluation. In more complex cases, human services (welfare), juvenile agencies, physicians, and others may be needed. For the most part, though, mental health services are not well coordinated. In recognition of this problem, the federal government has instituted the Child and Adolescent Service System Program (CASSP). Its function is to help coordinate services, as well as provide funds for training in mental health (Inouye, 1988). However, present funding of CASSP reportedly is inadequate to satisfy the needs of the states.

Children's mental health services have been criticized for not taking advantage of what is known about behavior problems and their treatment. For example, psychotherapy has shown itself effective for a variety of disorders in a variety of settings (Casey and Berman, 1985), and positive outcome for psychiatric hospitalization also has been reported (Saxe et al., 1988). As we have seen throughout this book, many knotty issues exist with regard to childhood behavior disorders, and it would be an injustice to oversimplify them. Nevertheless, there seems little doubt that children's development would be improved were more and better resources available.

Although diagnosis and treatment are the focus of mental health policy, some believe that prevention should be given more attention (Long, 1986). In fact, after studying the issue, the National Mental Health Association pinpointed four areas that hold particular promise for preventing mental and emotional disorders. These are: efforts to ensure wanted, healthy, full-term babies; prevention of adolescent pregnancy; school programs to foster mental health, including competency building; and alleviation of stress. Further, the Association noted that "a prudent investment in prevention research and services would dramatically lower the incidence and the toll of mental-emotional disabilities" (p. 828).

Children in the Global World

With mass transportation and media, the functional world becomes smaller day by day. Indeed, this fact more than many others will shape the lives of today's children.

One obvious implication of the shrinking world is the need for children to be able to deal with others of different color, face, clothes, and custom. The challenge of adapting to ethnic and racial differences is an age-old one, of course. In the United States, which is enormously heterogeneous, the issue has long been a concern. Prejudice and fears too often have had adverse effects

on peoples of various groups—American Indians, Irish, Afro-Americans, Poles, and Jews, to name a few. Being of "minority" status is a risk factor as it is linked to stress and reduced quality of life and opportunity (e.g., Albee, 1986). Indeed, in some cases official social policy can be seen as isolating children of certain groups (Laosa, 1984). We continue today to grapple with this issue, as shown by the controversy over adopting bilingualism in schools, hospitals, and other institutions. Although change will undoubtedly be gradual, a reasonable goal is to increase tolerance for those who are different from us and also recognize that heterogeneity can be enriching.

An important outgrowth of closer communication among the peoples of the world is increased cooperation in solving problems and optimizing conditions. Over the last decades world attention has been drawn to promoting the healthy development of children (Wagner, 1986). Thus, the United Nations has several agencies that focus on children's welfare, it declared 1979 the International Year of The Child, and it has written an official statement on the rights of children. The discipline of cross-cultural psychology, as well as others, continues to examine the cultural context of development, thereby enhancing understanding of the growth of children all over the world (e.g., Segall, 1986). In general, researchers and concerned citizens are increasingly addressing global issues such as the effects of poverty, high birth rates, infant mortality, gender bias, environmental pollution and destruction, and the lack of medical and mental health services. All of these can have dramatic influence on children.

SUMMARY

How children are cared for reflects what is known about development but also the social, political, and economic conditions in which they are living. Present-day concerns for the young recognize that they are shaped by a broad spectrum of influences.

Prevention of disordered development is widely conceptualized according to Caplan's model of primary, secondary, and tertiary prevention. Guidelines for prevention are clearer when reasonably well etiology is understood. Serious controversy still exists about primary intervention, but secondary prevention with high risk groups is relatively well accepted. Interventions vary enormously, based on what is known about risk factors.

The Mother-Infant Transaction Program has been successful in enhancing the welfare of mothers with low birth weight infants and the cognitive growth of the babies. Head Start, a comprehensive program for disadvantaged preschoolers and their families, can benefit children's health and facilitate short-term cognitive gains and school success. The long-term benefits of Head Start appear to operate through indirect effects on the school and on families. The Rochester Primary Mental Health Project intervenes with young elementary school children who are screened for school maladjustment. Research on the PMHP describes its successes and also provides data that is used as a basis for improvement.

Despite the success of many interventions, prevention still raises many issues. Ethical concerns are debated. Questions are also asked about the effectiveness of prevention, especially primary prevention and particularly when it calls for broad social improvements.

Concerns about transitions in the family are uppermost in the minds of many people. Much attention is given to the hugh increase in maternal employment and how it interacts with other variables to affect children. Studies of the impact of divorce so far indicate, among other things, that adverse short-term effects occur, age of the child may make a difference, boys tend to externalize while girls internalize, and divorce may be harder on boys and remarriage harder on girls. Research on child abuse shows that it occurs in diverse forms and is linked to socioeconomic stress, age of the child, and certain parental characteristics (but hardly to parental psychiatric disturbance and less than thought to parents' childhood maltreatment). Overall, research indicates that the effects of family transitions are multidetermined and that interventions can be effective.

As we look to the twenty-first century, several challenges to the optimal growth of children are apparent. Among them are increasing poverty, the lack of support for changing families and needed improvements in child foster placement, and inadequate and poorly coordinated medical and mental health services. Over the last few decades greater recognition has been given to the potential impact of global issues. International cooperation to better children's lives is reflected in the work of the United Nations and many professional and citizens' groups concerned about an array of global issues.

GLOSSARY

ABA′ (reversal) research design Single-subject quasi-experimental design in which the relevant behavior is measured during a baseline period (A), manipulation (B), and a period in which the manipulation is removed (A′). The reintroduction of the manipulation (B′) is added when treatment is the goal.

Accommodation In Piagetian theory, the process of adapting one's mental schemas of the world to fit with new experiences.

Adaptive behavior scales Psychological instruments that measure an individual's ability to perform in the everyday environment, for example, to wash one's hair, interact socially, and communicate. Used mostly for evaluation of retarded or severely disturbed persons.

Adoption studies In genetic research, the comparison of adopted children with their biological and their adoptive families to determine hereditary and environmental influences on characteristics.

Amniocentesis A procedure used to examine the development of the fetus. A long needle injected into the abdomen of the pregnant woman extracts fetal cells and amniotic fluid, which are evaluated for biochemical and chromosomal defects.

Amphetamines Drugs that act as stimulants, producing high levels of energy. Side effects such as sleeplessness and nervousness can result from large doses.

Anaclitic depression A period of withdrawal and sadness in very young children in reaction to prolonged separation from their parents.

Antisocial behavior A pattern of behavior that violates widely held social norms and brings harm to others (e.g., stealing, lying)

Aphasia A general term referring to language disturbances not caused by general intellectual deficiency. *Developmental aphasia* refers to receptive and expressive language disorders in childhood.

Assimilation In Piagetian theory, the process of taking in or interpreting new information according to existing mental schemas of the world.

Attachment A strong socioemotional bond between individuals. Usually discussed in terms of the child-parent or child-caretaker relationship, attachment is generally viewed as having a strong influence on a child's development.

Attribution of causality The assignment of causation to specific influences; for example, a child's attributing his or her school failure to lack of innate intelligence.

Autonomic nervous system A part of the nervous system that consists of ganglia along the spinal cord and nerves to peripheral organs (e.g., glands and blood vessels). It regulates functions usually considered involuntary, such as the operation of smooth muscles and glands. The system controls physiological changes associated with the expression of emotion.

Behavior modification An approach to the treatment of behavior disorders that is based primarily on learning principles. Also referred to as *behavior therapy*.

Biofeedback Procedures by which the individual is provided immediate information (feedback) about some aspect of physiological functioning (e.g., muscle tension, skin temperature). It is assumed that the individual can come to control bodily functioning through such feedback.

Case study Descriptive method of research in which an indivdual case is described. Case studies typically include behavioral manifestations, history and background of the person, test results, treatments, and outcome. The case study can be informative but cannot be generalized to other persons or situations with confidence.

Central nervous system In humans, the brain and spinal cord. (*See* autonomic nervous system)

Child guidance movement An early to mid-20th century effort in the U.S. to treat and prevent childhood mental disorders. Importance was given to influences of familial and wider social systems on the child.

Chromosome A threadlike structure in the cell nucleus that contains the genetic code. With the exception of the gametes, human cells possess 23 pairs, 22 pairs of autosomes and 1 pair of sex chromosomes. The gametes possess 23 single chromosomes.

Chromosome abnormalities Abnormalities in the number and/or structure of the chromosome complement that often lead to fetal death or anomalies in development.

Classical conditioning A form of learning, also referred to as Pavlovian conditioning. An individual comes to respond to a stimulus (conditioned stimulus or CS) that did not previously elicit a response. Classical conditioning occurs when a CS is paired with another stimulus (the unconditioned stimulus, or UCS) that does elicit the desired response (unconditioned response, or UCR). When this response is elicited by the conditioned stimulus alone it is called a conditioned response (CR).

Classificatory variable In research methodology, attributes of subjects (e.g., age, sex, diagnosis) that are investigated in some way. Classificatory variables are sometimes erroneously taken for independent variables (*See* mixed research design)

Clinical utility A criterion for judging the adequacy of a classification system, diagnosis, or assessment instrument. Judgments are based on how fully the observed phenomena are described and on how useful the descriptions are.

Cognitive strategies Information processing and memory strategies; for example, rehearsing and categorizing information.

Comorbidity Comorbidity exists when individuals simultaneously meet the criteria for more than one disorder (e.g., depression and anxiety).

Compulsions Behaviors the individual feels compelled to repeat over and over again, even though they appear to have no rational basis.

Concordant In genetic research, refers to individuals who are similar in particular attributes, for example, concordant for hair color or activity level.

Conditioned stimulus (CS) A neutral stimulus, which through repeated pairings with a stimulus (unconditioned stimulus) that already elicits a particular response, comes to elicit a similar response (conditioned response).

Contingency management Procedures that seek to modify behavior by altering the causal relationship between stimulus and response events, for example, between a behavior and its reinforcer.

Control group In an experiment, a group of subjects who are treated differently than subjects who receive the experimental manipulation and later compared with them. The purpose of control groups is to insure that the results of the experiment can be attributed to the manipulation rather than to other variables.

Correlation coefficient A number obtained through statistical analysis that reflects the presence or absence of a correlation, the strength of a correlation, and the direction (positive or negative) of a correlation. Pearson r is a commonly used coefficient. (*See* positive and negative correlation.)

Correlational research A research strategy aimed at establishing whether two or more variables covary, or are associated. (*See* positive correlation and negative correlation.) The establishment of a correlation permits prediction of one variable from the other, but does not establish a causal relationship.

Critical period A relatively limited period of development during which an organism may be particularly sensitive to specific influences. Strictly viewed, the critical period hypothesis postulates that certain inputs at certain times set up irreversible patterns of behavior.

Crossing over A genetic mechanism in which sections of a chromosome pair are exchanged in meiosis.

Cross-sectional research A research strategy that observes and compares different groups of subjects at one point in time. It is a highly practical way to gather certain kinds of information.

Cross-sequential research designs Various designs that combine the longitudinal and cross-sectional research strategies to maximize the strengths of these methods.

Defense mechanisms In psychoanalytic theory, psychological processes that distort or deny reality so as to control anxiety. Examples are repression, projection, reaction formation.

Deficit vs. difference model Antagonistic models to explain atypical functioning of poor children. The deficit model suggests that these children are deficient by reason of inheritance and/or inferior subculture. The difference model argues that poor children are not deficient but learn different content and styles that disadvantage them on intelligence tests and in institutions that stress middle-class values.

Delinquency A legal term that refers to an illegal act by a person under 18. Such behavior may be illegal for an adult as well, such as theft, or may only be illegal when committed by a juvenile, for example, truancy.

Delusion An idea or belief that appears contrary to reality and is not widely accepted in the culture (e.g., delusions of grandeur or persecution).

Dependent variable In the experimental method of research, the measure of behavior that may be influenced by the manipulation (independent variable).

Development Change in structure and function that occurs over time in living organisms. Typically viewed as change from the simple to the complex, development is the result of transactions between biological and environmental variables.

Developmental level The level at which an individual is functioning with regard to physical, intellectual, or socioemotional characteristics. Individuals can be assigned to a developmental level based on age-norms or theoretical constructions.

Developmental psychopathology The study of behavioral disorders within the context of developmental influences.

Developmental quotient (DQ) A measure of performance on infant tests of intelligence, paralleling the intelligence quotient (IQ) derived from intelligence tests for older children.

Developmental vs. difference controversy Theroetical dispute about atypical functioning, especially about mental retardation. The developmental view argues that retarded persons function intellectually in the same ways as do the nonretarded, but that they develop more slowly and perhaps reach a ceiling. The difference view maintains that the intellective processes of retarded persons are qualitatively different than normal processes.

Diathesis A constitutional predisposition toward a disease or disorder.

Differential reinforcement of other behaviors (DRO) In behavior modification, refers to applying relatively more reinforcement to desirable behaviors that are incompatible with specific undesirable behaviors.

Differentiation Process whereby growth becomes progressively refined. For example, motor development that initially involves global action of the arm comes to include refined movement of the wrist and fingers.

Discordant In genetic research, refers to individuals who are dissimilar in particular attributes, for example, discordant in hair color or activity level.

Discrimination The process by which an individual comes to learn that a particular stimulus, but not others, signals that a certain response is likely to be followed by a particular consequence.

Diversion programs This approach to delinquency attempts to intervene by providing services (e.g., education, vocational training) that will *divert* delinquent youth away from the juvenile justice system.

Dizygotic twins Twins resulting from two independent unions of ova and sperm that occur at approximately the same time. Dizygotic twins are genetically no more alike than are nontwin siblings.

DNA Deoxyribonucleic acid. The chemical carrier of the genetic code that is found in the chromosomes. The spiral-shaped DNA molecule is composed of sugar, phosphates, and nucleotides. The nucleotides carry the hereditary information that directs protein synthesis.

Dyscalculia General term for the inability to perform arithmetic operations. Many skills are involved, such as spatial and language abilities.

Dyslexia General term referring to the inability to read. *Developmental dyslexia* denotes problems in reading during childhood.

Echolalia The repetition of the speech of others, either immediately or delayed in time. A pathological speech pattern commonly found in infantile autism and psychoses.

Ego According to psychoanalytic theory, this is the structure of the mind that operates predominantly at the conscious level. It mediates between instinctual urges and reality and is responsible for decision making.

Electroencephalograph (EEG) A recording of the electrical activity of the brain.

Empirical The process of verification or proof by accumulating information or data through observation or experiment (in contrast to reliance on impression or theory).

Epidemiology The study of the occurrence of a (behavior) disorder within a specific population. Occurrence may be expressed as prevalence or incidence. (*See* prevalence, incidence)

Eros (libido) This is Freud's term for the id's impulse to seek pleasure and gratification. It is sometimes equated with sexual instinct.

Etiology The cause or origin of a disease or behavior disorder.

Eugenics Efforts to improve human characteristics through systematic control of reproduction and thus genetics.

Executive functions A term that refers to the ability to select, monitor, evaluate and revise strategies employed in memory. Includes metamemory.

Experimental research A research strategy that can establish causal relationships between variables. Subjects are treated by the independent variable to determine possible effects on the dependent variable. Comparison groups are included to control for extraneous influences and the procedures are carefully controlled by the researchers.

External validity In research, refers to the degree to which findings of an investigation can be generalized to other populations and situations.

Externalizing disorders Behavioral disorders in which the problems exhibited seem directed at others; for example, aggression and lying.

Extinction A weakening of a learned response that is produced when reinforcement that followed the response no longer occurs.

Factor analysis A statistical procedure that correlates each item with every other item, and then groups correlated items into factors.

Frustration-aggression hypothesis The proposition that frustration always leads to aggression and that aggression is only caused by frustration.

Gametes The sex cells that unite to form the zygote. In females the gametes are the ova (or eggs); in males the gametes are the spermatozoa (or sperm).

Gene The smallest unit of the chromosome that transmits genetic information. With the exception of the gametes, genes occur in pairs, one on each of the paired chromosomes.

Generalization The process by which a response is

made to a new stimulus that is different but similar to the stimulus present during learning.

Generalized imitation The tendency to imitate across persons, situations, and time.

Genotype The complement of genes that a person inherits; the genetic endowment.

Hallucination A sensory perception (e.g., hearing a noise, seeing an object) that occurs in the absence of any apparent environmental stimulation.

Hypothesis In science, a proposition or "educated guess" put forth for evaluation by some scientific method.

Id According to psychoanalytic theory this is developmentally the earliest of the structures of the mind—it is present at birth. The source of all psychic energy, the Id operates entirely at the unconscious level, seeking immediate gratification of all instinctual urges (the pleasure principle).

Impulsivity The tendency to act quickly without reflection. Hyperactive children are viewed as impulsive.

Incidence In studying the occurrence of a behavior disorder, incidence refers to the number of new cases in a given population in a given time period. (*See* prevalence)

Independent variable In the experimental method of research, the variable manipulated by the researcher.

Individual Education Plan (IEP) Detailed educational plan mandated by P.L. 94–142 for each child being served by special education.

Information processing Complex mental processes by which the organism attends to, perceives, interprets, and stores information. (*See* memory, executive functions, metamemory, cognitive strategies.)

Intelligence quotient (IQ), deviation A standard score derived from statistical procedures that reflects the direction and degree to which an individual's performance on an intelligence test deviates from the average score of the individual's age group.

Intelligence quotient (IQ), ratio The ratio of mental age (MA), derived from performance on tests of intelligence, to chronological age (CA), multiplied by 100. IQ = MA/CA × 100.

Interactional model of development The view that development is the result of the interplay of organismic and environmental variables. (*See* transactional model of development)

Internalizing disorders The large category of disorders—many of which are traditionally referred to as neuroses—in which the problems exhibited seem directed more at the self than at others; for example, fears, depression, and withdrawal.

Internal validity In research, refers to the degree to which findings can be attributed to certain factors. Frequently concerns the degree to which a result of an *experiment* can be attributed to the experimental manipulation (the independent variable), rather than to extraneous factors.

Interrater reliability The extent to which different raters agree on a particular diagnosis or measurement.

Introversion-extroversion A dimension of social behavior or personality. Introversion refers to the degree to which an individual is inner-oriented, shy, and uneasy in social situations. Extroversion is the degree to which an individual is outgoing and at ease socially.

In vivo A term referring to the natural context in which behavior occurs. For example, in vivo treatment is delivered in the setting in which the behavior problem occurs (e.g., the home rather than the clinic).

Learned helplessness Passivity and a sense of lack of control over one's environment that is learned through experiences where one's behavior was ineffective in controlling events.

Least restrictive environment A term that refers to the idea that handicapped individuals have a right to be educated with and to live with the nonhandicapped to the extent that is maximally feasible. (See Public Law 94–142.)

Libido The energy associated with Eros.

Longitudinal research A research strategy that observes the same subjects over a relatively long period of time, measuring behavior at certain points. It is particularly helpful in tracing developmental change.

Mainstreaming The placing of handicapped individuals into the least restrictive environments in which they are capable of functioning. More specifically, the placement of handicapped children in regular, rather than special, classes. (See Public Law 94–142)

Masked depression This term refers to cases in which a child's depression is "masked" by other problems such as hyperactivity or delinquency. These "depressive equivalents" are thought to be manifestions of the underlying depression.

Maturation Changes that occur in individuals of a species relatively independent of the environment provided that basic conditions are satisfied. For example, most humans will walk, given normal physical capacity, nourishment, and opportunity for movement.

Maturational lag A slowness or falling behind in development; often implies a lag in brain or nervous system development.

Mediational processes Strategies by which stimuli are connected so that learning and thinking are facilitated. Examples are the use of imagery, words, clustering, and rehearsal.

Meiosis In maturation of the gametes, the specialized cell division that results in the ova and sperm containing half of the number of chromosomes found in other cells.

Memory Complex process by which perceived information can be recalled in some way. According to a widely-held model, information is first taken in by a sensory register, is passed to short-term storage, and then to long-term storage.

Mental age (MA) The score corresponding to the chronological age (CA) of children whose intellectual test performance the examinee equals. For the average child, MA = CA.

Mental hygiene movement An effort organized in the United States early in the 20th century to bring effective, humane treatment to the mentally ill and to prevent mental disorders. Clifford Beers, who wrote *A Mind That Found Itself*, was a driving force in the movement, which was closely associated with the child guidance movement.

Metamemory The understanding or awareness of the working of one's memory or the strategies used to facilitate memory. (*See* Executive functions.)

Migraine headache A severe form of headache caused by sustained dilation of the extracranial arteries.

Minimal brain dysfunction (MBD) The hypothesis or assumption that the central nervous system or brain is functioning in a pathological way to a degree that is not clearly detectable. MBD is hypothesized as the cause of hyperactivity and learning disabilities, as well as other behavior disorders.

Mitosis The common type of cell division that results in two identical daughter cells. During mitosis each chromosome pair is duplicated, with one pair going to each daughter cell.

Mixed research design A research design in which subjects are assigned into groups on the basis of some attribute (i.e., a classificatory variable such as age), and then an experimental manipulation is applied. In interpretation of results, care must be taken not to view the classificatory variable as an independent variable.

Monozygotic twins Twins resulting from one union of an ovum and sperm. The single zygote divides early into two, with the new zygotes having identical genes (and thus being of the same sex).

Morphology In language, the study of word formation.

Mutation Spontaneous change in the genes that can be transmitted to the next generation. One of the genetic mechanisms that accounts for variation in species and individuals.

Nature vs. nurture controversy The continuing debate about the relative influence of innate and experiential factors on the shaping of the individual. Also known as the maturation vs. learning and heredity vs. environment controversy.

Negative correlation When two (or more) variables are negatively correlated they co-vary such that high scores on one variable are associated with low scores on the other, and vice versa.

Negative reinforcement The process whereby the withdrawal of a stimulus contingent on a particular response increases the probability of that response reoccurring.

Neuropsychological assessment The use of psychological tests and behavioral measures to *indirectly* evaluate the functioning of the nervous system. Performance on these measures is known or presumed to reflect specific aspects of the functioning of the brain.

Neurosis A traditional term employed to describe any of a group of nonpsychotic disorders that are characterized by unusual levels of anxiety and associated problems. Phobias, obsessions, and compulsions are examples of disorders in this category.

Neurotransmitter A chemical that carries the nerve impulse from one neuron across the synaptic space to another neuron. Examples are serotonin, dopamine, and norepinephrine.

Normal distribution (curve) The bell-shaped theoretical distribution or probability curve that describes the way in which many attributes (e.g., height, intelligence) are assumed to occur in the population. Extreme values of the attribute occur with less frequency than middle values of the attribute.

Normalization Assumption that the goal of treatment of behavior disorders should be behaviors that are as normal as possible, and that this goal should be reached by methods as culturally normal as possible. (*See* mainstreaming and least restrictive environment.)

Norms Data based on information gathered from a segment of the population that represents the entire population. Norms serve as standards to evaluate individual development or functioning.

Nuclear family A family unit consisting of the father, mother, and children.

Observational learning The learning that occurs through viewing the behavior of others. Modeled behavior can be presented in live or symbolic form.

Obsessions Recurring and intrusive irrational thoughts over which the individual feels no control.

Operant conditioning Learning processes by which responses are acquired, maintained, or eliminated as a function of consequences (e.g., reinforcement, punishment).

Operational criteria (definition) A specified set of observable operations that are measurable and allow one to define some concept. For example, maternal deprivation might be defined by measuring the time the child is separated from its mother.

Overcorrection Behavior modification technique in which an individual engaging in an undesirable behavior (e.g., self-injury, enuresis) must then practice a behavior that is incompatible with the undesirable act.

Overlearning The procedure whereby learning trials are continued beyond the point at which the child has completed the stated criteria. This is intended to increase the likelihood that the new behavior will be maintained.

Paired-associate learning Learning phenomenon in which an individual is initially presented paired stimuli (e.g., words, pictures) and later, when shown one stimulus of a pair, must recall or reproduce the other.

Paradigm The set of assumptions and conceptions shared by a group of scientists that is used in collecting data and interpreting the phenomena of interest.

Paradoxical drug effect An effect of a drug that contradicts the expected effect. An example is the quieting of many hyperactive children by stimulant medications.

Partial correlation statistical procedure A statistical procedure that aids in the interpretation of a demonstrated correlation by removing the effects of one or more specific variables.

Participant modeling A treatment method in which observation of a model is followed by the observer joining the model in gradual approximations of the desired behavior.

Perceptual-motor training Approach to rectify general and specific learning disabilities that is based on the assumption that basic perceptual and motor functioning have gone awry or have developed abnormally. Training emphasizes exercises in sensory reception and motor responses, such as practicing right/left orientation, balancing, and learning simple forms and shapes.

Perinatal The period of development at or around the time of birth.

Perspective *See* paradigm.

Phenotype The observable attributes of an individual that result from genetic endowment, developmental processes, and the transactions of these.

Phobia Anxiety about, and avoidance of, some object or situation that is judged to be an excessive, overly persistent, unadaptive, or inappropriate fear.

Phonology The study of speech sounds.

Pica The habitual eating of substances usually considered inedible such as dirt, paper, and hair.

Placebo A treatment—psychological or chemical—that alters a person's behavior because he or she expects that change will occur. Placebos are often employed as control treatments to evaluate whether a treatment being tested is effective for reasons other than the person's belief in it.

Polygenetic inheritance Inheritance of a characteristic that is influenced by many genes rather than a single one.

Positive correlation When two (or more) variables are positively correlated they co-vary with each other such that high scores on one variable are associated with high scores on the other variable, and low scores on the one variable are associated with low scores on the other.

Positive reinforcement A stimulus is presented following a particular response—and contingent upon that response—thereby increasing the likelihood that the response will occur in the future.

Pragmatics (of language) The use of speech and gesture in a communicative way, considering the social context. Pragmatic skills include using appropriate gestures and language style and not interrupting others.

Predictive validity The extent to which predictions about future behavior can be made by knowing an individual's diagnosis or performance on some test.

Premorbid adjustment This term refers to the psychological, social, and academic/vocational adjustment of a person prior to onset of the symptoms of a disorder or its diagnosis.

Prenatal The period of development that occurs during pregnancy.

Preparedness Refers to the idea that organisms are genetically influenced to learn particular responses or associations more readily than others. For example, an organism might be biologically predisposed to be sensitive to a certain object and more likely to learn a fear response to it.

Prevalence In studying the occurrence of a behavior disorder, prevalence refers to the number of cases in the population at a given time. It may be expressed by number of cases or percent of the population. (*See* incidence)

Primary prevention The prevention of disorders in the population by methods that preclude their occurrence. Examples are parent education in child management and prevention of poverty, which is associated with many disorders.

Projection A defense mechanism whereby the ego protects against unacceptable thoughts or impulses by attributing them to another person or some object.

Projective tests Psychological tests which present ambiguous stimuli to the person. The subject's response is presumed to reflect unconscious thoughts and feelings that are unacceptable to the ego and therefore cannot be expressed directly.

Pronoun reversal Deviant speech pattern in which speakers refer to themselves as "you" or "she" or "he" and refer to others as "I" or "me". Often found in autistic children.

Prospective research designs Designs that identify subjects and then follow them over time. (*See* retrospective research designs.)

Protective factors Variables that lessen the effects of risk; sometimes refered to as resiliencies.

Psychoactive drugs Chemical substances that influence psychological processes (e.g., behavior, thinking, emotions) by their influence on nervous system functioning. Examples are stimulants and tranquilizers.

Psychogenesis The view that development of a particular disorder is due to psychological influence.

Psychomotor retardation A slowing of movement often associated with depression that may involve slowed speech, slowed body movements, and decreased energy level.

Psychosis A general term for severe mental disorder that affects thinking, the emotions, and other psychological systems. The hallmark of a psychosis is disturbed contact with reality.

Psychosomatic disorders Disorders involving actual physical symptoms that are presumed to be caused, at least in part, by psychological factors such as stress.

Public Law 94–142 The federal *Education for all Handicapped Children Act of 1975*, that sets guidelines for the rights of handicapped children to appropriate education. It assures appropriate public education and services in the least restrictive environment, a role for parents in decision making, and assistance to the states.

Public Law 96–272 The federal *Adoption Assistance and*

Child Welfare Act of 1980 that is designed to provide better welfare services to children and to protect their rights in child adoption and placement.

Public Law 99–457 An amendment to the federal Public Law 94–142 that mandates the evaluation and special care of children from birth to three years of age.

Punishment A response is followed by either an unpleasant stimulus or the removal of a pleasant stimulus, thereby decreasing the frequency of that response.

Random assignment In research, the assignment of individuals to different groups in such a way that each individual has an equal chance of being assigned to any group. Such chance assignment helps make the groups comparable on factors that might influence the findings.

Recidivism The return to a previous undesirable pattern. The juvenile delinquent who returns to commit a crime after completing a treatment program illustrates recidivism.

Reflexes Automatic, unlearned responses to specific stimulation. Examples are the sucking, coughing, and Moro reflexes. Reflexes are considered relatively simple acts, some of which give way to voluntary, learned responses.

Regular Education Initiative (REI) Controversial proposal that learning handicapped children be educated in regular classrooms rather than special education classrooms.

Reinforcement A process whereby a stimulus presented contingent on the occurrence of a particular behavior results in an increase in the likelihood of that behavior. (*See* positive reinforcement and negative reinforcement.)

Relapse The reoccurrence of a problem after it has been successfully treated.

Reliability The degree to which an observtion is consistently made. The term can be applied to a test or other measurement or to a system of classification.

Repression According to psychoanalytic theory, the most basic defense mechanism. Thoughts or impulses unacceptable to the ego are forced back into the unconscious.

Response prevention A behavioral treatment procedure in which the person is not allowed to, or discouraged from, engaging in a compulsive ritual or behavior.

Retrospective research designs Designs that utilize information about past events; follow-back designs. (*See* prospective research designs.)

Risk The degree to which variables operate to increase the chance of behavior problems.

Rumination The voluntary regurgitation of food by infants.

Schema Mental concepts or constructions of the world. The development of complex schemas is central to Piaget's theory of cognitive growth.

School phobia An extreme reluctance to go to school which is frequently accompanied by somatic complaints. The term *school refusal* is preferred by some clinicians, since an actual fear of school may not be present.

Scientific method An empirical approach to understanding the wide array of natural phenomena. The scientific approach involves systematic observation, measurement and testing of relationships, and explanations of phenomena.

Secondary prevention The prevention of disorders in the population by shortening the duration of existing cases through early diagnosis and treatment, especially of at-risk populations.

Self-injurious behavior Repetitious action that damages the self physically, such as head banging, scratching the self, and pulling one's own hair. Often observed in psychotic and mentally retarded children, but occurs in a small percentage of young, normal children.

Self-stimulatory behavior Sensory-motor behavior that serves as stimulation for the child. Often refers to a pathological process, for example, as when an autistic child repetitiously flaps his or her hands.

Semantics The study of the meanings in language (or more generally, in signs).

Separation anxiety Excessive anxiety regarding separation from the mother or other major attachment figures.

Socioeconomic status (SES) Classification of people according to social class. Indices of SES include monetary level, amount of education, and occupational level. Many factors vary with SES, such as medical care and child-rearing practices.

Somatogenesis The viewpoint that development or a particular disorder is due to biological—rather than psychological—causes.

Stage theories of development Explanations of development that postulate that growth occurs in a recognizable order of noncontinuous stages or steps, which are qualitatively different from each other. Examples: Piaget's cognitive theory and Freud's psychosexual theory.

Statistical significance In research, refers to a low probability that the findings are merely chance occurrences. By tradition a finding is statistically significant when there is a 5 percent or less probability that it occurred by chance ($p \leq .05$).

Stimulant A drug which increases alertness and activity. Amphetamines are one example of stimulants.

Superego The third of Freud's three structures of the mind. It is the conscience or self-critical part of the individual that reflects society's morals and standards as they have been learned from parents and others.

Sympathetic nervous system A part of the autonomic nervous system which, among other things, accelerates heart rate, contracts blood vessels, inhibits intestinal activity, and in general seems to prepare the organism for stress or activity.

Symptom substitution The notion, derived largely from the psychodynamic perspective, that if one treats just the observed problem behavior, a new problem or symptom will occur since the underlying illness or psychological conflict has not been treated.

Syndrome　A group of behaviors or symptoms which tend to occur together in a particular disorder.

Syntax　The aspect of grammar that deals with the way words are put together to form phrases, clauses, and sentences.

Systematic desensitization　A behavioral treatment of anxiety. The client visualizes a hierarchy of scenes, each of which elicits more anxiety than the previous scene. These visualizations are paired with relaxation until they no longer produce anxiety.

Systematic direct observation　Observation of specific behaviors of an individual or group of individuals in a particular setting, with the use of a specific observational code or instrument.

Temperament　A variety of socioemotional behaviors viewed as relatively stable attributes of individuals, such as activity level, introversion-extroversion, and social responsiveness.

Teratogens　Conditions or agents that tend to cause developmental malformations, defects, or death of the fetus.

Tertiary prevention　The prevention of disorders in the population by reducing defective functioning that is residual to primary disorders. An example is support groups for persons who are returning to the community after hospitalization for mental disorders and who may face negative stereotyping.

Test-retest reliability　The degree to which a test or diagnostic system yields the same result when applied to an individual at different times.

Thanatos　According to psychoanalytic theory, it is the destructive, aggressive, death instinct. Thanatos and Eros are the two basic instincts of the id.

Theory　An integrated set of propositions that explains phenomena and guides research.

Theory of mind　The ability to infer mental states (e.g., beliefs, knowledge) in others or the self. Autistic children appear to show deficits in this ability.

Time-out　Behavior modification technique in which an individual displaying an undesirable behavior is removed from the immediate environment, usually by placement into an isolated room. Conceptually time-out is viewed as elimination of positive reinforcement or as punishment.

Time series quasi-experimental research designs　Various single-subject designs in which manipulation and measurement are made across time periods. Includes the ABA' and multiple baseline designs.

Token economy　A behavioral treatment procedure developed from operant conditioning principles. A system of behaviors that earn or cost reward points, given in the form of some scrip, such as poker chips, is set up. These tokens can then be exchanged for prizes, activities, or privileges.

Transactional model of development　The view that development is the result of the continuous interplay of organismic and environmental variables. It is conceptually similar to the interactional model of development but it emphasizes the ongoing, mutual influences of factors.

Tuberose sclerosis　A disorder, transmitted by an autosomal dominant gene, in which severe mental retardation and tumors of the skin and internal organs are exhibited.

Twin study　A type of research investigation frequently employed to examine the effects of hereditary and environmental variables. Pairs of genetically-identical monozygotic twins and genetically different dizygotic twins are examined to determine whether the former are more alike than the latter.

Unconditioned stimulus　A stimulus which elicits a particular response prior to any conditioning trials. The loud noise that causes an infant to startle is an example of an unconditioned stimulus.

Validity　A term used in several different ways, all of which address issues of correctness, meaningfulness, and relevancy. (See internal validity, external validity, predictive validity.)

Vulnerability factors　Variables that intensify the effects of risk.

Zeitgeist　A german word for the general viewpoint and attitudes of a given society at a particular time. A literal translation is *zeit* (time) *geist* (spirit).

Zygote　The cell mass formed by the joining of an ovum and sperm; the fertilized egg.

REFERENCES

A

Abel, E. L., & Lee, J. A. (1988). Paternal alcohol exposure affects offspring behavior but not body or organ weights of mice. *Alcoholism: Clinical and Experimental Research, 12,* 349–355.

Abikoff, H. (1985). Efficacy of cognitive training interventions in hyperactive children: A critical review. *Clinical Psychology Review, 5,* 479–512.

Abikoff, H., Ganeles, D., Reiter, G., Blum, C., Foley, C., & Klein, R. G. (1988). Cognitive training in academically deficient ADDH boys receiving stimulant medication. *Journal of Abnormal Child Psychology, 16,* 411–432.

Abikoff, H., & Gittelman, R. (1984). Does behavior therapy normalize the classroom behavior of hyperactive children? *Archives of General Psychiatry, 41,* 449–454.

Ablon, S. L., & Mack, J. E. (1979). Sleep disorders. In J. D. Noshpitz (Ed.), *Basic handbook of child psychiatry II.* New York: Basic Books.

Achenbach, T. M. (1974, 1982). *Developmental psychopathology.* New York: Wiley.

Achenbach, T. M. (1978). *Research in developmental psychology: Concepts, strategies, methods.* New York: Free Press.

Achenbach, T. M. (1985). *Assessment and taxonomy of child and adolescent psychopathology.* Beverly Hills: Sage.

Achenbach, T. M., Conners, C. K., Quay, H.C., Verhults, F. C., & Howell, C. T. (1989). Replication of empirically derived syndromes as a basis for taxonomy of child/adolescent psychopathology. *Journal of Abnormal Child Psychology, 17,* 299–323.

Achenbach, T. M., & Edelbrock, C. S. (1978). The classification of child psychopathology: A review and analysis of empirical efforts. *Psychological Bulletin, 85,* 1275–1301.

Achenbach, T. M., & Edelbrock, C. S. (1981). Behavioral problems and competencies reported by parents of normal and disturbed children aged four through sixteen. *Monographs of the Society for Research in Child Development, 46,* (Whole No. 188).

Achenbach, T. M., & Edelbrock, C. (1983). *Manual for the Child Behavior Checklist and Revised Child Behavior Profile.* Burlington: University of Vermont.

Achenbach, T. M., & Edelbrock, C. S. (1986). *Manual for the Teacher's Report Form and Teacher Version of the Child Behavior Profile.* Burlington: University of Vermont.

Achenbach, T. M., & Edelbrock, C. S. (1989). Diagnostic, taxonomic, and assessment issues. In T. H. Ollendick & M. Hersen (Eds.), *Handbook of child psychopathology* (2nd ed.). New York: Plenum.

Achenbach, T. M., McConaughy, S. H., & Howell, C. T. (1987). Child/adolescent behavioral and emotional problems: Implications of cross-informant correlations for situational specificity. *Psychological Bulletin, 101,* 213–232.

Ackerman, P. T., Anhalt, J. M., Dykman, R. A., & Holcomb, P. J. (1986). Effortful processing deficits in children with learning and attention disorders. *Brain and Cognition, 5,* 22–40.

Adams, J. A. (1984). Learning of movement sequences. *Psychological Bulletin, 96,* 3–28.

Adelman, H. S. (1989). Beyond the learning mystique: An interactional perspective on learning disabilities. *Journal of Learning Disabilities, 22,* 301–304; 328.

Adrien, J. L., Ornitz, E., Barthelemy, C., Sauvage, D., & Lelord, G. (1987). The presence or absence of certain behaviors associated with infantile autism in severely retarded autistic and nonautistic retarded children and very young normal children. *Journal of Autism and Developmental Disorders, 17,* 407–416.

Agras, W. S. (1988). Does early eating behavior influence later adiposity? In N. A. Krasnegor, G. D. Grave, & N. Kretchmer (Eds.), *Childhood obesity: A biobehavioral perspective.* Caldwell: The Telford Press.

Agras, W. S., & Kraemer, H. (1984). The treatment of anorexia nervosa: Do different treatments have different outcomes. In A. J. Stunkard & E. Stellar (Eds.), *Eating and its disorders.* New York: Raven Press.

Agras, W. S., Schneider, J. A., Arnow, B., Raeburn, S. D., & Telch, C. F. (1989). Cognitive-behavioral and response-prevention treatments for bulimia nervosa. *Journal of Consulting and Clinical Psychology, 57,* 215–221.

Ainsworth, M., Behar, M., Waters, E., & Wall, S. (1978). *Patterns of attachment.* Hillsdale, NJ: Erlbaum.

Akers, R. L., Krohn, J. D., Lanza-Koduce, L., & Radosevich, M. (1979). Social learning and deviant behavior: A specific test of a general theory. *American Sociological Review, 44,* 635–655.

Alanen, Y. (1960). Some thoughts of schizophrenia and ego development in the light of family investigations. *Archives of General Psychiatry, 3,* 650–656.

Albee, G. W. (1982). The politics of nature and nurture. *American Journal of Community Psychology, 10,* 4–36.

Albee, G. W. (1986).Toward a just society. Lessons from observations on the primary prevention of psychopathology. *American Psychologist, 41,* 891–898.

Alexander, A. B. (1980). The treatement of psychosomatic disorders. In B. B. Lahey & A. E. Kazdin (Eds.), *Advances in clinical child psychology,* Vol. 3. New York: Plenum.

Alexander, A. B., Cropp, G. J. A., & Chai, H. (1979). Effects of relaxation training on pulmonary mechanics in children with asthma. *Journal of Applied Behavior Analysis, 12,* 27–35.

Alexander, F. (1950). *Psychosomatic medicine.* New York: W. W. Norton and Co.

Alexander, J. F. (1973). Defensive and supportive communications in normal and deviant families. *Journal of Consulting and Clinical Psychology, 40,* 223–231.

Alexander, J. F., Barton, C., Schiavo, R. S., & Parsons, B. V. (1976). Systems-behavioral intervention with families of delinquents: Therapist characteristics, family behavior, and outcome. *Journal of Consulting and Clinical Psychology, 44,* 656–664.

Alexander, J. F., Haas, L. J., Klein, N. C., & Warburton, J. R. (1980, May). *Functional family therapy.* Paper presented at meeting of Western Psychological Association, Honolulu, Hawaii.

Alexander, J. F., & Parsons, B. V. (1973). Short-term behavioral intervention with delinquent families: Impact on family process and recidivism. *Journal of Abnormal Psychology, 81,* 219–225.

Alexander, J. F., & Parsons, B. V. (1982). *Functional family therapy: Principles and procedures.* Carmel, CA: Brooks/Cole.

Alexander, J. F., Waldron, H. B., Barton, C., & Mas, C. H. (1989). The minimizing of blaming attributions and behaviors in delinquent families. *Journal of Consulting and Clinical Psychology, 57,* 19–24.

Algozzine, B. (1977). The emotionally disturbed child: Disturbed or disturbing? *Journal of Abnormal Child Psychology, 5,* 205–211.

Algozzine, B., & Ysseldyke, J. E. (1986). The future of the LD field: Screening and diagnosis. *Journal of Learning Disabilities, 19,* 394–398.

Allen, D. A., Tennen, H., McGrade, B. J., Affleck, G., & Ratzan, S. (1983). Parent and child perceptions of the management of juvenile diabetes. *Journal of Pediatric Psychology, 8,* 129–141.

Allen, K., Hart, B., Buell, J., Harris, F., & Wolf, M. (1964). Effects of social reinforcement on isolated behavior of a nursery school child. *Child Development, 35,* 511–518.

Allen, M. G. (1976). Twin studies of affective illness. *Archives of General Psychiatry, 33,* 1476–1478.

Alpert-Gillis, L. J., Pedro-Carroll, J. L., & Cowen, E. L. (1989). The Children of Divorce Intervention Program: Development, implementation, and evaluation of a program for young urban children. *Journal of Consulting and Clinical Psychology, 57,* 583–589.

Aman, M. G., & Kern, R. A. (1989). Review of fenfluramine in the treatment of the developmental disabilities. *Journal of the American Academy of Child and Adolescent Psychiatry, 28,* 549–565.

American Humane Association. (1984). *Trends in child abuse and neglect: A national perspective.* Denver: Author.

American Psychiatric Association (1952, 1968, 1980). *Diagnostic and statistical manual of mental disorders.* Washington, DC: American Psychiatric Association.

American Psychiatric Association (1987). *Diagnostic and statistical manual of mental disorders,* 3rd ed., rev. Washington, DC: American Psychiatric Association.

Amiel, S. A., Sherwin, R. S., Simonson, D. C., Lauritano, A. A., & Tamborlane, W. V. (1986). Impaired insulin action in puberty: A contributing factor to poor glycemic control in adolescents with diabetes. *New England Journal of Medicine, 315,* 215–219.

Anastasi, A. (1982, 1988). *Psychological testing.* New York: Macmillan.

Anastopoulos, A. D., & Barkely, R. A. (1988). Biological factors in attention deficit-hyperactivity disorder. *Behavior Therapist, 11,* 47–53.

Anders, T. F. (1982). Neurophysiological studies of sleep in infants and children. *Journal of Child Psychology and Psychiatry, 23,* 75–83.

Anders, T. F., & Weinstein, P. (1972). Sleep and its disorders in infants and children: A review. *The Journal of Pediatrics, 50,* 311–324.

Anderson, J. C., Williams, S., McGee, R., & Silva, P. A. (1987). DSM-III disorders in preadolescent children: Prevalence in a large sample from the general population. *Archives of General Psychiatry, 44,* 69–76.

Anderson, K. E., Lytton, H., & Romney, D. M. (1986). Mothers interactions with normal and conduct-disordered boys: Who affects whom? *Developmental Psychology, 22,* 604–609.

Anderson, L. T., Campbell, M., Adams, P., Small, A. M., Perry, R., & Shell, J. (1989). The effects of haloperidol on discrimination learning and behavioral symptoms in autistic children. *Journal of Autism and Developmental Disorders, 19,* 227–239.

Andrasik, F., & Attanasio, V. (1985). Biofeedback in pediatrics: Current status and appraisal. In M. L. Wolraich & D. K. Routh (Eds.), *Advances in developmental and behavioral pediatrics,* Vol. 6. Greenwich, CT: JAI.

Andrasik, F., Blake, D. D., & McCarran, M. S. (1986). A biobehavioral analysis of pediatric headache. In N. A. Krasnegor, J. D. Arasteh, & M. F. Cataldo (Eds.), *Child health behavior: A behavioral pediatrics perspective.* New York: Wiley.

Andreasen, N. C., Rice, J., Endicott, J., Coryell, W., Grove, W. W., & Reich, T. (1987). Familial rates of affective disorder. *Archives of General Psychiatry, 44,* 461–472.

Angelino, H., Dollins, J., & Mech, E. V. (1956). Trends in the "fears and worries" of school children as related to socioeconomic status and age. *Journal of Genetic Psychology, 89,* 263–276.

Anthony, E. J. (1970). Behavior disorders. In P. H. Mussen (Ed.), *Carmichael's manual of child psychology,* Vol. II. New York: John Wiley.

Anthony, E. J. (1981). The psychiatric evaluation of the anxious child: Case record summarized from the clinic records. In E. J. Anthony & D. C. Gilpin (Eds.), *Three further clinical faces of childhood.* New York: S P Medical & Scientific Books.

Anthony, E. J. (1987). Risk, vulnerability, and resilience: An overview. In Anthony, E. J., & Cohler, B. J. (Eds.), *The invulnerable child.* New York: Guilford.

Anthony, E. J., &: Cohler, B. J. (Eds.) (1987). *The invulnerable child.* New York: Guilford.

Aoki, C., & Siekevitz, P. (1988). Plasticity in brain development. *Scientific American, 259,* 56–64.

Aragona, J., Cassady, J., & Drabman, R. S. (1975). Treating overweight children through parental training and contingency contracting. *Journal of Applied Behavior Analysis, 8,* 269–278.

Arbuthnot, J., & Gordon, D. A. (1986). Behavioral and cognitive effects of a moral reasoning development intervention for high-risk behavior-disordered adolescents. *Journal of Consulting and Clinical Psychology, 54,* 208–216.

Aristimuno, G. G., Foster, T. A., Voors, A. W., Srinivasan, S. R., & Berenson, G. S. (1984). Influence of persistent obesity in children on cardiovascular risk factors: The Bogalusa Heart Study. *Circulation, 69,* 895–904.

Asarnow, J. R., & Ben-Meir, S. (1988). Children with schizophrenia spectrum and depressive disorders: A comparative study of premorbid adjustment, onset pattern and severity of impairment. *Journal of Child Psychology and Psychiatry, 29,* 477–488.

Asarnow, J. R., Carlson, G. A., & Guthrie, D. (1987). Coping strategies, self-perceptions, hopelessness, and perceived family environments in depressed and suicidal children. *Journal of Consulting and Clinical Psychology, 55,* 361–366.

Asarnow, J. R, & Goldstein, M. J. (1986). Schizophrenia during adolescence and early adulthood: A developmental perspective on risk research. *Clinical Psychology Review, 6,* 211–235.

Asarnow, J. R., Goldstein, M. J., & Ben-Meir, S. (1988). Parental communication deviance in childhood onset schizophrenia spectrum and depressive disorders. *Journal of Child Psychology and Psychiatry, 29,* 825–838.

Asarnow, R., Sherman, T., & Strandburg, R. (1986) The search for the psychobiological substrate of childhood onset schizophrenia. *Journal of the American Academy of Child and Adolescent Psychiatry, 25,* 601–604.

Asarnow, R. F., Tanguay, P. E., Bott, L., & Freeman, B. J. (1987). Patterns of intellectual functioning in non-retarded autistic and schizophrenic children. *Journal of Child Psychology and Psychiatry, 28,* 273–280.

Association of Sleep Disorders Centers and the Association for the Psychological Study of Sleep. (1979). Diagnostic classification of sleep and arousal disorders. *Sleep, 2,* 1–137.

Atkinson, R. C., & Shiffrin, R. M. (1968). Human memory: A proposed system and its control processes. In K. W. Spence & J. T. Spence (Eds.), *The psychology of learning and motivation.* New York: Academic Press.

Attwood, A., Frith, U., & Hermelin, B. (1988). The understanding and use of interpersonal gestures by autistic and Down's Syndrome children. *Journal of Autism and Developmental Disorders, 18,* 241–257.

August, G. J., & Garfinkel, B. D. (1989). Behavioral and cognitive subtypes of ADHD. *Journal of the American Academy of Child and Adolescent Psychiatry, 28,* 739–748.

Axline, V. M. (1947). *Play therapy.* Boston: Houghton Mifflin.

Ayllon, T., Layman, D., & Kandel, H. J. (1975). A behavioral-educational alternative to drug control of hyperactive children. *Journal of Applied Behavior Analysis, 8,* 137–146.

Azar, S. T., & Wolfe, D. A. (1989). Child abuse and neglect. In E. J. Mash & R. A. Barkley (Eds.), *Treatment of childhood disorders.* New York: Guilford.

Azrin, N. H., Sneed, T. J., & Foxx, R. M. (1974). Dry bed: Rapid elimination of childhood enuresis. *Behaviour Research and Therapy, 12,* 147–156.

B

Baer, G. C., & Richards, H. C. (1981). Moral reasoning and conduct problems in the classroom. *Journal of Educational Psychology, 73,* 644–670.

Bahr, H. M. (1988). Family change and the mystique of the traditional family. In L. A. Bond & B. M. Wagner (Eds.), *Families in transition: Primary prevention programs that work.* Newbury Park, CA: Sage.

Bailey, G. W. (1989). Current perspectives on substance abuse in youth. *Journal of the American Academy of Child and Adolescent Psychiatry, 28,* 151–162.

Baker, B. L. (1969). Symptom treatment and symptom substitution in enuresis. *Journal of Abnormal Psychology, 74,* 42–49.

Baker, L., & Cantwell, D. P. (1980). Specific developmental disorders of childhood and adolescence: Developmental language disorder. In H. I. Kaplan, A. M. Freedman, & B. J. Sadock (Eds.), *Comprehensive textbook of psychiatry/III,* Vol. 3. Baltimore: Williams & Wilkins.

Baker, L., & Cantwell, D. P. (1989). Specific language and learning disorders. In T. H. Ollendick & M. Hersen (Eds.). *Handbook of child psychopathology.* New York: Plenum.

Bakwin, H. (1971). Enuresis in twins. *American Journal of Diseases in Childhood, 121,* 222–225.

Bakwin, H., & Bakwin, R. M. (1972). *Behavior disorders in children,* 4th ed. Philadelphia: Saunders.

Bancroft, J., Axworthy, D., & Ratcliffe, F. (1982). The personality and psycho-sexual development of boys with 47XXY chromosome constitution. *Journal of Child Psychology and Psychiatry, 23,* 169–180.

Band, E. B. (1990). Children's coping with diabetes: Understanding the role of cognitive development. *Journal of Pediatric Psychology, 15,* 27–41.

Band, E. B., & Weisz, J. R. (1988). How to feel better when it feels bad: Children's perspectives on coping with everyday stress. *Developmental Psychology, 24,* 247–253.

Bandura, A. (1965). Influence of models' reinforcement contingencies on the acquisition of imitative responses. *Journal of Personality and Social Psychology, 1,* 589–595.

Bandura, A. (1977a). Self-efficacy: Towards a unifying theory of behavior change. *Psychological Review, 84,* 191–215.

Bandura, A. (1977b). *Social learning theory.* Englewood Cliffs, NJ: Prentice Hall.

Bandura, A. (1982). Self-efficacy mechanisms in human agency. *American Psychologist, 37,* 122–147.

Bandura, A. (1986). *Social foundations of thought and action.* Englewood Cliffs, NJ: Prentice Hall.

Bandura, A., & Menlove, F. L. (1968). Factors determining vicarious extinction of avoidance behavior through symbolic modeling. *Journal of Personality and Social Psychology, 8,* 99–108.

Barbosa-Saldivar, J. L., & Van Italie, T. B. (1979). Semistarvation: An overview of an old problem. *Bulletin of the New York Academy of Medicine, 55,* 774–797.

Barkley, R. A. (1981). Hyperactivity. In E. J. Mash & L. G. Terdal (Eds.), *Behavioral assessment of childhood disorders.* New York: Guilford Press.

Barkley, R. A. (1988a). Attention deficit disorder with hyperactivity. In E. J. Mash and L. G. Terdal (Eds.), *Behavioral assessment of childhood disorders. Selected core problems.* New York: Guilford.

Barkley, R. A. (1988b). Child behavior rating scales and checklists. In M. Rutter, A. H. Tuma, & I. S. Lann (Eds.), *Assessment and diagnosis in child psychopathology.* New York: Guilford.

Barkley, R. A. (1988c). The effects of methylphenidate on the interactions of preschool ADHD children with their mothers. *Journal of the American Academy of Child and Adolescent Psychiatry, 27,* 336–341.

Barkley, R. A. (1989). Attention deficit-hyperactivity disorder. In E. J. Mash and R. A. Barkley (Eds.), *Treatment of childhood disorders.* New York: Guilford.

Barkley, R. A., & Edelbrock, C. S. (1987). Assessing situational variation in children's behavior problems: The Home and School Situations Questionnaires. In R. Prinz (Ed.), *Advances in behavioral assessment of children and families,* Vol. 3. Greenwich, CT: JAI.

Barkley, R. A., McMurray, M. B., Edelbrock, C. S., & Robbins, K. (1989). The response of aggressive and nonaggressive ADHD children to two doses of methylphenidate. *Journal of the American Academy of Child and Adolescent Psychiatry, 28,* 873–881.

Barlow, D. H. (1988). *Anxiety and its disorders: The nature of anxiety and panic.* New York: Guilford.

Barlow, D. H., & Hersen, M. (1984). *Single case experimental designs: Strategies for studying behavior change.* Elmsford, NY: Pergamon.

Barnes, G. G. (1985). Systems theory and family theory. In M. Rutter and L. Hersov (Eds.), *Child and adolescent psychiatry.* Boston: Blackwell Scientific Publications.

Baron—Cohen, S. (1988). Social and pragmatic deficits in autism: Cognitive or affective? *Journal of Autism and Developmental Disorders, 18,* 379–397.

Baron—Cohen, S. (1989). The autistic child's theory of mind: A case of specific developmental delay. *Journal of Child Psychology and Psychiatry, 30,* 285–297.

Baron—Cohen, S., Leslie, A. M., & Frith, U. (1985). Does the autistic child have a "theory of mind"? *Cognition, 21,* 37–46.

Barrera, M. E., Rosenbaum, P. L., & Cunningham, C. E. (1986). Early home intervention with low-birthweight infants and their parents. *Child Development, 57,* 20–33.

Barrios, B. A., & Hartmann, D. P. (1988). Fears and anxieties. In E. J. Mash & L. G. Terdal (Eds.), *Behavioral assessment of childhood disorders,* 2nd ed. New York: Guilford.

Barrios, B. A., & O'Dell, S. L. (1989). Fears and anxieties. In E. J. Mash & R. A. Barkley (Eds.), *Treatment of childhood disorders.* New York: Guilford.

Barton, C., Alexander, J. F., Waldron, H., Turner, C. W., & Warburton, J. (1985). Generalizing treatment effects of functional family therapy: Three replications. *The American Journal of Family Therapy, 13,* 16–26.

Bates, J. E. (1987). Temperament in infancy. In J. D. Osofsky (Ed.), *Handbook of infant development.* New York: Wiley.

Bateson, G., Jackson, D. D., Haley, J., & Weakland, J. (1956). Toward a theory of schizophrenia. *Behavioral Science, 1,* 251–264.

Bauer, D. H. (1976). An exploratory study of developmental changes in children's fears. *Journal of Child Psychology and Psychiatry, 17,* 69–74.

Baum, C. G. (1989). Conduct disorders. In T. H. Ollendick & M. Hersen (Eds.), *Handbook of child psychopathology,* 2nd ed. New York: Plenum.

Baumeister, A. A. (1987). Mental retardation: Some conceptions and dilemmas. *American Psychologist, 42,* 796–800.

Baumrind, D. (1964). Some thoughts on ethics of research—after reading Milgram's "Behavioral study of obedience." *American Psychologist, 19,* 421–423.

Baumrind, D. (1967). Child care practices anteceding three patterns of preschool behavior. *Genetic Psychology Monographs, 76,* 43–88.

Baumrind, D. (1986). Sex differences in moral reasoning: Response to Walker's (1984) conclusion that there are none. *Child Development, 57,* 511–521.

Bayley, N. (1969). *Bayley Scales of Infant Development: Birth to two years.* New York: Psychological Corporation.

Beardslee, W. R. (1986). The need for the study of adaption in the children of parents with affective disorders. In M. Rutter, C. E. Izard, & P. B. Read (Eds.), *Depression in young people: Developmental and clinical perspectives.* New York: Guilford.

Beardslee, W. R., Bemporad, J., Keller, M. B., & Klerman, G. L. (1983). Children of parents with major affective disorder: A review. *American Journal of Psychiatry, 140,* 825–832.

Beardslee, W. R., & Podorefsky, D. (1988). Resilient adolescents whose parents have serious affective and other psychiatric disorders: Importance of self-understanding and relationships. *American Journal of Psychiatry, 145,* 63–69.

Beck, A. T. (1967). *Depression: Clinical, experimental, and theoretical aspects.* New York: Harper & Row.

Beck, A. T., Ward, C. H., Mendelson, M., Mock, J. E., & Erbaugh, J. K. (1962). Reliability of psychiatric diagnosis: II. A study of consistency of clinical judgements and ratings. *American Journal of Psychiatry, 119,* 351–357.

Bell, R. (1985). *Holy anorexia.* Chicago: University of Chicago Press.

Bellak, L. (1971). *The Thematic Apperception Test and Children's Apperception Test.* New York: Grune & Stratton.

Belsky, J. (1980). Child maltreatment: An ecological integration. *American Psychologist, 35,* 320–335.

Belsky, J. (1988). The "effects" of infant day care reconsidered. *Early Childhood Research Quarterly, 3,* 235–272.

Belsky, J., Gilstrap, B., & Rovine, M. (1984). The Pennsylvania Infant and Family Development Project, I: Stability and change in mother-infant and father-infant interaction in a family setting at one, three, and nine months. *Child Development, 55,* 692–705.

Belsky, J., Rovine, M., & Taylor, D. G. (1984). The Pennsylvania Infant and Family Development Project, III: The origins of individual differences in infant-mother attachment: Maternal and infant contributions. *Child Development, 55,* 718–728.

Bem, S. L. (1985). Androgyny and gender schema theory: A conceptual and empirical integration. In T. B. Sonderegger (Ed.), *Nebraska symposium on motivation, 1984: Psychology and gender.* Lincoln, NE: University of Nebraska Press.

Bemis, K. M. (1978). Current approaches to the etiology and treatment of anorexia nervosa. *Psychological Bulletin, 85,* 593–617.

Bemporad, J. R. (1978). Encopresis. In B. B. Wolman, J. Egan, & A. O. Ross (Eds.), Handbook of treatments in childhood and adolescence. Englewood Cliffs, NJ: Prentice Hall.

Bemporad, J. R., & Schwab, M. E. (1986). The DSM-III and clinical child psychiatry. In T. Millon & G. L. Klerman (Eds.), *Contemporary directions in psychopathology: Toward DSM-IV.* New York: Guilford.

Bender, L. (1947). One hundred cases of childhood schizophrenia treated with electric shock. *Trans. American Neurological Association, 72,* 165–169.

Bender, L. (1972). Childhood schizophrenia. In S. I. Harrison & J. F. McDermott (Eds.), *Childhood psychopathology.* New York: International Universities Press.

Benedict, R. (1934a). Anthropology and the abnormal. *Journal of General Psychology, 10,* 59–82.

Benedict, R. (1934b). *Patterns of culture.* Boston: Houghton-Mifflin.

Benezra E., & Douglas, V. I. (1988). Short-term serial recall in ADDH, normal, and reading-disabled boys. *Journal of Abnormal Child Psychology, 16,* 511–525.

Bennett, W., & Gurin, J. (1982). *The dieter's dilemma: Eating less and weighing more.* New York: Basic Books.

Bennett, W. J. (1987). The role of the family in the nurture and protection of the young. *American Psychologist, 42,* 246–250.

Benton, A. L., & Sines, J. O. (1985). Psychological testing of children. In H. I. Kaplan & B. J. Sadock (Eds.), *Comprehensive textbook of psychiatry/IV,* 4th ed. Baltimore: Williams & Wilkins.

Berecz, J. M. (1968). Phobias of childhood: Etiology and treatment. *Psychological Bulletin, 70,* 694–720.

Bereiter, C. (1972). An academic preschool for disadvantaged children: Conclusions from evaluation studies. In J. C. Stanley (Ed.), *Preschool programs for the disadvantaged.* Baltimore, Md.: John Hopkins University Press.

Berg, I. (1976). School phobia in the children of agoraphobic women. *British Journal of Psychiatry, 128,* 86–89.

Berg, I., & Jackson, A. (1985). Teenage school refusers grow up: A follow-up study of 168 subjects ten years on average after inpatient treatment. *British Journal of Psychiatry, 147,* 366–370.

Berger, M. (1986). Toward an educated use of IQ tests: A reappraisal of intelligence testing. In B. B. Lahey & A. E. Kazdin (Eds.), *Advances in clinical child psychology,* Vol. 9. New York: Plenum.

Berger, M., & Yule, W. (1985). IQ tests and assessment. In A. M. Clarke, A. D. B. Clarke, & J. M. Berg (Eds.), *Mental deficiency. The changing outlook*. New York: The Free Press.

Berney, T., Kolvin, I., Bhate, S. R., Garside, R. F., Jeans, J., Kay, B., & Scarth, L. (1981). School phobia: A therapeutic trial with clomipramine and short-term outcome. *British Journal of Psychiatry, 138*, 110–118.

Bernstein, G. A., & Garfinkel, B. D. (1986). School phobia: The overlap of affective and anxiety disorders. *Journal of the American Academy of Child Psychiatry, 2*, 235–241.

Berry, P., Groeneweg, G., Gibson, D., & Brown, R. I. (1984). Mental development of adults with Down Syndrome. *American Journal of Mental Deficiency, 89*, 252–256.

Bersoff, D. N. (1981). Testing and the law. *American Psychologist, 36*, 1047–1056.

Bertenthal, B. J., & Campos, J. J. (1987). New directions in the study of early experience. *Child Development, 58*, 560–567.

Bettes, B. A., & Walker, E. (1987). Positive and negative symptoms in psychotic and other psychiatrically disturbed children. *Journal of Child Psychology and Psychiatry, 28*, 555–568.

Bettleheim, B. (1967a). *The empty fortress*. New York: Free Press.

Bettleheim, B. (1967b, Feb. 12). Where self begins. *New York Times*.

Biederman, J., Munir, K., Knee, D., Habelow, W., Armentano, M., Autor, S., Hoge, S. K., & Waternaux, C. (1986). A family study of patients with attention deficit disorder and normal controls. *Journal of Psychiatric Research, 20*, 263–274.

Bierman, K. ., & Furman, W. (1984). The effects of social skills training and peer involvement on the social adjustment of preadolescents. *Child Development, 55*, 151–162.

Bierman, K. L., & Schwartz, L. A. (1986). Clinical child interviews: Approaches and developmental considerations. *Journal of Child and Adolescent Psychotherapy, 3*, 267–278.

Bigler, E. D. (1987). Acquired cerebral trauma. *Journal of Learning Disabilities, 20*, 455–457.

Bijou, S. W., Peterson, R. F., Harris, F. R., Allen, K. E., & Johnston, M. S. (1969). Methodology for experimental studies of young children in natural settings. *The Psychological Record, 19*, 177–210.

Billings, A. G., & Moos, R. H. (1983). Comparisons of children of depressed and nondepressed parents: A social-environmental perspective. *Journal of Abnormal Child Psychology, 11*, 463–485.

Billings, A. G., & Moos, R. H. (1986). Children of parents with unipolar depression: A controlled 1-year follow-up. *Journal of Abnormal Child Psychology, 14*, 149–166.

Billings, A. G., Moos, R. H., Miller, J. J., & Gotlieb, J. E. (1987). Psychosocial adaptation in juvenile rheumatic disease: A controlled evaluation. *Health Psychology, 6*, 343–359.

Birmaher, B., Greenhill, L. L., Cooper, T. B., Fried, J., & Maminski, B. (1989). Sustained release methylphenidate: Pharmacokinetic studies in ADDH males. *Journal of the American Academy of Child and Adolescent Psychiatry, 28*, 768–772.

Birnbrauer, J. S. (1976). Mental retardation. In H. Leitenberg (Ed.), *Handbook of behavior modification and behavior therapy*. Englewood Cliffs, NJ: Prentice Hall.

Birns, B. (1976). The emergence and socialization of sex differences in the earliest years. *Merrill-Palmer Quarterly, 22*, 229–254.

Blasi, A. (1980). Bridging moral cognition and moral action: A critical review of the literature. *Psychological Bulletin, 88*, 1–45.

Blatcher, J. (1984). Sequential stages of parental adjustment to the birth of a child with handicaps: Fact or artifact? *Mental Retardation, 22*, 55–68.

Bleeker, E. R., & Engle, B. T. (1973). Learned control of cardiac rate and cardiac conduction in Wolff-Parkinson-White syndrome. *Seminars in Psychiatry, 5*, 465–479.

Bloom, B. L. (1981). The logic and urgency of primary prevention. *Hospital and community psychiatry, 32*, 839–843.

Bohman, M., Cloninger, R. C., Sigvardsson, S., & Knorring, A. von (1982). Predisposition to criminality in Swedish adoptees: I. Genetic and environmental heterogeneity. *Archives of General Psychiatry, 39*, 1233–1241.

Boivin, M., & Begin, G. (1989). Peer status and self-perception among early elementary school children: The case of the rejected children. *Child Development, 60*, 591–596.

Bond, M. A. (1989). Ethical dilemmas in context: Some preliminary questions. *American Journal of Community Psychology, 17*, 355–359.

Bootzin, R. R., & Chambers, M. J. (1990). Childhood sleep disorders. In A. M. Gross & R. S. Drabman (Eds.), *Handbook of clinical behavioral pediatrics*. New York: Plenum.

Borkovec, T. D. (1970). Autonomic reactivity to sensory stimulation in psychopathic, neurotic and normal delinquents. *Journal of Consulting and Clinical Psychology, 35*, 217–222.

Borkowski, J. G., & Cavanaugh, J. C. (1979). Maintenance and generalization of skills and strategies by the retarded. In N. R. Ellis (Ed.), *Handbook of mental deficiency*. Hillsdale, NJ: Erlbaum.

Borkowski, J. G., Johnston, M. B., & Reid, M. K. (1987). Metacognition, motivation, and controlled performance. In S. J. Ceci (Ed.), *Handbook of cognitive, social, and neuropsychological aspects of learning disabilities*. Hillsdale, NJ: Erlbaum.

Bornstein, B. (1949). Analyses of a phobic child. *Psychoanalytic Study of the Child*, Vol. III-IV, 181–226.

Bornstein, M., Bellack, A., & Hersen, M. (1977). Social skills training for unassertive children: A multiple baseline analysis. *Journal of Applied Behavior Analysis, 10*, 183–195.

Bornstein, M. H., Gaughran, J. M., & Homel, P. (1986). In C. E. Izard & P. B. Read (Eds.), *Measuring emotions in infants and children*, Vol. 2. New York: Cambridge Univ. Press.

Bouchard, T. J. (1983). Do environmental similarities explain the similarity in intelligence of identical twins reared apart? *Intelligence, 7*, 175–184.

Boucher, J., & Lewis, V. (1989). Memory impairments and communication in relatively able autistic children. *Journal of Child Psychology and Psychiatry, 30*, 99–122.

Bowen, M. (1980). Introduction: Family systems theory. In S. I. Harrison & J. F. McDermott, Jr. (Eds.), *New directions in child psychopathology*, Vol. 1. New York: International Universities Press.

Bowers, D. W., Clement, P. W. Fantuzzo, J. W., Sorenson. D. A. (1985). Effects of teacher-administered and self-administered reinforcers on learning disabled children. *Behavior Therapy, 16*, 357–369.

Bowlby, J. (1960). Grief and mourning in infancy and early childhood. *Psychoanalytic Study of the Child, 15*, 9–52.

Braddock, D., & Heller, T. (1985a). The closure of mental retardation institutions I: Trends in the United States. *Mental Retardation, 23*, 168–176.

Braddock, D., & Heller, T. (1985b). The closure of mental retardation institutions II: Implications. *Mental Retardation, 23*, 222–229.

Bradley, C. (1947). Early evidence of psychoses in children, with special reference to schizophrenia. *Journal of Pediatrics, 30*, 529–540.

Brandenburg, N. A., Friedman, R. M., & Silver, S. E. (1990). The epidemiology of childhood psychiatric disorders: Prevalence findings from recent studies. *Journal of the American Academy of Child and Adolescent Psychiatry, 29*, 76–83.

Brassard, M. R., Germain, R., & Hart, S. N. (Eds.). (1987). *Psychological maltreatment of children and youth*. New York: Pergamon.

Bregman, E. O. (1934). An attempt to modify the emotional

attitudes of infants by the conditioned response technique. *Journal of Genetic Psychology, 45,* 169–198.

Breznitz, Z., & Friedman, S. L. (1988). Toddler's concentration: Does maternal depression make a difference? *Journal of Child Psychology and Psychiatry, 29,* 267–279.

Bridger, W. H., & Mandel, I. J. (1965). Abolition of the PRE by instructions in GSR conditioning. *Journal of Experimental Psychology, 69,* 476–482.

Brier, N. (1989). The relationship between learning disability and delinquency: A review and reappraisal. *Journal of Learning Disabilities, 22,* 546–553.

Bronfenbrenner, U. (1974). *A report on longitudinal evaluations of preschool programs, Volume II: Is early intervention effective?* Washington, DC: Department of Health, Education, and Welfare.

Bronfenbrenner, U. (1986). Ecology of the family as a context for human development: Research perspectives. *Developmental Psychology, 22,* 723–742.

Bronheim, S. P. (1978). Pulmonary disorders: Asthma and cystic fibrosis. In P. R. Magrab (Ed.), *Psychological management of pediatric problems,* Vol. 1. Baltimore, MD: University Park Press.

Brown, G. W. (1988). Causal paths, chains and strands. In Rutter, M. (Ed.), *Studies of psychosocial risk: The power of longitudinal data.* New York: Cambridge University Press.

Brown, L., Branston, M., Hamre-Nietupski, S., Pumpian, I., Certo, N., & Grunenewald, L. (1979). A strategy for developing chronological age-appropriate and functional curricular content for severely handicapped adolescents and young adults. *Journal of Special Education, 13,* 81–90.

Brown, R. T., Borden, K. A., Wynne, M. E., Schleser, R., & Clingerman, S. R. (1986). Methylphenidate and cognitive therapy with ADD children: A methodological reconsideration. *Journal of Abnormal Child Psychology, 14,* 481–497.

Brownell, C. A. (1986). Convergent developments: Cognitive-developmental correlates of growth in infant/toddler peer skills. *Child Development, 57,* 275–286.

Bruch, H. (1973). *Eating disorders: Obesity, anorexia nervosa, and the person within.* New York: Basic Books.

Bruch, H. (1979). *The golden cage: The enigma of anorexia nervosa.* New York: Vintage Books.

Bruch, H. (1986). Anorexia nervosa: The therapeutic task. In K. D. Brownell & J. P. Foreyt (Eds.), *Handbook of eating disorders: Physiology, psychology, and treatment of obesity, anorexia, and bulimia.* New York: Basic Books.

Bruininks, R. H., Hauber, F. A., & Kudla, M. J. (1980). National survey of community residential facilities: A profile of facilities and residents in 1977. *American Journal of Mental Deficiency, 84,* 470–478.

Brumberg, J. J. (1986). "Fasting girls": Reflections on writing the history of anorexia nervosa. In A. B. Smuts & J. W. Hagen (Eds.), History and research in child development. *Monographs of the Society for Research in Child Development, 50*(4–5, Serial No. 211).

Bryan, T., & Bryan, J. (1990). Social factors in learning disabilities: An overview. In H. L. Swanson & B. Keogh (Eds.), *Learning disabilities. Theoretical and research issues.* Hillsdale, NJ: Erlbaum.

Bryan, T. H., & Bryan, J. H. (1975, 1986). *Understanding learning disabilities.* Palo Alto, CA: Mayfield.

Bryant, K. (1977). Speech and language development. In M. J. Krajicek & A. I. Tearney (Eds.), *Detection of developmental problems in children.* Baltimore: University Park Press.

Bryson, S. E., Clark, B. S., & Smith, I. M. (1988). First report of a Canadian epidemiological study of autistic syndromes. *Journal of Child Psychology and Psychiatry, 29,* 433–445.

Bryson, S. E., Smith, I. M., & Eastwood, D. (1988). Obstetrical suboptimality in autistic children. *Journal of the American Academy of Child and Adolescent Psychiatry, 27,* 418–422.

Bullock, M., & Russell, J. A. (1986). Concepts of emotion in developmental psychology. In C. E. Izard & P. B. Read (Eds.), *Measuring emotions in infants and children,* Vol. 2. New York: Cambridge Univ. Press.

Burchard, J. D., & Harig, P. T. (1976). Behavior modification and juvenile delinquency. In H. Leitenberg (Ed.), *Handbook of behavior modification and behavior therapy.* Englewood Cliffs, NJ: Prentice Hall.

Bureau of the Census (1985). *Current population reports: Marital status and living arrangements: March 1984.* (Series P–20, No. 399). Washington, DC: U.S. Government Printing Office.

Burke, A. E., & Silverman, W. K. (1987). The prescriptive treatment of school refusal. *Clinical Psychology Review, 7,* 353–362.

Busch-Rossnagel, N. A., & Vance, A. K. (1982). The impact of the schools on social and emotional development. In B. B. Wolman (Ed.). *Handbook of developmental psychology.* Englewood Cliffs, NJ: Prentice Hall.

Buss, A. H., & Plomin, R. (1986). The EAS approach to temperament. In R. Plomin and J. Dunn (Eds.), *The study of temperament: Changes, continuities, and challenges.* Hillsdale, NJ: Erlbaum.

Butler, L., Miezitis, S., Friedman, R., & Cole, E. (1980). The effect of two school-based intervention programs on depressive symptoms in preadolescents. *American Educational Research Journal, 17,* 111–119.

Butler, R. J., Brewin, C. R., & Forsythe, W. I. (1988). A comparison of two approaches to the treatment of nocturnal enuresis and the prediction of effectiveness using pretreatment variables. *Journal of Child Psychology and Psychiatry and Allied Disciplines, 29,* 501–509.

Butterfield, E. C., & Belmont, J. M. (1977). Assessing and improving the executive cognitive functions of mentally retarded people. In I. Bialer & M. Sternlicht (Eds.), *Psychological issues in mental retardation.* New York: Psychological Dimensions.

C

Caldwell, B. M., Bradley, R. H., & Elardo, R. (1975). Early stimulation. In J. Wortis (Ed.), *Mental retardation and developmental disabilities.* New York: Brunner/Mazel.

Cammann, R., & Miehlke, A. (1989). Differentiation of motor activity of normally active and hyperactive boys in schools: Some preliminary results. *Journal of Child Psychology and Psychiatry, 30,* 899–906.

Campbell, D. T., & Stanley, J. C. (1963). *Experimental and quasi-experimental designs for research.* Chicago: Rand McNally.

Campbell, M. (1988). Annotation. Fenfluramine treatment of autism. *Journal of Child Psychology and Psychiatry, 29,* 1–10.

Campbell, M., Adams, P., Small, A. M., Curren, E. L., Overall, J. E., Anderson, L. T., Lynch, N., & Perry, R. (1988). Efficacy and safety of fenfluramine in autistic children. *Journal of the American Academy of Child and Adolescent Psychiatry, 27,* 434–439.

Campbell, M., Cohen, I. L., Perry, R., & Small, A. M. (1989a). Psychopharmacological treatment. In T. H. Ollendick & M. Hersen (Eds.), *Handbook of child psychopathology.* New York: Plenum.

Campbell, M., Geller, B., & Cohen, I. L. (1977). Current status of drug research and treatment with autistic children. *Journal of Pediatric Psychology, 2,* 153–161.

Campbell, M., & Green, W. H. (1985). Pervasive developmental disorders of childhood. In H. I. Kaplan & B. J. Sadock (Eds.), *Comprehensive textbook of psychiatry/IV.* Baltimore: Williams and Wilkins.

Campbell, M., Overall, J. E., Small, A. M., Sokol, M. S., Spencer, E. K., Adams, P., Foltz, R. L., Monti, K. M., Perry, R., Nobler, M., & Roberts, E. (1989b). Naltrexone in autistic children: An acute open dose range tolerance trial. *Journal of the American Academy of Child and Adolescent Psychiatry, 28,* 200–206.

Campbell, M., & Spencer, E. K. (1988). Psychopharmacology in child and adolescent psychiatry: A review of the past five years. *Journal of the American Academy of Child and Adolescent Psychiatry, 27,* 269–279.

Campbell, S. B. (1985). Hyperactivity in preschoolers: Correlates and prognostic implications. *Clinical Psychology Review, 5,* 405–428.

Campbell, S. B. (1986). Developmental issues in childhood anxiety. In R. Gittleman (Ed.), *Anxiety disorders of childhood.* New York: Guilford.

Campbell, S. B. (1987). Parent-referred problem three-year-olds: Developmental changes in symptoms. *Journal of Child Psychology and Psychiatry, 28,* 835–845.

Campbell, S. B. (1989). Developmental perspectives. In T. H. Ollendick & M. Hersen (Eds.), *Handbook of child psychopathology.* New York: Plenum.

Campbell, S. B., Breux, A. M., Ewing, L. J., & Szumowski, E. K. (1986). Correlates and predictors of hyperactivity and aggression: A longitudinal study of parent-referred problem preschoolers. *Journal of Abnormal Child Psychology, 14,* 217–234.

Campos, J. J., Barrett, K. C., Lamb, M. E., Goldsmith, H. H., & Stenberg, C. (1983). Socioemotional development. In P. H. Mussen (Ed.), *Handbook of child development,* Vol. II. New York: Wiley.

Candy-Gibbs, S. E., Sharp, K. C., & Petrun, C. J. (1985). The effects of age, object, and cultural/religious background on children's concepts of death. *Omega Journal of Death and Dying, 15,* 329–346.

Canino, G. J., Bird, H. R., Rubio-Stipec, M., Woodbury, M. A., Ribera, J. C., Huertas, S. E., & Sesman, M. J. (1987). Reliability of child diagnosis in a hispanic sample. *Journal of the American Academy of Child and Adolescent Psychiatry, 26,* 560–565.

Cantor, S. (1988). *Childhood schizophrenia.* New York: Guilford.

Cantor, S., Evans, J., Pearce, J., & Pezzot-Pearce, T. (1982). Childhood schizophrenia: Present but not accounted for. *American Journal of Psychiatry, 139,* 758–762.

Cantor, S., & Kestenbaum, C. (1986). Psychotherapy with schizophrenic children. *Journal of the American Academy of Child Psychiatry, 25,* 623–630.

Cantwell, D. P. (Ed.). (1975). *The hyperactive child.* New York: Spectrum Publ.

Cantwell, D. P. (1980). The diagnostic process and diagnostic classification in child psychiatry: DSM-III. *Journal of the American Academy of Child Psychiatry, 19,* 345–355.

Cantwell, D. P. (1986). Attention deficit and associated childhood disorders. In T. Mellon & G.L. Klerman (Eds.), *Contemporary directions in psychopathology: Toward DSM-IV.* New York: Guilford.

Cantwell, D. P., & Baker, L. (1988). Issues in the classification of child and adolescent psychopathology. *Journal of the American Academy of Child and Adolescent Psychiatry, 27,* 521–533.

Cantwell, D. P., Baker, L., Rutter, M., & Mawhood, L. (1989). Infantile autism and developmental receptive aphasia. *Journal of Autism and Developmental Disorders, 19,* 19–31.

Cantwell, D. P., Russell, A. T., Mattison, R., & Will, L. (1979). A comparison of DSM-II and DSM-III in the diagnosis of childhood psychiatric disorders: I. Agreement with expected diagnosis. *Archives of General Psychiatry, 36,* 1208–1213.

Caplan, G. (1964). *The principles of preventive psychiatry.* New York: Basic Books.

Caplan, M., & Douglas, V. (1969). Incidence of parental loss in children with depressed mood. *Journal of Child Psychology and Psychiatry, 10,* 225–232.

Capute, A. J., Accardo, P. J., Vining, E. P. G., Rubenstein, J. E., & Harryman, S. (1978). *Primitive reflex profile.* Baltimore, MD: University Park Press.

Carlson, G. A., & Cantwell, D. P. (1980). Unmasking masked depression in children and adolescents. *American Journal of Psychiatry, 137,* 445–449.

Carnine, D. W., & Kameenui, E. J. (1990). The general education initiative and children with special needs: A false dilemma in the face of true problems. *Journal of Learning Disabilities, 23,* 141–144,148.

Carr, E. G. (1977). The motivation of self-injurious behavior: A review of some hypotheses. *Psychological Bulletin, 84,* 800–816.

Carr, E. G., & Durand, V. M. (1985). Reducing behavior problems through functional communication training. *Journal of Applied Behavior Analysis, 18,* 111–126.

Carr, E. G., Newsom, C. B., & Binkoff, J. A. (1976). Stimulus control of self-destructive behavior in a psychotic child. *Journal of Abnormal Child Psychology, 4,* 139–153.

Carr, J. (1985). The effect on the family of a severely mentally handicapped child. In A. M. Clarke, A. D. B. Clarke, & J. M. Berg (Eds.), *Mental deficiency: The changing outlook.* New York: The Free Press.

Carron, A. V., & Bailey, D. A. (1974). Strength development in boys from 10 through 16 years. *Monographs of the Society for Research in Child Development, 39* (4), No. 157, 1–37.

Casey, R. J., & Berman, J. S. (1985). The outcome of psychotherapy with children. *Psychological Bulletin, 98,* 388–400.

Caspi, A., Elder, G. H. Jr., & Bem, D. J. (1987). Moving against the world: Life-course patterns of explosive children. *Developmental Psychology, 23,* 308–313.

Caspi, A., Elder, G. H., Jr., & Bem, D. J. (1988). Moving away from the world: Life-course patterns of shy children. *Developmental Psychology, 24,* 824–831.

Cattell, P. (1960). *The measurement of intelligence of infants and young children.* New York: Psychological Corporation.

Ceci, S. J. (1990). A sideway glance at this thing called LD: A context X process X person framework. In H. L. Swanson & B. Keogh (Eds.), *Learning disabilities. Theoretical and research issues.* Hillsdale, NJ: Erlbaum.

Ceci, S. J., & Baker, J. G. (1987). Commentary: How shall we conceptualize the language problems of learning-disabled children? In S. J. Ceci (Ed.), *Handbook of cognitive, social and neuropsychological aspects of learning disabilities.* New York: Academic Press.

Ceci, S. J., & Baker, J. G. (1989). On learning . . . more or less: A knowledge X process X context view of learning disabilities. *Journal of Learning Disabilities, 22,* 90–99.

Chalfant, J. C. (1989). Learning disabilities: Policy issues and promising approaches. *American Psychologist, 44,* 392–398.

Chambers, W. J., Puig-Antich, J., Hirsch, M., Paez, P., Ambrosini, P. J., Tabrizi, M. A., & Davies, M. (1985). The assessment of affective disorders in children and adolescents by semi-structured interview: Test-retest reliability of the K-SADS-P. *Archives of General Psychiatry, 42,* 696–702.

Chandler, M. J. (1973). Egocentrism and antisocial behavior: The assessment and training of social perspective-taking skills. *Developmental Psychology, 9,* 326–332.

Charlesworth, R., & Hartup, W. (1967). Positive social reinforcement in the nursery school peer group. *Child Development, 38,* 993–1002.

Charlop, M. H. (1986). Setting effects on the occurrence of autistic children's immediate echolalia. *Journal of Autism and Developmental Disorders, 16,* 473–483.

Chatoor, I., Conley, C., & Dickson, L. (1988). Food refusal after an incident of choking: A posttraumatic eating disorder. *Journal of the American Academy of Child and Adolescent Psychiatry, 27,* 105–110.

Chess, S. (1988). Child and adolescent psychiatry come of age:

A fifty year perspective. *Journal of the American Academy of Child and Adolescent Psychiatry, 27,* 1–7.

Chess, S., & Thomas, A. (1972). Differences in outcome with early intervention in children with behavior disorders. In M. Roff, L. Robins, & M. Pollack (Eds.), *Life history research in psychopathology,* Vol. 2. Minneapolis: University of Minnesota Press.

Chess, S., & Thomas, A. (1977). Temperamental individuality from childhood to adolescence. *Journal of the American Academy of Child Psychiatry, 16,* 218–226.

Chiland, C. (1988). "Minimal brain dysfunction"—fact or fiction? In E. J. Anthony & C. Chiland (Eds.), *The child in his family,* Vol. 8. New York: Wiley.

Chinn, P. C., & Hughes, S. (1987). Representation of minority students in special education classes. *Remedial and Special Education, 8,* 41–46.

Christophersen, E. R., Barnard, J. D., Ford, D., & Wolf, M. M. (1976). The family training program: Improving parent-child interaction patterns. In E. J. Marsh, L. C. Handy, & L. A. Hamerlynck (Eds.), *Behavior modification approaches to parenting.* New York: Brunner/Mazel.

Cialdella, Ph., & Mamelle, N. (1989). An epidemiological study of infantile autism in a French Department (Rhone): A research note. *Journal of Child Psychology and Psychiatry, 30,* 165–175.

Cicchetti, D. (1984). The emergence of developmental psychopathology. *Child Development, 55,* 1–7.

Cicchetti, D. (1989). Developmental psychology: Some thoughts on its evolution. *Development and Psychopathology, 1,* 1–3.

Cicchetti, D., & Rizley, R. (1981). Developmental perspectives on the etiology, intergenerational transmission, and sequelae of child maltreatment. In R. Rizley & D. Cicchetti (Eds.), *New directions for child development: Developmental perspectives on child maltreatment.* San Francisco: Jossey-Bass.

Cicchetti, D., & Schneider-Rosen, K. (1986). An organizational approach to childhood depression. In M. Rutter, C. Izard, & P. Read (Eds.), *Depression in young people: Clinical and developmental perspectives.* New York: Guilford.

Cicchetti, D., Toth, S., & Bush, M. (1988). Developmental psychopathology and incompetence in childhood: Suggestions for intervention. In B. B. Lahey & A. E. Kazdin (Eds.), *Advances in clinical child psychology,* Vol. 11. New York: Plenum.

Clarke, A. D. B., & Clarke, A. M. (1984). Constancy and change in the growth of human characteristics. *Journal of Child Psychology and Psychiatry, 25,* 191–210.

Clarke, A. M. (1985). Polygene and environmental interactions. In A. M. Clarke, A. D. B. Clarke, & J. M. Berg (Eds.), *Mental deficiency. The changing outlook.* New York: The Free Press.

Clarke, A. M., & Clarke, A. D. B. (1985). Criteria and classification. In A. M. Clarke, A. D. B. Clarke, & J. M. Berg (Eds.), *Mental deficiency. The changing outlook.* New York: The Free Press.

Clarke-Stewart, K. A. (1978). And daddy makes three: The father's impact on mother and young child. *Child Development, 49,* 466–478.

Clarke-Stewart, K. A. (1989). Infant day care: Maligned or malignant? *American Psychologist, 44,* 266–273.

Clayton, R. R. (1986). Multiple drug use. *Recent Developments in Alcohol, 4,* 7–38.

Clements, P. R., Boft, L., DuBois, Y., & Turpin, W. (1980). Adaptive Behavior Scale, Part II: Relative severity of maladaptive behavior. *American Journal of Mental Deficiency, 84,* 465–469.

Cloninger, R. C., Sigvardsson, S., Bohman, M., Knorring, A. von (1982). Predisposition to petty criminality in Swedish adoptees: II. Cross-fostering analysis of gene-environment interaction. *Archives of General Psychiatry, 39,* 1242–1247.

Cohen, P., Velez, D. N., Brook, J., & Smith, J. (1989). Mechanisms of the relation between perinatal problems, early childhood illness, and psychopathology in late childhood and adolescence. *Child Development, 60,* 701–709.

Coie, J. D., Belding, M., & Underwood, M. (1988). Aggression and peer rejection in childhood. In B. B. Lahey & A. E. Kazdin (Eds.), *Advances in clinical child psychology,* Vol. 11. New York: Plenum.

Coles, G. S. (1987). *The learning mystique.* New York: Pantheon.

Coles, G. S. (1989). Excerpts from The Learning Mystique: A Critical Look at "Learning Disabilities." *Journal of Learning Disabilities, 22,* 267–273,277.

Combrinck-Graham, L. (1986). Family treatment for childhood anxiety disorders. In L. Combrinck-Graham (Ed.), *Treating young children in family therapy.* Rockville, MD: Aspen Publishers.

Combs, M., & Slaby, D. (1977). Social skills training in children. In A. Kazdin & B. Lahey (Eds.), *Advances in clinical child psychology.* New York: Plenum.

Cone, J. D. (1987). Behavioral assessment with children and adolescents. In M. Hersen & V. B. Van Hasselt (Eds.), *Behavior therapy with children and adolescents: A clinical approach.* New York: Wiley.

Conger, J., & Keane, S. (1981). Social skills intervention in the treatment of isolated or withdrawn children. *Psychological Bulletin, 90,* 478–495.

Conners, C. K. (1969). A teacher rating scale for use with drug studies with children. *American Journal of Psychiatry, 126,* 884–888.

Conners, C. K. (1973). Rating scales for use in drug studies with children. *Psychopharmacology Bulletin, 24*–29.

Conners, C. K. (1978). Psycotropic drug treatment of children. In J. G. Bernstein (Ed.), *Clinical psychopharmacology.* Littleton, MA: PSG Publishing.

Conners, C. K. (1980). Artificial colors in the diet and disruptive behavior. In R. M. Knights & D. J. Bakker (Eds.), *Treatment of hyperactive and learning disabled children.* Baltimore: University Park Press.

Conners, C. K., & Werry, J. S. (1979). Pharmacotherapy. In H. C. Quay & J. S. Werry (Eds.), *Psychopathological disorders of childhood.* New York: Wiley.

Coons, H. W., Klorman, R., & Borgstedt, A. D. (1987). Effects of methylphenidate on adolescents with a childhood history of attention deficit disorder: II. Information processing. *Journal of the American Academy of Child and Adolescent Psychiatry, 26,* 368–374.

Coovert, D. L., Kinder, B. N. & Thompson, J. K. (1989). The psychosexual aspects of anorexia nervosa and bulimia nervosa: A review of the literature. *Clinical Psychology Review, 9,* 169–180.

Corbett, J. A. (1985). Mental retardation: Psychiatric aspects. In M. Rutter & L. Hersov (Eds.), *Child and adolescent psychiatry.* Boston: Blackwell Scientific Publications.

Corley, D. L., Gevirtz, R., Nideffer, R., & Cummins, L. (1987). Prevention of post-infectious asthma in children by reducing self-inoculatory behavior. *Journal of Pediatric Psychology, 12,* 519–531.

Corman, L., & Gottlieb, J. (1978). Mainstreaming mentally retarded children: A review of the research. In N.R. Ellis (Ed.), *International review of research in mental retardation,* Vol. 9. New York: Academic Press.

Costello, E. J. (1989). Developments in child psychiatric epidemiology. *Journal of the American Academy of Child and Adolescent Psychiatry, 28,* 836–841.

Costello, E. J., Edelbrock, C. S., & Costello, A. J. (1985). Validity of the NIMH Diagnostic Interview Schedule for Children: A comparison between psychiatric and pediatric referrals. *Journal of Abnormal Child Psychology, 13,* 579–595.

Cotler, S. (1986). Epidemiology and outcome. In J. M. Reisman

(Ed.), *Behavior disorders in infants, children, and adolescents*. New York: Random House.

Cowan, W. M. (1979). The development of the brain. *Scientific American, 241*, 112–133.

Cowen, E., Pederson, A., Babigian, H., Izzo, L., & Trost, N. (1973). Long term follow-up of early detected vulnerable children. *Journal of Consulting and Clinical Psychology, 41*, 438–446.

Cowen, E. L. (1980). The wooing of primary prevention. *American Journal of Community Psychology, 8*, 258–284.

Cowen, E. L., Gesten, E. L., & Wilson, A. B. (1979). The Primary Mental Health Project (PMHP): Evaluation of current program effectiveness. *American Journal of Community Psychology, 3*, 293–303.

Cowen, E. L., & Hightower, A.D. (1989a). The Primary Mental Health Project: Alternatives in school based preventive interventions. In T. B. Gutkin & C. R. Reynolds (Eds.), *Handbook of school psychology*, 2nd ed. New York: Wiley.

Cowen, E. L., & Hightower, A. D. (1989b). The Primary Mental Health Project: Thirty years after. In R. E. Hess, & J. DeLeon (Eds.), *Prevention in human services*, Vol. 6, No. 2. New York: Haworth.

Cowen, E. L., Hightower, A. D., Johnson, D. B., Sarno, M., & Weissberg, R. P. (1989). State-level dissemination of a program for early detection and prevention of school maladjustment. *Professional Psychology: Research and Practice, 20*, 309–314.

Cowen, E. L., Trost, M. A., Lorion, R. P., Dorr, D., Izzo, L. D., & Issacson, R. V. (1975). *New ways in school mental health: Early detection and prevention of school maladaptation*. New York: Human Sciences Press.

Cowen, E. L., Zax, M., Izzo, L. D., & Trost, M. A. (1966). Prevention of emotional disorders in the school setting: A further investigation. *Journal of Consulting Psychology, 30*, 381–387.

Cox, A., & Rutter, M. (1985). Diagnostic appraisal and interviewing. In M. Rutter & L. Hersov (Eds.), *Child and adolescent psychiatry: Modern approaches*. Oxford: Blackwell Scientific Publications.

Cozby, P. C., Worden, P. E., & Kee, D. W. (1989). *Research methods in human development*. Mountain View, CA: Mayfield.

Craig, E. M., & McCarver, R. B. (1984). Community placement and adjustment of deinstitutionalized clients: Issues and findings. In N. R. Ellis & N. W. Bray (Eds.), *International review of research in mental retardation*. New York: Academic Press.

Creer, T. L. (1982). Asthma. *Journal of Consulting and Clinical Psychology, 50*, 912–921.

Creer, T. L., Harm, D. L., & Marion, R. J. (1988). Childhood asthma. In D. K. Routh (Ed.), *Handbook of pediatric psychology*. New York: Guilford.

Creer, T. L., & Reynolds, R. V. C. (1990). Asthma. In A. M. Gross & R. S. Drabman (Eds.), *Handbook of clinical behavioral pediatrics*. New York: Plenum.

Crisp, A. H. (1984). The psychopathology of anorexia nervosa: Getting the 'heat' out of the system. In A. J. Stunkard & E. Stellar (Eds.), *Eating and its disorders*. New York: Raven Press.

Crnic, K. A. (1988). Mental retardation. In E. J. Mash & L. G. Terdal (Eds.), *Behavioral assessment of childhood disorders. Selected core problems*. New York: Guilford.

Crnic, K. A., & Reid, M. (1989). Mental retardation. In E. J. Mash & R. A. Barkley (Eds.), *Treatment of childhood disorders*. New York: Guilford.

Croake, J. W., & Knox, F. H. (1973). The changing nature of children's fears. *Child Study Journal, 3*, 91–105.

Crockenberg, S. B. (1988). Infant irritability, mother responsiveness, and social support influences on the security of infant-mother attachment. In E. M. Hetherington & R. G. Parke (Eds.), *Contemporary readings in child psychology*. New York: McGraw*Hill*.

Cronbach, L. J. (1975). Five decades of public controversy over mental testing. *American Psychologist, 30*, 1–14.

Cushna, B. (1980). The psychological definition of mental retardation: A historical review. In L. S. Szymanski & P. E. Tanguay (Eds.), *Emotional disorders of mentally retarded persons*. Baltimore: University Park Press.

Cytryn, L., & Lourie, R. S. (1980). Mental retardation. In H. I. Kaplan, A. M. Freedman, & B. J. Sadock (Eds.), *Comprehensive textbook of psychiatry/III*, Vol. 3. Baltimore: Williams & Wilkins.

Cytryn, L., & McKnew, D. (1974). Factors influencing changing clinical expression of the depressive process in children. *American Journal of Psychiatry, 131*, 879–881.

Cytryn, L., McKnew, D. H., & Bunney, W. E. (1980). Diagnosis of depression in children: A reassessment. *American Journal of Psychiatry, 137*, 22–25.

Cytryn, L., McKnew, D. H., Zahn-Waxler, C., & Gershon, E. S. (1986). Developmental issues in risk research: The offspring of affectively ill parents. In M. Rutter, C. E. Izard, & P. B. Read (Eds.), *Depression in young people: Developmental and clinical perspectives*. New York: Guilford.

D

Dadds, M., Schwartz, S., Adams, T., & Rose, S. (1988). The effects of social context and verbal skill on the stereotypic and task-involved behavior of autistic children. *Journal of Child Psychology and Psychiatry, 29*, 669–676.

Dadds, M. R., Schwartz, S., & Sanders, M. R. (1987). Marital discord and treatment outcome in behavioral treatment of child conduct disorders. *Journal of Consulting and Clinical Psychology, 55*, 396–403.

D'Andrade, R. G. (1966). Sex differences and cultural institutions. In E. E. Maccoby (Ed.), *The development of sex differences*. Stanford, CA: Stanford Univ. Press.

Dangel, R. F., & Polster, R. A. (1984). *Parent training: Foundations of research and practice*. New York: Guilford.

Daniels, D., Moos, R. H., Billings, A. G., & Miller, J. J. (1987). Psychosocial risk and resistance factors among children with chronic illness, healthy siblings, and healthy controls. *Journal of Abnormal Child Psychology, 15*, 295–308.

Dare, C. (1985). Psychoanalytic theories of development. In M. Rutter & L. Hersov. (Eds.), *Child and adolescent psychiatry: Modern approaches*. Oxford: Blackwell Scientific Publications.

Davidson, W. S., & Basta, J. (1989). Diversion from the juvenile justice system: Research evidence and a discussion of issues. In B. B. Lahey & A. E. Kazdin (Eds.), *Advances in clinical child psychology*, Vol. 12. New York: Plenum.

Davidson, M. D., Kugler, M. M., & Bauer, C. H. (1963). Diagnosis and management in children with severe and protracted constipation and obstipation. *Journal of Pediatrics, 62*, 261–275.

Davidson, W. S., Redner, R., Blakely, C. H., Mitchell, C. M., & Emshoff, J. G. (1987). Diversion of juvenile offenders: An experimental comparison. *Journal of Consulting and Clinical Psychology, 55*, 68–75.

Davies, R. R., & Rogers, E. S. (1985). Social skills training with persons who are mentally retarded. *Mental Retardation, 23*, 186–196.

Davison, G. C., & Neale, J. M. (1978, 1982, 1990). *Abnormal psychology*. New York: Wiley.

Deaton, A. V. (1985). Adaptive noncompliance in pediatric asthma: The parent as expert. *Journal of Pediatric Psychology, 10*, 1–14.

Deaton, A. V., & Olbrisch, M. E. (1987). Adaptive noncompliance: Parents as experts and decision makers in the treatment of pediatric asthma patients. In M. Wolraich & D. K. Routh (Eds.), *Advances in developmental and behavioral pediatrics*. Greenwich, CT: JAI.

DeFries, J. C., Fulkner, D. W., & LaBuda, M. C. (1987). Evidence for a genetic aetiology in reading disability in twins. *Nature, 329,* 537–539.

DeFries, J. C., Plomin, R., & LaBuda, M. C. (1987). Genetic stability of cognitive development from childhood to adulthood. *Child Development, 23,* 4–12.

Deitz, D. E. D., & Repp, A. C. (1989). Mental retardation. In T. H. Ollendick & M. Hersen (Eds.), *Handbook of child psychopathology*. New York: Plenum.

Delamater, A. M. (1986). Psychological aspects of diabetes mellitus in children. In B. B. Lahey & A. E. Kazdin (Eds.), *Advances in clinical child psychology*, Vol. 9. New York: Plenum.

Delamater, A. M., & Lahey, B. B. (1983). Physiological correlates of conduct problems and anxiety in hyperactive and learning-disabled children. *Journal of Abnormal Child Psychology, 11,* 85–100.

Delfini, L. F., Bernal, M. E., & Rosen, P. M. (1976). Comparison of deviant and normal boys in home settings. In E. J. Mash, L. A. Hammerlynck, & L. C. Handy (Eds.), *Behavior modification and families*. New York: Brunner/Mazel.

Delprato, D. J. (1980). Hereditary determinants of fears and phobias: A critical review. *Behavior Therapy, 11,* 79–103.

Delprato, D. J., & McGlynn, F. D. (1984). Behavioral theories of anxiety disorders. In S. M. Turner (Ed.), *Behavioral treatment of anxiety disorders*. New York: Plenum.

DeMyer-Gapin, S., & Scott, T. J. (1977). Effects of stimulus novelty on stimulation-seeking in anti-social and neurotic children. *Journal of Abnormal Psychology, 86,* 96–98.

Denenberg, V. H. (1987). Animal models and plasticity. In J. J. Gallagher & C. T. Ramey (Eds.), *The malleability of children*. Baltimore: Paul Brookes.

Deno, E. (1970). Special education as developmental capital. *Exceptional children, 37,* 229–237.

deSilva, P., Rachman, S., & Seligman, M. E. P. (1977). Prepared phobias and obsessions: Therapeutic outcome. *Behavior Research and Therapy, 15,* 65–77.

Despert, J. L. (1940). A comparative study of thinking in schizophrenic children and in children of preschool age. *American Journal of Psychiatry, 97,* 189–213.

Devine, V. T. (1971). *The coercion process: A laboratory analogue.* Unpublished doctoral thesis. State University of New York at Stony Brook.

Dietz, W. H. (1988). Metabolic aspects of dieting. In N. A. Krasnegor, G. D. Grave, & N. Kretchmer (Eds.), *Childhood obesity: A biobehavioral perspective*. Caldwell, NJ: The Telford Press.

Dietz, W. H., Jr., & Gortmaker, S. L. (1985). Do we fatten our children at the television set? Obesity and television viewing in children and adolescents. *Pediatrics, 75,* 807–812.

Dimsdale, J. E. (1988). A perspective on Type A behavior and coronary disease. *New England Journal of Medicine, 318,* 110–112.

Dodge, K. (1985). Attributional bias in aggressive children. In P. C. Kendall (Ed.), *Advances in cognitive-behavioral research and therapy*, Vol. 4. New York: Academic Press.

Dodge, K. A. (1989). Problems in social relationships. In E. J. Mash & R. A. Barkley (Eds.), *Treatment of childhood disorders.* New York: Guilford.

Dodge, K. A. (1990). Developmental psychopathology in children of depressed mothers. *Developmental Psychology, 26,* 3–6.

Dodge, K. A., & Somberg, D. R. (1987). Hostile attributional biases among aggressive boys are exacerbated under conditions of threats to self. *Child Development, 58,* 213–224.

Doleys, D. M. (1988). Encopresis. In M. Hersen & C. G. Last (Eds.), *Child behavior therapy casebook*. New York: Plenum.

Doleys, D. M. (1989). Enuresis and encopresis. In T. H. Ollendick & M. Hersen (Eds.), *Handbook of child psychopathology*, 2nd ed. New York: Plenum.

Doleys, S., Stacy, D. M., & Knowles, S. (1981). Modification of grooming behavior in the adult retarded. *Behavior Modification, 5,* 119–128.

Dolgin, M. J., & Jay, S. M. (1989a). Childhood cancer. In T. H. Ollendick & M. Hersen (Eds.), *Handbook of child psychopathology*, 2nd ed. New York: Plenum.

Dolgin, M. J., & Jay, S. M. (1989b). Pain management in children. In E. J. Mash & R. A. Barkley (Eds.), *Treatment of childhood disorders*. New York: Guilford.

Doll, E. A. (1965). *Vineland Social Maturity Scale*. 1965 Edition. Circle Pines, MN: American Guidance Service.

Dollinger, S. J. (1986). Childhood sleep disturbances. In B. B. Lahey & A.E. Kazdin (Eds.), *Advances in clinical child psychology*, Vol. 9. New York: Plenum.

Doman, G., & Delacato, C. (1968). Doman-Delacato philosophy. *Human Potential, 1,* 112–116.

Douglas, J. (1975). Early hospital admissions and later disturbances of behaviour and learning. *Developmental Medicine and Child Neurology, 17,* 456–480.

Douglas, V. I. (1983). Attentional and cognitive problems. In M. Rutter (Ed.), *Developmental neuropsychiatry*. New York: Guilford.

Douglas, V. I., Barr, R. G., O'Neill, M. E., & Britton, B. G. (1986). Short term effects of methylphenidate on the cognitive, learning and academic performance of children with attention deficit disorder in the laboratory and the classroom. *Journal of Child Psychology and Psychiatry, 27,* 191–211.

Drotar, D. (1981). Psychological perspectives in chronic childhood illness. *Journal of Pediatric Psychology, 6,* 211–228.

Dubow, E. F., Huesmann, L. R., & Eron, R. D. (1987). Childhood correlates of adult ego development. *Child Development, 58,* 859–869.

Duffy, F. H., Mower, G., Jensen, F., & Als, H. (1984). Neural plasticity: A new frontier for infant development. In H. E. Fitzgerald, B. M. Lester, & M. W. Yogman (Eds.), *Theory and research in behavioral pediatrics*, Vol. 2. New York: Plenum.

Dulcan, M. K. (1986). Comprehensive treatment of children and adolescents with attention deficit disorders: The state of the art. *Clinical Psychology Review, 6,* 539–569.

Dulcan, M. K. (1989). Attention deficit disorders. In C. G. Last & M. Hersen (Eds.), *Handbook of child psychiatric diagnosis*. New York: Wiley.

Dumas, J. E. (1989). Treating antisocial behavior in children: Child and family approaches. *Clinical Psychology Review, 9,* 197–222.

Dunbar, J., & Wasak, L. (1990). Patient compliance: Pediatric and adolescent populations. In A. M. Gross & R. S. Drabman (Eds.), *Handbook of clinical behavioral pediatrics.* New York: Plenum.

Dunn, J. (1988). Annotation. Sibling influences on childhood development. *Journal of Child Psychology and Psychiatry, 29,* 119–127.

Dunn, L. M. (1968). Special education for the mildly retarded—is much of it justifiable? *Exceptional Children, 35,* 5–22.

Dunn, L. M., & Markwardt, F. C. (1970). *The Peabody Individual Achievement Test*. Circle Pines, MN: American Guidance Service.

Durand, V. M. (1986). Self-injurious behavior as intentional communication. In K. D. Gadow (Ed.), *Advances in learning and behavioral disabilities*, Vol. 5. Greenwich, CT: JAI Press.

Durand, V. M., & Carr, E. G. (1985). Self-injurious behavior: Motivating conditions and guidelines for treatment. *School Psychology Review, 14,* 171–176.

Durand, V. M., & Carr, E. G. (1988). Autism. In V. B. Van

Hasselt, P. S. Strain, & M. Hersen (Eds.), *Handbook of developmental and physical disabilities.* New York: Pergamon Press.

Durand, V. M., & Crimmins, D. B. (1987). Assessment and treatment of psychotic speech in an autistic child. *Journal of Autism and Developmental Disorders, 17,* 17–28.

Durand, V. M., & Crimmins, D. B. (1988). Identifying the variables maintaining self-injurious behavior. *Journal of Autism and Developmental Disorders, 18,* 99–117.

Durand, V. M., & Mindell, J. A. (1990). Behavioral treatment of multiple childhood sleep disorders: Effects on child and family. *Behavior Modification, 14,* 37–49.

Dush, D. M., Hirt, M. L., & Schroeder, H. E. (1989). Self-statement modification in the treatment of child behavior disorders. *Psychological Bulletin, 106,* 97–106.

du Verglas, G., Banks, S., & Guyer, K. E. (1988). Clinical effects of fenfluramine on children with autism: A review of the research. *Journal of Autism and Developmental Disorders, 18,* 297–308.

Dygdon, J. A., & Conger, A. J. (1990). A direct nomination method for the identification of neglected members in children's peer groups. *Journal of Abnormal Child Psychology, 18,* 55–74.

E

Earls, F., & Jung, K. G. (1987). Temperament and home environment characteristics as causal factors in the early development of childhood psychopathology. *Journal of the American Academy of Child and Adolescent Psychiatry, 26,* 491–498.

Edelbrock, C., & Costello, A. J. (1988a). Convergence between statistically derived behavior problem syndromes and child psychiatric diagnoses. *Journal of Abnormal Child Psychology, 16,* 219–231.

Edelbrock, C., & Costello, A. J. (1988b). Structured psychiatric interviews for children. In M. Rutter, A. H. Tuma, & I. S. Lann (Eds.), *Assessment and diagnosis in child psychopathology.* New York: Guilford.

Edelbrock, C., Costello, A. J., Dulcan, M. K., Kalas, R., & Conover, N. C. (1985). Age differences in the reliability of the psychiatric interview of the child. *Child Development, 56,* 265–275.

Edelbrock, C., & Rancurello, M. D. (1985). Childhood hyperactivity: An overview of rating scales and their applications. *Clinical Psychology Review, 5,* 429–445.

Egeland, B., Jacobvitz, D., & Sroufe, L. A. (1988). Breaking the cycle of abuse. *Child Development, 59,* 1080–1088.

Eggers, C. (1978). Course and prognosis of childhood schizophrenia. *Journal of Autism and Childhood Schizophrenia, 8,* 21–36.

Eisenberg, L. (1979). Hyperkinetic reactions. In J. D. Noshpitz (Ed.), *Basic handbook of child psychiatry,* Vol. 2. New York: Basic Books.

Ekman, P., & Friesen, W. V. (1975). *Unmasking the face.* Englewood Cliffs, NJ: Prentice Hall.

Ekstein, R., Friedman, S., & Carruth, E. (1972). The psychoanalytic treatment of childhood schizophrenia. In B. B. Wolman (Ed.), *Manual of child psychology.* New York: McGraw Hill.

Elias, M., Hayes, A., & Broerse, J. (1988). Aspects of structure and content of maternal talk with infants. *Journal of Child Psychology and Psychiatry, 29,* 523–531.

Elliot, C. H., Jay, S. M., & Woody, P. (1987). An observational scale for measuring children's distress during painful medical procedures. *Journal of Pediatric Psychology, 12,* 543–551.

Ellis, E. F. (1988). Asthma: Current therapeutic approach. *Pediatric Clinics of North America, 35,* 1041–1052.

Ellis, E. S., Deshler, D. D., & Schumaker, J. B. (1989). Teaching adolescents with learning disabilities to generate and use task-specific strategies. *Journal of Learning Disabilities, 22,* 108–119.

Ellis, P. L. (1982). Empathy: A factor in social behavior. *Journal of Abnormal Child Psychology, 10,* 123–134.

Eme, R. F. (1979). Sex differences in childhood psychopathology: A review. *Psychological Bulletin, 86,* 574–595.

Emerson, E. B. (1985). Evaluating the impact of deinstitutionalization on the lives of mentally retarded people. *American Journal of Mental Deficiency, 90,* 277–288.

Emery, R. E. (1982). Interparental conflict and the children of discord and divorce. *Psychological Bulletin, 92,* 310–330.

Emery, R. E. (1989). Family violence. *American Psychologist, 44,* 321–328.

Emery, R. E., Hetherington, E. M., & DiLalla, L. F. (1984). Divorce, children, and social policy. In H. W. Stevenson & A. E. Siegel (Eds.), *Child development research and social policy.* Chicago: Univ. of Chicago Press.

Empey, L. T. (1978). *American delinquency.* Homewood, IL: Dorsey.

English, H. B. (1929). Three cases of the "conditioned fear response." *Journal of Abnormal and Social Psychology, 24,* 221–225.

Entwisle, D. R., & Stevenson, H. W. (1987). Schools and development. *Child Development, 58,* 1149–1150.

Epple, W. A., Jacobson, J. W., & Janicki, M. P. (1985). Staffing ratios in public institutions for persons with mental retardation in the United States. *Mental Retardation, 23,* 115–124.

Epstein, L. H., & Cluss, P. A. (1986). Behavioral genetics of childhood obesity. *Behavior Therapy, 17,* 324–334.

Epstein, L. H., & Wing, R. R. (1987). Behavioral treatment of childhood obesity. *Psychological Bulletin, 101,* 331–342.

Epstein, L. H., Wing, R. R., Koeske, R., & Valoski, A. (1985). A comparison of lifestyle exercise, aerobic exercise, and calisthenics on weight loss in obese children. *Behavior Therapy, 16,* 345–356.

Erickson, M. T. (1987). *Behavior disorders of children and adolescents.* Englewood Cliffs, NJ: Prentice Hall.

Erlen, J. A. (1987). The child's choice: An essential component in treatment decisions. *Children's Health Care, 15,* 156–160.

Erlenmeyer-Kimling, L., Marcuse, Y., Cornblatt, B., Friedman, D., Rainer, J. D., & Rutschmann, J. (1984). The New York high-risk project. In N. F. Watt, E. J. Anthony, L. C. Wynne, & J. E. Rolf (Eds.), *Children at risk for schizophrenia: A longitudinal perspective.* New York: Cambridge University Press.

Erwin, R. J., Edwards, R., Tanguay, P. E., Buchwald, J., & Letai, D. (1986). Abnormal P300 responses in schizophrenic children. *Journal of the American Academy of Child Psychiatry, 25,* 615–622.

Evans, J. A., & Hammerton, J. L. (1985). Chromosomal anomalies. In A. M. Clarke, A. D. B. Clarke, & J. M. Berg (Eds.), *Mental deficiency. The changing outlook.* New York: The Free Press.

Evans, R. B., & Koelsch, W. A. (1985). Psychoanalysis arrives in America. *American Psychologist, 40,* 942–948.

Ewart, C. K., Harris, W. L., Iwata, M. M., Coates, T. J., Bullock, R., & Simon, B. (1987). Feasibility and effectiveness of school-based relaxation to lower blood pressure. *Health Psychology, 6,* 399–416.

Eysenck, H. J. (1986). A critique of contemporary classifications and diagnosis. In T. Millon & G. L. Klerman (Eds.), *Contemporary directions in psychopathology: Toward DSM-IV.* New York: Guilford.

F

Fagan, J. F., Singer, L. T., Montie, J. E., & Shepherd, P. A. (1986). Selective screening device for the early detection of normal or delayed cognitive development in infants at risk for later mental retardation. *Pediatrics, 78,* 1021–1026.

Fairburn, C. G. (1984). Bulimia: Its epidemilogy and management. In A. J. Stunkard & E. Stellar (Eds.), *Eating and its disorders.* New York: Raven Press.

Farrington, D. P. (1986). Stepping stones to adult criminal careers. In D. Olweus, J. Block, & M. R. Yarrow (Eds.), *Development of antisocial behavior and prosocial behavior.* New York: Academic Press.

Farrington, D. P. (1987). Early precursors of frequent offending. In J. Q. Wilson & G. C. Loury (Eds.), *From children to citizens: Vol. III. Families, schools, and delinquency prevention.* New York: Springer-Verlag.

Faust, D., Hart, K., & Guilmette, T. J. (1988). Pediatric malingering: The capacity of children to fake believable deficits on neuropsychological testing. *Journal of Consulting and Clinical Psychology, 56,* 578–582.

Faust, J. (1987). Correlates of the drive for thinness in young adolescent females. *Journal of Clinical Child Psychology, 16,* 313–319.

Feingold, B. F. (1975). *Why your child is hyperactive.* New York: Random House.

Felton, R. H., & Wood, F. B. (1989). Cognitive deficits in reading disability and attention deficit disorder. *Journal of Learning Disabilities, 22,* 3–13.

Ferguson, H. B., & Pappas, B. A. (1979). Evaluation of psychophysiological, neurochemical, and animal models of hyperactivity. In R. L. Trites (Ed.), *Hyperactivity in children.* Baltimore: University Park Press.

Ferguson, L. R. (1978). The competence and freedom of children to make choices regarding participation in research: A statement. *Journal of Social Issues, 34,* 114–121.

Fergusson, D. M., Fergusson, J. E., Horwood, L. J., & Kinzett, N. G. (1988a). A longitudinal study of dentine lead levels, intelligence, school performance, and behaviour—Part II. Dentine lead and cognitive ability. *Journal of Child Psychology and Psychiatry, 29,* 793–809.

Fergusson, D. M., Fergusson, J. E., Horwood, L. J., & Kinzett, N. G. (1988b). A longitudinal study of dentine lead levels, intelligence, school performance and behaviour—Part III. Dentine lead levels and attention/activity. *Journal of Child Psychology and Psychiatry, 29,* 811–824.

Ferrari, M. (1990). Developmental issues in behavioral pediatrics. In A. M. Gross & R. S. Drabman (Eds.), *Handbook of clinical behavioral pediatrics.* New York: Plenum.

Ferster, C. B. (1961). Positive reinforcement and behavioral deficits of autistic children. *Child Development, 32,* 437–456.

Ferster, C. B. (1966). The repertoire of the autistic child in relation to principles of reinforcement. In L. Gottschalk & A. H. Averback (Eds.), *Methods of research of psychotherapy.* New York: Appleton-Century-Crofts.

Ferster, C. B. (1974). Behavioral approaches to depression. In R. J. Friedman & M. M. Katz (Eds.), *The psychology of depression: Contemporary theory and research.* Washington, DC: Winston.

Field, T. (1981). Early peer relations. In P. S. Strain (Ed.), *The utilization of classroom peers as behavior change agents.* New York: Plenum.

Fine, D., Pennington, B., Markowitz, P., Braverman, M., & Waterhouse, L. (1986). Toward a neuropsychological model if infantile autism: Are the social deficits primary? *Journal of the American Academy of Child Psychiatry, 25,* 198–212.

Fine, R. (1985). Anna Freud. *American Psychologist, 40,* 230–232.

Finell, J. (1980). Psychoanalytic play therapy. In G. S. Belkin (Ed.), *Contemporary psychotherapies.* Chicago: Rand McNally.

Finkelhor, D. (1986). (Ed.) *A sourcebook on child sexual abuse.* Beverly Hills, CA: Sage.

Finkelstein, H. (1988). The long term effects of early parent death: A review. *Journal of Clinical Psychology, 44,* 3–9.

Finney, J. W., Russo, D. C., & Cataldo, M. F. (1982). Reduction of pica in young children with lead poisoning. *Journal of Pediatric Psychology, 7,* 197–207.

Fish, B. (1984). Characteristics and sequelae of the neurointegrative disorder in infants at risk for schizophrenia: 1952–1982. In N. F. Watt, E. J. Anthony, L. C. Wynne, & J. E. Rolf (Eds.), *Children at risk for schizophrenia: A longitudinal perspective.* New York: Cambridge University Press.

Fish, B. (1986). Antecedents of an acute schizophrenic break. *Journal of the American Academy of Child Psychiatry, 25,* 595–600.

Fish, B., & Ritvo, E. R. (1979). Psychoses of childhood. In J. D. Noshpitz (Ed.), *Basic handbook of child psychiatry,* Vol. 2. New York: Basic Books.

Fixsen, D. L., Wolf, M. M., & Phillips, E. L. (1973). Achievement place: a teaching-family model of community-based group homes for youth in trouble. In L. Hammerlynck, L. Handy, and E. Mash (Eds.), *Behavior change: Methodology, concepts and practice.* Champaign, IL: Research Press.

Flament, M., & Rapoport, J. L. (1984). Childhood obsessive compulsive disorder. In T. R. Insel (Ed.), *New findings in obsessive compulsive disorder.* Washington, DC: American Psychiatric Press.

Flament, M. F., Whitaker, A., Rapoport, J. L., Davies, M., Berg, C. Z., Kalikow, K., Sceery, W., & Shaffer, D. (1988). Obsessive compulsive disorder in adolescence: An epidemiological study. *Journal of the American Academy of Child and Adolescent Psychiatry, 27,* 764–771.

Flavell, J. H. (1963). *The developmental psychology of Jean Piaget.* New York: Van Nostrand.

Fleischman, M. J. (1981). A replication of Patterson's "Intervention for boys with conduct problems." *Journal of Consulting and Clinical Psychology, 49,* 342–351.

Fletcher, J. M. (1988). Brain-injured children. In E. J. Mash & L. G. Terdal (Eds.), *Behavioral assessment of childhood disorders,* 2nd ed. New York: Guilford.

Flicek, M., & Landau, S. (1985). Social status problems of learning disabled and hyperactive/learning disabled boys. *Journal of Clinical Child Psychology, 14,* 340–344.

Folstein, S., & Rutter, M. (1978). A twin study of individuals with infantile autism. In M. Rutter & E. Schopler (Eds.), *Autism: A reappraisal of concepts and treatment.* New York: Plenum.

Folstein, S. E., & Rutter, M. L. (1988). Autism: Familial aggregation and genetic implications. *Journal of Autism and Developmental Disorders, 18,* 3–30.

Forehand, R. (1977). Child noncompliance to parental requests: Behavioral analysis and treatment. In M. Hersen, R. M. Eisler, & P. M. Miller (Eds.), *Progress in behavior modification,* Vol. 5. New York: Academic Press.

Forehand, R., Brody, G., & Smith, K. (1986). Contributions of child behavior and marital dissatisfaction to maternal perceptions of child maladjustment. *Behavior Research and Therapy, 24,* 43–48.

Forehand, R., Furey, W. M., & McMahon, R. J. (1984). The role of maternal distress in a parent training program to modify child non-compliance. *Behavioral Psychotherapy, 12,* 93–108.

Forehand, R., King, H. E., Peed, S., & Yoder, P. (1975). Mother-child interactions: Comparisons of a noncompliant clinic group and a non-clinic group. *Behaviour Research and Therapy, 13,* 79–84.

Forehand, R., McCombs, A., & Brody, G. H. (1987). The relationship between parental depressive mood states and child functioning. *Advances in Behaviour Research and Therapy, 9,* 1–20.

Forehand, R., & McMahon, R. J. (1981). *Helping the noncom-*

pliant child: A clinician's guide to parent training. New York: Guilford.

Forehand, R., Wells, K. C., & Griest, D. L. (1980). An examination of the social validity of a parent training program. *Behavior Therapy*, *11*, 488–502.

Foreyt, J. P., & Kondo, A. T. (1985). Eating disorders. In P. H. Bornstein & A. E. Kazdin (Eds.), *Handbook of clinical behavior therapy with children*. Homewood, IL: Dorsey.

Foreyt, J. P., & McGavin, J. K. (1988). Anorexia nervosa and bulimia. In E. J. Mash & L. G. Terdal (Eds.), *Behavioral assessment of childhood disorders*, 2nd ed. New York: Guilford.

Foreyt, J. P., & McGavin, J. K. (1989). Anorexia nervosa and bulimia nervosa. In E. J. Mash & R. A. Barkley (Eds.), *Treatment of childhood behavior disorders*. New York: Guilford.

Forness, S. R. (1990). Subtyping in learning disabilities: Introduction to the issues. In H. L. Swanson & B. Keogh (Eds.), *Learning disabilities. Theoretical and research issues*. Hillsdale, NJ: Erlbaum.

Foster, G. G., & Salvia, J. (1977). Teacher response to the label of learning disabled as a function of demand characteristics. *Exceptional Children*, *43*, 533–534.

Foster, S. L., & Cone, J. D. (1986). Design and use of direct observation. In A. R. Ciminero, K. S. Calhoun, & H. E. Adams (Eds.), *Handbook of behavioral assessment*, 2nd ed. New York: Wiley.

Fowler, M. G., Johnson, M. P., & Atkinson, S. S. (1985). School achievement and absence in children with chronic health conditions. *Journal of Pediatrics*, *106*, 683–687.

Foxx, R. M., McMorrow, M. J., Storey, K., & Rogers, B. M. (1984). Teaching social/sexual skills to mentally retarded adults. *American Journal of Mental Deficiency*, *89*, 9–15.

Frankel, M. S. (1978). Social, legal, and political responses to ethical issues in the use of children as experimental subjects. *Journal of Social Issues*, *34*, 101–113.

Frederiksen, N. (1986). Toward a broader conception of human intelligence. *American Psychologist*, *41*, 445–452.

Freeman, E. H., Feingold, B. F., Schlesinger, K., & Gorman, F. J. (1964). Psychological variables in allergic disorders: A review. *Psychosomatic Medicine*, *26*, 543–575.

Freeman, B. J., Ritvo, E. R., Yokota, A., Childs, J., & Pollard, J. (1988). WISC-R and Vineland Adaptive Behavior Scale scores in autistic children. *Journal of the American Academy of Child and Adolescent Psychiatry*, *27*, 428–429.

French, T. M., & Alexander, F. (1941). Psychogenic factors in bronchial asthma. *Psychosomatic Medicine Monograph*, *4*, 2–94.

Freud, A. (1946). *The psycho-analytical treatment of children*. London: Imago.

Freud, S. (1949). *An outline of psycho-analysis*. Translated and newly edited by J. Strachey. New York: W. W. Norton and Co.

Freud, S. (1953). Analysis of a phobia in a five-year-old boy (1909). *Standard Edition*, Vol. 10. Ed. and trans. James Strachey. London: The Hogarth Press.

Freud, S. (1959). From the history of an infantile neurosis. In *Collected papers*. Vol. 3. New York: Basic Books. Originally published in 1918.

Friedman, H. S., & Booth-Kewley, S. (1988). Validity of the Type A construct: A reprise. *Psychological Bulletin*, *104*, 381–384.

Friedman, M., & Rosenman, R. (1974). *Type A behavior and your heart*. New York: Knopf.

Frostig, M., & Horne, D. (1964). The Frostig Program for the Development of Visual Perception. Chicago: Follett Corp.

Frostig, M., Lefever, W., & Whittlesey, J. R. B. (1966). *Administration and scoring manual for the Marianne Frostig developmental test of visual perception*. Palo Alto, CA: Consulting Psychologists Press.

Fultz, S. A., & Rojahn, J. (1988). Pica. In M. Hersen & C. G.

Last (Eds.), *Child behavior therapy casebook*. New York: Plenum.

Fundudis, T. (1986). Anorexia nervosa in a pre-adolescent girl: A multimodal behaviour therapy approach. *Journal of Child Psychology and Psychiatry*, *27*, 261–273.

Furman, W., Rahe, D., & Hartup, W. (1979). Rehabilitation of socially withdrawn preschool children through mixed-age and same-age socialization. *Child Development*, *50*, 915–922.

G

Gabrielli, W. F., & Mednick, S. A. (1983). Genetic correlates of criminal behavior. *American Behavioral Scientist*, *27*, 59–74.

Gadow, K. D. (1985). Relative efficacy of pharmacological, behavioral, and combination treatments for enhancing academic performance. *Clinical Psychology Review*, *5*, 513–533.

Galaburda, A. M. (1989). Learning disability: Biological, societal, or both? A response to Gerald Coles. *Journal of Learning Disabilities*, *22*, 278–282; 286.

Garbarino, J., & Vondra, J. (1987). Psychological maltreatment: Issues and perspectives. In M. R. Brassard, R. Germain, & S. N. Hart (Eds.), *Psychological maltreatment of children and youth*. New York: Pergamon.

Garcia, J. (1981). The logic and limits of mental aptitude testing. *American Psychologist*, *36*, 1172–1180.

Gardner, F. E. M. (1989). Inconsistent parenting: Is there evidence for a link with children's conduct problems? *Journal of Abnormal Child Psychology*, *17*, 223–233.

Garmezy, N. (1975). The experimental study of children vulnerable to psychopathology. In A. Davids (Ed.), *Child personality and psychopathology*, Vol. 2. New York: Wiley-Interscience.

Garmezy, N. (1983). Stressors of childhood. In N. Garmezy & M. Rutter (Eds.), *Stress, coping, & development in children*. New York: McGraw-Hill.

Garmezy, N. (1986). Developmental aspects of children's responses to the stress of separation and loss. In M. Rutter, C. E. Izard, & P. B. Read (Eds.), *Depression in young people: Developmental and clinical perspectives*. New York: Guilford.

Garn, S. M. (1986). Family-line and socioeconomic factors in fatness and obesity. *Nutrition Reviews*, *44*, 381–386.

Garn, S. M., & Clark, D. C. (1976). Trends in fatness and the origins of obesity: Ad hoc committee to review the ten-state nutrition survey. *Pediatrics*, *57*, 443–456.

Garn, S., Cole, P. E., & Baily, S. M. (1976). Effect of parental fatness levels on the fatness of biological and adoptive children. *Ecology of Food and Nutrition*, *6*, 1–34.

Garn, S. M., LaVelle, M., Rosenberg, K. R., & Hawthorne, V. M. (1986). Maturational timing as a factor in female fatness and obesity. *The American Journal of Clinical Nutrition*, *43*, 879–883.

Garner, D. M. (1988). Anorexia nervosa. In M. Hersen & C. G. Last (Eds.), *Child behavior therapy casebook*. New York: Plenum.

Garner, D. M., & Bemis, K. M. (1985). Cognitive therapy for anorexia nervosa. In D. M. Garner & P. E. Garfinkel (Eds.), *Handbook of psychotherapy for anorexia and bulimia*. New York: Guilford.

Garner, D. M., Garfinkel, P. E., & O'Shaughnessy, M. (1985). The validity of the distinction between bulimia with and without anorexia nervosa. *American Journal of Psychiatry*, *142*, 581–587.

Garner, D. M., Olmsted, M. P., Polivy, J., & Garfinkel, P. E. (1984). Comparison between weight-preoccupied women and anorexia nervosa. *Psychosomatic Medicine*, *46*, 255–266.

Garner, D. M., & Rosen, L. W. (1990). Anorexia nervosa and bulimia nervosa. In A. S. Bellack, M. Hersen, & A. E. Kazdin (Eds.), *International handbook of behavior modification and therapy*, 2nd ed. New York: Plenum.

Garnier, C., Comoy, E., Barthelemy, C., Leddet, I., Garreau, B., Muh, J. P., & Lelard, G. (1986). Dopamine-beta-hydroxylase (DBH) and homovanillic acid (HVA) in autistic children. *Journal of Autism and Developmental Disorders, 16*, 23–29.

Garvey, W. P., & Hegreves, J. P. (1966). Desensitization techniques in the treatment of school phobia. *American Journal of Orthopsychiatry, 36*, 147–152.

Gath, A. (1985). Chromosomal abnormalities. In M. Rutter & L. Hersov (Eds.), *Child and adolescent psychiatry: Modern approaches*, 2nd ed. Oxford: Blackwell Scientific Publications.

Gaylin, W. (1982). The "competence" of children: No longer all or none. *Journal of the American Academy of Child Psychiatry, 21*, 153–162.

Geller, E., Ritvo, E. R., Freeman, B.J., & Yuwiler, A. (1982). Preliminary observations on the effects of fenfluramine on blood serotonin and symptoms in three autistic boys. *New England Journal of Medicine, 307*, 165–169.

Geller, E., Yuwiler, A., Freeman, B. J., & Ritvo, E. (1988). Platelet size, number, and serotonin content in blood of autistic, childhood schizophrenic, and normal children. *Journal of Autism and Developmental Disorders, 18*, 119–126.

Gelles, R. J., & Straus, M. A. (1987). Is violence toward children increasing? A comparison of 1975 and 1985 national survey rates. *Journal of Interpersonal Violence, 2*, 212–222.

Genetic evidence for autism. (1989, June 3). *Science News, 135*, 349.

Gerard, M. W. (1939). Enuresis: A study in etiology. *American Journal of Orthopsychiatry, 9*, 48–58.

Gerrity, K. M., Jones, F.A., & Self, P.A. (1983). Developmental psychology for the clinical child psychologist. In C. E. Walker and M. C. Roberts (Eds.), *Handbook of clinical child psychology*. New York: Wiley.

Gesten, E. L. (1976). A Health Resources Inventory: The development of a measure of the personal and social competence of primary grade children. *Journal of Consulting and Clinical Psychology, 44*, 775–786.

Gesten, E. L., & Jason, L. A. (1987). Social and community interventions. In M. R. Rosenzweig and L. W. Porter (Eds.), *Annual review of psychology*, Vol. 38. Palo Alto, CA: Annual Reviews Inc.

Gholson, B., & Rosenthal, T. L. (Eds.) (1984). *Application of cognitive-developmental theory*. Orlando, FL: Acaademic Press.

Gibbons, D. C. (1976). *Delinquent behavior*, 2nd ed. Englewood Cliffs, NJ: Prentice Hall.

Gibbs, D. P., & Cooper, E. B. (1989). Prevalence of communication disorders in students with learning disabilities. *Journal of Learning Disabilities, 22*, 60–63.

Gillberg, C. (1988). The neurobiology of infantile autism. *Journal of Child Psychology and Psychiatry, 29*, 257–266.

Gillberg, C. (1990). Autism and pervasive developmental disorders. *Journal of Child Psychology and Psychiatry, 31*, 99–119.

Gillberg, I. C., & Gillberg, C. (1988). Generalized hyperkinesis: Follow-up study from age 7 to 13 years. *Journal of the American Academy of Child and Adolescent Psychiatry, 27*, 55–59.

Gilligan, C. (1982). *In a different voice*. Cambridge, MA: Harvard University Press.

Gillin, J. C., Duncan, W., Pettigrew, K. D., Frankel, B., & Snyder, F. (1979). Successful separtation of depressed, normal and insomniac subjects by EEG sleep data. *Archives of General Psychiatry, 36*, 85–90.

Ginsburg, H. (1972). *The myth of the deprived child: Poor children's intellect and education*. Englewood Cliffs, NJ: Prentice Hall.

Gittelman, R. (1980). The role of psychological tests for differential diagnosis in child psychiatry. *Journal of the American Academy of Child Psychiatry, 19*, 413–438.

Gittelman, R., Abikoff, H., Pollack, E., Klein, D. F., Katz, S., & Mattes, J. (1980). A controlled trial of behavior modification and methylphenidate in hyperactive children. In C. K. Whalen & B. Henker (Eds.), *Hyperactive children*. New York: Academic Press.

Gittleman, R., & Koplewicz, H. S. (1986). Pharmacotherapy of childhood anxiety disorders. In R. Gittleman (Ed.), *Anxiety disorders of childhood*. New York: Guilford.

Gittleman-Klein, R., & Klein, D. F. (1980). Separation anxiety in school refusal and its treatment with drugs. In L. Hersov & I. Berg (Eds.). *Out of school*. New York: Wiley.

Gladstone, M., Best, C. T., & Davidson, R. J. (1989). Anomalous bimanual coordination among dyslexic boys. *Developmental Psychology, 25*, 236–246.

Glidden, L. M. (1985). Semantic processing, semantic memory, and recall. In N. R. Ellis & N. W. Bray (Eds.), *International Review of Research In Mental Retardation*, Vol. 13. New York: Academic Press.

Glueck, S., & Glueck, E. T. (1968). *Delinquents and nondelinquents in perspective*. Cambridge, MA: Harvard University Press.

Glueck, S., & Glueck, E. (1970). *Towards a typology of juvenile offenders: Implications for therapy and prevention*. New York: Grune & Stratton.

Goddard, H. H. (1912). *The Kallikak family*. New York: Macmillan.

Goldberg, J. O., & Konstantareas, M. M. (1981). Vigilance in hyperactive and normal children on a self-paced task. *Journal of Child Psychiatry and Psychology, 22*, 55–63.

Goldfarb, W. (1970). Childhood psychosis. In P. H. Mussen (Ed.), *Carmichael's manual of child psychology*, Vol. 2. New York: Wiley.

Goldfarb, W., Spitzer, R. L., & Endicott, J. (1976). A study of psychopathology of parents of psychotic children by structured interview. *Journal of Autism and Childhood Schizophrenia, 6*, 327–338.

Goldfield, E. C. (1989). Transition from rocking to crawling: Postural constraints on infant movement. *Developmental Psychology, 25*, 913–919.

Goldsmith, H. H., Bradshaw, D. L., & Reiser-Danner, L. A. (1986). Temperament as a potential developmental influence on attachment. In J. V. Lerner & R. M. Lerner (Eds.), *Temperament and social interaction during infancy and childhood*. New Directions for Child Development, No. 31. San Francisco: Jossey-Bass.

Goldsmith, H. H., Buss, A. H., Plomin, R., Rothbart, M. K., Thomas, A., Chess, S., Hinde, R. A., & McCall, R. B. (1987). Roundtable: What is temperament? Four approaches. *Child Development, 58*, 505–529.

Goldstein, M. J., (1988). The family and psychopathology. *Annual Review of Psychology*. Palo Alto, CA: Annual Reviews Inc.

Goldston, S. E. (1986). Primary prevention. Historical perspectives and a blueprint for action. *American Psychologist, 41*, 453–460.

Goodman, R. (1989). Infantile autism: A syndrome of multiple primary deficits? *Journal of Autism and Developmental Disorders, 19*, 409–424.

Goodman, R., & Stevenson, J. (1989). A twin study of hyperactivity-II. The aetiological role of genes, family relationships and perinatal adversity. *Journal of Child Psychology and Psychiatry, 30*, 691–709.

Goodman, S. H., & Brumley, H.E. (1990). Schizophrenic and depressed mothers: Relational deficits in parenting. *Developmental Psychology, 26*, 31–39.

Gordon, D. A., & Arbuthnot, J. (1987). Individual, group, and family interventions. In H. C. Quay (Ed.), *Handbook of juvenile delinquency*. New York: Wiley.

Gortmaker, S. L., Dietz, W. H., Jr., Sobol, A. M., & Wehler, C. A. (1987). Increasing pediatric obesity in the United States. *American Journal of Diseases in Children, 141*, 535–540.

Gortmaker, S. L., & Sappenfield, W. (1984). Chronic childhood disorders: Prevalence and impact. *Pediatric Clinics of North America, 31*, 3–18.

Gottfried, A. E., & Gottfried, A. W. (1988). Maternal employment and children's development. An integration of longitudinal findings with implications for social policy. In A. E. Gottfried and A. W. Gottfried (Eds.), *Maternal employment and children's development.* New York: Plenum.

Gottman, J. M. (1983). How children become friends. *Monographs of the Society for Research in Child Development, 48* (3 Serial No. 201).

Gottman, J., Gonso, J., & Rasmussen, B. (1975). Social interaction, social competence and friendship in children. *Child Development, 46*, 709–718.

Gottman, J., Gonso, J., & Schuler, P. (1976). Teaching social skills to isolated children. *Journal of Abnormal Child Psychology, 4*, 179–186.

Gould, J. S. (1981). *The mismeasure of man.* New York: W. W. Norton.

Gould, M. S., Shaffer, D., & Kaplan, D. (1985). The characteristics of dropouts from a child psychiatric clinic. *Journal of the American Academy of Child Psychiatry, 24*, 316–328.

Goyette, C. H., Conners, C. K., & Ulrich, R. F. (1978). Normative data on revised Conners parent and teacher rating scales. *Journal of Abnormal Child Psychology, 6*, 221–236.

Grace, W. J., & Graham, D. T. (1952). Relationship of specific attitudes and emotions to certain bodily diseases. *Psychosomatic Medicine, 14*, 243–251.

Grannel de Aldaz, E., Vivas, E., Gelfand, D. M., & Feldman, L. (1984). Estimating the prevalence of school refusal and school-related fears: A Venezuelan sample. *Journal of Nervous and Mental Disease, 172*, 722–729.

Graves, T., Meyers, A. W., & Clark, L. (1988). An evaluation of parental problem-solving training in the behavioral treatment of childhood obesity. *Journal of Consulting and Clinical Psychology, 56*, 246–250.

Gray, J. W., Dean, R.S., & Lowrie, R. A. (1988). Relationship between socioeconomic status and perinatal complications. *Journal of Clinical Child Psychology, 17*, 352–358.

Graziano, A. M., DeGiovanni, I. S., & Garcia, K. A. (1979). Behavioral treatment of children's fears: A review. *Psychological Bulletin, 86*, 804–830.

Graziano, A. M., & Mooney, K. C. (1982). Behavioral treatment of "nightfears" in children: Maintenance of improvement at 2 1/2- to 3-year follow-up. *Journal of Consulting and Clinical Psychology, 50*, 598–599.

Green, W. H., Campbell, M., Hardesty, A. S., Grega, D. M., Padron-Gayol, M., Shell, J., & Erlenmeyer-Kimling, L. (1984). A comparison of schizophrenic and autistic children. *Journal of the American Academy of Child Psychiatry, 23*, 399–409.

Greenberg, M. T., & Crnic, K. A. (1988). Longitudinal predictors of developmental status and social interaction in premature and full-term infants at age two. *Child Development, 59*, 554–570.

Greenberger, E., & Goldberg, W. A. (1989). Work, parenting, and the socialization of children. *Developmental Psychology, 25*, 22–35.

Greenough, W. T., Black, J. E., & Wallace, C. S. (1987). Experience and brain development. *Child Development, 58*, 539–559.

Gresham, F. M., & Elliott, S. N. (1989). Social skills deficits as a primary learning disability. *Journal of Learning Disabilities, 22*, 120–124.

Griest, D. L., Forehand, R., Rogers, T., Breiner, J., Furey, W., & Williams, C. A. (1982). Effects of parent enhancement therapy on the treatment outcome and generalization of a parent training program. *Behaviour Research and Therapy, 20*, 429–436.

Griest, D. L., Forehand, R., Wells, K. C., & McMahon, R. J. (1980). An examination of differences between nonclinic and behavior-problem clinic-referred children and their mothers. *Journal of Abnormal Psychology, 89*, 497–500.

Griffin, B.S., & Griffin, C. T. (1978). *Juvenile delinquency in perspective.* New York: Harper & Row.

Grinder, R. E. (1967). *A history of genetic psychology.* New York: John Wiley.

Grolnick, W. S., & Ryan, R. M. (1990). Self-perceptions, motivation, and adjustment in children with learning disabilities: A multiple group comparison study. *Journal of Learning Disabilities, 23*, 177–183.

Gross, A. M. (1990). Behavioral management of the child with diabetes. In A. M. Gross & R. S. Drabman (Eds.), *Handbook of clinical behavioral pediatrics.* New York: Plenum.

Gross, A. M., & Drabman, R. S. (1990). Clinical behavioral pediatrics: An introduction. In A. M. Gross & R. S. Drabman (Eds.), *Handbook of clinical behavioral pediatrics.* New York: Plenum.

Gross, A. M., Heimann, L., Shapiro, R., & Schultz, R. (1983). Social skills training and hemoglobin A_{1C} levels in children with diabetes. *Behavior Modification, 7*, 151–184.

Gross, M. D., Tofanelli, R. A., Butzirus, S. M., & Snodgrass E. W. (1987). The effects of diets rich in and free from additives on the behavior of children with hyperkinetic and learning disorders. *Journal of the American Academy of Child and Adolescent Psychiatry, 26*, 53–55.

Grossman, H. J. (1983). *Classification in mental retardation.* Washington, DC: American Association on Mental Deficiency.

Group for the Advancement of Psychiatry. (1966). *Psychopathological disorders in childhood: Theoretical considerations and a proposed classification.* New York: Jason Aronson.

Guidubaldi, J., & Perry, J. D. (1985). Divorce and mental health sequelae for children: A two-year follow-up of a nationwide sample. *Journal of the American Academy of Child Psychiatry, 24*, 531–537.

Gunn, P., & Berry, P. (1985). Down's Syndrome temperament and maternal response to descriptions of child behavior. *Developmental Psychology, 21*, 842–847.

Gutterman, E. M., O'Brien, J. D., & Young, J. G. (1987). Structured diagnostic interviews for children and adolescents: Current status and future directions. *Journal of the American Academy of Child and Adolescent Psychiatry, 26*, 621–630.

H

Hafner, A. J., Quast, W., & Shea, M. J. (1975). The adult adjustment of one thousand psychiatric patients: Initial findings from a twenty-five year follow-up. In R. O. Wirt, G. Winokur, & M. Roff (Eds.), *Life history in psychopathology,* Vol. 4. Minneapolis: University of Minnesota Press.

Hagamen, M. B. (1980). Family adaptation to the diagnosis of mental retardation in a child and strategies of intervention. In L. S. Szymanski & P. E. Tanguay (Eds.), *Emotional disorders of mentally retarded persons.* Baltimore: University Park Press.

Hahn, W. K. (1987). Cerebral lateralization of function: From infancy through childhood. *Psychological Bulletin, 101*, 376–392.

Haley, J. (1976). *Problem-solving therapy.* San Francisco: Jossey-Bass.

Hallahan, D. P., & Kauffman, J. M. (1978). *Exceptional children: Introduction to special education.* Englewood Cliffs, NJ: Prentice Hall.

Halmi, K. A. (1985). Eating disorders. In H. I. Kaplan & B. J. Sadock (Eds.), *Comprehensive textbook of psychiatry,* 4th ed. Baltimore: Williams & Wilkins.

Hammill, D. D. (1990). On defining learning disabilities: An emerging consensus. *Journal of Learning Disabilities, 23*, 75–91.

Hansen, H., Belmont, L., & Stein, Z. (1980). Epidemiology. In J. Wortis (Ed.), *Mental retardation and development disabilities*, Vol. XI. New York: Brunner/Mazel.

Hardgrove, C. B. (1980). Helping parents on the pediatric ward: A report on a survey of hospitals with "living-in" programs. *Pediatrician, 9*, 220–223.

Haring, N. G. (1986). Introduction. In N. G. Haring and L. McCormick (Eds.), *Exceptional children and youth.* Columbus, OH: Charles E. Merrill.

Haring, N. G., & McCormick, L. (1986). *Exceptional children and youth.* Columbus, OH: Charles E. Merrill.

Harkavy, J., Johnson, S. B., Silverstein, J., Spillar, R., McCallum, M., & Rosenbloom, A. (1983). Who learns what at a diabetes summer camp. *Journal of Pediatric Psychology, 8*, 143–153.

Harley, J. P., & Matthews, C. G. (1980). Food additives and hyperactivity in children: Experimental investigations. In R. M. Knights and D. J. Bakker (Eds.), *Treatment of hyperactive and learning disordered children.* Baltimore: University Park Press.

Harlow, H. F., & Harlow, M. K. (1965). The affectional systems. In A. M. Schrier, H.F. Harlow, & F. Stolnitz (Eds.), *Behavior of nonhuman primates*, Vol. 2. New York: Academic Press.

Harper, L. V., & Huie, K. S. (1987). Relations among preschool children's adult and peer contacts and later academic achievement. *Child Development, 58*, 1051–1065.

Harrell, R. (1983). The effects of the Head Start program on children's cognitive development: Preliminary report of the Head Start evaluation, synthesis and utilization project. Washington, DC: U.S. Department of Health and Human Services.

Harris, S. L. (1979). DSM-III—Its implications for children. *Child Behavior Therapy, 1*, 37–46.

Harris, S. L. (1984). The family of the autistic child: A behavioral-systems view. *Clinical Psychology Review, 4*, 227–239.

Harris, S. L., (1986). Families of children with autism: Issues for the behavior therapist. *The Behavior Therapist, 9*, 175–177.

Harrison, N. S. (1979). *Understanding behavioral research.* Belmont, CA: Wadsworth.

Harrison, S. I., & McDermott, J. K. (1972). *Chldhood psychopathology.* New York: International Univ. Press.

Hart, S. N., & Brassard, M. R. (1987). A major threat to children's mental health: Psychological maltreatment. *American Psychologist, 42*, 160–165.

Harter, S. (1985). *Manual for the Self-Perception Profile for Children.* Denver, CO: University of Denver.

Hartmann, D. P., & Wood, D. D. (1990). Observational methods. In A. S. Bellack, M. Hersen, & A. E. Kazdin (Eds.), *International handbook of behavior modification and therapy*, 2nd ed. New York: Plenum.

Hartup, W. W. (1983). Peer relations. In P. H. Mussen (Ed.), *Handbook of child psychology*, Vol. IV. New York: Wiley.

Hartup, W. W. (1989). Social relationships and their developmental significance. *American Psychologist, 44*, 120–126.

Hartup, W. W., Glazer, J. A., & Charlesworth, R. (1967). Peer reinforcement and sociometric status. *Child Development, 38*, 1017–1024.

Haskins, R. (1989). Beyond metaphor: The efficacy of early childhood education. *American Psychologist, 44*, 274–282.

Hawkins, R. C., Fremouw, W. J., & Clement, P. F. (1984). *The binge-purge syndrome: Treatment, research, and theory.* New York: Springer.

Hawton, K., & Goldacre, M. (1982). Hospital admissions for adverse effects of medicinal agents (mainly self-poisoning) among adolescents in the Oxford region. *British Journal of Psychiatry, 140*, 118–123.

Haywood, H. C., Meyers, C. E., & Switzky, H. N. (1982). Mental retardation. In M. R. Rosenzweig & L. W. Porter (Eds.), *Annual review of psychology.* Palo Alto, CA: Annual Reviews Inc.

Heavey, C. L., Adelman, H. S., Nelson, P., & Smith, D. C. (1989). Learning problems, anger, perceived control, and misbehavior. *Journal of Learning Disabilities, 22*, 47–50.

Heffron, W. A., Martin, C. A., & Welsh, R. J. (1984). Attention deficit disorder in three pairs of monozygotic twins: A case report. *Journal of the American Academy of Child Psychology, 23*, 299–301.

Henker, B., & Whalen, C. K. (1980). The changing faces of hyperactivity: Retrospect and prospect. In C. K. Whalen & B. Henker (Eds.), *Hyperactive children.* New York: Academic Press.

Herjanic, B., & Reich, W. (1982). Development of a structured psychiatric interview for children: Agreement between child and parent on individual symptoms. *Journal of Abnormal Child Psychology, 10*, 307–324.

Hermelin, B., & O'Connor, N. (1970). *Psychological experiments with autistic children.* London: Pergamon.

Hermelin, B., O'Connor, N., & Lee, S. (1987). Musical inventiveness of five idiot-savants. *Psychological Medicine, 17*, 685–694.

Hernandez, D. J. (1988). Demographic trends and the living arrangements of children. In E. M. Hetherington & J. D. Arasteh (Eds.), *Impact of divorce, single-parenting, and stepparenting on children.* Hillsdale, NJ: Erlbaum.

Hersen, M. (1990). Single-case experimental designs. In A. S. Bellack, M. Hersen, & A. E. Kazdin (Eds.), *International handbook of behavior modification and therapy.* New York: Plenum.

Hersov, L. (1985). Emotional disorders. In M. Rutter & L. Hersov (Eds.), *Child and adolescent psychiatry.* Boston: Blackwell Scientific Publications.

Hersov, L. A. (1960). Persistent non-attendance at school. *Journal of Child Psychology and Psychiatry, 1*, 130–136.

Hertzler, A. A. (1983a). Children's food patterns—A review. I. Food preferences and feeding problems. *Journal of the American Dietetic Association, 83*, 551–554.

Hertzler, A. A. (1983b). Children's food patterns—A review. II. Family and group behavior. *Journal of the American Dietetic Association*, 555–560.

Heston, L. L. (1966). Psychiatric disorders in foster home reared children of schizophrenic mothers. *British Journal of Psychiatry, 112*, 819–825.

Hetherington, E. M. (1989). Coping with family transitions: Winners, losers, and survivors. *Child Development, 60*, 1–14.

Hetherington, E. M., & Camara, K. A. (1984). Families in transition: The process of dissolution and reconstitution. In R. D. Parke (Ed.), *Review of child development research: The family*, Vol. 7. Chicago: University of Chicago Press.

Hetherington, E. M., Cox, M., & Cox, R. (1982). Effects of divorce on parents and children. In M. E. Lamb (Ed.), *Nontraditional families: Parenting and child development.* Hillsdale, NJ: Erlbaum.

Hetherington, E. M., Cox, M., & Cox, R. (1985). Long-term effects of divorce and remarriage on the adjustment of children. *Journal of the American Academy of Child Psychiatry, 24*, 518–530.

Hetherington, E. M., & Martin, B. (1986). Family factors and psychopathology in children. In H. C. Quay & J. S. Werry (Eds.), *Psychopathological disorders of childhood*, 3rd ed. New York: Wiley.

Hetherington, E. M., Stanley-Hagan, M., & Anderson, E. R. (1989). Marital transitions: A child's perspective. *American Psychologist, 44*, 303–312.

Hightower, D. A., Cowen, E. L., Spinell, A. P., Lotyczewski, B. S., Guare, J. C., Rohrbeck, C. A., & Brown, L. P. (1987). The Child Rating Scale: The development and psychometric refinement of a socioemotional self-rating scale for young children. *School Psychology Review, 16*, 239–255.

Hinshaw, S. P. (1987). On the distinction between attentional deficits/hyperactivity and conduct problems/aggression in child psychopathology. *Psychological Bulletin, 101*, 443–463.

Hinshaw, S. P., Henker, B., & Whalen, C. K. (1984). Cognitive-behavioral and pharmacologic interventions for hyperactive boys: Comparative and combined effects. *Journal of Consulting and Clinical Psychology, 52*, 739–749.

Hinshaw, S. P., Henker, B., Whalen, C. K., Erhardt, D., & Dunnington, R. E. (1989). Aggressive, prosocial, and nonsocial behavior in hyperactive boys: Dose effects of methylphenidate in naturalistic settings. *Journal of Consulting and Clinical Psychology, 57*, 636–643.

Hobbs, N. (1975). *The futures of children.* San Francisco: Jossey-Bass.

Hobson, R. P. (1986). The autistic child's appraisal of expressions of emotions. *Journal of Child Psychology and Psychiatry, 27*, 321–342.

Hobson, R. P. (1989). Beyond cognition: A theory of autism. In G. Dawson (Ed.), *Autism: Nature, diagnosis, and treatment.* New York: Guilford.

Hodapp, R. M., & Mueller, E. (1982). Early social development. In B. B. Wolman (Ed.), *Handbook of developmental psychology.* Englewood Cliffs, NJ: Prentice Hall.

Hodapp, R. M., & Zigler, E. (1985). Placement decisions and their effects on the development of individuals with severe mental retardation. *Mental Retardation, 23*, 125–130.

Hodges, J., & Tizard, B. (1989a). IQ and behavioural adjustment of ex-institutional adolescents. *Journal of Child Psychology and Psychiatry, 30*, 53–75.

Hodges, J., & Tizard, B. (1989b). Social and family relationships of ex-institutional adolescents. *Journal of Child Psychology and Psychiatry, 30*, 77–79.

Hodges, K., McKnew, D., Cytryn, L., Stern, L., & Kline, J. (1982). The Child Assessment Schedule (CAS) diagnostic interview: A report on reliability and validity. *Journal of the American Academy of Child Psychiatry, 21*, 468–473.

Hoffman, L. W. (1989). Effects of maternal employment in the two-parent family. *American Psychologist, 44*, 283–292.

Hoffman, M. L. (1979). Development of moral thought, feeling, and behavior. *American Psychologist, 34*, 958–966.

Holden, G. W., Moncher, M. S., & Schinke, S. P. (1990). Substance abuse. In A. S. Bellack, M. Hersen, & A. E. Kazdin (Eds.), *International handbook of behavior modification and therapy,* 2nd ed. New York: Plenum.

Hollingsworth, C. E., Tanguay, P. E., Grossman, L., & Pabst, P. (1980). Long-term outcome of obsessive-compulsive disorder in childhood. *Journal of the American Academy of Child Psychiatry, 19*, 134–144.

Holmes, L. B. (1978). Genetic counseling for the older pregnant woman: New data and questions. *New England Journal of Medicine, 298*, 1419–1421.

Hops, H. (1983). Children's social competence and skill: Current research practices and future directions. *Behavior Therapy, 14*, 3–18.

Hops, H., Biglan, A., Sherman, L., Arthur, J., Friedman, L., & Osteen, V. (1987). Home observations of family interactions of depressed women. *Journal of Consulting and Clinical Psychology, 55*, 341–346.

Hops, H., & Greenwood, C. R. (1981). Social skills deficits. In E. J. Mash & L. G. Terdal (Eds.), *Behavioral assessment of childhood disorders.* New York: Guilford Press.

Hops, H., & Greenwood, C. R. (1988). Social skill deficits. In E. J. Mash & L. G. Terdal (Eds.), *Behavioral assessment of childhood disorders,* 2nd ed. New York: Guilford.

Horn, J. M. (1983). The Texas Adoption Project: Adopted children and their intellectual resemblance to biological and adoptive parents. *Child Development, 54*, 268–275.

Horne, A. M., & Van Dyke, B. (1983). Treatment and maintenance of social learning family therapy. *Behavior Therapy, 14*, 606–613.

Houts, A. C., Liebert, R. M., & Padawar, W. (1983). A delivery system for the treatment of primary enuresis. *Journal of Abnormal Child Psychology, 11*, 513–520.

Houts, A. C., Mellon, M. W., & Whelan, J. P. (1988). Use of dietary fiber and stimulus control to treat retentive encopresis: A multiple baseline investigation. *Journal of Pediatric Psychology, 13*, 435–445.

Houts, A. C., Peterson, J. K., & Whelan, J. P. (1986). Prevention of relapse in full-spectrum home training for primary enuresis: A components analysis. *Behavior Therapy, 17*, 462–469.

Hudson, J. I., Pope, H. G., Jonal, J. M., & Yurgelun-Todd, D. (1983). Family history of anorexia nervosa and bulimia. *British Journal of Psychiatry, 142*, 133–138.

Huesmann, L. R., Eron, L. D., Lefkowitz, M. M., & Walder, L. O. (1984). Stability of aggression over time and generations. *Developmental Psychology, 20*, 1120–1134.

Humphrey, L. L. (1989). Observed family interaction among subtypes of eating disorders using structured analysis of social behavior. *Journal of Consulting and Clinical Psychology, 57*, 206–214.

Humphreys, L., Forehand, R., McMahon, R., & Roberts, M. (1978). Parent behavioral training to modify child noncompliance: Effects on untreated siblings. *Journal of Behavior Therapy and Experimental Psychiatry, 9*, 235–238.

Humphreys, L. G., Rich, S. A., & Davey, T. (1985). A Piagetian test of general Intelligence. *Developmental Psychology, 21*, 872–877.

Hurtig, A. L., Koepke, D., & Park, K. B. (1989). Relation between severity of chronic illness and adjustment in children and adolescents with sickle cell disease. *Journal of Pediatric Psychology, 14*, 117–132.

Huse, D. M., Branes, L. A., Colligan, R. C., Nelson, R. A., & Palumbo, P. J. (1982). The challenge of obesity in childhood: I. Incidence, prevalence, and staging. *Mayo Clinic Proceedings, 57*, 279–284.

Huston, A. C. (1983). Sex-typing. In P. Mussen (Ed.), *Handbook of child psychology,* Vol. IV. New York: Wiley.

Hynd, G. W., & Semrud-Clikeman, M. (1989a). Dyslexia and brain morphology. *Psychological Bulletin, 106*, 447–482.

Hynd, G. W., & Semrud-Clikeman, M. (1989b). Dyslexia and neurodevelopmental pathology: Relationships to cognition, intelligence, and reading skill acquisition. *Journal of Learning Disabilities, 22*, 205–218.

Hynd, G. W., Snow, J., & Becker, M. G. (1986). Neuropsychological assessment in clinical child psychology. In B. B. Lahey & A. E. Kazdin (Eds.), *Advances in Clinical Child Psychology,* Vol. 9. New York: Plenum.

I

Ilg, F. L., & Ames, L. B. (1965). *School readiness: Behavior tests used at the Gesell Institute.* New York: Harper & Row.

Illingworth, R. S. (1971). The predictive value of developmental assessment in infancy. *Develop. Med. Child Neurology, 13*, 721–725.

Ingram, R. E., & Scott, W. D. (1990). Cognitive behavior therapy. In A. S. Bellack, M. Hersen, & A. E. Kazdin (Eds.), *International handbook of behavior modification and therapy,* 2nd ed. New York: Plenum.

Inouye, D. K. (1988). Children's mental health issues. *American Psychologist, 43*, 813–816.

Israel, A. C. (1988). Parental and family influences in the etiology and treatment of childhood obesity. In N. A. Krasnegor, G. D. Grave, & N. Kretchmer (Eds.), *Childhood obesity: A biobehavioral perspective.* Caldwell, NJ: The Telford Press.

Israel, A. C. (1990). Childhood obesity. In A. S. Bellack, M. Hersen, & A. E. Kazdin (Eds.), *International handbook of behavior modification and therapy*. New York: Plenum.

Israel, A. C., Pravder, M. D., & Knights, S. (1980). A peer-administered program for changing the classroom behavior of disruptive children. *Behavioural Analysis and Modification*, 4, 224–238.

Israel, A. C., & Shapiro, L. S. (1985). Behavior problems of obese children enrolling in a weight reduction program. *Journal of Pediatric Psychology*, 10, 449–460.

Israel, A. C., Silverman, W. K., & Solotar, L. C. (1986). An investigation of family influences on initial weight status, attrition, and treatment outcome in a childhood obesity program. *Behavior Therapy*, 17, 131–143.

Israel, A. C., Silverman, W. K., & Solotar, L. C. (1987). Baseline adherence as a predictor of dropout in a children's weight-reduction program. *Journal of Consulting and Clinical Psychology*, 55, 791–793.

Israel, A. C., Silverman, W. K., & Solotar, L. C. (1988). The relationship between adherence and weight loss in a behavioral treatment program for overweight children. *Behavior Therapy*, 19, 25–33.

Israel, A. C., & Solotar, L. C. (1988). Obesity. In M. Hersen, & C. G. Last (Eds.), *Child behavior therapy casebook*. New York: Plenum.

Israel, A. C., & Stolmaker, L. S. (1980). Behavioral treatment of obesity in children and adolescents. In M. Hersen, R. M. Eisler, & P. M. Miller (Eds.), *Progress in Behavior Modification*, Vol. 10. New York: Academic Press.

Israel, A. C., Stolmaker, L., & Andrian, C. A. G. (1985). The effects of training parents in general child management skills in a behavioral weight loss program for children. *Behavior Therapy*, 16, 169–180.

Israel, A. C., Stolmaker, L., Sharp, J. P., Silverman, W. K., & Simon, L. G. (1984). An evaluation of two methods of parental involvement in treating obese children. *Behavior Therapy*, 15, 266–272.

Israel, A. C., & Zimand, E. (1989). Obesity. In M. Hersen (Ed.), *Innovations in child behavior therapy*. New York: Springer.

Izard, C. E. (1986). Introduction. In C. E. Izard & P. B. Read (Eds.), *Measuring emotion in infants and children*, Vol. 2. New York: Cambridge Univ. Press.

J

Jacob, R. G., O'Leary, K. D., & Rosenblad, C. (1978). Formal and informal classroom settings: Effects on hyperactivity. *Journal of Abnormal Child Psychology*, 6, 47–59.

Jacobson, S. W., Jacobson, J. J., & Fein, G. G. (1986). Environmental toxins and infant development. In H. E. Fitzgerald, B. M. Lester, and M. W. Yogman (Eds.), *Theory and research in behavioral pediatrics*, Vol. 3. New York: Plenum.

Jacobvitz, D., Sroufe, L. A., Stewart, M., & Leffert, N. (1990). Treatment of attentional and hyperactivity problems in children with sympathomimetic drugs: A comprehensive review. *Journal of the American Academy of Child and Adolescent Psychiatry*, 29, 677–688.

James, A., & Taylor, E. (1990). Sex differences in the hyperkinetic syndrome of childhood. *Journal of Child Psychology and Psychiatry*, 31, 437–446.

Jarvie, G. J., Lahey, B., Graziano, W., & Framer, E. (1983). Childhood obesity and social stigma: What we know and what we don't know. *Developmental Review*, 3, 237–273.

Jastak, J. F., & Jastak, S. R. (1965). *The Wide Range Achievement Test*, rev. ed. Wilmington, DE: Guidance Associates.

Jastak, S., & Wilkinson, G. S. (1984). *Wide Range Achievement Test—Revised*. Wilmington, DE: Jastak Associates.

Jay, S. M. (1988). Invasive medical procedures: Psychological intervention and assessment. In D. K. Routh (Ed.), *Handbook of pediatric psychology*. New York: Guilford.

Jay, S. M., Elliot, C. H., Katz, E., & Siegel, S. E. (1987a). Cognitive behavioral and pharmacologic intervention for children's distress during painful medical procedures. *Journal of Consulting and Clinical Psychology*, 55, 860–865.

Jay, S. M., Elliot, C. H., Ozolins, M., Olson, R., & Pruitt, S. (1985). Behavioral management of children's distress during painful medical procedures. *Behavior Research and Therapy*, 23, 513–520.

Jay, S. M., Green, V., Johnson, S., Caldwell, S., & Nitschke, R. (1987b). Differences in death concepts between children with cancer and physically healthy children. *Journal of Clinical Child Psychology*, 16, 301–306.

Jeffrey, D. B., & Krauss, M. R. (1981). The etiologies, assessments, and treatments of obesity. In S. N. Haynes & L. A. Gannon (Eds.), *Psychosomatic disorders: A psychophysiological approach to etiology and treatment*. New York: Gardner.

Jeffrey, D. B., Lemnitzer, N. B., Hess, J. M., Hickey, J. S., McLellarn, R. W., & Stroud, J. (1979). *Children's responses to television food advertising: Experimental evidence of actual food consumption*. Paper presented at a meeting of the American Psychological Association, New York City, September.

Jennings, K. D., Connors, R. E., & Stegman, C. E. (1988). Does a physical handicap alter the development of mastery motivation during the preschool years? *Journal of Child and Adolescent Psychiatry*, 27, 312–317.

Jensen, A. R. (1969). How much can we boost IQ and scholastic achievement? *Harvard Educational Review*, 39, 1–123.

Jensen, P. S., Bloedau, L., Degroot, J., Ussery, T., & Davis, H. (1990). Children at risk I: Risk factors and child symptomatology. *Journal of the American Academy of Child and Adolescent Psychiatry*, 29, 51–59.

Jersild, A. T., & Holmes, F. B. (1935). Children's fears. *Child Development Monograph*, No. 20.

Jessor, R., & Jessor, S. L. (1977). *Problem behavior and psychosocial development*. New York: Academic Press.

Johnson, C., Connors, M. E., & Tobin, D. L. (1987). Symptom management of bulimia. *Journal of Consulting and Clinical Psychology*, 55, 668–676.

Johnson, J. H., Rasbury, W. C., & Siegel, L. J. (1986). *Approaches to child treatment: Introduction to theory, research, and practice*. New York: Pergamon.

Johnson, S. B. (1984). *Test of Diabetes Knowledge Revised—2*. Gainsville: University of Florida, Department of Psychiatry.

Johnson, S. B. (1988a). Chronic illness and pain. In E. J. Mash & L. G. Terdal (Eds.), *Behavioral assessment of childhood disorders*, 2nd ed. New York: Guilford.

Johnson, S. B. (1988b). Diabetes mellitus in childhood. In D. K. Routh (Ed.), *Handbook of pediatric psychology*. New York: Guilford.

Johnson, S. B. (1988c). Psychological aspects of childhood diabetes. *Journal of Child Psychology and Psychiatry*, 29, 729–738.

Johnson, S. B. (1989). Juvenile diabetes. In T. H. Ollendick & M. Hersen (Eds.), *Handbook of child psychopathology*, 2nd ed. New York: Plenum.

Johnson, S. B., Silverstein, J., Rosenbloom, A., Carter, R., & Cunningham, W. (1986). Assessing daily management in childhood diabetes. *Health Psychology*, 5, 545–564.

Johnson, S. M., Wahl, G., Martin, S., & Johansson, S. (1973). How deviant is the normal child? A behavioral analysis of the preschool child and his family. In R. D. Rubin, J. P. Brady, & J. D. Henderson (Eds.), *Advances in behavior therapy*, Vol. 4. New York: Academic Press.

Jones, F. R., Garrison, K. C., & Morgan, R. F. (1985). *The psychology of human development*. New York: Harper & Row.

Jones, M. C. (1924). A laboratory study of fear: The case of Peter. *Pedagogical Seminary, 31*, 308–315.

Jouriles, E. N., Murphy, C. M., & O'Leary, K. D. (1989). Interspousal aggression, marital discord, and child problems. *Journal of Consulting and Clinical Psychology, 57*, 453–455.

Joyce, K., Singer, M., & Isralowitz, R. (1983). Impact of respite care on parents' perceptions of quality of life. *Mental Retardation, 21*, 153–156.

Judd, L. J. (1965). Obsessive-compulsive neurosis in children. *Archives of General Psychiatry, 12*, 136–143.

Jurkovic, G. J. (1980). The juvenile delinquent as a moral philosopher: A structural-developmental perspective. *Psychological Bulletin, 88*, 709–727.

Jurkovic, G. J., & Prentice, N. M. (1977). Relation of moral and cognitive development to dimensions of juvenile delinquency. *Journal of Abnormal Psychology, 86*, 414–420.

Justice, E. M. (1985). Metamemory: An aspect of metacognition in the mentally retarded. In N. R. Ellis & N. W. Bray (Eds.), *International Review of Research In Mental Retardation, Vol. 13*. New York: Academic Press.

K

Kaffman, K., & Elizur, E. (1977). Infants who become enuretics: A longitudinal study of 161 Kibbutz children. *Monographs of the Society for Research in Child Development, 42* (4,Serial No. 170).

Kagan, J. (1984). *The nature of the child.* New York: Basic Books.

Kagan, J., Reznick, J. S., & Gibbons, J. (1989). Inhibited and uninhibited types of children. *Child Development, 60*, 838–845.

Kahn, E., & Cohen, L. H. (1934). Organic driveness: A brain syndrome and an experience—with case reports. *New England Journal of Medicine, 210*, 748–756.

Kallmann, F., & Roth, B. (1956). Genetic aspects of preadolescent schizophrenia. *American Journal of Psychiatry, 112*, 599–606.

Kalnins, I. V., Churchill, M. P., & Terry, G. E. (1980). Concurrent stresses in families with a leukemic child. *Journal of Pediatric Psychology, 5*, 81–92.

Kamin, L. J. (1974). *The science and politics of IQ.* Potomac, MD: Erlbaum.

Kandel, D. B. (1982). Epidemiological and psychosocial perspectives on adolescent drug use. *Journal of the American Academy of Child Psychiatry, 21*, 328–347.

Kanfer, F. H., Karoly, P., & Newman, A. (1975). Reduction of children's fear of the dark by competence-related and situational threat-related verbal cues. *Journal of Consulting and Clinical Psychology, 43*, 251–258.

Kanner, L. (1943). Autistic disturbances of affective contact. *Nervous Child, 2*, 217–250.

Kanner, L. (1972). *Child psychiatry*, 4th ed. Springfield, IL: Chas. C. Thomas.

Kanner, L. (1973). *Childhood psychoses: Initial studies and new insights.* Washington, DC: V. H. Winston & Sons.

Kanner, L., & Eisenberg, L. (1956). Early infantile autism, 1943–1955. *American Journal of Orthopsychiatry, 26*, 55–65.

Kaplan, A. S., & Woodside, D. B. (1987). Biological aspects of anorexia nervosa and bulimia nervosa. *Journal of Consulting and Clinical Psychology, 55*, 645–653.

Kaplan, B. J., McNicol, J., Conte, R. A., & Moghadam, H. K. (1989). Overall nutrient intake of preschool hyperactive and normal boys. *Journal of Abnormal Child Psychology, 17*, 127–132.

Kaplan, R. M. (1985). The controversy related to the use of psychological tests. In B. Wolman (Ed.), *Handbook of intelligence.* New York: Wiley.

Kaplan, S. L., Hong, G. K., & Weinhold, C. (1984). Epidemiology of depressive symptomatology in adolescents. *Journal of the American Academy of Child Psychiatry, 23*, 91–98.

Karoly, P., & Bay, R. C. (1990). Diabetes self-care goals and their relation to children's metabolic control. *Journal of Pediatric Psychology, 15*, 83–95.

Kashani, J. H., Carlson, G. A., Beck, N. C., Hoeper, E. W., Corcoran, C. M., McAllister, J. A., Fallahi, C., Rosenberg, T. K., & Reid, J. C. (1987). Depression, depressive symptoms, and depressed mood among a community sample of adolescents. *American Journal of Psychiatry, 144*, 931–934.

Kashani, J. H., Orvaschel, H., Rosenberg, T. K., & Reid, J. C. (1989). Psychopathology in a community sample of children and adolescents: A developmental perspective. *Journal of the American Academy of Child and Adolescent Psychiatry, 28*, 701–706.

Kaslow, N. J., & Racusin, G.R. (1990). Childhood depression: Current status and future directions. In A. S. Bellack, M. Hersen, & A. E. Kazdin (Eds.), *International handbook of behavior modification and therapy*, 2nd ed. New York: Plenum.

Kaslow, N. J., Rehm, L. P., & Siegel, A. W. (1984). Social-cognitive and cognitive correlates of depression in children. *Journal of Abnormal Child Psychology, 12*, 605–620.

Katz, E. R., Dolgin, M. J., & Varni, J. W. (1990). Cancer in children and adolescents. In A. M. Gross & R. S. Drabman (Eds.), *Handbook of clinical behavioral pediatrics.* New York: Plenum.

Kauffman, J. M., Gerber, M. M., & Semmel, M. I. (1988). Arguable assumptions underlying the regular education initiative. *Journal of Learning Disabilities, 21*, 6–11.

Kaufman, A. S., & Reynolds, C. R. (1984). Intellectual and academic achievement tests. In T. H. Ollendick & M. Hersen (Eds.), *Child behavioral assessment: Principles and procedures.* New York: Pergamon.

Kaufman, J., & Zigler, E. (1987). Do abused children become abusive parents? *American Journal of Orthopsychiatry, 57*, 186–192.

Kazdin, A. E. (1981). Drawing valid inferences from case studies. *Journal of Consulting and Clinical Psychology, 49*, 183–192.

Kazdin, A. E. (1985). *Treatment of antisocial behavior in children and adolescents.* Homewood, IL: Dorsey.

Kazdin, A. E. (1987). Treatment of antisocial behavior in children: Current status and future directions. *Psychological Bulletin, 102*, 187–203.

Kazdin, A. E. (1988). Childhood depression. In E. J. Mash & L. G. Terdal (Eds.), *Behavioral assessment of childhood disorders*, 2nd ed. New York: Guilford.

Kazdin, A. E. (1989a). Conduct and oppositional disorders. In C. G. Last & M. Hersen (Eds.), *Handbook of psychiatric diagnosis.* New York: Wiley.

Kazdin, A. E. (1989b). Identifying depression in children: A comparison of alternative selection criteria. *Journal of Abnormal Child Psychology, 17*, 437–454.

Kazdin, A. E. (1990a). Childhood depression. *Journal of Child Psychology and Psychiatry, 31*, 121–160.

Kazdin, A. E. (1990b). Conduct disorders. In A. S. Bellack, M. Hersen, & A. E. Kazdin (Eds.), *International handbook of behavior modification and therapy*, 2nd ed. New York: Plenum.

Kazdin, A. E., Esveldt-Dawson, K., Sherick, R. B., & Colbus, D. (1985). Assessment of overt behavior and childhood depression among psychiatrically disturbed children. *Journal of Consulting and Clinical Psychology, 53*, 201–210.

Kazdin, A. E., Esveldt-Dawson, K., Unis, A. S., & Rancurello, M. D. (1983). Child and parent evaluations of depression and aggression in psychiatric inpatient children. *Journal of Abnormal Child Psychology, 11*, 401–413.

Kazdin, A. E., & Kolko, D. J. (1986). Parent psychopathology and family functioning among childhood firesetters. *Journal of Abnormal Child Psychology, 14*, 315–329.

Kazdin, A. E., Rodgers, A., & Colbus, D. (1986). The Hopelessness Scale for Children: Psychometric characteristics and concurrent validity. *Journal of Consulting and Clinical Psychology, 54,* 241–245.

Kearney, C. A., & Silverman, W. K. (1990). A preliminary analysis of a functional model of assessment and treatment for school refusal behavior. *Behavior Modification, 14,* 340–366.

Kellerman, J. (1980). Rapid treatment of nocturnal anxiety in children. *Journal of Behavior Therapy and Experimental Psychiatry, 11,* 9–11.

Kelley, T. L., Madden, R., Gardner, E. F., & Rudman, H. C. (1964). *The Stanford Achievement Test.* New York: Harcourt Brace Jovanovich.

Kelly, M. L., & Heffer, R. W. (1990). Eating disorders: Food refusal and failure to thrive. In A. M. Gross & R. S. Drabman (Eds.), *Handbook of clinical behavioral pediatrics.* New York: Plenum.

Kelty, M. (1981). Protection of persons who participate in applied research. In G.T. Hannah, W. P. Christian, & H. B. Clark (Eds.), *Preservation of client rights.* New York: Free Press.

Kemph, J. P. (1987). Hallucinations in psychotic children. *Journal of the American Academy of Child and Adolescent Psychiatry, 26,* 556–559.

Kendall, P. C. (1985). Toward a cognitive-behavioral model of child psychopathology and a critique of related interventions. *Journal of Abnormal Child Psychology, 13,* 357–372.

Kendall, P. C. (1986). Comments on Rubin and Krasnor: Solutions and problems in research on problem solving. In M. Perlmutter (Ed.), Cognitive perspectives on children's social and behavioral development, Vol. 18. *Minnesota Symposium on Child Development.* Hillsdale, NJ: Erlbaum.

Kendall, P. C. (1987a). Ahead to basics: Assessment with children and families. *Behavioral Assessment, 9,* 321–332.

Kendall, P. C. (1987b). Cognitive processes and procedures in behavior therapy. In G. T. Wilson, C. M. Franks, P. C. Kendall, & J. P. Foreyt (Eds.), *Review of behavior therapy: Theory and practice,* 11th ed. New York: Guilford.

Kendall, P. C., & Braswell, L. (1985). *Cognitive-behavioral therapy for impulsive children.* New York: Guilford.

Kendall, P. C., & Braswell, L. (1986). Medical applications of cognitive-behavioral interventions with children. *Developmental and Behavioral Pediatrics, 7,* 257–264.

Kennedy, W. A. (1965). School phobia: Rapid treatment of 50 cases. *Journal of Abnormal Psychology, 70,* 285–289.

Kenny, T. J. (1980). Hyperactivity. In H. E. Rie & E. D. Rie (Eds.), *Handbook of minimal brain dysfunctions.* New York: John Wiley.

Keogh, B. (1988). Improving services for problem learners: Rethinking and restructuring. *Journal of Learning Disabilities, 21,* 19–22.

Kephart, N. C. (1960, 1971). *The slow learner in the classroom.* Columbus, OH: Chas. E. Merrill.

Kessler, J. W. (1966, 1988). *Psychopathology of childhood.* Englewood Cliffs, NJ: Prentice Hall.

Kessler, J. W. (1980). History of minimal brain dysfunctions. In H. E. Rie & E. D. Rie (Eds.), *Handbook of minimal brain dysfunctions.* New York: John Wiley.

Kiernan, C. (1985). Behaviour modification. In A. M. Clarke, A. D. B. Clarke, & J. M. Berg (Eds.), *Mental deficiency. The changing outlook.* New York: The Free Press.

King, N. J., & Ollendick, T. H. (1989). Children's anxiety and phobic disorders in school settings: Classification, assessment, and intervention issues. *Review of Educational Research, 59,* 431–470.

King, N. J., Ollendick, T. H., & Gullone, E. (1990). School-related fears of children and adolescents. *Australian Journal of Education, 34,* 99–112.

King, N. J., Ollier, K., Iacuone, R., Schuster, S., Bays, K., Gullone, E., & Ollendick, T. H. (1989). Fears of children and adolescents: A cross-sectional Australian study using the Revised-Fear Survey Schedule for Children. *Journal of Child Psychology and Psychiatry, 30,* 775–784.

Kirby, F. D., & Toler, H. C. (1970). Modification of pre-school isolate behavior: A case study. *Journal of Applied Behavior Analysis, 3,* 309–314.

Kirigin, K. A., Braukmann, C. J., Atwater, J. D., & Wolf, M. M. (1982). An evaluation of Teaching-Family (Achievement Place) group homes for juvenile offenders. *Journal of Applied Behavior Analysis, 15,* 1–16.

Kirk, S. A. (April 1963). *Behavioral diagnosis and remediation of learning disabilities.* Proceedings of the First Annual Meeting of the ACLD Conference on Exploration into the Problems of the Perceptually Handicapped Child. Chicago, IL.

Kirk, S. A. (1972). *Educating exceptional children.* Boston: Houghton Mifflin.

Kirk, S. A., & Gallagher, J. J. (1989). *Educating exceptional children.* Boston: Houghton Mifflin.

Kirk, S. A., McCarthy, J. J., & Kirk, W. D. (1968). *Illinois Test of Psycholinguistic Abilities.* Urbana, IL: University of Illinois Press.

Kirkpatrick, D. R. (1984). Age, gender, and patterns of common intense fears among adults. *Behaviour Research and Therapy, 22,* 141–150.

Klein, M. (1932). *The psycho-analysis of children.* London: Hogarth Press.

Klein, N. C., Alexander, J. F., & Parsons, B. V. (1977). Impact of family systems intervention on recidivism and sibling delinquency: A model of primary prevention and program evaluation. *Journal of Consulting and Clinical Psychology, 45,* 469–474.

Klesges, R. C., & Hanson, C. L. (1988). Determining the environmental causes and correlates of childhood obesity: methodological issues and future research directions. In N. A. Krasnegor, G. D. Grave, & N. Kretchmer (Eds.), *Childhood obesity: A biobehavioral perspective.* Caldwell, NJ: The Telford Press.

Klesges, R. C., Malott, J. M., Boschee, P. F., & Weber, J. M. (1986). The effects of parental influences on children's food intake, physical activity, and relative weight. *International Journal of Eating Disorders, 5,* 335–346.

Kliewer, W., & Weidner, G. (1987). Type A behavior and aspirations: A study of parents' and children's goal setting. *Developmental Psychology, 23,* 204–209.

Klorman, R., Coons, H. W., & Borgstedt, A.D. (1987). Effects of methylphenidate on adolescents with a childhood history of attention deficit disorder: I. Clinical findings. *Journal of the American Academy of Child and Adolescent Psychiatry, 26,* 363–367.

Knitzer, J. (1981). Child welfare: The role of federal policies. *Journal of Clinical Child Psychology, 10,* 3–7.

Knobloch, H., & Pasamanick, B. (1974). *Gesell and Amatruda's developmental diagnosis.* New York: Harper & Row Pub.

Koegel, R. L., O'Dell, M. C., & Koegel, L. K. (1987). A natural language teaching paradigm for nonverbal autistic children. *Journal of Autism and Developmental Disorders, 17,* 187–200. Plenum Pub. Corp.

Koegel, R., Schreibman, L., O'Neill, R. E., & Burke, J. C. (1983). The personality and family-interaction characteristics of parents of autistic children. *Journal of Consulting and Clinical Psychology, 51,* 683–692.

Kog, E., & Vandereycken, W. (1985). Family characteristics of anorexia nervosa and bulimia: A review of the research literature. *Clinical Psychology Review, 5,* 159–180.

Kohlberg, L. (1964). Development of moral character and moral ideology. In M. Hoffman & L. Hoffman (Eds.), *Review of child development research,* Vol. 1. New York: Russell Sage Foundation.

Kohlberg, L. (1976). Moral stages and moralization: The cognitive-developmental approach. In T. Lickona (Ed.), *Moral development and behavior: Theory, research and social issues*. New York: Holt, Rinehart and Winston.

Kohlberg, L., LaCrosse, J., & Ricks, D. (1972). The predictability of adult mental health from childhood behavior. In B. Wolman (Ed.), *Manual of child psychopathology*. New York: McGraw-Hill.

Kolata, G. B. (1978). Behavioral teratology: Birth defects of the mind. *Science, 202,* 732–734.

Kolko, D. J. (1985). Juvenile firesetting: A review and methodological critique. *Clinical Psychology Review, 5,* 345–376.

Kolko, D. (1987). Simplified inpatient treatment of nocturnal enuresis in psychiatrically disturbed children. *Behavior Therapy, 18,* 99–112.

Kolko, D. J. (1989). Fire setting and pyromania. In C. Last & M. Hersen (Eds.), *Handbook of child psychiatric diagnosis*. New York: Wiley.

Kolko, D. J., & Kazdin, A. E. (1986). A conceptualization of firesetting in children and adolescents. *Journal of Abnormal Child Psychology, 14,* 49–61.

Kolko, D. J., & Kazdin, A. E. (1989). Assessment of dimensions of childhood firesetting among patients and nonpatients: The Firesetting Risk Interview. *Journal of Abnormal Child Psychology, 17,* 157–176.

Kolko, D. J., Kazdin, A. E., & Meyer, E. C. (1985). Aggression and psychopathology in childhood firesetters: Parent and child reports. *Journal of Consulting and Clinical Psychology, 53,* 377–385.

Kolvin, I. (1971). Psychoses in childhood—a comparative study. In M. Rutter (Ed.), *Infantile autism: Concepts, characteristics, and treatments*. London: Churchill-Livingstone.

Koocher, G. P. (1973). Childhood, death, and cognitive development. *Developmental Psychology, 9,* 369–375.

Koocher, G. P. (1980). Pediatric cancer: Psychosocial problems and the high costs of helping. *Journal of Clinical Child Psychology, 9,* 2–5.

Koocher, G. P., & Sallan, S. E. (1978). Pediatric oncology. In P. R. Magrab (Ed.), *Psychological management of pediatric problems*, Vol. 1. Baltimore: University Park Press.

Koorland, M. A. (1986). Applied behavior analysis and the correction of learning disabilities. In J. K. Torgesen and B. Y. L. Wong (Eds.), *Psychological and educational perspectives on learning disabilities*. New York: Academic.

Kopp, C. B. (1983). Risk factors in development. In P. H. Mussen (Ed.), *Handbook of child psychology*, Vol. II. New York: Wiley.

Kopp, C. B. (1989). Health and development. Section introduction. *American Psychologist, 44,* 179.

Kopp, C. B., & Kaler, S. R. (1989). Risk in infancy: Origins and implications. *American Psychologist, 44,* 224–230.

Korn, S. J., & Gannon, S. (1983). Temperament, cultural variation, and behavior disorder in preschool children. *Child Psychiatry and Human Development, 13,* 203–212.

Kornblatt, E. S., & Heinrich, J. (1985). Needs and coping abilities in families of children with developmental disabilities. *Mental Retardation, 23,* 13–19.

Kotses, H., Glaus, K. D., Crawford, P. L., Edwards, J. E., & Scherr, M.S. (1976). Operant reduction of frontalis EMG activity in the treatment of asthma in children. *Journal of Psychosomatic Research, 20,* 453–459.

Kovacs, M. (1981). Rating scales to assess depression in school aged children. *Acta Paedopsychiatria, 46,* 305–315.

Kovacs, M. (1985). The Children's Depression Inventory (CDI). *Psychopharmacology Bulletin, 21,* 995–999.

Kovacs, M. (1989). Affective disorder in children and adolescents. *American Psychologist, 44,* 209–215.

Kovacs, M., & Beck, A. T. (1977). An empirical-clinical approach toward a definition of childhood depression. In J. G. Schulterbrandt & A. Raskin (Eds.), *Depression in children:*

Diagnosis, treatment, and conceptual models. New York: Raven Press.

Kovacs, M., Feinberg, T. L., Crouse-Novak, M. A., Paulauskas, S. L., & Finkelstein, R. (1984a). Depressive disorders in childhood: I. A longitudinal prospective study of characteristics and recovery. *Archives of General Psychiatry, 41,* 229–237.

Kovacs, M., Feinberg, T. L., Crouse-Novak, M., Paulauskas, S. L., Pollock, M., & Finkelstein, R. (1984b). Depressive disorders in childhood: II. A longitudinal study of the risk for a subsequent major depression. *Archives of General Psychiatry, 41,* 643–649.

Kraemer, S. (1987). Working with parents: Casework or psychotherapy? *Journal of Child Psychology and Psychiatry, 28,* 207–213.

Krasnegor, N. A., Grave, G. D., & Kretchmer, N. (Eds.) (1988). *Childhood obesity: A biobehavioral perspective*. Caldwell, NJ: The Telford Press.

Krug, D. A., Arick, J., & Almond, P. (1978). *Autism Screening Instrument For Educational Planning*. Portland, OR: ASIEP Education.

Krupski, A. (1986). Attention problems in youngsters with learning handicaps. In J. K. Torgesen & B. Y. L. Wong (Eds.), *Psychological and educational perspectives on learning disabilities*. New York: Academic Press.

Kuhn, T. S. (1962). *The structure of scientific revolutions*. Chicago: University of Chicago Press.

Kuhnley, E. J., Hendren, R. L., & Quinlan, D. M. (1982). Firesetting by children. *Journal of the American Academy of Child Psychiatry, 21,* 560–563.

Kuperman, S., Beeghly, J., Burns, T., & Tsai, L. (1987). Association of serotonin concentration to behavior and IQ in autistic children. *Journal of Autism and Developmental Disorders, 17,* 133–140.

Kuperman, S., Gaffney, G. R., Hamdan-Allen, G., Preston, D. F., & Venkatesh, L. (1990). Neuroimaging in child and adolescent psychiatry. *Journal of the American Academy of Child and Adolescent Psychiatry, 29,* 159–172.

Kydd, R. R., & Werry, J. S. (1982). Schizophrenia in children under 16 years. *Journal of Autism and Developmental Disorders, 12,* 343–357.

L

Ladd, G. (1981). Social skills and peer acceptance: Effects of a social learning method for training verbal social skills. *Child Development, 52,* 171–178.

Ladd, G. W., & Mize, J. (1983). A cognitive-social learning model of social-skill training. *Psychological Review, 90,* 127–157.

LaGreca, A. M. (1987). Diabetes in adolescence: Issues in coping and management. *Newsletter of the Society of Pediatric Psychology, 11,* 13–18.

LaGreca, A. M. (1988). Adherence to prescribed medical regimens. In D. K. Routh (Ed.), *Handbook of pediatric psychology*. New York: Guilford.

LaGreca, A., & Santogrossi, D. (1980). Social skills training with elementary school students: A behavioral group approach. *Journal of Consulting and Clinical Psychology, 48,* 220–228.

Lamb, H. R., & Zusman, J. (1981). A new look at primary prevention. *Hospital and Community Psychiatry, 32,* 843–848.

Lambert, N. M. (1988). Adolescent outcomes for hyperactive children: Perspectives on general and specific patterns of childhood risk for adolescent educational, social, and mental health problems. *American Psychologist, 43,* 786–799.

Landry, S. H., & Chapieski, M. L. (1989). Joint attention and infant toy exploration: Effects of Down Syndrome and prematurity. *Child Development, 60,* 103–118.

Landry, S. H., & Loveland, K. A. (1988). Communication behaviors in autism and developmental language delay. *Journal of Child Psychology and Psychiatry*, 29, 621–634.

Lang, P. J. (1984). Cognition in emotion: Concept and action. In C. E. Izard, J. Kagan, R. B. Zajonc (Eds.), *Emotions, cognition, and behavior*. New York: Cambridge University Press.

Lang, P. J., & Melamed, B. G. (1969). Avoidance conditioning therapy of an infant with chronic ruminative vomiting. *Journal of Abnormal Psychology*, 74, 139–142.

Langer, D. H. (1985). Children's legal rights as research subjects. *Journal of the American Academy of Child Psychiatry*, 24, 653–662.

Lansdown, R. (1986). Lead, intelligence, attainment and behaviour. In R. Lansdown and W. Yule (Eds.), *The lead debate: The environment and toxicology and child health*. London: Croom Helm.

Laosa, L. M. (1984). Social policies toward children of diverse ethnic, racial, and language groups in the United States. In H. W. Stevenson & A. E. Siegel (Eds.), *Child development research and social policy*. Chicago: University of Chicago Press.

Lapouse, R., & Monk, M. (1958). An epidemiologic study of behavior characteristics in children. *American Journal of Public Health*, 48, 1134–1144.

Lapouse, R., & Monk, M. A. (1959). Fears and worries in a representative sample of children. *American Journal of Orthopsychiatry*, 29, 803–818.

Last, C. G. (1989). Anxiety disorders. In T. H. Ollendick & M. Hersen (Eds.), *Handbook of child psychopathology*, 2nd ed. New York: Plenum.

Last, C. G., & Francis, G. (1988). School phobia. In B. B. Lahey & A. E. Kazdin (Eds.), *Advances in clinical child psychology*, Vol. 11. New York: Plenum Press.

Last, C. G., Francis, G., Hersen, M., Kazdin, A. E., & Strauss, C. C. (1987a). Separation anxiety and school phobia: A comparison using DSM-III criteria. *American Journal of Psychiatry*, 144, 653–657.

Last, C. G., Hersen, M., Kazdin, A. E., Finkelstein, R., & Strauss, C. C. (1987b). Comparison of DSM-III separation anxiety and overanxious disorders: Demographic characteristics and patterns of comorbidity. *Journal of the American Academy of Child and Adolescent Psychiatry*, 26, 527–531.

Last, C. G., & Strauss, C. C. (1990). School refusal in anxiety-disordered children and adolescents. *Journal of the American Academy of Child and Adolescent Psychiatry*, 29, 31–35.

Last, C. G., Strauss, C. C., & Francis, G. (1987). Comorbidity among childhood anxiety disorders. *Journal of Nervous and Mental Disease*, 175, 726–730.

Laufer, M. W., & Denhoff, E. (1957). Hyperkinetic behavior syndrome in children. *Journal of Pediatrics*, 50, 463–474.

Launay, J., Bursztejn, C., Ferrari, P., Dreux, C., Braconnier, A., Zarifian, E., Lancrenon, S., & Fermanian, J. (1987). Catecholamines metabolism in infantile autism: A controlled study of 22 autistic children. *Journal of Autism and Developmental Disorders*, 17, 333–347.

Lavigne, J. V., Burns, W. J., & Cotter, P. D. (1981). Rumination in infancy: Recent behavioral approaches. *International Journal of Eating Disorders*, 1, 70–82.

Lazar, I., Darlington, R., Murray, H., Royce, J., & Snipper, A. (1982). Lasting effects of early education: A report from the Consortium for Longitudinal Studies. *Monograph of the Society for Research in Child Development*, 47, (Serial No. 195).

Lazarus, A., & Abramavitz, A. (1962). The use of emotive imagery in the treatment of children's phobia. *Journal of Mental Science*, 108, 191–192.

Leach, G. M. (1972). A comparison of the social behaviour of some normal and problem children. In N. Blutron Jones (Ed.), *Ethological studies of child behaviour*. Cambridge: Cambridge University Press.

LeBow, M. D. (1984). *Child obesity: A new frontier of behavior therapy*. New York: Springer.

Le Couteur, A., Trygstad, O., Evered, C., Gillberg, C., & Rutter, M. (1988). Infantile autism and urinary excretion of peptides and protein-associated peptide complexes. *Journal of Autism and Developmental Disorders*, 18, 181–190.

Lee, M., & Prentice, N. M. (1988). Interrelations of empathy, cognition, and moral reasoning with dimensions of juvenile delinquency. *Journal of Abnormal Child Psychology*, 16, 127–139.

Lefkowitzz, M., & Burton, N. (1978). Childhood depression: A critique of the concept. *Psychological Bulletin*, 85 (4), 716–726.

Lefkowitz, M. M., & Tesiny, E. P. (1985). Depression in children: Prevalence and correlates. *Journal of Consulting and Clinical Psychology*, 53, 647–656.

Leitenberg, H., & Callahan, E. J. (1973). Reinforced practice and reduction of different kinds of fears in adults and children. *Behaviour Research and Therapy*, 11, 19–30.

Leitenberg, H., Gross, J., Peterson, J., & Rosen, J. C. (1984). Analysis of an anxiety model and the process of change during exposure plus response prevention treatment of bulimia nervosa. *Behavior Therapy*, 15, 3–20.

Leitenberg, H., Rosen, J. C., Gross, J., Nudelman, S., & Vara, L. S. (1988). Exposure plus response-prevention treatment of bulimia nervosa. *Journal of Consulting and Clinical Psychology*, 56, 535–541.

Lemert, E. M. (1971). *Instead of court: Diversion in juvenile justice*. Rockville, MD: National Institute of Mental Health.

Lemert, E.M. (1981). Diversion in juvenile justice: What hath been wrought. *Journal of Research in Crime and Delinquency*, 18, 34–46.

Leon, G. R., Kendall, P. C., & Garber, J. (1980). Depression in children: Parent, teacher, and child perspectives. *Journal of Abnormal Child Psychology*, 8, 221–235.

Leon, G. R., Lucas, A. R., Colligan. R. C., Ferdinande, R. J., & Kamp, J. (1985). Sexual, body-image, and personality attitudes in anorexia nervosa. *Journal of Abnormal Child Psychology*, 13, 245–257.

Leonard, H. L., Goldberger, E. L., Rapoport, J. L., Cheslow, D. L., & Swedo, S. E. (1990). Childhood rituals: Normal development or obsessive-compulsive symptoms? *Journal of the American Academy of Child and Adolescent Psychiatry*, 29, 17–23.

Lerner, J. V., & Galambos, N. L. (1986). Child development and family change: The influences of maternal employment on infants and toddlers. In L. P. Lipsitt and C. Rovee-Collier (Eds.), *Advances in infancy research*, Vol. 4. Norwood, NJ: Ablex.

Lerner, J. W. (1989). Educational interventions in learning disabilities. *Journal of the American Academy of Child and Adolescent Psychiatry*, 28, 326–331.

Lerner, R. M. (1987). The concept of plasticity in development. In J. J. Gallagher and C. T. Ramey (Eds.), *The malleability of children*. Baltimore: Brookes Publishing.

Levant, R. F. (1984). *Family therapy: A comprehensive overview*. Englewood Cliffs, NJ: Prentice Hall.

Levenstein, P. (1974). *VIP children reach school: Latest chapter*. Verbal Interaction Project. Progress Report.

Levine, H. G. (1985). Situational anxiety and everyday life experiences of mildly retarded adults. *American Journal of Mental Deficiency*, 90, 27–33.

Levine, M., & Perkins, D. V. (1987). *Principles of community psychology: Perspectives and applicatiion*. New York: Oxford University Press.

Levy, S., Zoltak, B., & Saelens, T. (1988). A comparison of obstetrical records of autistic and nonautistic referrals for psychoeducational evaluations. *Journal of Autism and Developmental Disorders*, 18, 573–581.

Lewis, M. (1986). Principles of intensive individual psychoanalytic psychotherapy for childhood anxiety disorders. In R. Gittleman (Ed.). *Anxiety disorders of childhood*. New York: Guilford.

Lewis, M., Feiring, C., McGuffog, C., & Jaskir, J. (1984). Predicting psychopathology in six-year-olds from early social relations. *Child Development, 55*, 123–136.

Lewis, S. (1974). A comparison of behavior therapy techniques in the reduction of fearful avoidance behavior. *Behavior Therapy, 5*, 648–655.

Lewinsohn, P. (1974). A behavioral approach to depression. In R. J. Freidman & M. M. Katz (Eds.), *The psychology of depression: Contemporary theory and research*. Washington, DC: Winston.

Liberman, I. Y., & Shankweiler, D. S. (1985). Phonology and the problems of learning to read and write. *Remedial and Special Education, 6*, 8–17.

Licht, B. G., & Kistner, J. A. (1986). Motivational problems of learning-disabled children: Individual differences and their implications for treatment. In J. K. Torgesen & B. Y. L. Wong (Eds.), *Psychological and educational perspectives on learning disabilities*. New York: Academic Press.

Lilly, M. S. (Ed.). (1979a). *Children with exceptional needs: A survey of special education*. New York: Holt, Rinehart and Winston.

Lilly, M. S. (1979b). Special education. Emerging issues. In M. S. Lilly (Ed.), *Children with exceptional needs*. New York: Holt, Rinehart and Winston.

Lilly, M. S. (1979c). Special education. Historical and traditional perspectives. In M. S. Lilly (Ed.), *Children with exceptional needs*. New York: Holt, Rinehart and Winston.

Lindquist, E. F., & Hieronymus, A. N. (1955–56). *Iowa Tests of Basic Skills Manuals*. New York: Houghton Mifflin.

Linscheid, T. R. (1978). Disturbances of eating and feeding. In P. R. Magrab (Ed.), *Psychological management of pediatric problems, Vol. 1: Early life conditions and chronic diseases*. Baltimore: University Park Press.

Linscheid, T. R., Iwata, B. A., Ricketts, R. W., Williams, D. E., & Griffin, J. C. (1990). Clinical evaluation of the self-injurious behavior inhibiting system (SIBIS). *Journal of Applied Behavior Analysis, 23*, 53–78.

Lobovits, D. A., & Handal, P. J. (1985). Childhood depression: Prevalence using DSM-III criteria and validity of parent and child depression scales. *Journal of Pediatric Psychology, 10*, 45–54.

Lobitz, G. K., & Johnson, S. M. (1975). Deviant and normal children. *Journal of Abnormal Child Psychology, 3*, 353–374.

Loeber, R. (1982). The stability of antisocial and delinquent child behavior: A review. *Child Development, 37*, 125–155.

Loeber, R. (1988). Natural histories of conduct problems, delinquency, and associated substance use: Evidence for developmental progressions. In B. B. Lahey & A. E. Kazdin (Eds.), *Advances in clinical child psychology*, Vol. 11. New York: Plenum.

Loeber, R. (1990). Development and risk factors of juvenile antisocial behavior and delinquency. *Clinical Psychology Review, 10*, 1–41.

Loeber, R., & Dishion, T. (1983). Early predictors of male delinquency: A review. *Psychological Bulletin, 94*, 68–99.

Loeber, R., & Schmaling, K. B. (1985). Empirical evidence for overt and covert patterns of antisocial conduct problems: A meta analysis. *Journal of Abnormal Child Psychology, 13*, 337–354.

Loney, J., & Milich, R. (1982). Hyperactivity, inattention, and aggression in clinical practice. In M. Wolraich & D. Routh (Eds.), *Advances in behavioral pediatrics*, Vol. 2. Greenwich, CT: JAI Press.

Long, B. B. (1986). The prevention of mental-emotional disabilities: A report from a national mental health association commission. *American Psychologist, 41*, 825–829.

Lopez, R. (1965). Hyperactivity in twins. *Canadian Psychiatric Association Journal, 10*, 421–426.

Lord, C., & Schopler, E. (1989). Stability of assessment results of autistic and non-autistic language-impaired children from preschool years to early school age. *Journal of Child Psychology and Psychiatry, 30*, 575–590.

Lorion, R. P., Cowen, E. L., & Caldwell, R. A. (1974). Problem types of children referred to a school based mental health program: Identification and outcome. *Journal of Consulting and Clinical Psychology, 42*, 491–496.

Lotter, V. (1966). Epidemiology of autistic conditions in young children. I. Prevalence. *Social Psychiatry, 1*, 124–137.

Lotter, V. (1974). Factors related to outcome in autistic children. *Journal of Autism and Childhood Schizophrenia, 4*, 263–277.

Lotter, V. (1978). Follow-up studies. In M. Rutter and E. Schopler (Eds.), *Autism: A reappraisal of concepts and treatment*. New York: Plenum.

Lovaas, O. I. (1987). Behavioral treatment and normal educational and intellectual functioning in young autistic children. *Journal of Consulting and Clinical Psychology, 55*, 3–9.

Lovaas, O. I., Koegel, R., & Schreibman, L. (1979). Stimulus overselectivity in autism: A review of research. *Psychological Bulletin, 86*, 1236–1254.

Lovaas, O. I., & Newsom, C. D. (1976). Behavior modification with psychotic children. In H. Leitenberg (Ed.), *Handbook of behavior modification and behavior therapy*. Englewood Cliffs, NJ: Prentice Hall.

Lovaas, O. I., & Simmons, J. Q. (1969). Manipulation of self-destruction in three retarded children. *Journal of Applied Behavior Analysis, 2*, 143–157.

Lovaas, O. I., & Smith, T. (1988). Intensive behavioral treatment for young autistic children. In B. B. Lahey & A. E. Kazdin (Eds.), *Advances in clinical child psychology*, Vol. 2. New York: Plenum.

Lovaas, O. I., Smith, T., & McEachin, J. J. (1989). Clarifying comments on the Young Autism Study: Reply to Schopler, Short, and Mesibov. *Journal of Consulting and Clinical Psychology, 57*, 165–167.

Lovaas, O. I., Young, D. B., & Newsom, C. D. (1978). Childhood psychosis: Behavioral treatment. In B. B. Wolman (Ed.), *Handbook of treatment of mental disorders in childhood and adolescence*. Englewood Cliffs, NJ: Prentice Hall.

Lovibond, S. H. (1964). *Conditioning and enuresis*. Oxford: Pergamon.

Lovko, A. M., & Ullman, D. G. (1989). Research on the adjustment of latchkey children: Role of background/demographic and latchkey situation variables. *Journal of Clinical Child Psychology, 18*, 16–24.

Lowe, K., & Lutzker, J. (1979). Increasing compliance to a medical regimen with a juvenile diabetic. *Behavior Therapy, 10*, 57–67.

Ludwick-Rosenthal, R., & Neufeld, R. W. J. (1988). Stress management during noxious medical procedures: An evaluative review of outcome studies. *Psychological Bulletin, 104*, 326–342.

Luxenberg, J. S., Swedo, S. E., Flament, M. F., Friedland, R., Rapoport, J. L., & Rapoport, S. I. (1988). Neuroanatomical abnormalities in obsessive-compulsive disorder detected with quantitative x-ray computed tomography. *American Journal of Psychiatry, 145*, 1089–1093.

Lynn, D. B. (1974). *The father: His role in child development*. Monterey, CA: Brooks/Cole.

Lyon, G. R., & Moats, L. C. (1988). Critical issues in the instruction of the learning disabled. *Journal of Consulting and Clinical Psychology, 56*, 830–835.

M

Maccoby, E. E., & Martin, J. A. (1983). Socialization in the context of the family: Parent-child interaction. In P. H.

Mussen (Ed.), *Handbook of child psychology*, Vol. IV. New York: Wiley.

MacDonald, L., & Barton, L. E. (1986). Measuring severity of behavior: A revision of Part II of the Adaptive Behavior Scale. *American Journal of Mental Deficiency, 90,* 418–424.

MacFarland, J. W., Allen, L., & Honzik, M. P. (1954). *A developmental study of the behavior problems of normal children between 21 months and 14 years.* Berkeley: University of California Press.

Machover, K. (1949). *Personality projection in the drawing of the human figure.* Springfield, IL: Chas. C Thomas.

MacMillan, D. L. (1982). *Mental retardation in school and society,* 2nd ed. Boston: Little-Brown.

MacMillan, D. L., & Kavale, K. A. (1986). Educational intervention. In H. C. Quay & J. S. Werry (Eds.), *Psychopathological disorders of childhood,* 3rd ed. New York: Wiley.

MacMillan, D. L., Keogh, B. K., & Jones, R. L. (1986). Special educational research on mildly handicapped learners. In M. C. Wittrock (Ed.), *Handbook of research on teaching.* New York: Macmillan.

Maddox, G. L., Back, K. W., & Liederman, V. R. (1968). Overweight as social deviance and disability. *Journal of Health and Social Behavior, 9,* 287–298.

Maerov, S. L., Brummett, B., Patterson, G. R., & Reid, J. B. (1978). Coding family interactions. In J. B. Reid (Ed.), *A social learning approach to family intervention: Vol. 2. Observation in home settings.* Eugene, OR: Castalia.

Magnuson, E. (1983). Child abuse: The ultimate betrayal. *Time* (Sept. 5), pp. 16–18.

Magnusson, D., Stattin, H., & Allen, V. L. (1988). Differential maturation among girls and its relationship to social adjustment: A longitudinal perspective. In E. M. Hetherington and R. D. Parke (Eds.), *Contemporary readings in child psychology.* New York: McGraw-Hill.

Maher, C. A., & Zins, J. E. (Eds.). (1987). *Psychoeducational interventions in the schools: Methods and procedures for enhancing student competence.* New York: Pergamon.

Mahler, M. S. (1952). *The psychoanalytic study of the child.* New York: International Universities Press.

Maisto, S. A., & Carey, K. B. (1985). Origins of alcohol abuse in children and adolescents. In B. B. Lahey & A. E. Kazdin (Eds.), *Advances in clinical child psychology,* Vol. 8. New York: Plenum.

Malatesta, C. Z., Grigoryev, P., Lamb, K., Albin, M., & Culver, C. (1986). Emotion socialization and expressive development in preterm and full-term infants. *Child Development, 57,* 316–330.

Malmquist, C. P. (1977). Childhood depression: A clinical and behavioral perspective. In J. G. Schulterbrandt & A. Raskin (Eds.), *Depression in childhood: Diagnosis, treatment, and conceptual models.* New York: Raven Press.

Mann, V. A. (1986). Why some children encounter reading problems: The contribution of difficulties with language processing and phonological sophistication to early reading disability. In J. K. Torgesen & B. Y. L. Wong (Eds.), *Psychological and educational perspectives on learning disabilities.* New York: Academic Press.

Mann, V. A., & Brady, S. (1988). Reading disability: The role of language deficiencies. *Journal of Consulting and Clinical Psychology, 56,* 811–816.

Mann, V. A., Cowin, E., & Schoenheimer, J. (1989). Phonological processing, language comprehension, and reading ability. *Journal of Learning Disabilities, 22,* 77–89.

Mansheim, P. (1979). Emotional and behavioral data in a case of the 48, XXYY syndrome. *Journal of Pediatric Psychology, 4,* 363–370.

Marans, S. (1989). Psychoanalytic psychotherapy with children: Current research trends and challenges. *Journal of the American Academy of Child and Adolescent Psychiatry, 28,* 669–674.

Marchi, M., & Cohen, P. (1990). Early childhood eating behaviors and adolescent eating disorders. *Journal of the American Academy of Child and Adolescent Psychiatry, 29,* 112–117.

Margalit, M. (1989). Academic competence and social adjustment of boys with learning disabilities and boys with behavior disorders. *Journal of Learning Disabilities, 22,* 41–45.

Mariner, R., Jackson, A. W., Levitas, A., Hagerman, R. J., Braden, M., McBogg, P. M., Berry, R., & Smith, A. C. M. (1986). Autism, mental retardation and chromosomal abnormalities. *Journal of Autism and Developmental Disorders, 16,* 425–440.

Marks, I. (1987). The development of normal fear: A review. *Journal of Child Psychology and Psychiatry and Allied Disciplines, 28,* 667–697.

Marlowe, H. A., & Weinberg, R. B. (Eds.) (1985). Is mental illness preventable? Pros and cons. *Journal of Primary Prevention, 5,* 207–312.

Marshall, P. (1989). Attention deficit disorder and allergy: A neurochemical model of the relation between the illnesses. *Psychological Bulletin, 106,* 434–446.

Marteau, T., Johnston, M., Baum, J. D., & Bloch, S. (1987). Goals of treatment in diabetes: A comparison of doctors and parents of children with diabetes. *Journal of Behavioral Medicine, 10,* 33–48.

Masek, B. J., Fentress, D. W., & Spirito, A. (1984). Behavioral treatment of symptoms of childhood illness. *Clinical Psychology Review, 4,* 561–570.

Masek, B. J., & Hoag, N. L. (1990). Headache. In A. M. Gross & R. S. Drabman (Eds.), *Handbook of clinical behavioral pediatrics.* New York: Plenum.

Mash, E. J. (1987). Behavioral assessment of child and family disorders: Contemporary approaches. *Behavioral Assessment, 9,* 201–205.

Mash, E. J., & Hunsley, J. (1990). Behavioral assessment: A contemporary approach. In A. S. Bellack, M. Hersen, & A. E. Kazdin (Eds.), *International handbook of behavior modification and therapy,* 2nd ed. New York: Plenum.

Mash, E., & Johnston, C. (1983). Sibling interactions of hyperactive and normal children and their relationship to reports of maternal stress and self-esteem. *Journal of Clinical Child Psychology, 12,* 91–99.

Mash, E. J., & Terdal, L. G. (1988). Behavioral assessment of child and family disturbance. In E. J. Mash & L. G. Terdal (Eds.), *Behavioral assessment of childhood disorders,* 2nd ed. New York: Guilford.

Mason, E. (1970). Obesity in pet dogs. *Veterinarian Record, 86,* 612–616.

Mason-Brothers, A., Ritvo, E. R., Guze, B., Mo, A., Freeman, B. J., Funderburk, S., & Schroth, P. C. (1987). Pre-, peri-, and postnatal factors in 181 autistic patients from single and multiple incidence families. *Journal of the American Academy of Child and Adolescent Psychiatry, 26,* 39–42.

Massman, P. J., Nussbaum, N. L., & Bigler, E. D. (1988). The mediating effect of age on the relationship between Child Behavior Checklist behavior hyperactivity scores and neuropsychological test performance. *Journal of Abnormal Child Psychology, 16,* 89–95.

Matarazzo, J. E. (1972). *Wechsler's measurement and appraisal of adult intelligence.* Baltimore: Williams & Wilkins.

Matson, J. L., Ollendick, T. H., & Adkins, J. (1980). A comprehensive dining program for mentally retarded adults. *Behavior Research and Therapy, 18,* 107–112.

Matthews, K. A. (1988). Coronary heart disease and Type A behaviors: Update on and alternative to the Booth-Kewley and Friedman (1987) quantitative review. *Psychological Bulletin, 104,* 373–380.

Matthews, K. A., & Rodin, J. (1989). Women's changing work roles: Impact on health, family, and public policy. *American Psychologist, 44,* 1389–1393.

Mattis, S., French, J. H., & Rapin, I. (1975). Dyslexia in children and young adults: The independent neuropsychological syndromes. *Developmental Medicine and Child Neurology, 17*, 150–163.

Mattison, R., Cantwell, D. P., Russell, A. T., & Will, L. (1979). A comparison of DSM-II and DSM-III in the diagnosis of childhood psychiatric disorders: II. Interrater agreement. *Archives of General Psychiatry, 36*, 1217–1222.

Maughan, B., Gray, G., & Rutter, M. (1985). Reading retardation and antisocial behaviour: A follow-up into employment. *Journal of Child Psychology and Psychiatry, 26*, 741–758.

Mazze, R. S., Lucido, D., & Shamoon, H. (1984). Psychological and social correlates of glycemic control. *Diabetes Care, 7*, 360–366.

McAdoo, W. G., & DeMyer, M. K. (1978). Personality characteristics of parents. In M. Rutter & E. Schopler (Eds.), *Autism: A reappraisal of concepts and treatment*. New York: Plenum.

McAlpine, C., & Singh, N. N. (1986). Pica in institutionalized mentally retarded persons. *Journal of Mental Deficiency Research, 30*, 171–178.

McBurnett, K., Hobbs, S. A., & Lahey, B. B. (1989). Behavioral treatment. In T. H. Ollendick & M. Hersen (Eds.), *Handbook of child psychopathology*, 2nd ed. New York: Plenum.

McCall, R. B., Applebaum, M. I., & Hogarty, P.S. (1973). Developmental changes in mental performance. *Monographs of the Society for Research in Child Development, 38* (Whole No. 150).

McCauley, E., Kay, T., Ito, J., & Treder, R. (1987). The Turner Syndrome: Cognitive deficits, affective discrimination, and behavior problems. *Child Development, 58*, 464–473.

McEvoy, R. E., Loveland, K. A., & Landry, S. H. (1988). The functioning of immediate echolalia in autistic children: A developmental perspective. *Journal of Autism and Developmental Disorders, 18*, 657–668.

McGarvey, B., Gabrielli, W. F., Jr., Bentler, P. M., & Mednick, S. A. (1981). Rearing social class, education, and criminality: A multiple indication model. *Journal of Abnormal Psychology, 90*, 354–364.

McGee, R., & Share, D. L. (1988). Attention deficit disorder-hyperactivity and academic failure: Which comes first and what should be treated? *Journal of the American Academy of Child and Adolescent Psychiatry, 27*, 318–325.

McGuffin, P. (1987). The new genetics and childhood psychiatric disorder. *Journal of Child Psychology and Psychiatry and Allied Disciplines, 28*, 215–222.

McKinney, J. D. (1986). The search for subtypes of specific learning disability. In S. Chess & A. Thomas (Eds.), *Annual progress in child psychiatry and child development*. New York: Brunner/Mazel.

McKinney, J. D. (1989). Longitudinal research on the behavioral characteristics of children with learning disabilities. *Journal of Learning Disabilities, 22*, 141–150.

McLean, J., & Ching, A. (1973). Follow-up study of relationships between family situation and bronchial asthma in children. *Journal of the American Academy of Child Psychiatry, 12*, 142–161.

McLoyd, V. C. (1990). The impact of economic hardship on black families and children: Psychological distress, parenting, and socioemotional development. *Child Development, 61*, 311–346.

McMahon, R. J. (1984). Behavioral checklists and rating scales. In T. H. Ollendick & M. Hersen (Eds.), *Child behavioral assessment: Principles and procedures*. New York: Pergamon.

McMahon, R. J., & Forehand, R. (1988). Conduct disorders. In E. J. Mash & L. G. Terdal (Eds.), *Behavioral assessment of childhood disorders*, 2nd ed. New York: Guilford.

McMahon, R. J., & Wells, K. C. (1989). Conduct disorders. In E. J. Mash & R. A. Barkley (Eds.), *Treatment of childhood disorders*. New York: Guilford.

McNabb, W. L., Wilson-Pessano, S. R., & Jacobs, A. M. (1986). Critical self-management competencies for children with asthma. *Journal of Pediatric Psychology, 11*, 103–117.

McNeal, E. T., & Cimbolic, P. (1986). Antidepressants and biochemical theories of depression. *Psychological Bulletin, 99*, 361–374.

McReynolds, P. (1987). Lightner Whitmer: Little-known founder of clinical psychology. *American Psychologist, 42*, 849–858.

Mednick, S. A., Gabrielli, W. F., & Hutchings, B. (1984). Genetic influences in criminal convictions: Evidence from an adoption cohort. *Science, 224*, 891–894.

Mednick, S. A., & Schulsinger, F. (1968). Some premorbid characteristics related to breakdown in children with schizophrenic mothers. In D. Rosenthal and S. S. Kety (Eds.), *The transmission of schizophrenia*. Elmsford, NY: Pergamon Press.

Meichenbaum, D. (1977). *Cognitive-behavior modification*. New York: Plenum.

Meichenbaum, D. H., & Goodman, J. (1971). Training impulsive children to talk to themselves: A means of developing self-control. *Journal of Abnormal Psychology, 77*, 115–126.

Meisels, S. J. (1984). Prediction, prevention, and developmental screening in the EPSTD program. In H. W. Stevenson & A. E. Siegel (Eds.), *Child development research and social policy*. Chicago: University of Chicago Press.

Melamed, B. G., & Siegel, L. J. (1975). Reduction of anxiety in children facing hospitalization and surgery by use of filmed modeling. *Journal of Consulting and Clinical Psychology, 43*, 511–521.

Melamed, B. G., & Siegel, L. J. (1980). *Behavioral medicine: Practical applications in health care*. New York: Springer.

Melton, G. B., & Davidson, H. A. (1987). Child protection and society: When should the state intervene? *American Psychologist, 42*, 172–175.

Mercer, J. (1973). *Labeling the mentally retarded*. Berkeley: University of California Press.

Mervis, C. B., & Cardoso-Martins, C. (1984). Transition from sensorimotor stage 5 to stage 6 by Down Syndrome children: A response to Gibson. *American Journal of Mental Deficiency, 89*, 99–102.

Mesibov, G. B., Schopler, E., Schaffer, B., & Michal, N. (1989). Use of the Childhood Autism Rating Scale with autistic adolescents and adults. *Journal of the American Academy of Child and Adolescent Psychiatry, 28*, 538–541.

Mesibov, G. B., Schroeder, C. S., & Wesson, L. (1977). Parental concerns about their children. *Journal of Pediatric Psychology, 2*, 13–17.

Mezzich, A. C., & Mezzich, J. E. (1985). Reliability of DSM-III vs. DSM-II in child psychopathology. *Journal of the American Academy of Child Psychiatry, 24*, 273–280.

Milgram, S. (1963). Behavioral study of obedience. *Journal of Abnormal and Social Psychology, 67*, 371–378.

Milich, R., & Loney, J. (1979). The role of hyperactivity and aggressive symptomatology in predicting adolescent outcome among hyperactive children. *Journal of Pediatric Psychology, 4*, 93–112.

Milich, R., Loney, J., & Roberts, M. (1986). Playroom observations of activity level and sustained attention: Two-year stability. *Journal of Consulting and Clinical Psychology, 54*, 272–274.

Miller, J. (1983). *National survey on drug abuse: Main findings, 1982*. (DHHS Pub. No. 83–1263) Washington, DC: U.S. Government Printing Office.

Miller, J. L. (1990). Apocalypse or renaissance or something in between? Toward a realistic appraisal of *The Learning Mystique. Journal of Learning Disabilities, 23*, 86–91.

Miller, L. C., Barrett, C.L., & Hampe, E. (1974). Phobias of childhood in a prescientific era. In A. Davids (Ed.), *Child* *personality and psychopathology: Current topics*, Vol. 1. New York: John Wiley.

Miller, L. C., Barrett, C.L., Hampe, E., & Noble, H. (1972). Comparison of reciprocal inhibition psychotherapy and waiting list control for phobic children. *Journal of Abnormal Psychology, 79*, 269–279.

Miller, N. E. (1969). Learning of visceral and glandular responses. *Science, 163*, 434–445.

Miller-Perrin, C. L., & Wurtele, S. K. (1988). The child sexual abuse prevention movement: A critical analysis of primary and secondary approaches. *Clinical Psychology Review, 8*, 313–329.

Millican, F. K., & Lourie, R. S. (1970). The child with pica and his family. In E. J. Anthony and C. Koupernik (Eds.), *The child in his family*, Vol. 1. New York: Wiley-Interscience.

Minderaa, R. B., Anderson, G. M., Volkmar, F. R., Harcherick, D., Akkerhuis, G. W., & Cohen, D. J. (1989). Whole blood serotonin and tryptophan in autism: Temporal stability and the effects of medication. *Journal of Autism and Developmental Disorders, 19*, 129–136.

Minuchin, P. P., & Shapiro, E. K. (1983). The school as a context for social development. In P. H. Mussen (Ed.), *Handbook of child psychology*, Vol. IV. New York: John Wiley.

Minuchin, S., Rosman, B. L., & Baker, L. (1978). *Psychosomatic Families: Anorexia nervosa in context.* Cambridge, MA: Harvard University Press.

Mishler, E. G., & Waxler, N. E. (1965). Family interactional processes and schizophrenia: A review of current theories. *Merrill-Palmer Quarterly, 11*, 269–315.

Mitchell, J., McCauley, E., Burke, P. M., & Moss, S. J. (1988). Phenomonology of depression in children and adolescents. *Journal of the American Academy of Child and Adolescent Psychiatry, 27*, 12–20.

Mitchell, J. E. (1986). Anorexia nervosa: Medical and physiological aspects. In K. D. Brownell & J. P. Foreyt (Eds.), *Handbook of eating disorders: Physiology, psychology, and treatment of obesity, anorexia, and bulimia.* New York: Basic Books.

Mitchell, J. E., & Eckert, E. D. (1987). Scope and significance of eating disorders. *Journal of Consulting and Clinical Psychology, 55*, 628–634.

Moffitt, T. E., Gabrielli, W. F., Mednick, S. A., & Schulsinger, F. (1981). Socioeconomic status, IQ, and delinquency. *Journal of Abnormal Psychology, 90*, 152–156.

Moore, D. R., & Arthur, J. L. (1989). Juvenile delinquency. In T. H. Ollendick & M. Hersen (Eds.), *Handbook of child psychopathology*, 2nd ed. New York: Plenum.

Moos, R. J., & Moos, B. S. (1981). *Family Environment Scale.* Palo Alto, CA: Consulting Psychologists Press.

Morgan, S. B., & Brown, T. L. (1988). Luria-Nebraska Neuropsychological Battery-Children's Revision: Concurrent validity with three learning disability subtypes. *Journal of Consulting and Clinical Psychology, 56*, 463–466.

Morris, R. D. (1988). Classification of learning disabilities: Old problems and new approaches. *Journal of Consulting and Clinical Psychology, 56*, 789–794.

Morris, R. J., & Kratochwill, T. R. (1983). *Treating children's fears and phobias: A behavioral approach.* Elmsford, NY: Pergamon Press.

Morris, S., Alexander, J. F., & Waldron, H. (1988). Functional family therapy: Issues in clinical practice. In I. R. H. Falloon (Ed.), *Handbook of behavioral family therapy.* New York: Guilford.

Morrison, M. M., & Smith, Q. T. (1987). Psychiatric issues of adolescent chemical dependence. *Pediatric Clinics of North America, 34*, 461–480.

Morrow-Bradley, C., & Elliot, R. (1986). Utilization of psychotherapy research by practicing psychotherapists. *American Psychologist, 41*, 188–197.

Moskowitz, D. S., Schwartzman, A. E., & Ledingham, J. E. (1985). Stability and change in aggression and withdrawal in middle childhood and early adolescence. *Journal of Abnormal Psychology, 94*, 30–41.

Mowrer, O. H. (1939). A stimulus-response analysis of anxiety and its role as a reinforcing agent. *Psychological Review, 46*, 553–565.

Mowrer, O. H., & Mowrer, W. M. (1938). Enuresis: A method for its study and treatment. *American Journal of Orthopsychiatry, 8*, 436–459.

Mundy, P., Sigman, M., Ungerer, J., & Sherman, T. (1987). Nonverbal communication and play correlates of language development in autistic children. *Journal of Autism and Developmental Disorders, 17*, 349–364.

Murray, H. A. (1943). *Thematic Apperception Test.* Cambridge, MA: Harvard University Press.

Murray, T. (1988). Learning to deceive. In J. Rubinstein & B. Slife (Eds.), *Taking sides.* Guilford, CT: Dushkin.

Myers, C. E., Nihira, K., & Zetlin, A. (1979). The measurement of adaptive behavior. In N. R. Ellis (Ed.), *Handbook of mental deficiency.* Hillsdale, NJ: Erlbaum.

N

National Institutes of Health Consensus Development Panel on the Health Implications of Obesity. (1985). Health implications of obesity: National Institutes of Health consensus development conference statement. *Annals of Internal Medicine, 103*, 1073–1077.

National Institute of Mental Health (1977). *Child abuse and neglect programs: Practice and theory.* Washington, DC: U.S. Government Printing Office.

Nelson, C. A. (1987). The recognition of facial expressions in the first two years of life: Mechanisms of development. *Child Development, 58*, 889–909.

Nelson, J. R., Smith, D. J., & Dodd, J. (1990). The moral reasoning of juvenile delinquents: A meta-analysis. *Journal of Abnormal Child Psychology, 18*, 231–239.

Nelson, K. (1981). Individual difference in language development: Implications for development and language. *Developmental Psychology, 17*, 170–187.

Nemiah, J. C. (1980). Phobic disorder (Phobic neurosis). In H. I. Kaplan, A. M. Freedman, & B. J. Sadock (Eds.), *Comprehensive textbook of psychiatry/III*, Vol. 2. Baltimore: Williams & Wilkins.

Neuchterlein, K. H. (1986). Childhood precursors of adult schizophrenia. *Journal of Child Psychology and Psychiatry, 27*, 133–144.

Newcomb, M. D., Maddahian, E., & Bentler, P. M. (1986). Risk factors for drug use among adolescents. *American Journal of Public Health, 76*, 525–531.

Newsom, C., Hovanitz, C., & Rincover, A. (1988). Autism. In E. J. Mash and L. G. Terdal (Eds.), *Behavioral assessment of childhood disorders. Selected core problems.* New York: Guilford.

Nichols, P. L. (1986). Familial retardation. In S. Chess & A. Thomas (Eds.), *Annual progress in child psychiatry and child development.* New York: Brunner/Mazel.

Ninio, A., & Rinott, N. (1988). Fathers' involvement in the care of their children and their attributions of cognitive competence to infants. *Child Development, 59*, 652–663.

Nisbett, R. E. (1972). Hunger, obesity, and the VMH. *Psychological Review, 79*, 433–453.

Noll, R. B., Bukowski, W. M., Rogosch, F. A., LeRoy, S., & Kulkarni, R. (1990). Social interactions between children with cancer and their peers: Teacher ratings. *Journal of Pediatric Psychology, 15*, 43–56.

Nordyke, N. S., Baer, D. M., Etzel, B. C., & Le Blanc, J. M. (1977). Implications of the stereotyping of modification of sex role. *Journal of Applied Behavior Analysis, 10*, 553–557.

Nowakowski, R. S. (1987). Basic concepts of CNS development. *Child Development, 58*, 568–595.

Nucci, L. P., & Herman, S. (1982). Behavioral disordered children's conceptions of moral, conventional, and personal issues. *Journal of Abnormal Child Psychology, 10,* 411–426.

O

O'Conner, H., & Hermelin, B. (1987). Visual memory and motor programmes: Their use by idiot-savant artists and controls. *British Journal of Psychology, 78,* 307–323.

O'Connor, N., & Hermelin, B. (1988). Annotation. Low intelligence and special abilities. *Journal of Child Psychology and Psychiatry, 29,* 391–396.

O'Connor, N., & Hermelin, B. (1990). The recognition failure and graphic success of idiot-savant artists. *Journal of Child Psychology and Psychiatry, 31,* 203–215.

O'Connor, N., & Tizard, J. (1956). *The social problems of mental deficiency.* New York: Pergamon Press.

O'Connor, R. D. (1969). Modification of social withdrawal through symbolic modeling. *Journal of Applied Behavior Analysis, 2,* 15–22.

O'Connor, R. D. (1972). The relative efficacy of modeling, shaping, and combined procedures. *Journal of Abnormal Psychology, 79,* 327–334.

Oden, S., & Asher, S. (1977). Coaching children in skills for friendship making. *Child Development, 48,* 495–506.

Odom, S. L., & Strain, P. S. (1984). Peer-mediated approaches to promoting children's social interaction: A review. *American Journal of Orthopsychiatry, 54,* 544–557.

Offer, D., Sabshin, M., & Marcus, D. (1965). Clinical evaluation of normal adolescents. *American Journal of Psychiatry, 121,* 864–872.

Offord, D. R., Adler, R. J., & Boyle, M. H. (1986). Prevalence and sociodemographic correlates of conduct disorder. *The American Journal of Social Psychiatry, 4,* 272–278.

Ogbu, J.U. (1981). Origins of human competence: A cultural-ecological perspective. *Child Development, 52,* 413–429.

Öhman, A., Erixon, G., & Löfberg, I. (1975). Phobias and preparedness: Phobic versus neutral pictures as conditioned stimuli for human autonomic responses. *Journal of Abnormal Psychology, 84,* 41–45.

Ohta, M. (1987). Cognitive disorders of infantile autism: A study employing the WISC, spatial relationship conceptualization, and gesture imitations. *Journal of Autism and Developmental Disorders, 17,* 45–62.

O'Keefe, A. (Ed.). (1979). *What Head Start means to families.* Washington, DC: U.S. Department of Health and Human Services.

O'Leary, K. D. (1972). Behavior modification in the classroom: A rejoinder to Winnett and Winkler. *Journal of Applied Behavior Analysis, 5,* 505–511.

O'Leary, K.D., & Emery, R. E. (1985). Marital discord and child behavior problems. In M. D. Levine & P. Satz (Eds.), *Developmental variation and dysfunction.* New York: Academic Press.

O'Leary, K. D., Pelham, W. E., Rosenbaum, M. A., & Price, G. H. (1976). Behavioral treatment of hyperkinetic children. *Clinical Pediatrics, 15,* 510–515.

O'Leary, K. D., Vivian, D., & Nisi, A. (1985). Hyperactivity in Italy. *Journal of Abnormal Child Psychology, 13,* 485–500.

O'Leary, K. D., & Wilson, G. T. (1987). *Behavior therapy: Application and outcome,* 2nd ed. Englewood Cliffs, NJ: Prentice Hall.

Ollendick, T. H. (1979). Fear reduction techniques with children. In M. Hersen, R. M. Eisler, & P. M. Miller (Eds.), *Progress in behavior modification,* Vol. 8. New York: Academic Press.

Ollendick, T. H. (1983). Reliability and validity of the Revised Fear Survey Schedule for Children (FSSC-R). *Behaviour Research and Therapy, 21,* 685–692.

Ollendick, T. H., & Cerny, J.A. (1981). *Clinical behavior therapy with children.* New York: Plenum.

Ollendick, T. H., King, N. J., & Frary, R. B. (1989). Fears in children and adolescents: Reliability and generalizability across gender, age and nationality. *Behaviour Research and Therapy, 27,* 19–26.

Ollendick, T. H., & Mayer, J. A. (1984). School phobia. In S. M. Turner (Ed.), *Behavioral treatment of anxiety disorders.* New York: Plenum.

Olweus, D. (1979). Stability of aggressive reaction patterns in males: A review. *Psychological Bulletin, 86,* 852–875.

Olweus, D. (1980). Familial and temperamental determinants of aggressive behavior in adolescent boys: A causal analysis. *Developmental Psychology, 16,* 644–660.

Orleans, C. T., & Barnett, L. R. (1984). Bulimarexia: Guidelines for behavioral assessment and treatment. In R. C. Hawkins, W. J. Fremouw, & P. F. Clement (Eds.), *The binge-purge syndrome: Diagnosis, treatment, and research.* New York: Springer.

Ornitz, E.M. (1985). Neurophysiology of infantile autism. *Journal of the American Academy of Child Psychiatry, 24,* 251–262.

Ornitz, E. M., & Ritvo, E. R. (1968). Perceptual inconstancy in early infantile autism. *Archives of General Psychiatry, 18,* 76–98.

Orris, J. B. (1969). Visual monitoring performance in three subgroups of male delinquents. *Journal of Abnormal Psychology, 74,* 227–229.

Orton, S. T. (1937). *Reading, writing, and speech problems in children.* New York: W. W. Norton and Co.

Orvaschel, H. (1983). Maternal depression and child dysfunction: Children at risk. In B. B. Lahey & A. E. Kazdin (Eds.), *Advances in clinical child psychology,* Vol. 6. New York: Plenum.

Orvaschel, H. (1990). Early onset psychiatric disorder in high risk children and increased family morbidity. *Journal of the American Academy of Child and Adolescent Psychiatry, 29,* 184–188.

Orvaschel, H., Walsh-Allis, G., & Ye, W. (1988). Psychopathology in children of parents with recurrent depression. *Journal of Abnormal Child Psychology, 16,* 17–28.

Oshima-Takane, Y., & Benaroya, S. (1989). An alternative view of pronominal errors in autistic children. *Journal of Autism and Developmental Disorders, 19,* 73–85.

Ozols, E. J., & Rourke, B. P. (1988). Characteristics of young learning-disabled children classified according to patterns of academic achievement: Auditory-perceptual and visual-perceptual abilities. *Journal of Clinical Child Psychology, 17,* 44–52.

P

Page, P., Verstraete, D. G., Robb, J. R., & Etzwiler, D. D. (1981). Patient recall of self-care recommendations in diabetes. *Diabetes Care, 4,* 95–98.

Palincsar, A. S., & Brown, A. L. (1986). Interactive teaching to promote independent learning from text. *The Reading Teacher, 39,* 771–777.

Palincsar, A. S., & Brown, D. A. (1987). Enhancing instructional time through attention to metacognition. *Journal of Learning Disabilities, 20,* 66–75.

Palmer, F. H., & Semlear, T. (1977). Early intervention: The Harlem study. In R. M. Liebert, R. W. Poulos, & G. D. Marmor (Eds.), *Developmental psychology.* Englewood Cliffs, NJ: Prentice Hall.

Papousek, H., & Papousek, M. (1983). Biological basis of social interactions: Implications of research for an understanding of behavioural deviance. *Journal of Child Psychology and Psychiatry, 24,* 117–129.

Parke, R. D., & Lewis, N. G. (1981). The family in context: A multilevel interactional analysis of child abuse. In R. W.

Henderson (Ed.), *Parent-child interaction—Theory, research, prospects.* New York: Academic Press.

Parker, J. G., & Asher, S. R. (1987). Peer relations and later personal adjustment: Are low-accepted children at risk? *Psychological Bulletin, 102,* 357–389.

Parks, S. (1983). The assessment of autistic children: A selective review of available instruments. *Journal of Autism and Developmental Disorders, 13,* 255–267.

Parsons, B. V., & Alexander, J. F. (1973). Short-term family intervention: A therapy outcome study. *Journal of Consulting and Clinical Psychology, 41,* 195–201.

Patterson, G. R. (1975). *Families.* Champaign, IL: Research Press.

Patterson, G. R. (1976a). *Living with children: New methods for parents and teachers,* rev. ed. Champaign, IL: Research Press.

Patterson, G. R. (1976b). The aggressive child: Victim and architect of a coercive system. In L. A. Hamerlynck, L. C. Handy, & E. J. Mash (Eds.), *Behavior modification and families.* New York: Brunner/Mazel.

Patterson, G. R. (1977). Naturalistic observation in clinical assessment. *Journal of Abnormal Child Psychology, 5,* 309–322.

Patterson, G. R. (1980). Mothers: The unacknowledged victims. *Monographs of the Society for Research in Child Development, 45,* (Serial No. 186).

Patterson, G. R. (1982). *Coercive family process: A social learning approach,* Vol. 3. Eugene, OR: Castalia.

Patterson, G. R. (1986). Performance models for antisocial boys. *American Psychologist, 41,* 432–444.

Patterson, G. R., Chamberlain, P., & Reid, J. B. (1982). A comparative evaluation of a parent-training program. *Behavior Therapy, 13,* 638–650.

Patterson, G. R., DeBaryshe, B. D., & Ramsey, E. (1989). A developmental perspective on antisocial behavior. *American Psychologist, 44,* 329–335.

Patterson, G. R., Littman, R. A., & Bricker, W. (1967). Assertive behavior in children: A step toward a theory of aggression. *Monographs of the Society for Research in Child Development, 32* (Serial No. 113).

Patterson, G.R., Reid, J. B., Jones, R. R., & Conger, R. E. (1975). *A social learning approach to family intervention,* Vol. 1. Eugene, OR: Castalia.

Patzer, G. L., & Burke, D. M. (1988). Physical attractiveness and childhood adjustment. In B. B. Lahey & A. E. Kazdin (Eds.), *Advances in clinical child psychology.* New York: Plenum.

Payton, J. B., Steele, M. W., Wenger, S. L., & Minshew, N. J. (1989). The fragile X marker and autism in perspective. *Journal of the American Academy of Child and Adolescent Psychiatry, 28,* 417–421.

Pearl, R., Donahue, M., & Bryan, T. (1986). Social relationships of learning-disabled children. In J. K. Torgesen & B. Y. L. Wong (Eds.), *Psychological and educational perspectives on learning disabilities.* New York: Academic Press.

Pelham, W. E. (1986). The effects of psychostimulant drugs on learning and academic achievement in children with attention-deficit disorders and learning disabilities. In J. K. Torgesen & B. Y. L. Wong (Eds.), *Psychological and educational perspectives on learning disabilities.* New York: Academic Press.

Peloquin, L. J., & Klorman, R. (1986). Effects of methylphenidate on normal children's mood, event-related potentials, and performance in memory scanning and vigilance. *Journal of Abnormal Psychology, 95,* 88–98.

Pennington, B. F., & Smith, S. D. (1983). Genetic influences on learning disabilities and speech and language disorders. *Child Development, 54,* 369–387.

Pennington, B. F., & Smith, S. D. (1988). Genetic influences on learning disabilities: An update. *Journal of Consulting and Clinical Psychology, 56,* 817–823.

Perlmutter, M. (Ed.). (1986). Cognitive perspectives on children's social and behavioral development, Vol. 18. *Minnesota Symposium on Child Development.* Hillsdale, NJ: Erlbaum.

Perner, J., Frith, U., Leslie, A. M., & Leekam, S. R. (1989). Exploration of the autistic child's theory of mind: Knowledge, belief, and communication. *Child Development, 60,* 689–700.

Perrin, E. C., & Perrin, J. M. (1983). Clinician's assessments of children's understanding of illness. *American Journal of Disease in Children, 137,* 874–878.

Perry, D. G., Perry, L. C., & Rasmussen, P. (1986). Cognitive social learning mediators of aggression. *Child Development, 57,* 700–711.

Perry, D. G., Perry, L. C., & Weiss, R. J. (1989). Sex differences in the consequences that children anticipate for aggression. *Developmental Psychology, 25,* 312–319.

Persson-Blennow, I., & McNeil, T. (1988). Frequencies and stability of temperament types in childhood. *Journal of the American Academy of Child and Adolescent Psychiatry, 27,* 619–622.

Peshkin, M. M. (1959). Intractible asthma of childhood: Rehabilitation at the institutional level with a follow-up of 150 cases. *International Archives of Allergy, 15,* 91–101.

Petersen, G. A. (1982). Cognitive development in infancy. In B. B. Wolman (Ed.), *Handbook of developmental psychology.* Englewood Cliffs, NJ: Prentice Hall.

Peterson, L. (1989). Latchkey children's preparation for self-care: Overestimated, underrehearsed, and unsafe. *Journal of Clinical Child Psychology, 18,* 36–43.

Peterson, L., Farmer, J., Harbeck, C., & Chaney, J. (1990). Preparing children for hospitalization and threatening medical procedures. In A. M. Gross & R. S. Drabman (Eds.), *Handbook of clinical behavioral pediatrics.* New York: Plenum.

Peterson, L., & Harbeck, C. (1990). Medical disorders. In A. S. Bellack, M. Hersen, & A. E. Kazdin (Eds.), *International handbook of behavior modification and therapy,* 2nd ed. New York: Plenum.

Peterson, L., & Magrab, P. (1989). Introduction to the special section: Children on their own. *Journal of Clinical Child Psychology, 18,* 2–7.

Peterson, L. J., & Mori, L. (1988). Preparation for hospitalization. In D. K. Routh (Ed.), *Handbook of pediatric psychology.* New York: Guilford.

Peterson, L., & Ridley-Johnson, R. (1980). Pediatric hospital response to survey on prehospital preparation for children. *Journal of Pediatric Psychology, 5,* 1–7.

Peterson, L., Schultheis, K., Ridley-Johnson, R., Miller, D. J., & Tracy, K. (1984). Comparison of three modeling procedures on the presurgical and postsurgical reactions of children. *Behavior Therapy, 15,* 197–203.

Peterson, L., & Shigetomi, C. (1982). One year follow-up of elective surgery child patients receiving preoperative preparation. *Journal of Pediatric Psychology, 7,* 43–48.

Petti, T. A. (1989). Depression. In T. H. Ollendick & M. Hersen (Eds.), *Handbook of child psychopathology,* 2nd ed. New York: Plenum.

Pfiffner, L. J., & O'Leary, S. G. (1987). The efficacy of all-positive management as a function of the prior use of negative consequences. *Journal of Applied Behavior Analysis, 20,* 265–271.

Phillips, E. L. (1968). Achievement Place: Token reinforcement procedures in a home-style rehabilitation setting for 'pre-delinquent' boys. *Journal of Applied Behavior Analysis, 1,* 213–223.

Phillips, R.D. (1985). Whistling in the dark?: A review of play therapy research. *Psychotherapy, 22,* 752–760.

Pick, H. L. (1989). Motor development: The control of action. *Developmental Psychology, 25,* 867–870.

Pierce, C. M. (1985a). Encopresis. In H. I. Kaplan & B. J. Sadock (Eds.), *Comprehensive textbook of psychiatry/IV*. Baltimore: Williams & Wilkins.

Pierce, C. M. (1985b). Enuresis. In H. I. Kaplan & B. J. Sadock (Eds.), *Comprehensive textbook of psychiatry/IV*. Baltimore: Williams & Wilkins.

Pless, I. B. (1984). Clinical assessment: Physical and psychological functioning. *Pediatric Clinics of North America, 31,* 33–45.

Pless, I. B., Roghmann, K., & Haggerty, R. J. (1972). Chronic illness, family functioning and psychological adjustment: A model for the allocation of preventive mental health services. *International Journal of Epidemiology, 1,* 271–277.

Plomin, R. (1989). Environment and genes: Determinants of behavior. *American Psychologist, 44,* 105–111.

Plomin, R. (1990). *Nature and nurture: An introduction to human behavioral genetics*. Pacific Grove, CA: Brooks/Cole.

Plomin, R., & Daniels, D. (1987). Why are children in the same family so different from one another? *Behavioral and Brain Sciences, 10,* 1–16.

Plomin, R., DeFries, J. C., & McClearn, G. E. (1990). *Behavioral genetics: A primer*, 2nd ed. New York: W. H. Freeman and Company.

Plomin, R., & Thompson, L. (1988). Life-span developmental behavioral genetics. In P. B. Baltes, D. L. Featherman, & R. M. Lerner (Eds.), *Life-span development and behavior*, Vol. 8. Hillsdale, NJ: Erlbaum.

Polivy, J., & Herman, C. P. (1985). Dieting and binging: A causal analysis. *American Psychologist, 40,* 193–201.

Polivy, J., Herman, C. P., Olmsted, M., & Jazwinski, C. (1984). Restraint and binge eating. In R. C. Hawkins, W. J. Fremouw, & R. F. Clement (Eds.), *The binge-purge syndrome: Treatment, research, and theory*. New York: Springer.

Pope, A. W., Bierman, K. L., & Mumma, G. H. (1987). Peer relations of hyperactive and aggressive boys. Paper presented at the Annual Meeting of the Society for Behavioral Pediatrics, April 27, Anaheim, CA.

Pope, H. G., Hudson, J. I., Jonas, J. M., & Yurgelun-Todd, D. (1983). Bulimia treated with imipramine: A placebo-controlled double-blind study. *American Journal of Psychiatry, 140,* 554–558.

Porrino, L. J., Rapoport, J. L., Behar, D., Sceery, W., Ismond, D. R., & Bunney, W. E. (1983). A naturalistic assessment of the motor activity of hyperactive boys: I. Comparison with normal controls. *Archives of General Psychiatry, 40,* 681–687.

Porter, J. E., & Rourke, P. B. (1985). Socioemotional functioning of learning-disabled children: A subtype analysis of personality patterns. In P. B. Rouke (Ed.), *Neuropsychology of learning disabilities: Essentials of subtype analysis*. New York: Guilford.

Potter, H. W. (1933). Schizophrenia in children. *American Journal of Psychiatry, 12,* 1253–1270.

Potter, H. W. (1972). Mental retardation in historical perspective. In S. I. Harrison & J. F. McDermott (Eds.), *Childhood psychopathology*. New York: International Universities Press.

Prechtl, H. F. R. (1981). The study of neural development as a perspective of clinical problems. In J. K. Connolly & H. F. R. Prechtl (Eds.), *Clinics in developmental medicine No. 77/78. Maturation and development*. Philadelphia: Lippincott.

Pressley, M., & Levin, J. R. (1987). Elaborative learning strategies for the inefficient learner. In S. J. Ceci (Ed.), *Handbook of cognitive, social and neuropsychological aspects of learning disabilities*. Hillsdale, NJ: Erlbaum.

Prinz, R. J., & Riddle, D. B. (1986). Associations between nutrition and behavior in five-year-old children. *Nutrition Reviews, 44,*(Suppl.), 151–157.

Prinz, R. J., Roberts, W. A., & Hantman, E. (1980). Dietary correlates of hyperactivity behavior in children. *Journal of Consulting and Clinical Psychology, 48,* 760–769.

Prior, M. (1986). Developing concepts of childhood autism: The influence of experimental cognitive research. In S. Chess & A. Thomas (Eds.), *Annual progress in child psychiatry and child development, 1985*. New York: Brunner/Mazel.

Prior, M., & Sanson, A. (1986). Attention deficit disorder with hyperactivity: A critique. *Journal of Child Psychology and Psychiatry, 27,* 307–319.

Prior, M., Sanson, A., Freethy, C., & Geffen, G. (1985). Auditory attentional abilities in hyperactive children. *Journal of Child Psychology and Psychiatry, 26,* 289–304.

Prior, M., & Werry, J. S. (1986). Autism, schizophrenia, and allied disorders. In H. C. Quay and J. S. Werry (Eds.), *Psychopathological disorders of childhood*. New York: Wiley.

Prout, H. T., & Chizik, R. (1988). Readability of child and adolescent self-report measures. *Journal of Consulting and Clinical Psychology, 56,* 152–154.

Public interest. Self-injury 'consensus' stirs strife, not accord. (1989, June). *APA Monitor*.

Puig-Antich, J. (1983). Neuroendocrine and sleep correlates of prepubertal major depressive disorder: Current status of the evidence. In D. P. Cantwell & G. A. Carlson (Eds.), *Affective disorders in childhood and adolescence: An update*. New York: Spectrum.

Puig-Antich, J. (1986). Psychobiological markers: Effects of age and puberty. In M. Rutter, C. E. Izard, & P. B. Read (Eds.), *Depression in young people: Developmental and clinical perspectives*. New York: Guilford.

Puig-Antich, J., & Gittelman, R. (1982). Depression in childhood and adolescence. In E. S. Paykel (Ed.), *Handbook of affective disorders*. New York: Guilford.

Puig-Antich, J., Perel, J., Lupatkin, W., Chambers, W. J., Tabrizi, M. A., King, J., Davies, M., Johnson, R., & Stiller, R. (1987). Imipramine in prepubertal major depressive disorders. *Archives of General Psychiatry, 44,* 81–89.

Purcell, K. (1975). Childhood asthma, the role of family relationships, personality, and emotions. In A. Davids (Ed.), *Child personality and psychopathology: Current topics*, Vol. 2. New York: John Wiley.

Purcell, K., Brady, K., Chai, H., Muser, J., Molk, L., Gordon, N., & Means, J. (1969). The effect on asthma in children of experimental separation from the family. *Psychosomatic Medicine, 31,* 144–164.

Q

Quay, H. C. (1986a). A critical analysis of DSM-III as a taxonomy of psychopathology in childhood and adolescence. In T. Millon & G. L. Klerman (Eds.), *Contemporary directions in psychopathology: Toward DSM-IV*. New York: Guilford.

Quay, H. C. (1986b). Classification. In H. C. Quay & J. S. Werry (Eds.), *Psychopathological disorders of childhood*, 3rd ed. New York: Wiley.

Quay, H. C. (1986c). Conduct disorders. In H. C. Quay & J. S. Werry (Eds.), *Psychopathological disorders of childhood*, 3rd ed. New York: Wiley.

Quay, H. C., & LaGreca, A. M. (1986). Disorders of anxiety, withdrawal, and dysphoria. In H. C. Quay & J. S. Werry (Eds.), *Psychopathological disorders of childhood*, 3rd ed. New York: John Wiley & Sons.

Quay, H. C., & Peterson, D. R. (1983). *Interim manual for the Revised Behavior Problem Checklist*. Unpublished manuscript. University of Miami and Rutgers University.

Quay, H. C., Routh, D. K., & Shapiro, S. K. (1987). Psychopathology of childhood: From description to validation. In M. R. Rosenzweig & L. W. Porter (Eds.), *Annual review of psychology*. Palo Alto, CA: Annual Reviews, Inc.

R

Rachman, S. J. (1977). The conditioning theory of fear-acquisition: A critical examination. *Behaviour Research and Therapy, 15,* 375–387.

Raine, A., & Venables, P. H. (1984). Tonic heart rate level, social class and antisocial behaviour in adolescents. *Biological Psychology, 18,* 123–132.

Rainer, J. D. (1980). Genetics and psychiatry. In H. I. Kaplan, A. M. Freedman, & B. J. Sadock (Eds.), *Comprehensive textbook of psychiatry/III,* Vol. 3. Baltimore: Williams & Wilkins.

Rainer, J. D. (1985). Genetics and psychiatry. In H. I. Kaplan & B. J. Sadock (Eds.), *Comprehensive textbook of psychiatry,* 4th ed. Baltimore: Williams and Wilkins.

Ramey, C. T., & Campbell, F. A. (1984). Preventive education for high-risk children: Cognitive consequences of the Carolina Abecedarian Project. *American Journal of Mental Deficiency, 88,* 515–523.

Ramey, C. T., & Campbell, F. A. (1987). The Carolina Abecedarian Project: An educational experiment concerning human malleability. In J. J. Gallagher & C. T. Ramey (Eds.), *The malleability of children.* Baltimore: Paul Brookes.

Rando, T. A. (1983). An investigation of grief and adaptation in parents whose children have died from cancer. *Journal of Pediatric Psychology, 8,* 3–20.

Rank, B. (1955). Intensive study and treatment of preschool children who show marked personality deviations or "atypical development" and their parents. In G. Caplan (Ed.), *Emotional problems of early childhood.* New York: Basic Books.

Rapoport, J. L. (1989). The biology of obsessions and compulsions. *Scientific American, 260,* 83–89.

Rapoport, J., Elkins, R., & Mikkelsen, E. (1980). Clinical controlled trial of clomipramine in adolescents with obsessive-compulsive disorder. *Psychopharmacology Bulletin, 16,* 61–63.

Rappaport, J. (1977). *Community psychology: Values, research, and action.* New York: Holt, Rinehart and Winston.

Rauh, V. A., Achenbach, T.M., Nurcombe, B., Howell, C. T., & Teti, D. M. (1988). Minimizing adverse effects of low birthweight: Four-year results of an early intervention program. *Child Development, 59,* 544–553.

Raymond, C. A. (1986). Biology, culture, and dietary changes conspire to increase incidence of obesity. *Journal of the American Medical Association, 256,* 2157–2158.

Reid, A. H. (1985). Psychiatric disorders. In A. M. Clarke, A. D. B. Clarke, & J. M. Berg (Eds.), *Mental deficiency: The changing outlook.* New York: The Free Press.

Reid, J. B., Kavanagh, K., & Baldwin, D. V. (1987). Abusive parents' perceptions of child problem behaviors: An example of parental bias. *Journal of Abnormal Child Psychology, 15,* 457–466.

Reid, W. J., & Crisafulli, A. (1990). Marital discord and child behavior problems: A meta-analysis. *Journal of Abnormal Child Psychology, 18,* 105–117.

Reiss, A. L., Egel, A. L., Feinstein, C., Goldsmith, B., & Borengasser-Caruso, M. A. (1988). Effects of fenfluramine on social behavior in autistic children. *Journal of Autism and Developmental Disorders, 18,* 617–625.

Rekers, G. A. (1984). Ethical issues in child behavioral assessment. In T. H. Ollendick & M. Hersen (Eds.), *Child behavioral assessment: Principles and procedures.* New York: Pergamon.

Rekers, G. A., & Lovaas, I. O. (1974). Behavioral treatment of deviant sex role behaviors in a male child. *Journal of Applied Behavior Analysis, 7,* 173–190.

Renne, C. M., & Creer, T. L. (1985). Asthmatic children and their families. In M. Wolraich & D. Routh (Eds.), *Advances in developmental and behavioral pediatrics,* Vol. 6. Greenwich, CT: JAI.

Reschly, D. J. (1981). Psychological testing in educational classification and placement. *American Psychologist, 36,* 1102.

Rest, J. (1983). Morality. In J. Flavell & E. Markman (Eds.), *Manual of child psychology: Vol. 3. Cognitive Development.* New York: Wiley.

Reynolds, C. R., & Richmond, B. O. (1978). What I think and feel: A revised measure of children's manifest anxiety. *Journal of Abnormal Child Psychology, 6,* 271–280.

Reynolds, W. M. (1985). Depression in childhood and adolescence: Diagnosis, assessment, intervention strategies, and research. In T. R. Kratchowill (Ed.), *Advances in school psychology,* Vol. 4. Hillsdale, NJ: Erlbaum.

Rice, J., Reich, T., Andreasen, N. N., Endicott, J. Eerdewegh, M. Van, Fishman, R., Hirschfeld, R. M. A., & Klerkman, G. L. (1987). The familial transmission of bipolar illness. *Archives of General Psychiatry, 44,* 451–460.

Richardson, E., Kupietz, S. S., Winsberg, B. G., Maitinsky, S., & Mendell, N. (1988). Effects of methylphenidate dosage in hyperactive reading-disabled children: II. Reading achievement. *Journal of the American Academy of Child and Adolescent Psychiatry, 27,* 78–87.

Richardson, S. A., & Koller, H. (1985). Epidemiology. In A. M. Clarke, A. D. B. Clarke & J. M. Berg (Eds.), *Mental deficiency: The changing outlook.* New York: The Free Press.

Richardson, S. A., Koller, H., & Katz, M. (1985). Relationship of upbringing to later behavior disturbance of mildly mentally retarded young people. *American Journal of Mental Deficiency, 90,* 1–8.

Richman, N. (1985). A double-blind drug trial of treatment in young children with waking problems. *Journal of Child Psychology and Psychiatry, 26,* 591–598.

Richman, N., Douglas, J., Hunt, H., Lansdown, R., & Levere, R. (1985). Behavioural methods in the treatment of sleep disorders—A pilot study. *Journal of Child Psychology and Psychiatry, 26,* 581–590.

Rickard, K. M., Forehand, R., Wells, K. C., Griest, D. L., & McMahon, R. J. (1981). Factors in the referral of children for behavioral treatment: A comparison of mothers of clinic-referred deviant, clinic-referred nondeviant, and nonclinic children. *Behaviour Research and Therapy, 19,* 201–205.

Rie, H. E. (1971). Historical perspectives of concepts of child psychopathology. In H. E. Rie (Ed.), *Perspectives in child psychopathology.* New York: Aldine-Atherton.

Rieder, R. O., Broman, S. H., & Rosenthal, D. (1977). The offspring of schizophrenics. *Archives of General Psychiatry, 34,* 789–799.

Rimland, B. (1984). Diagnostic Checklist Form E2: A reply to Parks. *Journal of Autism and Developmental Disorders, 14,* 343–345.

Ritter, D. R. (1989). Social competence and problem behavior of adolescent girls with learning disabilities. *Journal of Learning Disabilities, 22,* 460–461.

Ritvo, E. R., & Freeman, B. J. (1977). Current status of biochemical research in autism. *Journal of Pediatric Psychology, 2,* 149–152.

Ritvo, E. R., Freeman, B. J., Geller, E., & Yuwiler, A. (1983). Effects of fenfluramine on 14 outpatients with the syndrome of autism. *Journal of the American Academy of Child Psychiatry, 22,* 549–558.

Ritvo, E. R., Freeman, B. J., Mason-Brothers, A., Mo, A., & Ritvo, A. M. (1985). Concordance for the syndrome of autism in 40 pairs of afflicted twins. *American Journal of Psychiatry, 142,* 74–77.

Ritvo, E. R., Mason-Brothers, A., Jenson, W. P., Freeman, B. J., Mo, A., Pingree, C., Petersen, P. B., & McMahon, W. M. (1987). A report of one family with four autistic siblings and four families with three autistic siblings. *Journal of the American Academy of Child and Adolescent Psychiatry, 26,* 339–341.

Rivinus, T. M. (1980). Psychopharmacology and the mentally retarded patient. In L. S. Szymanski & P. E. Tanguay (Eds.), *Emotional disorders of mentally retarded persons*. Baltimore: University Park Press.

Roberts, J. A. M. (1989). Echolalia and comprehension in autistic children. *Journal of Autism and Developmental Disorders, 19*, 271–281.

Roberts, M. C., & Lyman, R. D. (1990). The psychologist as a pediatric consultant: Inpatient and outpatient. In A. M. Gross & R. S. Drabman (Eds.), *Handbook of clinical behavioral pediatrics*. New York: Plenum.

Robins, L. N. (1978). Sturdy childhood predictors of adult antisocial behavior: Replication from longitudinal studies. *Psychological Medicine, 8*, 611–622.

Robins, L. N., Murphy, G. E., Woodruff, R. A., Jr., & King, L. J. (1971). The adult psychiatric status of black school boys. *Archives of General Psychiatry, 24*, 338–345.

Robinson, E. A. (1985). Coercion theory revisited: Toward a new theoretical perspective on the etiology of conduct disorders. *Clinical Psychology Review, 5*, 597–625.

Robinson, N. M., & Robinson, H. B. (1976). *The mentally retarded child*. New York: McGraw-Hill.

Roff, J. D., & Wirt, R. D. (1984). Childhood aggression and social adjustment as antecedants of delinquency. *Journal of Abnormal Child Psychology, 12*, 111–126.

Roff, M. (1961). Childhood social interactions and young adult bad conduct. *Journal of Abnormal and Social Psychology, 63*, 333–337.

Roff, M., Sells, S., & Golden, M. (1972). *Social adjustment and personality development in children*. Minneapolis: University of Minnesota Press.

Rogeness, G. A., Jovors, M. A., Maas, J. W., & Macedo, C. A. (1989). Catecholamines and diagnosis in children. *Journal of the American Academy of Child and Adolescent Psychiatry, 29*, 234–241.

Rogoff, B., & Morelli, G. (1989). Perspectives on children's development from cultural psychology. *American Psychologist, 44*, 343–348.

Rolf, J., & Read, P. B. (1984). Programs advancing developmental psychopathology. *Child Development, 55*, 8–16.

Rolland-Cachera, M. F., Deheeger, M., Guilloud-Bataille, M., Avons, P., Patois, E., & Sempe, M. (1987). Tracking the development of adiposity from one month of age to adulthood. *Annals of Human Biology, 14*, 219–229.

Rosenberg, M. S. (1987). New directions for research on the psychological maltreatment of children. *American Psychologist, 42*, 166–171.

Rosenberg, R. P., & Beck, S. (1986). Preferred assessment methods and treatment modalities for hyperactive children among clinical child and school psychologists. *Journal of Clinical Child Psychology, 15*, 142–147.

Rosenthal, D. (1975). Heredity in criminality. *Criminal Justice and Behavior, 2*, 3–21.

Rosenthal, T. L. (1984). Some organizing hints for communicating applied information. In B. Gholson & T. L. Rosenthal (Eds.), *Applications of cognitive-developmental theory*. Orlando, FL: Academic Press.

Rosenthal, T., & Bandura, A. (1978). Psychological modeling: Theory and practice. In S. L. Garfield & A. E. Bergin (Eds.), *Handbook of psychotherapy and behavioral change: An empirical analysis*. New York: John Wiley.

Roshon, M. S., & Hagen, R. L. (1989). Sugar consumption, locomotion, task orientation, and learning in preschool children. *Journal of Abnormal Child Psychology, 17*, 349–357.

Ross, A. O. (1972). The clinical child psychologist. In B. J. Wolman (Ed.), *Manual of child psychopathology*. New York: McGraw-Hill.

Ross, A. O. (1981). *Child behavior therapy: Principles, procedures, and empirical basis*. New York: John Wiley.

Ross, D. M. (1988). Aversive treatment procedures: The school-age child's view. *Newsletter of the Society of Pediatric Psychology, 12*, 3–6.

Ross, D. M., & Ross, S. A. (1988). *Childhood pain: Current issues, research, and management*. Baltimore: Urban & Schwarzenberg.

Rothbart, M. K. (1986). Longitudinal observation of infant temperament. *Developmental Psychology, 22*, 356–365.

Rothblum, E. D., Solomon, L. J., & Albee, G. W. (1986). A sociopolitical perspective of DSM-III. In T. Millon & G. L. Klerman (Eds.), *Contemporary directions in psychopathology: Toward DSM-IV*. New York: Guilford.

Rourke, B. P. (1980). Neuropsychological assessment of children with learning disabilities. In S. B. Filskov & T. J. Boll (Eds.), *Handbook of clinical neuropsychology*. New York: Wiley-Interscience.

Rourke, B. P. (1988). Socioemotional disturbances of learning disabled children. *Journal of Consulting and Clinical Psychology, 56*, 801–810.

Rourke, B. P. (1989). Coles's learning mystique: The good, the bad, and the irrelevant. *Journal of Learning Disabilities, 22*, 275–277.

Rourke, B. P., & Finlayson, M. A. J. (1978). Neuropsychological significance of variations in patterns of academic performance: Verbal and visual-spatial abilities. *Journal of Abnormal Child Psychology, 6*, 121–133.

Rourke, B. P., Young, G. C., & Leenaars, A. A. (1989). A childhood learning disability that predisposes those afflicted to adolescent and adult depression and suicide risk. *Journal of Learning Disabilities, 22*, 169–175.

Routh, D. K. (Ed.), (1988). *Handbook of pediatric psychology*. New York: Guilford.

Routh, D. K., Schroeder, C. S., & Koocher, G. P. (1983). Psychology and primary health care for children. *American Psychologist, 38*, 95–98.

Rozin, P. (1988). Obesity and food preference: Measurements in search of meanings. In N. A. Krasnegor, G. D. Grave, & N. Kretchmer (Eds.), *Childhood obesity: A biobehavioral perspective*. Caldwell, NJ: The Telford Press.

Rozin, P., Fallon, A., & Mandell, R. (1984). Family resemblance in attitudes to foods. *Developmental Psychology, 20*, 309–314.

Rubin, K. H., Fein, G. G., & Vandenberg, B. (1983). Play. In P. H. Mussen (Ed.), *Handbook of child psychology: Vol. 4, Socialization, personality, and social behavior*. New York: Wiley.

Rubin, R. A., & Balow, B. (1979). Measures of infant development and socioeconomic status as predictors of later intelligence and school achievement. *Developmental Psychology, 15*, 225–227.

Ruderman, A. J. (1986). Dietary restraint: A theoretical and empirical review. *Psychological Bulletin, 99*, 247–262.

Rumsey, J. M., Rapoport, J. L., & Sceery, W. R. (1985). Autistic children as adults: Psychiatric, social, and behavioral outcomes. *Journal of the American Academy of Child Psychiatry, 24*, 465–473.

Russell, A. T., Bott, L., & Sammons, C. (1989). The phenomenology of schizophrenia occurring in childhood. *Journal of the American Academy of Child and Adolescent Psychiatry, 28*, 399–407.

Russell, G. F. M. (1985). Anorexia and bulimia nervosa. In M. Rutter & L. Hersov (Eds.), *Child and adolescent psychiatry: Modern approaches*. Oxford: Blackwell Scientific Publications.

Russo, D. C., Carr, E. G., & Lovaas, O. I. (1980). Self-injury in pediatric populations. In J. J. Ferguson & C. B. Taylor (Eds.), *The comprehensive handbook of behavioral medicine*, Vol. 3. New York: Spectrum Publications.

Rutter, M. (1978). Diagnosis and definition. In M. Rutter and E. Schopler (Eds.), *Autism: A reappraisal of concepts and treatments*. New York: Plenum.

Rutter, M. (1981). Psychological sequelae of brain damage in children. *The American Journal of Psychiatry, 138*, 1533–1544.

Rutter, M. (1983a). School effects on pupils progress: Research findings and policy implications. *Child Development, 54*, 1–29.

Rutter, M. (1983b). Stress, coping, and development. In N. Garmezy and M. Rutter (Eds.), *Stress, coping, and development in children*. New York: McGraw-Hill.

Rutter, M. (1985a). Infantile autism and other pervasive developmental disorders. In M. Rutter & L. Hersov (Eds.), *Child and adolescent psychiatry*. Boston: Blackwell Scientific Publications.

Rutter, M. (1985b). Psychopathology and development: Links between childhood and adult life. In M. Rutter and L. Hersov (Eds.), *Child and adolescent psychiatry*. Boston: Blackwell Scientific Publications.

Rutter, M. (1986a). Child psychiatry: Looking 30 years ahead. *Journal of Child Psychology and Psychiatry, 27*, 803–840.

Rutter, M. (1986b). Depressive feelings, cognitions, and disorders: A research postscript. In M. Rutter, C. E. Izard, & P. B. Read (Eds.), *Depression in young people: Developmental and clinical perspectives*. New York: Guilford.

Rutter, M. (1986c). The developmental psychopathology of depression: Issues and perspectives. In M. Rutter, C. E. Izard, & P. B. Read (Eds.), *Depression in young people: Developmental and clinical perspectives*. New York: Guilford.

Rutter, M. (1987). Psychosocial resilience and protective mechanisms. *American Journal of Orthopsychiatry, 57*, 316–331.

Rutter, M. (1989a). Child psychiatric disorders in ICD–10. *Journal of Child Psychology and Psychiatry, 30*, 499–513.

Rutter, M. (1989b). Isle of Wight revisited: Twenty-five years of child psychiatric epidemiology. *Journal of the American Academy of Child and Adolescent Psychiatry, 28*, 633–653.

Rutter, M. (1989c). Pathways from childhood to adult life. *Journal of Child Psychology and Psychiatry, 30*, 23–51.

Rutter, M. (1990). Commentary: Some focus and process considerations regarding effects of parental depression on children. *Developmental Psychology, 26*, 60–67.

Rutter, M., Bolton, P., Harrington, R., Le Couteur, A., Macdonald, H., & Simonoff, E. (1990a). Genetic factors in child psychiatric disorders—I. A review of research strategies. *Journal of Child Psychology and Psychiatry, 31*, 3–37.

Rutter, M., & Cox, A. (1985). Other family influences. In M. Rutter and L. Hersov (Eds.), *Child and adolescent psychiatry*. Boston: Blackwell Scientific Publications.

Rutter, M., & Garmezy, N. (1983). Developmental psychopathology. In P. H. Mussen (Ed.), *Handbook of child psychology*, Vol. IV. New York: Wiley.

Rutter, M., & Giller, H. (1984). *Juvenile delinquency: Trends and perspectives*. New York: Guilford.

Rutter, M., & Gould, M. (1985). Classification. In M. Rutter & L. Hersov (Eds.), *Child and adolescent psychiatry: Modern approaches*. Oxford: Blackwell Scientific Publications.

Rutter, M., Graham, P., & Yule, W. (1970). *A neuropsychiatric study in childhood*. Clinics in Developmental Medicine, Nos. 35/36. London: Heinemann.

Rutter, M., Izard, C. E., & Read, P. B. (Eds.). (1986). *Depression in young people: Developmental and clinical perspectives*. New York: Guilford.

Rutter, M., Macdonald, H., Le Couteur, A., Harrington, R., Bolton, P., & Baily, A. (1990b). Genetic factors in child psychiatric disorders—II. Empirical Findings. *Journal of Child Psychology and Psychiatry, 31*, 39–83.

Rutter, M., & Schopler, E. (1987). Autism and pervasive developmental disorders: Concepts and diagnostic issues. *Journal of Autism and Developmental Disorders, 17*, 159–186.

Rutter, M., & Shaffer, D. (1980). DSM-III: A step forward or back in terms of the classification of child psychiatric disorders? *Journal of the American Academy of Child Psychiatry, 19*, 371–394.

Rutter, M., Tizard, J., & Whitmore, K. (Eds.). (1970). *Education, health, and behavior*. London: Longmans.

Rutter, M., Tizard, J., Yule, W., Graham, P., & Whitmore, K. (1976). Research report: Isle of Wight studies, 1964–74. *Psychological Medicine, 6*, 313–332.

Rutter, M., & Tuma, A. H. (1988). Diagnosis and classification: Some outstanding issues. In M. Rutter, A. H. Tuma, & I. S. Lann (Eds.), *Assessment and diagnosis in child psychopathology*. New York: Guilford.

Rutter, M., Yule, W., & Graham, P. (1973). Enuresis and behavioral deviance: Some epidemiological considerations. In I. Kolvin, R. C. MacKeith, & S. R. Meadow (Eds.), *Bladder control and enuresis*. Philadelphia: Saunders.

Ryan, C., Vega, A., & Drash, A. (1985). Cognitive deficits in adolescents who developed diabetes early in life. *Pediatrics, 75*, 921–927.

Ryan, N. D., Puig-Antich, J., Cooper, T. Rabinovich, H., Ambrosini, P., Davies, M., King, J., Torrer, D., & Fried, J. (1986). Imipramine in adolescent major depression: Plasma level and clinical response. *Acta Psychiatrica Scandinavica, 73*, 275–288.

S

Saab, P. G., & Matthews, K. A. (1986). Type A behavior: Emergence, development, and implications for children. In M. Wolraich & D. K. Routh (Eds.), *Advances in developmental and behavioral pediatrics*, Vol. 7. Greenwich, CT: JAI.

Safer, D. J., & Allen, R. P. (1976). *Hyperactive children: Diagnosis and management*. Baltimore: University Park Press.

Sahley, T. L., & Panksepp, J. (1987). Brain opiods and autism: An updated analysis of possible linkages. *Journal of Autism and Developmental Disorders, 17*, 201–216.

Sajwaj, T., Libet, J., & Agras, S. (1974). Lemon-juice therapy: The control of life-threatening rumination in a six-month-old infant. *Journal of Applied Behavior Analysis, 7*, 557–563.

Sameroff, A. J. (1987). Transactional risk factors and prevention. In J. A. Steinberg & M. M. Silverman (Eds.), *Preventing mental disorders*. Washington, DC: Department of Health and Human Services, National Institutes of Mental Health.

Sameroff, A. J., & Chandler, M. J. (1975). Reproductive risk and the continuum of caretaking casualty. In F. D. Horowitz (Ed.), *Review of child development research.*, Vol. 4. Chicago: University of Chicago Press.

Santostefano, S. (1978). *A biodevelopmental approach to clinical child psychology*. New York: Wiley-Interscience.

Sattler, J. M. (1988). *Assessment of children*, 3rd ed. San Diego: Jerome M. Sattler, Publisher.

Satz, P., & Fletcher, J. M. (1980). Minimal brain dysfunctions: An appraisal of research concepts and methods. In H. E. Rie and E. D. Rie (Eds.), *Handbook of minimal brain dysfunctions*. New York: John Wiley.

Satz, P., & Fletcher, J. M. (1988). Early identification of learning disabled children: An old problem revisited. *Journal of Consulting and Clinical Psychology, 56*, 824–829.

Saxe, L., Cross, T., & Silverman, N. (1988). Children's mental health. *American Psychologist, 43*, 800–807.

Scarr, S. (1982). Testing for children: Assessment and the many determinants of intellectual competence. In S. Chess & A. Thomas (Eds.), *Annual Progress In Child Psychiatry and Child Development 1982*. New York: Brunner/Mazel.

Scarr, S., & Kidd, K. K. (1983). Developmental behavior genetics. In M. M. Haith & J. J. Campos (Eds.), *Handbook of Child Psychology*, Vol. 2, *Infancy and developmental psychobiology*. New York: John Wiley.

Scarr, S., & McCartney, K. (1983). How people make their own environments: A theory of genotype environment effects. *Child Development, 54*, 424–435.

Scarr, S., Phillips, D., & McCartney, K. (1989). Working mothers and their families. *American Psychologist, 44*, 1402–1409.

Scarr, S., & Weinberg, R. A. (1986). The early education enterprise. Care and education of the young. *American Psychologist, 41*, 1140–1146.

Scarr, S., Weinberg, R. A., & Levine, A. (1986). *Understanding development*. San Diego: Harcourt, Brace, Jovanovich.

Schacher, R., & Wachsmuth, R. (1990). Hyperactivity and parental psychopathology. *Journal of Child Psychology and Psychiatry, 31*, 381–392.

Schacht, T., & Nathan, P. E. (1977). But is it good for psychologists? Appraisal and status of DSM-III. *American Psychologist, 32*, 1017–1025.

Schaefer, C. E., & O'Connor, K. J. (1983). *Handbook of play therapy*. New York: Wiley.

Schafer, L. C., Glasgow, R. E., & McCaul, K. D. (1982). Increasing the adherence of diabetic adolescents. *Journal of Behavioral Medicine, 5*, 353–362.

Schaffer, D. (1973). The association between enuresis and emotional disorder: A review of the literature. In I. Kolvin, R. C. MacKieth, & S. R. Meadow (Eds.), *Bladder control and enuresis*. Philadelphia: J. B. Lippincott.

Schaughency, E. A., Lahey, B. B., Hynd, G. W., Stone, P. A., Piacentini, J. C., & Frick, P. J. (1989). Neuropsychological test performance and the attention deficit disorders: Clinical utility of the Luria-Nebraska Neuropsychological Battery-Children's Revision. *Journal of Consulting and Clinical Psychology, 57*, 112–116.

Scheerenberger, R. C. (1982). Public residential services, 1981: Status and trends. *Mental Retardation, 20*, 210–215.

Schloss, P. J., Sedlak, R. A., Elliott, C., & Smothers, M. (1982). Application of the changing-criterion design in special education. *Journal of Special Education, 16*, 359–367.

Schmidt, K., Solanto, M. V., & Bridger, W. H. (1985). Electrodermal activity of undersocialized aggressive children: A pilot study. *Journal of Child Psychology and Psychiatry, 26*, 653–660.

Schmidt, M. H., Esser, G., Allehoff, W., Geisel, B., Laucht, M., & Woerner, W. (1987). Evaluating the significance of minimal brain dysfunction—results of an epidemiology study. *Journal of Child Psychology and Psychiatry, 28*, 803–821.

School of Public Health—University at Albany (1989). Lead is more of a problem than we thought. *The Public Health Memo, 4*(2), 1–2.

Schopler, E. (1978). Limits of methodological differences in family studies. In M. Rutter & E. Schopler (Eds.), *Autism: A reappraisal of concepts and treatments*. New York: Plenum.

Schopler, E. (1987). Specific and nonspecific factors in the effectiveness of a treatment system. *American Psychologist, 42*, 376–383.

Schopler, E., & Mesibov, G. B. (Eds.). (1985). *Communication problems in autism*. New York: Plenum.

Schopler, E., Mesibov, G. B., & Baker, A. (1982). Evaluation of treatment for autistic children and their parents. *Journal of the American Academy of Child Psychiatry, 21*, 262–267.

Schopler, E., Reichler, R. J., DeVellis, R. F., & Daly, K. (1980). Toward objective classification of childhood autism: Childhood Autism Rating Scale (CARS). *Journal of Autism and Developmental Disorders, 10*, 91–103.

Schopler, E., Reichler, R. J., & Renner, B. R. (1988). The Childhood Autism Rating Scale (CARS). Los Angeles: Western Psychological Services.

Schopler, E., Short, A., & Mesibov, G. (1989). Relation of behavioral treatment to "normal functioning": Comment on Lovaas. *Journal of Consulting and Clinical Psychology, 57*, 162–164.

Schreibman, L., Koegel, R. L., Mills, D. L., & Burke, J. C. (1984). Training parent-child interactions. In E. Schopler and G. Mesibov (Eds.), *The effects of autism on the family*. New York: Plenum.

Schroeder, C. S. (1979). Psychologists in a private pediatric practice. *Journal of Pediatric Psychology, 4*, 5–18.

Schroeder, P. (1989). Toward a national family policy. *American Psychologist, 44*, 1410–1413.

Schroeder, S. R., Mulick, J. A., & Rojahn, J. (1980). The definition, taxonomy, epidemiology, and ecology of self-injurious behavior. *Journal of Autism and Developmental Disorders, 10*, 417–432.

Schumaker, J., Deshler, D., Alley, G., Warner, M., & Denton, P. (1984). Multipass: A learning strategy for improving reading comprehension. *Learning Disability Quarterly, 5*, 295–304.

Schumaker, J. B., Deshler, D. D., Ellis, E. S. (1986). Intervention issues related to the education of LD adolescents. In J. K. Torgesen and B. Y. L. Wong (Eds.), *Psychological and educational perspectives on learning disabilities*. New York: Academic Press.

Schwartz, D. M., & Thompson, M. G. (1981). Do anorectics get well?: Current research and future needs. *American Journal of Psychiatry, 138*, 319–323.

Scott, K. G., & Carran, D. T. (1987). The epidemiology and prevention of mental retardation. *American Psychologist, 42*, 801–804.

Sears, R. R. (1975). *Your ancients revisited: A history of child development*. Chicago: University of Chicago Press.

Segal, N. (1985). Monozygotic and dizygotic twins: A comparative analysis of mental ability profiles. *Child Development, 56*, 1051–1058.

Segall, M. H. (1986). Culture and behavior: Psychology in global perspective. In M. R. Rosenzweig & L. W. Porter (Eds.), *Annual review of psychology*, Vol. 37. Palo Alto, CA: Annual Reviews Inc.

Seidel, W. T., & Joschko, M. (1990). Evidence of difficulties in sustained attention in children with ADDH. *Journal of Abnormal Child Psychology, 18*, 217–229.

Seidman, E. (1987). Toward a framework for primary prevention research. In J. A. Steinberg & A. A. Silverman (Eds.), *Preventing mental disorders*. Rockville, MD: National Institute of Mental Health.

Seligman, M. E. P. (1971). Phobias and preparedness. *Behavior Therapy, 2*, 307–320.

Seligman, M. P., & Peterson, C. (1986). A learned helplessness perspective on childhood depression: Theory and research. In M. Rutter, C. E. Izard, & P. B. Read (Eds.), *Depression in young people: Developmental and clinical perspectives*. New York: Guilford.

Seligman, R., Gleser, G., Rauh, J., & Harris, L. (1974). The effect of earlier parental loss in adolescence. *Archives of General Psychiatry, 31*, 475–479.

Selman, R. (1976). Toward a structural analysis of developing interpersonal relations concepts: Research with normal and disturbed preadolescent boys. In A. D. Pick (Ed.), *Minnesota symposia on child psychology*, Vol. 10. Minneapolis: University of Minnesota Press.

Selye, H. (1956). *The stress of life*. New York: McGraw-Hill.

Semrud-Clikeman, M., & Hynd, G. W. (1990). Right hemispheric dysfunction in nonverbal learning disabilities: Social, academic, and adaptive functioning in adults and children. *Psychological Bulletin, 2*, 196–209.

Senf, G. M. (1986). LD research in sociological and scientific perspective. In J. K. Torgesen & B. Y. L. Wong (Eds.), *Psychological and educational perspectives on learning disabilities*. New York: Academic Press.

Serbin, L., & O'Leary, K. D. (1975, Dec.). How nursery schools teach girls to shut up. *Psychology Today*.

Shaffer, D. (1985). Brain damage. In M. Rutter & L. Hersov (Eds.), *Child and adolescent psychiatry: Modern approaches*, 2nd ed. Oxford: Blackwell Scientific Publications.

Shaffer, D., Campbell, M., Cantwell, D., Bradley, S., Carlson, G., Cohen, D., Denckla, M., Frances, A., Garfinkel, B.,

Klein, R., Pincus, H., Spitzer, R. L., Volkmar, F., & Widiger, T. (1989). Child and adolescent psychiatric disorders in DSM-IV: Issues facing the work group. *Journal of the American Academy of Child and Adolescent Psychiatry, 28*, 830–835.

Shantz, C. (1975). The development of social cognition. In E. M. Hetherington (Ed.), *Review of child development research*, Vol. 5. Chicago: University of Chicago Press.

Shapiro, D., Schwartz, G. E., & Tursky, B. (1972). Control of diastolic blood pressure in man by feedback and reinforcement. *Psychophysiology, 9*, 256–304.

Shaywitz, S. E., & Shaywitz, B. A. (1988). Attention deficit disorder: Current perspectives. In J. F. Kavanagh & T. J. Truss, Jr. (Eds.), *Learning disabilities: Proceedings of the National Conference*. Parkton, MD: York Press.

Shaywitz, S. E., Shaywitz, B. A., Cohen, D. J., & Young, J. G. (1983). Monoaminergic mechanisms in hyperactivity. In M. Rutter (Ed.), *Developmental neuropsychiatry*. New York: Guilford.

Sheldrick, C. (1985). Treatment of delinquents. In M. Rutter & L. Hersov (Eds.), *Child and adolescent psychiatry: Modern approaches*, 2nd ed. Oxford: Blackwell Scientific Publications.

Shinn, M. (1978). Father absence and children's cognitive development. *Psychological Bulletin, 85*, 295–324.

Sholevar, G. P., Burland, J. A., Frank, J. L., Etezady, M. H., & Goldstein, J. (1989). Psychoanalytic treatment of children and adolescents. *Journal of the American Academy of Child and Adolescent Psychiatry, 28*, 685–690.

Shultz, T. R., Wright, K., & Schleifer, M. (1986). Assignment of moral responsibility and punishment. *Child Development, 57*, 177–184.

Siegel, L. S. (1989). IQ is irrelevant to the definition of learning disabilities. *Journal of Learning Disabilities, 22*, 469–478,486.

Siegel, L. S. (1990). IQ and learning disabilities: R.I.P. In H. L. Swanson & B. Keogh (Eds.), *Learning disabilities. Theoretical and research issues*. Hillsdale, NJ: Erlbaum.

Siegel, O. (1982). Personality development in adolescence. In B. B. Wolman (Ed.), *Handbook of developmental psychology*. Englewood Cliffs, NJ: Prentice Hall.

Siervogel, R. M. (1988). Genetic and familial factors in human obesity. In N. A. Krasnegor, G. D. Grave, & N. Kretchmer (Eds.), *Childhood obesity: A biobehavioral perspective*. Caldwell, NJ: The Telford Press.

Sigman, M., & Mundy, P. (1989). Social attachments in autistic children. *Journal of the American Academy of Child and Adolescent Psychiatry, 28*, 74–81.

Sigman, M., & Ungerer, J. A. (1984). Attachment behaviors in autistic children. *Journal of Autism and Developmental Disorders, 14*, 231–244.

Silva, P. A., Hughes, P., Williams, S., & Faed, J. M. (1988). Blood lead, intelligence, reading attainment, and behaviour in eleven year old children in Dunedin, New Zealand. *Journal of Child Psychology and Psychiatry, 29*, 43–52.

Silver, L. B. (1987). The "magic cure": A review of the current controversial approaches for treating learning disabilities. *Journal of Learning Disabilities, 20*, 498–504.

Silver, L. B. (1989). Learning disabilities. Introduction. *Journal of the American Academy of Child and Adolescent Psychiatry, 28*, 309–313.

Silverman, W. K., Cerny, J. A., & Nelles, W. B. (1988). The familial influence in anxiety disorders: Studies on the offspring of patients with anxiety disorders. In B. B. Lahey & A. E. Kazdin (Eds.), *Advances in clinical child psychology*, Vol. 11. New York: Plenum.

Silverstein, A. B. (1982). Note on the constancy of the IQ. *American Journal of Mental Deficiency, 87*, 227–228.

Siperstein, G. N., & Bak, J. J. (1985). Effects of social behavior on children's attitudes toward their mildly and moderately mentally retarded peers. *American Journal of Mental Deficiency, 90*, 319–327.

Sisson, L. A., Egan, B. S., & Van Hasselt, V. B. (1988). Rumination. In M. Hersen & C. G. Last (Eds.), *Child behavior therapy casebook*. New York: Plenum.

Skinner, B. F. (1948). *Walden two*. London: Macmillan.

Skinner, B. F. (1953). *Science and human behavior*. New York: Macmillan.

Skinner, B. F. (1968). *The technology of teaching*. New York: Appleton-Century-Crofts.

Skrzypek, G. J. (1969). Effect of perceptual isolation and arousal on anxiety, complexity preference, and novelty preference in psychopathic and neurotic delinquents. *Journal of Abnormal Psychology, 74*, 321–329.

Skuse, D. (1984). Extreme deprivation in early childhood—II. Theoretical issues and a comparative review. *Journal of Child Psychology and Psychiatry, 25*, 543–572.

Skuse, D. (1987). Annotation. The psychological consequences of being small. *Journal of Child Psychology and Psychiatry, 28*, 641–650.

Slaby, R. G., & Guerra, N. G. (1988). Cognitive mediators of aggression in adolescent offenders: 1. assessment. *Developmental Psychology, 24*, 580–588.

Smith, L., & Hagen, V. (1984). Relationship between the home environment and sensorimotor development of Down Syndrome and nonretarded infants. *American Journal of Mental Deficiency, 89*, 124–132.

Smith, S. D., Pennington, B. F., Kimberling, W. J., & Ing, P. S. (1990). Familial dyslexia: Use of genetic linkage data to define subtypes. *Journal of the American Academy of Child and Adolescent Psychiatry, 29*, 204–213.

Smith, S. L. (1970). School refusal with anxiety: A review of 60 cases. *Canadian Psychiatric Association Journal, 15*, 257–264.

Snarey, J. R. (1985). Cross-cultural universality of social-moral development: A critical review of Kohlbergian research. *Psychological Bulletin, 97*, 202–232.

Snow, M. E., Hertzig, M. E., & Shapiro, T. (1987). Rate of development in young autistic children. *Journal of the American Academy of Child and Adolescent Psychiatry, 26*, 834–835.

Snow, M. E., Jacklin, C. N., & Maccoby, E. E. (1983). Sex-of-child differences in father-child interaction at one year of age. *Child Development, 54*, 227–232.

Solomon, S. (1985). Neurological evaluation. In H. I. Kaplan & B. J. Sadock (Eds.), *Comprehensive textbook of psychiatry/IV*, 4th ed. Baltimore: Williams & Wilkins.

Sparrow, S. S., Balla, D., & Cicchetti, D. V. (1984). *Vineland Adaptive Behavior Scales*. Circle Pines, MN: American Guidance Service.

Sperling, M. (1952). Animal phobia in a 2-year-old child. *Psychoanalytic Study of the Child, 7*, 115–125.

Spitz, R. A. (1946). Anaclitic depression. In *The psychoanalytic study of the child*, Vol. 2. New York: International Universities Press.

Spitzer, R. L., Forman, J. B. W., & Nee, J. (1979). DSM III field trials: I. Initial interrater diagnostic reliability. *American Journal of Psychiatry, 136*, 815–820.

Spivack, G., Marcus, J., & Swift, M. (1986). Early classroom behaviors and later misconduct. *Developmental Psychology, 22*, 124–131.

Spivack, G., & Shure, M. B. (1974). *Social adjustment of young children: A cognitive approach to solving real-life problems*. Washington, DC: Jossey-Bass.

Spock, B., & Rothenberg, M. B. (1985). *Dr. Spock's baby and child care*. New York: Pocket Books.

Spreen, O. (1988). Prognosis of learning disability. *Journal of Consulting and Clinical Psychology, 56*, 836–842.

Spring, B., Chiodo, J., & Bowen, D. J. (1987). Carbohydrates, tryptophan, and behavior: A methodological review. *Psychological Bulletin, 102*, 234–256.

Sroufe, L. A. (1979). The coherence of individual development. *American Psychologist, 34*, 834–841.

Sroufe, L. A. (1986). Appraisal: Bowlby's contribution to psychoanalytic theory and developmental psychology; attachment: separation: loss. *Journal of Child Psychology and Psychiatry, 27*, 841–849.

Sroufe, L. A., & Fleeson, J. (1986). Attachment and the construction of relationships. In W. W. Hartup & Z. Rubin (Eds.), *Relationships and development*. Hillsdale, NJ: Erlbaum.

Sroufe, L. A., & Rutter, M. (1984). The domain of developmental psychopathology. *Child Development, 55*, 17–29.

Stanley, L. (1980). Treatment of ritualistic behavior in an eight-year-old girl by response prevention: A case report. *Journal of Child Psychology and Psychiatry, 21*, 85–90.

Stanovich, K. E. (1986). Cognitive processes and the reading problems of learning-disabled children: Evaluating the assumption of specificity. In J. K. Torgesen and B. Y. L. Wong (Eds.), *Psychological and educational perspectives on learning disabilities*. New York: Academic Press.

Stanovich, K. E. (1989). Learning disabilities in broader context. *Journal of Learning Disabilities, 22*, 287–291,297.

Stark, K. D., Reynolds, W. M., & Kaslow, N. J. (1987). A comparison of the relative efficacy of self-control therapy and a behavioral problem-solving therapy for depression in children. *Journal of Abnormal Child Psychology, 15*, 91–113.

Stark, L. J., Dahlquist, L. M., & Collins, F. L., Jr. (1987). Improving children's compliance with diabetes management. *Clinical Psychology Review, 7*, 223–242.

Stefanik, M. E., Ollendick, T. H., Baldock, W. P., Francis, G., & Yaeger, N. J. (1987). Self-statements in aggressive, withdrawn, and popular children. *Cognitive Therapy and Research, 11*, 229–240.

Steffenburg, S., Gillberg, C., Hellgren, L., Andersson, L., Gillberg, I. C., Jakobsson, G., & Bohman, M. (1989). A twin study of autism in Denmark, Finland, Iceland, Norway and Sweden. *Journal of Child Psychology and Psychiatry, 30*, 405–416.

Steinberg, L. (1986). Stability (and instability) of Type A behavior from childhood to young adulthood. *Developmental Psychology, 22*, 393–402.

Steinhausen, H. C. (1988). Comparative studies of psychosomatic and chronic diseases among children and adolescents. In E. J. Anthony & C. Chiland (Eds.), *The child in his family*, Vol. 8. New York: Wiley.

Steinhausen, H. C., Schindler, H. P., & Stephan, H. (1983). Comparative psychiatric studies on children and adolescents suffering from cystic fibrosis and bronchial asthma. *Child Psychiatry and Human Development, 14*, 117–130.

Steketee, G., & Cleere, L. (1990). Obsessional-compulsive disorders. In A. S. Bellack, M. Hersen, & A. E. Kazdin (Eds.), *International handbook of behavior modification and therapy*, 2nd ed. New York: Plenum.

Stephan, C. W., & Langlois, J. H. (1984). Baby beautiful: Adult attributions of infant competence as a function of infant attractiveness. *Child Development, 55*, 576–585.

Stewart, R. B., Mobley, L. A., Van Tuyl, S. S., & Salvador, M. A. (1987). The first-born's adjustment to the birth of a sibling: A longitudinal assessment. *Child Development, 58*, 341–355.

Stipek, D., & McCroskey, J. (1989). Investing in children: Government and workplace policies for parents. *American Psychologist, 44*, 416–423.

St.James-Roberts, I. (1979). Neurological plasticity, recovery from brain insult, and child development. In H. W. Reese & L. P. Lipsitt (Eds.), *Advances in child development and behavior*, Vol. 14. New York: Academic Press.

Stolberg, A. L. (1988). Prevention programs for divorcing families. In L. A. Bond & B. M. Wagner (Eds.), *Families in transition: Primary prevention programs that work. Primary Prevention of Psychopathology*, Vol. XI. Beverly Hills, CA: Sage.

Stolberg, A. L., & Bush, J. P. (1985). A path analysis of factors predicting children's divorce adjustment. *Journal of Clinical Child Psychology, 14*, 49–54.

Stolberg, A. L., & Garrison, K. M. (1985). Evaluating a primary prevention program for children of divorce: The Divorce Adjustment Project. *American Journal of Community Psychology, 13*, 111–124.

Stone, W. L., & Greca, A. M. (1990). The social status of children with learning disabilities: A reexamination. *Journal of Learning Disabilities, 23*, 23–37.

Strauss, A. A., & Kephart, N. C. (1955). *Psychopathology and education of the brain-injured child*, Vol. II. New York: Grune & Stratton.

Strauss, A. A., & Lehtinen, L. (1947). *Psychopathology and education of the brain-injured child*. New York: Grune & Stratton.

Strauss, C. C. (1988). Social deficits of children with internalizing disorders. In B. B. Lahey & A. E. Kazdin (Eds.), *Advances in clinical child psychology*, Vol. 11. New York: Plenum.

Strauss, C. C., Last, C. G., Hersen, M., & Kazdin, A.E. (1988a). Association between anxiety and depression in children and adolescents. *Journal of Abnormal Child Psychology, 16*, 57–68.

Strauss, C. C., Lease, C. A., Last, C. G., & Francis, G. (1988b). Overanxious disorder: An examination of developmental differences. *Journal of Abnormal Child Psychology, 16*, 433–443.

Strean, H. S. (1970). *New approaches in child guidance*. Metuchen, NJ: The Scarecrow Press.

Streissguth, A. P., Barr, H. M., Sampson, P. D., Darby, B. L., & Martin, D. C. (1989). IQ at age 4 in relation to maternal alcohol use and smoking during pregnancy. *Developmental Psychology, 25*, 3–11.

Streissguth, A. P., Martin, D. C., Barr, H. M., Sandman, B. M., Kirchner, G. L., & Darby, D. L. (1984). Intrauterine alcohol and nicotine exposure: Attention and reaction time in 4-year-old children. *Developmental Psychology, 20*, 533–541.

Strober, M. (1986). Anorexia nervosa: History and psychological concepts. In K. D. Brownell & J. P. Foreyt (Eds.), *Handbook of eating disorders: Physiology, psychology, and treatment of obesity, anorexia and bulimia*. New York: Basic Books.

Strober, M., Green, J., & Carlson, G. (1981). The reliability of psychiatric diagnosis in hospitalized adolescents: Interrater agreement using the DSM III. *Archives of General Psychiatry, 38*, 141–145.

Strober, M., & Humphrey, L. (1987). Familial contributions to the etiology and course of anorexia nervosa and bulimia. *Journal of Consulting and Clinical Psychology, 55*, 654–659.

Strober, M., & Katz, J. L. (1987). Do eating disorders and affective disorders share a common etiology? *International Journal of Eating Disorders, 6*, 171–180.

Sullivan, A., & Brown, D. A. (1987). Enhancing instructional time through attention to metacognition. *Journal of Learning Disabilities, 20*, 66–75.

Suomi, S. J., & Harlow, H. H. (1972). Social rehabilitation of isolate-reared monkeys. *Developmental Psychology, 6*, 487–496.

Swaim, R. C., Oetting, E. R., Edwards, R. W., & Beauvais, F. (1989). Links from emotional distress to adolescent drug use: A path model. *Journal of Consulting and Clinical Psychology, 57*, 227–231.

Swanson, H. L. (1987). Information processing theory and learning disabilities: An overview. *Journal of Learning Disabilities, 20*, 3–7.

Swanson, H. L., Cochran, K. F., & Ewers, C. A. (1990). Can learning disabilities be determined from working memory performance? *Journal of Learning Disabilities, 23*, 59–67.

Swedo, S. E., Rapoport, J. L., Cheslow, D. L., Leonard, H. L., Ayoub, E. M., Hosier, D.M., & Wald, E. R. (1989b). High prevalence of obsessive-compulsive symptoms in patients with Sydenham's Chorea. *American Journal of Psychiatry, 146,* 246–249.

Swedo, S. E., Rapoport, J. L., Leonard, H., Lenane, M., & Cheslow, D. (1989c). Obsessive-compulsive disorder in children and adolescents: Clinical phenomenology of 70 consecutive cases. *Archives of General Psychiatry, 46,* 335–341.

Swedo, S. E., Schapiro, M. B., Grady, C. L., Cheslow, D. L., Leonard, H. L., Kumar, A., Friedland, R., Rapoport, S. I., & Rapoport, J. L. (1989a). Cerebral glucose metabolism in childhood-onset obsessive-compulsive disorder. *Archives of General Psychiatry, 46,* 518–523.

Szatmari, P., Bartolucci, G., Bremner, R., Bond, S., & Rich, S. (1989). A follow-up study of high-functioning autistic children. *Journal of Autism and Developmental Disorders, 19,* 213–225.

Szatmari, P., Boyle, M., & Offord, D. R. (1989). ADDH and conduct disorder: Degree of diagnostic overlap and differences among correlates. *Journal of the American Academy of Child and Adolescent Psychiatry, 28,* 865–872.

Szymanski, L. S. (1980). Individual psychotherapy with retarded persons. In L. S. Szymanski & P. E. Tanguay (Eds.), *Emotional disorders of mentally retarded persons.* Baltimore: University Park Press.

Szymanski, L. S., & Crocker, A. C. (1985). Mental retardation. In H. I. Kaplan & B. J. Sadock (Eds.), *Comprehensive textbook of psychiatry/IV.* Baltimore: Williams and Wilkins.

Szymanski, L. S., & Rosefsky, Q. B. (1980). Group psychotherapy with mentally retarded persons. In L. S. Szymanski & P. E. Tanguay (Eds.), *Emotional disorders of mentally retarded persons.* Baltimore: University Park Press.

T

Tager-Flusberg, H. (1981). On the nature of linguistic functioning in early infantile autism. *Journal of Autism and Developmental Disorders, 11,* 45–56.

Tager-Flusberg, H. (1985). Psycholinguistic approaches to language and communication in autism. In E. Schopler and G. B. Mesibov (Eds.), *Communication problems in autism.* New York: Plenum.

Tanguay, P. E., & Cantor, S. L. (1986). Introduction. Schizophrenia in children. *Journal of the American Academy of Child Psychiatry, 25,* 591–594.

Tanner, J. M. (1970). Physical growth. In P. H. Mussen (Ed.), *Carmichael's manual of child development,* Vol. 1. New York: John Wiley.

Tanner, J. M. (1978). *Foetus into man.* Cambridge, MA: Harvard Univ. Press.

Tannock, R., Schachar, R. J., Carr, R. P., Chajczyk, D., & Logan, G. D. (1989). Effects of methylphenidate on inhibitory control in hyperactive children. *Journal of Abnormal Child Psychology, 17,* 473–491.

Tanoue, Y., Oda, S., Asano, F., & Kawashima, K. (1988). Epidemiology of infantile autism in Southern Ibaraki, Japan: Differences in prevalence rates in birth cohorts. *Journal of Autism and Developmental Disorders, 18,* 155–166.

Tarjan, G., Wright, S. W., Eyman, R. K., & Keeran, C. V. (1973). Natural history of mental retardation: Some aspects of epidemiology. *American Journal of Mental Deficiency, 77,* 369–379.

Tarnowski, K. J., & Nay, S. M. (1989). Locus of control in children with learning disabilities and hyperactivity: A subgroup analysis. *Journal of Learning Disabilities, 22,* 381–383.

Taylor, E. (1988a). Attention deficit and conduct disorders syndromes. In M. Rutter, A. H. Tuma, & I. S. Lann (Eds.), *Assessment and diagnosis in child psychopathology.* New York: Guilford.

Taylor, H. G. (1988b). Learning disabilities. In E. J. Mash & L. G. Terdal (Eds.), *Behavioral assessment of childhood disorders,* 2nd ed. New York: Guilford.

Taylor, H. G. (1988c). Neuropsychological testing: Relevance for assessing children's learning disabilities. *Journal of Consulting and Clinical Psychology, 56,* 795–800.

Taylor, H. G. (1989). Learning disabilities. In E. J. Mash & R. A. Barkley (Eds.), *Treatment of childhood disorders.* New York: Guilford.

Taylor, H. G., Fletcher, J. M., & Satz, P. (1984). Neuropsychological assessment of children. In G. Goldstein & M. Hersen (Eds.), *Handbook of psychological assessment.* New York: Pergamon.

Tennant, C. (1988). Parental loss in childhood: Its effects in adult life. *Archives of General Psychiatry, 45,* 1045–1050.

Tennen, H., Affleck, G., Allen, D. A., McGrade, B. J., & Ratzan, S. (1984). Causal attributions and coping with insulin-dependent diabetes. *Basic and Applied Social Psychology, 5,* 131–142.

Thelen, E. (1986). Treadmill-elicited stepping in seven-month-old infants. *Child Development, 57,* 1498–1506.

Thelen, E., Skala, K. D., & Kelso, J. A. S. (1987). The dynamic nature of early coordination: Evidence from bilateral leg movements in young infants. *Developmental Psychology, 23,* 179–186.

Thomas, A., & Chess, S. (1984). Genesis and evolution of behavioral disorders: From infancy to early adult life. *The American Journal of Psychiatry, 141,* 1–9.

Thompson, R. A. (1986). Temperament, emotionality, and infant social cognition. In J. V. Lerner & R. M. Lerner (Eds.), *Temperament and social interaction during infancy and childhood.* New Directions for Child Development, No. 31. San Francisco: Jossey-Bass.

Thompson, R. A., Cicchetti, D., Lamb, M. E., & Malkin, C. (1985). Emotional responses of Down's Syndrome and normal infants in the Strange Situation. *Developmental Psychology, 21,* 828–841.

Thompson, R. A., Connell, J. P., & Bridges, L. J. (1988). Temperament, emotion, and social interactive behavior in the Strange Situation: A component analysis of attachment system functioning. *Child Development, 59,* 1002–1010.

Thompson, R. J., & Kronenberger, W. (1990). Behavior problems in children with learning problems. In H. L. Swanson & B. Keogh (Eds.), *Learning disabilities. Theoretical and research issues.* Hillsdale, NJ: Erlbaum.

Thompson, W. R., & Grusec, J. E. (1970). Studies of early experience. In P. H. Mussen (Ed.), *Carmichael's manual of child psychology,* Vol. 1. New York: John Wiley.

Thomson, G. O. B., Raab, G.M., Hepburn, W. S., Hunter, R., Fulton, M., & Laxen, D. P. H. (1989). Blood-lead levels and children's behaviour—results from the Edinburgh Lead Study. *Journal of Child Psychology and Psychiatry, 30,* 515–528.

Thorndike, E. L. (1905). *The elements of psychology.* New York: Seiler.

Thorndike, E. L. (1935). *The psychology of wants, interests, and attitudes.* New York: Appleton-Century-Crofts.

Thorndike, R. L., Hagen, E. P., & Sattler, J. M. (1986). *Stanford-Binet Intelligence Scale,* 4th ed. Chicago: Riverside.

Tolan, P. H. (1987). Implication of age of onset for delinquency risk. *Journal of Abnormal Child Psychology, 15,* 47–65.

Torgersen, S. (1986). Genetic factors in moderately severe and mild affective disorders. *Archives of General Psychiatry, 43,* 222–226.

Torgesen, J. K. (1986). Learning disabilities theory: Its current state and future prospects. *Journal of Learning Disabilities, 19,* 399–407.

Torgesen, J. K., & Morgan, S. (1990). Phonological synthesis tasks: A developmental, functional, and componential analysis. In H. L. Swanson & B. Keogh (Eds.), *Learning disabilities. Theoretical and research issues.* Hillsdale, NJ: Erlbaum.

Toro, P. A., Weissberg, R. P., Guare, J., & Liebenstein, N. L. (1990). A comparison of children with and without learning disabilities on social problem-solving skill, school behavior, and family background. *Journal of Learning Disabilities, 23,* 115–120.

Treffert, D. A. (1988). The idiot savant: A review of the syndrome. *American Journal of Psychiatry, 145,* 563–572.

Trites, R. L., Dugas, E., Lynch, G., & Ferguson, H. B. (1979). Prevalence of hyperactivity. *Journal of Pediatric Psychology, 4,* 179–188.

Tryphonas, H. (1979). Factors possibly implicated in hyperactivity. In R. L. Trites (Ed.), *Hyperactivity in children.* Baltimore: University Park Press.

Tuddenham, R. D. (1963). The nature and measurement of intelligence. In L. Postman (Ed.), *Psychology in the making.* New York: Knopf.

Tuma, J. M. (Ed.). (1982a). *Handbook for the practice of pediatric psychology.* New York: Wiley.

Tuma, J. M. (1982b). Pediatric psychology: Conceptualization and definition. In J. M. Tuma (Ed.), *Handbook for the practice of pediatric psychology.* New York: Wiley.

Tuma, J. M. (1989). Mental health services for children: The state of the art. *American Psychologist, 44,* 188–199.

Tuma, J. M., & Pratt, J. M. (1982). Clinical child psychology practice and training: A survey. *Journal of Clinical Child Psychology, 11,* 27–34.

Turkington, C. (1987, Sept.). Special talents. *Psychology Today,* 42–46.

Turnure, J. E. (1985). Communication and cues in the functional cognition of the mentally retarded. In N. R. Ellis & N. W. Bray (Eds.), *International Review of Research in Mental Retardation, Vol. 13.* New York: Academic Press.

Twardosz, S., & Nordquist, V. M. (1987). Parent training. In M. Hersen & V. B. Van Hasselt (Eds.), *Behavior therapy with children and adolescents: A clinical approach.* New York: Wiley.

Tyson, R. L. (1978). Notes on the analysis of a prelatency boy with a dog phobia. In A. J. Solnit, R. S. Eissler, A. Freud, M. Kris, & P. B. Neubauer (Eds.), *Psychoanalytic study of the child,* Vol. 33. New Haven, CT: Yale University Press.

Tyson, R. L. (1986). The roots of psychopathology and our theories of development. *Journal of the American Academy of Child Psychiatry, 25,* 12–22.

U

Ullmann, C. A. (1957). Teachers, peers, and tests as predictors of adjustment. *Journal of Educational Psychology, 48,* 257–267.

Ullmann, L. P., & Krasner, L. (1975). *A psychological approach to abnormal behavior,* 2nd ed. Englewood Cliffs, NJ: Prentice Hall.

United States Office of Education. (1977). Definition and criteria for defining students as learning disabled. *Federal Register,* 42:250, p. 65083. Washington, DC: U. S. Government Printing Office.

U.S. Department of Health and Human Services (1979). *Lasting effects after preschool.* Washington, D.C.: Superintendent of Documents. U.S. Government Printing Office.

U.S. Department of Health and Human Services (1980). *Head Start. A child development program.* Washington, DC: Superintendent of Documents, U.S. Government Printing Office.

Uzgiris, I. C. (1976). Organization of sensorimotor intelligence. In M. Lewis (Ed.), *Origins of intelligence.* New York: Plenum.

Uzgiris, I. C., & Hunt, J. McV. (1975). *Assessment in infancy: Ordinal scales of psychological development.* Urbana, IL: University of Illinois Press.

V

Valone, K., Goldstein, M. J., & Norton, J. P. (1984). Parental expressed emotion and psychophysiological reactivity in an adolescent sample at risk for schizophrenia spectrum disorder. *Journal of Abnormal Psychology, 93,* 448–457.

van der Meere, J., & Sergeant, J. (1988a). Controlled processing and vigilance in hyperactivity: Time will tell. *Journal of Abnormal Child Psychology, 16,* 641–655.

van der Meere, J., & Sergeant, J. (1988b). Focused attention in pervasively hyperactive children. *Journal of Abnormal Child Psychology, 16,* 627–639.

Van Dyke, D. C., & Fox, A. A. (1990). Fetal drug exposure and its possible implications for learning in the preschool and school-age population. *Journal of Learning Disabilities, 23,* 161–163.

Varni, J. W. (1983). *Clinical behavioral pediatrics: An interdisciplinary biobehavioral approach.* New York: Pergamon.

Varni, J. W., Katz, E., & Dash, J. (1982). Behavioral and neurochemical aspects of pediatric pain. In D. C. Russo & J. W. Varni (Eds.), *Behavioral pediatrics: Research and practice.* New York: Plenum.

Varni, J. W., Walco, G. A., & Wilcox, K. T. (1990). Cognitive-behavioral assessment and treatment of pediatric pain. In A. M. Gross & R. S. Drabman (Eds.), *Handbook of clinical behavioral pediatrics.* New York: Plenum.

Vega-Lahr, N., & Field, T. M. (1986). Type A behavior in preschool children. *Child Development, 57,* 1333–1348.

Vellutino, F. R. (1979). *Dyslexia. Theory and research.* Cambridge MA: MIT Press.

Vellutino, F. R. (1987). Dyslexia. *Scientific American, 256,* 34–41.

Vernon, D., Schulman, J., & Foley, J. (1966). Changes in children's behavior after hospitalization. *American Journal of Diseases in Children, 111,* 581–593.

Vicker, B., & Monahan, M. (1988). The diagnosis of autism by state agencies. *Journal of Autism and Developmental Disorders, 18,* 231–240.

Vikan, A. (1985). Psychiatric epidemiology in a sample of 1510 ten-year-old children—I. Prevalence. *Journal of Child Psychology and Psychiatry, 26,* 55–75.

Visintainer, P. F., & Matthews, K. A. (1987). Stability of overt Type A behaviors in children: Results from a two- and five-year longitudinal study. *Child Development, 58,* 1586–1591.

Volkmar, F. R. (1987). Annotation. Diagnostic issues in the pervasive developmental disorders. *Journal of Child Psychology and Psychiatry, 28,* 365–369.

Volkmar, F. R., Cicchetti, D. V., Dykens, E., Sparrow, S. S., Leckman, J. F., & Cohen, D. J. (1988). An evaluation of the Autism Behavior Checklist. *Journal of Autism and Developmental Disorders, 18,* 81–97.

Volkmar, F. R., & Cohen, D. J. (1988). Diagnosis of pervasive developmental disorders. In B. B. Lahey & A. E. Kazdin (Eds.), *Advances in clinical child psychology,* Vol. 2. New York: Plenum.

Volkmar, F. R., Sparrow, S. S., Goudreau, D., Cicchetti, D. V., Paul, R., & Cohen, D. J. (1987). Social deficits in autism: An operational approach using the Vineland Adaptive Behavior Scales. *Journal of the American Academy of Child and Adolescent Psychiatry, 26,* 156–161.

Vyse, S. A., & Rapport, M. (1989). The effects of methylphenidate on learning in children with ADDH: The stimulus equivalence paradigm. *Journal of Consulting and Clinical Psychology, 57,* 425–435.

W

Wagner, D. A. (1986). Child development research and the third world. *American Psychologist, 41,* 298–301.

Wagner, R. K., & Torgesen, J. K. (1987). The nature of phonological processing and its causal role in the acquisition of reading skills. *Psychological Bulletin, 101*, 192–212.

Wagner, W. G., Smith, D., & Norris, W. R. (1988). The psychological adjustment of enuretic children: A comparison of two types. *Journal of Pediatric Psychology, 13*, 33–38.

Wahler, R. G., & Dumas, J. E. (1984). Changing the observational coding styles of insular and noninsular mothers: A step towards maintenance of parent training effects. In R. F. Dangel & R. A. Polster (Eds.), *Parent training: Foundations of research and practice.* New York: Guilford.

Wahler, R. G., & Dumas, J. E. (1986). Maintenance factors in coercive mother-child interactions: The compliance and predictability hypotheses. *Journal of Applied Behavior Analysis, 19*, 13–22.

Wahler, R. G., & Dumas, J. E. (1989). Attentional problems in dysfunctional mother-child interactions: An interbehavioral model. *Psychological Bulletin, 105*, 116–130.

Waisbren, S., Mahon, B. E., Schnell, R. R., & Levy, H. L. (1987). Predictors of intelligence quotient and intelligence quotient change in persons treated for phenylketonuria early in life. *Paediatrics, 79*, 351–355.

Walker, C. E., Kenning, M., & Faust-Companile, J. (1989). Enuresis and encopresis. In E. J. Mash & R. A. Barkley (Eds.), *Treatment of childhood behavior disorders.* New York: Guilford.

Walker, C. E., Milling, L., & Bonner, B. (1988). Incontinence disorders: Enuresis and encopresis. In D. Routh (Ed.), *Handbook of pediatric psychology.* New York: Guilford.

Walker, H., Greenwood, C., Hops, H., & Todd, N. (1979). Differential effects of reinforcing topographic components of social interaction. *Behavior Modification, 3*, 291–321.

Walker, L. J. (1984). Sex differences in the development of moral reasoning: A critical review. *Child Development, 55*, 677–691.

Walker, L. J. (1986). Sex differences in the development of moral reasoning: A rejoinder to Baumrind. *Child Development, 57*, 522–526.

Wallander, J. L., Feldman, W. S., & Varni, J. W. (1989). Physical status, and psychosocial adjustment in children with spina bifida. *Journal of Pediatric Psychology, 14*, 89–102.

Wallander, J. L., Varni, J. W., Babani, L., Banis, H. T., & Wilcox, K. T. (1988). Children with chronic physical disorders: Maternal reports of their psychological adjustment. *Journal of Pediatric Psychology, 13*, 197–212.

Wallerstein, J. S. (1984). Children of divorce: Preliminary report of a ten-year follow-up of young children. *American Journal of Orthopsychiatry, 54*, 444–458.

Wallerstein, J. S. (1985). Children of divorce: Preliminary report of a 10-year follow-up of older children and adolescents. *Journal of the American Academy of Child Psychiatry, 24*, 538–544.

Wallerstein, J. S., & Blakeslee, S. (1989). *Second chances.* New York: Tichnor and Fields.

Wallerstein, J., & Kelly, J. (1980). Effects of divorce on the visiting father-child relationship. *American Journal of Psychiatry, 137*(12), 1534–1539.

Warm, J. S., & Berch, D. B. (1985). Sustained attention in the mentally retarded: The vigilance paradigm. In N. R. Ellis & N. W. Bray (Eds.), *International review of research in mental retardation, Vol. 13.* New York: Academic Press.

Warren, R. P., Margaretten, N. C., Pace, N. C., & Foster, A. (1986). Immune abnormalities in patients with autism. *Journal of Autism and Developmental Disorders, 16*, 189–197.

Waterman, J. M., Sobesky, W. E., Silvern, L., Aoki, B., & McCaulay, M. (1981). Social perspective-taking and adjustment in emotionally disturbed, learning-disabled, and normal children. *Journal of Abnormal Child Psychology, 9*, 133–148.

Waters, E., & Sroufe, L. A. (1983). Social competence as a developmental construct. *Developmental Review, 3*, 79–97.

Waters, E., Wippman, J., & Sroufe, A. (1980). Social competence in preschool children as a function of the security of earlier attachment to the mother. *Child Development, 51*, 208–216.

Watkins, J. M., Asarnow, R. F., & Tanguay, P. E. (1988). Symptom development in childhood onset schizophrenia. *Journal of Child Psychology and Psychiatry, 29*, 865–878.

Watson, J. B. (1913). Psychology as the behaviorist views it. *Psychological Review, 20*, 158–177.

Watson, J. B. (1963). *Behaviorism.* Chicago: University of Chicago Press.

Watson, J. B., & Rayner, R. (1920). Conditioned emotional reactions. *Journal of Experimental Psychology, 3*, 1–14.

Webster-Stratton, C. (1985a). Predictors of treatment outcome in parent training for conduct-disordered children. *Behavior therapy, 16*, 223–243.

Webster-Stratton, C. (1985b). The effects of father involvement in parent training for conduct problem children. *Journal of Child Psychology and Psychiatry, 26*, 801–810.

Webster-Stratton, C., Hollinsworth, T., & Kolpacoff, M. (1989). The long-term effectiveness and clinical significance of three cost-effective training programs for families with conduct-problem children. *Journal of Consulting and Clinical Psychology, 57*, 550–553.

Wechsler, D. I. (1974). *WISC-R manual. Wechsler Intelligence Scale for Children-Revised.* New York: Psychological Corporation.

Weidner, G., Sexton, G., Matarazzo, J. S., Pereira, C., & Friend, R. (1988). Type A behavior in children, adolescents and their parents. *Developmental Psychology, 24*, 118–121.

Weinberg, R. A. (1989). Intelligence and IQ: Landmark issues and great debates. *American Psychologist, 44*, 98–104.

Weinrott, M. R., Jones, R. R., & Howard, J. R. (1982). Cost-effectiveness of teaching family programs for delinquents: Results of a national evaluation. *Evaluation review, 6*, 173–201.

Weintraub, S., & Neale, J. (1984). The Stony Brook high-risk project. In N. F. Watt, E. J. Anthony, L. C. Wynne, & J. E. Rolf (Eds.), *Children at risk for schizophrenia: A longitudinal perspective.* New York: Cambridge University Press.

Weintraub, S., Winters, K. C., & Neale, J. M. (1986). Competence and vulnerability in children with an affectively disordered parent. In M. Rutter, C. E. Izard, & P. B. Read (Eds.), *Depression in young people: Developmental and clinical perspectives.* New York: Guilford.

Weiss, B. (1982). Food additives and environmental chemicals as sources of childhood behavior disorders. *Journal of Child Psychiatry, 21*, 144–152.

Weiss, B., Weisz, J. R., & Bromfield, R. (1986). Performance of retarded and nonretarded persons on information-processing tasks: Further tests of the similar structure hypothesis. *Psychological Bulletin, 100*, 157–175.

Weiss, G., & Hechtman, L. T. (1986). *Hyperactive children grown up.* New York: Guilford.

Weissberg, R. P., Cowen, E. L., Lotyczewski, B. S., & Gesten, E. L. (1983). The primary mental health project: Seven consecutive years of program outcome research. *Journal of Consulting and Clinical Psychology, 51*, 100–107.

Weissman, M. M., Kidd, K. K., & Prusoff, B. A. (1982). Variability in rates of affective disorders in relatives of depressed and normal probands. *Archives of General Psychiatry, 39*, 1397–1403.

Weissman, M. M., Warner, V., Wichramaratne, P., & Prusoff, B. A. (1988). Onset of major depression in adolescence and early adulthood: Findings from a family study of children. *Journal of Affective Disorders, 15*, 269–277.

Weisz, J. R., Suwanlet, S., Chaiyasit, W., Weiss, B., Walter, B. R., & Anderson, W. W. (1988). Thai and American perspectives on over- and undercontrolled child behavior problems: Exploring the threshold model among parents, teachers, and psychologists. *Journal of Consulting and Clinical Psychology, 56,* 601–609.

Weisz, J. R., Weiss, B., Alicke, M. D., & Klotz, M. L. (1987). Effectiveness of psychotherapy with children and adolescents: A meta-analysis for clinicians. *Journal of Consulting and Clinical Psychology, 55,* 542–549.

Weisz, J. R., & Yeates, K. O. (1981). Cognitive development in retarded and nonretarded persons: Piagetian tests of the similar structure hypothesis. *Psychological Bulletin, 90,* 153–178.

Weisz, J. R., Yeates, K. O., & Zigler, E. (1982). Piagetian evidence and the developmental-difference controversy. In E. Zigler & D. Balla (Eds.), *Mental retardation: The developmental-difference controversy.* Hillsdale, NJ: Erlbaum.

Weisz, J. R., & Zigler, E. (1979). Cognitive development in retarded and nonretarded persons: Piagetian tests of the similar sequence hypothesis. *Psychological Bulletin, 86,* 831–851.

Weithorn, L. A. (1987). Informed consent for prevention research involving children: Legal and ethical issues. In J. A. Steinberg & M. M. Silverman (Eds.), *Preventing mental disorders.* Rockville, MD: U.S. Department of Health and Human Services.

Weizman, R., Gil-Ad, I., Dick, J., Tyano, S., Szekely, G. A., & Laron, Z. (1988). Low plasma immunoreactive beta-endorphin levels in autism. *Journal of the American Academy of Child and Adolescent Psychiatry, 27,* 430–433.

Wells, K. (1987). Annotation. Scientific issues in the conduct of case studies. *Journal of Child Psychology and Psychiatry, 28,* 783–790.

Wells, K. C., & Forehand, R. (1985). Conduct and oppositional disorders. In P. H. Bornstein & A. E. Kazdin (Eds.), *Handbook of clinical behavior therapy with children.* Homewood, IL: Dorsey.

Wells, K. C., Forehand, R., & Griest, D. L. (1980). Generality of treatment effects from treated to untreated behaviors resulting from a parent training program. *Journal of Clinical Child Psychology, 9,* 217–219.

Wenar, C. (1982). Developmental psychology: Its nature and models. *Journal of Clinical Child Psychology, 11,* 192–201.

Wenar, C., Ruttenberg, B. A., Kalish-Weiss, B., & Wolf, E. G. (1986). The development of normal and autistic children: A comparative study. *Journal of Autism and Developmental Disorders, 16,* 317–333.

Wender, P. H., Kety, S. S., Rosenthal, D., Schulsinger, F., Ortmann, J., & Lunde, I. (1986). Psychiatric disorders in the biological and adoptive families of adopted individuals with affective disorders. *Archives of General Psychiatry, 43,* 923–929.

Werkman, S. (1980). Anxiety disorders. In H. I. Kaplan, A. E. M. Freedman, & B. J. Sadock (Eds.), *Comprehensive textbook of psychiatry/III,* Vol. 3. Baltimore: Williams & Wilkins.

Werner, E. E. (1980). Environmental interaction. In H. E. Rie & E. D. Rie (Eds.), *Handbook of minimal brain dysfunctions.* New York: Wiley.

Werner, E. E., & Smith, R. S. (1982). *Vulnerable but invincible.* New York: McGraw-Hill.

Werry, J. S. (1968). Studies of the hyperactive child: IV. An empirical analysis of the minimal brain dysfunction syndrome. *Archives of General Psychiatry, 19,* 9–16.

Werry, J. S. (1979a). Organic factors. In H. C. Quay & J. S. Werry (Eds.), *Psychopathological disorders of childhood,* 2nd ed. New York: John Wiley.

Werry, J. S. (1979b). The childhood psychoses. In H. C. Quay & J. S. Werry (Eds.), *Psychopathological disorders of childhood,* 2nd ed. New York: John Wiley.

Werry, J. S. (1986). Physical illness, symptoms and allied disorders. In H. C. Quay & J. S. Werry (Eds.), *Psychopathological disorders of childhood,* 3rd ed. New York: Wiley.

Werry, J. S., Methven, R. J., Fitzpatrick, J., & Dixon, H. (1983). The interrater reliability of DSM III in children. *Journal of Abnormal Child Psychology, 11,* 341–354.

Wertlieb, D., Hauser, S. T., & Jacobson, A. M. (1986). Adaptation to diabetes: Behavior symptoms and family context. *Journal of Pediatric Psychology, 11,* 463–479.

West, D. J. (1982). *Delinquency: Its roots, careers, and prospects.* London: Heinemann.

West, D. J. (1985). Delinquency. In M. Rutter & L. Hersov (Eds.), *Child and adolescent psychiatry: Modern approaches,* 2nd ed. Oxford: Blackwell Scientific Publications.

West, M. O., & Prinz, R. J. (1987). Parental alcoholism and childhood psychopathology. *Psychological Bulletin, 102,* 204–218.

Wetherby, A. M. (1986). Ontogeny of communicative functions in autism. *Journal of Autism and Developmental Disorders, 16,* 295–316.

Whalen, C. K. (1989). Attention deficit and hyperactivity disorders. In T. H. Ollendick & M. Hersen (Eds.), *Handbook of child psychopathology.* New York: Plenum.

Whalen, C. K., & Henker, B. (1985). The social worlds of hyperactive (ADDH) children. *Clinical Psychology Review, 5,* 447–478.

Whalen, C. K., Henker, B., Buhrmester, D., Hinshaw, S. P., Huber, A., Laski, K. (1989). Does stimulant medication improve the peer status of hyperactive children? *Journal of Consulting and Clinical Psychology, 57,* 545–549.

Whalen, C. K., Henker, B., & Dotemoto, S. (1980). Methylphenidate and hyperactivity: Effects on teacher behaviors. *Science, 208,* 1280–1282.

Whalen, C. K., Henker, B., & Granger, D. A. (1990). Social judgment processes in hyperactive boys: Effects of methylphenidate and comparisons with normal peers. *Journal of Abnormal Child Psychology, 18,* 297–316.

Whalen, C. K., Henker, B., & Hinshaw, S. P. (1985). Cognitive-behavioral therapies for hyperactive children: Premises, problems, and prospects. *Journal of Abnormal Child Psychology, 13,* 391–409.

White, J. L., Moffitt, T. E., & Silva, P. A. (1989). A prospective replication of the protective effects of IQ in subjects at high risk for juvenile delinquency. *Journal of Consulting and Clinical Psychology, 57,* 719–724.

Whitehill, M., DeMyer-Gapin, S., & Scott, T. J. (1976). Stimulation-seeking in antisocial pre-adolescent children. *Journal of Abnormal Psychology, 85,* 101–104.

Whitehurst, G. J. (1982). Language development. In B. B. Wolman (Ed.), *Handbook of developmental psychology.* Englewood Cliffs, NJ: Prentice Hall.

Whitehurst, G. J., & Valdez-Menchaca, M. C. (1988). What is the role of reinforcement in early language acquisition? *Child Development, 59,* 430–440.

Williams, C. A., & Forehand, R. (1984). An examination of predictor variables for child compliance and noncompliance. *Journal of Abnormal Child Psychology, 12,* 491–504.

Williams, C. D. (1959). The elimination of tantrum behavior by extinction procedures: Case report. *Journal of Abnormal and Social Psychology, 59,* 269.

Williams, L. (1988, Jan. 15). Parents and doctors fear growing misuse of drug used to treat hyperactive kids. *Wall Street Journal,* 21.

Williamson, D. A., Davis, C. J., & Kelly, M. L. (1989). Headaches. In T. H. Ollendick & M. Hersen (Eds.), *Handbook of child psychopathology,* 2nd ed. New York: Plenum.

Williamson, D. A., McKenzie, S. J., Gorecany, A. J., & Faulstich, M. (1987). Psychophysiological disorders. In M. Hersen & V. B. Van Hasselt (Eds.), *Behavior therapy with children and adolescents.* New York: Wiley.

Willner, A.G., Braukmann, C. J., Kirigin, K. A., & Wolf, M. M. (1978). Achievement Place: A community model for youths in trouble. In D. Marholin (Ed.), *Child behavior therapy*. New York: Gardner.

Wilson, C. C., & Haynes, S. N. (1985). Sleep disorders. In P. H. Bornstein & A. E. Kazdin (Eds.), *Handbook of clinical behavior therapy with children*. Homewood, IL: Dorsey.

Wilson, G. T. (1986). Cognitive-behavioral and pharmacological therapies for bulimia. In K. D. Brownell & J. P. Foreyt (Eds.), *Physiology, psychology, and treatment of eating disorders*. New York: Basic Books.

Wilson, G. T. (1989). The treatment of bulimia nervosa: A cognitive-social learning analysis. In A. J. Stunkard & A. Baum (Eds.), *Perspectives in behavioral medicine: Eating, sleeping, and sex*. Hillsdale, NJ: Lawrence Erlbaum.

Wilson, G. T., Rossiter, E., Kleifield, E., & Lindholm, L. (1986). Cognitive-behavioral treatment of bulimia: A controlled evaluation. *Behaviour Research and Therapy, 24,* 277–288.

Wilson, R. S. (1983). The Louisville Twin Study: Developmental synchronies in behavior. *Child Development, 54,* 298–316.

Wilson, R. S., & Matheny, A. P. (1986). Behavior-genetics research in infant temperament: The Louisville Twin Study. In R. Plomin & J. Dunn (Eds.), *The study of temperament: Changes, continuities and challenges*. Hillsdale, NJ: Erlbaum.

Windle, M. (1990). A longitudinal study of antisocial behaviors in early adolescence as predictors of late adolescent substance use: Gender and ethnic group differences. *Journal of Abnormal Psychology, 99,* 86–91.

Wing, L., & Gould, J. (1979). Severe impairments of social interaction and associated abnormalities in children: Epidemiology and classification. *Journal of Autism and Developmental Disorders, 9,* 11–29.

Wohlwill, J. F. (1980). Cognitive development in childhood. In O. G. Brim & J. Kagan (Eds.), *Constancy and change in human development*. Cambridge, MA: Harvard University Press.

Wolf, M. M., Braukmann, C. J., & Ramp, K. A. (1987). Serious delinquent behavior as part of a significantly handicapping condition: Cures and supportive environments. *Journal of Applied Behavior Analysis, 20,* 347–359.

Wolfe, B. E. (1979). Behavioral treatment of childhood gender disorders. *Behavior Modification, 4,* 550–575.

Wolfe, D. A. (1985). Child-abusive parents: An empirical review and analysis. *Psychological Bulletin, 97,* 462–482.

Wolfe, D. A. (1988). Child abuse and neglect. In E. J. Mash & L. G. Terdal (Eds.), *Behavioral assessment of childhood disorders*, 2nd ed. New York: Guilford.

Wolfe, D. A., & St. Pierre, J. (1989). Child abuse and neglect. In T. H. Ollendick & M. Hersen (Eds.), *Handbook of child psychopathology*, 2nd ed. New York: Plenum.

Wolfe, P. H. (1981). Normal variations in human maturation. In K: J. Connolly & H. F. R. Prechtl (Eds.), *Clinics in developmental medicine No. 77/78. Maturation and development*. Philadelphia: Lippincott.

Wolfe, V. V., & Wolfe, D. A. (1988). The sexually abused child. In E. J. Mash & L. G. Terdal (Eds.), *Behavioral assessment of childhood disorders*, 2nd ed. New York: Guilford.

Wolfensberger, W. (1980). *The principle of normalization in human services*. Toronto: National Institute on Mental Retardation.

Wolff, S., Narayan, S., & Moyes, B. (1988). Personality characteristics of parents of autistic children: A controlled study. *Journal of Child Psychology and Psychiatry, 29,* 143–153.

Wolkind, S., & Rutter, M. (1985). Sociocultural factors. In M. Rutter and L. Hersov (Eds.), *Child and adolescent psychiatry*. Boston: Blackwell Scientific Publications.

Wolman, B. B. (1972). Psychoanalytic theory of infantile development. In B. B. Wolman (Ed.), *Handbook of child psychoanalysis: Research theory and practice*. New York: Van Nostrand Reinhold.

Wolock, I., & Horowitz, B. (1984). Child maltreatment as a social problem: The neglect of neglect. *American Journal of Orthopsychiatry, 54,* 530–543.

Wolraich, M., Milich, R., Stumbo, P., & Schultz, F. (1985). The effects of sucrose ingestion on the behavior of hyperactive boys. *Journal of Pediatrics, 106,* 675–682.

Woodcock, R. W. (1973). *Woodcock Reading Mastery Tests*. Circle Pines, MN: American Guidance Services.

Woodcock, R. W., & Johnson, M. B. (1978). *Woodcock-Johnson Psycho-Educational Battery*. Allen, TX: DLM/teaching Resources.

Woodhead, M. (1988). When psychology informs public policy. The case of early childhood intervention. *American Psychologist, 43,* 443–454.

Woodward, W. M. (1979). Piaget's theory and the study of mental retardation. In N. R. Ellis (Ed.), *Handbook of mental deficiency*. Hillsdale, NJ: Erlbaum.

Woody, E. Z. (1986). The obese child as a social being and developing self. *Canadian Psychology, 27,* 286–298.

World Health Organization (1978). *International Classification of Diseases*, 9th revision. Geneva: World Health Organization.

Wright, H. F. (1960). Observational child study. In P. H. Mussen (Ed.), *Handbook of research methods in child development*. New York: John Wiley.

Wright, L. (1988). The Type A behavior pattern and coronary artery disease: Quest for the active ingredients and the elusive mechanism. *American Psychologist, 43,* 2–14.

Wright, L., & Walker, C. E. (1976). Behavioral treatment of encopresis. *Journal of Pediatric Psychology, 4,* 35–37.

Y

Yates, A. (1989). Current perspectives on the eating disorders: I. History, psychological and biological aspects. *Journal of the American Academy of Child and Adolescent Psychiatry, 28,* 813–828.

Yates, A. (1990). Current perspectives on the eating disorders: II. Treatment, outcome, and research directions. *Journal of the American Academy of Child and Adolescent Psychiatry, 29,* 1–9.

Young, J. G., O'Brien, J. D., Gutterman, E. M., Cohen, P. (1987). Research on the clinical interview. *Journal of the American Academy of Child and Adolescent Psychiatry, 26,* 613–620.

Ysseldyke, J., & Algozzine, B. (1984). *Introduction to special education*. Boston: Houghton Mifflin.

Yule, W., & Rutter, M. (1985). Reading and other learning difficulties. In M. Rutter & L. Hersov (Eds.), *Child and adolescent psychiatry*. Boston: Blackwell Scientific Publications.

Z

Zametkin, A. J., & Rapoport, J. L. (1986). The pathophysiology of attention deficit disorder with hyperactivity: A review. In B. B. Lahey & A. E. Kazdin (Eds.), *Advances in clinical child psychology*, Vol. 9. New York: Plenum.

Zametkin, A. J., & Rapoport, J. L. (1987). Neurobiology of attention deficit disorder with hyperactivity: Where have we come in 50 years? *Journal of the American Academy of Child and Adolescent Psychiatry, 26,* 676–686.

Zaslow, M. J., & Hayes, C. D. (1986). Sex differences in children's response to psychosocial stress: Toward a cross-context analysis. In M. E. Lamb, A. L. Brown, & B. Rogoff (Eds.), *Advances in developmental psychology*, Vol. 4. Hillsdale, NJ: Erlbaum.

Zax, M., & Cowen, E. L. (1967). Early identification and prevention of emotional disturbance in a public school. In E. L. Cowen, E. A. Gardner, & M. Zax (Eds.), *Emergent approaches to mental health problems*. New York: Appleton-Century-Crofts.

Zeaman, D., & House, B.J. (1979). A review of attention theory. In N. R. Ellis (Ed.), *Handbook of mental deficiency*. Hillsdale, NJ: Erlbaum.

Zeanah, C. H., Anders, T. F., Seifer, R., & Stern, D. N. (1989). Implications of research on infant development for psychodynamic theory and practice. *Journal of the American Academy of Child and Adolescent Psychiatry, 28*, 657–668.

Zentall, S.S. (1985). A context for hyperactivity. In K. Gadow (Ed.), *Advances in learning and behavioral disabilities*, Vol. 4. Greenwich, CT: JAI Press.

Zentall, S. S., & Meyer, M. J. (1987). Self-regulation of stimulation for ADD-H children during reading and vigilance task performance. *Journal of Abnormal Child Psychology, 15*, 519–536.

Zigler, E. (1978). The effectiveness of Head Start: Another look. *Educational Psychologist, 13*, 71–77.

Zigler, E. F. (1987). Formal schooling for four-year-olds? *American Psychologist, 42*, 254–260.

Zigler, E., & Balla, D. (1982). Motivation and personality factors in the performance of the retarded. In E. Zigler & D. Balla (Eds.), *Mental retardation: The developmental-difference controversy*. Hillsdale, NJ: Erlbaum.

Zigler, E., Balla, D., & Hodapp, R. (1984). On the definition and classification of mental retardation. *American Journal of Mental Deficiency, 89*, 215–230.

Zigler, E., & Trickett, P. K. (1978). IQ, social competence, and evaluation of early childhood intervention programs. *American Psychologist, 33*, 789–798.

NAME INDEX

Flicek, M., 190
Folstein, S.E., 278
Forehand, R., 6, 39, 66, 144, 145, 156, 161, 172, 173
Foreyt, J.P., 304, 306, 308, 310
Forman, J.B.W., 90
Forness, S.R., 264
Forsythe, W.I., 312
Foster, G.G., 95
Foster, S.L., 100
Fowler, M.G., 331
Fox, A.A., 254
Foxx, R.M., 232, 313
Francis, C.G., 124, 126
Frankel, M.S., 83
Frary, R.B., 113
Frederiksen, N., 215
Freeman, B.J., 280
Freeman, E.H., 326
Fremouw, W.J., 308
French, T.M., 326
Freud, S., 9, 12, 13, 34, 51, 52, 53, 54, 62, 115, 116, 139, 307
Freuda, 9, 64–65
Friedman, H.S., 338
Friedman, M., 338
Friedman, S., 281, 295
Friedman, S.L., 145
Friedman, R.M., 7
Friesen, W.V., 26
Frith, U., 274, 276
Fromm, E., 54
Frostig, M., 102, 257, 260–61
Fulkner, D.W., 255
Fultz, S.A., 300
Fundudis, T., 308
Furey, W.M., 66
Furman, W., 151–52

G

Gabrielli, W.F., 165, 166
Gadow, K.D., 202, 207
Galaburda, A.M., 256
Galambos, N.L., 28
Gallagher, J.J., 244
Gannon, S., 3–5
Garbarino, J., 363
Garber, J., 139
Garcia, J., 227
Garcia, K.A., 114
Gardner, F.E.M., 161,
Garfinkel, B.D., 108, 188, 192
Garfinkel, P.E., 305
Garmezy, N., 35, 36, 37, 140
Garn, S.M., 301
Garner, D.M. 305, 308
Garnier, C., 279
Garrison, K.C., 18
Garrison, K.M., 362
Garvey, W.P., 124
Gath, A., 46
Gaughran, J.M., 24
Gaylin, W., 83
Geller, E., 279, 282, 295
Gelles, R.J., 363, 366
Gerard, M.W., 312
Gerber, M.M., 263
Germain, R., 363

Gerrity, K.M., 32
Gesell, A., 12, 13, 102
Gesten, E.L., 354, 355, 366
Gholson, B., 58
Gibbons, D.C., 181
Gibbons, J., 148
Gibbs, D.P., 250
Gillberg, C., 192, 271, 272, 278
Gillberg, I.C., 192
Giller, H., 161, 166 , 176, 177, 178, 180, 181
Gilligan, C., 163
Gillin, J.C., 141
Gilstrap, B., 28
Ginsburg, H., 355
Gittelman, R., 98, 121, 133, 207
Gittleman-Klein, R., 121
Gladstone, M., 255
Glasgow, R.E., 336
Glazer, J.A., 149
Glidden, L.M., 231
Glueck, E.T., 161, 177
Glueck, S., 161, 177
Goddard, H.H., 212–13, 225–26
Goldberg, J.O., 28, 79
Golden, M., 148
Goldfarb, W., 267, 291, 292–93
Goldfield, E.C., 21
Goldsmith, H.H., 24, 26
Goldstein, M.J., 293, 294
Goldston, S.E., 355
Gonso, J., 149, 150
Goodman, J., 59
Goodman, R., 194, 196, 277
Goodman, S.H., 144
Gordon, D.A., 161, 164
Gortmaker, S.L., 301, 303, 323, 332
Gottfried, A.E., 28, 357
Gottfried, A.W., 28, 357
Gottleib, J., 237
Gottman, J., 149, 150
Gould, J.S., 8, 14, 91, 95, 213, 227, 276
Goyette, C.H., 199
Grace, W.J., 321
Graham, D.T., 321
Graham, P., 106, 312
Granell de Aldaz, 122
Granger, D.A., 190, 201
Grave, G.D., 302
Graves, T., 304
Gray, G., 177
Gray, J.W., 49
Graziano, 114, 121
Green, J., 90
Green, W.H., 271, 289
Greenberg, M.T., 32
Greenberger, E., 28
Greenough, W.T., 19
Greenwood, C.R., 150
Gresham, F.M., 250, 251–52
Griest, D.L., 171, 172, 173
Griffin, B.S., 181
Griffin, C.T., 181
Grinder, R.E., 11
Grolnick, W.S., 254
Gross, A.M., 298, 335, 336
Gross, M.D., 195
Grossman, H.J., 211, 216 , 218, 219, 226, 233
Grusec, J.E., 34
Guerra, N.G., 164
Guidubaldi, J., 161, 359, 360

Kraemer, S., 14
Krasnegor, N.A., 302
Krasner, L., 339
Kratochwill, T.R., 118
Krauss, M.R., 303
Kretchmer, N., 302
Kronenberger, W., 252
Krug, D.A., 280
Krupski, A., 245
Kudla, M.J., 235
Kugler, M.M., 315
Kuhn, T., 42
Kuhnley, E.J., 174
Kuperman, S., 103, 104, 279
Kydd, R.R., 291, 294

L

LaBuda, M.C., 32, 255
LaCrosse, J., 39
Ladd, G., 150–51
Ladd, G.W., 150
LaGreca, A., 150
LaGreca, A.M., 108, 251, 333, 334, 336
Lahey, B.B., 66, 166
Lamb, H.R., 355
Lambert, N.M., 36, 37
Landau, S., 190
Landry, S.H., 222, 274, 275
Lang, P.J., 109–10, 300
Langer, 83, 84
Langlois, J.H., 21
Lansdown, R., 196
Laosa, L.M., 368
Lapouse, R., 7, 113, 114
Last, C.G., 91, 124, 126
Laufer, M.W., 193
Launay, J., 279
Lavigne, J.V., 300
Layman, D., 205–6
Lazar, I., 352
Lazarus, A., 342
Le Couteur, A., 279
Leach, G.M., 71–72
LeBow, M.D., 301
Ledingham, J.E., 148, 159
Lee, J.A., 49
Lee, M., 163
Leenaars, A.A., 252
Lefever, W., 102
Lefkowitz, M., 136
Lefkowitz, M.M., 133, 142
Lehtinen, L., 193, 254
Leitenberg, H., 119, 309
Lemert, E.M., 181
Leon, G.R., 139, 306, 310
Leonard, H.L., 127
Lerner, J.V., 28
Lerner, J.W., 245, 256, 262
Lerner, R.M., 38
Leslie, A.M., 276
Levenstein, P., 352
Leventhal, 124
Levin, J.R., 248
Levine, A., 303
Levine, H.G., 232
Levine, M., 349
Levy, S., 278

Lewinsohn, P., 139
Lewis, M., 35, 121
Lewis, N.G., 363
Lewis, S., 119–20
Lewis, V., 272
Libet, J., 300
Licht, B.G., 253–54
Liebert, R.M., 311, 313
Liederman, V.R., 301
Lilly, M.S., 60, 61, 96, 237
Lindquist, E.F., 103
Linscheid, T.R., 285, 299, 300
Littman, R.A., 167, 169
Lobitz, G.K., 172
Lobovits, D.A., 133
Loeber, R., 158, 159, 168
Loney, J., 189, 191
Long, B.B., 173, 368
Lopez, R., 194
Lord, C., 272
Lorion, R.P., 354
Lotter, V., 271, 279
Lourie, R.S., 8, 223–24, 234, 300, 301
Lovaas, O.I., 2, 15, 272, 282, 283, 284, 285, 286, 287
Loveland, K.A., 274, 275,
Lovibond, S.H., 313
Lovko, A.M., 358
Lowe, K., 337
Lowrie, R.A., 49
Lucido, D., 331
Ludwick-Rosenthal, R., 342
Lutzker, J., 337
Luxenberg, J.S., 129
Lyman, R.D., 298
Lynn, D.B., 26
Lyon, G.R., 261, 262
Lytton, H., 161

M

McAdoo, W.G., 277
McAlpine, C., 300
McBurnett, K., 66
McCall, R.B., 215
McCarran, M.S., 339
McCarthy, J.J., 103, 257
McCartney, K., 33, 41, 147, 357
McCarver, R.B., 235
McCaul, K.D., 336
McCauley, E., 223
McClearn, G.E., 46
Maccoby, E.E., 26, 28
McCombs, A., 144
McConaughy, S.H., 102, 134
McCormick, L., 242, 247
McCroskey, J., 357
McDermott, J.K., 210
MacDonald, L., 217
McEachin, J.J., 287
McEvoy, R.E., 275
MacFarland, J.W., 113, 114, 136, 148
McGarvey, B., 177
McGavin, J.K., 304, 306, 310
McGee, R., 189
McGlynn, F.D., 116
McGuffin, P., 44
Machover, K., 99
Mack, J.E., 318

S

SUBJECT INDEX

Behavior disorders
  defined, 1–6
  predicting, 38–39
  protection factors in, 37–38
  risk factors in, 36–37
  vulnerability factors in, 37
Behavior modification, for ADHD, 203, 205–6
Behavior-personality assessment, 96–102
  checklists, 101–2
  dimensional rating scales, 101–2
  interviews, 96–98
  psychological tests, 98–101
Behavior Problem Checklist, Revised, 93, 96
Behaviorism/social learning theory, 9–10
Bender Visual-Motor Gestalt Test, 104, 105
Beta commands, 172
Binet Scales, 212–13
Biofeedback, 339
Biological/physiological perspective, 43–51
  biochemical influences, 46–47
  genetic influences, 43–46
  structural/physiological damage, 47–50
Brain
  abnormalities, in dyslexia, 255
  damage, 47–51, 192–93
  development, 19
Bulimia, 304–10

C

Case study, as research method, 70–71
Cattell Intelligence Tests for Infants and Young Children, 102
Child abuse, 362–66
  intervention/treatment, approaches to, 365
Child and Adolescent Service System Program (CASSP), 368
Child Behavior Checklist, 92, 93, 101, 135, 142, 330
Child guidance movement, 10–11
Childhood Autism Rating Scale (CARS), 280
Childhood disorders
  age of onset and, 8
  historical influences on, 8–12
  incidence/prevalence of, 6–7
  interdisciplinary approach to, 12–15
  sex differences in, 7–8
Childhood schizophrenia, 287–96
  developmental course, 291–92
  DSM-III-R criteria, 288
  etiology, 292–94
  prevalence, 289
  prognosis, 294–95
  psychological/behavioral functioning, 289–91
  treatment, 295–96
Children's Apperception Test (CAT), 99
Children's Asthma Research Institute and Hospital (CARIH), study by, 326–28
Children's Depression Inventory, 133, 134, 142
Chromosome, 18, 221
  abnormalities, 46, 221–23
Chronic illness, psychological consequences of, 329–32
  disease status, adjustment and, 330–31
  family functioning, adjustment and, 331–32
Classification, 87–106
  age/sex categories and, 92
  clinically derived, 88–91
  dangers of, 95–96
  empirically derived, 91–95
  similarity of derived syndromes and, 92

Classificatory variable, 79
Clinical utility, 88
Cognition, Piagetian theory of, 22–23
Cognitive self-management strategies, phobias and, 120–21
Cohort effects, 81
Communication deviance (CD), 293
Comorbidity, 109
Compulsions, 127
Computerized tomography (CT), 104–4
Concordance
  defined, 45
  schizophrenia and, 292
Conditioning
  classical, 55–56, 116
  operant, 56–57, 116, 228, 287
  two-factor theory of, 116–17
Conduct disorders, 155–83
  aggression, 167–71
  biological influences, 165–66
  classification, 156–58
  developmental course, 158–59
  family influences and, 160–62
  firesetting, 173–75
  juvenile delinquency, 175–83
  oppositional/noncompliant behavior, 171–73
  prevalence, 156
  social-cognitive influences, 162–65
  stability of, 159–60
Conner's Parent Questionnaire, 93
Conner's Parent Rating Scale, 199
Conner's Teacher Rating Scale, 101, 199
Continuity
  cumulative, 39
  interactional, 39
Continuous Performance Test (CPT), 187, 201
Control group, 75
Controlled observations, as research method, 79
Correlation coefficient, 73
Correlational research method, 73–75
Critical period hypothesis, 34–35
Cross-sectional research, 81
Cultural-familial retardation, 224–26
Cumulative continuity, 39

D

Defense mechanisms, 53
Deficit model, of atypical functioning, 355
Delusion, 290
Dementia praecox, 267
Dependent variable, 75–76
Depression, 132–53
  description/classification, 135–39
  maternal, as risk factor, 144–47
  peer relations and, 147–53
  prevalence, 133–35
  theories of, 139–43
  treatment of, 143–44
Desensitization, systematic, 118–19, 124
Development
  change/continuity in, 38–39
  defined, 16–17
  Freudian view of, 9
  genetic context of, 17–18
  intellectual, 21–23
  nature/nurture and, 31–32
  physical, 18–21
  risk factors in, 36–37

Genetic influences
   and ADHD children, 194
   in autism, 278
   on conduct disorders, 165–66
   on human behavior, 43–46
   in learning disabilities, 254–55
Genital stage, 52–53
Gesell Developmental Schedules, 102
Group for the Advancement of Psychiatry (GAP), 88

H

Hallucination, 289
Halstead Neuropsychological Test Battery for Children, 104
Head Start, 351–53, 355
Heredity, sex-linked pattern of, 44–45
   and environment, in mental retardation, 225–26
Heritability, 45
Home Situations Questionnaire, 199–200
Home Start, 351–52
Hospitalization, 343–44
Human Figure Drawing Test, 99
Huntington's chorea, 44
Hyperactivity, *See* Attention-Deficit Hyperactivity Disorder (ADHD)
Hypothesis, 69

I

Id, 52
Illinois Test of Psycholinguistic Abilities, 103
Impulsivity, 188
In vivo desensitization, 119
Incidence, defined, 6–7
Independent variable, 75–76
Individualized education program, 237
Information processing, 229–31
Intellectual-educational assessment, 102–3
   ability/achievement tests, 102–3
   developmental scales, 102
   intelligence tests, 102
Intelligence quotient (IQ), 213
Intelligence tests
   score stability, 215–16
   validity of, 214–15
Interactional continuity, 39
Intermittent alarm procedure, for enuresis, 313
   overlearning and, 313
Internal validity, 76
Internalizing disorders
   anxiety disorders, 108–31
   childhood depression, 132–47
   peer relationship problems, 147–53
Interpersonal relations, conduct disorders and, 164–65
Intervention, *See* Prevention
Interviews
   as assessment technique, 96–98
   in identifying ADHD child, 198–99
Iowa Test of Basic Skills, 103

J

Joint attention interactions, in autism, 274
Juvenile delinquency, 175–83
   causes/correlates of, 176
   definition, problem of, 175–76
   socioeconomic status and, 177–78

subtypes of, 177–78
treatment of, 179–83

K

Klinefelter's syndrome, 223

L

Language deficits, learning disabilities and, 248
Latency stage, 52
Law of Effect (Thorndike), 9–10, 56
Lead exposure, and ADHD, 196
Learned helplessness, 140
Learning
   autism and, 272
   behavioral/social, 54–58
   classical conditioning and, 55–56, 228
   cognition and, in mental retardation, 228–31
   discrimination, 230
   observational, 57–58
   operant conditioning and, 56–57, 228
   paired-associate, 230–31
   processes, 22
Learning disabilities, (LD), 241–64
   academic performance and, 244–45
   assessment of, 257–59
   cognitive deficits and, 245–49
   defined, 241–42
   developmental course, 256–57
   educational efforts/policy, 262–63
   etiology of, 254–56
   exclusionary criteria for, 243–44
   fundamental issues about, 263–64
   prevalence, 244
   social/motivational factors and, 250-54
   specific criteria for, 242–43
   treatment, 259–62
Learning Disabilities Association of America, 243
Learning Mystique: A Critical Look at "Learning Disabilities", The (Coles), 256
Least restrictive environment, 237–39, 262–63
   See also Public Law 94–142
Leiter International Performance Scale, 280
Lesch-Nyhan Syndrome, 44, 284
Libido, 51
Little Albert, 55, 115
Little Hans, 53, 62, 115, 116
Longitudinal research, 80–81
Luria-Nebraska Neuropsychological Battery—Children's Revision, 104

M

Mainstreaming, 238–39
Marital discord, conduct disorders and, 161–62
Masked depression, 135
Matching Familiar Figures Test (MFFT), 188, 201
Maternal employment, 356–59
Maturation, 12
   milestones of, 21
Medical treatment, psychological influences on, 332–44
   See also Physical conditions, psychological factors affecting
Meiosis, 18
Memory, learning disabilities and, 247–48